"Worship has been described as the source and summit of the entire Christian life. Orthodoxy in its foundational etymology is 'right or true doxology or glory.' Or more simply, it is 'right worship.' The intimate marriage of biblical theology with worship theology and practice is therefore a most crucial and relevant endeavor. *Biblical Worship: Theology for God's Glory* is truly an invaluable compendium to that end, outlining the scriptural foundations for the expression of right theology in the worship of God's people throughout the entire biblical narrative. The theological, devotional, and moral/ethical formation in which God's people are, and have always been, called to participate in worship is indeed for the very life of the world and the advancement of God's kingdom."

—James R. Hart, President,
Robert E. Webber Institute for Worship Studies

"Christ followers have been called to submit their whole lives as a living sacrifice. *Biblical Worship: Theology for God's Glory* provides a wealth of information that facilitates just that—theology unto the glory of God. The authors accomplish their purpose of developing biblical doxology, submissive homage, and worshipful response to the revelation of the Almighty. By looking both backward to the worship of the Old Testament and forward to the worship of the New Testament, readers are able to see the consistency and seamlessness of God's design for worship and make practical applications to present-day doxology, aiding the spiritual act of worship which is holy and pleasing to God."

—Hanna Byrd, Director of Practica,
Liberty University School of Music

"In a world that is driven by pragmatics and the appearance of success, I welcome any and all efforts to recover a biblical theology of worship and to demonstrate its importance for the church today. This volume makes an extremely important contribution to that project. The editors have given us access to a magnificent collection of essays by more than thirty scholars, all writing from their areas of expertise, and covering most of the genres of Scripture. The result is a kaleidoscope of images of biblical worship ranging from essays that focus on the function of liturgy and cult to daily life as worship, but all drawing on the Scriptures for their portrayal of worship that pleases and glorifies God."

—Daniel Block, Guenther H. Knoedler Professor of Old Testament,
Wheaton College Graduate School

"*Biblical Worship: Theology for God's Glory* is a comprehensive guide that's deeply rooted in Scripture and grounded in solid exegesis, while also eminently approachable for worship leaders—which I mean in its broadest sense. The thirty-four men and women whose scholarship comprise this work have explored the topic with a depth and breadth that few resources can claim. It's an excellent book."

—Sandra Glahn, Professor of Media Arts and Worship,
Dallas Theological Seminary

"In the revelation within the Bible, there is an inexhaustible beauty to God. As nothing limits God's power or love, there seems to be no limits to the proper wonder and awe of the Lord God, too. *Biblical Worship: Theology for God's Glory* helps us see this amazing breadth of how biblical people have worshiped the God revealed in the Scriptures. Come, read how biblical authors have been 'lost in wonder, love, and praise' and be drawn into the same with them."

—Lester Ruth, Research Professor of Christian Worship,
Duke Divinity School

"As believers we are called upon to worship the Lord, and this volume helps us grasp what the biblical writers mean by worship. We are treated to a guided tour of the canon by the contributors to the volume, and thereby we are enriched by the diverse expressions of worship in the Scriptures. The significance of the biblical teaching is applied to the contemporary world, and I am grateful for this fine work which reminds us afresh that we are called upon to worship in spirit and truth."

—Thomas R. Schreiner,
James Buchanan Harrison Professor of New Testament
Interpretation, Professor of Biblical Theology,
The Southern Baptist Theological Seminary

"Worship is at the heart of the Bible, but the changing patterns of worship through the biblical story can be a challenge for readers. This book leaves no part of the biblical canon out of account and consistently develops the implications for our personal and corporate prayer and worship today."

—Richard Bauckham, Professor Emeritus of New Testament Studies,
University of St. Andrews

BIBLICAL THEOLOGY FOR THE CHURCH

BIBLICAL WORSHIP

Theology for God's Glory

BENJAMIN K. FORREST,
WALTER C. KAISER JR.,
AND VERNON M. WHALEY
EDITORS

KREGEL
ACADEMIC

Biblical Worship: Theology for God's Glory

Published by Kregel Academic, an imprint of Kregel Publications, 2450 Oak Industrial Dr. NE, Grand Rapids, MI 49505-6020.

Scripture quotations not marked are the author's own translation.

ISBN 978-0-8254-4556-9

Printed in the United States of America

21 22 23 24 25 / 5 4 3 2 1

To Reagan Adeline Forrest,
may you raise your voice and spend your
life in worship of our wonderful Savior!
—BKF

To my wife Nancy Elizabeth,
who loves to sing with me the songs of
praise and worship to our Lord every day!
—WCK

To Dr. Paul Rumrill,
lover of "the Most High God," powerful prayer
partner, student of worship, true friend, and comrade.
—VMW

CONTENTS

WORSHIP IN THE NEW TESTAMENT

ACKNOWLEDGEMENTS

Nearly all of the authors of this project readily admitted their appreciation for and dependence on the work of Dan Block, Allen Ross, and Greg Beale. To these scholars we want to specifically extend our thanks—for their continued faithfulness in exposing and teaching the biblical text. Their valuable contribution to biblical theology and the study of worship forms much of the basis for the research and chapters herein, and we hope that this project continues in the vein of adding to and clarifying what biblical worship looks like in practice and posture. We also want to thank the contributing authors who committed to this project in its nascent form many years ago. At the beginning of this project, few of the authors knew each of us. Yet, they readily saw the value in thinking deeply about worship followed by research and writing as they extended their teaching ministries beyond their classrooms and into the hands and hearts of readers everywhere. Their response and partnership has been a tremendous joy, encouragement, and blessing. We are thankful for what each has taught us and hope that readers will find similar enjoyment throughout.

We are extremely thankful for all those at Kregel who saw the potential in such a project, and for their continued patience in waiting for its long-anticipated submission. Laura Bartlett, Dennis Hillman, Paul Hillman, Robert Hand, and Shawn Vander Lugt labored behind the scenes to bring this book to fruition, and much of its success is due to their hard work. Francis Watson was a bibliography machine, helping us to track sources and put them together. We appreciate her willingness to jump in and help out!

From Ben: I would like to thank my wife Lerisa, who models daily a love and enjoyment of Jesus. She is a godly woman who is a blessing to her family. I am encouraged each morning by her faithful pursuit of Christ through his Word. I also want to thank my good friend John R. Markley, who was an early supporter of this project. He saw the value of and advocated for this project from the beginning. Your friendship, encouragement, and assistance are greatly appreciated.

From Walter: I would like to thank all of the writers of the chapters in this wonderful manuscript on worship. It has been a joy reading how diligently you have undertaken your essays on each of the portions of Scripture. May this work be a landmark in the history of worship in the evangelical church around the world and may all praise go to the Lord our God.

From Vernon: I would like to thank Beth Smith Whaley, my companion, soul mate, partner, and wife for more than forty-five years—she is my rock, prayer partner, and confidence builder; Jeremy Whaley, our son, and his helpmeet, Kenya—forever teaching me principles of good communication; Laurie Whaley Roe, our daughter, and her husband Jeremy (JRoe)—always looking for ways to encourage; our six grandchildren—Carter, Luca, Noah, Daisy, Eliza, and Aliyana—I pray that they grow up to be faithful worshipers of Jesus; Ben Forrest—for giving me opportunity to be part of this significantly powerful book project; Alissa Passburg, Kim Witt, Becky McKennett, Tim Williamson, Becca Stegall, Christy Solomon, Hanna Byrd, Patrick Shorts, Kevin Williams, Pat Edmiston, Kaitlyn Collier, Stephanie Gates, and Stephanie Pritchard—the best staff and partners in ministry ever! And last, the Liberty University School of Music faculty—totally committed to the mission of equipping students as worshipers of "the Most High God."

Last, and mostly, we want to thank our Lord for calling us as his own and inviting us to spend our lives worshiping him, and teaching others how to be worshipers.

ABBREVIATIONS

BIBLICAL ABBREVIATIONS

ANE	Ancient Near East
BHS	*Biblia Hebraica Stuttgartensia*
BSB	Berean Study Bible
ESV	English Standard Version
HCSB	Holman Christian Standard Bible
LXX	Septuagint
MT	Masoretic Text
NA^{28}	*Novum Testamentum Graece*, Nestle-Aland, 28th ed.
NASB	New American Standard Bible
NET	New English Translation
NETS	New English Translation of the Septuagint
NIV	New International Version
NKJV	New King James Version
NLT	New Living Translation
NRSV	New Revised Standard Version
TNIV	Today's New International Version

JOURNALS, SERIES, REFERENCE WORKS

ABD	*Anchor Bible Dictionary*. Edited by David Noel Freedman. 6 vols. New York: Doubleday, 1992.
AbrN	*Abr-Nahrain*
AnBib	Analecta Biblica
ANF	*The Ante-Nicene Fathers*. Edited by Alexander Roberts and James Donaldson. 1885–1887. 10 vols. Repr., Peabody, MA: Hendrickson, 1994.
AOTC	Apollos Old Testament Commentary
AUSS	*Andrews University Seminary Studies*
A(Y)B	Anchor (Yale) Bible
BA	*Biblical Archaeologist*
BAFCS	The Book of Acts in Its First Century Setting

BAGD	Bauer, Walter, William F. Arndt, F. Wilbur Gingrich, and Frederick W. Danker. *Greek-English Lexicon of the New Testament and Other Early Christian Literature*. 2nd ed. Chicago: University of Chicago Press, 1979.
BAR	*Biblical Archaeological Research*
BASOR	*Bulletin of the American Schools of Oriental Research*
BBR	*Bulletin for Biblical Research*
BBRSup	Bulletin for Biblical Research, Supplements
BCOTWP	Baker Commentary on the Old Testament Wisdom and Psalms
BDAG	Danker, Frederick W., Walter Bauer, William F. Arndt, and F. Wilbur Gingrich. *Greek-English Lexicon of the New Testament and Other Early Christian Literature*. 3rd ed. Chicago: University of Chicago Press, 2000.
BHQ	Biblia Hebraica Quinta
Bib	*Biblica*
BR	*Biblical Research*
BSac	*Bibliotheca Sacra*
BSL	Biblical Studies Library
BTCP	Biblical Theology for Chrstian Proclamation
BTNT	Biblical Theology of the New Testament
BZNW	Beihefte zur Zeitschrift für die neutestamentliche Wissenschaft
CBC	Cornerstone Biblical Commentary
CBQ	*Catholic Biblical Quarterly*
CC	Continental Commentaries
Chm	*Churchman*
COS	*The Context of Scripture*. Edited by William W. Hallo. 3 vols. Leiden: Brill, 1997–2002.
CTM	*Concordia Theological Monthly*
DCH	*Dictionary of Classical Hebrew*. Edited by David J. A. Clines. 9 vols. Sheffield: Sheffield Phoenix Press, 1993–2014.
DLNT	*Dictionary of the Later New Testament and Its Developments*. Edited by R. P. Martin and P. H. Davids. Downers Grove, IL: InterVarsity Press, 1997.
DOTWPW	*Dictionary of the Old Testament: Wisdom, Poetry and Writings*. Edited by Tremper Longman III and Peter Enns. Downers Grove, IL: InterVarsity Press, 2008.
ECC	Eerdmans Critical Commentary
ECL	Early Christianity and Its Literature
EDT	*Evangelical Dictionary of Theology*. Edited by Walter Elwell. Grand Rapids: Baker, 2001.
EvQ	*Evangelical Quarterly*
FAT	Forschungen zum Alten Testament
FOTL	Forms of the Old Testament Literature

GTJ	*Grace Theological Journal*
HALOT	*The Hebrew and Aramaic Lexicon of the Old Testament.* Ludwig Koehler, Walter Baumgartner, and Johann J. Stamm. Translated and edited under the supervision of Mervyn E. J. Richardson. 4 vols. Leiden: Brill, 1994–1999.
HAT	Handbuch zum Alten Testament
HSM	Harvard Semitic Monographs
HTR	*Harvard Theological Review*
ICC	International Critical Commentary
Int	*Interpretation*
ITC	International Theological Commentary
JAOS	*Journal of the American Oriental Society*
JATS	*Journal of the Adventist Theological Society*
JBL	*Journal of Biblical Literature*
JESOT	*Journal for the Evangelical Study of the Old Testament*
JETS	*Journal of the Evangelical Theological Society*
JHebS	*Journal of Hebrew Scriptures*
JHS	*Journal of Hellenic Studies*
JNES	*Journal of Near Eastern Studies*
JNSL	*Journal of Northwest Semitic Languages*
JPT	*Journal of Pentecostal Theology*
JSNT	*Journal for the Study of the New Testament*
JSNTSup	Journal for the Study of the New Testament Supplement Series
JSOT	*Journal for the Study of the Old Testament*
JSOTSup	Journal for the Study of the Old Testament Supplement Series
L&N	Louw, Johannes P., and Eugene A. Nida, eds. *Greek-English Lexicon of the New Testament: Based on Semantic Domains*. 2nd ed. New York: United Bible Societies, 1989.
LHBOTS	The Library of Hebrew Bible/Old Testament Studies
LNTS	Library of New Testament Studies
LSJ	Liddell, Henry George, Robert Scott, Henry Stuart Jones. *A Greek-English Lexicon*. 9th ed. with revised supplement. Oxford: Clarendon, 1996.
NAC	New American Commentary
NCB	New Century Bible
NEA	*Near Eastern Archaeology*
Neot	*Neotestamentica*
NICNT	New International Commentary on the New Testament
NICOT	New International Commentary on the Old Testament
NIDNTTE	*New International Dictionary of New Testament Theology and Exegesis*. Edited by Moisé Silva. 2nd ed. 5 vols. Grand Rapids: Zondervan, 2014.

NIDOTTE	*New International Dictionary of Old Testament Theology and Exegesis*. Edited by Willem A. VanGemeren. 5 vols. Grand Rapids: Zondervan, 1997.
NIGTC	New International Greek Testament Commentary
NIVAC	NIV Application Commentary
NovT	*Novum Testamentum*
NovTSup	Supplements to Novum Testamentum
NSBT	New Studies in Biblical Theology
NTL	New Testament Library
NTS	*New Testament Studies*
OTL	Old Testament Library
PiNTC	Pillar New Testament Commentary
RINAP	Royal Inscriptions of the Neo-Assyrian Period
SBJT	*Southern Baptist Journal of Theology*
SCS	Septuagint and Cognate Studies
SHBC	Smyth & Helwys Bible Commentary
SJT	*Scottish Journal of Theology*
SNTSMS	Society for New Testament Studies Monograph Series
StBibLit	Studies in Biblical Literature (Lang)
STDJ	Studies on the Texts of the Desert of Judah
TDNT	*Theological Dictionary of the New Testament*. Edited by Gerhard Kittel and Gerhard Friedrich. Translated by Geoffrey W. Bromiley. 10 vols. Grand Rapids: Eerdmans, 1964–1976.
TDOT	*Theological Dictionary of the Old Testament*. Edited by G. Johannes Botterweck and Helmer Ringgren. Translated by John T. Willis et al. 8 vols. Grand Rapids: Eerdmans, 1974–2006.
TJ	*Trinity Journal*
TLOT	*Theological Lexicon of the Old Testament*. Edited by Ernst Jenni, with assistance from Claus Westermann. Translated by Mark E. Biddle. 3 vols. Peabody, MA: Hendrickson, 1997.
TNTC	Tyndale New Testament Commentaries
TOTC	Tyndale Old Testament Commentaries
TynBul	*Tyndale Bulletin*
UBCS	Understanding the Bible Commentary Series
VT	*Vetus Testamentum*
WBC	Word Biblical Commentary
WTJ	*Westminster Theological Journal*
WUNT	Wissenschaftliche Untersuchungen zum Neuen Testament
ZAW	*Zeitschrift für die alttestamentliche Wissenschaft*
ZECNT	Zondervan Exegetical Commentary on the New Testament

CONTRIBUTORS

Kenneth Berding (PhD, Westminster Theological Seminary) is professor of New Testament at Talbot School of Theology.

Craig L. Blomberg (PhD, University of Aberdeen) is distinguished professor of New Testament at Denver Seminary.

Greg Couser (PhD, University of Aberdeen) is senior professor of Bible and Greek at Cedarville University.

Ben R. Crenshaw is a doctoral student at Hillsdale College.

Benjamin K. Forrest (EdD, Liberty University) is associate dean of the College of Arts and Sciences and professor of Christian education at Liberty University.

R. Alan Fuhr (PhD, Southeastern Baptist Theological Seminary) is associate professor of Old Testament at Liberty University.

Benjamin L. Gladd (PhD, Wheaton College) is associate professor of New Testament at Reformed Theological Seminary in Jackson.

N. Blake Hearson (PhD, Hebrew Union College) is associate professor of Old Testament at Midwestern Baptist Theological Seminary.

Ted Hildebrandt (PhD, Grace Theological Seminary) is professor of biblical studies at Gordon College.

Andrew Hill (PhD, University of Michigan) is professor of Old Testament at Wheaton College.

Edward E. Hindson (ThD, Trinity Graduate School; DMin, Westminster Theological Seminary; DPhil, University of South Africa) is the founding dean of the John W. Rawlings School of Divinity and Distinguished Research Professor at Liberty University.

JoAnna M. Hoyt (PhD, Dallas Theological Seminary) is an adjunct professor at Dallas International University, a visiting professor at Dallas

Theological Seminary, and assistant editor for the Evangelical Exegetical Commentary Series.

Karen Jobes (PhD, Westminster Theological Seminary) is professor of New Testament Greek and exegesis, emerita, at Wheaton College.

Walter C. Kaiser Jr. (PhD, Brandeis University) is the Colman M. Mockler Distinguished Professor of Old Testament and president emeritus of Gordon-Conwell Theological Seminary.

Andreas Köstenberger (PhD, Trinity Evangelical Divinity School; Dr. rer. soc. oec., Vienna University of Economics) is research professor of New Testament and biblical theology and director of the Center for Biblical Studies at Midwestern Baptist Theological Seminary.

Peter Y. Lee (PhD, Catholic University of America) is professor of Old Testament and dean of students at Reformed Theological Seminary in Washington, DC.

Donald Roe Love III (PhD, Southeastern Baptist Theological Seminary) is associate professor of New Testament at Liberty University.

Eugene Merrill (PhD, Columbia University; PhD, Bob Jones University) is distinguished professor emeritus of Old Testament studies at Dallas Theological Seminary.

Erika Moore (PhD, Westminster Theological Seminary) is academic dean, professor of Old Testament and Hebrew, and director of the STM program at Trinity School for Ministry.

Dickson Ngama (PhD, Westminster Theological Seminary; PhD ABD, Liberty University) is instructor of Old Testament and theology at Liberty University.

William R. Osborne (PhD, Midwestern Baptist Theological Seminary) is associate professor of Biblical and Theological Studies at the College of the Ozarks.

John Oswalt (PhD, Brandeis University) is visiting distinguished professor of Old Testament at Asbury Seminary. He is author of *Isaiah* in the NIVAC.

Christine Elizabeth Palmer (PhD, Hebrew Union College) is instructor of Old Testament exegesis and biblical theology at Gordon-Conwell Theological Seminary.

Donna Petter (PhD, University of Toronto) is director of the Hebrew Language Program and associate professor of Old Testament at Gordon-Conwell Theological Seminary.

Thomas Petter (PhD, University of Toronto) is Senior Pastor, Trinitarian Congregational Church, Wayland, MA, and associate professor of Old Testament, Gordon-Conwell Theological Seminary.

Mark Rooker (PhD, Brandeis University) is senior professor of Old Testament at Southeastern Baptist Theological Seminary.

Jillian L. Ross (PhD, Trinity Evangelical Divinity School) is associate professor of biblical studies and director of biblical languages programs at Liberty University.

Jinsung Seok (PhD, Trinity Evangelical Divinity School) is an adjunct professor at Sungkyul University and a pastor in South Korea.

Monte Shanks (PhD, Southern Baptist Theological Seminary) is assistant professor of New Testament at Liberty University.

Brian J. Tabb (PhD, London School of Theology) is the academic dean and associate professor of Biblical Studies at Bethlehem College & Seminary.

J. Michael Thigpen (PhD, Hebrew Union College) is executive vice president, provost, and professor of Old Testament at Phoenix Seminar.

A. Chadwick Thornhill (PhD, Liberty University) is graduate program director of biblical and theological studies as well as associate professor of biblical studies.

Willem A. VanGemeren (PhD, University of Wisconsin) is professor emeritus of Old Testament and Semitic languages at Trinity Evangelical Divinity School.

Ray Van Neste (PhD, University of Aberdeen) is dean and professor of biblical studies, School of Theology and Missions at Union University.

Vernon M. Whaley (PhD, University of Oklahoma) is associate vice president of program development and professor of worship at the School of Music and Worship Arts at Trevecca Nazarene University.

Gary Yates (PhD, Dallas Theological Seminary) is professor of Old Testament at Liberty University.

INTRODUCTION: WORSHIP AS THEOLOGY FOR GOD'S GLORY

Benjamin K. Forrest, Walter C. Kaiser Jr., and Vernon M. Whaley

The story of biblical worship is one where the common is made sacred by proximity to that which is uncommon. From the beginning God sought to call out a people for a unique relationship from among creation. Time and again, however, humankind tarnished the sacred, but God in his providence has offered redemption. Redemption ultimately comes through Christ, but the story leading to Christ takes us through a journey spread over thousands of years where sacred places were constructed (Exod. 26), moved (Num. 1:51), built (1 Kings 6), and torn down (2 Kings 25), all leading to a the wonderful revelation in John 4, where Christ tells of a day when place will not matter for worship (John 4:19–22) because the people of God will become his dwelling place (1 Cor. 3:16; Acts 1:8), as we worship in Spirit and truth (John 4:23–24). This story leading to Christ through worship also travels through paths showing the need for sacred people who perform sacred rituals. Here mediators intercede on behalf of a sinful people to propitiate the sin of individuals and of a nation (Exod. 30:1–10; Lev. 6, 16). These rituals are filled with meaning (Lev. 1), symbolism (Lev. 16:20–22), and significance (Exod. 12:21–28; cf. Num. 19:1–10; Heb. 9:11–28), and the people divinely chosen to carry these out have been set apart for this work (Num. 8:5–26). But both the people and the ritual fail to bring about lasting worship—for these are imperfect pictures of what is only perfected in Christ, who is the "only mediator between God and man" (2 Tim. 2:15) and the only sacrifice that wholly cleanses from all unrighteousness (1 John 1:9). Last, we also see that throughout this story, time too is sacred. Seasons are set apart for feasts and fasts, where strict observance of worship is not only expected but also required. Yet as the story continues from the wilderness to the kingdoms to exile and return, we see a people falling short of the expectations clearly laid out in the law (Ezra 9–10). As Christ came, however, he ushered in a new dispensation that will ultimately find its fulfillment in a heavenly feast where bride and groom join together forever (Rev. 19:6–9). This is the story of biblical worship. It begins with a commission, in the beginning, to worship (Gen. 1–3; cf. Exod. 20; Deut. 5), and it ends in the culmination of a heavenly host singing the eternal praise of the one who is worthy (Rev. 19:1–8).

If this is the story of biblical worship, it is proper to situate ourselves within this story, learning from both righteous and wayward worship that we might faithfully join in the song of the redeemed (Ps. 107:1–3; Rev. 5:9; 14:1–5). Worship then is not dictated by those who bring it, but by the one who commissions it and is worthy of its reception (Exod. 25–31; 2 Sam. 6:1–7; 1 Chron. 29; 1 Kings 6:11–13; 8:1–66). Therefore, what God has said about worship must be our pursuit for our worshiping. And so to understand our call to worship, we must turn to Scripture humbly and honestly asking that we might understand our calling to worship well. This pursuit is not one we can master in our own endeavoring, but an obedient response to that which has been laid out in the pages of Scripture for the people of God. Right worship is thus eternal, for the object of our worship has no end, and this worship in which we now join will be our vocation throughout eternity.

THEOLOGY *UNTO* THE GLORY OF GOD

Humanity was made to worship and this truth is ingrained on our hearts for, as Augustine noted, "our heart is restless until it rests in you."[1] Worship of God, rightly expressed, satisfies our deepest hungers and thirsts because this is what we were made for. God has revealed himself to humanity in his written Word and the Word that became flesh. J. I. Packer has said, "Theology is for doxology." Understanding the Word and the Word ultimately is for worship. For Packer, doxology is "glorifying God by praise and thanks, by obedient holiness, and by laboring to extend God's kingdom, church, and cultural influence."[2] And it is this idea that stands behind the conviction of this project. We believe that theology is worship, and that worship must be theological. Therefore, biblical worship is theology *unto* the glory of God. Nothing less is acceptable. But what is worship, and how to do we understand the way that places, people, ritual, and time play into our rightful worshiping? Two helpful definitions can begin to answer this first question, and we hope that the following chapters begin to answer the second. Daniel Block defines worship as "reverential human acts of submission and homage before the divine Sovereign in response to his gracious revelation of himself and in accord with his will,"[3] while Allen

1. Augustine, *Confessions* 1.1.1
2. J. I. Packer, "Reading the Bible Theologically," in *Understanding Scripture: An Overview of the Bible's Origin, Reliability, and Meaning*, eds. Wayne Grudem, C. John Collins, and Thomas R. Schreiner (Wheaton, IL: Crossway, 2012), 34.
3. Daniel I. Block, *For the Glory of God: Recovering a Biblical Theology of Worship* (Grand Rapids: Baker Academic, 2014), 23.

Ross says that worship is an "appropriate response to the revelation of the holy God of glory."[4] If worship is theology as we have proposed, submission as Block has stated, and a response to summarize Ross's definition, then our exploration in the coming chapters must cultivate these three dispositions at the very least, and that surely is our goal. We hope that readers will grow in their theology as doxology, their submissive homage, and their responsiveness to God's revelation of himself.

EDITORIAL CONVICTIONS

Our pursuit of accomplishing such lofty goals is imperfect at best, but nonetheless, it is our best attempt at faithfully accomplishing such a holy aim. What will soon follow is a series of chapters working out from Scripture what various portions of the biblical text have to say about worship. Each chapter has organizational similarities while allowing for the voices of each author to tell their story from their study and their expertise. Authors were tasked to tell this story using the organizational tools of context, theology, and significance, and so each chapter is built around these three headings so as to situate the theology of worship in the context of the text so that application could faithfully follow. There is much more to say on each of these chapters—these surely will not be the final word on worship in their corresponding portions of Scripture—but we hope that readers will find them encouraging to their souls and useful in their teaching, preaching, and practice. This book is aimed at Christians who want to worship well, according to Scripture. It does not discuss stylistic or denominational approaches to worship. Instead it is a biblical-theological approach to the text to ask how the context of a passage bears on the theology and what this theology then leads to with regard to significance. It is our belief that this approach compels our worship in the right direction, and then allows for cultures and denominations to decide on its practice from an informed position.

If the story of biblical worship intends to include us in its composition, then we must turn to the text and ask how we might posture ourselves to worship well according to all that God has laid out. It is our hope that readers will situate themselves within this story and learn from it, so that we might join early with the heavenly hosts singing praises to the Lamb who sits on the throne (Rev. 5).

4. Allen P. Ross, *Recalling the Hope of Glory: Biblical Worship from the Garden to the New Creation* (Grand Rapids: Kregel Academic, 2006), 50.

WORSHIP
in the
OLD TESTAMENT

CHAPTER 1

WORSHIP: A CONCEPT STUDY IN BIBLICAL HEBREW

Peter Y. Lee

Worship is at the very heart of the Old Testament. There seems very little doubt about this assertion. To be in the presence of the Lord in his house of worship represented one of the highest expressions of the blessed life, if not *the* highest. The psalmist in Psalm 84:10 describes such contentment that comes from worship when he says, "For a day in your courts is better than a thousand elsewhere. I would rather be a door-keeper in the house of my God than dwell in the tents of wickedness."[1] A similar sense of bliss is mentioned in Psalm 27:4: "One thing have I asked of the LORD, that will I seek after: that I may dwell in the house of the LORD all the days of my life, to gaze upon the beauty of the LORD and to inquire in his temple." These two poetic declarations are samples of countless others in the pages of Scripture that state the genuine joy found in the true, godly worship of God (see Ps. 36:7–9; 47:1–12; Isa. 2:2–3; 44:28; Jer. 3:17–18; Mic. 4:1–3).

In many ways, the entire direction and flow of the history of Israel pivots on this aspect of worship. When Israel was properly worshiping the Lord, all was well. It is when they engaged in improper worship that their life began to collapse. The zeal that the Lord had for his own glory would not permit such impropriety in the worship life of his chosen people (see Exod. 20:3; Isa. 43:25; 48:9–11; 49:3; Ezek. 36:22–23; Ps. 106:7–8; Rom. 9:17). He revealed to them set standards on how worship is to be done, and he would not settle for anything less. Above all else, Israel's worship was required to be in accordance to his revealed Word.

1. In the MT, this is verse 11.

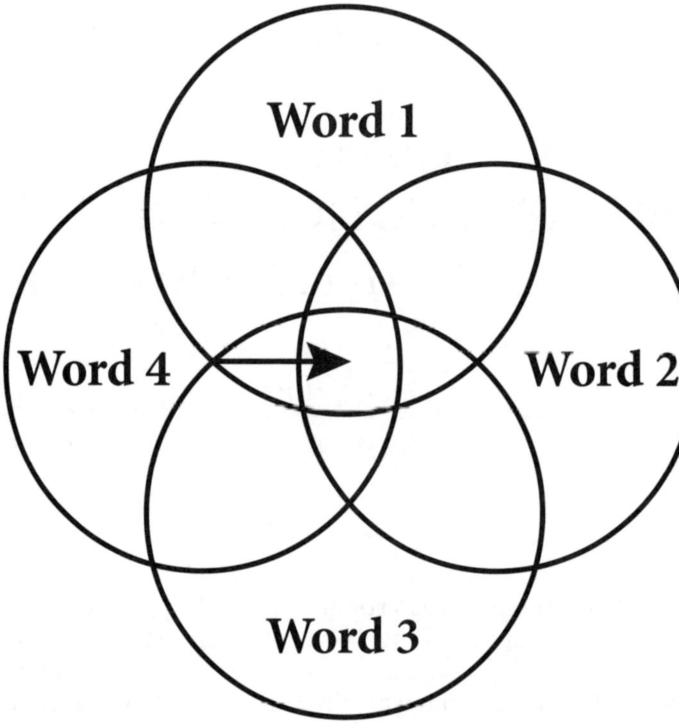

But what was that biblical standard of worship? The intent of this volume is to answer that very question. This opening chapter will introduce key concepts that make up a biblical understanding of worship by examining key words and translational methodologies in Biblical Hebrew. Although there is some semantic overlap, certain words in Biblical Hebrew provide a particular contribution to comprehending the Israelites' worship life. It is the combination of these words that clarifies the concept of worship in the Old Testament (see diagram). The investigation of these words will reveal what it meant for the people of the Old Testament to participate in proper worship of the Lord. Although such an approach cannot address every detail in the worship life of ancient Israel, it will nonetheless give a framework on which Israel engaged in their devotions to their Sovereign. From this study, we will see the following five principles clarified as we explore the semantic domains that make up a study of worship: (1) sacred journey, (2) sacred structures, (3) sacred practices, (4) sacred disposition, (5) and a sacred goal.

WORSHIP AS CONCEPT IN TRANSLATIONAL PRACTICE

Before our study begins, we begin with two brief comments on methodology. The first is regarding the choice of Hebrew words examined below. There are words in Biblical Hebrew that can be properly translated "worship."

However, there are a number of other words that cannot be translated as such yet are included in this study. The reason for this is because the concept of "worship" is broader than words that can be translated as "worship." If we were to narrow our research to only those few words that mean "worship," we would have an extremely limited and unhelpful picture of Israel's worship life. This is because the domain of words related to worship is larger than the singular usage of words expressly translated from Hebrew to English as "worship." This would mean such an approach would fail to include analysis or evaluation of the "fear of God" because these three words are not technically translated as "worship" when moving from Hebrew to English, even though the context and meaning of this phrase has great implications for worship, both in the time of the Israelites and today. Failing to study these related words, therefore, will hinder our final goal—which is to gain an accurate concept of worship in the Old Testament.

Second, the words under examination should not be taken as representing concepts. Rather, each word is part of an overall schematic (mosaic) that contributes to a general holistic understanding of worship. Each "word" provides an aspect of understanding worship. It is only when they are systematized that we are offered a "concept" of worship. This distinction has been the battle of lexicographers ever since the publication of James Barr's seminal work *The Semantics of Biblical Language*.[2] In it he criticized biblical theologians for "overload[ing] the word with meaning in order to relate it to the 'inner world of thought.'"[3] By "inner world of thought," Barr meant the mistaken way in which scholars did conceptual studies in the name of lexicography. His point is that this is not lexicography. The statement "God is love" captures a conceptual idea that cannot be inserted in every occurrence of the word "love" or "God." Such an approach obscures the meaning of a word in any given context. All of the words studied below have a wide range of meanings, one of which is related to worship. Thus it is the *meaning* associated with worship that is the focus of our interest. More than a vocabulary lesson, my goal is to gain a clearer understanding of the theme of worship by examining the use of these key words in the literary context of worship. Therefore, we will begin this study to see what lies beneath it to aid in understanding worship in biblical Hebrew.

Sacred Journey

Worship in biblical Israel required that Yahweh's followers journey to him. There is a connotation that requires their seeking him in the place where he would reveal himself.

The word *darash* has the general meaning "to seek." The nuance of the word is often effected by the context and the object of what is sought. In

2. James Barr, *The Semantics of Biblical Language* (Oxford: Oxford University Press, 1961).
3. Barr, *Semantics*, 246.

cases where the object being sought is God or objects and/or places associated with God, there is a sense in which the purpose of the seeking is for the sake of worship. Andrew Hill points out two examples where *darash* is even translated as "worship" in the RSV (Ezra 4:2; 6:21).[4] What this word tells us is that there are certain locations that the Lord himself designates as the only proper places for worship.

Perhaps the best example of this sacred use of *darash* is in Deuteronomy 12:5. The first four verses describe the Deuteronomic mandate placed on Israel to destroy the foreign pagan worship sites once they have settled in the land of Canaan. In addition to this, verse 5 states that the Lord will choose the place where he is to be worshiped. Israel is to "seek" this place. Regardless of which portion of the land they are allotted as their inheritance (Num. 32; Josh. 13–19), worship will be centralized at one place and the Israelites are to journey to this place for worship. The use of the verb *bo* (to enter), which immediately follows *darash*, confirms this expectation to travel to a particular location. This is also reinforced in verse 11, which is nearly identical to verse 5. Where the verb *darash* and *bo* are both used in verse 5, only the verb *bo* is used in verse 11. This suggests that the two different words communicate the same concept of a sacred place.

The word *darash* occurs prominently in 1 and 2 Chronicles with God as the direct object (1 Chron. 10:14; 13:3; 15:13; 16:11; 21:30; 2 Chron. 1:5; 7:14; 12:14). It frequently occurs in combination with the related verb *biqqesh*, which also means "to seek" (1 Chron. 16:10, 11; 2 Chron. 11:16; 15:15). Second Chronicles 7:14 is particularly helpful as it affirms that when the people of God suffered the consequences of their covenant violation (i.e., exile), there was still hope of restoration if they only "seek" the Lord with sincerity and humility. In fact, the Chronicler measures the success of the past Judean kings based on whether they "sought" the Lord (2 Chron. 14:4; 15:12) or not (2 Chron. 25:15, 20). The message to the postexilic community who received this book was clear: as difficulties arise in their task to rebuild the ancient cult center in Jerusalem, the Lord would bless those who "seek" him but reject those who do not.

Without a doubt, the notion of "seeking" this central place of worship is behind the rationale for the pilgrim festivals mentioned in Deuteronomy 16:1–17, where the three annual Feasts of Unleavened Bread, Weeks, and Booths are described. Verse 16 states explicitly the necessity of travel and even alludes to Deuteronomy 12: "Three times a year all your males shall appear before the LORD your God at the place that he will choose." Notice the reference to the "place that he will choose" is similar to Deuteronomy 12:5: "the place that the Lord your God will choose." Although the verb *darash* does not occur in chapter 17, the verb *bo* does, thus reinforcing the necessity to seek the Lord by "going" to this centralized site of worship.

4. Andrew E. Hill, *Enter His Courts with Praise: Old Testament Worship for the New Testament Church* (1993; repr., Grand Rapids: Baker, 1996), 2.

In contrast to this centralization of worship was the practice of the patriarchs. It was not uncommon for them to build altars at various locations where God performed a significant, redemptive act (Gen. 12:7, 8; 13:18; 22:9, 13; 26:25; 33:20; 35:1, 7). Since the patriarchs were sojourners (not residents) in the land of Canaan, they were not required to localize their place of worship. Once their children claimed that land as their covenantal inheritance, however, worship was no longer to be done at numerous locations. Instead, there would be one central place with one central altar that they must "seek."

This singular place of worship contrasted with the worship of Canaanite deities, which required numerous worship sites. Since Israel was strongly committed to monotheism (Deut. 6:4), this was paralleled with the one site of worship. This was the reason that Joshua panicked when the Transjordanian tribes of Reuben, Gad, and Manasseh built an altar at the frontier of the land of Canaan. It was only after they explained that this was a memorial, not a cultic center, that the remaining tribal groups held off any formal acts of judgment against them (Josh. 22:10–34).

This was also the reason that Jeroboam's act in 1 Kings 12:25–33 was abominable. In this passage, Jeroboam established not just one illegitimate worship site but two, one in Dan and the other in Bethel. He knew that in order to establish a new northern Israelite nation, his people could not continue to go to Jerusalem to offer worship at the central shrine, where their allegiance to him would be challenged. He needed to establish his own religious practice; thus he constructed the two false places of worship. It was due to this practice that the Lord condemned him and eventually rejected his kingship (1 Kings 13).

Thus in the word *darash* we read about the call to the ancient Israelites to "seek" their God by journeying to their central cult site, which would eventually be the temple of Solomon in the city of Jerusalem. Worship, therefore, could only be done in one proper place. Anywhere else would be a disgrace.

Sacred Structures

Worship was done at specially designated locations, in specific structures of worship. Prior to the establishment of the temple and thus the required pilgrimage described above, the lone structure of worship was the tabernacle. There were various Hebrew terms used for the tabernacle, each of which highlighted particular aspects of the structure. The most prominent section dedicated to the tabernacle is Exodus 25–31 and 35–40, which gives a detailed description of its architectural design and construction. The first term used in reference to the tabernacle was *miqdash* (see Exod. 25:8; cf. Lev. 16:33). There had been an increasing anticipation for this structure ever since the redemptive event in Exodus 14–15, where the Lord divided the waters of the Red Sea to provide a way of salvation for his people (Exod. 14). This colossal event was celebrated in song in Exodus 15, which praises the Lord as the Divine Warrior who freed his people so that they may worship him at the mountain of his inheritance in his "sanctuary" (*miqdash*, v.17). There was thus an expectation for this coming "sanctuary." It is fulfilled in Exodus 25:8 as the Lord builds this structure through the Israelites at Mount Sinai.

The root of this word is derived from *quiddesh*, which means "to be holy." Thus it seems that the holy character of God is accentuated by this term. Although the word *miqdash* occurs only in Exodus 25:8 within the tabernacle sections of chapters 25–31 and 35–40, the fact that this is the first word used in reference to the tabernacle gives the reader the primary understanding of its intrinsic character. Above all else, it is a *holy* structure. Its holy characteristic is further emphasized by the fact that the word *qodesh*, meaning "holiness," is frequently used instead of *miqdash* throughout the remainder of the construction sections (Exod. 30:13, 24; 36:1, 3, 4, 6; 38:24, 25, 26, 27). To add further emphasis, the heart of the tabernacle is called the "most Holy Place," literally "the holiness of the holinesses" (*qodesh haqqodashim*, Exod. 26:33, 34). If there were any doubts about its holy character, they were erased by the use of this word *qodesh* as a substitute for *miqdash*. The fact that both words are translated as "sanctuary" shows the interconnection between the two and the overarching holiness of this place.

The reason for the emphasis on this holy attribute of the "sanctuary" is due to the fact that the "holy" God (see Lev. 19:2; Isa. 6:3) is the one who dwells within it. This is confirmed in Exodus 40:35, which states the "glory of the Lord filled the tabernacle" at its completion. This awe-inspiring, holy presence of God is also what made Mount Sinai holy (Exod. 3:5) as well as the land of Canaan (Josh. 5:15) and the Israelites themselves (Exod. 12:16; 19:6). This is also the rationale as to why the Israelites were to live as holy people (Lev. 19:2).

The blessed reality is that this all-holy God does not remain distant and far off. Instead, he abides within the midst of his covenant people. This is what we read in Exodus 25:8. Immediately after Israel is instructed to build this *miqdash* "sanctuary," they are told for whom and why they are building it: "that I may dwell in their midst." The verb "I may dwell" is from the verb *shakan*, which means "to abide, settle down, dwell." It can be used in reference to the dwelling of people (see Num. 24:2; Deut. 33:20). When the subject is the Lord, it is much more significant since this holy God is no longer far off but is "in their midst." This notion of the Lord "dwelling" in the midst of the Israelite community is further underscored by the fact that the word *mishkan*, which is based on the root *shakan*, is constantly used (more common than *qodesh*) in reference to the tabernacle. It appears immediately in verse 9, then an additional fifty-seven times in Exodus 25–31 and 35–40.

The fact that *miqdash* is the first word to appear in reference to the tabernacle provides the proper understanding of the transcendent nature of God and this holy sanctuary. This is further emphasized by the repeated use of the word *qodesh*. The Lord, however, does not want to be distant from his covenant people, whom he had just liberated from centuries of enslavement under Egyptian taskmasters. He is nearby and "dwells [*shakan*] in their midst" (Exod. 25:8). The imminence of this holy God is then further highlighted by the overwhelming use of the word *mishkan*. Therefore, the interplay between these two words, *miqdash* and *mishkan*, in the book of Exodus reveals to the reader a blessed theological truth—the transcendent God is also imminent and in their midst.

In addition to the terms above, the tabernacle is also repeatedly referred as an *ohel moed*, "tent of meeting" (Exod. 33:7; cf. 27:21; 28:43). It occurs approximately 150 times in the Old Testament, with the highest concentration in the Pentateuch (i.e., Exodus, Leviticus, and Numbers). The reference to a "tent" (*ohel*) tells us that this structure was portable. It could be disassembled, transported, and rebuilt as needed (Exod. 40:34–38). The three sons of Levi (Kohath, Gershon, Merari) were assigned to care for and manage the various components of the tabernacle during their wilderness wanderings (Num. 4–5). By its very name, this tent was for a *moed*, "meeting" or "assembly." Given the proximity with his people, this would be the location where the Lord would meet with them through mediatorial intercessors (Lev. 8:3–4; Num. 2:17; 14:10; Josh. 18:1). The ritual function of this structure is evident from its close association with the Aaronic priesthood. They were the ones charged with its maintenance and care (Exod. 27:21; 30:16). This would also be the location where sacrifices would be offered to the Lord by the priests (Exod. 29:10–11, 42; Lev. 1:3, 5). It thus had a significant cultic purpose, which easily made this the most important sacred structure during the wilderness era of Israel's history.

The "assembly" may also anticipate a similar type of gathering that occurs later in the history of salvation. This is brought out when the *ohel moed* is compared to the similar phrase *har moed*, "mount of assembly," which occurs only in Isaiah 14:13. In that passage, the "mount of assembly" appears in apposition to the "heights of the north." According to Psalm 48:3, the "heights of the north" is the location of "Mount Zion," the "city of the great king," which is the ultimate location of the tabernacle in the temple of Solomon (1 Kings 8:4 = 2 Chron. 5:5).[5] In fact, there are certain places where only the word *moed*, "assembly," is used as a reference to the temple and the worship of God in the temple (Ps. 74:4; Lam. 2:6). Therefore, this supports the cultic and worshipful purpose of the "assembly" in the tabernacle. The fact that the word "assembly" can also be used in reference to the temple shows that there is an organic and linguistic connection between these two sacred structures.[6]

---

5. See C. C. Torrey, "Armageddon," *HTR* 31 (1938): 237–248. In this article, Torrey persuasively demonstrates that the illusive phrase "Armageddon" in Revelation 16:16 is derived from the Hebrew *har moed*.
6. For further details on the furnishings and theology of the tabernacle, see Richard E. Averbeck, "Tabernacle," in *Dictionary of the Old Testament: Pentateuch*, eds. T. Desmond Alexander and

When the Israelites settled in the land of Canaan, the tabernacle was no longer mobile. Instead, it was placed in particular locations for long (yet unspecified) durations of time. It began in Shiloh (Josh. 18:1; 19:51; 1 Sam. 2:22). For reasons not recorded within the historical books, the tabernacle ultimately made its way to Gibeon (2 Sam. 6:17; 1 Chron. 16:1), where it stayed until the temple of the Lord was constructed (1 Kings 8). During this time, Israelites were most likely required to "seek" out the Lord for worship at these specified locations (1 Sam. 3:3; 1 Kings 3:4). This was their practice until the construction of the temple in the city of Jerusalem. After that, the new centralized location of worship was permanently at this newly built cultic site.

Like the tabernacle, various different Hebrew terms are used in reference to the temple. One word in particular is *hekal*. This word was most likely a loanword from the Akkadian *ekallu*, which in turn was a loanword from the Sumerian *E.GAL* (meaning "great house"). The Akkadian and Sumerian words were used for the "palace" of monarchs and the "temple" of gods. Thus it is not surprising to find that the Hebrew *hekal* can have the same uses (for "palace," see 1 Kings 21:1; 2 Kings 20:18 = Isa. 38:17; 2 Chron. 36:7; Dan. 1:4). When it is used to mean a "temple," it is often in construct with the divine name YHWH, thus the *hekal of Yahweh* (see Isa. 6:1; 2 Kings 18:16; 2 Chron. 26:16; Jer. 7:4; Zech. 6:12–13). Given this semantic range, we must discern the use of the word *hekal* cautiously. It can refer to the temple as a place of sacrifice and worship (1 Kings 6:1, 17), but also as a divine "palace," which reflects the Lord as the monarch over Israel (Ps. 11:3; 18:7 = 2 Sam. 22:7; Mic. 1:2; Hab. 2:20; Zech. 6:12–13) and over all of creation.

This notion that the God whom Israel worships is also their divine Sovereign comes from 2 Samuel 7, where the Lord made a covenant of perpetual kingship with David and his sons. According to this passage, David reached a place of power and prominence in a united Israel. He felt that it was inappropriate that the Lord would remain in a meager abode when he was in a grander home (v. 2). For that reason, he wanted to build for the Lord a *bayit*, "house." The Lord responded by saying that David would not build for him a "house," but rather the Lord himself will build David a "house," meaning a "household" of royal monarchs. In turn, it would be one of these sons of David who would build a "house" for the Lord. We know from the history of Israel that Solomon was the Davidic son, who would build this "house" for the Lord (1 Kings 8). This wordplay with the Hebrew *bayit* became the basis for referring to the temple as "the house [*bayit*] of the Lord" (1 Kings 7:12, 40, 45, 51) or "the house [*bayit*] of God" (1 Chron. 9:11, 13, 26). Therefore, when Solomon completed the construction of this temple not only did this make the city of Jerusalem

David W. Baker (Downers Grove, IL: Intervarsity Press, 2003), 807–27. For further details on the archeological studies, see Richard E. Friedman, "Tabernacle," in *ABD* 6:292–300.

the new central location of all Israelite worship but it also became the theological center of the entire cosmos.

The Lord was the true heavenly king of Israel who was seated in his "house [*bayit*] of exaltedness" (1 Kings 8:13). He was also the thrice-holy God who was the center of Israel's worship (Isa. 6:3). Interestingly, the word *miqdash*, which was used in reference to the tabernacle, is also used in numerous occasions for the temple of the Lord (Ps. 74:7; 2 Chron. 20:8; 26:18; 29:21). Second Chronicles 36:17 even uses the phrase "house [*bayit*] of their sanctuary [*miqdash*]."

The most meaningful use of *miqdash* as a place of temple worship may be Psalm 73. The psalmist begins in a state of confusion as he wrestles with the prosperity of the wicked while he suffers in spite of his faithfulness to the Lord. He is unable to reconcile this logical incoherency, and as a result, he falls into a state of intellectual and emotional turmoil. It is only after he enters into the "sanctuary [*miqdash*] of God" that he is able to discern the truth of life. The wicked, who appeared to enjoy the materialism of the world, live in a state of instability, and are ultimately rejected by the Lord. The psalmist, on the other hand, comes to realize that the Lord was always with him and that "God is the strength of my heart and my portion forever" (Ps. 73:26). This is a valuable lesson, perhaps one that Israel also needed to be reminded of on a regular basis: the wicked do not escape the judgment of the king of the cosmos who sits enthroned on his "house." At the same time, Israel is freed to give their hearts in worship to the Lord, who is more precious than silver, gold, or even all the wisdom of this world.

Sacred Practices

I have established the concept of the sacred journey, where the Israelites were called to "seek" the Lord on a regular basis for worship. I have also described the sacred structures, where worship was done. The practice of worship in these sacred locations is the subject of the next section of this study. Although we have very little description of an actual service of worship in the Old Testament, several words give us a small glimpse into the practice of worship in these sacred places.

The Hebrew verb *hishtahawa* is the word most commonly translated as "worship." It was a long-held view that this verb was from the *hithpael* (reflexive) stem of the root *shahah*. Once the ancient texts from Ugarit were studied, the root *haway*, meaning "to prostrate oneself," was discovered. It did not take long for Hebraists to realize that this was the root behind *hishtahawa*.[7] This verb occurs more than 170 times in the Old Testament.

7. The general consensus now is that the verb is from an archaic infixed-t causative *saphel* stem of this root. As is often the case when the sibilant *sh* is adjacent to the prefixed *t*, the two consonants metathesize, thus *hishtahawa* as opposed to *hitshahawa*. It is not certain whether the ancient Hebrew writers were aware of the historical origins of this verb. The comments above

The basic meaning of this verb is "to prostrate oneself" or "to bow down." This gesture of prostration is not necessarily an act of worship. It can be a form of greeting of a stranger (Abraham before the three men in Gen. 18:2; Lot in 19:1; Moses to Jethro in Exod. 18:7), a gesture among family members (Jacob bows before Esau in Gen. 33:3; Joseph before Jacob in Gen. 48:12; Solomon to his mother Bathsheba in 1 Kings 2:19), submission before a person of stature and honor (Ruth before Boaz in Ruth 2:10), an act of respect (David before Jonathan in 1 Sam. 20:41), even begging (1 Sam. 28:14). It is a common act that is done before figures of royalty (David prostrates himself before Saul in 1 Sam. 24:9 [Eng. 8]); see also 2 Sam. 1:2; 9:6; 14:4, 22; 15:5; 16:4; 18:28; 1 Kings 1:23, 53; 2 Chron. 24:17). The expectation that inferiors bow down before high-ranking officials is seen in Esther 3:2, where all the king's servants bowed to Haman with the exception of Mordecai, who did not bow nor "pay homage" (*hishtahawa*) to him. This enraged Haman and led to his bloodlust against Mordecai. The most frequent use of this verb in the Old Testament, however, is as an act of worship before the Lord (1 Sam. 1:3; Ps. 29:2; 95:6; 96:9; 99:5, 9; 132:7; Jer. 7:2; Ezek. 46:9). It was strictly forbidden for Israel to "worship" (*hishtahawa*) other gods or idols, although their history records their constant violation of this mandate (Exod. 20:5; 23:34; 34:14; Lev. 26:1; Deut. 5:9). There are many times when worship is done by the actual gesture of bowing down (Josh. 5:14), while in other cases it refers to a general sense of worship (Gen. 26:24). In these cases, *hishtahawa* usually occurs with a verb meaning "to bow down" (*qadad*: Gen. 24:48; Exod. 4:31; 12:27; 2 Chron. 20:18; cf. Num. 22:31, where both mean "bow down"; *sagad*: Isa. 44:17; 46:6; *kara*: 2 Chron. 7:3; 29:29).

The Old Testament does not limit this act of worship to Israel alone. The prophets frequently depict the foreign nations also coming to the Lord to "worship" him and recognize his sovereign rule over all nations (Ps. 22:28, 30 [Eng. 27, 29]; 89:9; 96:9; Isa. 45:14; 49:7; Zeph. 2:11; Zech. 14:16). Even the angelic realm bows down before the Lord in worship (Ps. 29:2; 97:7). The use of this verb extends beyond the confines of earthly peoples to include even the angelic counsel. The vision of worship in the Old Testament is thus universal in its scope.

In addition to *hishtahawa*, another prominent word used to refer to the act of worship is the verb *abad*. The basic meaning of this word is "to make, do, serve." It is frequently used to mean working the ground (Gen. 2:15) or a general sense of service (Exod. 20:9; 21:6; Deut. 5:13; 15:12, 18). This is the verb used to describe the Israelite labors under the harsh conditions in Egypt (Exod. 1:13; 5:18). It is also commonly used in a cultic

---

follow a diachronic analysis. There is another possible approach, a synchronic one. Here, the verb could be reanalyzed as deriving from the *hithpael* stem from a rare quatra-literal root *sh-H-w-y*, meaning "to prostrate oneself." Depending on the perspective (synchronic or diachronic), either analysis is linguistically sound.

context, which is where the meaning "worship" is brought out. That this word is closely associated with *hishtahawa* is evidenced by the numerous times the two occur together in parallelism.[8]

Several specific uses of this verb *abad* as "worship" are noteworthy. Exodus 3:12 states that the reason why the Lord commissioned Moses to free the Israelites and to bring them to Sinai was so that they could "worship" (*abad*) him on his holy mountain. In fact, Moses stresses this point constantly to Pharaoh (Exod. 4:23; 8:1, 20: 9:1, 13; 10:3, 7, 24, 26). This act of *abad* is further described as an act of "sacrifice" (Exod. 3:18; 5:3), thus confirming its use as an act of worship. Consider, also, how this verb is used for observance of the Feast of Passover in Exodus 13:5: "you shall perform [*abad*] this service [*aboda*]." In addition to the verb *abad*, the noun form of the verb also occurs in this passage in reference to Passover: *aboda*, "this service." It is even used in reference to the sacrifices associated with the central altar at the temple (Isa. 19:21). Just as Israel was called not to "worship" (*hishtahawa*) idols and false gods (see above), so they were also called not to "worship, serve" (*abad*) them either (Exod. 23:33; Deut. 4:28; Josh. 23:7).

The verb *abad* can also be used to refer to the maintenance, upkeep, and transporting of the tabernacle. In this regard, the verb has a close association with the Levitical priests. Numbers 3:6–8 is helpful in this understanding as it says that the Levites were brought to Aaron to keep his duties and the duties of the assembly of Israel before the "tent of meeting" by "serving [*abad*] the service [*aboda*] of the tabernacle" (cf. Num. 16:9). The following chapters in Numbers proceed to describe in detail the specific duties of each of the three sons of Levi and their responsibilities regarding the packing and transporting of the tabernacle during their wilderness wanderings. The Levites had a similar task with the temple (Ezek. 44:11; 45:5; 46:24). In this sense, *abad* has a strong affinity with the verb *sheret* (*piel* only). The verb *sheret* generally means to serve as an assistant to a superior (Joshua to Moses in Exod. 24:13; Josh. 1:1; Elisha to Elijah in 1 Kings 19:21; Levites to Aaron in Num. 3:6; 13:2). It is also used similarly to *abad* in the context of the worship life of Israel, specifically in connection to the tabernacle (Num. 1:50; 3:31; 8:26; Deut. 18:7) and the temple (1 Kings 8:11).

Whereas the uses of *sheret* appear to be limited to the cultic institution of Israel, so *abad* seems to have a broader aspect that views life as a whole as a worship to the Lord. Deuteronomy 10:12–13 is outstanding in this regard as Israel is instructed to "walk in all his ways, to love him, to serve [*abad*] the LORD your God with all your heart and with all your soul, and to keep the commandments and statutes of the LORD, which I am commanding you today for your good." Joshua gives Israel the same charge in a covenant renewal ritual as they drew near to the conquest of the land of

8. Exod. 20:5; 23:34; Deut. 4:19; 5:9; 8:19; 11:16; 17:3; 29:25 (Eng. 26); 30:17; Josh. 23:7, 16; Judg. 2:19; 1 Kings 9:6, 9; 2 Kings 17:35; 21:3, 21; Jer. 8:2; 13:10; 16:11; 22:9; 25:6; 2 Chron. 7:19, 22; 33:3.

Canaan to possess their long-awaited homeland (Josh. 22:5). Notice the extent to which Israel is called to "serve" the Lord—"with all your heart and with all your soul," alluding to the great commandment of Deuteronomy 6:4. Concerning this comprehensive use of *abad*, David Peterson states, "Although cultic service to the living God is clearly involved, some contexts set this service within the broader framework of fearing him, walking in all his ways, and observing all his commands and decrees."[9]

Sacred Disposition

The reference to loving and serving "with all your heart and with all your soul" highlights that biblical worship cannot be limited to superficial acts of ritual practice. Such religious formalism was detestable to the Lord (Isa. 1:11–14). Whether Israel were to "bow down" (*hishtahawa*) before the Lord or "serve" (*abad*) him in their cultic life or general living, genuine worship must be done from the heart and soul. Thus, along with these sacred practices, a sacred disposition was needed within the heart and soul of Israel.

Deuteronomy 10:12 stresses how sincere devotion to the Lord comes from the inner core of Israel by stating that they are to "fear [*yare*] the Lord your God" as well as walk, love, serve, and obey him. Although the fear of the Lord is more associated with Wisdom Literature (e.g., Prov. 1:7), it is still an important part in true worship as it establishes the proper awe-inspired deference needed when coming before their covenant Lord (see Exod. 3:6). Later in Deuteronomy 10:16, the heart-centeredness of worship is further underscored when Moses states that Israel must circumcise their hearts. This stresses that outward circumcision is nothing unless it is accompanied with a genuine heart of devotion. Much later, Deuteronomy proclaims that what they cannot do on their own merit (circumcise the heart), the Lord will do for them as a blessing of the new covenant (Deut. 30:6, 14; Jer. 32:39; Ezek. 11:19; 36:26; Rom. 10:8) and thus give them the ability to do what they could not do prior—worship the Lord with all their heart.

Sacred Goal

Thus far I have discussed the *sacred journey* toward the *sacred structures* where the people of God would engage in *sacred practices* of worship with a *sacred disposition*. The final noteworthy comment is the goal. What is all this to accomplish?

It is not difficult to observe the sinfulness of Israel in the Old Testament. They were reminded of this on a daily basis and their need for a restored covenantal relationship with their God. The way to accomplish this was by implementing the various types of sacrifices as outlined in Leviticus 1–7. Although it is tempting to engage in a full discussion on

9. David Peterson, *Engaging with God: A Biblical Theology of Worship* (Downers Grove, IL: InterVarsity Press, 2002), 65–66.

the theology of the atonement in this extraordinary book, we must limit our thoughts specifically in answer to one question: What was the goal of the sacrifices?[10] This is an important question to answer with regard to worship since sacrifices were central to the worship experience for Israel.

There were five specific types of sacrifices implemented in ancient Israel. The burnt offering, *ola* (Lev. 1:3–17), and grain offering, *minha* (Lev. 2:1–16), were offered in total to the Lord and represented atonement for sin and "complete consecration to God."[11] The peace offering, *shelamim* (Lev. 3:1–17), where Israel partook of the sacrificial meal, represented the restored covenantal relationship between the Lord and his covenant people. The sin offering, *hattat* (Lev. 4:1–5:13), and guilt offering, *asham* (Lev. 5:14–6:7), dealt with the need to expiate the sins of Israel.

According to Peterson, the ordination of Aaron and his sons to the priesthood (Lev. 8) inaugurated the sacrificial system and established the pattern on which the sacrifices would be implemented "to make atonement" (from *kipper*, Lev. 1:4; 4:20; 5:6; 6:7) for the sins of the people (Lev. 9:7–21). The first sacrifice was a sin and guilt offering to deal with the issue of sin. This was followed by the burnt and grain offering as an act of consecration to the Lord.[12] With this new endowed state of ritual holiness, Israel reaches their spiritual apex in the peace offering. Peterson states, "The peace offering could symbolize the restoration of communion or fellowship with God and with others in the community of his people."[13] This interpretation is confirmed by the word used for "peace offering," *shelamim*, which is based on the word *shalom*, meaning "peace." In other words, the sacrificial system was intended to consecrate the people of God (i.e., make them holy) so that they could come before the presence of their holy God in order to engage in an intimate act of fellowship, the sharing of a meal.[14] This work of atonement is also the basis for why Israel was called to "declare his glory among the nations, his marvelous works among the peoples" (Ps. 96:3; cf. Ps. 57:9 = 108:3; 105:1).

CONCLUSION

Through the study of key words related to the worship life of ancient Israel, several prominent concepts arise. During their tenure in the land of Canaan, the Israelites were called to embark on a sacred journey three times a year (Exod. 23; Lev. 23) to "seek" the Lord to worship at his presence

10. For further reading in the book of Leviticus, see Jacob Milgrom, *Leviticus 1–16*, AB 3; *Leviticus 17–22*, AB 3a; *Leviticus 23–27*, AB 3b (New York: Doubleday, 1991–2001); and Nobuyoshi Kiuchi, *Leviticus*, AOTC (Downers Grove, IL: InterVarsity Press, 2007).
11. Peterson, *Engaging with God*, 39.
12. Cf. Leviticus 14:31 for the same order concerning uncleanness due to leprosy; 15:30 for uncleanness caused by bodily emissions.
13. Peterson, *Engaging with God*, 39.
14. For further support on the significance of this order in the sacrificial system, see Anson Rainey, "The Order of Sacrifices in Old Testament Ritual Texts," *Biblica* 51 (1970): 485–98.

within the sacred structure of his temple that he himself designed. Prior to this era of Canaanite settlement, such a journey was not necessary since the sacred structure of the tabernacle traveled with them during their long forty-year trek to their promised homeland. One could say, however, that the entire wilderness era was a journey to Canaan, where the Lord planned to establish "his name for his dwelling" (Deut. 12:5). Regardless, the names of these sacred places of worship express both the transcendence and imminence of the God of Israel.

Whether within a mobile tent or a permanent temple, Israel was called to "bow down" in worship before their God. The Levites were especially called on to "serve" the tabernacle/temple. In a general sense, such a call was placed upon every Israelite to live a life of "service" to the Lord with all their heart and soul. Within these sacred structures, the most significant act of worship was done—namely, the sacrificing of animals/grain. This system was the means by which the people were made holy so that they could draw near to their holy God in peace. Such peace is only a glimpse, however, of the true "peace with God" that comes only "through our Lord Jesus Christ" (Rom. 5:1).

BIBLIOGRAPHY

Averbeck, Richard E. "Tabernacle." In *Dictionary of the Old Testament: Pentateuch*, edited by T. Desmond Alexander and David W. Baker, 807–27. Downers Grove, IL: InterVarsity Press, 2003.

Barr, James. *The Semantics of Biblical Language*. Oxford: Oxford University Press, 1961.

Friedman, Richard E. "Tabernacle." In *ABD* 6:292–300.

Hill, Andrew E. *Enter His Courts with Praise: Old Testament Worship for the New Testament Church*. 1993. Reprint, Grand Rapids: Baker, 1996.

Kiuchi, Nobuyoshi. *Leviticus*. AOTC. Downers Grove, IL: InterVarsity Press, 2007.

Milgrom, Jacob. *Leviticus 1–16*. AB 3. New York: Doubleday, 1991.

______. *Leviticus 17–22*. AB 3a. New York: Doubleday, 2000.

______. *Leviticus 23–27*. AB 3b. New York: Doubleday, 2001.

Peterson, David. *Engaging with God: A Biblical Theology of Worship*. Downers Grove, IL: InterVarsity Press, 2002.

Rainey, Anson. "The Order of Sacrifices in Old Testament Ritual Texts." *Bib* 51 (1970): 484–98.

Torrey, C. C. "Armageddon." *HTR* 31 (1938): 237–48.

CHAPTER 2

ROYAL PRIESTS CREATED TO WORSHIP

Worship in the Garden . . . and Beyond

William R. Osborne

"The assumption that God exists is the Old Testament's greatest gift to mankind."

CONTEXT OF WORSHIP IN CREATION

In the beginning, God existed. However, he not only existed but also spoke. He created, calling forth reality in holy utterances that forever linked the divine word to the world that it produced. The first chapter of Genesis records God's mighty voice commanding the universe, along with its prompt obedience. Waters divide, mountains explode from the seas, the swarming things swarm, the growing things bloom, and God says that it is all *good*! In response to the "formless and empty" (*tohu wabohu*) state of the world (Gen. 1:2), the chapter demonstrates God's work in forming what was formless and filling what was empty, with climactic emphasis being placed on the creation of humanity—his image bearers.[1]

1. *Epigraph*. Ludwig Köhler, *Old Testament Theology*, trans. A. S. Todd (London: Lutterworth, 1957; repr. Cambridge: James Clarke, 2002), 19.

While the narrative clearly moves the reader toward the holy and blessed seventh day, McConville notes that the structure of the seven-day account is not completely symmetrical: "The sixth day of creation is substantially longer than those of the other days. In narrative terms, the story slows down and becomes expansive. . . . There is a particular focus on the subject matter of the sixth day, on which God creates humans" (J. Gordon McConville, *Being Human in God's Image: An Old Testament Theology of Humanity* [Grand Rapids: Baker

The reader is introduced to this pinnacle of creation on day six in Genesis 1:26, when God declares, "Let us make humanity in our image, according to our likeness." The verses that follow help provide a clearer description, albeit a brief one, of what it means to be made in God's image. The Lord first commissions his creatures to rule as his vice regents over all creation (v. 26) and then blesses them to multiply and fill the earth in verse 28. The universal scope of chapter 1 presents humanity through the functional lens of dominion—both categorically and numerically. Humanity's rule was to reflect the character of the Creator.

While the text does not explicitly speak to a relational aspect of the *imago Dei* (image of God) in chapter 1, many have noted that the language of "image" and "likeness" encountered in Genesis denotes a unique status and is not unusual in its broader ancient Near Eastern context. Robin Routledge writes, "This idea is reflected elsewhere in the ANE, where the expression 'the image of god' might be applied to kings, as the earthly representatives of the deity. God has created human beings with the authority and responsibility to rule over his world on his behalf."[2] However, the relationship extends outward because as God relates to his image bearers, his image bearers are to relate to all creation as his representatives. The *imago Dei* simultaneously speaks to substantive, functional, relational, and representative realities that are unique to men and women in God's created order.

Genesis 1, while failing to satisfy many of our modern scientific queries,[3] reveals several undeniable theological truths about our Creator and his creation. First, all that exists finds its source in God (cf. John 1:3). God is the only necessary being that exists; all else is fundamentally contingent on his existence. Unlike many comparable ancient texts, the Hebrew Scriptures offer no origin story for God (called a theogony). Second, as the Creator and Sustainer of creation, God is sovereign over its boundaries and aims, including humanity (cf. Acts 17:24–27). Human beings exist because God does, and therefore all anthropologies are necessarily theological anthropologies. We can only understand what it means to be human in that we understand how we were created to reflect the image of our Creator. Third, Genesis 1 reveals that these two—God and his image bearers—were designed to live in relationship with one another. God did not create the world to only observe it as a cosmic spectator. Fourth, God infused the cosmos with his character not only through creating humans

Academic, 2016], 13). So also Gordon J. Wenham, *Genesis 1–15*, WBC 1 (Waco, TX: Word, 1987), 38.

2. Robin Routledge, *Old Testament Theology: A Thematic Approach* (Nottingham, UK: Apollos, 2013), 140.
3. To say that Genesis 1 is a premodern text written about the creation of the world is not to say that it is false, mythical, or inadequate. The simple fact is that Genesis was not written to answer modern scientific questions, and many of the debates swirling around Genesis 1–3 are probing an ancient text with modern questions. I believe the best way to begin any reading of the creation account is to first read it on its own terms and in its own context, historically, literarily, and theologically.

in his image but also through blessing and sanctifying time—namely, the seventh day. This act of commemoration is woven throughout Israel's story as God's Sabbath, by which "God and his creatures share in the celebration of his good creation, and God's people are enjoined to enter into the rhythm of work and joyful rest."[4]

The early chapters of Genesis are foundational to the Christian faith. Like a ramp launching a stunt rider through the air, these early chapters establish the trajectory we follow through the rest of the biblical narrative. Allen Ross aptly notes the connection between the creation account and Christian worship: "The first two chapters of the Bible provide an unparalleled revelation of the LORD, who is the majestic and sovereign God of creation. This revelation is not only foundational to the faith but is also essential for worship: The LORD God alone must be worshipped because he is sovereign over all things—he was before all things, and by him all things exist."[5] As people living in a world shaped and distorted by sin, a regular revisiting of the created design for worship revealed in the Eden narrative is beneficial, if not necessary. Turning our attention to worship in the garden of Eden, we can observe characteristics of worship established between God and man in this primeval time that reverberate throughout the Scriptures and the rest of human history.

THEOLOGY OF WORSHIP IN THE GARDEN

Worship is always carried out as a creaturely response to the divine initiative of the sovereign Creator. Worship exists because God exists and he created people for his glory. Ultimately, we only come to know God's initial will for his people through the opening chapters of Genesis, and it is to these chapters that we now turn. Careful study of the garden narrative in Genesis 2 reveals three important theological themes that can guide our reflection on how this pre-fallen state of being sets a trajectory for humanity's relationship with God. As creatures made in his image, we come to know and worship God relationally (creation and relation), within a certain location (creation and location), and finally with a purpose or telos (creation and vocation). These themes then serve as a foundation for the significance of biblical worship as humanity moves beyond the garden and into the *world.*

Creation and Relation

The garden narrative begins in Genesis 2:4 with an important narrative formula: "these are the generations . . ." (*eleh toledot*) encountered in ten other locations in Genesis (5:1; 6:9; 10:1; 11:10, 27; 25:12, 19; 36:1, 9; 37:2). The *toledot* formulas serve as a significant literary feature shaping

4. Kenneth A. Mathews, *Genesis 1–11:26*, NAC 1A (Nashville: Broadman & Holman, 1996), 179.
5. Allen P. Ross, *Recalling the Hope of Glory: Biblical Worship from the Garden to the New Creation* (Grand Rapids: Kregel Academic, 2006), 78.

the structure of the book, and the reference in 2:4 provides a formulaic introduction to the garden narrative in chapter 2.[6] However, with the narrative break in chapter 1, the reader need not be confused as to whether this is a separate creation account. Nahum Sarna notes, "Chapter 2 is not another creation story. As such it would be singularly incomplete. In fact, it presupposes a knowledge of much of the preceding account of Creation. Many of the leading ideas in the earlier account are here reiterated, though the mode of presentation is different. Thus, in both narratives God is the sovereign Creator, and the world is the purposeful product of His will."[7]

The account after 2:4 focuses the reader's attention on the events described in day six of the previous chapter, highlighting the terrestrial nature of humanity and showing how those events relate to the following account of human origins.[8] Verse 5 explains that we were made *for* the earth ("and there was no man to work the ground"), while verse 7 reveals we were made *from* it ("then the LORD God formed the man from the dust of the ground"). His making of the man and the woman seems to be a deliberate act of God drawing near and engaging with his good world. Humanity was made for the world but also made for God.

The man is described as a "living creature" because God breathed the "breath of life" into the man he formed. If Genesis 1 depicts the Creator as the majestic, reality-speaking, universe-making God, then chapter 2 demonstrates that such power does not necessitate distance (a stark contrast from religious notions of the ancient world). With intimacy and care, God forms the man by breathing into his nostrils his life-giving breath. This same concern and precision characterizes the creation of woman also, as God takes a rib from the man and creates Eve to be a suitable partner and helper for Adam. Genesis 1:26–28 describes both male and female as being made in God's image, and the picture of intimacy and closeness is further illustrated in the narrative of chapter 2. The essence of humanity is not found in autonomy, but in right relation to our Creator.

Creation and Location

After describing the creation of humanity, the narrative turns to describe a garden planted by the Lord God in Eden.[9] While frequently referred to as "the garden of Eden," leading many listeners to assume that Eden and the garden are one and the same, the text describes the setting as "a garden *in* Eden." Genesis 2:8 tells us that "the LORD God planted" this garden,

6. See Sarah Schwartz, "Narrative *Toledot* Formulae in Genesis: The Case of Heaven and Earth, Noah, and Isaac," *JHebS* 16 (2016): DOI:10.5508/jhs.2016.v16.a8.
7. Nahum M. Sarna, *Genesis*, JPS Torah Commentary (Philadelphia: JPS, 1989), 16.
8. Mathews, *Genesis 1:1–11:26*, 191.
9. Generally, no attempt is made by scholars at arriving at a historic location of the actual garden. The reference to the "east" has prompted some to offer conjectures about locations in Mesopotamia. However, the prominent mountain-garden theme in the ancient Near East and OT makes precision an impossibility.

thereby setting up and establishing its design, inhabitants, and boundaries (both geographical and moral). In a special act of creation, God creates a place for his creatures to dwell and flourish in his good world.

Trees both beautiful and fruitful sprung up from the ground, including the enigmatic tree of life and tree of the knowledge of good and evil. The description of the vegetation in the garden is life-giving and sustaining compared to the "thorns and thistles" outside the garden that would wage war against the man in his post-fallen state.[10] Verse 10 describes a river that flowed out of Eden, seeming to divide into four large branches once it nourished the garden. One thing is clear: the Lord God is a gardening God.

At first glance, as a modern interpreter, the mention of God planting a garden might simply seem like a quirky divine hobby. However, when compared with the literature and imagery of the ancient Near East, the planting of a garden is highly significant.[11] From Babylon to Ugarit, myths associating various deities with garden dwellings encircled the ancient world.[12] Analyzing several divine-garden texts in the ancient Near East, Howard Wallace provides the following important similarities to the Eden narrative in Genesis 2, such as (1) unmediated presence of the deity; (2) the issuing of divine decrees; (3) the source of subterranean, life-giving water; abundant fertility; and (4) trees of supernatural qualities and beauty.[13]

Gardens also played a significant role in and around ancient temples and royal palaces.[14] Ancient Mesopotamian kings frequently gave reports of the luxurious and expansive nature of their royal gardens. Sennacherib's annals read:

> By divine will, vines, all kinds of fruit trees, olive trees, and aromatic trees flourished greatly in (those) gardens. . . . I created a marsh to moderate the flow of water for (those) gardens and had a canebrake planted (in it).[15]

The annals go on to describe the abundance of wildlife that flourished in the royal park in a way that is not dissimilar to the portrait painted in the biblical narrative. Frequently, royal building projects would also include the construction and consecration of temples, temple gardens, and palaces. The garden was a mini-cosmos established by the king for the deity

10. Howard N. Wallace, *The Eden Narrative*, HSM 32 (Atlanta: Scholars Press, 1985), 70–71.
11. Reading the Eden narrative alongside the traditions of the ancient Near East is not intended to diminish the historical veracity of the account, but to wrestle with the significance of the text for its original ancient audience.
12. Wallace, *Eden Narrative*, 70–89.
13. Howard N. Wallace, "Garden of God," in *ABD* 2:907.
14. See William R. Osborne, *Trees and Kings: A Comparative Analysis of Tree Imagery in Israel's Prophetic Tradition and the Ancient Near East*, BBRSup 18 (University Park, PA: Eisenbrauns, 2018), 31–75.
15. A. Kirk Grayson and Jamie Novotny, *The Royal Inscriptions of Sennacherib, King of Assyria (704–681 BC), Part 1*, RINAP 3/1 (Winona Lake, IN: Eisenbrauns, 2012), 51–52.

that represented world order and creative power (cf. Eccl. 2:1–11). The opulence and beauty of the garden served as the backdrop for divine-human interactions transpiring between deity and king,[16] and as noted earlier, kings were also described as being the "image" of the deity on earth, or the offspring of a deity. Adam and Eve were commissioned in Genesis 1:28 to serve as YHWH's royal vice regents, exercising his cosmic agenda in his royal garden as his image bearers. And later on in chapter 2, Adam exercises his creative dominion by naming all other living things.

The garden in Eden was not simply green space; it was sacred space. It was the place established by God for his interactions with humanity. This notion of sacred space resurfaces throughout the book of Genesis as we see God call the leaders of a new nation to a new land. In Genesis 12:7–8 we read, "Then the LORD appeared to Abram. . . . So he [Abram] built there an altar to the LORD, who had appeared to him."[17] The altar marked out a location where God had made himself known to his people, and it also commemorated the event that took place at this location (cf. Gen. 35:7). However, this activity indicated more than the patriarch's penchant for construction projects. As Richard Hess notes, "Noah, Abram, and the successive leaders of his family built altars, made sacrifices, and functioned in the role of priests."[18] These pockets of sacred space, initiated by God in theophanies and commemorated by men with altars, created new opportunities for the leaders of God's people to call on the name of YHWH, intercede for their families, and worship the living and active God.

As Abram's little family grew into a great nation, the trappings of Israel's sacred space would change from tabernacle to temple. However, images of the garden continue to reappear. Gordon Wenham has pointed out the archetypal nature of the garden for later institutions of Israel's worship noting the following: (1) God walked in the garden (Gen. 3:8: cf. Lev. 26:12; Deut. 23:15; 2 Sam 7:6–7); (2) cherubim were present east of the garden and in the tabernacle and temple with the entrance being from the east (1 Kings 6:23–28; Exod. 26:31); (3) the tabernacle menorah was possibly a stylized

16. D. J. Wiseman, "Palace and Temple Gardens in the Ancient Near East," in *Monarchies and Socio-religious Traditions in the Ancient Near East*, ed. T. Mikasa, Bulletin of the Middle East Center in Japan 1 (Wiesbaden: Harrossowitz, 1984), 37–43.

17. The first record of YHWH-directed worship through altar worship is in Genesis 8:20, when we are told that Noah built an altar after the flood and worshiped YHWH. Other accounts of altar building in Genesis include 13:18; 22:9; 26:25; 33:20; 35:1, 5. It is quite interesting that these first altars built by Abram were in close proximity to noteworthy trees: the oak of Moreh (12:8) and the oaks of Mamre (13:18). The first is located near Shechem, where we are told resided a large stand of trees that is later mentioned in Genesis 35:4, when Jacob buries idols there, and it seems to be the tree that stood "in the sanctuary of YHWH" where the stone was erected in Joshua 24:26 (see Roland de Vaux, *Ancient Israel: Its Life and Institutions* [New York: McGraw-Hill, 1961], 279). It is possible that these divine encounters at sacred sites associated with trees are theological and cultural echoes ringing out of humanity's beginnings with God in a garden.

18. Richard S. Hess, *Israelite Religions: An Archaeological and Biblical Survey* (Grand Rapids: Baker Academic, 2007), 193.

image of the tree of life; (4) the description of the man's job in the garden to "work and keep it" is the same as the priest's job description (see Num. 3:7–8; 8:26; 18:5–6); (5) the river watering the garden is comparable to the river in Ezekiel's temple vision in Ezekiel 47; and (6) the sacred items and decorations of the tabernacle and temple are prefigured.[19] These intentional reappearances of the garden imagery in Israel's priestly traditions warrant our thinking of the garden less as a paradisiacal botanical reserve to more of a temple-garden. The garden was not simply an ancient arboretum for human flourishing; it was the dwelling place of God with man. And in this garden we see God's plans for his creatures and the world.

Creation and Vocation

Human beings have been striving for millennia to unlock the meaning of life, from the ancient epics of man versus the gods to Douglas Adams's much less compelling "42" in *The Hitchhiker's Guide to the Galaxy*. Most long to know their purposes in this world, and the garden narrative suggests that mankind's purpose is actually a calling—a glorious, priestly, co-reigning calling. Genesis 2:15 says that after God completed his garden project he "took the man and placed him in the garden to work it and watch over it."[20] This was the man's vocation, or calling, placed on him by his Creator. As highlighted by Wenham, the verbs describing the man's duties in the garden are not insignificant. The verbs *abad* (to work) and *shamar* (to guard) are found together describing the work of the priests in the tabernacle in the book of Numbers. T. D. Alexander writes, "Because they met God face to face in a Holy Place, we may assume that Adam and Eve had a holy or priestly status. Only priests were permitted to serve within the sanctuary or temple."[21] As priestly workers in the temple-garden, the man and woman were to serve the garden and its resident Sovereign by watching over it and cultivating it. Combining the priestly orientation of the temple-garden with the royal description of the *imago Dei* in 1:26–28, a visage of humanity emerges from Genesis 1 and 2 as royal priests commissioned to create, subdue, cultivate, and worship.

SIGNIFICANCE OF THE GARDEN FOR BIBLICAL WORSHIP

Worship Is Personal

Stating that worship is personal does not mean that it is purely private. The driving force of the creation narrative in Genesis 1 and 2 is that, as cre-

19. Gordon J. Wenham, "Sanctuary Symbolism in the Garden of Eden Story," in *Proceedings of the Ninth World Congress of Jewish Studies, Division A: The Period of the Bible* (Jerusalem: World Union of Jewish Studies, 1986), 19–25. See also T. Desmond Alexander, *From Eden to the New Jerusalem: An Introduction to Biblical Theology* (Grand Rapids: Kregel Academic, 2008), 20–31.
20. Author's translation.
21. Alexander, *From Eden to New Jerusalem*, 25.

ated beings, our relationship to the sovereign Lord of the universe is not merely a matter of personal preference! We live in a culture that frequently divides the subjective and objective along the lines of what is considered private and public. Seemingly objective areas like math and science can be discussed in the public arena, but religion or worship is considered a "personal matter" and should not be permitted public or corporate discussion.

Through God's self-revelation in the Scriptures we come to know a person—more specifically three persons with one essence. As God breathes the breath of life into the lungs of his image bearers, he endows them with the necessary abilities to live in relationship to himself. God is not an otherworldly "it" to be studied or examined. He is not another created entity to be explored and subdued.

There is only one being in existence worthy of our worship. When we allow any other thing in existence to sit on the throne of our hearts, we immediately align ourselves with Paul's dismal assessment of humanity in Romans 1:25: "they exchanged the truth about God for a lie and worshiped and served the creature rather than the Creator, who is blessed forever! Amen."

As a personal God, he is known and loved in much the same way we come to know and love another person. He is knowable to his creatures because he reveals himself to them. In a self-motivated act of disclosure, the Creator creates and initiates the relationship with his creatures. The man and the woman come to know God truly, and they can only respond to him rightly so long as they know him truly. We generally do not love—much less worship—things or persons we do not know. The relational and personal nature of the covenant-making God of creation grounds worship in the epistemological as much as the existential. Indeed, our experiences in relation to other persons are often shaped and formed by what we know about them (or perceive to know about them). And what we know about God comes through his revelation of himself through creation, Holy Writ, and—ultimately—the incarnation.

Worship Is Active

While the garden narrative in Genesis is certainly less than comprehensive, the role of humanity in response to God was intended to be one of activity. They were to *do* things—have children, exercise dominion, cultivate a temple-garden, and obey. Peter Leithart writes, "*Worship is an act not an attitude*. The vocabulary of worship in the Bible emphasizes this, for the biblical words are all active, with literal meanings like 'bow down' and 'serve.'"[22] In a culture in which we often associate worship with a passive "being present" in a worship service where we often spend the majority of our time looking at a person or a screen, the active nature of worship is an important corrective. Leithart helpfully connects the active nature of

22. Peter J. Leithart, "Transforming Worship," *Foundations* 38 (1997): 28.

our worship to our creaturely status: "God made us as physical beings and that, the Lord himself declared, is a good thing. It is so good for us to have bodies that we will have bodies forever. There is no biblical reason whatsoever for being ashamed of having a body, for thinking that our bodiliness is somehow a detriment to communion with God, or for feeling that, to be close to God, we have to shed our bodies or at least pretend they are not there. Less bodily worship is not more pleasing to God than more bodily worship and Paul says that our true spiritual worship involves offering our bodies."[23] Ultimately, the downfall of our first parents played out in an improper action. While there were obvious intellectual and emotive precursors to the act of taking the fruit, the ultimate judgment was reserved for the completed deed, not the temptation. Worship is not simply a feeling experienced during a song, nor is it double-mindedly believing the right things about God while ignoring his revealed Word (see James 1:8, 22–25). Spiritual worship is not spiritual because it carries us away from this world, but because the Holy Spirit is breaking into this present world and transforming the created minds, wills, affections, and actions of those united with Christ by faith.

Worship Is Comprehensive

The active nature of worship means not only that our worship should be active but also that all of our activities should be worshipful. When God placed man in the garden to care for it, this was his God-given vocation—that is, his job. The man was created for a purpose, and when he lived that purpose out faithfully as YHWH's royal priest in his temple-garden, everything he did was act of worship. Despite many of our Monday-morning sentiments, work is not an unintended product of human rebellion against God; it is a part of God's good design for the world. In a pre-fall world, caring for plants, naming animals, and even the sexual relationship between Adam and Eve were worshipful acts of obedience to mankind's image-bearing vocation. Not only are we to be active within the compartments of worship we have instituted in our lives and cultures; we must allow the comprehensive nature of our relationship with the Creator to affect all of our activities (see 1 Cor. 10:31).[24]

For many in our complex modern society it is difficult to recognize the worshipful aspects of our various occupations. Sometimes this is because we fail to see the connection between our jobs—which we do to make money to live—and our God-given calling as image bearers in God's good world. While there are some ways that people can make money that are deeply immoral and feed on the brokenness of humanity, many people

23. Leithart, "Transforming Worship," 29.
24. See James M. Todd III, "Edenic Endeavors: Sacred Service in the Garden of Eden," *Faithful Lives: Christian Reflections on the World—Faithful Work* 1 (2016): 11–20, http://images.cofo.edu/cofo/about/FaithfulLivesFaithfulWork.pdf.

make a living in various kinds of service industries, providing goods and services for those willing and able to offer payment. Even the burgeoning technological field creatively offers novel ways of rearranging, reordering, and ultimately subduing (i.e., making more convenient) aspects of the created world. When we are engaged in these image-bearing activities of creating, reordering, and subduing, the question of worship arises not so much from the nature of the task but the motivations and orientation of the heart. When we create things (like stringing words together in a chapter), for whom are we working? When we interject new order into the world, to whose standard are we seeking to conform? As Christians, we can indeed offer up every area of our lives as worship when we recognize our image-bearing role as royal priests employed as ambassadors for God's reconciliation program (2 Cor. 18–20).

Worship Is Responsive

There is no greater scene of divine initiative than creation, and worship is fundamentally the proper anthropological response to theological disclosure. All that Adam and Eve are to do is in direct response to the immediate revelation of the divine "Thou." In fact, God's activity in creation provoked Israel's psalmists to worship over and over again, with Psalm 33 being one example:

> By the word of the Lord the heavens were made,
> and by the breath of his mouth all their host.
> He gathers the waters of the sea as a heap;
> he puts the deeps in storehouses.
> Let all the earth fear the Lord;
> let all the inhabitants of the world stand in awe of him!
> For he spoke, and it came to be;
> he commanded, and it stood firm.
> (Ps. 33:6–9)

In these verses the responsive nature of worship emerges. All of the earth should fear God and be in awe of him because "he spoke, and it came to be; he commanded and it stood firm." The very act of creation and the majesty revealed therein should prompt universal worship. However, the previous verse shows not only that such worship is grounded in God's raw power revealed in creation but also the value and character of his work:

> For the word of the Lord is upright,
> and all his work is done in faithfulness.
> He loves righteousness and justice;
> the earth is full of the steadfast love of the Lord.
> (Ps. 33:5)

Creation reveals both God's greatness and his goodness, and both should lead us to respond rightly with worship as his creatures.

Worship Is in God's Presence

In the garden, God spoke directly with the man and woman with no need for mediation. Humanity was created for direct access to the presence of God, and it was only because of the rebellion of our first parents that such access would be severed. The garden was designed as God's dwelling place with humanity, and the presence of God remains a central theme throughout the rest of the Bible. From theophanies in the desert to smoke filling the temple, Israel's worship orbited around manifestations of YHWH's presence. God delivered his covenant people out of Egypt in order to bring them to himself (Exod. 19:4), and Moses would not depart from Mt. Sinai without the presence of the Lord: "If your presence will not go with me, do not bring us up from here. For how shall it be known that I have found favor in your sight, I and your people? Is it not in your going with us, so that we are distinct, I and your people, from every other people on the face of the earth?" (Exod. 33:15–16). God's presence resided in the Holy of Holies in the center of Israel's camp when all the tribes of Israel traveled through the wilderness (Num. 1:47–2:2). Centuries later in Israel's history the presence of YHWH would fill Solomon's temple (1 Kings 8:11), only to depart it on the brink of Babylonian destruction due to the wickedness of the people (Ezek. 1:4–28; 8:1–10:22). Just like the eastward exit from Eden (Gen. 3:24), God's glory would depart eastward from the temple (Ezek. 10:18–19) and his people would depart to the east of his holy city to the city of Babylon.[25]

While prophets like Ezekiel and Isaiah hold out hope for a future time when God will dwell once again with his people (see Ezek. 48:35; Isa. 65:17–25), it is not until the incarnation of Christ that we see God once again dwelling so closely among his image bearers. The gospel of John describes this as the preexistent Word taking on human flesh and dwelling (i.e., "tabernacling") among humanity so that they can see his glory, full of grace and truth (1:14). The divine presence of the garden, Old Testament tabernacle, and temple is now a man walking around Galilee.

For this reason, Jesus denounces the legitimacy of the temple as the central feature of worship for God's people (Mark 13; John 2:18–22; 4:20–26), and instead presents himself as the way to proper worship of the Father (John 5:19–24). In the Old Testament Scriptures worship was inseparably tied to the tragic reality of Adam and Eve's rebellion and sin,

25. Werner Berg identifies the garden of Eden a prototype (*Urbild*) for the land of Canaan. However, the theological significance of the garden in later Israelite perspective does not necessitate the garden story as a later etiological invention. See Werner Berg, "Israels Land, der Garten Gottes: Der Garten als Bild des Heiles im Alten Testament," in *Das Kleid der Erde: Pflanzen in der Lebenswelt des Alten Israel*, eds. Ute Neumann-Gorsolke and Peter Riede (Stuttgart: Calwer, 2002), 75–76.

and in the New Testament Scriptures worship is inseparably linked to the redemptive cross-work of the second Adam (see Rom. 5:12–17).

While Christians presently worship separated from the bodily presence of the resurrected Christ, the apostle Paul instructs us that we have received the firstfruits of our eternal inheritance—the Spirit of Christ (Rom. 8:9–25). And this abiding Spirit is building the people of God into a living temple, built on the cornerstone of Christ, the foundation of the prophets and apostles, so that God may dwell once again with his people (Eph. 2:19–22). The church worships now as the already/not-yet kingdom citizens who live under the reign of God yet are separated from their true homeland. Because of Jesus Christ—the second Adam—God's people will one day dwell in his presence, worshiping their Maker forever.

WORSHIP IN THE FUTURE GARDEN

The divine-human relationship described in Genesis 1–2 is paradigmatic for all of Israel's encounters with her God in the Old Testament. The notion of God as sovereign Creator who formed a people for himself to dwell with him in a sacred space undergirds the entire Old Testament.[26] However, this theological thread extends across the canon, culminating in the ministry, death, and resurrection of Jesus Christ. The work of Christ forever changed the way God's people would dwell in his presence. The idyllic worship of the first garden finds its ultimate fulfillment and embodiment in a future garden-city described in Revelation 22.

In the final chapter of John's vision, the apostle is taken to a garden and a river flowing through the new Jerusalem and issuing forth from the throne of God and of the Lamb (22:1). The tree of life once again appears, though interestingly there seem to be multiple trees with one on each side of the river. The throne is not located in a temple, but is simply found in the city because there is no need for a temple when the glory of the Lord fills the streets. Similar to the man's original commission in the garden of Eden, John records that the servants of the Lord will worship him before his throne, seeing him face-to-face (vv. 3–4). As Ross states, "What is 'new' about all of this is the reality of the presence of God with people. The waiting will finally be over, the alienation and separation ended."[27]

The word translated "worship" (*latreuō*) in verse 3 is the same word used to translate the work of the Levites in Numbers 8:28. The holy, consecrated, and priestly nature of our worship established in the first garden will not be done away with in the future garden-city; it will be perfected. John's final vision not only alludes back to the priestly nature of humanity's creation mandate but also reiterates the royal role we are intending to play in God's good design. Verse 5 describes the citizens of the garden-city, stating, "and

26. This is aptly captured in Graeme Goldsworthy's definition of the kingdom of God as "God's people, in God's place, under God's rule and blessing."

27. Ross, *Recalling the Hope of Glory*, 496.

they will reign forever and ever." However, there is no threat of usurpation or abuse of power in this new garden for all evil will have been eradicated.

Seated on the throne, God's reign and order will be universally established through the new heavens and the new earth—his kingdom will be on earth as it was in heaven. The worship of God's people will once again comprehensively embrace all areas of life as they exercise dominion over the new heavens and new earth. Revelation 21:2–3 summarize the perfection of Christian worship achieved in God's future cosmic sacred space: "And I saw the holy city, new Jerusalem, coming down out of heaven from God, prepared as a bride adorned for her husband. And I heard a loud voice from the throne saying, 'Behold, the dwelling place of God is with man. He will dwell with them, and they will be his people, and God himself will be with them as their God.'"

BIBLIOGRAPHY

Alexander, T. Desmond. *From Eden to the New Jerusalem: An Introduction to Biblical Theology*. Grand Rapids: Kregel Academic, 2008.

Berg, Werner. "Israels Land, der Garten Gottes: Der Garten als Bild des Heiles im Alten Testament." In *Das Kleid der Erde: Pflanzen in der Lebenswelt des Alten Israel*, edited by Ute Neumann-Gorsolke and Peter Riede, 61–79. Stuttgart: Calwer, 2002.

Grayson, A. Kirk, and Jamie Novotny. *The Royal Inscriptions of Sennacherib, King of Assyria (704–681 BC), Part 1*. RINAP 3/1. Winona Lake, IN: Eisenbrauns, 2012.

Hess, Richard S. *Israelite Religions: An Archaeological and Biblical Survey*. Grand Rapids: Baker Academic, 2007.

Köhler, Ludwig. *Old Testament Theology*. Translated by A. S. Todd. London: Lutterworth, 1957. Reprint, Cambridge: James Clarke, 2002.

Leithart, Peter J. "Transforming Worship." *Foundations* 38 (1997): 27–34.

Mathews, Kenneth A. *Genesis 1–11:26*. NAC 1a. Nashville: Broadman & Holman, 1996.

McConville, J. Gordon. *Being Human in God's Image: An Old Testament Theology of Humanity*. Grand Rapids: Baker Academic, 2016.

Osborne, William R. *Trees and Kings: A Comparative Analysis of Tree Imagery in Israel's Prophetic Tradition and the Ancient Near East*. BBRSup 18. University Park, PA: Eisenbrauns, 2018.

Ross, Allen P. *Recalling the Hope of Glory: Biblical Worship from the Garden to the New Creation*. Grand Rapids: Kregel Academic, 2006.

Routledge, Robin. *Old Testament Theology: A Thematic Approach*. Nottingham, UK: Apollos, 2013.

Sarna, Nahum M. *Genesis*. JPS Torah Commentary. Philadelphia: JPS, 1989.

Schwartz, Sarah. "Narrative *Toledot* Formulae in Genesis: The Case of Heaven and Earth, Noah, and Isaac." *JHebS* 16 (2016): DOI:10.5508/jhs.2016.v16.a8.

Todd, James M., III. "Edenic Endeavors: Sacred Service in the Garden of Eden." *Faithful Lives: Christian Reflections on the World—Faithful Work* 1 (2016): 11–20.

Vaux, Roland de. *Ancient Israel: Its Life and Institutions*. New York: McGraw-Hill, 1961.

Wallace, Howard N. *The Eden Narrative*. HSM 32. Atlanta: Scholars Press, 1985.

______. "Garden of God." In *ABD* 2:906–7.

Wenham, Gordon J. "Sanctuary Symbolism in the Garden of Eden Story." In *Proceedings of the Ninth World Congress of Jewish Studies, Division A: The Period of the Bible*, 19–25. Jerusalem: World Union of Jewish Studies, 1986.

______. *Genesis 1–15*. WBC 1. Waco, TX: Word, 1987.

Wiseman, Donald J. "Palace and Temple Gardens in the Ancient Near East." In *Monarchies and Socio-religious Traditions in the Ancient Near East*, edited by T. Mikasa, 37–43. Bulletin of the Middle East Center in Japan 1. Wiesbaden: Harrossowitz, 1984.

CHAPTER 3

DRAWING NEAR TO A HOLY GOD

Priestly Worship in the Tabernacle

Christine Elizabeth Palmer

CONTEXT OF WORSHIP BEYOND EDEN

Exile from Eden left its mark. The image of God in humanity was marred by sin, a life of flourishing became choked by thorns and thistles, the sacred relationship of husband and wife was challenged by struggle and strife, and direct communion with the Lord was broken through disobedience. While worship in the garden was personal, intimate, and unmediated, the worship of God's people was now on the other side of guardian cherubim wielding a flaming sword. There was a palpable distance between a sinful humanity and a holy God. And yet, grace abounded. The Lord purposed to redeem a people and design a way for them to regain fellowship with him. This new season of worship after Eden is marked by (1) the election of a people called to worship, (2) the creation of a priesthood to mediate worship, and (3) the construction of the tabernacle as the place of worship. The portable sanctuary, its sacrifices, and the priests who attended it were Yahweh's act of grace to draw a nation to himself in covenant relationship. He was at work creating a holy people and consecrating holy ground as a bridgehead from which to extend his rule throughout the world. Israel was set apart for the Lord's indwelling and called to worship by the way forged into his presence through blood sacrifice and priestly mediation.

A People Called to Worship

The Lord would reclaim the worship of a fallen humanity through the election of Abraham and his descendants, making them conduits of redemptive blessing to the world (Gen. 12:2–3). Their enslavement in Egypt and cry for deliverance culminated in a high-stakes battle for true worship, the transfer of allegiance from Pharaoh's reign to Yahweh's, and the freedom to serve the living God rather than the powers of this world. Ultimately, Yahweh redeemed Abraham's descendants to be *worshipers*: "Let my son go, so he may worship me" (Exod. 4:23 NIV). The Lord took for himself a people among whom he would dwell, sanctify by his presence, and through whom he would make himself known to the nations. He entered into covenant with them, fulfilling his promises to their forefathers, and on solemn oath promised that he would be their God and they his people (Gen. 17:7; Lev. 26:45; Jer. 31:33; Ezek. 14:11). At Sinai, Israel was given a charter that defined their identity and mission in the world to be "a kingdom of priests and a holy nation" (Exod. 19:5–6). They were to be a unique people because God's presence was among them (Exod. 33:15–16). They were elevated from slaves to Yahweh's own personal treasure, an image rich with the value and worth he ascribes to his very own. Among all the nations of the earth, Israel was called to a priestly vocation, holy to the Lord and invited to worship in his presence, as John Davies reflects: "The essence of the priestly prerogative consisted in access to the presence of God, particularly the presence of God associated with the altar, and above all the sanctuary."[1]

A Priesthood to Mediate Worship

Though the entire nation was a kingdom of priests, their worship was mediated by God-appointed leaders who were called to "draw near to Yahweh" (Lev. 10:3). In response to the Lord's command, Moses instituted the priesthood to approach God's holy presence at the altar on behalf of the nation: "Then *bring near* to you Aaron your brother, and his sons with him, from among the people of Israel, to serve me as priests" (Exod. 28:1, emphasis added).

The pattern for the nation's worship was set at Sinai when Yahweh entered into covenant with Israel. As his presence descended on the mountain, it became holy ground; it could not be touched but had to be guarded by a fence around its base (Exod. 19:23). An altar was constructed at the foot of the mountain for the congregation to worship through sacrifice, while a select group of Israel's representatives—Moses, Aaron and his sons, and seventy elders—were invited to approach halfway up the mountain and there enjoy the covenant hospitality of the Lord. They were granted access to the place of his feet and they ate and drank in his presence (Exod. 24:9–11). As intimate as the fellowship was, this was as far as Aaron and his sons were able to go. Only one man and mediator, Moses, was invited to ascend and enter the cloud to meet with the Lord. At the summit, Moses received the inscribed tablets of the covenant and the blueprint for covenant worship. Yahweh's dwelling place was to be constructed *according to the pattern* shown him on the mountain (Exod. 25:9, 40).

1. John A. Davies, *A Royal Priesthood: Literary and Intertextual Perspectives on an Image of Israel in Exodus 19.6*, eds. Claudia V. Camp and Andrew Mein, JSOTSup 395 (New York: T&T Clark, 2004), 162.

The Sinai encounter was replicated in the pattern of tabernacle worship: the three stages of ascent up the mountain were re-created in the layout of the tent where all Israel was invited to approach *representatively* through the priesthood. A linen screen marked the boundaries of holy ground as the fence had surrounded the base of the mountain. The altar in the outer court corresponded to the altar at the foot of the mountain where worshipers could approach to offer sacrifice. The priests, serving as the nation's representatives, gained access to eat and drink at the Lord's table in the Holy Place as the elders had feasted halfway up the mountain. The high priest's privileged entrance to the Holy of Holies once a year retraced Moses's ascent to the summit. When the tabernacle was completed, the glory of the Lord that had settled on Sinai now descended to fill the sanctuary and consecrate it by his presence (Exod. 40:34–35).

A Place Consecrated for Worship

The tabernacle was the means by which a transcendent God whom the highest heavens could not contain became "God with us." Yahweh set his dwelling in the midst of his people as the climax of the covenant: "I will dwell among the people of Israel and will be their God" (Exod. 29:45). The tabernacle extended an invitation to commune with the Lord in a re-created heaven on earth.[2] Architecture was put to the service of theology: the outer court was a reflection of the land and sea of the habitable world represented by a mountain-like "altar of earth" (Exod. 20:24), and a standing water basin called the "sea" (1 Kings 7:23). The tent was designed to evoke an Eden-like setting, providing shelter and shade like the lush garden canopy where God walked with Adam in the "cool of the day" (Gen. 3:8). Yahweh was said to walk among his people once again in the tabernacle as he had in the garden sanctuary (Lev. 26:12; Deut. 23:14).[3] The sanctuary faced east, just as the garden of Eden was in the east (Gen. 2:8). It was adorned with gold and precious stones recalling the environs of Eden, where the gold was good and precious stones were in abundance (Gen. 2:12). Housed inside the tent was a golden lampstand shaped into branches, blossoms, calyxes, and flowers that visually re-created a stylized tree aflame with the glory of God (Exod. 25:31–37; cf. Exod. 3:2). Its artistic crafting suggests that it may have represented the tree of life in the midst of the garden. The most prominent echoes of Eden were found in the replication of heavenly creatures throughout the sacred tent. Cherubim of hammered gold flanked the ark, and their figures were woven into the embroidered hangings that sealed off the divine throne room from view, barring the way into the life-giving presence of God (Gen. 3:24).

2. Gregory K. Beale, *The Temple and the Church's Mission: A Biblical Theology of the Dwelling Place of God*, NSBT 17 (Downers Grove, IL: InterVarsity Press, 2004), 32–36.
3. The form of the Hebrew verb "to walk" (*hithallek*) is a rare reflexive, making the connection between creation and sanctuary most explicit in the original language.

If the tabernacle replicates the world through its symbols, then the worship of God's people in its courts reverberates with significance for the entire world. And if the sacred tent is an intentional replica of Eden's garden sanctuary, then priestly ministry enacts a theology of reconciliation that is envisioned as regaining access to Eden. Not surprisingly, the language chosen to describe priestly ministry is the very same expression used of Adam's cultivation of the garden (Gen. 2:15).[4] The Hebrew terms *'abad* and *shamar* may be translated as "to work and to keep," but they may also be translated as "to minister and to guard" the garden sanctuary. Looking backward, it brings into view Adam's role as a priest; looking forward, it brings into clearer perspective that the priesthood is called to be a "second Adam."

Worship of the Lord in the tabernacle is envisioned as being rooted in creation with the priesthood fulfilling humanity's original vocation. Humanity was created to worship. To root worship in Eden, before the nation even comes into existence, speaks to a theology of worship that is eternal. Worship of the Lord exists apart from the creation of the nation, but the nation was created to worship.

THEOLOGY OF WORSHIP

At the heart of covenant is the gift of God's presence: "I will make my dwelling among you, and I will not abhor you. I will walk among you and be your God, and you will be my people" (Lev. 26:11–12). Priests were consecrated to approach the altar of sacrifice so they could mediate the worship of the nation before the presence a holy God. The priesthood put on display Israel's priestly call to live *restored to God's presence.*

Worship through Mediators

The tribe of Levi was set apart to serve Yahweh in the sanctuary on behalf of a nation set apart to serve him in the world. Israel's mediators were divinely chosen, appointed, and consecrated for service.[5] Aaron and his sons ministered in the tabernacle and its altar, while the rest of the clans transported and guarded the sacred tent. Each was brought into the service of the Lord through the performance of ritual that transferred them from the realm of the common to the realm of the holy and qualified them to stand in God's presence.

The Levites were chosen to serve in the place of all firstborn males whom the Lord had redeemed at the exodus: "On the day that I struck down all the firstborn in the land of Egypt I consecrated them for myself, and I have taken the Levites instead of all the firstborn among the people

4. The only instances where the Hebrew verbs *'abad* and *shamar* occur together are in relation to Adam's cultivation of the garden (Gen. 2:15) and to priestly service in the tabernacle (Num. 3:7–8; 8:26; 18:5–6).

5. See Hebrews 5:1–4 for the New Testament implications.

of Israel" (Num. 8:17–18). The Levites were ceremoniously brought into the service of the Lord as *elevation offerings*, a type of offering that required gifts to be placed in the palms of the worshipers' hands and raised before Yahweh to symbolize a giving over to him in total dedication.[6] The people gathered around the Levites at the entrance to the tabernacle and laid hands on them as they would sacrificial offerings. Their gesture in essence communicated, "Take them in our place." In a very concrete way, the Levites served as *living sacrifices* on behalf of the nation, as they lived out their lives fulfilling Israel's covenant vocation to worship their Redeemer.

Aaron and his sons were consecrated to serve on holy ground through a seven-day ordination ceremony. They were made holy by washing, anointing with oil, investiture with holy garments, and the sprinkling of the blood of sacrifice. Some of the blood of the ordination sacrifice was applied to their right ear lobe, right thumb, and right toe, while the remainder was splashed against the altar (Lev. 8:23–24). The blood that touched their bodies also touched the altar, forging a bond between the priests and the altar at which they served. They alone were granted access to the altar where a holy God met with his people and they alone were qualified to handle the shed blood that atoned for sin and reconciled the worshiper to Yahweh. The priesthood's sacred duties positioned them at the very meeting place of heaven and earth to mediate between them.

The priesthood's role as mediators between Yahweh and his set-apart people was woven into the "holy garments" that ordained them to service (Exod. 28:2). Ordinary priests were clad in pure, white linen and extolled in the psalms as "priests . . . clothed with righteousness" (Ps. 132:9; cf. Rev. 19:8). The high priest was set above the rest in sumptuous apparel that mirrored the textiles of the sanctuary in embroidered fabrics of deep blue, purple, and crimson, golden threads, and floral embellishments. His garments were woven of a mixture of fine linen and woolen yarns that was otherwise forbidden to lay Israelites (Lev. 19:19). The sacral fabrics that draped Yahweh's holy dwelling also clothed the high priest, displaying that the intersection of heaven and earth was to be found in the tent of worship as well as in the man who mediates between these two worlds.[7] In fact, it was only inasmuch as God's chosen mediator shared in both worlds that he could bridge them by bringing them together in his person.

On his forehead, the high priest wore a gold frontlet inscribed with the words "Holy to Yahweh" (Exod. 28:36). In Old Testament worship, to be holy to the Lord referred to that which had been wholly dedicated to him

6. Also referred to as "wave offerings" (Num. 8:11, 13, 15). The action represented here is not a right-to-left waving motion, but rather a lifting heavenward in a gesture of presentation to Yahweh.
7. See Christine Palmer, "Israelite High Priestly Apparel: Embodying an Identity between Human and Divine," in *Fashioned Selves: Dress and Identity in Antiquity*, ed. Megan Cifarelli (Oxford: Oxbow, 2019), 117–27.

and belonged to him as his exclusive possession.[8] Yahweh's claim of ownership was written on the priest's forehead, where slaves were branded in the ancient world.[9] To be inscribed with the divine name visually and unmistakably communicated the high priest's role as God's earthly representative.

Inasmuch as he stood on behalf of the Lord, he also stood on behalf of the people. Attached to a golden, apron-like garment known as the ephod was a breastpiece adorned with twelve stones in gold-plaited settings representing the twelve tribes of Israel. Mounted on the shoulder straps of the ephod were two more stones etched with the names of six tribes each. The precious stones were engraved as signet seals, customarily strung from a cord and pinned over the heart to betoken identity (Song 8:6). The engraved signets laid a different claim of ownership than that of the gold frontlet; they marked the priest as the people's proxy as he drew near to Yahweh to bring them to remembrance (Exod. 28:12, 29). When the Lord was called on to remember his people, he did so in the context of his covenant promises for salvation and for blessing (Lev. 26:45). Though Israel was barred from entering the sanctuary, they were daily brought before the presence of the Lord as the high priest carried them on his shoulders and over his heart. The two covenant partners met as they were brought together in the man who was inscribed with the names of both on his body. Mediated worship in the tabernacle illustrated there is only *one way* into Yahweh's presence and only *one man* who is appointed to bring God's people near. As the apostle Paul would later reflect, "there is one God, and there is one mediator between God and men, the man Christ Jesus" (1 Tim. 2:5).

Worship as Liturgy

Priestly ministry in the tabernacle was governed by *liturgy*—that is, the regular performance of acts of worship decreed by the Lord at the appointed times and in the appointed ways. For Israel, this experience of worship was as natural as the liturgy of creation with its regular patterns of evening and morning, springtime and harvest. Creation's imprint was visible in the tabernacle's architecture as well as in its rhythms of sacred time.

Twice daily, at morning and at twilight, the high priest offered a yearling lamb as a burnt offering on the altar (Num. 28:3–8). He then entered the Holy Place to offer incense on the golden altar before the veil and to

---

8. These can be goods such as the tithe of produce or flock (Lev. 27:30–32), sacrificial meat offered on the altar (Lev. 6:17), or vessels for ritual use (Ezra 8:8) that are all given to the Lord. Most significantly, Israel shares a holy status by belonging to Yahweh as a "people holy to the Lord" (Deut. 7:6).

9. All of Israel is enjoined to wear Yahweh's words as a "headband" to distinguish them as people belonging to him among the nations (Deut. 6:8). The Lord's marking for redemption has deep resonances within the Bible: Cain is singled out for protection (Gen. 4:15), those who grieve over the sin of the nation are marked to be spared from God's judgment (Ezek. 9:4), and at the culmination of all human history, those who are the Lord's very own will bear his name on their foreheads (Rev. 14:1).

tend the lamps that burned from "evening to morning." The order and regularity of this ritual act echoed the original ordering of creation, where cycles of "evening to morning" were defined by the great "lampstands" in the sky (Gen. 1:14).[10] On the Sabbath, the daily liturgy picked up a greater weekly liturgy: two yearling lambs were offered on the sacrificial altar, and twelve fresh loaves of bread were set out on the golden table (Lev. 24:8). The priests ate the old loaves on behalf of a holy nation invited to fellowship at the Lord's table. The Sabbath was a day for all Israel to cease from their labors, but for Yahweh it was a day to feed his people. Weekly liturgies picked up annual celebrations constructed around the remembrance of Yahweh's saving acts so that built within the unfolding of time was an ever-enduring call to worship.[11]

Daily service at the tabernacle testified to a God who was present among his people and who promised to meet them in worship, especially in the daily sacrifice: "It shall be a regular burnt offering throughout your generations at the entrance of the tent of meeting before the LORD, where I will meet with you, to speak to you there" (Exod. 29:42). Israel heard the awe-inspiring voice of Yahweh for themselves only once (Exod. 20:18–19). At all other times when they approached the Lord with their offerings, they did so in faith that he was present to receive them. The daily ordering of his house, the preparation of his table, the kindling of the lamps, and priests to serve in the divine estate were signs of Yahweh's covenant dwelling (2 Chron. 13:11). These signs were the seemingly mundane tasks of daily life that nevertheless profoundly testified to the real, abiding presence of God. It is in the daily living that the Lord meets with his people and invites his worship to pervade their lives.

The daily liturgy concluded as the creation account concludes, with God's blessing over humanity (see Gen. 1:28). The priest stood at the altar, raised his hands, and pronounced the benediction:[12] "The LORD bless you and keep you; the LORD make his face to shine upon you and be gracious to you; the LORD lift up his countenance upon you and give you peace" (Num. 6:24–26). The priest blessed in the divine name, invoking the protection, grace, and peace that came from a covenant relationship with the Lord. It was in the pronouncement of the benediction that Yahweh's name was said to be placed on the worshipers, marking them as belonging to him: "So shall they put my name upon the people of Israel, and I will bless them" (Num. 6:27). The people mirrored the name inscribed on the forehead of the high priest who representatively lived out the nation's holy calling. The priest spoke Yahweh's life-giving, covenantal blessing over the

---

10. The Hebrew literally reads "lampstands." This unusual lexical choice draws a connection between the great heavenly lights and the tabernacle's lampstand.
11. See chapter 4 in this volume, JoAnna Hoyt, "The Calendar for Worship in Ancient Israel: Worship in the Feasts and Celebrations."
12. See Lev. 9:22; Deut. 10:8; 2 Chron. 30:27.

people, restoring them to the fellowship humanity enjoyed in Eden and marking them as belonging to God (see Rev. 14:1).

The significance of blessing for the worshiping community was not simply as a parting ceremonious word, but one that was believed to have power to shape the life of every Israelite. Blessing is woven into the Lord's relationship with humanity since creation and blessing continues to be felt in the world as a result of covenant worship.[13] Divine blessing actualizes God's purposes for his creation—the fruitfulness, flourishing, and filling of the land with a reflection of his image and name. As the priest stood in the courts of the tabernacle that were, in effect, a re-created Eden, he stood on behalf of Yahweh to proclaim blessing as his earthly representative.

Worship in Holiness

Worship in the tabernacle makes theological realities concrete, like a drama enacted on a grand stage displaying the character of Yahweh for all to see. Holiness to us may seem like an abstract idea.[14] In Israel's worship, however, holiness was *personal*, anchored in the person of Yahweh, who alone is inherently holy and the fountainhead of all holiness. The only way for God's people to be made holy was through *relationship* with him: "I am the Lord who sanctifies you" (Lev. 20:8). The Lord's dwelling among his people sanctified them, but it also threatened them with destruction (Lev. 10:1–3). God's presence is like a consuming fire in the crucible of sanctification: "Of the elements of nature there is none of such spiritual and mighty energy as Fire: what it consumes it takes and changes into its own spiritual nature, rejecting as smoke and ashes what cannot be assimilated. And so the Holiness of God is that infinite Perfection by which He keeps Himself free from all that is not Divine, and yet has fellowship with the creature, and takes it up into union with Himself, destroying and casting out all that will not yield itself to Him."[15]

Holiness was given tangible expression through the tabernacle's architecture. The tent of worship was constructed along three concentric zones of holiness, each deriving its sanctity from proximity to God's presence.[16] The Holy of Holies, where the Lord was enthroned in the midst of

13. Gen. 1:28; 12:1–3; Deut. 28:1–13. As illustration of its significance in the life of God's people, the earliest surviving biblical text is a variation of Numbers 6:24–26. Two miniature silver scrolls (1 × 3.75 in. and .5 × 1.5 in.) incised with the priestly blessing were excavated in the context of a Jerusalem cemetery dating to the seventh century BC.
14. To define the Hebrew *qadosh*, "holy," presents a challenge because Israel learned holiness through the performance of ritual rather than as a concept disconnected from its enactment. Holiness primarily denotes Yahweh's otherness and transcendence, his character in its moral excellence and perfection, and by extension, anything that has been brought into his sphere. Space and time may also be regarded as holy because they are set apart for a manifestation of the Lord.
15. Andrew Murray, *Holy in Christ* (Edinburgh: Morrison & Gibb, 1888), 39.
16. For the definitive study on graded holiness see Philip Peter Jenson, *Graded Holiness: A Key to the Priestly Conception of the World*, JSOTSup 106 (Sheffield: JSOT Press, 1992).

his people, was the sphere of the greatest density of holiness. The objects of worship in this space (the ark, its cover, and the golden cherubim attached to it) were made of the purest gold. Only the high priest, the holiest man in all Israel, could minister in this sphere when once a year he approached the Lord to secure atonement. One step removed on the other side of a drawn veil was the Holy Place. The furnishings here (altar of incense, lampstand, and table) were also crafted of pure gold, but unlike the ark of the covenant, which could not be seen or touched, these articles could be touched by the priests who engaged in sacred service to the Lord. Priests had access to the Holy Place for tending to the Lord's house, but Levites and lay Israelites were restricted from entering. One step further removed was the courtyard where priests served at the bronze altar of sacrifice. Lay Israelites were granted access to the courts of the Lord to offer their worship through sacrificial gifts and dedicated offerings. Yet, if they approached in a state of impurity, the Levites were charged with putting them to death (Num. 1:53)![17] The Levites encamped around the perimeter of the sanctuary guarding God's holiness and casting out all impurity, a task that recalls Adam's priestly service in the garden.

Priests were not only guardians of sacred space but also guardians of the sacred covenant relationship, entrusted with guiding the nation in worship by teaching them to live in holiness (Lev. 10:10–11). The Lord makes demands of his people that are *transformative*: "You must be holy to me, for I the Lord am holy and have separated you from the peoples that you should be mine" (Lev. 20:26). Since Israel belonged to Yahweh in covenant relationship, they were to live out the implications of his sanctifying presence in their midst by consecrating themselves in obedience to him (see Phil. 2:12–13). Their obedience in everyday life took the shape of separation from impurity and of conformity to the ethical demands of the covenant (Lev. 17–26). Physical and ethical holiness were inseparable as both body and soul were trained toward godliness. The God who created the world by separating light from darkness and land from sea required that his people make distinctions that maintained the boundaries he marked out by his law, distinguishing between holy and common, true worship from false, and good from evil. Israel was invited to share in God's holiness and thereby be transformed into a holy people who reflected his image to the world.

The priesthood lived out Israel's call to holiness and embodied sanctification that was visible in the physical wholeness of their bodies, their white linen robes, and the purity of their relationships. Since holiness was nonnegotiable for access into God's presence, priests had to live according to stricter standards than that of lay Israelites. They had to present their bodies

---

17. This challenges us to reevaluate our own priorities and affections regarding the Lord's worth. Phineas is commended for his zeal and granted an eternal priesthood because he treasured Yahweh's honor above all else (Num. 25:6–9). Jesus's cleansing of the temple must be understood in this priestly tradition (John 2:17).

as whole and unblemished in the very same way that the sacrifices they offered on the altar were without blemish.[18] They were forbidden from coming into contact with death or displaying the signs of mourning. They were not to take a wife who had been defiled, as they were called to live lives above reproach. The Lord claims all areas of life, even the most personal, for those who draw near to him in worship. In the sight of all Israel, the priesthood embodied the reality that those who are called to draw near to Yahweh will be cleansed and made whole. In this way, their worship is prophetic.

Worship through Sacrifice

Sacrifice was the center of gravity in Israel's worship—its daily, communal, and most visible act of worship. Through his offering (*qorban*), the worshiper drew near (*qarab*) to Yahweh to commune with him at the altar. The portrait of Old Testament sacrificial worship was full-orbed—worshipers drew near to the Lord to offer their thanksgiving, acknowledge his sovereignty, enjoy covenant fellowship, and to restore relationship through sacrifices of atonement (Lev. 1–7). Certain offerings were given over to Yahweh in their entirety (Lev. 1:9), while others were shared in fellowship with him through a meal in the courtyard of the tabernacle (Lev. 7:15). In every case, the offering was more than what it seemed; the gift represented the worshiper. Every sacrificial act of worship was a giving of one's *self* to the Lord.[19]

The priesthood was entrusted with mediating worship at the altar and preparing the people to meet with Yahweh through the ritual of sacrifice. They had a prominent role as the only ones who were able to approach the altar and handle the blood provided for atonement (Lev. 17:11). When a worshiper brought his offering to the tent, he laid his hand on the head of the animal in identification with the life that was being offered up in his place. He actively engaged in worship as he himself slaughtered the animal. The priest caught the blood in a basin and dashed it against the altar to return it to the ground in acknowledgment that all life belongs to the Lord (Lev. 4:24–26). The worshiper then skinned and flayed the animal, and the priestly mediator arranged it on the altar, where it would be "turned to smoke" and ascend to the Lord as a "pleasing aroma."[20] The

---

18. The blemishes that disqualify priests from serving at the altar (Lev. 21:17–20) are nearly identical to the blemishes that disqualify animals from being offered as a sacrifice to the Lord (Lev. 22:20–25).
19. While this is most clearly seen in the offerings that secure atonement, it is the case that every sacrifice (fruit of the womb or yield of the earth) is offered out of one's livelihood. Often, it is the firstborn male animal or the firstfruits of the harvest that are offered. These are meant to symbolically acknowledge that all the worshiper owns and all that he is belongs to the Lord.
20. The Lord receives all sacrifices that he requires as a "pleasing aroma." This is another way of saying he is pleased with worship offered to him in obedience by coming to him on his terms for his acceptance. In the same way, Christ gave his life for ours out of obedience to the Father as a "fragrant offering and sacrifice to God" (Eph. 5:2).

offering of sacrifice (both voluntary and required) was never meant to be a going through the motions of ritual, but a faith-filled and heartfelt act of obedience to please the Lord who ordained the altar as the meeting place between God and man.

The high point of the priesthood's sacrificial ministry came on the Day of Atonement, a yearly ritual that purified the tabernacle and enacted the removal of sin from the nation. In the Old Testament, sin was conceived as a physical burden borne by the sinner. Far from being private, its effects were a pollution that defiled the individual, the community, the land, and the sanctuary where Yahweh dwelled. Sin accrued in the sanctuary, clung to the horns of the sacrificial altar, and spilled out onto the land until it had to be dealt with in judgment (Lev. 18:24–28). Sin was not taken lightly; it endangered a people's relationship with their God and threatened their very existence. Were it not for the provision of the sacrificial system, Israel's sin would accumulate like that of the nations whom the Lord had judged and expelled from the land before them. Sacrifice provided the means for setting aright the relationship between a wayward people and a holy God. At this time in redemptive history, though inadequate in itself, the blood of animals would serve to communicate that only a life may atone for a life and that the blood of the innocent will ransom the guilty. The Day of Atonement was one of the clearest pictures of the Lord's provision to atone for his people's sin and to cleanse them from all unrighteousness through a substitutionary sacrifice. The high priest's role was central to the ritual, ultimately prefiguring the offering of the High Priest who would secure a lasting atonement (Heb. 10:11–14).

The solemnity of the day was felt by all. The high priest laid aside his sumptuous garments in favor of a humble, white linen robe. Worship for the people on this day meant denying themselves in fasting and repentance (Lev. 16:29, 31). They were commanded to be in a posture of sorrow over their sin, teaching them "a godly grief produc[ing] a repentance that leads to salvation" (2 Cor. 7:10). Anyone who did not humble himself in repentance before the Lord or who did any work was to be cut off from his people: "For whoever is not afflicted on that very day shall be cut off from his people. And whoever does any work on that very day, that person I will destroy from among his people" (Lev. 23:29–30). The severity of this command underscored the necessity of repentance for forgiveness and that atonement was not man's work but the Lord's.

On this day alone the high priest was granted access into the Holy of Holies behind the cherubim-embroidered veil that re-created the separation between God and humanity since the guardian cherubim were first stationed at Eden's threshold (Gen. 3:24). It was only by Yahweh's invitation that anyone dared approach the inner sanctuary where he was enthroned in holiness. No one else was permitted access during the purification of the sanctuary; it was exclusively the work of the man who interceded between God and his people (Lev. 16:17). As Israel's mediator entered behind the veil to cleanse the Holy of Holies by the sprinkling of sacrificial blood, he had to create his own protective veil and shield himself behind a cloud of incense. Before the mercy seat, he sprinkled the blood of a bull offered for his own sins and those of his household, as well as the blood of a goat taken by lot for the sin of the nation. He drew near in faith that the Lord would appear over the mercy seat on the appointed day to be approached for forgiveness (Lev. 16:2). The high priest then made his way from the throne room to the outer court, purifying the Holy Place and its articles of worship and the court's sacrificial altar with the blood of cleansing. In all, blood was sprinkled forty-nine times (7 × 7) within the sanctuary. In Israelite ritual, the number seven symbolized completion, and multiplied by itself, it signified the comprehensive ritual cleansing of all Israel's sin.[21]

The ceremony continued with the second of the two goats presented to the Lord. While the first was offered on the altar to atone for the nation and cleanse the sanctuary through the sprinkling of its blood, the second goat also made atonement for the nation, but as a *live sacrifice*. The ritual involved a national confession of sin performed by the high priest on behalf of the people. Placing his hands on the goat's head, he confessed over it all the sins of Israel, thereby transferring them onto its head. Israel's mediator stood in the place of all sinners: "Aaron is to lay both his hands on the head of the live goat and confess over it all the *iniquity* and *transgressions* of the Israelites—all their *sins*—and put them on the goat's head" (Lev. 16:21, author translation). The language is comprehensive regarding the totality of sins the animal substitute took on itself, repeating the very same language of the totality of Yahweh's forgiveness: "forgiving *iniquity* and *transgression* and *sin*" (Exod. 34:7 BSB, emphasis added).

After the confession of sin, there was an unexpected departure from the typical order of sacrifice Israelites observed every other day of the year. The expected course was to ritually slaughter the animal, drain its blood, and offer it on the altar. Instead, the goat on whose head Israel's sins had come to rest was driven out into the wilderness. This departure from every other ritual offering was like a plot twist highlighting the remarkable. By driving the animal away from the community and in the opposite direction of God's presence, sin itself was cast out into the wilderness realm of chaos.[22] Before their very eyes, the people saw their sin being physically removed from their midst! Relationship with a holy God was restored, and his covenant presence would continue to abide among them. There was a day written into Israel's calendar—the tenth day of the seventh month—where sin was banished from God's presence and forgiveness won for the repentant through a substitutionary sacrifice offered by a humbled high priest. Israel needed only repent, believe, and see the Lord's work on their

21. Jacob Milgrom, *Leviticus 1–16*, AB 3 (New York: Doubleday, 1991), 1039.
22. Frank H. Gorman Jr., *Divine Presence and Community: A Commentary on the Book of Leviticus*, ITC (Grand Rapids: Eerdmans, 1997), 97–98.

behalf. The significance of this day cannot be overstated. If we understand the tabernacle as a re-creation of heaven and earth, then the atonement effected in its courts brims with significance for the entire world. Worship through sacrifice is worship that anticipates the cross.

SIGNIFICANCE OF THE PRIESTHOOD FOR BIBLICAL WORSHIP

Priestly worship in the tabernacle answers the question of how exile from Eden will be overcome and humanity be restored to God's presence. Its rich theological vision scripts worship around substitutionary sacrifice and the ministry of the anointed high priest who bridges the gap between God and man. For this reason, it continues to reverberate with relevance for the church—revealing Christ, urging us toward personal sanctification, and compelling a communal worship that puts on display the saving acts of God.

Worship through Christ Our Great High Priest

In tabernacle worship, we encounter Christ in the sublime shadows of the person of the high priest. Chosen, anointed, and invested with authority, the high priest is ritually qualified to draw near to God's presence on behalf of the nation. No one can come to the Lord except through his divinely appointed intercessor: "I am the way, and the truth, and the life. No one comes to the Father except through me" (John 14:6). Christ our High Priest mediates at the intersection of heaven and earth, inhabiting both worlds so that he could reconcile them in his flesh. The mystery of the incarnation is writ large on his body—inscribed with the divine name on his forehead and the names of God's own people over his heart, he brings together heaven and earth, sharing in both a human and divine nature. He perfectly represents the Father whose fullness indwells him (Col. 2:9). He perfectly represents humanity whose flesh and blood he fully partakes (Heb. 2:14).

Under the old covenant, there was only one place where the Lord and his people were brought together in union without barriers, and that was on the body of the high priest. There was only one time when that was made possible, and that was during worship. As the high priest entered the sanctuary for daily worship carrying the nation's signets, Israel entered God's presence *through him*. Yet their access was limited before a veiled Holy of Holies. In Christ, we have access to the heavenly throne room "by the new and living way that he opened for us through the curtain, that is, through his flesh" (Heb. 10:20). The "living way" is none other than our living Mediator. Through Christ's sinless life that was poured out unto death and his triumph over the grave, we are restored to God's presence and "sanctified through the offering of the body of Jesus Christ once for all" (Heb. 10:10). We have confidence to come before our heavenly Father with our prayers and petitions because Jesus's high priestly ministry extends beyond officiating at the altar to also becoming the perfect unblemished sacrifice that atones for sin. When he came before the Father to offer up his life in full, foreshadowed by the 7 × 7 sprinklings of blood, he did not turn to go back out because there will never have to be another sacrifice (Heb. 10:14). Jesus Christ remained in the heavenly throne room to share the throne of his Father and to intercede for us forever. He is our eternal Advocate at the mercy seat of God.

As the altar was the centerpiece of Old Testament worship, the atonement is at the heart of Christian worship. We orient our confession, our worship, and our very lives around the cross as Israel did around the altar. Resting on the finished work of Christ, we come to see that the language of sacrifice, far from having faded with time, has now become the metaphor that characterizes our own discipleship in Christian community. We are called to worship with a radical self-giving that embraces all of life: "present your bodies as a living sacrifice, holy and acceptable to God, which is your spiritual worship" (Rom. 12:1). We have been bought with a price to offer ourselves back to the Lord by living lives that take the shape of his own obedient and sacrificial self-offering. When we speak of offering ourselves to the Lord, it may be helpful to have in our minds the image of worshipers bringing their animal sacrifices to the altar. Their act of worship was physical, participatory, and fully engaged. Should ours be less so? Am I offering up songs of praise in joyful participation? Am I present and engaged at the preaching of God's Word? Do I serve out of a heartfelt obedience, seeking to please the Lord as Jesus pleased the Father? Old covenant worship was costly. New covenant worship is costlier still, as we are called to offer ourselves *fully*, imitating Christ who offered himself for us all.

Worship as a Holy Priesthood

Tabernacle worship after Eden's template ordained a priesthood restored to God's presence. New Testament authors would find this a most compelling expression of Christian identity: "But you are a chosen people, a royal priesthood, a holy nation, God's special possession, that you may declare the praises of him who called you out of darkness into his wonderful light" (1 Peter 2:9 NIV). Priestly identity is rooted in having been rescued and chosen to draw near to God in worship.

The Old Testament priesthood was called to a life of worship that has surprising affinity to our own call of discipleship: their identity was shaped through being known as God's own (cf. John 1:12–13), they embodied a higher standard of holiness (cf. Matt. 5:20), their daily service revolved around sacrifice at the altar (cf. Gal. 2:20), and they were called to live in this world as ministers of reconciliation (cf. 2 Cor. 5:20). Priestly ministry fundamentally brought Israel into communion with a holy God. The offering of sacrifice was never an end in itself, but the means to a worshiper's *reconciliation with God*. Their ministry of reconciliation translates for us into the proclamation of the gospel (see Rom. 3:23–25). As a redeemed people, we bridge the gap between heaven and earth as we proclaim in our worship that relationship with God has been restored through the substitutionary sacrifice of Jesus Christ: "All this is from God, who through Christ reconciled us to himself and gave us the ministry of reconciliation; that is, in Christ God was reconciling[a] the world to himself, not counting their trespasses against them, and entrusting to us the message of reconciliation" (2 Cor. 5:18–19).

The Lord invites us into worship that defines our very being. In the tabernacle, this was made concrete on the high priest's golden frontlet inscribed with the words "Holy to Yahweh" that conferred on him an identity as dedicated to God and citizen of heaven. What is foreshadowed in the Old Testament reaches its climax in the work of Christ, who makes us citizens of heaven (Phil. 3:20) and invites us to share in his holiness (Heb. 2:11). Whereas the priesthood of the old covenant displayed purity in the physical wholeness of their bodies and white linen garments, holiness is most evident in our worship by transformed lives that reflect the unblemished character of the One who calls us to be holy as he is holy (Lev. 19:2; 1 Peter 1:16). This is more than living a moral life; it is an invitation to a life lived in *communion* with the Holy One. Holiness comes only through relationship with Jesus Christ, whose indwelling presence transforms us and re-creates us after his own image. As far as Christian worship is transformational, it is also missional, putting the gospel on display for the world to see.

Worship as a Life Liturgy

Most of us are not accustomed to thinking of our worship as liturgy. We are apt to regard liturgy as something formal and distant, or associate it with a certain style of high church service.[23] And yet, every worship tradition is shaped by a "liturgy"—regular patterns of gathering as a congregation, fixed ways of telling the story of redemption, weekly or monthly celebrations of being hosted at the Lord's Table, and rhythms within the calendar year that prepare our hearts to encounter the God of our salvation. Liturgy is worship in a rhythm of sacred repetition that aims at honoring the Lord and shaping the worshiper by cultivating the heart's affections heavenward.

Regular patterns of worship are formative in our discipleship and in the shaping of our theology. Living out our faith in daily and weekly rhythms shapes our beliefs, our expectations, and our very identity. Rhythms of life can all too easily be built around competing liturgies such as work schedules and sports calendars that ultimately supplant our worship of the Lord. James K. A. Smith insightfully explains, "Cultural liturgies are

---

23. Liturgy, in fact, is a very "earthy" word. In the Old Testament, *'abodah* (rendered as *leitourgia* in the Old Greek translation) refers to the daily priestly service of caring for God's house. Liturgy as regular, ordained worship is rooted as far back as Adam's priestly charge "to work [*'abad*] and to keep" the garden sanctuary.

not just one-off events that you unwittingly do; more significantly, they are formative practices that do something *to* you, unconsciously but effectively tuning your heart to the songs of Babylon rather than the songs of Zion (Ps. 137)."[24] When we gather as the body of Christ, we proclaim that we are a people created to worship as opposed to a people created to consume, compete, or be entertained. We are the people of God called to commune with him. Regular rhythms of worship do more than tell the narrative of the faith (Christmas-Easter-Pentecost); they embed us into the true story of the world.

Intentional rhythms further serve to habituate us to God's presence in our lives. Tabernacle liturgy cultivated the expectation of meeting with Yahweh in worship: the altar's fire was burning and the table was set for communion with the Lord. Worshipers drew near in faith that the God who dwelt in their midst was present to share life with them as they participated in rhythms of worship scripted and blessed by him. This invites us to reflect on our own sense of anticipation in worship. What kind of liturgies do we intentionally cultivate as individuals to care for our souls? Are there daily habits that incline our hearts to our Savior's life-giving words?[25] When we gather to worship as a community of faith, do we come expectant to meet with the Lord? How do we attune ourselves to the Lord's presence among us—present in the preached Word, present at the table, and present in the fellowship of the redeemed? What vision of God does our worship cultivate in us, and how does it empower us for a life lived in fellowship with him?

Daily liturgy at the tabernacle is eschatological: it is a rehearsal of what is to come, forming a people who belong in the world to come. In a very tangible way, priestly worship puts on display things as they ought to be—an ordered world where God is enthroned over his creation, priests clothed in righteousness, and worshipers cleansed and made whole. Those who drew near to worship at the sacred tent entered a world where Yahweh is sovereign, sin is being defeated, and forgiveness is won by the shed blood of sacrifice. It is a world that reclaims the imagination and infuses it with godly hope. It is a world where being human is being restored to God's presence. Our worship forms us into a people whose ultimate destiny is to be participants in the eternal liturgy of the heavenly kingdom: "Worthy are you . . . for you were slain, and by your blood you ransomed people for God from every tribe and language and people and nation, and you have made them a kingdom and priests to our God" (Rev. 5:9–10).

24. See James K. A. Smith, *You Are What You Love: The Spiritual Power of Habit* (Grand Rapids: Brazos, 2016), 37.

25. For a thoughtful reflection, see Tish Harrison Warren, *Liturgy of the Ordinary: Sacred Practices in Everyday Life* (Downers Grove, IL: InterVarsity Press, 2016).

BIBLIOGRAPHY

Beale, Gregory K. *The Temple and the Church's Mission: A Biblical Theology of the Dwelling Place of God*. NSBT 17. Downers Grove, IL: InterVarsity Press, 2004.

Cheung, Alex T. M. "The Priest as the Redeemed Man: A Biblical-Theological Study of the Priesthood." *JETS* 29 (1986): 265–75.

Davies, John A. *A Royal Priesthood: Literary and Intertextual Perspectives on an Image of Israel in Exodus 19.6*. JSOTSup 395. New York: T&T Clark, 2004.

Gorman, Frank H., Jr. *Divine Presence and Community: A Commentary on the Book of Leviticus*. ITC. Grand Rapids: Eerdmans, 1997.

Jenson, Philip Peter. *Graded Holiness: A Key to the Priestly Conception of the World*. JSOTSup 106. Sheffield: JSOT Press, 1992.

Milgrom, Jacob. *Leviticus 1–16*. AB 3. New York: Doubleday, 1991.

Murray, Andrew. *Holy in Christ*. Morrison & Gibb, 1888.

Palmer, Christine. "Israelite High Priestly Apparel: Embodying an Identity between Human and Divine." In *Fashioned Selves: Dress and Identity in Antiquity*, edited by Megan Cifarelli, 117–27. Oxford: Oxbow, 2019.

Smith, James K.A. *You Are What You Love: The Spiritual Power of Habit*. Grand Rapids: Brazos, 2016.

Warren, Tish Harrison. *Liturgy of the Ordinary: Sacred Practices in Everyday Life*. Downers Grove, IL: InterVarsity Press, 2016.

CHAPTER 4

THE CALENDAR FOR WORSHIP IN ANCIENT ISRAEL

Worship in the Feasts and Celebrations

JoAnna M. Hoyt

The ancient Israelites worshiped our same God, in part through feasts and celebrations described in the Mosaic Covenant. Leviticus 23 lists the seven feasts and celebrations as well as the sabbath, calling them the "appointed times of the Lord".[1] God specially ordained each of these eight events as worship to him. Though the majority of modern Christians do not celebrate the Israelite feasts and celebrations, their underlying theology of worship is consistent with what God still desires from us today. As we worship the Triune God today, we do so with the ancient Israelites as they worshiped him through their feasts and celebrations.

CONTEXT OF WORSHIP IN THE FEASTS AND CELEBRATIONS

The Israelite feasts and celebrations existed in a wider context where such religious events were common. It was in this culture that God established the Israelite feasts and celebrations. He redeemed this common feature of the surrounding culture by changing aspects of the feasts and placing them within a different theological context as worship to him. The following survey of ancient Near Eastern feasts followed by a survey of the Israelite feasts describe the cultural context and features of the feasts, which provide a foundation for the later discussion of their theology of worship.

1. The Hebrew word *ḥag* is best translated as "festival," but the term "feast" is used here because that is the traditional term used to describe these events. And, even though the Feast of Trumpets and the Day of Atonement are not addressed as "feasts/festivals" in the Old Testament, they are included in this chapter's use of the word "feasts" for ease of discussion.

Feasts and Celebration in the Ancient Near East

Religious feasts and celebrations were a part of life for each cultural group in the ancient Near East and are not unique to the ancient Israelites. Some specific feasts were common throughout the ancient Near East, such as new year feasts, feasts concerning the dead and/or the netherworld, agricultural feasts, and feasts celebrating the seventh day of the seventh month.[2] Some feasts were tied to a culture's understanding of their gods' relationship with nature such as celebrations of the winter solstice "in honor of the resurrection of the sun-god."[3] Many feasts praised the gods for providing food, favor, protection, and so on and asked them for further provisions.

The vast number of ancient Near Eastern feasts make a full survey impossible for this setting. Instead, a survey of the most well-known feast will suffice for a general understanding of some of their basic features. The most well-known ancient feast is the yearly Babylonian *Akitu* feast for purification and celebrating the new year. Its focus on purification shares many similarities to the Israelite Day of Atonement. The *Akitu* feast would last twelve days, as opposed to the one day of the Day of Atonement. The first half was a private component celebrated among individuals and families, while the second half was a communal celebration that included processions of the Marduk idol, banquets, and other public rituals. The Babylonian king was key to the feast since he was reigning on behalf of the gods. For example, as a sign of humility, the priest would slap the king, who would then kneel before the idol of Marduk and perform an oath.[4]

Though composed of both private and communal elements, the underlying focus was on the temple. With regard to the temple, the purification rites included a cleansing of the priest, sprinkling of the sanctuary, sacrificed animals, and confession, all of which are also included in the Israelite Day of Atonement. The differences, though, include exorcising a demon guilty of causing the defilement (as opposed to purifying the results of the sins of the people), offering a burnt offering to cleanse the temple (as opposed to also sending away a goat as sin-bearer), and focusing on the king's worthiness (as opposed to the people's purity).[5]

Versions of the *Akitu* feast were found throughout the surrounding cultures, including Ugarit. While much is unknown about the Ugaritic

---

2. For more details concerning the ancient Near Eastern feasts please see Mark Cohen, *The Cultic Calendars of the Ancient Near East* (Bethesda, MD: CDL Press, 1993), 389–481. The seventh day of the seventh month was considered "unfavorable" and "unlucky." Thus the festivals on that day were intended to counteract that by having the people "cleanse themselves" of evil on that day (Cohen, *Cultic Calendars*, 391).
3. Cohen, *Cultic Calendars*, 394.
4. Stephen Bertman, *Handbook to Life in Ancient Mesopotamia* (New York: Facts on File, 2003), 130–32.
5. Jacob Milgrom, *Leviticus: A Book of Ritual and Ethics*, CC (Minneapolis: Fortress, 2004), 163–165.

ritual, it demonstrates similarities such as the inclusion of sacrifices and the focus on purity, though there is no indication it was concerned with the purity of the temple.[6]

By celebrating the religious feasts, Israel was taking part in the wider culture of the ancient Near East. The similarities between their feasts illustrate that God revealed himself within a culture, and the differences illustrate how God took the secular and re-created it into something holy as worship to himself. The Israelites participated in their surrounding culture while also standing apart from it.

The Biblical Feasts and Celebrations

Leviticus 23 lists, and briefly describes, the "appointed times of the Lord" (*mo'ade yhwh*), which include the seven feasts and the Sabbath. The seven are referred to in this manuscript as "feasts," the Old Testament addresses neither the Feast of Trumpets nor the Day of Atonement as a "feast" (*ḥag*). The seven feasts can be divided into three groups: (1) those that occur in the first month: The Passover and the Feast of Unleavened Bread; (2) those that occur in the seventh month: the Feast of Trumpets, the Day of Atonement, and the Feast of Booths (or Tabernacles, or *Sukkot*); and (3) agricultural feasts: the Feast of the Firstfruits and the Feast of the Ingathering (or Harvests).

Feasts in the first month

While the Passover and the Feast of Unleavened Bread are two separate feasts, they are intricately tied together both in timing and purpose (Exod. 12:1–28, 42–49; 13:3–10; 23:15; 34:18; Lev. 23:5–8; Num. 9:1–14; Deut. 16:1–7). The Passover occurs first, at twilight on the fourteenth day of the first month, and lasts only one day. The Feast of Unleavened Bread begins the following day, on the fifteenth, and lasts for seven days. The Passover recounts the night of the final plague on the Egyptians, which led to Pharaoh setting the people free, and the Feast of Unleavened Bread celebrates their hasty departure. These feasts celebrate the past, not to live in the past, but to worship the God who acted in the past (see Exod. 12:14).

Feasts in the seventh month

The three feasts of the seventh month include the Feast of Trumpets, the Day of Atonement, and the Feast of Booths.[7] The Feast of Trumpets is a day of "remembrance" (*zikkaron*) and a time for the blowing of trumpets

6. N. Nick Wyatt, *Religious Texts from Ugarit: The Words of Ilimilku and His Colleagues* (Sheffield: Sheffield Academic, 1998), 342–47.

7. Interestingly, even though there are three feasts in the seventh month, none fall on the seventh day of the month. As mentioned in the survey of ancient Near Eastern feasts, the seventh day of the seventh month was a common feast day. It was intended to counteract the perceived unluckiness of the day. This difference from their neighbors may indicate a refusal to endorse such a feast, while also acknowledging the cultural significance of the seventh month.

(Lev. 23:23–25; Num. 29:1–6). Little is said about the purpose and function of this feast in the biblical text.[8] Today, this feast is known as Rosh Hashanah (New Year), though that connection is not in the biblical description.[9]

The second event in this grouping is the Day of Atonement (Lev. 16; 23:26–32; Num. 29:7–11). Though the Day of Atonement is an "appointed time of Yahweh," it is not a time for feasting or celebrating, but a time of ceasing, a complete refrain from all work, and a time of humbling one's soul before God (Lev. 16:31; 23:32). Though the purpose is often considered a day of purification of the people, its primary focus is the cleansing of the temple from the effects of the people's sin (Lev. 16:16). Even though the Israelites offered sacrifices throughout the year for their sins, and God responded to their faith (evidenced in their obedience), the sacrifices were inadequate (see Heb. 10:1–18). Thus, even with the sacrifices, the sins of the people tarnished the holiness of the temple. As the place where the holy God chose to meet with Israel, it was important for the temple to remain holy and pure. For this reason, this is a somber day set aside to acknowledge and address how their sin affects their relationship with God.

The last feast of this grouping is the Feasts of Booths (or Tabernacles or *Sukkot*) which occurs in the seventh month, just after the grape harvest. It calls for the people to gather foliage and live in tents/booths for seven days as a reminder of their ancestors who lived in the wilderness while waiting to enter the Promised Land (Lev. 23:33–43; Num. 29:12–40; Deut. 16:13–15; 31:10–13). This feast celebrates God's past actions (guidance into the land) and his present provisions (the harvest). By combining these two purposes into one feast, the Israelites worshiped God as the God of the past and present, with hope for the future.

Feasts concerning agriculture

The third group of "appointed times" includes the Feast of Firstfruits and the Feast of Ingathering.[10] While these are two distinct feasts, they are

---

8. Milgrom connects this feast with the use of trumpets (or, as he calls them, "alarm blasts") in the ancient Near East to gain a deity's attention to fulfill a need of the people. Combining this with the types of sacrifices and the timing of the feast, Milgrom proposes that the purpose of this feast was to "beseech God for adequate and timely rain in the forthcoming agricultural year" (Milgrom, *Leviticus*, 280–81).
9. The surrounding ancient Near Eastern religions often had a second New Year's feast at the beginning of the seventh month to celebrate the agricultural year, which makes such a connection possible (Milgrom, *Leviticus*, 280).
10. The distinction between these two feasts in the biblical text is not always clear. The Feast of Firstfruits in Exodus 23:16a and 34:22a is described with the words "firstfruits" (*bikkure*) and "weeks" (*shabuot*), yet the feast in Leviticus 23:15–22 and Deuteronomy 16:9–12, which most identify with the Feast of Ingathering, uses "firstfruits" and "weeks." This study identifies the Feast of Ingathering in Exod. 23:16b, 34:22b; Lev. 23:15–22; and Deut. 16:9–12; and the Feast of Firstfruits in Exod. 23:16a; 34:22a; Lev. 23:9–14; Num. 28:26–31; Deut. 26.

closely related. The Feast of Firstfruits occurs at the beginning of the barley harvest,[11] and the Feast of Ingathering occurs at the end of the wheat harvest.[12] Each of the two feasts is one day long and celebrates God's provision through the produce of the land. The biblical text states that the first is celebrated at the "turning of the year" (*tequpat hashshana*) and at the "harvest" (*qasir*), and the second is observed fifty days after the first.[13] This fifty-day period later earned the second feast the title "Pentecost," which means "fifty." The biblical text says surprisingly little about these two feasts.

Sabbath as celebration

Even though the Sabbath is not called a "feast" or "celebration" it is not only included but also begins the list of "appointed times of the LORD" in Leviticus 23. As an "appointed time" it reveals much about Israel's worship. The weekly day of ceasing stands unique in the ancient Near East. In agricultural societies ceasing from work once a week is a ludicrous idea. Yet God called the Israelites to do just that. This weekly ceasing requires the people to demonstrate complete trust that God will provide even though they stop working. The Israelites were to observe the Sabbath as a way to remember that God alone is the one who made them holy (Exod. 31:13). As the one who made them holy, he gave them the Sabbath for themselves and for himself (Exod. 31:14–15).

THEOLOGY OF WORSHIP

Throughout the "appointed times of the LORD" there are seven common elements that reveal pieces of Israel's theology of worship. Each of these elements communicate the same underlying theology: Israel was in a relationship with the holy God, who had provided and protected them in the past, and on whom they were still dependent for provision and protection; all of which compelled Israel to worship him.

The Community's Role in Worship

Six of the seven feasts, as well as the Sabbath, call for a "holy assembly" (*miqra qodesh*).[14] On these occasions, the Israelites were to gather together

11. Milgrom, *Leviticus*, 277.
12. Milgrom, *Leviticus*, 278.
13. Exod. 34:22; Lev. 23:15–16. These two agricultural feasts are tied closely to the observance of the Passover and Feast of Unleavened Bread, with the first traditionally celebrated at the end of the Feast of Unleavened bread. This connection is explained by some through the (yeast-raised) grain offerings of the Feast of Firstfruits as "a sign of the fullness of God's blessing in comparison to the earlier week-long consumption of unleavened bread, the sign of poverty and affliction" (R. Dennis Cole, "Numbers," in *Zondervan Illustrated Bible Backgrounds Commentary: Old Testament*, vol. 1, *Genesis, Exodus, Leviticus, Numbers, Deuteronomy*, ed. John Walton (Grand Rapids: Zondervan, 2009), 389.
14. The Passover does not call for a "holy assembly," but it is intertwined with the Feast of Unleavened Bread, which calls for a holy assembly on the day following the Passover.

(not necessarily in Jerusalem[15] in a manner that is characterized as "holy" (*qodesh*). This holiness did not come through any ritual or action. The assembly was holy because a people already declared holy (Deut. 7:6) were gathering to worship the holy God in submission and obedience to him.

Holy assemblies highlight two things about the Israelites' worship. First, there are special types and times of worship that require God's people, who are declared holy, to worship together. Worship is often communal. Holy assemblies were so important to worship that they were required not only for special occasions but also weekly at the Sabbath. Second, assembling together is worship when it is a holy assembling. Their feasts and celebrations were worship not because they gathered, but because they did so as people called to be holy, and in accord with the holy God's instructions. When the people come together as holy people dedicated and obedient to God, the assembly stands apart from other assemblies.

Remembrance and Teaching as Worship

Remembrance and teaching are integral parts of Israelite worship in the feasts. In both of the first-month feasts (Passover and Unleavened Bread), the first and last of the seventh-month feasts (Trumpets and Booths), and the last of the agricultural feasts (Ingathering), the Israelites were instructed to use the occasions as a remembrance and/or teaching tool.[16] Each of the five feasts with this element called the Israelites to remember either God's actions and provisions in the past or his provisions in the present.

The descriptions primarily use either the verb "remember" (*zakar*) or the related noun "reminder" (*zikkaron*) to describe this purpose. Both of these words describe not a recalling of something forgotten, but a calling to mind of an event that is known. In other words, the purpose is to keep what is to be remembered at the forefront of one's mind. This drawing to mind is similar to dwelling and meditating on God and his past actions. This type of remembering is vital to one's relationship with God and the resulting worship. One must continually call to mind what one knows about God in order to worship him.

In the Israelite mind-set, the future was behind them (because it was unknown) and the past was before them (because it was known).[17] This same mindset was integral to the feasts. As they celebrated, they looked at the past because it gave them the reason for the celebration (e.g., the

15. They were called to Jerusalem only three times a year. See discussion below in the section "Commitment in Worship."
16. Only two of the seven feasts do not mention teaching or remembrance: Firstfruits and the Day of Atonement. Though it is not specifically mentioned for the Feast of the Firstfruits, it is mentioned for the first observance of the feast when they enter the land (Deut. 26). And the Day of Atonement does not call for teaching or remembering the distant past; rather, its focus is on solemnity for the consequences of their recent sins.
17. Cf. John H. Walton, *Ancient Near Eastern Thought and the Old Testament: Introducing the Conceptual World of the Hebrew Bible*, 2nd ed. (Grand Rapids: Baker Academic, 2018), 195.

Exodus) and helped them to trust the God who they could see in the past, but could not (yet!) see in the future, and to understand and recognize his actions in their present.

Three descriptions of remembrance and teaching in the feasts are especially important. First, God specifically mentions that children will ask questions about the purpose of the Passover and Feast of Unleavened Bread. He instructs the adults to take advantage of this teaching opportunity and explain not just the past event of the exodus but also what that past event teaches about God (Exod. 13:14–15). Second, though not listed as a perpetual feature, the first Feast of Firstfruits in the land included everyone reciting the history of Israel, from Abram down through their entrance into the land and its first harvest (Deut. 26:3–11). And, finally, the Feast of Booths calls for a full reading of the law to all the Israelites every seven years so that everyone may "learn" (*lamad*) to fear the Lord (Deut. 31:10–13). This word for "learn" refers not merely to the gathering of head knowledge but to a learning that necessitates acting on the knowledge. To worship God, one must know who God is. Yet it is not head knowledge that prompts worship but an engagement with that knowledge.

Sacrifices and Offerings as Worship

As the Israelites brought their various sacrifices and offerings to the Levites and priests, the people were continually reminded of their brokenness before God. The sacrifices never ceased. Though there were daily and occasional sacrifices and offerings, the feasts required even more. The feasts in the seventh month and the agricultural feasts required burnt offerings, grain offerings, and sin offerings. The Feast of Ingathering also required a freewill offering and a peace offering. The Feast of Booths required the most amount of sacrifices and offerings, tallying a total of 189 animals over seven days.[18]

The sacrifices and offerings of the feasts did not restore their relationship to God but were acts of obedience and worship carried out in faith which God responded to with grace and mercy. Their inclusion in the feasts highlighted their continual need for God's grace in the face of their sin. Part of their worship during the feasts included remembering their sin, their brokenness, and God's mercy. This aspect of the worship in the feasts required obedience, humility, and repentance.

Commitment in Worship

A study of the Israelite feasts reveals a deep level of commitment. Three times a year Israelites were to leave their land and their work and

18. See Num. 29:12–40. For each of the seven days they were to sacrifice two rams, fourteen male lambs, and one male goat for a total of fourteen rams, ninety-eight male lambs, and seven male goats. Additionally, on the first day they sacrificed thirteen bulls, and on each subsequent day they were to offer one less bull (e.g., twelve bulls on the second day, and eleven on the third day), for a total of seventy bulls.

in celebration of feasts travel to the place where God caused his name to dwell; Shiloh initially, then Jerusalem.[19] This worship required a high level of commitment that left their land unprotected, a commitment to endure a journey, a commitment to part with their material possessions such as animals and grains for sacrifices, and a commitment to relinquish their tithes.

To leave one's land and travel to Jerusalem (or, initially, Shiloh) left the land vulnerable to invaders. In calling the people to leave their land, God's command was a call for them to trust him to protect their land. In Exodus 34:23–24 God addressed this concern: they were free to travel because God would drive out the other nations (those who would be tempted to invade in their absence), and he assured them that no one would covet their land.

In addition to leaving their land vulnerable, they must act on their commitment to God by traveling. While today it takes mere hours to travel to Jerusalem from any part of Israel, travel for the ancient Israelites was more involved. If one lived, say, in Dan and traveled to Jerusalem the distance is approximately 150 miles (depending on the route). If one traveled twenty miles a day, then that would take seven and a half days—one way. Such a journey required the sacrifice not just of leaving one's land but of time and physical exertion as well.

And, last, their worship through the feasts required a commitment of their material possessions. Not only did they relinquish portions of their flocks and harvests as sacrifices and offerings, but they also relinquished portions as tithes. While the biblical text does not clearly delineate tithes as a part of the feasts, some tithes were a tenth of the produce of the land and several of the feasts occurred at the end of the harvests when the tithes would have been gathered. The instructions for tithes directed that they were to be given to the Levites (see Num. 18:21), used for celebrating in Jerusalem (see Deut. 14:23–26), and contributed as support for the poor and needy (see Deut. 14:28–29). This relinquishing of a tenth of their flocks and harvests required the people to show their commitment through their material possessions.

The commitment required for worship in the feasts is weighty. God called for the people to fully commit themselves to worship him by leaving their land, traveling, and relinquishing material possessions. None of these were easy feats. This aspect of their worship required that they commit all they had (their land, time, and possessions) to God and value worshiping God above them all.

Rejoicing as Worship

The Israelites were commanded to rejoice (*samaḥ*) at the three feasts connected to agriculture: Feast of Ingathering, Feast of Booths, and the

19. See Exod. 23:13–17; 34:23–24; Deut. 16:16–17. Exod. 23:13–17 states that the feasts are the Feast of Unleavened Bread, the Feast of Firstfruits, and the Feast of the Ingathering. Deuteronomy 16:16–17, however, replaces the Feast of Ingathering with the Feast of Booths.

first celebration in the land of the Feast of Firstfruits.[20] The description of each of these three feasts also shares another unique description: they are to celebrate the feast "for" themselves (*ta'ase lek*, "do/celebrate [the feast] for yourselves," Exod. 34:22, Num. 29:12, Deut. 16:13). Every harvest was a reminder of God's promise for their possession of the land and the bountiful produce of the land. The harvests, then, were a time to rejoice, not only in God but also in the fulfillment of God's promises. They were to rejoice "for" themselves because they had received blessings.

It may seem strange that God would command people to rejoice, since rejoicing is often viewed as an expression of positive emotion, often conflated with happiness, which is organic and not produced on command. Yet, this very instruction demands that we shift our perspective. The Hebrew verb describes a "concrete expression" and "articulated expressions of joy" not an abstract emotion.[21] At these harvest feasts, the people were to chose to find joy in God's provision of the harvest and express that joy in celebration. The command to rejoice did not come with an exception clause if a person was filled with grief or another emotion. Rather, when God's provisions were received the people were to choose to rejoice regardless of their other life situations. This does not negate emotions such as grief, anger or sadness, but it places them secondary for a time in order to focus on God's provisions.

Ceasing as Worship

Most of the feasts required a ceasing from work. Five of the feasts (Unleavened Bread, Firstfruits, Ingathering, Trumpets, and Booths) state that no "laborious work" (*kal-meleket aboda*) may be done. This type of work includes both a skill/craft and the work of a job (Exod. 36:1, 3; 1 Chron. 9:13; 28:13; 28:20; 2 Chron. 24:12). This stands in contrast to the commands for the Day of Atonement and Sabbath, which specify that no work of any kind (*kal-melaka*) should be done. The Mosaic law specifies that this type of ceasing includes a restriction against even gathering firewood (see Exod. 31:14–15; 35:2–3; Num. 15:32–36), which is neither a skill nor a job. This indicates that there are two types of ceasing work. Once a week and for an additional day during the year the people were to completely stop working in order to worship, and as worship. However, the other five feasts merely limited the types of work but do not limit things such as gathering firewood. Theologically this causes us to consider not just that ceasing is part of worship but also that there are different levels of such ceasing. While there are

20. All feasts are described as a time of rejoining in Numbers 10:10, and elsewhere it is commanded specifically for the Feasts of Booths (Lev. 23:40, Deut. 16:15), Ingathering (Deut. 16:11), and the first celebration of the Feast of Firstfruits (Deut. 26:11). The Feast of Booths is not listed in the grouping of agricultural feasts at the beginning of this chapter because its primary focus is on remembrance of the exodus journey, but it is also tied to the agricultural calendar.

21. G. Vanoni, "*śāmaḥ*," in TDOT 14:147, 149.

times to cease all work, other instances of worship may only require that we limit our work, such as in taking a break from our jobs. In both instances, the absence of work is not laziness but worship. Ceasing from work in order to worship demonstrates a trust that God is the one who provides—not us.

Humility in Worship

The Day of Atonement stands apart from the other six feasts because it commands the people to "humble [their] soul" (*tannu et-napshotekem*; see Lev. 16:29, 31; 23:27, 32; Num. 29:7). While there is an implied humbling in gathering for a holy assembly (gathering as people called to be holy with the holy God requires humility), this is the only feast which commands that the people "humble [their] soul." To humble oneself is to acknowledge one's dependence on God by deeming oneself as lesser in regard to power and worth.[22] The humbling of a soul requires going beyond the head knowledge of one's dependence on God to the reality evidenced in how one approaches and responds to God. The Day of Atonement required the people to acknowledge who they were (sinners) and who God is (holy) and that it was merely by God's grace and mercy that they were able to know him because their sin tarnished them and his temple. The forbearance of God to still meet the people where they were, and to dwell among them in the tabernacle/temple, even though their sin tarnished the tabernacle/temple, truly is a humbling reality.

Significance of the Feasts and Celebrations for Biblical Worship

Here we turn our attention to how the theological elements discussed above, which are part of the fulfilled Mosaic covenant, have significance for how we worship today as we live in the new covenant. The Israelite feasts may seem a distant reality that have no bearing on our worship today. Yet the theology of worship that underlies their feasts are applicable because we worship the same God.

Worship within Community

The holy assemblies of Israel's feasts teach us about the community and holiness aspects of worship. While we can worship alone, God, at times, calls us to worship together. For the Israelites that was weekly (in Sabbath observance), as well as for most of the feasts. This idea remains consistent in the New Testament as well (Heb. 10:25; Acts 2:42). Additionally, like the Israelites, we are God's holy people, declared holy by his grace and mercy (see 2 Cor. 7:1; 1 Thess. 4:7; 1 Peter 1:15–16). When we gather to worship as holy people worshiping the holy God, our assemblies should be characterized by that holiness.

There are a variety of ways Christians "do" worship when we gather. While some of us are liturgical, and others of us flee from liturgy, may we

22. Cf. R. Martin-Archard, "*ʿnh*," in *TLOT* 2:933.

never lose sight of the underlying foundation of our community worship as *holy*. As we participate in, or are involved in leading, our weekly and special assemblies, we should each ask ourselves whether it is a holy assembly. A holy assembly is identifiable by the reason and result of gathering. The New Testament provides clarity for the holy assemblies in its discussion on the church's unity. Assemblies are holy when they are composed of those God declares holy (i.e., Christians), are founded on Christ, and bring glory to God (Rom. 15:5–6; John 17). We must always remember that the assemblies will not be holy because of how we craft the service, or how loud we sing, or even how much we participate; rather, they are holy because we are a holy people gathered in unity to worship the holy God. Relatedly, we must reject any elements that are unholy or bring disunity for they do not glorify God.

Worship through Remembrance and Teaching

To worship well we must live in the past. Not in a negative sense and not with longing, but with the benefit of hindsight and proclamation. A major component of the feasts and celebrations was remembering the past and teaching the past. The past is where we see God with a clarity that's difficult (or impossible) to obtain for the present and future. As we worship, we must do what the Israelites did: remember and teach the past (see 2 Tim. 3:14; Titus 1:9; 1 Peter 2:2; 2 Peter 3:2). Jesus himself instructed us to do this in his last observance of the Passover, which became the church's Eucharist celebration, in which he declared "do this in remembrance of me" (Luke 22:7–20; 1 Cor. 11:23–26).

Remembering and teaching the past begins with teaching Scripture. The remembering and teaching should expand beyond Sunday school, Bible studies, and sermons. While those are great places for remembering and teaching, do not forget that the teaching of the feasts often happened as they were observing various aspects of the feasts. For example, their children would ask what the feasts meant, and the parents would answer. If our churches relegate teaching only to classes and sermons we will miss out on a vast number of opportunities. The teaching need not (and should not) only be formal teaching. Here the instructions of Deuteronomy 6:4–9 ring loudly. Teaching should be as much a part of our lives as breathing.

Additionally, our remembering and teaching should expand to the church's history and our own history. How has God been at work in the church for the past two thousand years? Those who have gone before us have much they can teach us. How have you seen God revealed in your life? Find ways to set up memorials. Not so you can live in the past, but to remember how God intervened in your life so you can have confidence and hope that he can and will do so in the future. Your memorials will help you worship, and when shared as testimonies, they can help the community worship.

Let us not be afraid to boldly stand and face the past: the past of the Israelites, the New Testament believers, the early church, the church throughout history, and our own past. And let us not fear the unpleasant parts of the past, but rather remember and teach how God was there too. It is that teaching and remembering which will help propel our worship.

Worship Knowing the Sacrifices Are Complete

One cannot deny that sacrifices and offerings were worship; but comprehending the reality of this when we live after the cross and the empty grave is difficult. We have no action today that is similar.[23] And that's for good reason! We no longer offer sacrifices, but rather rejoice in the sacrifice of Jesus Christ. Even still, the sacrifices at the Israelite feasts should influence our worship today.

Every time the Israelites brought their sacrifices, whether during a feast or otherwise, they faced the reality of their sin and their need for God's grace and mercy. Though as Christians we approach God knowing that our sins have been removed from us, we should never forget that we approach God in worship through the sacrifice of Jesus Christ (see Heb. 10:1–22). A friend once asked what our church services would look like if we had to sacrifice a lamb on our way into the sanctuary. Perhaps we would not walk so casually. Perhaps we would stop texting. Perhaps we would stop critiquing the songs. Perhaps we would stop being distracted. Perhaps being faced with a physical reminder of our sin and our need for God's grace and mercy would help us worship. Thankfully, though, we do not offer sacrifices. But as we gather to worship, we should meditate on and celebrate Jesus Christ's sacrifice so that we are not tempted to lose our focus in worship.

Worship Requires Counting the Cost

There is often a tendency to think of worship a bit selfishly, as something we enjoy doing. We choose our churches based on whether we like their style of worship. And perhaps we only go to church services or events when they are convenient. Yet what we learn from the feasts is that there were times when God called the people to do something decidedly inconvenient as worship for him. They had to leave their homes unprotected three times a year and undertake, for many of them, a long and arduous journey, and then part with material possessions as part of their worship. The New Testament affirms this cost of worship (see Luke 14:26–35; Rom. 12:1; Eph. 4:1; 1 Peter 2:11; Heb. 13:5). As those who live after the cross and the empty grave, we are not required to travel to Jerusalem three times a year, but we are called to fully commit our lives to the obedience and worship of God. Worship requires commitment; it requires us to consider the cost of worship. If our worship is never inconvenient, it would perhaps be good to ask why.

---

23. Let us not fall into the trap of referring to forgoing our favorite indulgence as a "sacrifice." To do so is to demean, to cheapen, and to misunderstand the purpose and role of sacrifices in the Hebrew Bible.

Worship with Rejoicing

The idea of God commanding us to rejoice is, perhaps, the most difficult of all of these elements of worship. This command calls us to reconsider how we integrate our emotions into our worship. It is far too easy to fall into the trap of thinking that worship is founded on emotions, that we only worship if we "feel like it." Yet that is not the case. In the context of the feasts, the command to rejoice was contextually fitting because of the receipt of God's blessings. So, too, should we rejoice when we receive blessings (see Rom. 12:15; 1 Cor. 12:26, 13:6; Phil. 4:4; 1 Thess. 5:16; 1 Peter 4:13). Instead, I fear, we find it far too easy to receive the blessings and forget to rejoice. It is also important to note that even though the Israelites were commanded to rejoice in these feasts, this command did not negate the other, very real emotions and their role in worship. While worship sometimes calls for rejoicing, do not forget the lament psalms that prove one can worship with grief (see Pss. 10; 26; 38; 74; 120; 137).

Worship by Ceasing

Christians debate whether Sabbath observance is required within the new covenant.[24] Regardless of whether one observes the Sabbath, the ceasing from work present in the Sabbaths and the feasts has much to contribute to our worship today. Ceasing required the ancient Israelites to wholly rely on God to provide, and it allowed them the opportunities to set aside distractions and focus on worshiping God. Our society has conditioned us to be busy and self-reliant. While not inherently wrong, busyness distracts us from worship. And self-reliance conditions us to look to ourselves and not God, which is the opposite of worship. How often do you sit in a church service and think about work or responsibilities? Or about how you are going to solve some problem or situation? For many of us, that is a constant struggle. Even if you do not choose to fully observe the Sabbath, the discipline of setting aside our busy and self-reliant lives to worship God is a worthy endeavor (see Matt. 6:25–34). And let us not forget that an even greater ceasing is promised at the completion of the new covenant (see Heb. 4:1–11).

Worship in Humility

Humbling oneself does not come naturally to us. But that is what God asks of us. While the Israelites were specifically told to humble themselves once a year, humility before God is required in all worship. One cannot worship God without understanding who he is (even if only in part). And the more we understand who he is, the more we understand who we are, which is a humbling process. Yet there is a way in which we can "stall out" in our humility as we worship and become comfortable with who

24. For a discussion of various perspectives on the Sabbath see Charles P. Arand and Christopher John Donato, eds., *Perspectives on the Sabbath: 4 Views* (Nashville: B&H Academic, 2011).

we are in relation to him. Just as the Israelites paused once a year and intentionally focused on humbling themselves before him, so too should we intentionally focus on humbling ourselves (see James 4:10). It is good to periodically pause and consider the magnitude of who God is and the magnitude of our sin (which has been removed from us!), and the magnitude of his grace and mercy.

CONCLUSION

As we worship the Triune God in our various contexts and styles let us never forget that we are worshiping with the Israelites. Their worship in the feasts echoes through history and encourages and guides us in our worship. The underlying theology of worship in their feasts is consistent with what God desires of us who live after the cross and the empty grave. Let us worship as holy assemblies who remember and teach who God is. Let us celebrate Christ's ultimate fulfillment of the sacrifices while counting the cost of worshiping our Triune God. And let us rejoice in his blessings, while ceasing from our striving to do and provide, and humble ourselves before our God. Let us worship together with the ancient Israelites.

BIBLIOGRAPHY

Arand, Charles P, and Christopher John Donato. *Perspectives on the Sabbath: 4 Views*. Nashville: B&H Academic, 2011.

Bertman, Stephen. *Handbook to Life in Ancient Mesopotamia*. New York: Facts on File, 2003.

Cohen, Mark. *The Cultic Calendars of the Ancient Near East*. Bethesda, MD: CDL Press, 1993.

Cole, R. Dennis. "Numbers." In *Zondervan Illustrated Bible Backgrounds Commentary: Old Testament*, vol. 1, *Genesis, Exodus, Leviticus, Numbers, Deuteronomy*, edited by John Walton, 338–417. Grand Rapids: Zondervan, 2009.

Martin-Archard, R. "*'nh*." In *TLOT* 2:931–37.

Milgrom, Jacob. *Leviticus: A Book of Ritual and Ethics*. CC. Minneapolis: Fortress, 2004.

Vanoni, G. "*samaḥ*." In *TDOT* 14:142–57.

Walton, John H. *Ancient Near Eastern Thought and the Old Testament: Introducing the Conceptual World of the Hebrew Bible*. 2nd ed. Grand Rapids: Baker Academic, 2018.

Wyatt, N. Nick. *Religious Texts from Ugarit: The Words of Ilimilku and His Colleagues*. Sheffield: Sheffield Academic, 1998.

CHAPTER 5

TRUST AND OBEDIENCE AS WORSHIP TO YAHWEH

Worship in the Book of Joshua

J. Michael Thigpen

CONTEXT OF WORSHIP IN JOSHUA

Although many popular definitions of worship can be found, there are two works that have consistently helped me understand worship biblically: Allen Ross's *Recalling the Hope of Glory* and Daniel Block's *For the Glory of God*.[1] Both works pursue worship with a long lens seeking the widest possible idea of worship—not just worship in our organized communal and private devotional practices. Each work contributes uniquely to a definition and theology of worship, yet there is an amazing set of commonalities in their definitions. Ross defines true worship as "the celebration of being in covenant fellowship with the sovereign and holy triune God, by the means of the reverent adoration and spontaneous praise of God's nature and works, the expressed commitment of trust and obedience to the covenant responsibilities, and the memorial reenactment of entering into covenant through ritual acts, all with the confident anticipation of the fulfillment of the covenant promises in glory."[2]

Let me highlight a few key items from Ross's work. First the attitude or demeanor of worship is celebratory, reverent, adoring, spontaneous, praiseful, trusting, and expectant. Second, the context of worship is a covenant relationship with God, who is holy and sovereign, and who reveals

1. Allen P. Ross, *Recalling the Hope of Glory: Biblical Worship from the Garden to the New Creation* (Grand Rapids: Kregel Academic, 2006); Daniel I. Block, *For the Glory of God: Recovering a Biblical Theology of Worship* (Grand Rapids: Baker Academic, 2014).
2. Ross, *Recalling the Hope of Glory*, 67–68.

himself. Third, the actions of worship include trust and obedience, and memorial reenactment.[3]

These highlights are helpful when approaching a book like Joshua in order to learn about worship. If you are like me, my default view of worship tends to include many of the attitudes Ross enumerates along with the relational context. But when it comes to the actions of worship, memorial enactment is the only one that regularly comes to mind. As I worked on this chapter, I came to see that too often I left trust and obedience out of my definition of worship. Joshua has relatively few memorial reenactments. And although attitudes are certainly addressed, the book has a decided emphasis on trust and obedience—the very items I am prone to neglect in my own practicing definition of worship.

My oversight fared no better when I looked to Block for help. His effort to reflect the "complexity of the biblical picture" of worship leads to this definition: "True worship involves reverential human acts of submission and homage before the divine Sovereign in response to his gracious revelation of himself and in accord with his will."[4] As Block unpacks his definition he notes that we must "recognize that true worship involves actions that demonstrate covenant commitment to and love for God, and that our daily lives [must be] characterized by reverence and awe before him. As the prophets declare . . . and Jesus himself affirms . . . obedience to the revealed ethical will of God must take priority over cultic ritual expression."[5]

The prophets make it clear that the prescribed rituals of worship are not true worship if they are not accompanied by genuine trust and obedience. Yet, as I began to work through the book of Joshua, it became abundantly clear that trust and obedience are not merely necessary accompaniments to worship; they *are* acts of worship. I might even be so bold as to say that in Joshua they are *the* acts of worship at the heart of the book.

The Cultural Context of Joshua

Joshua is set in the midst of a significant transition in the life of Israel. Moses, the one to whom God spoke face-to-face as a friend (Exod. 33:11), is dead. Joshua, Moses's faithful attendant, is now leading the nation. But Joshua is as yet unproven. The people understood his proximity to Moses and had seen Moses designate Joshua as his successor (Deut. 34:9). But Joshua was not a prophet like Moses (Deut. 34:10), nor had the Lord demonstrated signs and wonders through him as he had Moses. Life was very different in Israel now.

---

3. I include trust as both an attitude and an action. It is part of the action of obedience as displayed in the Scriptures. Obedience that is mere formality or ritual is not what the followers are commanded to display. Rather, obedience is an action born of trust in the goodness and wisdom of Yahweh. So here I have included "trust and obedience" as actions of worship.
4. Block, *For the Glory of God*, 23.
5. David M. Howard Jr., *Joshua*, NAC 5 (Nashville: B&H, 1998), 31.

The change in leadership is not the only transition Israel faced. Camped on the edge of the Promised Land, the people were about to wage war against the "giants of the land" in their fortified cities (Num. 13:28–29). They were going where their fathers had been unwilling to go, afraid for their lives (Num. 13:30–14:4). They were going across the Jordan to undo the great weight of shame that had accompanied them in the wilderness as the prior generation slowly died.

They were becoming a landed nation. Abraham, Isaac, and Jacob had lived in the land, but it had not been theirs to possess as a nation. Following Joseph, the family and burgeoning nation had sojourned for centuries in a land not their own. They had been slaves and then refugees on the run from one of the most powerful rulers in the world. Now they would be living in the land promised to Abraham (Gen. 12). They would be home, but it was a home none of them had ever known.

As in any time of transition, questions must have been swirling in their minds and in their conversations. Would God fulfill his promises? Would they be successful where their parents had failed? Would Joshua lead them like Moses? What would happen when Joshua died? What would happen if Joshua fell in battle? What if they could not defeat the people of the land? If they conquered the land, what then? Was their sojourning truly over? Would they find rest in the Promised Land? This was the context of the people we read about. In addition to the people's context, the book of Joshua, as a literary work, also has a context. It was written as "the fitting resolution of issues left unresolved at the end of the Pentateuch." It interprets and provides the context for "Israel's inheriting and settling in the land," which "are the focal points toward which the Pentateuch moves in a purposeful and consistent way."[6] It settles the literary uncertainty that began with Genesis 12, describing the fulfillment of God's promise of a land to Abraham's descendants. Yet Israel's receipt of the land as a gift from the Lord raises other questions that the book will need to address for the readers looking back on this part of their history. What is required of us now? How do we live successfully in this place? What does it mean to be the people of God here and now?

The book of Joshua is God's revelation to Israel to show "who she had been, who she was supposed to be, and who she could become."[7] It would lead her ultimately to see the importance of the threads of the past for who she is to be today and who she would become in the future. This rich tapestry of past, present, and future would be used by God to teach Israel to look for a new Moses—a new Joshua, a new leader—"who would bring the people to follow God all his days and to confess once and for all that this God fulfilled all his promises to his people."[8]

6. Howard, *Joshua*, 30–31.
7. Trent C. Butler, *Joshua*, WBC 7 (Grand Rapids: Zondervan, 1983), xlii.
8. Butler, *Joshua*, xlii.

Worship is about God—who he is and what he does in the past, present, and future. So although our past, present, and future differs in many details from theirs, the basic plot is much closer than we might think. God has revealed himself to us in the past. We worship God in response to his past revelation and his current provisions, by trusting and obeying him in the present. As we trust and obey in the present, we wait with eager expectation for him to fulfill all he has promised in the future. Where Israel struggled to move from past, to present, to hope in the future, we can learn about pitfalls we might face in similar circumstances.

THEOLOGY OF WORSHIP

The Biblical Basis of Worship: Joshua 1:1–9

The book of Joshua opens with the Lord preparing the newly appointed leader. Now that Moses is dead, Joshua will have to take command of the people and lead them into the Promised Land. The Lord encourages Joshua by promising he will use him to bring them into the land, be with him as he was with Moses, and defeat the enemies Israel will encounter (1:1–5). The response required of Joshua does not seem surprising at first glance. He should be strong, read the Scriptures, and be obedient (1:6–9). These requirements seem almost commonplace and unworthy of comment. Yet consider them again; Joshua is to respond with trust and he is not to turn to the right or the left from the book that Moses wrote.

Joshua saw the miracles in the wilderness. He was nearby when Moses spoke with God in the tent of meeting. He had been obedient and called for the people to trust and obey at Kadesh-Barnea (Num. 13–14). Joshua had heard the law given at Mount Sinai, and he had personally affirmed submission to it. He had heard Moses's exposition of the law just before his death. He had all the experience he needed to believe God would keep his promises, to prompt him to be courageous, to be obedient, and to spend a lifetime meditating on God's great acts.

But God never once mentions Joshua's experiences or memories. Instead, God points him to the Scriptures that existed at his time—the *book* of the law of Moses. This sets the tone for the rest of Joshua, emphasizing that the word of God, the Scriptures, are the bedrock of all worship. God teaches Joshua that his call to trust and obey is founded on his meditation on the Scriptures and his attentive obedience to them. His actions will flow from this lifelong orientation to the Scriptures.

The attention to the Scriptures emphasizes past revelation and the record of fulfilled promises as guidance for Joshua's present trust and obedience and his hope for future fulfillment. The Lord also motivates Joshua by connecting his obedience to the written word with his future success. God will reward Joshua's trust and obedience, his worship according to the Scriptures, with divine blessing.

The attention to the Scriptures does not dismiss the revelation Joshua is receiving in the events recorded in the first chapter, nor his personal testimony of his past walk with God. God is speaking to him, and he is right to obey this revelation and to remember and testify to the great acts he saw God do in the past. The emphasis on the Scriptures, as opposed to his personal testimony, serves to bring two issues front and center. First as taught in Deuteronomy 13 and 18, the nation would have to weigh a prophecy or a dream from time to time. True revelation would always lead them to worship the Lord, and thus to live by what had been provided in the Scriptures.[9] As the authoritative revelation, Scripture would serve as the filter through which other prophecies and dreams would be judged. Second, there is the issue of continuity. It is the Scriptures that will carry forward for the next generation the record and interpretation of God's great acts and the record of his will for their lives.[10] Thus Joshua is to worship by the book. His life of worship, his life of trust in God and obedience to his word, will be for his good and for God's glory.

Worship Is a Matter of Life and Death: Joshua 2:1–22; 7:1–26; 23:1–24:33

Part of God's encouragement to Joshua was his assurance that obedience would be rewarded with success.[11] Although it is unstated here the question naturally arises: What are the consequences of disobedience? What if Joshua does not meditate on and obey the word of God, deviating to the left or right of his revealed will? He would clearly not be worshiping, but what would that mean?

We get a hint of an answer to this question almost immediately when the spies encounter Rahab. In Joshua 2:10 she tells the spies that the people of the land are aware of how the Lord revealed himself in the miracle of the Red Sea crossing and in the defeat of Sihon and Og. She now chooses to respond to the Lord's self-revelation by trusting that his sovereignty is as advertised, and that, should she oppose him by opposing his people, she

9. The New Testament also indicates that the Scriptures, both the Old Testament and the apostolic teachings, should be used to weigh private revelation (see 1 Thess. 5:21; 2 Thess. 2:2; 1 John 4:1–3). Paul and John indicate that only a false spirit would "give a message that is contrary to known apostolic teaching" (Gary S. Shogren, *1 and 2 Thessalonians*, ZECNT [Grand Rapids: Zondervan, 2012], 226).

10. See Howard, *Joshua*, 86, for a discussion of the written nature of Scripture and for other examples of texts that indicate the written texts are for posterity.

11. To be sure, the promise of success here is specific to the task at hand. The wider portrait of the Old Testament, especially the Wisdom Literature and Job, is clear that due to sin, the righteous will at times suffer and the wicked will at times prosper. This is in the words of Ecclesiastes an "under the sun" problem. It will ultimately be corrected by God's just actions, but potentially not in our lifetime. Against the broader teaching, we must then understand the promise to Joshua as more limited in scope than a universal promise of success for obedience. For a concise survey of the issues see Howard, *Joshua*, 86–87.

will die. So she trusts and obeys what she knows of him by respecting his power and his people.

Thus she helps the spies escape capture and becomes a heroine of the faith (Heb. 11:31). She responded to God's revelation with acts of submission and homage, acknowledging him as the divine Sovereign[12] and expressing a commitment of trust and obedience.[13] Based on what she knew at this point, she chose to worship the Lord, who had revealed himself to her in the report of his victory, and her life was spared. The story of Jericho shows the opposite outcome for the rest of her town. Their lives were lost in battle as they chose to rely on their gods and to reject the offer of salvation that came in the advance notice of God's prior acts and his impending visitation.

If the story of Rahab helps to confirm the life-and-death nature of worship, the account of Achan inscribes it in stone. Not worshiping the Lord, not trusting and obeying, is deadly. In this well-known story, Achan refuses to trust in God's promises of blessing and instead selfishly takes some of the devoted items. His actions bring death on fellow Israelites who fell in the first battle against Ai, on himself, and on his family.[14]

When Joshua confronts Achan, he encourages him to give glory to God by confessing and not hiding his sin: "Joshua was not instructing Achan to indulge in a disengaged act of glorifying and praising God and then to confess his sin; rather, by his very confession, he was glorifying God."[15] Achan had failed to trust and obey God, and it would cost him his life.

In assessing the life-and-death aspect of worship we must be cautious. The Scriptures do not clarify the eternal destiny of every individual involved. They focus on the Mosaic covenant and the curses and blessings given there. Death was the penalty for many items, but physical death, though often a symbol for eternal damnation, is not the equivalent of it. So here we might rightly question Achan, but how do we understand his willingness to be truthful in the face of imminent punishment? How do we understand the destiny of those Israelites killed in battle as a result of Achan's sin but who had no knowledge of it and were not complicit with him?

On the other side, however, we are able to see a bit more clearly. Rahab definitely moves from the kingdom of darkness to the kingdom of light as she trusts and obeys the revelation she has. In this way worship, as a matter of life and death, looks a lot like Romans 1. Failing to acknowledge the revelation one has—failing to worship the Creator—leads to death. Regardless of whether we know the final state of all the people mentioned,

---

12. Cf. Block's definition of worship.
13. Cf. Ross's definition of worship.
14. On the complex issue of the guilt or innocence of Achan's family and the nation in this incident, see Marten H. Woudstra, *The Book of Joshua*, NICOT (Grand Rapids: Eerdmans, 1981), 130–31.
15. Howard, *Joshua*, 197. Howard notes the same wording is used in John 9:24, when the Pharisees want a blind man to testify truthfully.

the narratives of Joshua make it clear that worship—that is to say, trusting and obeying God—is a matter of life and death.

The book of Joshua concludes with an extended passage that explores the life-and-death realities of worship and calls each Israelite to choose whom they will worship. In an extended discourse running from 23:1 to 24:33, Joshua begins to prepare the people for his death. They are now back in a period of transition, and the very life of the nation is again at stake. However, unlike the beginning of the book, no heir apparent to leadership has been named. Each Israelite is called to worship and to lead in worship by trusting and obeying God as they continue the work of the conquest, taking full possession of their tribal territories.

Joshua begins by reminding them of all that God has done by fighting for them (23:1–3). He goes on to encourage them to continue trusting God by obeying the book of the law of Moses, not deviating from it, just as God had commanded him in the first chapter. Their obedience, completing the conquest as they have been commanded, is a life-or-death task of worship. Joshua tells them that they must drive out the remnants of the nations and not mix with them, lest they turn from the Lord and begin to worship other gods (23:7–8). He presses further and tells them explicitly that, should they fail to worship the Lord, should they refuse to trust and obey this command, the Lord will stop defeating the nations and will instead use them to discipline Israel. Idolatry will lead to the nation perishing from "this good ground that Yahweh gave to you" (23:13).[16]

Now we reach the core of Joshua's argument and the key idea the book brings forward about worship as trust and obedience. In 23:14–16, Joshua teaches them that it is not possible to look back on the good promises God made and kept and not believe his clear warning of certain future judgment for disobedience. If the Israelites accept only the blessings of God without believing and obeying in light of the warning of the curses, they are in fact choosing to reject God. Just as he revealed himself to Moses in Exodus 34:6–7 in a holistic fashion, the Lord refuses to be subdivided into the attributes we like and the attributes we want to reject. He is who he is (Exod. 3:13–22), and each person must accept or reject him as he is.[17] Joshua then reminds the Israelites of their story again in chapter 24 and presses them to choose whether they will worship the Lord. The people acknowledge that they must choose to worship the Lord, and they commit to serving him by trusting and obeying his word, because he is their God. They willingly vow to celebrate the covenant fellowship they have with God by trusting and by obeying the covenant responsibilities

16. All translations are mine unless otherwise noted.

17. For more on how God reveals himself and rejects our attempts to rely on a single attribute while rejecting the totality of who he is, see J. Michael Thigpen, *Divine Motive in the Hebrew Bible: A Comprehensive Survey and Analysis*, Gorgias Biblical Studies (Piscataway, NJ: Gorgias, 2015), 80–81, 178–182, 199–204.

he has revealed to them in the Scriptures. In the words of Deuteronomy 30:19–20, they choose life; they choose to love God by obeying his word.[18]

God's Intentions and Our Motivation to Worship

One important but often-overlooked aspect of the revelation of God in the Old Testament is the declaration of God's motives. God's self-revelation includes record of his actions and his instructions for his people. But this is not all it gives us. It also tells us quite often, and quite explicitly, exactly what motivates God to act the way he does. This self-disclosure of motive serves as a point of motivation for those in covenant relationship with God. The covenant and Israel's obedience to it is not merely a contractual agreement. It is also very much a personal relationship between the sovereign, Yahweh, and his people, Israel. It is a relationship in which the Lord knows his people perfectly and discloses himself to his people. One of the most important ways he does this is to disclose what motivates him.[19]

The theme of divine motive presents itself in several key passages related to trust and obedience in the book of Joshua. A good place to begin is the crossing of the Jordan in Joshua 3–4. There God announces that his motives for the miracle of the Jordan crossing include confirming for Joshua that he will be with him as he was with Moses (3:7); demonstrating to the people that he, not Baal, is a living God, and that he is active in their midst (3:9–10); and affirming that he will accomplish all he has promised with regard to the conquest of the land (3:9–10).[20] What is significant for our purposes is how this disclosure is intended to affect the Israelites. By announcing the miracle and his purposes for the miracles in advance, God is actively supporting them in their worship of him. By giving this present revelation he is affirming his past revelation and prompting them with tangible evidence to bolster their future trust and obedience. Thus we might say that God is motivated to support his people's worship of him, knowing that they are weak and incapable without his enabling work (Josh. 24:19).

Later, in Joshua 4:23–24, when Joshua is instructing the nation in the catechetical use of the twelve stones set up after the crossing, he tells them to teach their children that God's intent for the miracles of the Red Sea and Jordan crossings was twofold. First, he wanted all the peoples of the earth to know that the Lord's hand is powerful. Second, God wanted to lead the

---

18. It is important say explicitly that worship, trust, and obedience flows from the relationship and is not the basis for the relationship. Even here in the old covenant, Israel does not earn the relationship by obedience. They express the relationship by obedience. So failing to worship, choosing not to trust and obey, is an expression of rejection of the covenant relationship. Choosing to trust and obey is an expression of love that is based on the already established relationship. For more on this important distinction see Joe M. Sprinkle, "Law and Narrative in Exodus 19–24," *JETS* 47, no. 2 (2003): 235–52.
19. For more on this aspect of Old Testament theology, see Thigpen, *Divine Motive*.
20. For more on the Baal polemic in the crossing account see J. Michael Thigpen, "Lord of All the Earth: Yahweh and Baal in Joshua 3," *TJ*, n.s. 27, no. 2 (2006): 245–54.

people of Israel and their children to fear him forever. God is motivated to reveal himself to the world and to Israel, so that the world and Israel might respond rightly by worshiping him. In the words of Block, he wants to motivate people to respond with humble acts of submission and homage by his self-revelation.[21]

Finally, in multiple texts there is a subtle but powerful repetition of the idea that God's intentions toward Israel are good and generous. Consider the following partial list: God will be with Joshua to support his leadership (1:5, 9; 3:7, 14; 6:27); God's promises are good and he fulfills them (3:10; 14:13; 23:5, 10, 14–15; 24:20); the land is a gift (1:11, 13, 15; 23:15; 24:13); the land is a place of goodness, abundance, and rest (1:13, 15; 5:10–12; 14:15; 18:1; 22:4; 23:13, 15–16; 24:14); and God acted for the sake of Israel (22:3, 10; 24:14).

Notice how these places that highlight the goodness of God's intentions toward Israel frame the central narrative of the conquest and distribution of the land. This framing functions to ensure that the reader correctly understands and responds to the conquest account. Israel was given a good land, by the grace of God, not on the basis of any merit. The framing ensures that the reader walks away responding "God is good." In the words of Ross's definition, the narrative is designed to prompt "spontaneous praise of God's nature and works."[22] These revelations were intended to function the same way in the life of Israel, who received them before and after the conquest. They served to properly frame the miraculous years of the conquest so that it might lead to worship and praise rather than pride. God is motivated to lead his people to worshipfully respond to his self-revelation.

Testimony and Memorial Reenactment

Although I began this study by outlining the way Joshua teaches the biblical basis of worship, that does not mean that there is no place for personal and corporate testimony in worship. In fact, the memorial reenactments, and the planned future memorial testimonies, are designed to wed together the biblical foundation and the personal experience of God's goodness, and our worshipful response of trust and obedience.

In Joshua 4:6, we see that the memorial stones are intended to prompt the children's question, "What are these stones to you?" This invites personal testimony of the meaning of the stones, the retelling of the experience of the great miracle of the Jordan crossing. Yet this is not all. Later,

21. Block, *For the Glory of God*, 23. For more on the theme of God's self-revelation and the proper response to it see Walther Zimmerli, "Knowledge of God according to the Book of Ezekiel," in *I Am Yahweh*, ed. Walter Brueggemann (Atlanta: John Knox, 1982), 29–98; and Zimmerli, "The Word of Divine Self-Manifestation (Proof Saying): A Prophetic Genre," in Brueggemann, *I Am Yahweh*, 99–110.

22. Ross, *Recalling the Hope of Glory*, 67.

in 4:21–24, they are to retell the crossing of the Jordan in light of the prior generation's experience of the crossing of the Red Sea. The language used in 4:24 is very reminiscent of Exodus 14:31. With this connection, the personal testimony is founded on and interpreted by the scriptural testimony of the earlier miracle. The legacy of worship that the memorial inspires is uniquely tied both to personal testimony and to the Scriptures.

In Joshua 5:2–12 we encounter memorial reenactments that exhibit the past, present, and future orientation outlined at the beginning of the study. In this chapter the men of Israel are circumcised. The older generation had been circumcised, but those who were born in the wilderness had not been. The chapter highlights that the older, circumcised generation had died in the wilderness because they did not obey the Lord. This led to the Lord's promising that they would not enter the Promised Land. As with all his promises, God made good, and the original exodus generation died, with the exception of Joshua and Caleb, before entering the land.

Notice that the chapter highlights two promises of God, and they are side by side in the narrative. The Lord swore that the exodus generation would not enter the Promised Land. He also promised that the land he had sworn to give to the patriarchs would be given to the next generation. God solemnly fulfilled both oaths. The exodus generation, through their refusal to worship God with trust and obedience at Kadesh-Barnea, forfeited their opportunity to receive the fulfillment of the promise to the patriarchs. Their sin did not ultimately thwart God's promise, but it did move its fulfillment to their children. So it was the children that the Lord had established in their place, who were circumcised that day.

The conquest generation was forced to ponder the implications of God's past actions for their present situation. Once before the people had been on the edge of the land and had failed because they refused to trust and obey. In this moment they must own their faith and express their trust individually through obedience.

In the present they also experienced the removal of the shame and reproach Israel had borne since the failure to enter the land at Kadesh-Barnea in Numbers 13–14. The release from the past shame is highlighted in the memorial of Passover. In Gilgal, the place where they were circumcised, the nation would eat the fruit of the Promised Land, no longer living on the wilderness staple of manna.[23] The wilderness era and its shame had ended.

Their freedom from reproach, and the personalization of faith in the face of the tests that lay in their future, is a beautiful picture of how their worship response is shaped by God's past, present, and future interactions with them. This same pattern is found again in Joshua 8 and the memorial reading of the blessings and curses on Ebal and Gerizim. They gave public testimony to the past revelation of God, which was a present act

23. See Richard S. Hess, *Joshua: An Introduction and Commentary*, TOTC 6 (Downers Grove, IL: InterVarsity Press, 1996), 137–38.

of obedience to the commands of Deuteronomy 11:39 and 27:11–13. In this memorial they also gave testimony that their future would be tied to continued trust and obedience, to continued worship of the Lord. They testified that they were accepting all of God's self-revelation. They testified that they must worship.

SIGNIFICANCE OF JOSHUA FOR BIBLICAL WORSHIP

There is so much to wrestle with as we consider how Joshua's theology of worship might inform our worship today. Each passage in the survey could be mined for its implications. But I have chosen to focus on just two areas. As I pored over the material, I kept coming back to two aspects of worship in Joshua that are most needed today: meditating on the Scripture and the life-and-death nature of worship.

Meditating on the Scriptures

The Scriptures provide the foundation for worship. The Scriptures provide the core content that leads us to worship—the inspired revelation of God and his great works. His self-revelation is what leads us to adore and praise him. It is his character and nature that prompt us to trust and obey him. It is his gracious covenant and offer of salvation that allows us to be in relationship with him. It is his record of fulfilled promises that lead us to have hope for the future.

Worship, both corporate and individual, must begin with meditation on the Scriptures. David Howard wisely clarifies what biblical meditation is and what it is not:

> The idea of meditating here is not the one commonly familiar . . . namely, of emptying the mind and concentrating on nothing or on self or on visualizations of various types; much of this type of meditation is indebted to Eastern mystic religions. Rather, the Old Testament concept of meditation involves two things: First, a focus upon God himself (Ps. 63:6[Hb.7]), his works (Pss. 77:12[Hb. 13]; 143:5), or his law (Josh. 1:8; Ps. 1:2), and second, an activity that was done aloud. This is why God told Joshua that this lawbook should not leave his mouth (as opposed to, e.g., his heart or his mind).[24]

So, whatever else we include in our worship, be it our personal devotional time, our spontaneous praise, our acts of homage, or our corporate services, it should all be founded on our meditation on Scripture. Mere citation of the Bible is not enough. Only worship derived from the deep penetration and impact of Scripture will begin to look like biblically defined worship.

Three practical implications arise from this. First, we should view our time in Scripture as an integral part of worship. In some cases we may

24. Howard, *Joshua*, 186.

need to adjust our language in corporate settings where often we segregate worship (prayer, praise, and song) from teaching. Meditation on the word is in fact a necessary component of worship and should be thought of and taught as such.

Second, we ought to think about the other elements of worship in relation to the Scripture. Are lyrics (whether sung by the congregation or listened to by the individual) reflective of a deep and meaningful interaction with Scripture? This does not mean lyrics should be limited to quotations or paraphrases of Scripture but that they should be so influenced by Scripture that they too help us meditate on Scripture and how we trust and obey it in our lives.

Third, genuine meditation on Scriptures leads to trust and obedience. Joshua affirms that worship is the proper fruit of meditation. Study of the Scriptures that leads to knowledge about God, but not knowledge of God, is *not* biblical mediation. J. I. Packer in his classic spiritual work, *Knowing God*, speaks against meditation that leads only to knowledge about God. In meditation our aim must be "to know God himself better."[25] In meditation we "turn each truth we learn *about* God into matter for meditation *before* God, leading to prayer and praise *to* God."[26] As we meditate "in communion with God" we are applying the content of our meditation to ourselves, and we "let his truth make its full and proper impact on one's mind and heart."[27]

We can confirm this understanding by remembering the definition of eternal life that Jesus gave his disciples in John 17:3: "that they know you, the only true God, and Jesus Christ whom you have sent" (ESV). Eternal life is knowing God, not merely knowing about him. This does not mean that we do not need knowledge about God, but that the *knowledge about* must serve the *knowing of* God. The relational purpose of meditation must inform our own personal study of the Scripture and our corporate teaching if we are truly to worship God and to have the eternal life he offers.

You Are What You Worship

The weighty significance of the desperate need we have to know God, and not just know about him, is intimately connected to the second aspect of worship in Joshua that has deep significance for our worship today: Worship is a matter of life and death.

Psalm 115:4–7 lays out the folly of worshiping idols. They are made by humans, and though they have mouths, eyes, ears, noses, hands, and feet, they cannot speak, see, hear, smell, act, or walk. They are lifeless despite being made as an imitation of life. In 115:8, this familiar anti-idolatry

25. J. I. Packer, *Knowing God* (Downers Grove, IL: InterVarsity Press, 1993), 20th-Anniversary Edition, 23.
26. Packer, *Knowing God*, chap. 1 (emphasis original).
27. Packer, *Knowing God*, chap. 1.

exposition turns in a unique way. The psalmist warns Israel that those who make idols and those who trust in them will become like them. What does he mean? They will be lifeless, just like the dead idols. Life comes from God, the creator of all. Seeking life anywhere else can bring only death.[28] You are what you worship.[29] You are either intimately connected to the creator and giver of life or you are connected to death. There is no other option. Worship—that is to say, trusting and obeying—is a matter of life and death.

As I considered the effect this truth should have on our worship, it became clear that it raises the importance of confession and discipline. Confession and the willing acceptance of the Lord's discipline bring glory to God. For most of us, sin, discipline, and confession are things we only think about and talk about in hindsight. "There was a time when . . ." It is not inappropriate to share past accounts for the edification of others, but should we not also confess our sins to each other and pray for one another (James 5:16)? Should we not provide meaningful times of confession and repentance in our corporate gatherings and close personal relationships?

As I considered this, I initially pushed back on the idea in light of the celebratory nature of worship. But as I thought more, what is more worthy of celebration than the reality that God disciplines his children as a sign of his love, and that we can have full assurance of his forgiveness when we confess (see Heb. 12:6; Rev. 3:19)? Freedom from the fear of rejection is indeed worthy of celebration, not an occasion for hiding and shame. The trust and obedience involved in confessing our sins does indeed bring glory to God (Josh. 7:19).

If we are truly meditating on the Scriptures, we will have plenty of occasions to worship through confession. We will be able to express our trust and obedience through confession with confident hope in the promise of his forgiveness and healing. Worshiping the Lord, especially through confession, is life-giving and should play a much larger role in our personal and corporate worship than it typically does, because worship is truly a matter of life and death.[30]

---

28. Interestingly, some ancient manuscripts link Psalms 114 and 115. See Leslie C. Allen, *Psalms 101–150*, WBC 21 (Nashville: Thomas Nelson, 2002), 147. Psalm 114 recounts the Red Sea and Jordan crossings. In the plague and exodus account we have a strong polemic against idolatry (see Exod. 12:12; Num. 33:4). The polemic against idolatry is also present in the Jordan crossing as well. See Thigpen, "Lord of All the Earth." As such we have hints of a connection between a psalm that references anti-idolatry polemics and a psalm that explicitly declares that idolaters can only receive death from their supposed gods. These psalms, like Joshua, clearly assert that worship is a matter of life and death.
29. See G. K. Beale, *We Become What We Worship: A Biblical Theology of Idolatry* (Downers Grove, IL: InterVarsity Press, 2008); and James K. A. Smith, *You Are What You Love: The Spiritual Power of Habit* (Grand Rapids: Brazos, 2016).
30. One might think here of how everyone approaching the temple to worship brought sacrifices to deal with sin and then celebrated peace with God that had been achieved through trust and obedience in his provision of sacrifice for forgiveness.

CONCLUSION

Joshua 22:5 reads, "Only be very careful to observe the commandment and the law that Moses the servant of the Lord commanded you, to love the Lord your God, and to walk in all his ways and to keep his commandments and to cling to him and to serve him with all your heart and with all your soul" (ESV). Here Joshua calls Israel to love their God by walking in his ways and being obedient to the Scriptures, clinging to him with all their heart and with all their soul.[31] In this summary statement of their worship of the Lord, Joshua reminds them of God's great past actions when he called them into covenant and gave them the law that would guide them in how to worship. He reminds them of their present acts of trust and obedience. They are to be like God, walking in his ways, which are defined by the Scriptures he gave them. He reminds them that this is not a matter of mere legal adherence. They must cling to him as a husband and wife cling together (Gen. 2:24). This is a call to a deep, life-giving relationship. It is a call to serve their sovereign Lord with all that they are (Deut. 6:4–6). And it is a call that orients them toward the future. Soon Joshua will not be with them, but God will be. As he kept his word to Moses and Joshua, he will continue to keep his word to them. Worship is intimately related to the past, present, and future acts of God as he shows us who he is and how we might be rightly related to him.

We love and worship God by trusting and obeying. Just as Christ commanded his disciples, there is no tension between love and obedience (John 14:15).[32] Rather in the Scriptures they are wedded together. Trust and obedience are at the core of biblical worship and at the center of Joshua's portrayal of Israel's worship. May we learn to truly celebrate our covenant fellowship with God through our praise, adoration, trust, and our obedient acts of submission and homage in great expectation of the promised fulfillment of our salvation.

BIBLIOGRAPHY

Allen, Leslie C. *Psalms 101–150.* WBC 21. Nashville: Thomas Nelson, 2002.

Beale, G. K. *We Become What We Worship: A Biblical Theology of Idolatry.* Downers Grove, IL: IVP Academic, 2008.

31. It is stirring to read in Jeremiah 32:41 that after the exile the Lord would rejoice to do good to them, planting them back in the land in faithfulness, with all his heart and with all his soul. The deep tenderness of God is perhaps best revealed here as he acts toward them in the very same manner he commands them to love him. For an exploration of this theme in the context of judgment and salvation in Jeremiah, see J. Michael Thigpen, "The Storm of YHWH: Jeremiah's Theology of God's Heart and Motives," *BSac* 176 (2019): 418–28.

32. For an excellent review of the ways in which God's love for us, our love for God, and our obedience are intertwined, see Jon D. Levenson, *The Love of God: Divine Gift, Human Gratitude, and Mutual Faithfulness in Judaism*, Library of Jewish Ideas (Princeton: Princeton University Press, 2015).

Block, Daniel I. *For the Glory of God: Recovering a Biblical Theology of Worship.* Grand Rapids: Baker Academic, 2014.

Butler, Trent C. *Joshua.* WBC 7. Waco: Word, 1983.

Hess, Richard S. *Joshua: An Introduction and Commentary.* TOTC 6. Downers Grove, IL: InterVarsity Press, 1996.

Howard, David M., Jr. *Joshua.* NAC 5. Nashville: B&H, 1998.

Levenson, Jon D. *The Love of God: Divine Gift, Human Gratitude, and Mutual Faithfulness in Judaism.* Library of Jewish Ideas. Princeton, NJ: Princeton University Press, 2015.

Packer, J. I. *Knowing God.* 20th-Anniversary Edition. Downers Grove, IL: InterVarsity Press, 1993.

Ross, Allen P. *Recalling the Hope of Glory: Biblical Worship from the Garden to the New Creation.* Grand Rapids: Kregel Academic, 2006.

Shogren, Gary S. *1 and 2 Thessalonians.* ZECNT. Grand Rapids: Zondervan, 2012.

Smith, James K. A. *You Are What You Love: The Spiritual Power of Habit.* Grand Rapids: Brazos, 2016.

Sprinkle, Joe M. "Law and Narrative in Exodus 19–24." *JETS* 47, no. 2 (2003): 235–52.

Thigpen, J. Michael. "Lord of All the Earth: Yahweh and Baal in Joshua 3." *TJ*, n.s. 27, no. 2 (2006): 245–54.

______. *Divine Motive in the Hebrew Bible: A Comprehensive Survey and Analysis.* Gorgias Biblical Studies. Piscataway, NJ: Gorgias, 2015.

______. "The Storm of YHWH: Jeremiah's Theology of God's Heart and Motives." *BSac* 176 (2019): 418–28.

Woudstra, Marten H. *The Book of Joshua.* NICOT. Grand Rapids: Eerdmans, 1981.

Zimmerli, Walther. "Knowledge of God according to the Book of Ezekiel." In *I Am Yahweh*, edited by Walter Brueggemann, 29–98. Atlanta: John Knox, 1982.

______. "The Word of Divine Self-Manifestation (Proof Saying): A Prophetic Genre." In *I Am Yahweh*, edited by Walter Brueggemann, 99–110. Atlanta: John Knox, 1982.

CHAPTER 6

DETERIORATING DEVOTION AMONG GOD'S PEOPLE

Worship in the Book of Judges

Jillian L. Ross

"Everyone did that which is right in his own eyes." So concludes the book of Judges, and with that many readers exclaim, "Good riddance!" The haunting tails of gang rape, child sacrifice, and unfettered violence leave believers feeling sullied by merely reading the text.[1] These "texts of terror" appear so extreme and removed from "common, decent living" that few find any relevance for them, and certainly little application to Christian worship practices.[2] Such natural reactions may explain the dearth of sermon series on the book of Judges. Moreover, if some brave pastor even preaches a series on Judges, it focuses mainly on typological relationships among the flawed major deliverer-judges and the sinless Great Deliverer Jesus Christ. In the end, the application is akin to "worship Jesus because he is the sinless Savior and perfect Judge and be ever so thankful that you are not under the yoke of a reprobate judge like Jephthah or Samson."

Thanksgiving for Christ, though laudable and highly appropriate, is but one application from the book of Judges. Although the "dark days of the judges" occurred more than three millennia ago, the entire book of Judges provides contemporary Christians with a robust theology of worship.

---

1. I wish to thank Liberty University for the release time to write this essay and my colleague Don Fowler for his helpful comments on an earlier draft of this essay.
2. The term "text of terror" comes from Phyllis Trible, *Texts of Terror: Literary-Feminist Readings of Biblical Narratives*, eds. Walter Brueggemann and Christopher R. Seitz, Overtures to Biblical Theology 13 (Philadelphia: Fortress, 1984).

CONTEXT OF WORSHIP IN THE JUDGES

The difficulty in understanding the theology of Judges stems largely from the fact that the narrator rarely offers commentary about the merits or demerits of the characters' actions. Instead, the author deftly uses the biblical law, particularly the book of Deuteronomy, as the interpretive key to the book. Thus the book functions like a parable in which those who have ears to hear—those who know the Torah—can hear and heed the book of Judges.

The identity of these hearers has been a subject of much debate. Those who affirm the general unity of the book tend to date its composition to the late preexilic period or early exilic period. Two internal clues appear in the prologue and epilogue of Judges. First, the structure of Judges 1 follows the pattern of an Assyrian conquest account.[3] This suggests a time when Israel would be familiar with the genre. Second, Judges 17–18 closes with a report that the priesthood, established by Jonathan the descendant of Moses, remained in Dan until "the day of the captivity of the land" (Judg. 18:30).[4] This event most likely refers to the Assyrian deportation of the northern kingdom led by Tiglath-pileser III in 734–732 BC (2 Kings 15:29; cf. 1 Chron. 5:26).[5]

In my estimation, a few other factors, when taken together, suggest that the primary audience were preexilic Israelites, living in the southern kingdom after the northern kingdom's fall. First, the author is conversant in Genesis–Joshua.[6] Second, the author seems generally pro-monarchy. He dates Israel's lawlessness to when "there was no king in Israel" (17:6; 18:1; 19:1; 21:25).[7] Third, the book exhorts the people to worship Yahweh and refrain from idolatry.[8]

---

3. K. Lawson Younger Jr., "Judges 1 in Its Near Eastern Literary Context," in *Faith, Tradition, and History: Old Testament Historiography in its Near Eastern Context*, eds. A. R. Millard, James K. Hoffmeier, and David W. Baker (Winona Lake, IN: Eisenbrauns, 1994), 207–27.
4. All translations are the author's unless otherwise stated. For the suspended *nun* related to the phrase "Jonathan the son of Gershom the son of Moses," see Natalio Fernández Marcos, *Judges*, ed. A. Schenker, BHQ 7 (Stuttgart: Deutsche Bibelgellschaft, 2011), 104–5.
5. For an alternate view, see J. Gordon McConville, *Grace to the End: A Study in Deuteronomic Theology*, Studies in Old Testament Biblical Theology (Grand Rapids: Zondervan, 1993), 109–10.
6. This is point is neutral in and of itself, but the points the author makes about idolatry lead me to view the work as preexilic.
7. Block observes that "[the Books of Kings] place responsibility for the exile squarely on the shoulders of kings who led the people into sin. An exilic author would hardly have looked upon the monarchy as an institution to be the solution for the problems reflected in the book" (Daniel Block, *Judges, Ruth*, NAC 6 [Nashville: B&H, 1999], 66). It should be noted that the author is not absolutely pro-monarchy. A king should follow Deuteronomy's laws for kings (Deut. 17:14–20). The author looks ill upon Gideon's pseudo-kingship (Judg. 8:22–35) and Abimelech's attempts at such (Judg. 9). If the minor judges are to be interpreted by the center of the book—namely, the Gideon account—then the author is likely denouncing their violations of Deuteronomy 7:14–17. Still, by strategically placing the refrain throughout the epilogue, the author appears to suggest that the monarchy militates unabated lawlessness.
8. Similarly, Block, *Judges, Ruth*, 67.

At structurally significant points in the work, the author addresses false places of worship (esp. Judg. 2:1–5; 6:25–35; 8:22–28; 17:1–18:31). The book itself is arranged to illustrate Israel's progressive spiritual deterioration, predominantly as it pertains to warfare and worship.[9] These themes are arranged chiastically at three major sections of Judges: the prologue, central judge account (Gideon), and epilogue.[10]

Table 1. Judges' Chiastic Structure of Warfare and Worship[11]

Prologue	A	Warfare against Foreigners (1:1–2:5)*
	B	Worship of Foreign Idols (2:1–3:6)
Center of Judges: Gideon	B	Worship of Foreign Idols (6:1–32)
	A	Warfare against Foreigners (6:33–7:25)
	A′	Warfare against Israelites (8:1–21)
	B'	Worship of Israelite Idols (8:22–32)
Epilogue	B'	Worship of Israelite Idols (17:1–18:31)
	A′	Warfare against Israelites (19:1–21:25)

Each worship unit (B) addresses aberrant worship sites, whether foreign idolatrous cultic sites (2:2; 6:25–32) or Israelite synchronistic cultic sites (8:27; 17:1–18:31).[12] The concept also appears in the Ehud, Abimelech, and Samson accounts (Judg. 3:19, 26; 9:4, 27, 46; 16:23–30). It stands to reason that if the intended audience were from the exilic or postexilic periods, cultic sites would not figure as prominently in the text. "Anxious for the revival of pure and orthodox Yahwism, and the spiritual rejuvenation of his people, this preacher [the author of Judges] draws upon the dark days of the judges to warn his people of the peril of their ways."[13] Idolatry leads to exile, the seeds of which were sown in

9. This is the central thesis of my dissertation; see Jillian L. Ross, "A People Heeds Not Scripture: A Poetics of Pentateuchal Allusions in the Book of Judges" (PhD diss., Trinity Evangelical Divinity School, 2015).

10. K. C. Way, "The Literary Structure of Judges Revisited: Judges as a Ring Composition," in *Windows to the Ancient World of the Hebrew Bible: Essays in Honor of Samuel Greengus*, eds. Bill T. Arnold, Nancy L. Erickson, and John H. Walton (Winona Lake, IN: Eisenbrauns, 2014), 247–60.

11. Jillian L. Ross, "The Ring Composition of Judges Revisited: Allusive Texts in the Book of Judges" (paper presented at the Annual Meeting of the IBR, Boston MA, November 17, 2017), 2. This table is an adaptation of Way's arrangement, which views Israel and Gideon more positively than reflected above. It should also be noted that I view 2:1–5 as transitional; it closes one unit and opens the next. See Way, "Literary Structure," 254.

12. The worship units contain the crux of Judges' theology of worship. For this reason, each narrative often contains multiple aspects of what makes the book's theology of worship. This will become apparent in the theology section.

13. Block, *Judges, Ruth*, 67.

the wilderness (Exod. 32; Num. 25; cf. Amos 5:25–27) and matured in the judges' period.

THEOLOGY OF WORSHIP

Despite the attention given to warfare in Judges, the book is not primarily about *conquest* but about the *consequences* of forsaking the Lord and his covenant (Judg. 2:2–3, 12–13). Indeed, as the prologue teaches, idolatry is the cause for the oppressions: "they forsook Yahweh and worshiped [*abad*] other gods" (Judg. 2:12–13).[14]

Contemporary Christians typically regard worship primarily as an *action*; the author of Judges, however, associates it more with *reverence* toward Yahweh that results in active covenant fidelity.[15] Judges teaches that if the people revere Yahweh, then all the rest will fall into place. They will refrain from idolatry, offer sacrifices and praises rightly, and receive God's blessings.[16] This theological treatment will address concepts associated with reverence toward Yahweh followed by practices of worship.

Worship with Reverence to the Lord

Israelites first and foremost should be "those who love him" (Judg. 5:31; cf. Deut. 6:5). Loving Yahweh constitutes a covenant commitment to him marked by unwavering fidelity.

Worship the Lord alone

Yahweh expects and deserves exclusive worship (see Judg. 2:1–3; 6:8–10; 10:10–16; cf. 6:24–32). Judges' first words about worship teach this and serve as a "theological key" to the book.[17]

> I brought you up from Egypt and I brought you to the land that I swore to your fathers. And I said, "*I will never break my covenant with you*," and as for you, "*you shall not make a covenant with the inhabitants of this land; you shall tear down their altars*." But *you have not obeyed my voice*; what is this you have done? Indeed, I said "I will no longer drive them out from you. They shall become thorns in your sides, and *their gods shall become a snare*." (Judg. 2:1–3, emphasis added)

---

14. When collocated with deities or images, *abad* means to "serve (in a religious sense), worship" (David J. A. Clines, ed., "*'bd*," *DCH* 6:211).
15. The Oxford English Dictionary defines worship of the supernatural in a twofold manner: "Reverence or veneration paid to a being or power regarded as supernatural or divine; the action or practice of displaying this by appropriate acts, rites, or ceremonies" ("worship, n.," OED Online, Oxford University Press, June 2017).
16. Idolatry is "false worship, involving reverential human acts of submission and homage before beings or objects in the place of the one true God" (Daniel I. Block, *For the Glory of God: Recovering a Biblical Theology of Worship* [Grand Rapids: Baker Academic, 2014], 29).
17. Carolyn Pressler, *Joshua, Judges, and Ruth*, Westminster Bible Companion (Louisville: Westminster John Knox, 2002), 134.

The speaker grounds Yahweh's expectations by contrasting the deity's stalwart commitment to Israel and the nation's lackluster posture toward him. Israel shall suffer the consequences of their breech: calamity and enticing gods.[18]

Covenant fidelity

Israel is under covenant obligation to heed Yahweh "the God of Israel" because of what he has done and because he has not reneged on the covenant (2:2). Deliverances from Egypt of old (2:1; 6:10) and from contemporary oppressors (10:11–12) bind Israel to "Yahweh the one of Sinai" (5:5). Israel's God fights for them (5:4–5; cf. 4:15). Consequently, Yahweh's mighty deeds for Israel should result in service (*abad*) to him. It did so for Joshua's generation (2:7; 6:13), not so for the judges' generation (2:10–12) except under duress (10:14–16).

Contrary to Yahweh's warning (2:3), Israel erroneously expects Yahweh to perform mighty deeds even when they disobey him. Just after the prophet appeals to the exodus and rebukes Israel for "fearing the gods of the Amorites," Gideon chides the Envoy of Yahweh (6:8–10).[19] "If Yahweh were with us, then why is all this happening to us? And where are all his mighty deeds which our fathers recounted to us, saying 'Indeed Yahweh brought us up from Egypt.' But now Yahweh has abandoned us and given us into the hand of Midian" (6:13; cf. 6:9–10).[20] The heart of the matter is that "the Israelites *did not see how the worship of the gods surrounding them* angered the Israelite deity they were supposed to be worshipping."[21]

Yahweh's loving fidelity to Israel should have impelled the people to action for Yahweh. Israel is to tear down pagan altars, thereby eradicating non-Yahwistic worship (2:2). The command also aims to keep Israel from corrupting worship of Yahweh by adopting practices that the Canaanites do to their gods (cf. Deut. 12:29–31). Israel's failures on this point include Gideon's ephod (6:7), Jephthah's human sacrifice (11:34–40), and Micah's idols and shrine (Judg. 17).

Apostasy

Tragically, covenant infidelity in the form of apostasy infects Israel. Israel makes Baal Berit—that is, Baal of the covenant—"their god" and erects his temple in Shechem (8:33; 9:4). Worshiping Baal Berit constitutes

18. Similarly, Trent C. Butler, *Judges*, WBC 8 (Nashville: Nelson, 2009), 198.
19. Many use the word "Angel" instead of "Envoy."
20. From a literary standpoint, Gideon's contempt of Yahweh is absurd not only because he stands face-to-face with the Envoy of Yahweh but also because Deborah and Barak had just sung of a new mighty deed of the Lord, for "Yahweh had confounded Sisera, all the chariots, and all the army before Barak" (4:15; chap. 5). Moreover, the song has an exodus motif that links Yahweh's present actions for Israel in the land with their exodus from Egypt.
21. Tammi J. Schneider, *Judges*, Berit Olam: Studies in Hebrew Narrative and Poetry (Collegeville, MN: Liturgical Press, 2000), 107 (emphasis added).

spiritual prostitution (*zonah*) (8:33). The same term is used of Gideon's ephod (8:27) and worshiping "other gods" (2:17).[22]

In a similar vein, forsaking Yahweh involves a transfer of allegiance, not simply a void. Whenever Israel "abandons" Yahweh, the people worship other gods (2:11–12, 13; 10:6, 13). Worshiping other gods is tantamount to "not worship[ing] him" (10:6); Judges leave no room for a both/and.[23] The defection is poignantly depicted when Israel's zeal for Baal lead the citizens of Ophrah to demand the death penalty for Gideon because he desecrated Baal's altar and hewed the Asherah pole beside it (6:27–32). Ironically, the town's treason is the capital offense (Deut. 13:12–17 [Heb. 13:13–18]), yet God spares them. Judges 6 teaches that idolatry constitutes a grievous sin (cf. 10:10, 15), but not "the unpardonable sin" because Gideon and his clan lead Israel in Yahweh war against Midian (6:34–35).

Aside from their alluring nature, rival gods are impotent, and Baal is no match for Yahweh. Baal cannot protect Sisera and his men from Yahweh (4:15; 5:4–5, 19–22).[24] Baal cannot contend against Yahweh's deliverer Gideon "because he tore down his altar" (6:25–32). Asherah likewise falls. Gideon hews down the Asherah (pole) beside Baal's altar, and its wood stokes an altar for Yahweh (6:26–28). Dagon cannot save himself or his worshipers. His temple falls with three thousand Philistine devotees inside it (16:23–27, 30). To highlight Dagon's impotence, Yahweh overthrows him with a blind man (16:28–30). The gods of seven nations lack the power to deliver Israel when the nation faces severe oppression (10:6–16). Yahweh, in contrast, gives the enemy into Israel's hand and decidedly defeats Ammon (11:32–33).[25] In the end, gods are

---

22. The precise form of Gideon's ephod evades scholars. Most frequently, ephods refer to linen garments worn by priests (see Exod. 28:6–14, 31–34; 39:2–7, 22–26), the most elaborate of which is reserved for the high priest and has the Urim and Thummim over it (Exod. 28:6–30). In light of this, ephods are associated with oracles. Ephods may also refer to cultic objects for oracular rituals. Gideon's ephod must be of this nature because it is made of approximate forty-five pounds of gold (probably overlaying an image). What is unclear is if these objects are idols with ephods on them or separate objects altogether (Judg. 8:24–27; Isa. 30:22). Judges 8:22–27, however, is less concerned with the object's physical form than with its (unintended?) function, idolatry. The narrative recounts the manufacturing of Gideon's golden ephod in a manner that alludes to the manufacturing of Israel's golden calf (see Exod. 32:1–6). Even though the ephod's shape is unknown, its nature is not—it is an idol on par with the golden calf. For the allusion, see Ross, "A People Heeds Not Scripture," 218–22. For more details about the ephod, see P. Jenson, "ʾepiyd," in *NIDOTTE* 1:476–77; Jack M. Sasson, *Judges 1–12: A New Translation and Commentary*, AYB 6D (New Haven, CT: Yale University Press, 2014), 336–37; Daniel I. Block, "Judges," in *Zondervan Illustrated Bible Backgrounds Commentary: Old Testament*, vol. 2, *Joshua, Judges, Ruth, 1 & 2 Samuel*, ed. John Walton (Grand Rapids: Zondervan, 2009), 166.

23. Israel "chooses" foreign gods (10:14).

24. Baal is not mentioned in Judges 4–5; however, the depiction of Yahweh as a divine warrior coming from a mountain and the cosmic imagery suggests such (Block, *Judges, Ruth*, 237; cf. 223). The song may contain a polemic against Anat as well (Stephen G. Dempster, "Mythology and History in the Song of Deborah," *WTJ* 41 [1978]: 33–53).

25. Jephthah's statement to the Ammonite king suggests he espouses henotheism: "Do you not possess *what Chemosh your god* gives you to possess? And everything that Yahweh our G/god causes us to

manmade objects (18:24).[26] They can be stolen and carted off to another location, as Micah declares: "My gods [*elohay*] that I made, you have taken, and the priest!" (18:24). Powerless to save themselves or their followers, the gods are wholly unworthy of worship. It is treason and folly to worship other gods.

Worship by doing right in the Lord's eyes

Worshippers should practice doing right in the eyes of the Lord. The phrase appears frequently in Deuteronomy and Kings; however, it never occurs in Judges.[27] Instead, the people do "evil in the eyes of Yahweh" or do "right in their own eyes."[28] Judges 2:11–13 defines doing evil in the eyes of Yahweh as apostasy by making "doing evil" the introduction to the text's chiastic arrangement.[29]

Table 2. Doing Evil—Apostasy in Israel (Judg. 2:11–13)

Intro	***The Israelites did evil in the eyes of Yahweh.***
A	And they *worshiped* [*abad*] the Baals.
B	And *forsook* [*azab*] Yahweh who brought them out of Egypt.
	And they walked after other gods of the surrounding peoples
C	And bowed in worship to [*histaphal hvh*] them.
	And provoke Yahweh to anger [*hiphil k's*].
B′	And they *forsook* [*azab*] Yahweh.
A′	And *worshiped* [*abad*] the Baal and the Asherahs/Astartes.

The components of the chiasm characterize practicing evil as serving the Baals (and Asherahs), forsaking Yahweh, and paying homage to gods. The center emphasizes the fact that aberrant worship provokes Yahweh's anger.[30] Elsewhere in Judges the phrase collocates with "forgetting/forsaking Yahweh" (3:7; 10:6), "not worshiping Yahweh" (10:6), and "worshiping" various deities (3:7; 10:6). Israel thus failed to worship Yahweh and intentionally replaced him with other gods.

---

possess, we will possess" (11:24). Whatever Jephthah's intent for the statement, he belittles Yahweh by suggesting that other gods have any power to bequeath land. Yahweh gave Ammon their land (Deut. 2:19–22); Yahweh's power extends beyond the borders of Israel (Judg. 5:4–5).

26. In like manner, idols are manufactured by a (silver)smith (17:4), yet also made by those for whom it is commissioned (17:5; 18:24, 31). Idols and icons can ensnare (8:27; cf. 18:14–31).

27. The Israelites do beg Yahweh to "do whatever is good in your eyes; only deliver us today" (10:15).

28. Samson seeks to marry the Timnite because "she is right in my eyes" (Judg. 15:3; cf. v. 7). This phrase is "an anticipatory link" with the refrain "each did that which is right in his own eyes" (17:6; 21:21) (K. Lawson Younger Jr., *Judges/Ruth*, NIVAC [Grand Rapids: Zondervan, 2002], 301).

29. The table below is an adaptation from Younger, *Judges/Ruth*, 88.

30. Younger, *Judges/Ruth*, 88.

At the end of the book, Israel shifts from "doing evil in Yahweh's eyes" to "doing right in their own eyes." The latter pertains not only to lawless living but also to worshiping wherever (and however) one pleases. In the Micah story the phrase points back to Deuteronomy 12's regulations about destroying Canaanite worship centers and worshiping God at his chosen place. Deuteronomy 12's "prime concern is not to mandate a single centralized location . . . as it is to eliminate idolatry and guard against syncretism" by tearing down rival sites.[31] Judges 17 serves as its foil by narrating precisely what the law prohibits: creating idols, worshiping Yahweh like a Canaanite god, and founding a "house of gods" (17:5).

Micah continues to do right in his own eyes by appointing his Ephraimite son as priest (17:5). According to the law, only *Aaronic* Levites can serve as priests.[32] The Levite who replaces his son also does what is right in his own eyes.[33] He chooses Micah's place over Yahweh's place. [34] Contentedly, this non-Aaronic Levite takes an illegitimate priestly post for mercenary gains: receiving silver, clothing, and sustenance (17:10–11). When a more prestigious and economic post is offered, "the heart of the priest was glad" (18:20). He leaves Micah's shrine to serve as the Danites' priest and found the (illegitimate) rival cultic site at Dan (18:20). Doing right in one's own eyes serves only self, which leaves no room for serving God rightly or doing right in his eyes.

Worship by knowing and teaching the Lord

Right worship of God begins with knowing him and what he has done. The corollary to this is teaching others about him. To know God is not about mental assent. "To know God is to be in a right relationship with him."[35] According to the prologue, "The people *served Yahweh* all the days of Joshua and all the days of the elders who outlived Joshua, who saw all the *works of Yahweh* that he *had done* for Israel" (2:7). But the next generation "knew neither Yahweh nor the *works* that he *had done* for Israel" (2:10). In the

31. Michael Grisanti, "Deuteronomy," in *The Expositor's Bible Commentary*, vol. 2, *Genesis–Leviticus*, eds. Tremper Longman III and David E. Garland, rev. ed. (Grand Rapids: Zondervan, 2012), 617.
32. All priests are Levites, but not all Levites are priests. From the tribe of Levi, God appointed Aaron and his descendants to serve him as priests (see Lev. 8). Only Aaron and his descendants can officiate sacrificial activities; the rest of the Levites are not priests (see Num. 3–4). For them to approach the sanctuary is a capital offense (see Num. 3:10). They support the Aaronic priesthood by taking care of the sanctuary furnishings (esp. during the wilderness wanderings; see Num. 8:14). Once Israel is in the land and God sets up his chosen place of worship, the non-Aaronic Levites may elect to move from their designated cities (Num. 35:1–8; Josh. 21) to assist the Aaronic priesthood at the chosen place (Deut. 18:6–8). Even there, they do not become priest but rather continue to aid with the upkeep of the daily furnishings.
33. Similarly, Yairah Amit, *The Book of Judges: The Art of Editing*, trans. Jonathan Chipman, VTSup 38 (Leiden: Brill, 1999), 327.
34. According to Deuteronomy 18:6–8, the non-Aaronic Levites who elects to serve Yahweh at his chosen place receive the same amount of food as the Aaronic priest despite their different roles.
35. Terence E. Fretheim, "*yd*'," in *NIDOTTE* 2:413.

Hebrew Bible the phrase "did not know Yahweh" means "to be unfaithful, guilty of harlotry, [and] 'sleeping around' with other gods.'"[36] Judges defines it the same way by placing the cyclical refrain directly afterward. To not know is to practice apostasy: *doing evil* in the eyes of Yahweh by *worshiping/serving Baal(s) and Asherah, forsaking* Yahweh, *walking after other gods* from the surrounding peoples, and *bowing in worship* to them (2:11–13).

Instead of venerating Yahweh for what he has done for Israel as Joshua's generation had (2:10, 17), each generation in the judges' period acts more corruptly than the prior one (2:19). The book's progressive decline bears this out. Israel becomes less and less adept at responding to the covenant curses. With no one training the next generation in the ways of Yahweh (contra Deut. 6:7, 20–25), the generations either fail to worship Yahweh (Judg. 2:17, 19) or worship him wrongly (e.g., Gideon, Jephthah, Samson, Micah, Jonathan).

The Gideon cycle combines these two points. Yahweh sends a prophet to explain the covenant curses; his voice goes unheeded (6:9–10). In the next paragraph, Gideon encounters the Envoy of Yahweh and fails to grasp it. Gideon's father bears some guilt in this because he sponsors a thriving Baal center (Judg. 6:25), thereby neglecting to diligently teach his children Yahweh's commands (Deut. 6:7; cf. Prov. 22:6). After defeating the Midianites, Gideon worships Yahweh syncretistically with the ephod and leads his sons into apostasy by it (Judg. 8:27). Worship totally degenerates with Gideon's son Abimelech. He accepts blood money from the temple of Baal Berit and massacres his seventy brothers (9:4–6).[37]

The epilogue furnishes the most remarkable case of intergenerational, idolatrous ignorance. Micah's mother exclaims, "I wholly consecrate to Yahweh the silver from my hand to my son in order to make a graven image and molten image" (17:3). Micah makes the idol(s) and appoints his son as priest over his "house of gods." Three generations share in the sin. When Jonathan replaces Micah's son, Micah's words betray his own ignorance of Yahweh's ways: "Now I know that Yahweh will prosper me [*hiphil 'tb*] because I have a Levite as priest" (17:13). Tragically, lineage alone proves sufficient for Micah to ordain the Levite as spiritual father to his household (17:10). The sin of wayward worship does not remain in the household. It spreads to and infects a tribe. This spiritual head leads the tribe of Dan into an illegitimate conquest and makes his progeny the priests of Dan's aberrant sanctuary.

Jonathan stands in stark contrast to Deborah, who serves as a spiritual mother to Israel (5:7), leading the people in praise to Yahweh for his mighty work against Jabin and Sisera (Judg. 5). With her and Barak, the land has rest (5:31). Jonathan and his descendants lead Israel into syncretism. With them, the land has unrest because the northern tribes go into

36. Fretheim, "*yd*'," 2:413.

37. Space does not permit a treatment of Jephthah or Samson. For a superb treatment on Jephthah's vow and the people's culpability as those ignorant of Torah, see David Janzen, "Why the Deuteronomist Told about the Sacrifice of Jephthah's Daughter," *JSOT* 29 (2005): 339–57.

exile (18:30). Failing to know Yahweh and teach his ways leads to worshiping Yahweh wrongly or failing to worship him at all. These failures bring death and deportation. Ignorance is not bliss; ignorance is destructive.

Reverential Worship Practices

The narratives of Judges are replete with examples of worship practices. Some are praiseworthy; many are contemptible. The author sanctions but a few. He relies on his audience's knowledge of Torah, a knowledge hopefully greater than those from the time of Judges. Nevertheless, he clearly affirms two worship practices: worship Yahweh at sanctioned sites and in divine warfare. The latter may disturb our modern sensibilities, but it represents a core practice that must be addressed and contextualized. Other actions include offering sacrifices to Yahweh, praying to him, and praising him.

Worship at sites sanctioned by the Lord

Israel is to worship the Lord exclusively and rightly by tearing down rival cultic sites (2:1–3). The command exists because worship centers represent the cosmic stage. In other words, cultic centers attest to the deity's authority and hegemony over a city, territory, or nation. Canaanite sites left standing suggest that other gods preside over the Promised Land, thus Yahweh strictly charges Israel to eradicate them.

By Gideon's day, the Israelites have gone from allowing Canaanite cultic places in the land to erecting their own Baal site. The cause-and-effect nature of the narrative helps reveal its message.

Table 3. Gideon's Worship Centers

Gideon accepts his divine commission to deliver Israel from the Midianites.	*Introduction*
Yahweh commands Gideon to desecrate the Baal-Asherah worship center.	Command
Gideon desecrates the Baal-Asherah worship site *in Ophrah.*	Obedience
Gideon and his men miraculously defeat the Midianites.	Blessing
Gideon consecrates plundered gold and makes an ephod.	Violates second commandment
Gideon (re-)creates a corrupted Yahwistic worship site *in Ophrah.*	Disobedience
Gideon and his sons succumb to idolatry with the ephod.	Curse
Gideon's sons die.	Curse

The twofold story teaches a core doctrinal point. Yahweh blesses those who depose foreign gods, and he punishes those who worship him like foreign gods. Obedience brings martial success, resulting in rest in the land (Judg. 7; 8:28; cf. Lev. 26:6; Deut. 28:7). Disobedience yields idolatry and physical death (Judg. 8:27; 9:1–6). Ultimately, fidelity brings the covenant blessings and infidelity brings the covenant curses.

The epilogue reinforces the cause-and-effect relationship of syncretism. Judges 17 recounts the founding of an Israelite cultic shrine that begins in an Ephraimite's home, close to Yahweh's chosen place in Shiloh. The shrine features a graven image, molten image, ephod, and teraphim (17:4–5; 18:14, 17). These idols were manufactured to aid in worshiping g/God and hearing from him. Despite their intent, the practice of divining through these mediums is strictly forbidden in Scripture and is grounds for execution (Deut. 17:2–6; cf. Deut. 13). This home has thus become a rival worship center, albeit a small one. Nonetheless, this center will become Israel's downfall.

When some wayfaring Danite scouts arrive at the home and receive lodging, they do not cringe at Micah's idolatry but rather seize the opportunity for his priest to "inquire of God that [they] may know whether their way will prosper" (Judg. 18:5). So impressed with the shrine and the Levite, the Danites scouts return to Micah's after their journey with six hundred armed Danites to confiscate the priest and the paraphernalia (18:14–20, 27). Micah's neighbors, who should have stoned Micah and his household for idolatry (Deut. 13:6–11 [Heb. 13:7–12]), actually pursue the Danites with Micah (Judg. 18:21–26). The Danites, with the Levite on their side, retain the cultic furnishing and erect a site in the city of Dan (18:20). The author reports that Micah's idol had remained at Dan "the entire time the house of God was in Shiloh," Yahweh's true site (18:31). The text recriminates all parties because at one point or another they are all close to the chosen place and elected to void it. In fact, they all support a rival place. Parent, child, Levite, tribe, and neighbor are all too busy doing "what was right in his eyes" to worship Yahweh rightly at his place.[38] Their spiritual malaise results in tribal and national idolatry with a rival priesthood officiating over a tribe (and northern Israel) "until the day of the land's captivity" (18:30).[39] The cause, idolatry, led to the effect, exile.

Thus the book teaches that Israel's ambivalence toward pagan worship sites leads to the nation's demise, spiritually and physically. Acceptance

38. Israel had struggles with false gods and places of worship on other occasions in Judges. Ehud did not tear down the idols at Gilgal (3:19, 26), and Shechem had made a temple (house) to Baal-Berit (9:4, 27, 46).

39. The Aaronic priesthood serves at the sanctuary in Shiloh (and later Jerusalem); Jonathan's (the descendant of Moses) priesthood serves at Dan. Being a descendant of Moses does not permit Jonathan to serve as a priest. In fact, his lineage should make him all the more aware of the distinction between "priests and Levites"—that is, between Aaronic Levites and the rest of the Levites.

of the Canaanite places led to creating their own pagan places (Judg. 6:25–32; cf. 9:4, 27, 46), which led to constructing syncretistic rival sites (Judg. 8:27; 17–18), which led to the ultimate covenant curse—Israel's exile (Deut. 28:64; Lev. 26:27–32).

Worship by participating in the Lord's battles

Judges begins at the opposite end of Israel's history: the conquest of the Promised Land with its blessings. "The Israelites inquire of Yahweh, 'Who shall go up for us against the Canaanites to fight against them?'" (1:1). The inquiry pertains to Yahweh's command to defeat the Canaanites, avoid covenants with them, and refrain from intermarrying (esp. Deut. 7:1–6). The Torah stipulates that failure in divine warfare, or *herem* warfare, results in apostasy (Deut. 7:4; Exod. 23:32–33; 34:15–16). Judges 1:16–31 reports Israel's conquest failures; the next pericope warns of apostasy (Judg. 2:1–5).[40] The cyclical framework and the narratives wed the two as well.

The actions of *herem* warfare must not be viewed solely on terrestrial grounds. Divine warfare involves cosmic battles where Yahweh/the Envoy of Yahweh functions as the commander and chief of one side (2:1–3; 6:11–23; 16:5; cf. 5:23) and the Canaanite deities on the other.[41] The cosmos itself joins forces, as "stars fought from heaven" and "the torrent of Kishon washed away" the kings of Canaanites (5:21). Humans, specifically Israelites and their oppressors, act as subjects to and warriors for their respective deities. The Canaanites, therefore, are not solely "inhabitants of the land" (2:2) but are Yahweh's "enemies" (5:31) who promote idolatrous worship on Yahweh's terrain (3:3–6).

The cosmic aspect of the war is why the book highlights Yahweh's victory over the gods in the longer narratives of the major judges.[42] The Samson story lacks a bona fide terrestrial battle because Samson chooses to fornicate rather than fight foreigner oppressors. Nevertheless, Yahweh proves mighty in the temple of Dagon, thereby demonstrating that Dagon did not deliver Samson into the Philistines' hands. Yahweh does not need human warriors (cf. Judg. 7:3; Deut. 20:8). Nevertheless, Israelites and

---

40. Anthony F. Campbell and Mark A. O'Brien, *Unfolding the Deuteronomistic History: Origins, Upgrades, Present Text* (Minneapolis: Fortress, 2000), 183n12.

41. The Envoy of Yahweh acts as the commander of the army (Exod. 23:20–23; cf. Josh. 9:13–15). It is the Envoy who charges Israel with infidelity after the failed conquest (Judg. 2:1–3). He commissions Gideon (6:11–23) and announces Samson's birth and role "to begin to deliver Israel from the hand of the Philistines" (16:5). The Envoy curses Meroz "because [its inhabitants] did not come to Yahweh's aid, to Yahweh's aid against the warriors" (5:23).

42. Baal (Deborah-Barak, in battle), Baal and Asherah (Gideon, pre-battle), all regional gods (Jephthah because of battle), and Dagon (Samson, no battle). Judges 10:6 lists seven deities. Seven apparently expresses totality here. It suggests that Israel has come to worship all the gods of the region—all except Yahweh. Thus Yahweh's ability to defeat the Ammonites trumpets his superiority above all the gods of the land.

non-Israelites (e.g., Jael) who participate receive praise (5:9, 12–15, 18, 31; cf. 8:35) and God's blessing (5:24–27, 31). Willful nonparticipation constitutes a dereliction of duty (5:16–17; 15:11–13), at times resulting in a divine curse (5:23).

Whereas Samson is apprehensive to participate in Yahweh-sanctioned *herem*, others in Judges go to the opposite extreme—they go beyond Yahweh's directives about what circumstances allow for *herem*.[43] The Danites conquer a people beyond their tribal allotment, if not beyond that of Israel (Judg. 18). In Judges 20, "all Israel" nearly annihilates one of its tribes on the testimony of a single witness, contra Deuteronomy 17:6, which requires two or three witnesses.[44] To "patch things up" and preserve Benjamin, the nation utterly destroys Jabesh-Gilead, sparing only four hundred virgins (Judg. 21:8–12).[45] Gideon and Abimelech also participate in unholy, civil war (Judg. 8:13–17; 9:34–57). Israel either avoids or adulterates the sacred rite of *herem* warfare. It results in excessive violence and God's displeasure.[46]

Worship by sacrificing to the Lord

Judges assumes that worshipers of a deity venerate him or her by offering sacrifices. The Israelites are portrayed as stingy in their sacrifices to Yahweh. At Bochim the Israelites weep and "offer sacrifices" to Yahweh after Yahweh rebukes them (2:1–5; cf. 20:26). The phraseology is generic. No mention is made of burnt offerings or sin offerings. Curiously, no mention is made of sacrifice whenever Israel "cries out to Yahweh" (3:9, 15; 6:6, 7; 10:10). One would expect sacrifices and festivals of praise to Yahweh after one of his great deliverances.[47] There are none.[48] The Philistines, in contrast, readily "assemble to offer a great sacrifice to Dagon their god" after

---

43. *Herem* warfare is restricted to Israelite cities that apostatize (Deut. 13:12–17 [Heb. 13:13–18]), Canaanite cities in the Promised Land (Deut. 7:1–5; 20:17–18), and cities outside the Promised Land that eschew peaceful relations with Israel (Deut. 20:10–16).

44. Judges 20 intimates that Israel is correct in the main for applying Deuteronomy 13:12–17 to Gibeah. It is in the secondary details of the law that they "do what is right in their own eyes."

45. This city's "crime" was nonparticipation in the battle against Gibeah (Judg. 21:8–12).

46. "Judges does not simply give us raw violence, but interpreted violence. The challenge for those of us who read it as Scripture is not whether we can identify with the violence, but whether we can identify with theology that frames and interprets it" (Barry G. Webb, *The Book of Judges*, NICOT [Grand Rapids: Eerdmans, 2012], 61).

47. The name Eglon ("young calf/bull") and the narrative's "sacrificial overtones" seem to portray Eglon as "a fatted calf ready for sacrifice" (Younger, *Judges/Ruth*, 115, 117; *pace* Lawson G. Stone, "Eglon's Belly and Ehud's Blade: A Reconsideration," *JBL* 128 [2009]: 654–56).

48. Judges gives an account of Shiloh's annual festival for Yahweh (21:19), but the event is utterly profaned. When the "daughters of Shiloh" come out to dance (presumably in worship to Yahweh), the Benjaminites "lie in wait," then "each snatches [*ḥṭp*] one for a wife" (21:20–23). Put simply, these men rape women to acquire them as wives. The atrocity occurs at the sacred site of Shiloh when Israelites were supposed to be worshiping Yahweh. What is more, the elders devised the plan (21:16, 22). Defiling holy war led to defiling a holy day, which led to defiling "the daughters of Shiloh."

capturing Samson (16:23–24). The statement excoriates Israel. "The uncircumcised Philistines" lavishly adore Dagon for his supposed triumph over a single enemy, whereas Israelites forgo a festival for Yahweh, who has defeated thousands of foes.

Israel's miserliness takes other forms. Gideon's preparations of food (or offering?) before the Envoy are elusive.[49] Manoah offers a goat and a grain offering to Yahweh at the Envoy's suggestion (13:16, 19, 23), but Manoah, unlike Gideon, does not build an altar to Yahweh after the encounter. The Israelites fighting Benjamin also appear out of step with ceremonial rites. Israel waits until the eve of the third battle before fasting and offering burnt offerings and peace offerings (20:26; cf. 21:4) even though offerings are part of prebattle preparations.

Unquestionably the worst sacrifice in Judges is Jephthah's daughter.[50] Part of the difficulty with Jephthah's vow involves the primacy of two Torah regulations, one related to making and fulfilling vows and the other prohibiting human sacrifices. The characters in the story seem fully aware of the former: "If someone vows a vow to the Lord or swears an oath, binding himself by obligation, he shall not break his word; he shall do all that proceeded from his mouth" (Num. 30:2 [Heb. 30:3]; cf. Deut. 23:21–22 [Heb. 23:22–23]; Eccl. 5:5 [Heb. 5:4]). In contrast, the characters seem unawares of the latter: "Do not worship [*asah*] [like the Canaanites] to the Lord your God for every abomination that the Lord hates they do to their gods; for even their sons and daughters they burn with fire to their gods" (Deut. 12:31; cf. Lev. 18:32; 20:1–5; 2 Kings 16:3).

The biblical text, in my estimation, recriminates Jephthah for going through with such a foolhardy oath and sacrifice. Jephthah should not have offered his daughter because "to obey is better than to sacrifice" (1 Sam. 15:22).[51] Sacrifices must be done according to Yahweh's commandments, not as one pleases and not in contradiction with Yahweh's explicit stipulations in the Torah.[52]

49. Sasson, *Judges 1–12*, 334–35; Richard D. Nelson, *Judges: A Critical & Rhetorical Commentary* (New York: T&T Clark, 2017), 131–33. Positively, Gideon builds an altar to Yahweh out of gratitude (6:24). When instructed by Yahweh, he builds another altar and offers a whole burnt offering from the demolished Asherah pole (6:25–27).

50. Space does not permit a thorough treatment of the grammatical construction of the vow and the vow's implementation. Some suggest that Jephthah never sacrifices his daughter because the text does not explicitly say so and the passage emphasizes the daughter's virginity rather than her death. However, the grammar of the conditional statement ("if X, then Y"), though challenging, supports the traditional reading (Ross, "A People Heeds Not Scripture," 243n42). Moreover, the book of Judges has frequently shown Israel's syncretistic ways, Israel's ignorance of Torah, and a propensity to refrain from critiquing by the narrator. Thus "he did as he said" is better taken as circumlocution for "offered it/him as a whole burnt offering" rather than as a dedication to Yahweh of the daughter as a celibate woman. For the celibacy view, see David Marcus, *Jephthah and His Vow* (Lubbock: Texas Tech Press, 1986).

51. Janzen, "The Sacrifice of Jephthah's Daughter," 345.

52. Janzen, "The Sacrifice of Jephthah's Daughter," 345–46.

Excursus on Jephthah's Vow and Sacrifice[53]

Even if Jephthah did not intend for the vow to include human sacrifice, his vow is wrongheaded on many fronts.[54] *First, victory was sure. The Spirit had already "come upon" Jephthah and was moving him across the region (11:29) when the vow interrupts the movement (11:30–31), which resumes after the vow is made (11:32a).*[55] *Second, it evades ordinate Yahwistic worship.*

On the other hand, if the vow intended to include humans, then Jephthah is playing with someone's life. Even if the vow envisaged animal sacrifice only, questions remain. Any (domestic) animal could come out of the house (11:31). What would happen if a lame ox came out? Is Jephthah required to offer it (contra Deut. 17:1; Lev. 22:18–23)? What if it were a cow, or any other female animal (contra Lev. 22:19)? How would the reader respond if Jephthah offered a lame animal so that he could "do what came out from his mouth"? The reader would likely be outraged that Jephthah would commit an abomination to Yahweh by offering an unacceptable animal, an animal other than "an unblemished male from the cattle, sheep, or goats" (Lev. 22:19–20). The reader may suggest that Jephthah find an appropriate substitute and (also?) give the monetary value for the lame animal (Lev. 27:27). If the reader would make such suggestions about animals for acceptable sacrifices to Yahweh, why not do so for a human?

Surely it is more sinful to commit an abomination against Yahweh than to incur the guilt from not following a defunct, ill-crafted vow. The vow's composition reveals that Jephthah has forgotten Yahweh while concomitantly paying homage to him. Vows are designed to offer the deity something that pleases him—not something he hates (cf. Deut. 12:31).[56] *Therefore, the biblical laws on vows have the deity's delights, not his disdains, in view. The biblical texts on vows expect that the payment will be something of which Yahweh approves. Vows are serious, and as the above example sought to illustrate, Jephthah should have provided an apt substitute for his daughter's life, perhaps ten shekels (Lev. 27:5) or an unblemished bull.*[57] *Instead, Jephthah committed a capital offense and became an abomination to Yahweh. His daughter and the people of Gilead are culpable to some extent as well. They had two months to come to terms with the law, but they did not (Lev. 20:2–5).*[58] *Apparently, they too had forgotten it. The Israelites may have "removed the foreign gods from among them to serve Yahweh" (Judg. 10:16),*

---

53. This section is an adaptation of Ross, "A People Heeds Not Scripture," 256–57.
54. For a compelling case that Jephthah only intended a human sacrifice, see Sasson, *Judges 1–12*, 444–47.
55. Barry G. Webb, *The Book of the Judges: An Integrated Reading*, JSOTSup 46 (Sheffield: JSOT Press, 1987), 62.
56. Similarly, Tony W. Cartledge, *Vows in the Hebrew Bible and the Ancient Near East*, JSOTSup 147 (Sheffield: JSOT Press, 1992), 28.
57. Cartledge discusses how cash substitutes are not a change in the original promise (Cartledge, *Vows*, 32–33).
58. Similarly, Janzen, "The Sacrifice of Jephthah's Daughter," 347–48.

but they have not worshiped him rightly by offering acceptable sacrifices and heeding his Torah. The story teaches what David Janzen considers "the most important theological motif: when Israel worships like foreigners, it will act like foreigners."[59]

Worship by praying to the Lord

Despite the relative paucity of sacrifices in Judges, the book has many prayers and petitions to Yahweh. The Israelites inquire of Yahweh/God (1:1; 18:5–6; 20:18, 23, 27–28), cry out to Yahweh (3:9, 15; 6:6, 7; 10:10), and confess their sin (10:15–16). Manoah offers supplication (13:8), Samson calls out to Yahweh (15:18; 16:28), and the elders raise a lament (21:3). Numbers are not everything. Most of these petitions lack the proper knowledge of Yahweh's ways or posture toward him (especially in the epilogue).[60]

Though not a prayer, one positive example appears with Gideon. Gideon is the only Israelite in Judges to bow in worship to Yahweh (7:15; *histaphal hvh*). His homage comes after the "fleecing" when Yahweh has him overhear the Midianites' dream and its interpretation that foretells of Gideon's victory. Unlike Gideon, Israel perpetually bows in worship to "the other gods" (2:12, 17, 19).

Israel frequently "cried out" (*tsʿq/zʿq*) to Yahweh. The term refers to "the loud agonized 'crying' of someone in acute distress"[61] and is associated with "large-scale calamity."[62] When Israel cries out, Yahweh sends a deliverer. He sends the deliverer even though Israel fails to inquire of him, listen to the prophet, repent, or bring an offering (6:7–10). Only once does Israel cry out, confess its sin, and put away its idols; it represents "a conversion of convenience" void of authentic repentance (10:10–16).[63] Without penitential prayers, Israel's prayer life falls short of pleasing worship.

Worship by praising the Lord

Singing songs to Yahweh allows worshipers to jubilantly praise Yahweh for who he is and what he has done (Judg. 5). Victory hymns call the assembly to recount the mighty works of Yahweh and teach others of his deeds, particularly his martial successes. Because "the battles were a divinely willed holy war . . . the only proper response, upon recognition that the victory was God's gift to his people, was praise."[64] The Song of Deborah constitutes the only victory hymn in Judges. By incorporating the hymn into the book, the

---

59. Janzen, "The Sacrifice of Jephthah's Daughter," 341.
60. For example, Manoah asks the Envoy's name. To modern sensibilities, the inquiry is benign. The request, however, is steeped in ancient practices that seek "to get control of the [numinous] and be able to use it" (H. F. Fuhs, "sha'al," in *TDOT* 14:258).
61. G. Hasel, "*zʿq*," in *TDOT* 4:115.
62. A. H. Konkel, "*zʿq*," in *NIDOTTE* 1:1131.
63. Block, *Judges, Ruth*, 349.
64. Tremper Longman III and Daniel G. Reid, *God Is a Warrior*, Studies in Old Testament Biblical Theology (Grand Rapids: Zondervan, 1995), 43.

author highlights Deborah and Barak's ordinate worship and sets up a contrast between these singers and the last judge. Samson sings a victory song crediting himself: "With a jawbone of a donkey, bones upon bones, with a jawbone of a donkey *I smote* a thousand soldiers" (15:16).[65] In the next breath, he rebuffs Yahweh (in prayer), intimating that Yahweh will cause him to die of thirst (15:18). Replacing a victory hymn with a self-aggrandizing jingle robs Yahweh of the glory due his name and smacks of irreverence inasmuch as Samson had neglected to worship Yahweh in any form after Yahweh delivers him from certain death (15:16–18). Judges condemns Samson's words and deeds with the words of Deborah and Barak (Judg. 5). True worshipers praise the Lord (5:3).

SIGNIFICANCE OF JUDGES FOR BIBLICAL WORSHIP

Before applying the finding of Judges' theology of worship to the church, the "elephant in the sanctuary" must be addressed. How did "Gideon, Barak, Samson, [and] Jephthah" ever make it into Hebrews' "Hall of Faith" (11:32)? Their fittingness to serve as role models and "witnesses" for Christians is hard to reconcile with Judges' censuring of them. Nonetheless, it can be done without compromising the integrity of either book's message. Hebrews 11 emphasizes faith and acts of faith. Judges emphasizes inordinate worship. The two are separate yet related ideas.

Hebrews 11:3–38 recounts stories of Old Testament heroes of faith. The unit with the judges involves post-Joshua heroes and classifies saints as "triumphant heroes" (Heb. 11:32–35a) or "suffering heroes" (Heb. 11:35b–38).[66] The judges fall within the heroes with (martial) victories.[67] The staccato list of victorious acts of faith points to individuals specifically mentioned in the list and those unmentioned, like "the prophets."[68] Several praiseworthy acts of faith can be attributed to the four judges: "overcame kingdoms" (Barak, Gideon, Jephthah, and Samson), "obtained things that were promised" (Barak and Gideon, if the promise includes victories), "shut mouths of lions" (Samson?), "were made powerful in weakness" (Gideon and "captive and blind" Samson), "became powerful in battle," and "routed enemy armies" (esp. Gideon) (Heb. 11:33–34).[69]

Each of these judges had exercised faith in God at the "critical moment."[70] It takes extraordinary faith in the Lord to *actively* believe that three hundred men will route 135,000 or that a blind man, using his bare hands, can breakdown an edifice holding three thousand people. Credit must be given where credit is due. The presence of these flawed figures in

65. Literally, "heaps upon heaps."
66. Craig R. Koester, *Hebrews*, AB 36 (New York: Doubleday, 2001), 517–19.
67. The suffering heroes experience martyrdom. See David L. Allen, *Hebrews: An Exegetical and Theological Exposition of Holy Scripture*, NAC 35 (Nashville: Broadman & Holman, 2010), 539.
68. Koester, *Hebrews*, 516–17.
69. Koester, *Hebrews*, 512–13.
70. William L. Lane, *Hebrews 9–13*, WBC 47B (Dallas: Word Books, 1991), 384.

Hebrews can warn and encourage Christians, even those tempted to apostatize. "If faith is possible despite Jephthah's rashness and Barak's hesitancy, then faith is also possible for the listeners, despite their shortcomings."[71]

Worship the Lord Reverently and Rightly

The shortcomings of these judges will be addressed from the perspective of worship in Judges, but it is appropriate first to cast a wider vision for the significance of worship in the church. Judges integrates the nature of God, specifically his love and covenant fidelity, into its theology of worship. Perhaps the church should follow suit and do more of this as well. What God has done for sinners should impel believers to unwavering loyalty to him. The Lord had delivered Israel from Egypt and its oppressors in Judges. In the New Testament, Christ died for our sins and rose again. "Our Savior Christ Jesus abolished death and brought life and immortality to light through the gospel" (2 Tim. 1:10). In view of this, Christians should worship the Great Deliverer Jesus Christ. As the book of Judges clearly details, humans cannot deliver and neither can false gods. Jesus is the unrivaled Savior of the world.

Along these lines, Judges teaches that there is no such thing as worshiping nothing. People replace God with something. It may be another god like Allah, Asherah, or Baal, but in the West it is more often a person, thing, or idea. Like the gods of the surrounding nations, secularism, sex, and social media seduce. Pluralism, politics, and pleasures compete with pure religion. Like the gods of old, they can neither save nor satisfy. Those who worship such things must repent, turn to the Lord, and revere him.

Churches have less risk of outright apostasy than they do of corrupt worship. "One of the greatest dangers to the community of faith is an insidious, creeping syncretism, where the power of this age infiltrates and corrupts genuine faith and worship. That danger always looms large and demands constant vigilance."[72]

Know Him and Make Him Known

Judges recommends a guard against syncretism and apostasy: knowing the Lord and teaching the next generation about him. "To know him and to make him known" is more than a Christian creed. It is a sacred rite. Time and again, Judges has shown that God's people tailspin into all kinds of sin when they do not know him, his word, or his mighty works. For Israel, training was an act of worship. Is it for the church? Christian parents bear the brunt of the training for their children. The stories of Micah's mother, Jephthah, and Gideon's father are enough to sober most

71. Koester, *Hebrews*, 517–18.

72. Phillip E. McMillon, "Worship in Judges 17–18," in *Worship and the Hebrew Bible: Essays in Honour of John T. Willis*, eds. M. Patrick Graham, Rick R. Marrs, and Steven L. McKenzie, JSOTSup 284 (Sheffield: Sheffield Academic, 1999), 242.

parents seeking to "diligently teach [their] children" God's Word (Deut. 6:7; cf. 11:19).

The local church shares in the responsibility because each one is a spiritual family (1 Tim. 5:1–2; Titus 2:1–10). Deborah was a spiritual mother in Israel. Jonathan, though a spiritual father, was a fatal choice, leading generations of Israelites into false worship of Yahweh.[73] Churches would do well to have some form of catechism for children because to know and love God is to rightly worship him. Since we live in a "post-Christian" society, venerating God by training young Christians demands a lot of time and energy, especially for those tasked with shepherding a generation, who in the words of Judges "do not know God or the works he has done" (Judg. 2:10). Thus the task of the local church is larger than that of Israel's in Judges. The church must teach primarily Jesus and his saving work but secondarily the rest of the Trinity and his works found in the entire Old and New Testament and throughout church history.

Worship at True Churches

According to Judges, right worship requires worshiping at the right place: Shiloh, not at Micah's shrine, not at Dan's sanctuary, not at the temples of Baal Berit or Dagon. The practice was rarely implemented despite the fact that worshiping at the chosen place was a sacred rite. In Micah's day even those living near Shiloh could not be bothered. The characters preferred the convenience of their own home (Micah and his family), the economic prosperity of other places (Jonathan), religious "latitude" (all parties), and flashy accoutrements (esp. the Danites).

More than three thousand years have gone by and God's people still struggle with these temptations. Although believers no longer have to worship at the "chosen place" (John 4:24), the church is God's chosen vehicle for believers' growth in Christ and the spread of the gospel. Thus, although sacred space is not as geographically localized in the New Testament as in the Old, the principles about Yahweh's chosen place aptly function as a warning for the Christian community. A growing number of Christians are replacing, rather than augmenting, corporate worship with listening to a sermon on the radio or online, watching a preacher, or participating in a parachurch activity. Others prefer going nowhere, which is tantamount to erecting a false place. Some attending a church allow convenience of

73. Along these lines, the Micah story urges God's people to consider carefully who they appoint as their spiritual leaders. These individuals oversee the assembly's worship. Jonathan the descendant of Moses demonstrates that who your relatives are or where you came from does not determine spirituality. The qualifications of 1 Timothy 3 and Titus 1 must be met, wherever one stands of the issue of women. Jonathan was a "lover of money" who was neither "above reproach" nor "upright" nor "holy." He claimed to give a message from the Lord, but it was against the Lord's word (Judg. 18:5–7); therefore, he failed "to teach sound doctrine" (cf. Rev. 2:14–17). Nonetheless he rose in influence, advancing from a small "church" to a "megachurch," and brought its people into apostasy.

location or programs to trump doctrinal fidelity. This mentality is dangerous. Orthodoxy and orthopraxy are the chief factors for choosing a local church to embrace. Believers need to attend the right houses of God, and churches must teach sound doctrine. Otherwise believers will fail to serve God or serve him crookedly.

Worshipers Arm Themselves for Battle

Wayward worship also evidences itself in wrongheaded warfare, according to Judges. Earlier Israelites paid homage to the Lord by tearing down rival sites and driving out the Canaanites from the Promised Land. Christians do not have the same mandates, "for our fight is not against flesh and blood" (Eph. 6:12). Nevertheless, both Israelites and Christians are charged with the task to engage in war for the Lord (2 Cor. 10:2–4; Eph. 6:11–17; 2 Tim. 2:3–4).[74] Because Israel's war had a spiritual dimension, Judges' warfare texts have application for worshipers of Christ. The Christian's warfare, like that of Israel's, is rigorous. Those who treat it lightly get "entangled in the affairs of daily life" (2 Tim. 2:4 NASB) and are blindsided by Satan's fiery darts, as Samson was.[75] However, the fully armed Christian soldier can "cast down" Satan's "strongholds" (2 Cor. 10:4). The defeat involves standing firm, exercising faith, taking the Word of God, and praying in the Spirit (Eph. 6:14–18).

Worship the Lord with One's Being

When believers forget their armor and calling, they become selfish ingrates. Samson proves instructive. Samson's escapades were self-centered and worldly. He spurned his sacred rite, the Nazarite vow, and its commitment to holiness. Christians, especially those called to the ministry, should reflect soberly. By pursuing worldly pleasures, practicing unchastity, or neglecting to grow in holiness, Christians can spurn their sacred act of worship—that is, "offering [their] bodies as a living sacrifice, holy and pleasing to God" (Rom. 12:1–2).

Because Christ is the paschal lamb, the Old Testament sacrificial system has been abolished and a Christian's sacrifice does not involve offering animals or grain (Heb. 9:12–22), as in the days of Judges. Judges gives concrete examples of God's disappointment and wrath when worshipers profane sacrifices and thereby displease God (esp. Jephthah's daughter). If Samson can be used as an example of defiling one's body, then his blindness and imprisonment can testify to the seriousness with which God takes blatant sin.

---

74. It is unclear when the mandate ceased for Israel, but the *terminus ad quem* would be 586 BC.
75. To Hughes, "A secularized Church is a Church which, having adopted the standards of the world, has ceased to fight and is herself overshadowed by the powers of darkness" (Philip Edgcumbe Hughes, *Paul's Second Epistle to the Corinthians*, NICNT [Grand Rapids: Eerdmans, 1962], 350).

Worship the Lord with Our Lips

Prayers show reverence, love, and dependence on God. Thus prayerlessness is not an option. Crying out and requesting things of God are acceptable but not to the exclusion of confession or repentance. Worshiping with the right posture rarely occurs in the texts of Judges. Gideon bows in worship only once to the Lord. On one desperate occasion, Israel confesses its sin (10:10). Yet its repentance was fleeting, if it ever existed. Confession and repentance have a long tradition in Christendom. Notwithstanding, contemporary culture hinders this practice by undermining and underemphasizing sin. In this environment, it is easy for Christians to listen to the world and forget to confess their sins or turn from their ways. Perhaps nonliturgical worshipers, like myself, can learn from their liturgical brethren by implementing some of their practices of corporate and individual confession.[76]

Praise is another aspect of worship that the Israelites frequently omitted. Samson praised himself because he forgot the power of God (15:16). In Judges 5, praise focuses mainly on who God is and what he has done. God had delivered Israel from Egypt and Canaanite kings, and Deborah cannot contain herself: "I to Yahweh, I will sing" (5:3). Because the Lord receives praise for these great acts, it stands to reason that believers in Christ should burst forth with praise to Jesus Christ, the sinless Savior, who conquered death and rose victoriously (cf. 1 Cor. 15:54–55). God's greatest act of deliverance, as well as other acts, should regularly be part of the liturgy of the church. The author of Judges would concur with the author of Hebrews: "Through him, let us continually offer up a sacrifice of praise [*ainesis*] to God, namely the fruit of the lips that praise [*homologeō*] his name" (Heb. 13:15).

BIBLIOGRAPHY

Allen, David L. *Hebrews*. NAC 35. Nashville: B&H, 2010.

Amit, Yairah. *The Book of Judges: The Art of Editing*. Translated by Jonathan Chipman. VTSup 38. Leiden: Brill, 1999.

Block, Daniel I. *For the Glory of God: Recovering a Biblical Theology of Worship*. Grand Rapids: Baker Academic, 2014.

______. "Judges." In *Zondervan Illustrated Bible Backgrounds Commentary: Old Testament*, vol. 2, *Joshua, Judges, Ruth, 1 & 2 Samuel*, edited by John H. Walton, 94–241. Grand Rapids: Zondervan, 2009.

76. Gideon's "fleecing" can be a source of confusion for believers. In the narrative, Gideon continually asked God for signs to prove that Yahweh would save Israel through him (6:17, 36–40). "Gideon in these passages might seem reminiscent of many believers who, uncertain of God's will, have sought a 'sign' by 'laying out a fleece' (6:37). But Gideon's desire for a sign marked his lack of faith (cf. Matt. 16:4). . . . The fleece [for him] is not a means of finding God's will, but possibly a maneuver by one who knew God's will but simply did not want to do it" (Lawson G. Stone, "Judges," in *Joshua, Judges, Ruth*, by Joseph Coleson, Lawson G. Stone, and Jason Driesbach, CBC 3 [Carol Stream, IL: Tyndale, 2012], 280). When God's will is clear (6:14), there is no reason to try God's patience. Christians would do well to approach "sign seeking" with great caution and with grounding in Scripture. For more details, see Stone, "Judges," 280.

______. *Judges, Ruth*. NAC 6. Nashville: Broadman & Holman, 1999.
Butler, Trent C. *Judges*. WBC 8. Nashville: Thomas Nelson, 2009.
Campbell, Anthony F., and Mark A. O'Brien. *Unfolding the Deuteronomistic History: Origins, Upgrades, Present Text*. Minneapolis: Fortress, 2000.
Cartledge, Tony W. *Vows in the Hebrew Bible and the Ancient Near East*. JSOTSup 147. Sheffield: JSOT Press, 1992.
Dempster, Stephen G. "Mythology and History in the Song of Deborah." *WTJ* 41 (1978): 33–53.
Fernández Marcos, Natalio. *Shofṭim: Judges*. BHQ 7. Stuttgart: Deutsche Bibelgesellschaft, 2011.
Grisanti, Michael. "Deuteronomy." In *The Expositor's Bible Commentary*, vol. 2, *Genesis–Leviticus*, edited by Tremper Longman III and David E. Garland, 457–814. Rev. ed. Grand Rapids: Zondervan, 2012.
Hughes, Philip Edgcumbe. *Paul's Second Epistle to the Corinthians*. NICNT. Grand Rapids: Eerdmans, 1962.
Janzen, David. "Why the Deuteronomist Told about the Sacrifice of Jephthah's Daughter." *JSOT* (2005): 339–57.
Koester, Craig R. *Hebrews*. AB 36. New York: Doubleday, 2001.
Lane, William L. *Hebrews 9–13*. WBC 47B. Dallas: Word, 1991.
Longman, Tremper, III, and Daniel G. Reid. *God Is a Warrior*. Studies in Old Testament Biblical Theology. Grand Rapids: Zondervan, 1995.
Marcus, David. *Jephthah and His Vow*. Lubbock: Texas Tech Press, 1986.
McConville, J. Gordon. *Grace to the End: A Study in Deuteronomic Theology*. Studies in Old Testament Biblical Theology. Grand Rapids: Zondervan, 1993.
McMillon, Phillip E. "Worship in Judges 17–18." In *Worship and the Hebrew Bible: Essays in Honour of John T. Willis*, edited by M. Patrick Graham, Rick R. Marrs, and Steven L. McKenzie, 225–43. JSOTSup 284. Sheffield: Sheffield Academic, 1999.
Nelson, Richard D. *Judges: A Critical & Rhetorical Commentary*. New York: T&T Clark, 2017.
Pressler, Carolyn. *Joshua, Judges, and Ruth*. Westminster Bible Companion. Louisville: Westminster John Knox, 2002.
Ross, Jillian L. "The Ring Composition of Judges Revisited: Allusive Texts in the Book of Judges." Paper presented at the Annual Meeting of the IBR, Boston MA, November 17, 2017.
______. "A People Heeds Not Scripture: A Poetics of Pentateuchal Allusions in the Book of Judges." PhD diss., Trinity Evangelical Divinity School, 2015.
Sasson, Jack M. *Judges 1–12*. AYB 6D. New Haven, CT: Yale University Press, 2014.
Schneider, Tammi J. *Judges*. Berit Olam: Studies in Hebrew Narrative and Poetry. Collegeville, MN: Liturgical Press, 2000.
Stone, Lawson G. "Eglon's Belly and Ehud's Blade: A Reconsideration." *JBL* 128 (2009): 649–63.

______. "Judges." In *Joshua, Judges, Ruth*, by Joseph Coleson, Lawson G. Stone, and Jason Driesbach, 185–494. CBC 3. Carol Stream, IL: Tyndale, 2012.

Trible, Phyllis. *Texts of Terror: Literary-Feminist Readings of Biblical Narratives*. Overtures to Biblical Theology 13. Philadelphia: Fortress, 1984.

Way, K. C. "The Literary Structure of Judges Revisited: Judges as a Ring Composition." In *Windows to the Ancient World of the Hebrew Bible: Essays in Honor of Samuel Greengus*, edited by Bill T. Arnold, Nancy L. Erickson, and John H. Walton, 247–60. Winona Lake, IN: Eisenbrauns, 2014.

Webb, Barry. G. *The Book of Judges*. NICOT. Grand Rapids: Eerdmans, 2012.

______. *The Book of the Judges: An Integrated Reading*. JSOTSup 46. Sheffield: JSOT Press, 1987.

Younger, K. Lawson, Jr. "Judges 1 in Its Near Eastern Literary Context." In *Faith, Tradition, and History: Old Testament Historiography in its Near Eastern Context*, edited by A. R. Millard, James K. Hoffmeier, and David W. Baker, 207–27. Winona Lake, IN: Eisenbrauns, 1994.

______. *Judges/Ruth*. NIVAC. Grand Rapids: Zondervan, 2002.

CHAPTER 7

SACRED PLACES, ACTS, TIMES, AND PEOPLE IN THE WORSHIP OF YAHWEH

Worship in Israel's United Monarchy

Eugene Merrill

Theologies of biblical principles and propositions abound, but theologies of divine and human activities are rare. Their scarceness, however, does not invalidate them as objects of theological thought. Hence, the undertaking here is not the theology of doctrine or of liturgy or prayer, but the theology of the mood, reflection, inner impulses, and ritual of worship itself as action, movement, choreography, and even the stasis of place and time.

CONTEXT OF WORSHIP IN THE UNITED MONARCHY

Following the exodus from Egypt in 1446 BC, the encounter with Yahweh at Sinai, the giving of the covenant and its law, and the conquest of Canaan led by Joshua, Israel at last settled into the land promised to Abraham and commenced life as a sedentary people (c. 1350). Yahweh had commanded Moses that he, Yahweh, must be worshiped in a communal manner in only the places "where he made his name to dwell"[1] (Deut. 12:5–14, 18, 26; 14:23; 16:2–11; 26). This could be a solitary altar (Gen. 12:7; 13:3–4; 35:1–8, 14–15; Exod. 20:24), the tabernacle in the desert (Exod. 25:22), and finally at or near Jerusalem, including, first, David's quasi-temple on Mount Zion (2 Sam 6:1–19) and then Solomon's temple,

1. The idea of "where my name shall dwell" has at least two nuances: (1) the name of Yahweh as a figure of speech, a metonymy, in which God's name stands for God himself, i.e., God is where his name is praised; and (2) his name embodies all he is as divine; in Israel's case, the "I AM."

also known as the First Temple (1 Kings 8:1–9:25). Strictly forbidden were alien gods, random places, and man-originated rituals.

The era of the united monarchy of Israel is specifically defined by the reigns of Saul (1051–1011 BC[2]), David (1011–971), and Solomon (971–931).[3] Before the unification under the monarchy, Israel was led by judges as representative rulers who acted on behalf of Yahweh for about three hundred years. Eventually, however, the people of Israel rebelled against Yahweh alone as king, and demanded that Samuel provide for them a king "like all the [other] nations" (1 Sam. 8:1–9).

Israel was a small state geographically, politically, and militarily among the great nations of the ancient Near Eastern world such as Egypt, Assyria, Babylonia, and Hatti (the Hittites). The apogee of its power and influence was doubtless in the latter part of the 120 years of the united monarchy, under Solomon (1071–1031 BC). Israel's location in the eastern Mediterranean Levant made it a natural route for commerce and trade, though it was narrowly pressed between the eastern deserts and the sea. That advantage was, however, frequently offset by the tramping feet of armies at war, most between the surrounding powers, but some whose purpose was to defeat Israel and incorporate it into their respective empires.

Historians label this period variously but usually in archaeological terms it is labeled the Late Bronze–Early Iron Age (c. 1550–900 BC). The great nations contending for supremacy at the time were Egypt to the south and southwest; Hatti and Mitanni to the northwest and northeast; and Assyria-Babylonia to the east and northeast.[4] The kings of the united monarchy never engaged any of these major powers since in this period (1150–950) most of the kingdoms were mutually stalemated. Assyria dominated Mesopotamia from around 1100 to 605, long after the Israelite

2. Unfortunately, the text at 1 Samuel 13:1, where the age of Saul and the length of his tenure are recorded, is defective. It reads literally, "Saul's inauguration [to kingship] a year, and he reigned over Israel two years," obviously an incorrect reading based on scribal error. Certain Old Greek (Septuagint) versions omit the verse altogether whereas others suggest thirty for Saul's age or (with the Syriac Peshitta) twenty-one. The Peshitta also omits the length of Saul's reign. For a proffered solution that grants Saul a forty-two-year kingship, see Eugene H. Merrill, *Kingdom of Priests: A History of Old Testament Israel*, 2nd ed. (Grand Rapids: Baker Academic, 2008), 210–12.

3. For the transition of Israel from a tribal to a monarchic state, see Bruce C. Birch, *The Rise of the Israelite Monarchy: The Growth and Development of I Samuel 7–15* (Missoula, MT: Scholars Press, 1976); M. Tsevat, "The Emergence of the Israelite Monarchy: Eli, Samuel, and Saul," in *The World History of the Jewish People* (Jerusalem: Masada Press, 1979), 4/1:61–75.

4. Helpful discussions and descriptions of this era and Israel's place in it may be found in such works as Lester Grabbe, *Israel in Transition: From the Late Bronze II to Iron IIA (c. 1250–850 BCE)*, vol. 2, *The Texts* (Edinburgh: T&T Clark, 2012); Yair Amit, *Essays on Ancient Israel in Its Near Eastern Context: A Tribute to Nadav Na'aman* (Winona Lake, IN: Eisenbrauns, 2009); Shirly Ben-Dor Evian, "Egypt and Israel: The Never-Ending Story," *NEA* 80, no. 1 (2017): 30–39; Amit, Yair, *Essays on Ancient Israel in Its Near Eastern Context: A Tribute to Nadav Na'aman* (Winona Lake, IN: Eisenbrauns, 2009); Ben-Dor Evian, "Egypt and Israel," 30–39.

united monarchy, during which time Egypt was staggering through the so-called Third Intermediate Period, a time of relative impotence.[5]

Israel, as a state and people, was in many ways not unique among its neighbors. Countries had innate political, social, and religious norms that made up their context and culture. With regard to religion, Israel, like many other peoples, had rich theological symbolism ingrained in the performance of worship and the liturgy of the priests and other officiants. What made Israel stand apart from among the nations, however, was the content of their faith and their theological presuppositions, and how their theology influenced their social and political norms. Only Israel was monotheistic in a world of thousands of imaginary deities worshiped in vain by millions of devout adherents. Only Israel claimed their God was directly involved in the daily affairs of his people. And only Israel confessed and maintained that it had been called by God out from the nations to become a beacon of light among the nations.

Other peoples of the ancient Near Eastern world held that within their religious systems there was a sort of government of the gods, an assembly, as it were, consisting of ranks and titles headed by a supreme being, the lord of the pantheon and the king universal.[6] The various states and their leaders often say in their texts—especially the royal inscriptions—that their kings were called by a special god to whom they owed their privilege and by whom they exercised authority.[7] Such gods were customarily referred to as X, the god of Y. But these ideologies fail in comparison to the majesty, logic, and purity of Israel's monotheistic faith in a God too transcendent to be humanized and so immanent as to be accessible to everyone.

All organized religions of the world, ancient and modern, share in common certain irreducible elements though, of course, they vary greatly in the symbolism, expression, and significance of what they do. Most, if not all, religions of the world have sacred places, sacred acts, sacred times, and sacred

5. Eugene H. Merrill, *Kingdom of Priests: A History of Old Testament Israel*, 2nd ed. (Grand Rapids: Baker Academic, 2008), 317–27.

6. The Akkadian term *puhur ilani*, "assembly of the gods," envisions a parliamentary conclave of lesser gods over which presided the great god, in the case of Babylonia the god Marduk with his consort Ishtar. Though he was thought to have ultimate power, he depended on the counsel of his "cabinet" and the assembly in general for counsel in making wise decisions. Thorkild Jacobsen went so far as to propose that this form of governance represented the most "primitive" form of democracy. See his "Primitive Democracy in Ancient Mesopotamia," *JNES* 2, no. 3 (1943): 159–72. The Ugaritic texts from Ras Shamra attest the same concept with El, the chief god, contesting with Baal for headship over the assembly. A reflection of this appears in the Old Testament, where Yahweh convenes an assembly of angels, among whom is Satan who "walks up and down" in a show of dominion contrary to God (Job 1:6–12). This, of course, is the true and original shape of things of which pagan exemplars were perverted imitations.

7. For Egypt, see "Daily Ritual of the Temple of Amun-Re at Karnak," *COS* 1:55–57; for the Hittites, "Ritual and Prayer to Ishtar of Nineveh," 1:164–165; for Ugarit, see "Ugaritic Liturgy Against Serpents and Sorcerers," 1:295–98; and for Sumerian/Akkadian Emar, see "The Installation of the Storm God's High Priestess," 1:427–31.

persons. This is true too of Israel. For we see throughout the history of Israel the importance of the sacred places, the tabernacle and the temple, the consequences for worshiping in locations other than that which was declared right by Yahweh, and Jesus's foreshadowing of the day that was to come where worship would no longer be found in a location, but in spirit and truth (John 4).

THEOLOGY OF WORSHIP

Sacred Places

After Joshua's conquest was finished (c. 1350), a place was sought for the location of the ark of God.[8] For reasons not explained, Joshua and the tribes determined that the "Tent of Meeting"[9] should be at Shiloh, some twenty-five miles north of Jerusalem in the tribal territory of Ephraim (Josh. 18:1).[10] There the ark remained for about 350 years, until the destruction of Shiloh by the Philistines in 1104.[11] Eli, of the line of Ithaman Ithamarite,[12] was a priest in Shiloh, as was Samuel, Eli's apt pupil, but there was no ark. It had been "spared," ironically, from destruction by the Philistines, who destroyed everything else including the tabernacle, having been taken as booty. The Philistines kept the ark for only a brief season because it, a representative of Yahweh himself, caused great havoc among them (1 Sam. 5:1–5). This event began an irregular and checkered series of travels—from Ekron to Beth-Shemesh (1 Sam. 6:14–22) to Kiriath-Jearim (1 Sam. 7:1–3) to the home of Obed-Edom in Gath (2 Sam. 6:1–11) to Jerusalem (2 Sam. 6:12–19).[13] All this time the ark was separated from the tabernacle. Since Samuel's day, the tabernacle had been located first in Mizpah[14] (1 Sam. 7:5–11; 9:14; 10:17–25), then at Gibeah (1 Sam. 14:2–3). This untenable situation prevailed until David built a tent/temple on Mount Zion. Other remedies had been sought, such as the erection of a tabernacle in Nob,[15] where Ahimelech (or Ahijah), great-grandson of Eli

8. The ark of the covenant (*aron habbrit*) was the most symbolically significant object of all the panoply of furnishings in and about the temple (Exod. 25:10–22). It was a chest that contained the stone tablets of the law (Ten Commandments) and that was covered by a lid called the *kipporeth*, literally, "the covering." The *kipporeth* served two functions: (1) as the place where the blood of atonement was applied on the Day of Atonement—that is, as a quasi-altar (Lev. 16:15); and (2) and as a "throne" on which sat invisible Yahweh, King of kings, above whom were cherubim who unceasingly sang his praises (Exod. 25:22; 1 Sam. 4:4; 2 Sam. 6 :2; 2 Kings 19:15; 1 Chron. 13:6).
9. The phrase refers to the theophanic glory of God that filled the tent (and the temple later) as a palpable sign of his presence and his communion with the priests on behalf of the nation.
10. Now called Seilun in Arabic, it lies on an imposing hill in the tribal territory of Ephraim twelve miles south of Shechem and c. thirty-five miles north of Jerusalem.
11. The destruction of Shiloh, "the first place Yahweh had appeared" in the land (Jer. 7:12), became proverbial and a sign of the destruction of Jerusalem in the day of Jeremiah (v. 14).
12. Ithamar was a son of Aaron, as was Eleazar (Exod. 6:23). They were both anointed as high (or chief) priests a result of their patrimony (Exod. 28:1–43).
13. G. W. Ahltrom, "The Travels of the Ark: A Religio-political Composition," *JNES* 43 (1984):141–49.
14. This was ten miles northwest of Jerusalem, in the tribal area of Benjamin, as was Gibeah.
15. On the slope of the Mount of Olives.

the Ithamarite, served as priest (1 Sam. 21:1–10; 22:20–23). However, the legitimate high priest must descend from Eleazar through Zadok, hence David's ultimate selection of Zadok and his line as high priests of his tent/temple (2 Sam. 8:17).[16] Abiathar the Ithamarite did indeed serve alongside Zadok for a time, but when Solomon became king he rejected Abiathar as ineligible and dismissed him from service (1 Kings 2:26–27).

In David's final years, he challenged his legitimate heir Solomon to keep covenant with Yahweh,[17] warning that failure to do so could bring God's judgment, even so much as to jeopardize the continuation of the God-chosen Davidic dynasty (1 Kings 2:1–4). The fuller transition narrative (1 Chron. 22:1–29:25) deals with (1) preparation for building a temple (22:1–16); (2) acceptance of Solomon by the royal family and others and to assist him as needed (22:17–19); (3) reorganization of the Levitical order (23:1–32); (4) establishment of the priesthood (1 Chron. 24:1–31); (5) the order of temple services (1 Chron. 25:1–26:32); (6) military preparedness (27:1–15); and (7) civil administration (27:16–34).

Finally, in one of the most important theological treatises in the Old Testament (1 Chron. 28:1–29:25), David the theologian explains his messianic role and that of all his successors. He presents himself as one called by God (via his son Solomon) to build a temple to house the ark of the covenant (28:1–8) and then affirms the same to Solomon (vv. 9–10). In an unusual density of technical terms, the verb "choose" or "chosen" occurs four times in three verses (vv. 4–6).[18] David was chosen to be king (v. 4), Judah was chosen to be prince (v. 4), Solomon was chosen to succeed David (v. 4), and Yahweh chose Solomon to be his son (v. 6).

Sacred Acts

The Holy One of Israel must be approached in a holy manner. There is no place for pride, self-righteousness, frivolity, or irreverence in approaching him, as the Old Testament amply illustrates (Exod. 3:5–7; 19:20–24; Lev. 10:1–2; Deut. 10:12–22; 2 Chron. 26:16–20). He is the Creator, Redeemer, Sovereign, who alone must be worshiped and who demands obedience in a spirit of profound reverence and in ways and means ordained by him for his own glory.

Sacrifice

The offering of sacrifices to deity is a feature of many religious traditions, ancient and modern. It represents the giving up of something

---

16. The choice of Eleazar's line to be high priest came about directly through the heroism and theological zeal of his son Phinehas in punishing certain Israelite men for engaging in the perverted sexual rituals of the Moabite god Baal (Num. 25:1–13). First, it had to be a clean animal—that is, one without blemish or defect.
17. The choice of verbiage—"statutes, commandments, ordinances, testimonies"—puts beyond doubt that David is referring to the book of Deuteronomy (5:31; 6:1, 20; 7:11; 11:1; 17:14–20).
18. Heb. *bahar*, in this sense, as elected by God's predetermination. Cf. Deut. 7:6; 14:2; 18:5; 21:5; *HALOT*, 119–120; *TDOT*.

precious by the worshiper to a god who is pleased not so much with the offering but with the piety of the giver. Especially significant is the offering of animals or, in some benighted cultures, of human beings. The latter is, of course, severely condemned in the Old Testament as a pagan practice that has no understanding of the sanctity of human life in the eyes of God (Lev. 18:21; 20:2–4). Animals meeting certain criteria were offered in the united monarchy not for the meat but for the blood.[19] Israel seems to have been unique among the cultures of the world in recognizing that blood is symbolic of life. When the blood drains out, the life drains out. Moses had taught that "the life of the flesh is in the blood" long before William Harvey (1578–1657) learned that principle of basic medicine in only relatively recent times. When the blood of animals was applied to the altar and *kipporeth* (or "mercy seat") of the tabernacle and temple, it was viewed as a substitute for the person who presented the animal to the priest. In this manner, the animal paid the price for the man or woman's sin. The fundamental idea in Israelite offerings in David's time was as a kind of tax due the King of kings for the generous support of the poor, sick, and helpless; for the maintenance of government including the monarchy and its bureaucracy; and for defense against nations that would do harm to the kingdom.

Prayer

The Bible has much to say about prayer in general as individual spiritual exercise, but little or nothing about its place in the temple. For example, Hannah, mother of Samuel, prayed a personal prayer for children, and she did so in the precinct of the Shiloh tabernacle, but it was not part of temple liturgy (1 Sam 2:1–10). Samuel's prayer for the people of his troubled times had no temple connection either. David, of course, composed many prayers that constitute large parts of the book of Psalms, including some that were clearly intended for congregational worship.[20] The great prayers of the united kingdom period are by the kings themselves, usually intercessory on behalf of the citizens for whom they were responsible (1 Kings 8:22–66; 2 Kings 19:14–19; 2 Chron. 30:18).

Music

It is impossible to overestimate the importance of music in worship, particularly in the period of the united monarchy, and most particularly

---

19. The Torah criteria are as follows: the sacrificial animal must (1) be free of physical defect; (2) be domesticated, not wild game; (3) chew the cud; (4) have cleft hooves. Moreover, the best parts of the animal, those that belong to Yahweh, must be wholly consumed in the flames, indicating its "consumption" by the Lord; other parts could be roasted as table fare for the family making the offering. These instructions are rather generic; each kind of sacrifice or offering had its own meaning, set of rituals, and purposes.
20. Information about the psalms and their possible temple connections is found primarily in their titles, the accuracy of which should be taken *prima facie* unless proved wrong. See, e.g., Pss. 5–9; 12–14; 19–22; 30–31; 36; 39; 41–42; 44–49; 51–62; 65–70; 109; 139–140.

under the leadership of King David, the "sweet singer of Israel." The composer of a great number of the psalms in the Psalter (some seventy-three), others are scattered throughout the narratives of Samuel-Kings and Chronicles as well.[21] These arose largely out of David's own life experiences from the time of his youth until the day of his death. They celebrate military success, praise to God for protection, and thanks for meeting needs in his life and that of his nation.

David was renowned as a youth for his skill on the harp, which he played from time to time at Saul's request to soothe him and control the demons that haunted him (1 Sam. 16:15–23; 18:10; 19:9). In the later years of his reign he organized and appointed leaders for instrumental and vocal music. As for the former, they consisted of harps, cymbals, and psalteries under the baton of sons of Asaph and Heman (1 Chron. 25:1–5). The vocalists, male and female alike, constituted great choirs, 288 members in all, under Heman (v. 5). Both instrumentalists and choristers, divided into twenty-four groups, alternated in their service in the temple month by month. The blending of strings, brass, percussion, and voice must have sounded like heaven on earth.

Sacred Times

The calendar of the period was arranged according to festival times, so much a part of everyday life was Israel's faith. Month names are rare in the Bible, but the names of religious events proliferate. Life in all its aspects was a drama in which all members of the community were expected to play their roles at designated times and in prescribed manners.

Sabbath

The first of these and most common was the Sabbath (*shabbat*), "cease," "stop," "rest," "celebrate."[22] This was first enjoined by Moses, first as a day to celebrated the creation of heaven and earth in six days and God's "rest" from it on the seventh (Exod. 6:8–11); and second to remember the Lord's deliverance of Israel from Egyptian slavery and consequently the need for human masters to free their servants and slaves also one day a week from their labors (Deut. 5:12–15). As God desisted from his "labors" so men ought also to desist from theirs. Sabbath was taken for granted in the united monarchy, it seems, for hardly a word is said of it in narratives of the period. David did issue lengthy instructions to the clergy about proper observance of the Sabbath and other temple functions (1 Chron. 23:1–26:32), but Sabbath per se receives only passing attention as though

21. Seventy-three psalms bear his name in the titles. There are other psalms of no attribution that are thought to by some scholars also to come from David's hand and a few embedded in Samuel and Chronicles. For the latter, see "Lamentation over Saul and over Jonathan" (2 Sam. 2:19–27); "Deliverance from His Enemies" (2 Sam. 22:2–51); "Last Words of David" (2 Sam. 23:1–7); and "Song of the Ark" (1 Chron. 16:8–36).

22. *HALOT*, 1407.

no specifics were necessary (23:31). Stranger still, the Sabbath is never referred to in all the psalms from David's hand.

New moon festival

The new moon festival is mentioned in the Torah in two places only, Numbers 10:10 and 28:14, suggesting its relative unimportance to biblical theology. Otherwise it is noted by David, who discussed with Jonathan the problem he might face should he celebrate the new moon by sitting at Saul's bountiful table (1 Sam. 20:5, 18). When the day came, David was absent (v. 24), as he was on the second and following days, confirming Saul's suspicions about David's disloyalty. Other instances of new moon reference are (1) in the narrative of the Shunammite woman's husband who questioned the likelihood of the prophet's coming to heal her son on a day that was neither the Sabbath nor new moon (2 Kings 4:23) and (2) in David's final address, in which he urged ongoing observance of the Sabbath and new moons (1 Chron. 24:31). Though secondary to Sabbath, new moon continued to the very end of Israel's history as evidenced in both Ezra 3:5 and Nehemiah 10:33 and sparsely in the Prophets (for a reference in Psalms, see 81:3; for the Prophets see Isa. 1:14; 66:23; Ezek. 46:1; Hos. 5:7; Amos 8:5). In fact, Paul hints that the new moon was part of the festal calendar in his own day (Col. 2:16).

Its significance lies, we suggest, in the creation narrative where the sun "rules the day" and the moon "rules the night" (Gen. 1:14–19). The seventh day (Sabbath) celebrates the week and the other (new moon) celebrates the month. Rosh Hashanah, of course, celebrates the year. Aside from the brief narrative mentioned above, this festival is missing in the united monarchy literature.

Festivals

By "festivals"[23] is meant the other sacred times in the year when the whole community of Israel by divine edict was required to appear before the Lord at the temple, and in post-temple times, at the synagogue or other special places of assembly.

Rosh Hashanah

They begin with Rosh Hashanah,[24] on the first day of the month Tishri in the fall of the year.[25] Like other sacred times, this is strangely lacking in texts of the united monarchy.

---

23. Hebrew *hag* bears the meaning of "celebration," "festivity," even "reckless abandon." It usually signifies a joyful approach to Yahweh, though Yom Kippur is a striking exception.
24. *Ro'sh hashanah*, "head of the year."
25. The Hebrew calendar of ancient times reckoned with two calendrical systems, the Tishri New Year in the autumn and the Nisan in the spring. The Old Testament mandates the latter for the observance of the festivals, though in time the Nisan calendar became universally accepted and the New Year fell in the spring. Thus Rosh Hashanah in the Old Testament falls on Tishri 1.

The Day of Atonement

On the tenth day of Tishri, the Day of Atonement,[26] the whole community was to be in repentant mourning for their sins. On that day once a year the chief priest only was permitted to enter the *qodesh haqqodashim*, "the most holy [place]." On behalf of the nation he offered a sacrifice that could not, of course, atone for the sins of the whole nation to say nothing of the sins of the world. It served as a prototype of the Melchizedek Priest who, 1,400 years later and with his own shed blood, entered the throne room of his Father, where his offering was received, making available salvation to all who believe (Heb. 9:11–28). This is not specifically singled out in the united monarchy narratives or injunctions.

Sukkoth

Five days later marked the beginning of a two-week-long festival called, *sukkoth*—that is, "Booths" or "Tabernacles"—the purpose of which was to remember and celebrate the exodus and the forty years in the deserts where the Lord sustained them until they reached the Promised Land. In years to come the tradition was to erect replicas of the huts in which the ancestors found refuge in the desert and to stay in them until the two weeks had passed. This was the last of the Tishri festivals and, like others, seemed to receive no particular attention in the united monarchy.

Passover

In the month of Nisan in the spring the festival season was inaugurated by the celebration of *pesah*, Passover, on the fifteenth through twenty-second days. It was set apart as a time to remember the exodus from Egypt in 1446 BC. This deliverance had been revealed to Abraham six hundred years earlier: "Know for certain that your offspring will be sojourners in a land that is not theirs and will be servants there, and they will be afflicted for four hundred years. But I will bring judgment on the nation that they serve, and afterward they shall come out with great possessions" (Gen. 15:13–14). Moses, of course, knew of this ancient pledge and was later informed by Yahweh in the burning bush that the time had come for him to lead his people to freedom: "Come, I will send you to Pharaoh that you may bring my people, the children of Israel, out of Egypt" (Exod. 3:10). Yahweh then proceeded to inflict judgment on Egypt by a series of plagues, thus weakening and demoralizing them to the point that Pharaoh relented and told Moses the Israelites could leave (Exod. 7:14–12:32). However, he changed his mind, a blunder that moved Yahweh to afflict Egypt with one more plague, the death of all of Egypt's firstborn children. The children of the Israelites could be spared but

---

26. *Yom kippur*, "day of covering." The term comes from the theological concept of the blood of an "innocent" animal being shed in the place of sinful human beings and then applied to the cover of the ark, the *kipporet*, which implicitly served also as the throne of Almighty God (Lev. 16:3–28; cf. Exod. 25:17–22).

only by the application of blood to their doorposts. Only then would he pass over[27] his own people and lead them to the land of promise.

Amazingly enough, the celebration of the Passover is mentioned in the Bible only once in the era of Joshua (Josh. 5:10–11), but never in Judges, Ruth, and Samuel. In fact, David, Solomon, and all their royal successors seem to have ignored it until Hezekiah sent out letters throughout Judah and the North inviting the populace to Jerusalem for is observance (2 Chron. 30:1). It had been neglected, as far as the record shows, since the conquest period, over six hundred years earlier.[28] The second recorded celebration of Passover was at the instigation of another godly ruler, King Josiah (640–609), a century after Hezekiah. Finally, Ezra, the postexilic priest, notes that a Passover occurred "on the fourteenth day of the first month"—that is, in 538 (Ezra 6:19–22).

Feast of Unleavened Bread

Associated with the Passover is the Feast of Unleavened Bread[29] (Exod. 12:17; 23:15), to be observed from the fifteenth through twenty-second days of Nisan. It harks back to the edict of Moses that the escapees from Egypt should carry with them bread that could not wait to be baked, so urgent was the need for haste. Like Passover, not a word is said of its observance in the united monarchy era.

Feast of Firstfruits

Fifty days (seven weeks) after Passover–Unleavened Bread marked the Feast of Firstfruits (or of Weeks) to celebrate with joyful thanksgiving God's bountiful blessings of agricultural produce, the first or best of which must be returned to him (Exod. 23:16, 19; 34:22, 26; Deut. 26:2–11). This is lacking in the united monarchy texts. With this the full agenda of biblical holy days and festivals comes to an end.

Very likely, the assumption is that David, a man fully committed to Yahweh and Torah,[30] not only would have observed the festivals himself but by example and unwritten edict (at least in the inspired record) would have mandated their observance by the priests and Levites and, hence, by the general population (again, see 1 Chron. 22:1–23:32).

Sacred Persons

To this point, the emphasis has been on location, acts, and times. The root *qdsh* in its various forms has the meaning of "cutting," "separating,"

27. This term in a technical sense occurs first in Exod. 12:11. Its noun form, *pesah*, is a derivative of the verb meaning "limp by," "pass by," "skip over" (*HALOT*, 947).
28. Joshua's Passover can be dated to c. 1400, and Hezekiah's reign is securely set at 729–686. See Merrill, *Kingdom of Priests*, 126–28, 422–26.
29. *Matzoth*, derived from the verb *matzah*, "to be flat, tasteless."
30. For these traits, see, in addition to the Psalms, 2 Sam. 22:1–23:7; 1 Kings 2:3; 3:6; 9:4; 11:6, 12–13; 14:7–8.

"setting apart."[31] The issue is not one of inner or outer personal righteousness but of being dedicated to serving and worshiping the Holy One of Israel and him only. Thus, persons, places, objects, and the like can all be considered holy in that highly refined sense of the word. From the very beginning God was to be found in special locales that he had set apart as meeting points between himself and those who worshiped him. Abraham, Isaac, and Jacob were all conscious of this (Gen. 12:6; 13:4, 18; 22:9; 26:25; 28:13; 32:1–2, 30; 35:3, 14), as were Moses (Exod. 3:5) and Joshua (Josh. 5:15; 24:26). The tabernacle in the desert epitomized the concept of holy space what with its Holy Place and most Holy Place. These were set apart respectively for various ministries of the priests and Levites (Exod. 26:33; 28:29, 43; 29:30; 31:11; Leviticus passim) and for the high (or chief) priests (Exod. 26:33, 34; Lev. 16:2–33; 1 Kings 6:16; 7:50; 8:6, 8; 1 Chron. 6:49; 2 Chron. 3:8, 10; 4:22; 5:7, 9).

Also from the onset of sacred history God chose persons from within the body of his people to represent them before him as ministers and servants. In descending order of responsibility and authority were the high priest, attending priests, Levites, and Nethinim, each now to be examined as to qualifications and function.

The high priest

The priests of Israel were required to come from the tribe of Levi so in a sense they were all Levites. However, not all Levites were priests. These latter were required to be direct descendants of Aaron, brother of Moses, as opposed to other Levites whose descent from Levi through other sons was sufficient. The first hint of Aaron's primacy is Yahweh's command that he and his sons must "forever" be in charge of the central places of worship (Exod. 27:21). Then he is called to minister in "the priest's office," a clear clue to his peculiar and special priestly function (Exod. 28:1, 3, 4; 40:13–15). His subsequent apparel strongly implied dominance in priestly affairs (28:2–43; 29:5–9), and his consecration with a lavish sacrifice and anointing (29:10–46) led inexorably to the position of what is popularly called "high priest" or "chief priest," terms never used in the Old Testament but strongly implied.

Eleazar and Ithamar, sons of Aaron, were "priests during the lifetime of their father Aaron" (Num. 3:4). The line of Ithamar led to Eli and Samuel and worship at Shiloh (1 Sam. 14:3). The Eli priesthood ended with the term of Abiathar, who was sent home to Anathoth (a Levitical city in the territory of Benjamin) during the early reign of Solomon (see 1 Kings 1:7; 2:26–27), thus fulfilling God's curse on Eli and his descendants (see 1 Sam. 2:12–17; 27–36; 1 Kings 2:27). The true, Aaronic line ran through Eleazar, Phinehas, and Zadok to David's time. Zadok, along with Abiathar from the Eli priesthood, served as the high priest during the reigns of David (see

31. *HALOT*, 1072–73.

2 Sam 8:17; 15:27, 35–36; 20:25; 1 Chron. 18:16) and Solomon, and the construction of Solomon's Temple (1 Kings 1:32, 34; 4:4; 1 Chron. 29:22). Solomon eventually removed Abiathar from office (1 Kings 1:26–27), thus bringing to completion the Lord's judgment on the house of Eli and the Eli priesthood (1 Sam. 2:27–36). The Aaron-Eleazar-Phinehas-Zadok line of high priests who served in Solomon's temple in Jerusalem are traditionally referred to as the "Zadokite heirs" or the "Zadokite priesthood."

The attending priest

Though never described in precisely these terms, attending priests were all priests other than the "sons of Aaron" in the limited sense described above. They were all of the tribe of Levi, and they could undertake all priestly duties in and about the tabernacle, then temple, as they pleased, with the exceptions of (1) access to the Holy of Holies and (2) ministering with respect to the ark of the covenant. They also were forbidden use of the Urim and Thummim and obviously were dressed in much less elaborate attire. Also, as opposed to the high priests, attending priests are rarely mentioned by name or even referred to except in very general terms such as "the priests" or "a priest" who may appear in narratives, always anonymous.

The Levites

All other descendants of Levi were also invested with certain liturgical and ritualistic privileges. They were responsible for the care and maintenance of the temple and its furnishings (Num. 1:47–54); they could and were expected to assist the priests in their cultic duties, they were exempt from military and other secular requirements (Num. 2:33–34), and they were provided and owned homes in forty-eight villages throughout the land where they could live more or less normal lives until their time in the rotation of temple employment rolled around again (Lev. 25:32–34). Levites were gifted with a kind of "lay" ministry whether in Jerusalem or elsewhere in the land (Deut. 18:6–8; 27:14–15).

The Nethinim[32]

This servant class was dedicated as a gift to Yahweh for temple service, but since the same term is used for secular servants in the employ of kings and other persons of prestige and affluence, there is nothing particularly significant in a theological sense to be attributed to them as temple servants. They are not clearly referred to in early texts and times except as those Levites who had been totally dedicated to service under Aaron and his sons (Num. 3:9; 18:6). After the return from exile they appear again but as virtual slaves to Solomon's servants (Ezra 2:43, 58, 70; 7:7; 8:17) who are able to reclaim their homes near the temple (Neh. 3:26, 31; 7:46, 60, 72; 11:3, 21).

---

32. This noun plural (*netiynim*) derives from the passive plural participle verb *ntn*, "to give," here, "those who have been given."

SIGNIFICANCE OF THE UNITED MONARCHY FOR BIBLICAL WORSHIP

Worship in the era of the united monarchy underwent significant changes from what had preceded Moses through the judges' administration (c. 1450–1100) to the inauguration of kingship under Saul, David, and Solomon (c. 1051–931).

1. First of all and for the first time, Israel was a rooted and settled nation among nations with a clear sense of identity. Gone were the days, indeed years, of virtual nomadic tent life, moving from place to place with flocks and herds and the uncertainties brought by weather, unrest, fatigue, and enemy threat that on occasion brought actual conflict.

2. With the transition to urbanity, especially in Jerusalem, came transition also in worship practice. The tabernacle gave way to the temple, first that of David on Mount Zion[33] and then the magnificent palace of Yahweh the King, as it were, known commonly as the Temple of Solomon (1 Kings 6:1–38).

3. Despite the merciful and abundant grace of God, there was always the possibility of corruption in the priesthood (2 Kings 16:10–16), resort to paganism by the royalty (2 Kings 11:17), and spiritual indifference among the multitudes of the population, scattered as they were in sometimes isolated places.

4. Nevertheless, at least a remnant always remained bound closely to Yahwistic faith and Mosaic Torah observance, sometimes under severe opposition even from within the populace to say nothing from without. Prophets of God began to rise up with conviction and courage to withstand an always present opposition, and sometimes paid with their lives (see 2 Chron. 24:20–22) .

5. The united monarchy was designed to reflect the kingdom of God on earth, which explains why Yahweh was formally, at least, seen to be enthroned in glory over the *Kipporet*, manifesting his

---

33. Mount Zion was a stronghold on the southeast corner of the old city of Jerusalem that was built by the indigenous Jebusites to protect Jerusalem from incursion by enemies. By a stratagem described in detail in 1 Chronicles 11:4–9, David took the city in 1004 BC and proceeded to refortify it and build on Mount Zion a "temple" that was a tentlike replica of the wilderness tabernacle and, in fact, is called a tent, *ohel*. David was not ordained to build the temple for he was a warrior; the privilege would go, in fact, to Solomon, whose name is related to *shalom*, the word for "peace." The site, also called Ophel, has been excavated for a number of years resulting in what the lead excavator, Eilat Mazar, claims to be recovery of David's palace. See her "Did I Find King David's Palace?," *BAR* 32, no. 1 (2006): 16–27, 70.

regency through the monarchs whom had had called and authenticated. Their failure was not his failure, nor could their triumphs be really theirs, for God is sovereign and has at last manifested it in the person of his Son, the Lord Jesus Christ, who has triumphed over death and who even now sits at the right hand of the Father awaiting to day when he shall come again and reign in fact over all the earth as even now he reigns in heaven.

BIBLIOGRAPHY

Albertz, Rainer. *A History of Israelite Religion in the Old Testament Period.* Louisville: Westminster John Knox, 1994.

Albright, William F. *Yahweh and the Gods of Canaan*. Garden City, NY: Doubleday, 1969.

Anderson, G. W., "Israel's Creed: Sung, Not Signed." *SJT* 16 (1963): 277–85.

Eakin, Frank E., Jr. *The Religion and Culture of Israel*. Boston: Allyn and Bacon, 1971.

______. "Yahwism and Baalism before the Exile." *JBL* 84 (1965): 407–14.

Fohrer, Georg. *History of the Israelite Religion*. Nashville: Abingdon, 1972.

Friedman, Richard E., "The Tabernacle in the Temple." *BA* 43 (1980): 241–48.

Greenberg, Moshe. "Religion: Stability and Ferment." In *The World History of the Jewish People*, vol. 4/2, *The Age of the Monarchies: Culture and Society*, edited by Abraham Malamat, 79–123. Jerusalem: Masada, 1979.

Heiser, Michael S. "Does Divine Plurality in the Hebrew Bible Demonstrate an Evolution from Polytheism to Monotheism in Israelite Religion?" *JESOT* 1, no. 1 (2012): 1–24.

Hendrix, Ralph E. "*Miškān* and *'Ôhel Mô'ēd*: Etymology, Lexical Definitions, and Extra-biblical Usage." *AUSS* 29 (1991): 213–24.

Kitchen, Kenneth A. "The Desert Tabernacle: Pure Fiction or Plausible Account?" *BR* 16, no. 6 (2000): 14–21.

Kitz, Anne Marie. "The Plural Form of *'ûrîm* and *tummîm*." *JBL* 116 (1997): 401–10.

Lipinski, Edward. "Cult Prostitution in Ancient Israel?" *BAR* 40, no. 1 (2014): 48–56, 70.

Price, Randall. "Where Was the Temple Located?" *The Chosen People* 22, no. 7 (2016): 4–5.

Rooke, Deborah W. *Zadok's Heirs: The Role and Development of the High Priesthood in Ancient Israel*. New York: Oxford University Press, 2012.

Routledge, Robin. "'My Spirit' in Genesis 6.1–4." *JPT* 20 (2011): 232–51.

Smith, Mark. "The Three Bodies of God in the Hebrew Bible." *JBL* 134, no. 3 (3015): 471–88.

Ussishkin, David. "The Sacred Area of Early Bronze Megiddo: History and Interpretation." *BASOR* 373 (2015): 69–104.

Widengren, Geo. "Israelite-Jewish Religion." *Historia Religionum*, vol. 1, *Religions of the Past*, edited by C. Jonco Bleeker and Geo Widengren, 223–317. Leiden: Brill, 1969.

Samuel

Carlson, R. A. *David, the Chosen King: A Traditio-historical Approach to the Second Book of Samuel.* Stockholm: Almqvist & Wiksell, 1964.
Davies, P. R. "The History of the Ark in the Books of Samuel." *JNSL* 5 (1976): 9–18.
Hood, Jared. "YHWH Tsevaot in Samuel: God of the Davidic Age." *JETS* 62, no. 3 (2019): 495–513.
Klein, R. W. "The Song of Hannah." *CTM* 41 (1970): 674–84.
Kleven, Terence. "Hebrew Style in 2 Samuel 6." *JETS* 35 (1992): 299–314.
Lawlor, John I. "Theology and Art in the Narrative of the Ammonite War (2 Samuel 10–12)." *GTJ* 3 (1982): 193–205.
Maucline, J. *1 and 2 Samuel.* NCB. London: Oliphants, 1971.
Mayes, A. D. H. "The Rise of the Israelite Monarchy." *ZAW* 90 (1978): 1–19.
McCarter, P. Kyle, Jr. "The Apology of David." *JBL* 99 (1980): 489–504.
______. "The Historical David." *Int* 40 (1986): 117–29.
______. "Plots, True or False: The Succession Narratives as Court Apologetic." *Int* 35 (1981): 355–67.
McCarthy, Dennis J. "II Samuel 7 and the Structure of the Deuteronomic History." *JBL* 84 (1965): 131–38.
______. "The Inauguration of Monarchy in Israel: A Form-critical Study of 1 Sam 8–12." *Int* 27 (1973): 401–22.
McKenzie, Steven L. "Elaborated Evidence for the Priority of 1 Samuel 26." *JBL* 129, no. 3 (2010): 437–44.

Kings

Davis, Andrew R. "Rereading 1 Kings 17:21 in Light of Ancient Medical Texts." *JBL* 135, no. 3 (2016): 465–81.
Grabbe, Lester L. *1 and 2 Kings: History and Story in Ancient Israel.* London: Bloomsbury, 2017.
Kitchen, Kenneth A. "How We Know When Solomon Ruled." *BAR* 27, no. 4 (2001): 32–37, 58.
Knoppers, Gary N. "The Historical Study of the Monarchy: Developments and Detours." In *The Face of Old Testament Studies*, edited by David W. Baker and Bill T. Arnold, 207–35. Grand Rapids: Baker, 1999.
______. "'There Was None Like Him': Incomparability in the Books of Kings." *CBQ* 54 (1992): 411–31.
Koopmans, W. T. "The Testament of David in 1 Kings ii 1–10." *VT* 41 (1991): 429–49.
Lemaire, Andre. "Solomon and Sheba, Inc." *BAR* 36, no. 1 (2010): 54–59.
McConville, J. G. "1 Kings viii 46–53 and the Deuteronomic Hope." *VT* 42 (1992): 67–79.

______. "Narrative and Meaning in the Books of Kings." *Bib* 20 (1989): 31–49.

McKenzie, Steven L. "The Source for Jeroboam's Role at Shechem (1 Kgs ii:43–12:3, 12, 20)." *JBL* 106 (1987): 297–300.

Parker, Kim Ian. "Repetition as a Structuring Device in 1 Kings 1–11." *JSOT* 42 (1988): 19–27.

Schley, Donald G., Jr. "1 Kings 10:26–29: A Reconsideration." *JBL* 106 (1987): 595–601.

Tomes, Roger. "'Our Holy and Beautiful House': When and Why Was 1 Kings 6–8 Written?" *JSOT* 70 (1996): 33–50.

Young, Rodger C. "Solomon and the Kings of Tyre." *Bible & Spade* 30, no. 3 (2017): 66–73.

Walsh, Jerome T. "The Characterization of Solomon in First Kings 1–5." *CBQ* 57 (1995): 471–493.

______. "Methods and Meanings: Multiple Studies of 1 Kings 21." *JBL* 111 (1992): 193–211.

Willis, Timothy M. "The Text of 1 Kings 11:43–12:3." *CBQ* 53 (1991): 37–44.

Yeivin, Sh. "Administration." In *The World History of the Jewish People*, vol. 4/2, *The Age of the Monarchies: Culture and Society*, edited by Abraham Malamat, 147–71. Jerusalem: Masada, 1979.

Zipor, Moshe A. "On the Presentation of the Synoptic Accounts of the Monarchies (Samuel, Kings, and Chronicles)." *AbrN* 28 (1990): 127–35.

Zuidhof, Albert. "King Solomon's Molten Sea and (π)." *BA* 45 (1982): 179–84.

Chronicles

Ackroyd, Peter R. *I and II Chronicles, Ezra, Nehemiah*. London: SCM, 1973.

______. *The Chronicler in His Age*. JSOTSup 101. Sheffield: JSOT Press, 1991.

Braun, Roddy. *I Chronicles*. WBC 14. Waco: Word, 1986.

______. "The Message of Chronicles: Rally Round the Temple." *CTM* 42 (1971): 502–13.

Dillard, Raymond B. "The Chronicler's Solomon." *WTJ* 43 (1981): 289–300.

______. "The Literary Structure of the Chronicler's Solomon Narrative." *JSOT* 30 (1984): 85–93.

Dumbrell, William J. "The Purpose of the Book of Chronicles." *JETS* 27 (1984): 257–66.

Japhet, Sara. "The Historical Reliability of Chronicles." *JSOT* 33 (1985): 436–42.

______. *I & II Chronicles*. OTL. Louisville: Westminster John Knox, 1993.

Merrill, Eugene H. *1, 2 Chronicles*. Bible Study Commentary. Grand Rapids: Zondervan, 1988.

______. *A Commentary on 1 & 2 Chronicles*. Kregel Exegetical Library. Grand Rapids: Kregel Academic, 2015.

Williamson, H. G. M. *Israel in the Books of Chronicles*. New York: Cambridge University Press, 1977.

Wright, John W. "The Legacy of David in Chronicles: The Narrative Function of 1 Chronicles 23–27." *JBL* 110 (1991): 229–42.

CHAPTER 8

KINGSHIP AND FAITHFULNESS

Worship and the Divided Kingdom

N. Blake Hearson

CONTEXT OF WORSHIP IN THE DIVIDED KINGDOM

At its core, biblical worship is relational.[1] To properly worship God is to live life in proper relationship with him. The fact that total devotion to God is required is evident in Deuteronomy 6:5, which states, "You shall love the LORD your God with all your heart and with all your soul and with all your might."[2] This law, given to the people of Israel, provided a foundation for worship articulating that their love for God should move from the inner person to the whole person and then influence everything one does in life.[3] While this idea of whole-life worship is a noble goal, such a life of worship was not always lived out by the people of God, and this improper worship grew, with small exceptions, the further they got chronologically from Moses. More often than not, the people of Israel lived a double life of public worship and private rebellion. In fact, it was this sort of dichotomy between public worship and selfish living that characterized the divided kingdom period in the Old Testament. The response of the prophets and biblical writers to such inconsistency in worship indicates what God really desires from his people—our faithfulness to his kingship.

1. One term often associated with worship in Hebrew is *avad*, which can also be understood as "serve." Thus the idea of worship is usually tied to service that is relational. See Andrew Hill, *Enter His Courts with Praise: Old Testament Worship for the New Testament Church* (Nashville: Star Song, 1993), xviii–xx.
2. Unless otherwise noted, all Scripture references come from the New American Standard Bible.
3. See N. Blake Hearson, "'And with All Your Strength'? A Reassessment of the Translation and Meaning of Deuteronomy 6:5," in *The Unfolding of Your Words Gives Light: Studies on Biblical Hebrew in Honor of George L. Klein*, ed. Ethan C. Jones (University Park, PA: Eisenbrauns, 2018), 203–16.

In order to understand the complicated ideas of worship in the divided kingdom, it is best to begin at the end of Solomon's reign, before the kingdom split. For those who grew up in the church, the stories of Solomon's vast wisdom are familiar. So too is the fact that Solomon's reign was one of great prosperity for the kingdom of Israel. Yet religiously, it was a period of great compromise. In addition to marrying foreign women, Solomon allowed his wives and concubines to worship their pagan gods in Israel (1 Kings 11:1–8). The people followed his example. From the top down, then, Solomon allowed religious syncretism among the people. For all his wisdom, Solomon lacked the desire or discipline or both to please God that characterized his father David.[4] In fact, by the end of his reign, Solomon failed to meet any of the requirements of the ideal king described in Deuteronomy 17:14–20. His concern for the Torah, and therefore his relationship with God, was not high on his list of priorities, and the epitaph of his reign reflected not the faith of his father David as it was said: "For when Solomon was old, his wives turned his heart away after other gods; and his heart was not wholly devoted to the Lord his God, as the heart of David his father had been" (1 Kings 11:4).

This attitude had a significant effect on his economic and military policies as well. Solomon was very successful by earthly standards, but at the cost of the satisfaction of the people he ruled. If the reasons for the division of the kingdom are any indicator, the northern tribes in particular felt that Solomon's policies and manner of ruling the country were burdensome.[5] When Rehoboam, Solomon's son, took the advice of the younger counselors rather than the elders, it was the proverbial straw that broke the camel's back. The division of the country of Israel into two kingdoms—Israel in the north and Judah in the south—became a foregone conclusion. Solomon's religious and administrative policies caused significant divisions among the people—divisions whose long-lasting effects would be felt until both kingdoms fell to invading empires.

When Rehoboam refused to lighten the people's workload, the northern tribes rebelled, and Jeroboam became king of the new kingdom of Israel (1 Kings 12:1–19). One of Jeroboam's first acts as king was to establish two new shrines where his people could worship. He did this, at least in part, in order to secure his own reign, because he feared that otherwise the people in the north would continue to worship at the temple in Jerusalem. Jeroboam reasoned that such worship would result in continued ties with the southern kingdom of Judah—ties that would lead to a desire to be reunified into one country.

---

4. David's desire to please God and his trust in the Lord is well documented (Ps. 16:2; 18:1; 25:11; 119:34). These descriptions are largely absent with respect to Solomon.
5. Solomon ignored the tribal boundaries and organized the kingdom into twelve districts. Based on the numbers of supplies required for the court/government, the tax burden on the people was very heavy. Additionally, his standing army was large, and he required public service from most of the people for various governmental projects. See 1 Kings 4.

In an attempt to avoid this outcome, Jeroboam set up cult centers at Dan and Bethel, which were roughly at the northern and southern borders of the new kingdom of Israel (1 Kings 12:26–29). Bethel had a long tradition of being a place at which it was appropriate to worship God. Jeroboam's choice of this site made perfect sense, and provided the people of his kingdom with a certain amount of continuity with their past patterns of worship.[6] During the time of the patriarchs, Jacob had experienced the place of Bethel as a connection point between heaven and earth, and had made the place his primary spot for worshiping God (Gen. 28:10–22). Bethel, then, was a logical choice. The city of Dan, on the other hand, was quite different. It had no special connection with divine revelation, and seems to have been chosen simply for its geographical location near the northern border.

At these two locations, Jeroboam set up golden calves for the people to worship (1 Kings 12:26–33). It is not entirely clear whether he intended these calves to be representative of the God of Israel or of some other deity. Clearly, he did intend for the calves to be reminiscent of the episode when Aaron made a calf for the people to worship after they became restless, waiting for Moses to return from the mountain (1 Kings 12:28). Even Jeroboam's declaration, "'Look! Your god(s), O Israel, who brought you up from the land of Egypt!'" clearly reflects the statement of the people in Exodus 32:4: "These are your gods, O Israel, who brought you up from the land of Egypt."[7] Naturally, the reader understands that this connection cannot be good, given the Lord's assessment of the original calf (Exod. 32:7–10). It seems likely that Jeroboam, much like the people in both the southern and northern kingdoms in general, was syncretistic in his worship. In other words, even if he saw some connection between the calves at Dan and Bethel and the Lord, he did not hold to a religious conviction of worshiping God in purity and truth. Instead, he blended past and present pagan elements with the worship of the God of Israel, and viewed worship as a means to an end—namely, as a way to secure his own future. This syncretistic and self-serving perspective would characterize the period of the divided kingdom, no matter how much the prophets and certain righteous kings tried to stamp it out and encourage God's people to worship God alone.

THEOLOGY OF WORSHIP

The period of the divided kingdom covered hundreds of years and many generations. As such, it is difficult to describe the worship of the era concisely without oversimplifying. With that being said, we can identify three primary themes. The first is the tendency toward syncretism in human worship. The second is the tendency for people to lean on the external trappings of worship while failing to have a heart for God. And

6. See N. Blake Hearson, "Bethel: Where Is the House of God? Defining Sacred Space in the Bible," *Midwestern Journal of Theology* 15, no. 1 (Spring 2016): 66–83.
7. Both translations mine.

the third is the fact that God is always in control even when our worship falters. Therefore, there is always hope for the faithful.

North and South: Same Trajectory, Different Speeds

When we look at the first theme, the evidence of Israel's and Judah's syncretism was readily apparent in the form of rampant idolatry. As noted above, Solomon was at least partially responsible for this trend among the people. First Kings 11:1–8 states,

> Now King Solomon loved many foreign women along with the daughter of Pharaoh: Moabite, Ammonite, Edomite, Sidonian, and Hittite women, from the nations concerning which the LORD had said to the sons of Israel, "You shall not associate with them, nor shall they associate with you, for they will surely turn your heart away after their gods." Solomon held fast to these in love. He had seven hundred wives, princesses, and three hundred concubines, and his wives turned his heart away. For when Solomon was old, his wives turned his heart away after other gods; and his heart was not wholly devoted to the LORD his God, as the heart of David his father had been. For Solomon went after Ashtoreth the goddess of the Sidonians and after Milcom the detestable idol of the Ammonites. Solomon did what was evil in the sight of the LORD, and did not follow the LORD fully, as David his father had done. Then Solomon built a high place for Chemosh the detestable idol of Moab, on the mountain which is east of Jerusalem, and for Molech the detestable idol of the sons of Ammon. Thus also he did for all his foreign wives, who burned incense and sacrificed to their gods.

With Solomon publicly endorsing these other deities, it is no surprise that the people would begin to worship them as well. Indeed, in all likelihood the foreign wives of Solomon came with their own retinues of servants who would have been adherents to the worship of other gods. The high places that Solomon set up would have had images of the gods worshiped there as well as people ready to instruct newcomers in the worship of these gods. After the institution of such false worship and idolatry, its influence would only accelerate over time. After the division of Solomon's kingdom, the northern kingdom (Israel) would eventually outpace the southern kingdom (Judah) in its proclivity to turn away from the worship of God alone. As a result, it would also be the first to suffer God's judgment through destruction and exile by the Assyrians in 722 BCE.

The worship of the people became a tool for Jeroboam to abuse rather than a means of actual relationship with the Lord.[8] As king, Jeroboam

8. Jeroboam's actions are largely pagan ideologically in that they are attempting to coerce the people and the god(s) to do something he wants. In reality, the rituals in ancient Israel "are performed not in order to coerce God, but to bring the worshipper to God by the means that He is

continued the trend of false worship started by Solomon, by instituting false worship at Bethel and Dan.[9] This move on Jeroboam's part was his attempt to maintain control; he wanted to make sure he retained his power as king over the northern kingdom. In fact, all of the kings of the northern kingdom seemed to operate by using religious worship as a means to an end, rather than out of any genuine heart for the God of Israel (or even the pagan gods they entertained in the high places and cult sites). The example of Ahab is relevant here. First Kings 16:30–33 makes it clear that Ahab was cast from the same mold as Jeroboam:

> Ahab the son of Omri did evil in the sight of the LORD more than all who were before him. It came about, as though it had been a trivial thing for him to walk in the sins of Jeroboam the son of Nebat, that he married Jezebel the daughter of Ethbaal king of the Sidonians, and went to serve Baal and worshiped him. So he erected an altar for Baal in the house of Baal which he built in Samaria. Ahab also made the Asherah. Thus Ahab did more to provoke the LORD God of Israel than all the kings of Israel who were before him.

Like Jeroboam, Ahab moved in ways that would secure his power. Like Solomon, he married a foreign woman that gained him an ally in Sidon, but also incorporated the worship of Baal, the Canaanite storm god, into the worship at the capital city of the northern kingdom. Ahab wanted control, and directing the worship of the people helped him maintain that control.

Ahab's decisions in this case yield two illustrative points. First, Ahab was worse than those who came before him with respect to provoking the anger of the Lord. The movement toward idolatry and syncretism grew worse over time. Eventually this progression would reach a sort of critical mass, and God would bring judgment to wipe out the sinful state of the kings and the nation. Indeed, 2 Kings 17:7–23 summarizes the pattern of progressive sinful worship that culminated in the destruction of the northern kingdom by the Assyrian Empire. The false worship that originated with the kings had made its way among the people, who followed their bad example. This false worship was, of course, a direct violation of God's commands. First Kings 17:10 is just one passage that makes this clear. The phrase "they set for themselves sacred pillars and Asherim on every high hill and under every green tree" is an allusion to Deuteronomy 12:2–3, in which God commands the people to destroy the high places "under every green tree" and not to worship God in those locations. Ironically, the people of Israel were now the ones setting up the very pagan

---

believed to have commanded" (A. S. Herbert, *Worship in Ancient Israel*, Ecumenical Studies in Worship 5 [Richmond, VA: John Knox Press, 1959], 15).

9. Note that there are two King Jeroboams in the history of the northern kingdom of Israel. Unless otherwise noted, we are referring to Jeroboam I and not Jeroboam II.

objects, such as the Asherahs, that they were told to destroy.[10] What is more, the kings had led them to this behavior, when their role was to immerse themselves in Torah and obediently follow God (Deut. 17:14–20). All in all, the "worship" of both kings and people was offensive to God rather than truly worshipful.

Second, Ahab viewed religion as a tool for independence. True worship of the God of Israel required submission and obedience. From the time of the garden of Eden, however, the human temptation has been to establish independence from God.[11] The temptation to be independent of God is a strong one—a theme common to the stories of most of the kings in Israel and Judah. There can be no doubt that the possibility of being completely in control would be tantalizing to a king who already had a taste of such power and independence by virtue of his position. Like Jeroboam before him and the kings who would follow him, Ahab wanted power more than he wanted a true relationship with God.

In contrast with Israel's rush to syncretism, the southern kingdom of Judah would be slower in its move away from the exclusive worship of God. No doubt this reduced speed had much to do with the presence of the temple in Jerusalem, and the fact that some of the kings of the South followed Yahweh, while none of the kings of the North did. After all, the temple was dedicated to the God of Israel. While Solomon set up high places to other gods, the primary God of the kingdom remained the Lord.[12] The identity of the people of Judah as a nation was tied to God and their history as a people remained visually present in the presence of the temple structure. By virtue of being Judahites, they were the people of the Lord God, who had brought them out of Egypt and given them the land in which they were dwelling. In the northern kingdom, Jeroboam actively sought to remove this history from the minds of his people by creating a new history and story, complete with new places of worship.[13] In the southern kingdom, however, the kings in the line of David owed their position to God, and could not escape that fact without rejecting their claim to the throne.

---

10. Asherah was a mother goddess associated with fertility and was often paired with Baal as his consort.
11. The promise of the fruit, in the words of the serpent, was that the man and woman would become like God in their knowledge. In other words, they would not need to depend on God. They could rule beside him.
12. High places were chosen for worship by virtue of their being closer to the heavenly realm, where the gods dwelled. This is why Jacob is so shocked to find a connection point between heaven and earth at a nondescript rocky plain (Gen. 28:10–22). There was no geographic feature that would indicate the connection to a god or heaven there. See Menahem Haran, *Temples and Temple Service in Ancient Israel: An Inquiry into Biblical Cult Phenomena and the Historical Setting of the Priestly School* (Winona Lake, IN: Eisenbrauns, 1985), 18–25.
13. The idea Jeroboam seems to be after is tying the history to the golden calf episode so that Israel is still connected to its existing history, but this connection predates the establishment of the kingdom under Saul, David, and Solomon. Therefore, Israel is connected to but also different from Judah.

Yet inevitably, it seems, many of the kings and most of the people of Judah eventually followed the same path as their northern brothers. Slowly but surely, the people of Judah became strangers to the God they supposedly worshiped. In 2 Kings 22, for example, we read of the finding of the book of the law in the temple by Hilkiah the priest. The fact that things had gone so far that the Torah—or at least some portion of it—had been completely lost to memory and buried in a storeroom is telling. God had become just another one of Judah's gods. He may have still been their national God in some form, but any unique relationship with him had long since disappeared.

There were, of course, some bright spots here and there, as illustrated by Josiah's response to the finding of the scroll.[14] He realized that the status of the people before God was not a good one. Second Kings 22:11–13 shows Josiah's deep concern:

> When the king heard the words of the book of the law, he tore his clothes. Then the king commanded Hilkiah the priest, Ahikam the son of Shaphan, Achbor the son of Micaiah, Shaphan the scribe, and Asaiah the king's servant, saying, "Go, inquire of the LORD for me and the people and all Judah concerning the words of this book that has been found, for great is the wrath of the LORD that burns against us, because our fathers have not listened to the words of this book, to do according to all that is written concerning us."

Josiah's tearing of his robe was a sign of genuine worship, one that reflected the heart of the king. He was genuinely upset and repentant as he realized just how far off the kingdom had wandered from the proper worship of God. Reading the Torah made Josiah realize that Judah was in line for a similar fate to that of her northern sister: destruction and exile. As a result, Josiah sent messengers to Huldah the prophetess to see what could be done. The answer, while not entirely encouraging, revealed that Josiah had what God really desired in terms of worship: a tender heart. Second Kings 22:19–20 states,

> "Because your heart was tender and you humbled yourself before the LORD when you heard what I spoke against this place and against its inhabitants that they should become a desolation and a curse, and you have torn your clothes and wept before Me, I truly have heard you," declares the LORD. "Therefore, behold, I will gather you to your fathers, and you will be gathered to your grave in peace, and your eyes will not see all the evil which I will bring on this place." So they brought back word to the king.

---

14. For a discussion of the date and extent of the reforms of Josiah see Rainer Albertz, "Why a Reform Like Josiah's Must Have Happened," in *Good Kings and Bad Kings*, ed. Lester L. Grabbe, LHBOTS (New York: T&T Clark, 2005), 27–46.

As described in Deuteronomy, true worship of God originates in the heart (Deut. 6:5; 10:16). Josiah's heart was committed to the Lord, and this was evident in his reaction to the word from God. Instead of simply accepting that he was personally off the hook, Josiah chose to do his best to return the people to the proper worship of God. Even though he had a certain word of inevitable destruction, Josiah did what God had commanded in the book of the law. He and the people renewed the covenant with God, committing to worship only God. In addition, Josiah removed the symbols of the false deities from the temple and destroyed the worship site at Bethel, since it had become profane from the cult of the calf that Jeroboam had set up there. Josiah also destroyed all the other high places at which other gods were worshiped.[15] Finally, he reinstituted the celebration of Passover, which had been long abandoned.[16] The young king was fully committed to the Lord no matter the final outcome in the fate of the nation. He worshiped the Lord and led the people in worship out of a love for God.

Unfortunately, of course, the reforms of Josiah would not be enough. God's anger at the sins of the nation remained unabated. Josiah may have bought the nation some more time, but on a fundamental level the hearts of the people remained unchanged. All Josiah could do was change the outward face of public worship. Without a fundamental change of heart among the people of Judah, however, the core problem of insincere worship remained.

Ritual in Worship: The Good and the Bad

The insincerity of the worship in both kingdoms is a recurring theme found throughout the books of Kings, Chronicles, and the preexilic prophets. While Josiah enacted public reforms of rituals and worship, the people continued to worship foreign deities in the privacy of their own homes: "The children gather wood, and the fathers kindle the fire, and the women knead dough to make cakes for the queen of heaven; and they pour out drink offerings to other gods in order to spite Me" (Jer. 7:18).[17] Thus, even during those brief times in which the worship of false gods was publicly outlawed, the worship of these gods continued in private, and the hearts of the people remained cold toward the Lord.

Indeed, the people saw no problem with worshiping the Lord in a ritualistic way while simultaneously worshiping other gods. One of the most glaring examples of this practice is found in Jeremiah 7:1–15. In this

---

15. See Lisbeth Fried, "The High Places (Bāmôt) and the Reforms of Hezekiah and Josiah: An Archaeological Investigation," *JAOS* 122, no. 3 (2002): 437–65.

16. On the uniqueness of the Passover celebration when compared to other sacrifices see H. H. Rowley, *Worship in Ancient Israel: Its Forms and Meanings* (London: SPCK, 1967), 117.

17. "The Queen of Heaven" most likely refers to the Babylonian and Assyrian goddess Inanna-Ishtar. She was associated with sex/love, the practice of justice, and war. See Jeremy A. Black and Anthony Green, eds., *Gods, Demons and Symbols of Ancient Mesopotamia: An Illustrated Dictionary* (Austin: University of Texas Press, 1992).

passage, God describes the actions of those who came to the temple to worship. The first issue the Lord brings before the people is that they were trusting in the temple itself to keep them safe from harm. The people were declaring, "This is the temple of the LORD, the temple of the LORD, the temple of the LORD" (7:4). Repeating something three times in the Bible is a way of expressing the superlative.[18] In other words, the people were emphasizing the superiority of the temple. The focus, then, was on the building rather than the God of the temple.

This raises the question of why the people would have such a focus. Of course, God indwelled the temple and made it the place at which the people could interact with him through worship. Yet their emphasis in this verse was not on God. There are two primary reasons that the people's worship had gone astray here. The first reason is rooted in the events that occurred during the reign of King Hezekiah.

During his time as king, Hezekiah rebelled against Assyria, trusting in Egypt for help against the Assyrian army when the reprisal came. Egypt failed to deliver any aid, however, and Sennacherib, ruler of Assyria, invaded Judah and destroyed many of the towns and cities before laying siege to Jerusalem. At this point, in desperation, Hezekiah finally threw himself on the mercy of God. In all these actions, Hezekiah served as a perfect example of the attitude of the people of God at the time. Ultimately, Hezekiah trusted in foreign powers and political manipulation until all other resources were exhausted. Only then, when there were no other options, did Hezekiah turn to God and beg for help. For the sake of his promises to Hezekiah's ancestor David, the Lord did intervene and destroyed a large part of Sennacherib's army, rescuing Jerusalem from the enemy.

Unfortunately, however, it seems that the people did not learn the correct lesson from these events. Instead of viewing God's deliverance of Jerusalem as a response to Hezekiah's humble submission, the people attributed it to the idea that God needed his temple. This conclusion was an example of the syncretism that had crept into the worship of the Lord. Among the pagan religions of Judah's neighbors, it was a common belief that worship was carried out to meet the needs of the gods. In this worldview, the gods were part of creation and needed to be fed and housed. As a result, they were in a very real sense dependent on their temples and servants, which provided for these needs.[19] This view of the gods gave their worshipers a certain sense of security, because they knew that the gods would defend their sources of food and shelter—their temples. It is very likely that the people of Judah had fallen into this sort of thinking about

18. For another example, see Isaiah 6:3, in which the angels declare God to be "holy, holy, holy."

19. For example, after the flood in the Babylonian flood epic, the gods were starving and crowded like flies around the smoke from the first sacrifice made by the survivor, Utnapishtim. See Tablet XI of the Gilgamesh Epic in *Myths from Mesopotamia: Creation, the Flood, Gilgamesh, and Others*, ed. and trans. Stephanie Dalley (Oxford: Oxford University Press, 2009).

the Lord as well; they assumed that God would not let his temple be destroyed because he needed it. They saw God's defense of Jerusalem and the temple during Hezekiah's reign in this false, syncretistic light, rather than understanding that the Lord was not like pagan gods. The irony that the people thought their God was limited and dependent on his temple, while they also trusted that he could defend his temple, should not be missed.

The second issue that God raises against Judah in Jeremiah 7 is that there is no moral or ethical connection between the ritualistic worship and the behavior of the people. In Jeremiah 7:9–10, God asks, "Will you steal, murder, and commit adultery and swear falsely, and offer sacrifices to Baal and walk after other gods that you have not known, then come and stand before Me in this house, which is called by My name, and say, 'We are delivered!'—that you may do all these abominations?" Most of the listed sins are drawn directly from the Ten Commandments. These are not violations of ritual, but sins related to the inner character and heart condition of the people. While it may seem strange to us that God would need to call out this sort inconsistent behavior, the disconnect between ritual and inner character seems to have been normalized in Judah's syncretistic culture.

The pagan influence did not stop with the idea that God somehow needed his temple. The people of Judah applied pagan, polytheistic notions to their worship in general. In the polytheistic worldview, the gods had to share. Because there were multiple gods, worshipers did not typically worship only one. There was usually a god or goddess designated as the head of the pantheon, and that deity received the top billing, so to speak, but he or she was still not worshiped exclusively. Accordingly, in the theology of worship among the peoples surrounding Israel and Judah, there was no expectation that worshiping multiple gods was a problem. In addition, worship of pagan gods was operated on a tit-for-tat principle. In other words, the gods did not expect ethical behavior from their worshipers. Instead, "worship" was a transactional agreement, a mutually beneficial exchange between worshiper and the deities. The worshiper gave the deities what they needed through ritual enactment, and in turn the gods would provide their adherents with safety and blessing. The gods did not particularly care whether the worshiper was holy.[20] This is a far cry from the purpose of worship described in the Pentateuch (Exod. 20:1–17; Lev. 19:3–17). As noted, biblical worship had its aim and purpose in a genuine heart-based relationship with God (Deut. 6:4–5). Unfortunately, the people had missed this goal, instead applying the more transactional idea of the surrounding nations to their worship of the Lord. They came to

20. This description is somewhat oversimplified, as most such discussions must be. Ancient Near Eastern religion was not completely devoid of morality, but any such code of behavior was not a primary motivating factor in worship. In the creation epics of the ancient Near East, humankind is created as a source of cheap labor rather than as a creature made in the image of God who would reflect God's character and live in relationship with him.

the temple and went through the prescribed motions, thinking this would affect God in the same way it would the pagan deities. Their hearts were far from God, however, and this manifested in the form of immoral and self-serving behavior. The worship of the people was deceptive and manipulative.[21] In the end, this false worship was more insulting to God than abstaining from ritualistic worship altogether would have been.

Naturally, such worship would not be allowed to continue. In Jeremiah 7, God warned the people of their forthcoming doom by telling them to visit Shiloh. This place had once been the semi-permanent home to the tabernacle, and yet by the time of Jeremiah Shiloh was in ruins. The object lesson was straightforward. God did not need his temple. He would and could do the same thing to Jerusalem and the temple that he had done to his sanctuary at Shiloh. Moreover, God declared that he destroyed the sanctuary at Shiloh "because of the wickedness of My people Israel" (7:12). Ritualistic worship was not enough. Indeed, God had pleaded with his people to change their ways, but they did not listen (7:13). God sought relational worship and a heart tuned toward pleasing him. Given the pagan, polytheistic notions Jeremiah's audience held, this message no doubt sounded startling and even heretical; the ritual worship they engaged in would not save them.

It would be a mistake, however, to assume that this rejection of ritual worship by God was a rejection of ritual in general. It is true that there are many times in which God declares his distaste for the cultic celebrations and rituals of the people. In Isaiah 1:14, for example, God declares, "I hate your new moon festivals and your appointed feasts, they have become a burden to Me; I am weary of bearing them." Likewise, in Amos 5:21–22, God states, "I hate, I reject your festivals, nor do I delight in your solemn assemblies. Even though you offer up to Me burnt offerings and your grain offerings, I will not accept them; and I will not even look at the peace offerings of your fatlings." But in both cases, context is crucial. In both Isaiah and Amos, the ritualistic worship of the people was akin to what we saw with the temple worship in Jeremiah above: empty, transactional, and manipulative. God rejected empty ritualistic worship. He did not reject ritual in worship. In fact, God was the one who had commanded such ritual and sacrifice in the first place (see, e.g., Lev. 1–7). The key was this: only with love for God and the resulting godly behavior would such worship be accepted. Amos goes on to state, "But let justice roll down like waters and righteousness like an ever-flowing stream" (5:24). In other words, love for the Lord was to motivate worship. But fairness in the treatment of others was just as much a part of true worship as rituals at the temple, since a

21. An analogy of a vending machine is helpful here. God was seeking a relationship with the people, but, based on the pagan theology, the people were treating him as a vending machine. If they had the right code and correct change, they could get what they wanted, and God would receive what he wanted.

love for God would lead God's people to love one another and to practice justice. Isaiah clarifies this in 1:16–20:

> Wash yourselves, make yourselves clean;
> Remove the evil of your deeds from My sight.
> Cease to do evil, Learn to do good;
> Seek justice, Reprove the ruthless,
> Defend the orphan, Plead for the widow.
> "Come now, and let us reason together," says the LORD,
> "Though your sins are as scarlet, they will be as white as snow;
> Though they are red like crimson, they will be like wool.
> If you consent and obey, you will beat the best of the land;
> But if you refuse and rebel, you will be devoured by the sword."
> Truly, the mouth of the LORD has spoken.

Before any formal worship that involved sacrifice could take place, a love for God that manifested itself in the positive treatment of the less fortunate in society had to be present. God was not looking for empty ritual, but for transformed hearts and lives.

The prophet Micah sums up God's requirements for worship succinctly but comprehensively. In 1:16–20, the prophet records a covenantal lawsuit between God and his people.[22] This lawsuit not only illustrates the fact that the people were in the wrong while God had been faithful to the covenant but also makes clear just how far the people really were from understanding what God wanted from his worshipers. This is most clearly evident in the people's offer to sacrifice their firstborn to God in order to compensate for their sin when they ask, "Shall I present my firstborn for my rebellious acts, the fruit of my body for the sin of my soul?" (6:7). That the people would even offer such a thing shows just how much they had been influenced by the pagan religions of the people around them.[23] Micah responds with the well-known statement in verse 8: "He has declared to you, O Man, what is good and what it is the LORD is seeking from you, only to do justice, and to love covenantal faithfulness, and to live humbly in relationship with your God."[24] This statement encapsulates the type of worship God expected and thus bears unpacking. First of all, God's expectations should not have been new to the people living in the kingdoms of Judah and Israel. God's requirements for worship had been declared time and time again. Second, the requirement for justice among his people was part and parcel of proper

22. The covenant lawsuit was a formulaic method used by several of the prophets to show the people of the divided kingdoms how they had breached their agreement with God while he had remained faithful to them.
23. The Canaanite and Ammonite god Molech required child sacrifice as part of his worship rites.
24. My translation.

worship. As we saw with the list of sins in Jeremiah 7, God rejected worship that was preceded or followed by unjust acts. The third requirement both trumps the previous one and includes it. Loving covenantal faithfulness, or *hesed*, could not happen without justice. Yet such love went beyond mere justice in that it put the needs of others above one's own. Ruth and Boaz were stellar examples of this type of love for God's covenant, for their behavior put the needs of others first. They obeyed the Torah with a heart that went beyond mere justice. Finally, God required his worshipers to be in a relationship with him. The more literal rendering of the Hebrew is "to walk humbly with your God," but the idea behind this idiom is living life in a positive relationship with the Lord. Thus the requirements listed in Micah 6:8 move from the lesser to the greater without eliminating the lesser commands. True worship in the divided kingdom—and throughout the whole Bible—was worship that had its origin in a heart that pleased God and actions that reflected that heart in the totality of one's life. Ritual remained a part of this worship, but it was an outworking of a love for God, not an end in and of itself.

God Is Always in Control

A final theme of worship in the divided kingdom is the idea that God is always in control. God's people always faced a choice: would they trust God or doubt him? Their actions inevitably reflected their decision. Two examples from the period of the divided kingdom illustrate this idea. First, the faithful worshipers were usually under pressure to desert God because they were the human minority during the period of the divided kingdom. Elijah was a well-known prophet of God during the divided kingdom period. Yet as recorded in 1 Kings 19:10, right after God's major victory over the prophets of Baal, Elijah lost hope. He believed that he was the only one that truly remained faithful to the Lord, and told God as much. Elijah was discouraged by the rampant, state-sponsored paganism he saw around him and began to feel that there was no reason to go on. Yet God told Elijah that he was not, in fact, alone; there were seven thousand people who were still loyally worshiping the God of Israel. While this was still a minority of Judah's people, it gave Elijah hope. He was not alone, and he was reminded that God was in control.

Likewise, the prophet Habakkuk complained about the way in which the wicked majority of Judahites were persecuting the righteous minority. God's response was twofold. First, he made it clear that he was, in fact, in control of the situation despite appearances to the contrary (1:5–11). The faithful were a minority, but their lack of numbers in no way hindered his power. Second, God told Habakkuk that he was bringing the Babylonians to punish his wayward and wicked people. God's control extended much farther than just Judah; even the Babylonians were tools in his hands, whether they recognized this fact or not. On the one hand, Habakkuk was glad to know that the wickedness of the people would not go unpunished. On the other hand, the prophet struggled with the way God planned to bring judgment on his people. And this leads to the second key idea: our faith is to remain, even in seemingly difficult situations. In Habakkuk's case, the prophet was faced with God's plan and did not like it. In using the Babylonians to punish the wicked among Judah, it appeared to Habakkuk that God was using a greater evil to punish a lesser evil. How was this just? God's response to Habakkuk's questions focuses on the distinctions between the true worshiper and one oriented toward self. In 2:4, God states, "Look! The one puffed up with pride, his soul is not right within him. By contrast, the righteous one, by his faith he will live."[25] As the representative of the faithful worshipers of God, Habakkuk had to choose whether to submit to God. He knew difficult times were ahead, and he was left with a choice to make: he could place his trust in God, or he could try to fix things in his own power. Ultimately, Habakkuk chose to follow God, a decision detailed in his song of faith (3:1–19). The prophet's fear was not completely erased, but he decided to trust God to bring justice to those who deserved it. Part of worshiping God, therefore, was trusting him in difficult situations without having all the answers.

Third, and finally, those who faithfully worshiped God with their whole being were given hope for the future. Because God is in control, his worshipers could trust that judgment was not the end. Those who failed to worship truly and fully, however, would inevitably seek to control things themselves. For example, when God told Isaiah to go to King Ahaz of Judah and offer him a sign that God was in control and trustworthy, Ahaz refused to accept the sign. While his refusal was couched in pious terms ("I will not ask, nor will I test the Lord!"), Isaiah called it out for what it was: a lack of faith (7:12–13). Ahaz had already decided to appeal to the Assyrians for help instead of trusting in God. As with Hezekiah's trust in the Egyptians, Ahaz's decision would have disastrous results for the kingdom of Judah. Yet even with impending doom hanging over the nations of Israel and Judah at the hands of the Assyrians and Babylonians, there was still a note of hope. God was still in control, and so there was hope for the future. As noted above, when Hezekiah completely humbled himself before God in worship and asked for help, God responded by destroying much of the Assyrian army. While the northern and southern kingdoms would fall as a result of their sins, this fall was not the end. In the final episode of the book of Kings, Jehoiachin was released from prison in Babylon. He was elevated by the Babylonian ruler to a favored status and remained there for the rest of his life. God was in control. The Davidic line was preserved. There was hope for the future.

25. My translation.

SIGNIFICANCE OF THE DIVIDED KINGDOM FOR BIBLICAL WORSHIP

So, what significance can we draw from the theological ideas about worship during the divided kingdom? First, we must recognize that the ideal worship described in Scripture is something that must govern our entire life. Most of the time, the people living in the divided kingdoms missed this ideal because they had incorporated pagan ideas into their practice of worship. However, as we see in Deuteronomy 6:5 and Micah 6:8, worship is intended to be a way of living life rather than just a ritual to perform, a time of music, or a ministry restricted to Sunday mornings. Jesus himself describes the true worshiper as one who completely denies himself in order to follow God (Matt. 16:24–26).

Second, we should regularly check our ideas and choices against Scripture. The best way to do this is to know God's Word backward and forward. This is the way the kings of Israel were to know Scripture (Deut. 17:14–20), and when they failed in this task—going so far as to even forget about the existence of God's written commands—they quickly went astray, leading the people along with them. We are not immune to this same issue. It is very easy, humanly speaking, to justify our own ideas or to be influenced by worldviews that are not compatible with the revelation of God if we are unfamiliar with Scripture. Knowing God's Word, then, is essential to staying true in our worship. In addition, as is evident in several examples throughout the time of the divided kingdom, it is human nature to desire control and to only humble ourselves before God only as a last resort. Yet much grief and sorrow could be avoided if we make humble worship our first action instead of our last act of desperation when all else fails.

Third, in order to properly worship God, our motivation for everything we do in life should be a deep love for God and a resulting desire to please him. Josiah did what would please the Lord, even though he knew it would not avert the judgment God had ordained for Judah. His motivation for complete and proper worship was not selfish. Instead, he sought to please God by doing justice, keeping the covenant, and maintaining a humble relationship with God. This is the pattern that is set before us when we look at worship in the divided kingdom. We can choose to trust God and live our lives in worship, or we can try to maintain control of our lives and seek to benefit ourselves. It is not enough to go to church once or twice a week. It is not enough to serve in some ministry in the church. As with the rituals in Old Testament worship, these things are important and good. Yet, unless we are truly seeking to please God in everything we do and motivated by love for him, we are failing to truly worship the Lord.

Fourth and finally, we must continue to have faith in the Lord and his control, even in the face of difficult circumstances and overwhelming odds. Like Habakkuk and the righteous remnant in Judah, we may question why God is doing things the way he is. Like Elijah, we may feel like we are all alone in our efforts to follow God and worship him. However, we must not give up or turn to our own solutions in these times. Instead, we must seek to be faithful, turning to God and worshiping him, even in the midst of difficulty. Like Habakkuk, we can remind ourselves of God's past faithful actions and know that we can count on him to come through in the same way in the future (Hab. 3). Even in dark and difficult times when the world appears to falling apart, we can choose to worship God and acknowledge that he is in control. And this gives us hope.

CONCLUSION

The divided kingdom period of Israel's history was a relatively dark time, as God's people grew further and further away from him. There were glimmers of the way things should have been, but by and large, it was a difficult time to be a faithful worshiper of the one true God of Israel. The challenge both then and now lies in the fact that corrupting influences abound from the culture both outside and within the community of faith. Yet there is hope, and it manifests in two ways. First, as Josiah's actions illustrated, there is hope in knowing that the current situation, however challenging, is not the end. God is in control, and the faithful can and should worship him because we know that redemption is coming by his hand. Second, the faithful are never alone. The life of Elijah demonstrates that it is discouraging to see a culture in which there is only a nominal service to God by many claiming to be God's people. Even as Jeremiah grieved over the public worship in the temple by people who had no real devotion to God in their everyday lives, we can become discouraged by seeing so much of our own culture corrupting ourselves and our fellow believers in various ministry settings. Additionally, an effort to be faithful in such contexts often leads to persecution. Still, God calls us to live out our worship in all we do, even in the face of difficulty, knowing that God is in control. The transformation of culture is not our primary concern. Rather, pleasing God through faithful worship and obedience is our calling. When oriented toward the love of God in all our efforts and interactions, we will have hope in the source of all hope and may even end up transforming the culture after all. In the end, the same principle holds true for us as it did for the ancient Israelites: do justice, and love covenantal faithfulness, and live humbly in relationship with our God.

BIBLIOGRAPHY

Ackroyd, Peter R. *The Chronicler in His Age*. JSOTSup 101. Sheffield: JSOT Press, 1991.

Anderson, Gary A., and Saul M. Olyan. *Priesthood and Cult in Ancient Israel*. JSOTSup 125. Sheffield: JSOT Press, 1991.

Arnold, Bill T., and Brent A. Strawn, eds. *The World around the Old Testament: The People and Places of the Ancient Near East*. Grand Rapids: Baker Academic, 2016.

Black, Jeremy A., and Anthony Green, eds. *Gods, Demons and Symbols of Ancient Mesopotamia: An Illustrated Dictionary*. Austin: University of Texas Press, 1992.

Bright, John. *Jeremiah*. AB 21. New York: Doubleday, 1965.

Dalley, Stephanie. *Myths from Mesopotamia: Creation, the Flood, Gilgamesh, and Others*. Oxford: Oxford University Press, 2009.

Dever, William G. *The Lives of Ordinary People in Ancient Israel: Where Archaeology and the Bible Intersect*. Grand Rapids: Eerdmans, 2012.

Fried, Lisbeth. "The High Places (*Bāmôt*) and the Reforms of Hezekiah and Josiah: An Archaeological Investigation." *JAOS* 122, no. 3 (2002): 437–65.

Grabbe, Lester L, ed. *Good Kings and Bad Kings*. LHBOTS. New York: T&T Clark, 2005.

Haran, Menahem. *Temples and Temple Service in Ancient Israel: An Inquiry into Biblical Cult Phenomena and the Historical Setting of the Priestly School*. Winona Lake, IN: Eisenbrauns, 1985.

Hearson, N. Blake. "'And with All Your Strength'? A Reassessment of the Translation and Meaning of Deuteronomy 6:5." In *The Unfolding of Your Words Gives Light: Studies on Biblical Hebrew in Honor of George L. Klein*, edited by Ethan C. Jones, 203–16. University Park, PA: Eisenbrauns, 2018.

______. "Bethel: Where Is the House of God? Defining Sacred Space in the Bible." *Midwestern Journal of Theology*, volume 15, no. 1 (Spring 2016): 66–83.

Herbert, A. S. *Worship in Ancient Israel*. Ecumenical Studies in Worship 5. Richmond, VA: John Knox, 1959.

Hill, Andrew E. *Enter His Courts with Praise: Old Testament Worship for the New Testament Church*. Nashville: Star Song, 1993.

House, Paul R. *1, 2 Kings*. NAC 8. Nashville: Broadman & Holman, 1995.

Japhet, Sara. *The Ideology of the Book of Chronicles and Its Place in Biblical Thought*. Winona Lake, IN: Eisenbrauns, 2009.

Jensen, Philip Peter. *Graded Holiness: A Key to the Priestly Conception of the World*. JSOTSup 106. Sheffield: JSOT Press,1992.

Kiuchi, N. *The Purification Offering in the Priestly Literature: Its Meaning and Function*. JSOTSup 56. Sheffield: JSOT Press, 1987.

Kleinig, John L. *The Lord's Song: The Basis, Function, and Significance of Choral Music in Chronicles*. JSOTSup 156. Sheffield: JSOT Press, 1993.

Lowery, R. H. *The Reforming Kings: Cults and Society in First Temple Judah*. JSOTSup 120. Sheffield: JSOT Press, 1991.

Lynch, Matthew. *Monotheism and Institutions in the Book of Chronicles: Temple, Priesthood, and Kingship in Post-exilic Perspective*. FAT 2. Reihe 64. Tübingen: Mohr Siebeck, 2014.

McComiskey, Thomas Edward, Raymond Dillard, and Jeffrey Niehaus. *Hosea, Joel, Amos*. The Minor Prophets: An Exegetical & Expository Commentary 1. Grand Rapids: Baker, 1992.

Motyer, J. Alec, Thomas McComiskey, and Douglas Stuart. *Zephaniah, Haggai, Zechariah, Malachi*. The Minor Prophets: An Exegetical & Expository Commentary 3. Grand Rapids: Baker, 1998.

Niehaus, Jeffrey, Joyce Baldwin, Bruce Waltke, Tremper Longman III, and F. F. Bruce. *Obadiah, Jonah, Micah, Nahum, Habakkuk*. The Minor Prophets: An Exegetical & Expository Commentary 2. Grand Rapids: Baker, 1993.

Oswalt, John N. *The Book of Isaiah: Chapters 1–39*. NICOT. Grand Rapids: Eerdmans, 1986.

______. *The Book of Isaiah: Chapters 40–66*. NICOT. Grand Rapids: Eerdmans, 1998.

Riley, William. *King and Cultus in Chronicles: Worship and the Reinterpretation of History*. JSOTSup 160. Sheffield: JSOT Press, 1993.

Rowley, H. H. *Worship in Ancient Israel: Its Forms and Meanings*. London: SPCK, 1967.

Thompson, J. A. *1, 2 Chronicles*. NAC 9. Nashville: Broadman & Holman, 1994.

______. *The Book of Jeremiah*. NICOT. Grand Rapids: Eerdmans, 1980.

Wheeler, Samuel Billings. "Prayer and Temple in the Dedication Speech of Solomon, 1 Kings 8:14–61." PhD diss., Columbia University, 1977.

CHAPTER 9

THE CONTEXT OF WORSHIP IN THE PSALTER

Walter C. Kaiser Jr.,
Willem A. VanGemeren, and Erika Moore

The book of Psalms has been treasured in the history of the church. Throughout the centuries devout Christians met with the Lord Jesus Christ by dwelling in the Psalter. The Psalms taught them the prayers of Christ, gave them a deeper apprehension of the life of Jesus Christ, and provided insights into a life of wisdom by their dwelling in the Psalms.[1] The Desert Fathers worshiped God by singing the Psalms throughout the day. Jerome observed how Christians sang the Psalms while working in the fields. Augustine cited the Psalms more frequently than any book of Scripture. Luther and Calvin experienced spiritual renewal through their study of the Psalms. Indeed, this book is "God's prescription for a complacent church. It reveals how great, wonderful, magnificent, wise, and utterly awe-inspiring he is. If God's people before the incarnation could have such faith in the Lord . . . how much more should this be true among twenty-first century Christians! The book of Psalms can revolutionize our devotional life, our family patterns, and the fellowship and witness of the church of Jesus Christ."[2]

The text of the Psalms need not be spiritualized. It is open to interpretation, and its interpretation is reliable when the focus is on the God of the psalmists. It does require sensitivity to the poetic nature of the Hebrew

1. Willem A. VanGemeren, "The Reformation and the Appropriation of Scripture: Dwelling in the Psalms," plenary lecture given at the occasion of the International Congress of the Korean Evangelical Theological Society, Seoul, South Korea, November 11, 2017.
2. Willem A. VanGemeren, *Expositor's Bible Commentary*, vol. 5, *Psalms*, eds. Tremper Longman III and David E. Garland, rev. ed. (Grand Rapids: Zondervan, 2008), 23.

text, however.[3] In becoming a student of the text, the reader learns to enter the presence of God, to apprehend the Triune God by "seeing" the Psalms, and to dwell in a metaphorical world.

Unlike many other Old Testament books, which tend to be ignored by the church, down through the centuries the Psalms have been recognized, appreciated, and utilized as a deep repository for developing worship postures, languages, and practices that are pleasing to the Lord.[4] Certainly, a large part of this appeal stems from the way the poems of the Psalter speak to the various expressions of the human condition. In the preface to his Psalms commentary, Calvin sagely underscores two aspects of the Psalter that account for its enduring appeal. First, he observes, "I have been accustomed to call this book, I think not inappropriately, 'An Anatomy of all the Parts of the Soul'; for there is not an emotion of which anyone can be conscious that is not here represented as in a mirror. Or rather, the Holy Spirit has here drawn to the life all the griefs, sorrows, fears, doubts, hopes, cares, perplexities, in short, all the distracting emotions with which the minds of men are wont to be agitated."[5]

The Psalms speak to us where we are at, no matter what our emotional location (exuberant joy, grief, fear, perplexity, frustration, anger, deep sorrow). Despite the distance of time (the Psalms were written more than two millennia ago), culture (the Psalms are the product of ancient Near Eastern thinking and poetic conventions), and theology (before the incarnation), this collection of poems uniquely conveys the wide array of our innermost feelings and emotions, including those typically ignored in contemporary Christian poetry and song.

Second, Calvin notes,

> There is no other book in which there is to be found more express and magnificent commendations, both of the unparalleled liberality of God towards his Church, and of all his works; there is no other book in which there is recorded so many deliverances, nor one in which the evidences and experiences

3. Psalm 145 as the last Davidic psalm forms a bridge to the hallelujah psalms (146–50). Marvin Sweeney reads Psalms 145–50 as a unit. See *Tanak: A Theological and Critical Introduction to the Jewish Bible* (Minneapolis: Fortress, 2012), 394–95. On the hallelujah psalms, see Willem A. VanGemeren, "God's Faithfulness, Human Suffering, and the Concluding Hallel Psalms (146–150): A Canonical Study," in *Building on the Foundations of Evangelical Theology: Essays in Honor of John S. Feinberg*, eds. Gregg R. Allison and Stephen J. Wellum (Wheaton, IL: Crossway, 2015), 263–84.

4. William Holladay, *The Psalms through Three Thousand Years: Prayerbook of a Cloud of Witnesses* (Minneapolis: Fortress, 1996).

5. Luther expressed similarly: "The Psalter is the favorite book of all the saints. . . . [Each saint], whatever his circumstances may be, finds in [the book] psalms and words which are appropriate to the circumstances in which he finds himself and meet his needs as adequately as if they were composed exclusively for his sake, and in such a way that he himself could not improve on them nor find or desire any better psalms or words" (quoted by Arthur Weiser, *The Psalms* [Philadelphia: Westminster, 1962], 20).

> of the fatherly providence and solicitude which God exercises towards us, are celebrated with such splendor of diction, and yet with the strictest adherence to truth; in short, there is no other book in which we are more perfectly taught the right manner of praising God, or in which we are more powerfully stirred to the performance of this religious exercise.[6]

Because the Psalter provides us with numerous examples of old covenant saints' responses to the Lord's unfailing love toward them, the Psalter can serve as a primer helping us to develop vocabulary and postures for our own responses to the Lord.

Many of the psalms were composed by individual Israelites and pressed into service for Israel's worship where they were chanted or sung at the temple.[7] Later these psalms were assembled into three books, including the Davidic, Korahite, and Asaphite collections.[8] Other psalms were added, many of them anonymous. David again becomes a significant voice in book 5 (Pss. 108–10; 122; 124; 131; 133; 138–45). The rabbis noted, "As Moses gave five books of law to Israel, so David gave five books of Psalms to Israel."[9] As the songbook and prayer book of ancient Israel, the Psalms are a deep well from which to draw and develop our understanding of what type of worship pleases God. They offer us glimpses into how Old Testament saints approached the Lord in repentance (Pss. 6; 31; 37) protestations of innocence (Ps. 26), exuberant praise (Pss. 18; 21; 30; 32; 34), petitions for deliverance (Pss. 4; 10; 13; 17; 22), and confidence (Pss. 11; 16; 23; 27) among other things. By becoming more familiar with the book of Psalms, we can gain wisdom regarding the place that worship (private and corporate) ought to have in our lives. The New Testament authors recognized the importance of the Psalter for the life of the church as evidenced in their quoting the Psalter more than any other Old Testament book (Psalm 110:1 being the most quoted Old Testament verse in the New Testament).

Our English word *psalms* is derived from the Vulgate's Greek (*psalmoi*), which denotes music and songs sung to the accompaniment of a stringed instrument. It is a translation of the Hebrew word *mizmor* (from the root *zmr*), meaning "praise," "sing," or "music." The rabbis gave the entire collection of Psalms the title of *tehillim* (praises) even though there are more lament psalms than praise psalms in the Psalter. This is because even though the Psalter is frontloaded with laments, they recognized the consistent

6. Weiser, *The Psalms*, xxxviii–xxxix.
7. For example, the superscription of Psalm 30 reads, "For the dedication of the temple" and the superscription for Psalm 38 links the psalm with the memorial offering.
8. According to 1 Chronicles 25:1; 2 Chronicles 5:12; Ezra 2:41; 3:10; and Nehemiah 7:44; 11:22, Asaph was a leading musician and member of the guild of temple musicians during the reign of David.
9. Bruce K. Waltke with Charles Yu, *Old Testament Theology: An Exegetical, Canonical, and Thematic Approach* (Grand Rapids: Zondervan, 2007), 884.

movement from lament to praise both in individual psalms of lament[10] and throughout the entire book, building to a crescendo in Psalms 145–50. Additionally, a doxology punctuates each of the five books of the Psalter (Pss. 41:13; 72:18–19; 89:52; 106:48; 150:6). Gordon Wenham observes, "It is as though the more you pray, the more you will realize God's goodness."[11]

THEOLOGICAL ORGANIZATION OF THE PSALMS

All too frequently it is assumed that each chapter in the book of Psalms stands on its own as an independent psalm with little or no attention paid the context or the overall plan of that psalm within each of the five books of the Psalms, or even within the entire Psalter. However, in recent Psalms studies, especially following the lead of O. Palmer Robertson's book *The Flow of the Psalms: Discovering Their Structure and Theology*,[12] there has come a major impetus for reading the Psalms with a holistic contextual appreciation. This approach has emphasized placing each individual psalm in its broader context and interpreting the specific psalm in the context of the other psalms surrounding it in order to gain a more accurate picture of what that psalm meant. This new movement in Psalms studies has taken place despite almost universal skepticism of ever finding any such significant order, or an intentional structure within neighboring psalms, or even within the five books of the Psalter.

A good number of biblical scholars have adopted the modern form-critical approach as the best way of exegeting the meaning of each psalm instead of starting the examination of each psalm by inspecting its context in its neighboring psalms. In the form-critical approach, the meaning of a psalm is sought in its genre, and how it relates to the cultural and social circumstances of the times in which it was written. For example, the evangelical Old Testament scholar John Goldingay comments, "The Psalter as a whole does not have a structure that helps us get a handle on its contents. . . . [Instead, we must rely on the] more traditional critical approach.[13]

But we must ask, as does Robertson, "Is there such a thing as a flow [a plan or a purpose in] the book of Psalms?"[14] Robertson answers positively, though he takes the minority position on this question among scholars. Yet there are a few others who agree with him. For example, John H. Walton argues that the context functions as a major key in detecting the Psalter's structure, especially if it is placed alongside of the Davidic covenant

---

10. Psalms 39 and 88 are exceptions to this progression from lament to praise.
11. Gordon Wenham, *The Psalter Reclaimed: Praying and Praising with the Psalms* (Wheaton, IL: Crossway, 2013), 43.
12. O. Palmer Robertson, *The Flow of the Psalms: Discovering Their Structure and Theology* (Phillipsburg, NJ: P&R), 2015.
13. John Goldingay, *Psalms*, vol. 1, *Psalms 1–41*, BCOTWP (Grand Rapids: Baker Academic, 2006), 36–37.
14. Robertson, *Flow of the Psalms*, 50.

in 2 Samuel 7.[15] Nevertheless, Walton and Robertson have chosen a difficult path to tread, for even the great evangelical scholar Franz Delitzsch (1813–1890) warned, after examining the attempt of the church father Gregory of Nyssa (335–395) to argue that the five books of Psalms lead to five steps of perfection, that "we fear that in this direction, investigation has set before itself an unattainable end."[16]

The point we wish to make is that the Psalms are not to be viewed as a random, disembodied assembly of variously isolated contributions that can be detached from the other psalms as stand-alone pieces. Instead, they make up an orchestrated plan and structure that builds as it progresses in each book, a conclusion that is not to be found in the Psalms according to some scholars. It is true of course that the 150 Psalms spanned some five hundred years in their composition and are not, nor do they claim to be, the work of a single writer.

SIGNIFICANCE OF GENRE FOR WORSHIPING THROUGH THE PSALMS

Attempts have been made throughout history to identify the genre and types of poetic content in the Psalter. Each of these attempts has contributed to the literary base and our understanding of the Psalms, which utilize broad Hebraic poetry constructions (e.g., *mizmor, higgayon, miktam, tepillah, maskil, shir, shir hamma'alot, tehillah, yedidot*, and perhaps *'edut*). Hermann Gunkel, however, recognized five categories of psalms: praise, laments (both individual and communal), and thanksgiving (again, both individual and communal), albeit these are not the only categories possible for classification.[17] Yet with these prominent categories we can begin to see how genre directly affects worshiping through the Psalms, for worship must entail praise, thanksgiving, and the submissive posture of trust necessary to entrust God with our laments.

It is noteworthy to recognize the congruity between Gunkel's proposed forms and 1 Chronicles 16:4, where we are told that David appointed some of the Levites to "serve before the ark of the Lord, to *offer prayers, songs of thanks, and hymns* to the Lord God of Israel" (NET, emphasis added). The prayers that were offered (lit., "to bring to remembrance") corresponds broadly to the psalms of lament and petition. Thus, one of their jobs was to bring the community or the afflicted individual to God's remembrance—just as Hannah prays to God "remember me" (1 Sam. 1:11). The songs of thanks (lit., "to confess in the sense of give acknowledgment, to give voice") relate to the public confession of what God has done for you. This corresponds to

---

15. John H. Walton, "Psalms: A Cantata about the Davidic Covenant," *JETS* 34 (March 1991): 21–31.
16. Franz Delitzsch, *Biblical Commentary on the Psalms* (Grand Rapids: Eerdmans, 1959), 1:19. We must add that the route chosen for a structure by Gregory of Nyssa was far off the mark.
17. Hermann Gunkel, *The Psalms: A Form-Critical Introduction* (Philadelphia: Fortress, 1967); Gerald H. Wilson, *Psalms Volume 1*, NIVAC (Grand Rapids: Zondervan, 2002), 79.

Gunkel's category of thanksgiving psalms. Last, the hymns (lit., "to praise") correspond with Gunkel's category of praise psalms—that is, they are psalms that praise God for who he is and what he has done in creation and the salvation history of God's people, rather than in particular events in the life of the individual. This remarkable agreement between the internal and external evidences for three forms of psalms puts beyond reasonable doubt that Israel's poets were conscious of them. The Chronicler's sequence is intentional: petition leads to declarative praise, and this to descriptive praise.

These genres of the Psalms were written, crafted, implemented, and ordered into the five books of the Psalter, which was written over a five-hundred-year time period. The fact that God is the One who stands behind the book of Psalms and is the source for its contents should not be surprising for those who hold that the Scriptures have come to us as a revelation from God. Seeing how genre and order have been related to an ordained flow of the Psalms' unified meaning across its divisions was not to be seen as a purely chronological feature, but it is instead one with a clear shared theme of the Bible's total purpose and plan. For example, Robertson begins his exposition by showing how Psalm 1 was a "Torah" or "Teaching Psalm" that was coupled with Psalm 2, which was a "Messianic Psalm."[18] The contents of these two psalms supply the reader with the major themes and a sample of the genre that guides the entire corpus that is sustained across all 150 Psalms.

Accordingly, the narrative Robertson traces begins in book 1 (Pss. 1–41) with the theme of "Confrontation," where David meets a multitude of enemies while attempting to establish God's kingdom of righteousness and peace. That narrative was continued as a theme of "communication" with foreign nations and peoples as the psalmist used the name "Elohim," instead of "Yahweh" for God in book 2 (Pss. 42–72). The narrative in the Psalter continued on with the theme of "Devastation" of the people for their lack of faith in the Lord in the seventeen Psalms of book 3 (Pss. 73–89). Book 4 (Pss. 90–106) features the rejuvenation of the Lord's kingdom in the "Maturation" of God's plan in the theology of the Psalms and its narrative. Finally, book 5 (Pss. 107–50) gives us the "Consummation" of the narrative and conclusion of the theme flow of the Psalms as a "Torah" or "Teaching Psalm" (Ps. 119), which is once again matched with a "Messianic Psalm," thereby paralleling how the Psalms began in Psalm 1 and Psalm 2 with these two "Poetic Pillars."

One rather outstanding structural element is the fact that each of the five books ends with its own doxology, four of which are quite similar.

> ***Doxology of book 1:***
> "Praise be to the LORD, the God of Israel,
> From everlasting to everlasting. Amen and Amen" (Ps. 41:13 TNIV).

18. See Robertson, *Flow of the Psalms*, chap. 2.

> ***Doxology of book 2:***
> "Praise be to the LORD God, the God of Israel,
> Who alone does marvelous deeds.
> Praise be to his glorious name forever;
> may the whole earth be filled with his glory. Amen and Amen" (Ps. 72:18–19 TNIV).
> ***Doxology of book 3:***
> "Praise be to the LORD forever! Amen and Amen" (Ps. 89:52 TNIV).
> ***Doxology of book 4:***
> "Praise be to the LORD, the God of Israel,
> from everlasting to everlasting.
> Let all the people say, 'Amen!'
> Praise the LORD" (Ps. 106:48 TNIV).

The doxology of the fifth book of the Psalter concludes with five hallelujah psalms (Pss. 146–50), which appropriately climaxes the doxologies of all the books in Psalms. And, as Gerald Wilson has noted regarding this fifth doxology, "the final Hallel (Pss. 146–150) stands at the conclusion of the whole Psalter collection and admirably fulfills the role of concluding praise of Yahweh."[19] Accordingly, the significance of the Psalms' poetic structure that features the "poetic pillars" of Psalm 1 and Psalm 2 is that they escort the reader into the temple of the book of Psalms. These poetic pillars anticipate the major themes that permeate the whole book of Psalms, and conclude with resounding and repetitive praise of Yahweh.

BIBLIOGRAPHY

Delitzsch, Franz. *Biblical Commentary on the Psalms*. Grand Rapids: Eerdmans, 1959.

Goldingay, John. *Psalms*. Vol. 1, *Psalms 1–41*. BCOTWP. Grand Rapids: Baker Academic, 2006.

Gunkel, Hermann. *The Psalms: A Form-Critical Introduction*. Philadelphia: Fortress, 1967.

Holladay, William. *The Psalms through Three Thousand Years: Prayerbook of a Cloud of Witnesses*. Minneapolis: Fortress, 1996.

Robertson, O. Palmer. *The Flow of the Psalms: Discovering Their Structure and Theology*. Phillipsburg, NJ: P&R, 2015.

Sweeney, Marvin. *Tanak: A Theological and Critical Introduction to the Jewish Bible*. Minneapolis: Fortress, 2012.

VanGemeren, Willem A. "The Reformation and the Appropriation of Scripture: Dwelling in the Psalms." plenary lecture given at the occasion of the International Congress of the Korean Evangelical Theological Society, Seoul, South Korea, November 11, 2017.

19. Wilson, *Psalms*, 1:77.

______. *The Expositor's Bible Commentary*. Vol. 5, *Psalms*. Edited by Tremper Longman III and David E. Garland. Rev. ed. Grand Rapids: Zondervan, 2008.

______. "God's Faithfulness, Human Suffering, and the Concluding Hallel Psalms (146–150): A Canonical Study." In *Building on the Foundations of Evangelical Theology: Essays in Honor of John S. Feinberg*, edited by Gregg R. Allison and Stephen J. Wellum, 263–84. Wheaton, IL: Crossway, 2015.

Waltke, Bruce K., with Charles Yu. *Old Testament Theology: An Exegetical, Canonical, and Thematic Approach*. Grand Rapids: Zondervan, 2007.

Walton, John H. "Psalms: A Cantata about the Davidic Covenant." *JETS* 34 (March 1991): 21–31.

Weiser, Arthur. *The Psalms*. OTL. Philadelphia: Westminster, 1962.

Wenham. Gordon. *The Psalter Reclaimed: Praying and Praising with the Psalms*. Wheaton, IL: Crossway, 2013.

Wilson, Gerald H. *Psalms Volume 1*. NIVAC. Grand Rapids: Zondervan, 2002.

CHAPTER 10

COVENANT HOPE IN THE KING REGARDLESS OF CIRCUMSTANCES

Worship in Book 1 (1–41) of the Psalter

Erika Moore

CONTEXT OF WORSHIP IN BOOK 1 OF THE PSALTER

In book 1 of the Psalter (Pss. 1–41), often referred to as the "Yahwistic Psalter"[1] or the "Davidic Collection,"[2] there is a sustained emphasis on the reign of God (a theme revisited in book 4) through his chosen servant David, amid the opposition that the Lord's anointed faces to establish his reign. Closely aligned with this is the Lord's covenantal commitment to David that he not only hears the psalmist's petitions and laments but also assures him of protection in light of all the threats from various crises and enemies.

Since the patristic era, there have been those who have understood Psalms 1 and 2 as the gateway not just to book 1 but also to the entire Psalter.[3] Psalm 1, with its contrast between the righteous and the wicked, opens the Psalter with a wisdom theme: ultimately, righteousness leads to blessing and wickedness leads to destruction. Psalm 2 underscores that because the Lord reigns supreme through his Davidic king, this assures the righteous that a life of covenant faithfulness is not an exercise in futility but ultimately will be rewarded. Furthermore, the scope is universal: "all who take refuge in him" (Ps. 2:12). These two psalms provide the foundation and set the

1. Due to the fact that God is referred to as "Yahweh" (Lord in English versions) more than 278 times and as Elohim (God in English versions) fifteen times. This pattern is reversed in book 2 (Psalms 42–72) with Yahweh occurring forty-four times and Elohim 201 times.
2. For a discussion on the various meanings of the Hebrew preposition *lamed*, see Bruce K. Waltke and James M. Houston with Erika Moore, *The Psalms as Christian Worship: A Historical Commentary* (Grand Rapids: Eerdmans, 2010), 89–90.
3. Waltke and Houston with Moore, *Psalms as Christian Worship*, 118–28; 160–61.

tone for the rest of the Psalter. The poetry of book 1 reflects that the Lord's reign does not go unchallenged. Psalm 3 begins the prayers of King David,[4] with a dramatic shift in tone as a number of David's enemies are referenced throughout his petitions for deliverance (e.g., his son Absalom's attempted coup [Ps. 3]; members of the seditious upper class [Ps. 4]; and rebellious liars [Ps. 5]). The high frequency of laments in book 1 evidences David's struggles, as the Lord's vice regent, to establish his reign over a united Israel.

Psalms 1 and 41 form an *inclusio* around book 1, which begins and ends with the nominal exclamation *ʾashre* ("blessed"; 1:1 and 41:1), denoting the idea not so much of happiness but rather fortunate—that is, "people who experience life optimally, as the Creator intended."[5] Both psalms also contain the word *hgh* ("meditate" in Ps. 1:2; "pleased" in 41:11). Mark David Futato notes:

> While Psalm 41 acknowledges that inheriting the promises of Psalm 2 involved David in struggles with his enemies (vv. 5–9 . . .), the psalm celebrates David's victories over those enemies. . . . Since David delighted in the Lord *à la* Psalm 1, the Lord is pleased with David, and this pleasure is experienced in David's triumphing over his enemies. By the end of book 1, David is inheriting the nations, just as Psalm 2 promised he would.[6]

Book 1 encourages the believer to pursue covenantal righteousness and worship the Lord in the midst of intense struggles while waiting for the final consummation of all things. Because the Lord reigns, believers can be confident as they bring their petitions and laments and seek refuge in him. As such, book 1 ends on a note of victory (41:12).

THEOLOGY OF WORSHIP

Worship the King

First, the royal psalms[7] in book 1 (Pss. 2, 11, 18, 20, 21) assured the Davidic king of the Lord's protection in the face of numerous foes. The Lord's promises to David (2 Sam. 7; 1 Chron. 17) would be fulfilled in spite of persistent opposition. The placement of Psalm 19, a psalm extolling the Lord's kingship, in the midst of the cluster of royal Psalms (18, 20, and 21) serves to underscore the close nexus between divine and human rule: the

4. Virtually all the psalms in book 1 have superscriptions ascribing authorship to David. The lack of superscriptions in Psalms 1 and 2 has already been discussed. Additionally, Psalm 10 lacks a superscription because it forms an (albeit somewhat imperfect) acrostic with Psalm 9, and Psalm 33's lack may be the result of the close similarity between Psalms 32:11 and 33:1.
5. Waltke and Houston with Moore, *The Psalms as Christian Worship*, 133.
6. Mark David Futato, *Interpreting the Psalms: An Exegetical Handbook* (Grand Rapids: Kregel, 2007), 81.
7. The designation "royal psalms" refers not so much to a particular genre, but rather a select group of psalms connected by a common theme.

Lord reigned though his Davidic king. However, in the ideological presentation of David in Psalm 2, there are already proleptic indicators that an ideal king, someone greater that David, is ultimately needed. As such, in the exilic and postexilic period, the focus sharpened to the messianic thrust of these psalms. The christocentric interpretation of these psalms (and the entire Psalter) by New Testament authors teaches believers today, united to Israel's ultimate king, to find in these psalms a source of confidence and security when they encounter unrelenting suffering and oppression. The covenant theology of kingship in these psalms should lead Christians today to extoll Christ as King, and continually remind us where our ultimate hope lies.

Psalm 2 provides a case study, becoming a go-to psalm throughout history. Erasmus saw his own struggles mirrored within the laments of the psalm; Luther applied the psalm to the turbulence of his time as manifested in the Peasants' War (1525), to his conflict with Zwingli, to the Turkish invasion of eastern Europe, and of course his conflict with Rome. Even Sir Walter Raleigh, hardly known for his biblical literacy, quoted Psalm 2 in light of the approaching threat of the Spanish Armada in 1588.[8] Psalm 2 is a coronation poem structured around four clearly defined stanzas of three verses each. The first stanza (vv. 1–3) begins with a rhetorical question, "Why?" Here the psalmist is not so much seeking information as expressing his utter astonishment at the actions of this hostile worldwide confederation of nations. Whereas the godly "meditate" (*hlh*) on the Lord's Torah (Ps. 1:2), the picture painted here is of the nations meditating (*hlh*), plotting their evil schemes in their futile attempts to overthrow the Lord's rule. In verse 2 we see that the tumultuous raging of the nations is not merely aimless restlessness, but "against the LORD and against his anointed." In verse 3 the psalmist quotes these insurrectionists urging one another on in their evil plot to overthrow the Lord's rule as they express their desire to be freed from any restraint the Lord places on them. They view his holy laws as an oppressive burden detrimental to their best interests, and they view the Lord as a tyrant.

In stanza 2 (vv. 4–6), the focus shifts to the corresponding scene in heaven and, as we see in the Lord's rejoinder, all their schemes are laughably ridiculous in his sight. He is not at all flustered, wringing his hands in anxiety, but views the actions of the rebellious nations as he sits enthroned in his sovereign security and declares, "I have set my King on Zion, my holy hill." In stanza 3 (vv. 7–9) the anointed king speaks of the decree given him and the authority given him, thus underscoring that the Lord has inextricably bound himself to the Davidic dynasty (2 Sam. 7) as his sovereign means of fulfilling the covenant to Abraham. Here the outcome of the continued opposition to the Lord is not in doubt as the king's rule is portrayed as extending to the ends of the earth as the nations become

8. Waltke and Houston with Moore, *The Psalms as Christian Worship*, 154–57.

his inheritance. In the fourth and final stanza (vv. 10–12), the psalmist once again speaks, holding out mercy to the rebels and summoning a call to allegiance in acknowledging that Israel's covenant God is Lord of all. Those who do not submit will kindle the Son's anger and face destruction. The psalm ends on a reassuring note: all who take refuge in him will find blessing and satisfaction in him.

This is all well and good, but those familiar enough with the record of the Davidic dynasty in the Old Testament recognize that the Southern Kingdom was often at war with her neighbors and often subject to foreign rule. In the sixth century BCE, the Davidic dynasty languished in Babylonian exile, returning home only to enjoy small provincial status in the vast Persian Empire as the Old Testament drew to a close. The picture represented in Psalm 2 never became a historical reality. In fact, according to the superscription of Psalm 3, David is fleeing from his son Absalom. How could he crush the rebellious nations when he was unable to subdue his own son? While speaking of a Davidic king, the true nature of this Psalm is christological. The language of this psalm spills over its banks, so to speak, pointing to someone much greater. In the redemptive-historical development of the concept of the Messiah, the ideal king, we understand that the psalm is now being fulfilled in David's greater son, Jesus, and will be consummated at the second coming.

Psalm 2 was also a go-to psalm for the New Testament authors. It is quoted or alluded to around eighteen times. In fact, it is quoted in the first recorded prayer of the church (Acts 4:23–29). Peter and John had been apprehended by the temple police and rulers of Jerusalem and were threatened with execution if they persisted in preaching about Jesus. When set free, they immediately found their fellow believers and reported what had happened. The account in Acts 4 indicates that as soon as their fellow believers heard the report, they began to pray, quoting from Psalm 2: "And when they heard it, they lifted their voices together to God and said, 'Sovereign Lord, who made the heaven and the earth and the sea and everything in them, who through the mouth of our father David, your servant, said by the Holy Spirit, "Why did the Gentiles rage, and the peoples plot in vain? The kings of the earth set themselves, and the rulers were gathered together, against the Lord and against his Anointed"'" (Acts 4:24–26).

In this way, the early church encourages us during times of duress and suffering to find solace and fortitude in proclaiming the reign of Jesus. The eschatological tension characteristic of where the church currently dwells in redemptive history leads us to confess this by faith, recognizing the temporal disjunction between the promise and the reality.

The psalm's message of hope and confidence is a message that both the early church and the contemporary church need to affirm in the midst of the strife and vehement opposition to Christ and his kingdom. The chaos all around can tempt us to conclude that God is not in control. But Psalm 2 can help fortify us, inviting us to affirm the truth that the Lord reigns and that he intends to bless those who put their trust in him. In this present age conflict and hostility toward Jesus and his kingdom remain, and that should not surprise us. But we can face this reality in the knowledge that the Lord reigns. Jesus is building his own kingdom in the hearts and minds of those who believe in him. The present age will not continue forever. Jesus will return in majesty and power, and the church can worship in eschatological hope knowing that no power can deprive Jesus of his throne. The church will someday share in his dominion because Jesus's power is infinitely greater than all the powers of evil.[9]

Worship Is Covenantal

Second, book 1 of the Psalter also reminds us that our worship is covenantal, and as such it is a response to the Lord's prior redeeming actions on behalf of his people. In our responses to the Lord's redeeming love, we are not left to our own imaginations, but we pray the Lord's words back to him. Because our worship is covenantal, it is not a monologue but must of necessity be a dialogue.[10] One way the church develops this dialogical worship is through meditation on the Lord's Torah "day and night" (Ps. 1:2). Torah encompasses much more than the law given through Moses. It is derived from the root *yrh*, meaning "to teach, instruct," and is better glossed as "catechetical instruction."[11] As Christians immerse themselves in God's revealed Word and meditate on it, they learn what is pleasing to him and develop a biblical vocabulary and grammar for worship. Biblical meditation is not an emptying of the mind in an attempt to enter some sort of transcendental spiritual state, but is rather a concerted focusing on the Lord and his Word for the purposes of appreciating and understanding. *Hgh*, the Hebrew word translated "meditate(s)" (Ps. 1:2) is used of the low murmuring and cooing of animals (Isa. 31:4; 38:14), and so carries the connotation of murmuring, speaking softly. Eugene Peterson observes, "This (*hgh*) is quite different from merely reading God's word, or thinking about it. This is not so much an intellectual process, figuring our meanings, as it is a physical process, hearing and rehearing these words as we sound them again, letting the sounds sink into our muscle and bones. Meditation is mastication."[12] Biblical meditation is not an end in itself. The outcome of the righteous engaging in this sort of mediation is a profound

9. In many liturgical traditions (e.g., Anglican, Orthodox, Lutheran, Roman Catholic), Christ the King Sunday is the last Sunday of the Christian Year, followed by Advent. One of the collects for the day reads, "*Almighty and everlasting God, whose will it is to restore all things in your well-beloved Son, the King of kings and Lord of lords: Mercifully grant that the peoples of the earth, divided and enslaved by sin, may be freed and brought together under his most gracious rule; who lives and reigns with you and the Holy Spirit, one God, now and for ever. Amen.*"
10. John D. Witvliet, *The Biblical Psalms in Christian Worship* (Grand Rapids: Eerdmans, 2007), 16.
11. Waltke and Huston with Moore, *The Psalms as Christian Worship*, 136.
12. Eugene Peterson, *Answering God: The Psalms as Tools for Prayer* (San Francisco: Harper & Row, 1989), 26.

understanding of the Lord's moral will, which then results in faithful covenant living based on what one has learned.

Because our worship is grounded in our covenant relationship with the Lord, the practice of remembrance should have a significant and integral role in our worship. Regularly rehearsing the Lord's deeds on behalf of his people in time and history can serve to encourage us to look to the Lord ourselves especially during times of deep anguish and distress. Established times of remembrance in worship can serve to fortify our confidence and trust in the Lord.

Psalm 23 is an example of a song of trust and confidence in the Lord's care.[13] The point is not that life is good and carefree. According to the superscription, this is a psalm of David, and the historical books of the Old Testament testify that David's life was far from carefree. King Saul tried to kill him. The Philistines pursued him. His own estranged son Absalom usurped the throne, causing David to flee for his life. He lost his son whom Bathsheba bore after their illicit affair. Life for David was hard, filled with crises, deprivation, and loss. Some crises were caused by his own doing, but not all, and yet in light of all this, David declares, "I shall not want" (v. 1). David could declare this not because the Lord gave him everything that he wanted but because the Lord gave him contentment in the midst of life's hardships, challenges, and frustrations.

We do not know the particulars of what David was thinking when he wrote about walking through the valley of the shadow of death (v. 4), evil threatening him (v. 4), enemies pursuing him (v. 5), but there is some sort of crisis that generated these words of confidence and trust. Perhaps that is part of the beauty of this pure declaration of confidence and trust in the Lord: the metaphorical language can be adapted to and speak to a wide variety of troubling situations. This psalm encourages God's people that as we encounter the dangers and evils and crises of this world, the Lord is with us and we will lack nothing that we need. Further, Psalm 23 reminds us that the Lord's protection and care are "for his name's sake" (v. 3). This is a claim on the Lord's promises and his character, reminding us that the Lord is committed to maintaining the relationship that he has established with his covenant people, for it is his own reputation and integrity that are at stake. Bruce Waltke succinctly observes, "We live in a universe where God's interests and his people's interests cohere, not compete."[14] At the close of the poem (v. 6) David leaves behind the imagery of shepherd, sheep, and banqueting table (v. 5) to reflect on dwelling in the Lord's house. Ironically, the covenantal words "goodness" (*tov*) and "mercy" (*hesed*), and not the enemies of verse 5, are here personified as the Lord's agents in hot pursuit of his loved one.[15] The Lord's people

13. Psalm 30 is another example of a psalm of remembrance in book 1.

14. Waltke and Huston with Moore, *The Psalms as Christian Worship*, 440.

15. The Hebrew word *yirdephuni* (from the root *radaph*) is better translated "pursue" rather than "follow."

cannot escape his unfailing desire and commitment to do good all the days of our lives.

So also in Psalm 13, after repeatedly petitioning the Lord with questions of "How long?" (v. 1 [×2]; v. 2 [×2]) the psalm ends on a note of confidence: "But I have trusted in your steadfast love; my heart shall rejoice in your salvation. I will sing to the LORD, because he has dealt bountifully with me" (vv. 5–6).

Remembrance in worship is not merely a pining for the "good old days" but rather is closely tethered to eschatological anticipation. Remembrance of the Lord's past saving actions in the midst of various dangers and trials builds confidence and trust for the present, and glorious expectation of the Lord's future interventions. David's cries in Psalm 9:13, "Be gracious to me, O LORD! See my affliction from those who hate me, O you who lift me up from the gates of death" is preceded by remembering the Lord's acts of deliverance on the psalmist's behalf in the past (vv. 3–6, 9, 12) and followed by confident declarations that ultimately the Lord's justice will prevail (vv. 16–20). Psalm 22 follows a similar pattern in which reminders of the Lord's past faithfulness (vv. 4, 5, 9, 10) and assured pronouncements of future justice (vv. 22–29) shore up David in the midst of his agonizing distress.[16]

The superscription to Psalm 18 identifies the psalm as a song sung by David "on the day when the LORD rescued him from the hand of all his enemies, and from the hand of Saul."[17] The lengthy poetic recounting of the Lord's deliverance leads David to confidently proclaim concerning the future: "He gives his king great victories; he shows unfailing kindness to his anointed, to David and his descendants forever" (v. 50 NIV). Once again, in the midst of the psalmist's petitions, we can discern a melody of eschatological joy and hope because of the assurance that the future is not in doubt.

This nexus between remembrance, petition, and anticipation can also be seen in the macro-structure of the Psalter, in the movement from lament and suffering to blessing and glory. This movement assures us that "while the truly happy life held out in the teaching of Psalm 1 and guaranteed by the reign of God in Psalm 2 may not be experienced at every point along the path of life, the truly happy life is certainly the destiny of Israel and the nations. Our destiny is glory."[18]

Worship in Petition

Last, these psalms remind us that our glorious destiny will not be realized without much sorrow and distress. Suffering followed by glory was the experience of Jesus and so this will be the pattern for his followers

16. See also Psalm 31 for another example of this sort of relationship between remembrance, petition, and anticipation.
17. See 2 Samuel 22 for this song (with minor variation) linked to its historical context.
18. Futato, *Interpreting the Psalms*, 80.

(Luke 24:26, 46; Acts 14:22). More specifically, the language of book 1 in particular is steeped in lament.[19] The common terms "lament" or "complaint" psalm can be confusing, for the psalmist is not merely interested in the Lord "feeling his pain" but is crying out for the Lord to intervene and bring relief.[20] As such, the term "petition" is to be preferred.[21] Biblical lament is not to be confused with contemporary notions of psychological complaint. The psalmist is not merely interested in venting his frustrations. Rather, the laments are petitions for deliverance. Psalms of lament/petition have the following elements:

1. An initial address to the Lord: usually (the Elohistic psalter is an obvious exception) the covenant name Yahweh is used because the psalmist is a member of the covenant community, and on the basis of the relationship is petitioning the one who can rectify the situation (Pss. 5:1; 6:1; 7:1).

2. A description of the psalmist's dire circumstances: the culprits include enemies (10:2–11; 12; 28:3), illness (6:2; 22:14–15; 31; 35; 38:3–10, 17; 39), false accusers (4:2; 5:6–9; 7; 17; 26; 27; 38:11–12, 19–20), persecution (3; 9; 10; 35); and personal sin (25:7; 38:18; 39:8).

3. A confession of trust in the Lord (7:10–11; 13:5; 28:7–8; 31:14).

4. A petition to the Lord for deliverance: based on the Lord's unfailing goodness, the psalmist pleads for relief (3:7; 22:19–21; 35:17, 22–24).

5. An expression of confidence that the Lord will come and provide relief (6:8–10; 7:10; 13:5–6; 22:24; 28:6).

6. A proclamation of praise in light of expected answer to prayer (7:17; 13:5–6; 22:22–31; 28:6–7).

Lamenting, however, does not necessarily lead to dour, sullen worship. For example, Psalm 25 has been identified as an individual lament of struggle.[22] It is a psalm of great sorrow in which David expresses loneliness, affliction, and deep distress. In particular, David is struggling on three different fronts: pressure from formidable enemies (vv. 2–3, 19–20),

19. The lament psalms are most heavily concentrated in books 1–3.
20. Hermann Gunkel's pioneering work on the literary analysis of the Psalter greatly enabled scholars to recognize groupings of psalms that shared both a distinctive structure as well as affinities in content.
21. Bruce K. Waltke's preference is for the term *petition* rather than *lament.*
22. Psalm 25 is an acrostic. There are twenty-two verses corresponding in order to the twenty-two consonants of the Hebrew alphabet.

the burden of guilt for past sin (vv. 6–7, 11, 18), and a deep-seated need for the Lord's guidance (vv. 4–5, 12b, 14b). In this particular psalm, David does not specifically indicate who the enemies are from whom he seeks relief. Perhaps this is intentional as a means of allowing future generations of saints to appropriate his petitions for their own struggles even though the specifics may vary for each one. David is also conscious of past sin, particularly the sins of his youth (v.7). Certainly, David knows the sweetness of the Lord's forgiveness; perhaps he is still suffering from the consequences of his youthful waywardness. Finally, David recognized his need for guidance from the Lord. He asks the Lord to "show" and "teach" (vv. 4–5), to "guide" (v. 5), to "instruct" (v. 12b). If David is to persevere to the end, he must receive instruction from the Lord. Perseverance does not take place on autopilot. In the midst of his deep anguish, David confidently expresses his settled trust in the Lord. Twice in the psalm we see David move from petition to meditation. He turns his gaze from dwelling on himself and the source of his problems and reorients himself to focus on the Lord and his goodness (vv. 7–8); his uprightness (v. 8); his willingness to guide, teach, and instruct the humble and upright (vv. 9, 12); and his covenant promises (vv. 12–15). The psalm ends with an abrupt and unexpected reference to the nation as David petitions the Lord to "redeem Israel, O God, out of all his troubles" (25:22). Certainly as king, David is in corporate solidarity with and often speaks on behalf of the nation. Perhaps David's petitioning the Lord in his time of deep anguish softened and enlarged his heart, giving him the capacity to sympathize with others.

SIGNIFICANCE OF PSALMS BOOK 1 FOR BIBLICAL WORSHIP

Worship Christ the King

First, book 1 reminds us that the Lord is sovereign King over all. As Abraham Kuyper notes, "There is not a square inch in the whole domain of our human existence over which Christ, who is Sovereign over all, does not cry, Mine!"[23] Our God truly has "the whole world in his hands," and recognition of this biblical truth ought to infuse our worship with praise and confidence. Certainly the theme of pilgrimage and alienation in this world is a truth taught in Scripture (Gal. 4:26; Heb. 11:1, 13; 1 Peter 2:11; 1 John 2:15). There is indeed something "off" and disjointed about the world in which we live, and the church, in seeking to work against this, becomes alienated from the system and those who have bought into this system of evil. The consequences of such alienation can wear us down, tempting us to want to give in or simply quit. On the other hand, Scripture also teaches us that the Lord sovereignly rules over all, and as such the church has a "home-field advantage" in the battle against evil. Jesus reigns. Now. Today. And his kingdom will endure forever. The current satanic

23. See James D. Bratt, ed., *Abraham Kuyper: A Centennial Reader* (Grand Rapids: Eerdmans, 1998).

opposition to the kingdom of God is formidable, powerful, and *limited*. Even when our opponents seem most successful, the situation is not out of hand. In this present age conflict will remain, and the church ought not to be surprised by this. But we can face this ongoing conflict in the knowledge that the Lord reigns and will come again to consummate what was established at his first coming. These truths, so beautifully celebrated in book 1, are invaluable truths in which the church can anchor her soul.

Extolling the kingship of Christ in word, sacrament, and song ought to nurture a sense of biblical confidence in the church no matter what is happening in society around us and the world in general. The church can flourish no matter what the context, under the sovereign rule of Jesus. This is a far cry from the cultural triumphalism that has often plagued the church, and is rather grounded in the reality of our current state of affairs in a fallen world in light of the glorious future that is to come.

Worship in Light of Our New Covenant Position

Second, many of the psalms in book 1 remind us that, as our worship is grounded in our covenantal relationship with the Lord, it is appropriate to include the art of remembrance in worship. As such, book 1 of the Psalter opens with an encouragement to meditate on God's Word (Ps. 1:2). One time-tested way of doing this has been through *lectio divina*, a receiving and dwelling within the text, thus allowing oneself to become immersed in the text. In the midst of our busy lives it is tempting to read Scripture in a rushed and careless way. It is good to ask ourselves, "In the midst of my own struggles have I developed the habit of slowly reading?" In comparing the consignment approach of many modern readers with the approach of religious readers, Gordon Wenham observes, "As a reader memorizes a text, he becomes textualized; that is, he embodies the work he has committed to memory. So too, one hopes that this is the experience of many as they sing and pray the psalms. They mold one's character and heighten one's love of God."[24] This remembrance is a far cry from the sentimental longing for "olden days" and is rather a robust recognition that the covenant Lord is committed to his people. Focusing on the ways in which he has rescued his people in the past provided the church with a deep-seated sense of security and confidence as well as a healthy anticipation of the glories that are yet to come.

Worship with an Eschatological Hope

Finally, book 1 of the Psalter can help the church to learn the lost art of lamenting. Book 1 of the Psalter begins and ends with a declaration of "blessing" (*'ashre*) on the righteous (1:1; 41:1), and yet there are not many hymns of praise in book 1. The most prevalent type of psalm in book 1 is

24. Gordon Wenham, *The Psalter Reclaimed: Praying and Praising with the Psalms* (Wheaton, IL: Crossway, 2013), 22–23.

the lament (petition), a prayer for deliverance from some crisis. Much of the Western church has lost the practice of lament in corporate worship, and in so doing, this has left individual Christians and the church at large impoverished in their understanding of the need for lament, the words of lament, and the power of lament. The Western church in particular needs to retrieve the practice of corporate lament in order to combat the alienation that derives from the tendency of believers to put on a happy face and suffer in silence in the midst of much pain and suffering, and also to live in solidarity with the church at large that suffers greatly. Even when life is going well, praying the laments can help us learn to sympathize with those who are hurting, beset by many afflictions, and with our persecuted brothers and sisters around the world. Praying the lament psalms encourages us to find our refuge in the Lord during times of trouble. When we come to the Lord amid various crises and troubles that threaten us, we are acknowledging and worshiping him as our king, no matter what challenging circumstances we may be facing. Repeatedly finding refuge in our sovereign king enables us identify and renounce the insidious pastime of self-reliance.[25]

Incorporating the laments of book 1 in public worship can also serve to help the church speak a word of reorienting truth to an American culture that embraces Disney endings, victory being snatched out of the jaws of defeat, and Hallmark plot lines. These are just a few of the seductive obstacles embraced and lauded by our Western culture that the church needs to overcome as we attempt to retrieve the lost art of biblical lament. For many reading this, not being oppressed can put us at a disadvantage; we rarely need to cry out as the psalmist does about being treated unjustly, being the victim of prejudice and violence. In such cases, we can pray on behalf of our brothers in sisters around the world who suffer greatly because of their faith and circumstances. As we pray in solidarity with and for them, we also prepare ourselves for the times, should they come, "when all around my soul gives way, he then is all my hope and stay."[26] For Jesus's sake, the Lord hears us when we cry out to him.

The fact is, life in a fallen world is not always enjoyable, for believers and nonbelievers alike. Failure to redress this false optimism regularly doled out in media and pop culture by embracing the need for lament can leave the church ill-equipped to minister to those who are suffering. The gathering of the saints in public corporate worship before the Lord ought to be one safe place where disappointments, frustrations, confusion, and despair can be

25. While researching and writing this chapter, the house of one of the board members of the seminary where I teach was attacked. The Nigerian bishop and his wife Gloria have sixty adopted children that they have rescued. One person was killed in the attack. My life is going well. There are few complaints at the Moore house, but we can come before the Lord and pray these laments in concert with our afflicted brothers and sisters locally and around the globe who are suffering greatly because they name the name of Jesus.

26. Edward Mote, "My Hope Is Built on Nothing Less" (1834).

acknowledged. How many people sitting in the pews Sunday after Sunday have "put on a happy face" but are inwardly groaning in despair?

Incorporating in our public worship the laments in Psalms 3, 6, 7, 9, 10, 12, 17, 26, 27, 38, and 39 can also help us resist several tendencies plaguing the church today. One such destructive impulse is offering premature solutions to the problems facing us. Perhaps the Lord's answer will not be to remove the lamentable situation, but to give his children the strength to bear up in the midst of unrelenting assaults. When the church laments, she does not minimize the problems but rather admits that the scale of the problems facing her are overwhelming and that she cannot face them without divine aid. This recognition can in turn serve to reorient those in dire straits from deep despair, anger, or revenge. What better place than the saints united together in worship to express corporately our griefs, sorrows, and sufferings?

A second benefit of embracing lament in corporate worship is that it can serve as a means of combating the danger of individualism that infects so much of Western worship. When we join in corporate lament during personal times of joy and shalom, we learn to sympathize with and remember those who are suffering. Praying the psalms of lament is one way we can fulfill the command to "weep with those who weep" (Rom. 12:15). As we pray in solidarity with and for them, we also prepare ourselves for the times, should they come, "when all around my soul gives way, he then is all my hope and stay."[27] For Jesus's sake, the Lord hears us when we cry out to him.

Third, the retrieval of corporate lament in our communal liturgies can catechize Christians in a truly biblical response to suffering that will resist the deeply ingrained impulse to prematurely rush to praise. Biblical lament is an *expression of faith* as the petition is made to the Lord to come and rescue those in dire need. Book 1 teaches us how to worship while we wait, how to find refuge in God. The optimistic Western, can-do culture provides a wide array of unhelpful distractions such as work, sports, entertainment in which individuals can hide themselves in an attempt to deny either their own pain and suffering or the misery and destitution of others. As the beloved George Herbert, seventeenth-century priest of the Church of England, wrote in his poem "Bitter-Sweet,"

> Ah my dear angry Lord,
> Since thou dost love, yet strike;
> Cast down, yet help afford;
> Sure I will do the like.
> I will complain, yet praise;
> I will bewail, approve:
> And all my sour-sweet days
> I will lament and love.

27. Mote, "My Hope Is Built on Nothing Less."

BIBLIOGRAPHY

Bratt, James D., ed. *Abraham Kuyper: A Centennial Reader.* Grand Rapids: Eerdmans, 1998.

Futato, Mark David. *Interpreting the Psalms: An Exegetical Handbook.* Grand Rapids: Kregel, 2007.

Peterson, Eugene. *Answering God: The Psalms as Tools for Prayer.* San Francisco: Harper & Row, 1989.

Waltke, Bruce, James M. Houston, and Erika Moore. *The Psalms as Christian Lament: A Historical Commentary.* Grand Rapids: Eerdmans, 2015.

______. *The Psalms as Christian Worship: A Historical Commentary.* Grand Rapids: Eerdmans, 2010.

Wenham, Gordon. *The Psalter Reclaimed: Praying and Praising with the Psalms.* Wheaton, IL: Crossway, 2013.

Witvliet, John D. *The Biblical Psalms in Christian Worship.* Grand Rapids: Eerdmans, 2007.

CHAPTER 11

THE CALL AND CAUSE TO PRAISE
Worship in Book 2 (42–72) of the Psalter

Ted Hildebrandt

CONTEXT OF WORSHIP IN BOOK 2 OF THE PSALTER: PSALMS 42–72

In this chapter we explore the praise of God in book 2 (Pss. 42–72) of the Psalter. By way of introduction, I begin with a description of the three main characters: king, psalmist, and enemy. The divine-human king rescues, protects, and renders justice; the psalmist cries out for deliverance and protection, then praises the king; and the treacherous enemy taunts, shames, and seeks to trap, devour, and destroy the psalmist. I then demonstrate that lament is often a basis for praise and even imprecation is frequently linked with praise. Next, the praises themselves are examined in discussions on the call to praise, the cause of praise, how to praise, and the place of praise. Finally, the chapter comes to a close with drawing implications for modern worship from the praise of God in book 2 of the Psalter.

Book 2 flows from the initial lament of God's absence and distance from the place of praise (42/43), to Zion, the "city of God" (46–48), to wisdom (49), and dips into sacrifices (50; 51) and sin (52–53). It returns to laments (54–64) with a pair of "Be merciful" psalms (56–57) and an echo of the thirsting-for-God motif (63; cf. 42:1). It then moves on to several hymns of praise (65–68). Book 2 concludes with a transition from a feeble and aged psalmist (71; cf. 1 Kings 1) to the vibrant King Solomon (72). It ends in a way characteristic of many of the "books" of Psalms, with a double "praise" and a double "Amen."

Having briefly surveyed the canonical context and flow of book 2, it is important to understand the three characters that dominate the book: king, psalmist/suppliant, and enemy. Each of these can be described via the metaphors used, their characteristic actions, and the accompanying virtues/vices they exhibit.

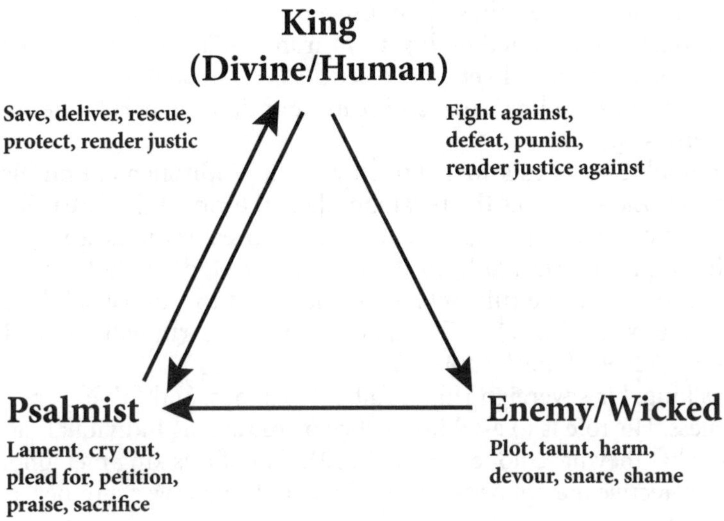

The King (human-divine)

The king is the predominant metaphor for God in the Psalms.[1] This kingship characterization of God is prominent in book 2 and plays a foundational role for the notion of praise. Immediately after the opening introductory pair of Psalms 42 and 43, Psalm 44, a communal lament, directs its address to God saying, "You are my King and my God, who decrees victories for Jacob. Through you we push back our enemies" (44:4–5; cf. 55:16–19).[2] Here the three main characters emerge in their roles: God, as king, saves or delivers; the needy psalmist, who petitions/laments; and the oppressing enemy who is defeated. After the king's deliverance the psalmist responds, "we will praise your name forever" (44:8).

Psalm 47:2–3, an imperatival call to praise, acknowledges the awesome Lord Most High as "the great King over all the earth." His victory over and subduing of the nations results in the psalmist's clapping hands in praise (47:1). The sons of Korah sound the trumpets amid shouts of joyful praise, thereby issuing the call to praise in Psalm 47:6–8: "Sing praises to God, sing praises; sing praises to our King, sing praises." This "call to

1. J. H. Eaton, *Kingship and the Psalms* (London: SCM-Canterbury Press, 1976); James L. Mays, *The Lord Reigns: A Theological Handbook to the Psalms* (Louisville: Westminster John Knox, 1994); Hans Kraus, *Theology of the Psalms* (Minneapolis: Fortress, 1992); J. Clinton McCann Jr., *A Theological Introduction to the Book of Psalms* (Nashville: Abingdon, 1993); and James Grant, *The King as Exemplar: The Function of Deuteronomy's Kingship Law in the Shaping of the Book of Psalms* (Williston, VT: Academia Biblica, 2004).

2. All translations here are NIV, unless otherwise noted.

praise" is rooted in God's role as king rescuing the psalmist and manifesting his sovereign rule over the nations. The "call to praise" is followed by a "cause to praise" that explains why one is called on to praise: "For God is the King of all the earth; sing to him a psalm of praise. God reigns over the nations; God is seated on his holy throne" (47:7–8). The divine king's role seems to be the deliverance, rescue, salvation, and protection of the psalmist from the plots, snares, threats, and damage perpetrated by the treacherous enemy.

In book 2, God as king is linked with his enthronement on his holy mountain. Zion receives the regal moniker "the city of the Great King." It is there that the divine king receives praise: "Great is the Lord, and most worthy of praise [*mehullal*], in the city of our God, his holy mountain" (48:1). From Zion the rule of God emanates out to a universal dominion from sea to sea (72:8–11). Ultimately, the whole earth will be filled with his glory (72:19; cf. John 4:20–23).

As king, his sovereign rule is full of loyal love, faithfulness, and righteousness. His role is to establish justice by rewarding individuals according to what they have done (58:11; 62:12). Out of this king metaphor spin other protective metaphors such as God as a strong tower, a refuge, a rock, and a fortress.

The Psalmist or Suppliant

The psalmist is shown as thirsting for God (42:1–2; 63:1). He desires to meet with God but is haunted by the enemy's ridicule, "Where is your God?" He is comforted by the repeated refrains of God's presence (46:7, 11) and the hope of praising him (42:5, 11; 43:5).

The psalmist's emotions are diverse and clearly expressed. Feelings cover a broad range—from a sense of being abandoned and rejected by God, being downcast and disturbed, anxious, fearful, crushed, forgotten, sorrowful, and repentant over the need of cleansing. The psalmist faces situations that put him on the edge of death and betrayal by a most intimate friend (44:25; 55:13). Yet the psalmist remains hopeful, reflective, full of praise and joy. The enemy has devoured, attacked, taunted, insulted, shamed, and scorned the psalmist. The psalmist longs for God's presence and his dwelling, which is in Zion, the city of God, God's holy mountain. That is where God's house, the temple, is located. The zeal for God's house consumes the psalmist (69:9; quoted in John 2:17; cf. Jer. 7).

The Enemy

The enemy is the third major character described in great detail in book 2. While the psalmists portray themselves as sheep, the enemies are portrayed as ravenous beasts, lions, venomous snakes, and prowling dogs. They are deceivers who trust in their wealth and are wicked, hating instruction. They join with thieves and throw in their lots with adulterers. They are ruthless killers who conspire against and attack the psalmists, spreading a net to trap their feet. The enemies cast scorn, disgrace, and shame on the righteous. It is against these wicked foes that the psalmists pray to God for protection and deliverance, and call for justice to be meted out. In short, there is an identification of the wicked and evildoers with the enemy (64:1–6; 59:1–2).

In the context of the psalmists' deliverance from the enemy, the divine king receives the vow to praise and later declarative praise. Just as the acts of the deliverance from Egypt and God's involvement in creation had formerly called forth praise so the psalmists rehearse the mighty acts of God done on their behalf.

THEOLOGY OF WORSHIP

Call to Praise

The "call to praise" is an imperative statement, often at the beginning of a hymn, that invites the audience to praise God. The hymn Psalm 66 begins, "Shout for joy to God, all the earth! Sing the glory of his name; make his praise glorious. Say to God, 'How awesome are your deeds!'" (vv. 1–2). Each line begins with an initial imperative verb ("shout," *hariy'u*; "sing," *zammru*; "make," *simu*; "say," *'imru*) that calls on the worshipers to express their praise to God with exuberance (cf. 47:1, 6; 66:8; 68:4, 26, 32, 34). The call to praise in Psalm 67:3–5 utilizes *inclusio* bookends beginning and ending with the imperfect tense, which has a jussive sense seen in the translation "may": "May the peoples praise you, God; may all the peoples praise you. May the nations be glad and sing for joy. . . . May the peoples praise you, God; may all the peoples praise you."

Closely related is the psalmist's "vow to praise" in Psalm 61:7–8: "May [the king] be enthroned in God's presence forever. . . . Then I will ever sing in praise of your name and fulfill my vows day after day." Previously, the psalmist had reflected, "For you, God, have heard my vows" (61:5).

The psalmist states his commitment, determination, and hope to praise in the three refrains of the opening psalm pair of book 2: "Put your hope in God, for I will yet praise him, my savior and my God" (42:5, 11; 43:5). Book 2 closes with a doubled "praise be" to the Lord/his glorious name (72:18–19) and a doubled "Amen."

Cause for Praise

Often connected with an initial "call to praise" is a statement that develops the cause for praise. Hence in Psalm 47:1 there is a call to praise, "clap your hands, shout to God with cries of joy," followed by a *ki* (for/because) clause giving the rationale or cause for why one is being called on to praise God: "For [*ki*] the Lord Most High is awesome, the great King over all the earth. He subdued nations. . . . He chose our inheritance" (47:2–4; cf. 63:7; 66:10; 69:35). Similarly, Psalm 57 offers a cause to praise, "For [*ki*] great is your love, reaching to the heavens," followed by a vow to praise, "I will praise you, Lord, among the nations" (57:9–10).

Sometimes the explanatory "for" is not added but the cause is simply concatenated with the call to praise without an intervening causal particle. Often descriptive praise is the reason for the initial call, as in Psalm 66:8–9: "Praise our God, all peoples, . . . he has preserved our lives." This could also have taken the form "[for] he has preserved our lives," giving the reason or cause for praising God with the causal particle "for." The psalmist sees praise as caused by God's answer to his prayer (66:20), although, again, without the explicit use of "for."

There is often a blending of the "cause for praise" with the content of the praise itself. Patrick Miller notes that "the reasons for praise indeed become expressions of praise."[3] For example, Psalm 63:3 gives a cause to praise that itself is praise with an initial *ki*: "Because [*ki*] your love is better than life, my lips will glorify you. I will praise you as long as I live." Then in verse 7 another *ki* initial cause for praise offers praise: "Because [*ki*] you are my help, I sing in the shadow of your wings" (cf. 57:10). A major cause for praise is the acknowledgment that God has listened to one's prayer (66:19–20).

How to Praise

The underpinning of praise, according to book 2, seems to be finding delight in God, which then manifests itself in praise (42:4; 43:4). There are also moral prerequisites—the reciting of God's covenant by a wicked person is unacceptable to God, but the upright and righteous freely rejoice in God (50:16; 66:17–18). The tongue, lips, and mouth are the bodily parts used in praise along with clapping and uplifted hands. Musical instruments are often mentioned in the means of praise (especially harp, lyre [71:22–23], trumpets [47:5], and timbrels [68:25]). When praise is offered it is frequently in song (*zmr*) or with a joyful shout (*rnn*). Erhard Gerstenberger is correct when he observes that "a joyful service in the ancient world was a noisy affair."[4]

The Israelites regularly gathered in processions of worship in a "festive throng" (42:4). Psalm 68 describes such a procession in detail:

> Your procession, God, has come into view,
> the procession of my God and King into the sanctuary.
> In front are the singers, after them the musicians;
> with them are the young women playing the timbrels.
> Praise God in the great congregation;
> praise the LORD in the assembly of Israel.
> There is the little tribe of Benjamin, leading them. (68:24–27)

3. Patrick D. Miller, *They Cried to the Lord: The Form and Theology of Biblical Prayer* (Minneapolis: Fortress, 1994), 360. See also J. Kenneth Kuntz, "Grounds for Praise: The Nature and Function of the Motive Clause in the Hymns of the Hebrew Psalter," in *Worship and the Hebrew Bible: Essays in Honor of John T. Willis*, eds. M. Patrick Graham, Rick R. Marrs, and Steven L. McKenzie, JSOTSup 284 (Sheffield: Sheffield Academic, 1999), 159, 166, 169.

4. Erhard Gerstenberger, *Psalms, Part 1: With an Introduction to Cultic Poetry*, FOTL 14 (Grand Rapids: Eerdmans, 1988), 18.

The individual offers up praise, often with an accompanying sacrifice "in the presence of your faithful people" (52:9; 54:6). The Israelites, in procession, walk as a collective congregation to the sanctuary (55:14).

Finally, praise is something that is declared, proclaimed, and told. As the psalmist states, "My mouth will tell of your righteous deeds, of your saving acts all day long" (71:15, 16, 18). Many times the next generation is invited to praise as narrated in the historical deliverances by those of the previous generations (44:1–5).

Place of Praise

Book 2 opens with the taunting question: "Where is your God?" (42:3, 10). In response, the psalmist remembers, "How I used to go to the house of God . . . with shouts of joy and praise among the festive throng" (42:5; cf. 52:9). Later, there is a procession linking God and the king (68:24). In that opening psalm pair (42/43) the psalmist says, "Let them [God's light and faithful care] bring me to your holy mountain, to the place where you dwell. Then I will go to the altar of God" (43:3–4). Zion and the temple are the cultic loci to which praise is directed. Sacrifices and the altar are repeatedly mentioned in the context of praise. Praise is at times connected with one's vow to praise and the fulfillment of that vow. So the Psalms portray cultic aspects as the setting for praise. "I will come to your temple with burnt offerings and fulfil my vows to you—vows my lips promised and my mouth spoke when I was in trouble. I will sacrifice fat animals to you . . . let me tell you what he has done for me. . . . Praise be to God" (66:13–16, 20).

The procession of God as King from Sinai into the sanctuary at Jerusalem is described in Psalm 68 (vv. 17, 24, 35). Praise is described as awaiting God in Zion, expressed by worshipers who have been "filled with good things of your house, of your holy temple" (65:1, 4). Psalm 61:4 reflects back before the First Temple when the psalmist longs "to dwell in [God's] tent forever." It is in his sanctuary that God is "seen" by the psalmist (63:2), and it is the exiled psalmist's desire to be brought "to your holy mountain, to the place where you dwell" (43:3). After having been taunted by the enemy, "Where is your God?" the psalmist remembers "how I used to go to the house of God" (42:4).

There is a strong nexus between God and Jerusalem. In the psalms of Zion, the psalmist links the notion of "city of God, the holy place where the Most High dwells" with God's fortress-like defense of Zion against attacks from the nations (46:4–7). The psalmist tells worshipers to "walk about Zion, go around her, count her towers . . . that you may tell of them [the ramparts] to the next generation. For this God is our God for ever and ever" (48:12–14). Indeed, it is from "Zion, perfect in beauty, God shines forth" (50:2). It is to the temple the psalmist says, "I will come . . . and fulfill my vows to you—vows my lips promised [vow to praise] and my mouth spoke when I was in trouble" (66:13–14). Even in exile the psalmist expresses his longing for the return to divine presence and protection and vows to praise God's name forever (61:7; 61:2; 42:6–7).

Many point to Jesus's words to the Samaritan woman in John 4 that focus on the character of the worshiper rather than the geographical conflict between Mount Zion and Mount Gerizim. The decentralization of worship in the global church is taken as an opportunity to ignore or downplay the rich statements linking worship at the temple on Zion. This bypasses a major theme in book 2 of the Psalter that clearly places their worship in Zion. The significance of God's presence and worship shine forth from Zion. Indeed, the psalmist sees Zion as the center from which praise emanates universally to all nations, which is part of Jesus's point in John 4:19–24 for us (Ps. 46:4, 10; cf. 48 and 57).

Language of Praise

Book 2 models the language important for praise, some of which is readily recognized in our modern worship contexts. Other language is now often forgotten. These are lament/petition and imprecation.

Descriptive/declarative praise

Claus Westermann splits praise into what he labels "descriptive praise" and "declarative praise." Descriptive praise is reflected in a hymn that "praises God for his actions and his being as a whole." Declarative praise is a thanksgiving song that "praises God for a specific deed which the one who has been delivered recounts or reports in his song."[5] Leopold Sabourin, in describing hymns, says, "God is described by what he has done and by what he is."[6]

"All people will fear; they will proclaim the works of God" (64:9). That statement demonstrates that praise is often rooted in the mighty acts of God manifested in the deliverance of Israel and celebrated in worship contexts. The psalmist directs worshipers, "Say to God, 'How awesome are your deeds!'" (66:3).

The praise of God for his majestic power in creation is seen in Psalm 65:6–8: "who formed the mountains by your power . . . who stilled the roaring of the seas. . . . The whole earth is filled with awe at your wonders; where morning dawns, where evening fades, you call forth songs of joy." Ironically, the disciples, having witnessed Jesus stilling the "roaring of the seas," ask in astonishment, "Who then is this, that even the wind and sea obey him?" (Mark 4:41).

Both the exodus miracles (Ps. 66:6) and the conquest of Canaan provide bases for praise (44:2–8; 68:14). The shekinah glory of God's movement from Sinai to Zion is narrated in Psalm 68:17 (cf. 68:7–8). In a more generic sense of deliverance God is praised as the king who "rides on the

5. Claus Westermann, *Praise and Lament in the Psalms* (Richmond, VA: John Knox, 1981), 31.
6. Leopold Sabourin, *The Psalms: Their Origin and Meaning* (Staten Island, NY: Alba House, 1969), 177.

clouds. . . . A father to the fatherless, a defender of widows is God in his holy dwelling . . . leading out the prisoners with singing" (68:5–6).

Praise also expresses a hope in God's future mighty acts of deliverance: "But may all who seek you rejoice and be glad in you; may those who long for your saving help always say, 'The Lord is great!'" (70:4). This hope/praise link opens book 2 in the thrice-repeated refrain "Put your hope in God, for I will yet praise him, my Savior and my God" (42:5, 11; 43:5). It also concludes book 2 in the petition of the aged: "For you have been my hope . . . since my youth. From birth I have relied on you. . . . I will ever praise you" (71:5–6). God's acts of saving and protection are also highlighted in the cluster of metaphors by which he is addressed: rock, refuge, strong tower, and fortress.

Though praise is done in the congregation, yet it is often a witness of the unique way in which each individual has experienced God's greatness and goodness. In a most intimately personal manner the psalmist extols God for his forgiveness of his transgressions, iniquity, and sin (51:15). The psalmist, with thankful heart, praises God for having "delivered me from all my troubles" (54:7) and, after gathering, the congregation declares, "all you who fear God; let me tell you what he has done for me" (66:16; cf. 52:9).

In many of these statements of praise there is a very close joining of the declaration of God's character to the manifestation of some particular act of rescuing. So Psalm 54:6 praises the name of the Lord "for it is good. You have delivered me." Unfailing love (*hesed*) is an attribute that is praised (62:12). His power and glory (*kavod*) are also extolled (63:2; 66:3). Often God's "name" is cited as a metonymy for God himself receiving praise (48:10; 54:6; 61:8; 66:4; 68:4; 69:30; 72:19). Note how often the attributes of God are not isolated or abstracted but carefully linked to the divine actions that manifest those attributes in the lives of his people. So when the psalmist is going to praise God for his uniqueness and righteousness he declares, "Your righteousness, God, reaches to the heavens, you have done great things. Who is like you, God?" (71:19). Thus, while the difference between descriptive and declarative praise is a helpful cognitive distinction, one must be cautious about separating what the text itself organically connects.

Lament/petition as the basis of praise

Book 2 features many psalms of lament/petition. Literary genre alone classifies the various psalms as psalms of lament/petition of the individual (42/43; 51; 54–57; 59; 61; 64; 69–71) or community (44; 60), Zion hymn (46; 48) hymns (47; 65–68), or instructional psalms (49; 50; 52; 53; 58). The problem with focusing on genre, however, is that it is easy to overlook elements of praise embedded in nonhymn types of psalms. Book 2 has many laments and complaints from which the postmodern Christian community stands to learn much. Often a religious atmosphere is constructed as supporting aspects of the prosperity gospel, where religion is used as an escape from the reality of suffering and as a talisman or good luck charm. Lament is a lost art for Christians, yet it is featured prominently in book 2 of the Psalter.

As a result of the perception of having been forgotten by God, the lament of the downcast soul in the opening psalm pair (42/43) manifests itself in "tears have been my food day and night" (42:3). The taunting jabs of the foes ("Where is your God?") and the personal lament ("Why, my soul, are you downcast?") are eased by the thrice-repeated refrain of hope of praise: "I will yet praise him, my Savior and my God" (42:5, 11; 43:5). Praise arises out of a context of lament.

Psalm 57 talks of God's sending forth his love (*hesed*) and faithfulness (*emet*) as God rebukes those who "hotly pursue" the psalmist. Even though the psalmist is in the midst of ravenous beasts and lions (enemies) who spread a net for his feet, yet, he vows, "I will praise you, Lord, among the nations; . . . for great is your love, reaching to the heavens. . . . Be exalted, O God, above the heavens; let your glory be over all the earth" (57:9–11). The struggles of lament set the context for meaningful praise. Having been rescued from life-threatening enemies results in the psalmists' personally witnessing the mighty acts of God on their behalf. The psalmists then bear witness within the community in songs of praise.

Even the messianic Psalm 69 calls for divine salvation from the miry depths and engulfing floods of those who hate the psalmist without reason (69:1–4). The psalmist is covered in scorn, mocking and shame (69:6–12, 19–20) with the enemy putting "gall in my food and gave me vinegar to drink" (69:21). He hopes to witness God's salvation and vows to "praise God's name in song and glorify him with thanksgiving" (69:30). He then calls on heaven and earth to praise God for saving Zion (69:34–35).

Psalm 66:17–20 exemplifies the lament/praise nexus saying,

> I cried out to him with my mouth;
> his praise was on my tongue.
> If I had cherished sin in my heart,
> the Lord would not have listened;
> but God has surely listened
> and has heard my prayer.
> Praise be to God,
> who has not rejected my prayer
> or withheld his love from me!

In Psalm 50:15 God himself describes the movement from lament, to deliverance, to praise: "call on me in the day of trouble; I will deliver you, and you will honor me."

Thus, while there are majestic hymns (145–50), book 2 features psalms of lament/petition that demonstrate the sequence of lament, God's deliverance, and resultant praise. Lament adds a strong dose of reality and personalization to praise, utilizing the dark colors of lament to focus one's attention on the contrasting vibrant hues of praise. In psalms of lament, there is almost a universal shift from the depths of tragedy and despair to the heights of praise (see 54–59; 64; 66; 69).

Imprecation as the basis of praise

The basis of lament as foundational to praise opens the door for the further exploration of imprecations. Imprecations are rejected by some, explained away by others, or cordoned off into a locked trunk of Old Testament unspeakables. However, the text of Psalms itself often employs imprecations as a background and basis for praise.

How is it that imprecations are often connected with, and provide the basis for, praise? A brief survey of examples in the larger context, the destruction of the wicked, may perhaps be best understood in relation to the divine King's rendering salvation/rescue/deliverance for the psalmist (68:20) who was faced with attacks, traps, harm, scorn, and shame from the fangs of the enemies. Psalm 44:6–7 states, "but you [God] give us the victory over our enemies, you put our adversaries to shame. In God we make our boast all day long, and we will praise your name forever." Even "Mount Zion rejoices, the villages of Judah are glad" (48:11). Why? "Because of your judgments." Verse 7 provides the specifics: "You destroyed them like ships of Tarshish shattered by an east wind." In contrast to his own flourishing like an olive tree in the house of God, the psalmist notes, "Surely God will bring you [wicked/Doeg] down to everlasting ruin" (52:5, 8). The psalmist then reflects back on God's mighty acts—both positive and imprecatory in nature—and concludes, "For what you have done I will always praise you" (52:9).

The nexus of praise and imprecation is also drawn close in Psalm 54:4–7: "Surely God is my help. . . . Let evil recoil on those who slander me; in your faithfulness destroy them. . . . I will praise your name. . . . You have delivered me." God vindicates/saves the psalmist, rebuking those who hotly pursue him, and causing those who have dug a pit in his path to fall into it themselves (57:6). This results in the psalmist's singing and vowing to praise (57:5, 11).

Even after the strong imprecation in Psalm 58, in which the psalmist requests that God "break the teeth in their mouths" and "let them vanish like water that flows away" (58:6–7), the response to the destruction of the wicked is that the righteous will be glad, and people will exclaim, "Surely the righteous still are rewarded; surely there is a God who judges the earth" (58:11). This is a statement of praise based on the divine display of salvation/deliverance. It is when the enemy is turned back that the psalmist "will know that God is for me" (56:9).

Perhaps Psalm 59:13 connects this imprecation/praise nexus more concisely, after giving a detailed description of the enemy: "consume them in your wrath, consume them till they are no more. Then it will be known to the ends of the earth that God rules over Jacob." The psalm concludes, "You are my strength, I sing praise to you; you, God, are my fortress" (59:17; cf. 64:7–9). The concatenation of imprecation and joyful praise is also seen in Psalm 68:2–4: "May you blow them away like smoke. . . . But may the righteous be glad and rejoice before God. . . . Sing to God, sing in praise of his name, extol him who rides on the clouds."

Similarly, Psalm 69:27–30 states:

> Charge them with crime upon crime;
> do not let them share in your salvation.
> May they be blotted out of the book of life
> and not be listed with the righteous.
> But as for me, afflicted and in pain—
> may your salvation, God, protect me.
> I will praise God's name in song
> and glorify him with thanksgiving.

Salvation comes through the destruction of the enemy and causes the powerless suppliants to give praise for God's deliverance and the display of divine justice (70:2–4). Psalm 64 describes the destruction of the enemy/wicked as something God will do in the natural course of the future (64:7–8). As a result of the divine actions to ruin the enemy, praise emerges: "they will proclaim the works of God" and "the righteous will rejoice in the Lord" (64:9–10).

Psalm 71 also links petition/lament, imprecation, and praise (vv. 9–14). The editors drew book 2 to a close with the lament not to be cast "away when I am old . . . be not far from me, my God" (cf. 42:3, 9). This is followed by an imprecation, "May my accusers perish in shame," which is then juxtaposed by a vow to praise: "I will always have hope; I will praise you more and more. My mouth will tell of your righteous deeds of your saving acts all day long" (71:14–15; cf. 71:18). The hope to praise in Psalm 71 provides a book-closing *inclusio* with the opening Psalm-pair refrain (42:5, 11; 43:5). The psalmist concludes his psalm with a vow to praise rooted in the demise called for in the imprecation (71:13, 24). Other psalms also relate imprecation as a motive for praise (59:11–13; cf. 64:7–9; 63:7–11; 68:14–23). Indeed, at times, imprecation is part of praise itself (55:22, 23).

The point of this section is not to explore all aspects of this imprecation/praise connection, but merely to raise it as an area for further exploration. Rather than rising up and taking vengeance against the enemy into their own hands, the helpless and poor have committed it to the divine King who rules and executes justice. For this deliverance the divine King is to be praised. There is no smug triumphalism here but rather gratefulness for God's deliverance and justice executed on the wicked resulting in the psalmists' praise of his mighty acts of rescue and salvation.

Lament/petition and imprecation thus play integral roles in the praise of God. Praise is thereby connected to struggles in real life. The downplaying of lament and the virtual banning of imprecation in the modern church reduces the praise of God to declarations of his attributes, but rarely includes his acts of deliverance against evildoers. Erich Zenger, in his excellent study, suggests that the church needs to change its worship praxis to include imprecational cries for justice. Zenger concludes,

> The psalms of enmity offer us neither a dogmatic doctrine of God nor a summary of biblical ethics. These are poetic prayers that hold up a mirror to the perpetrators of violence, and they are prayers that can help the victims of violence, by placing on their lips a cry for justice and for the God of vengeance, to hold fast to their human dignity and to endure nonviolently, in prayerful protest against a violence that is repugnant to God, despite their fear in the face of their enemies and the images of enmity. The transfer of vengeance to God that is indicated in the psalms implies renouncing one's own revenge.[7]

Elsewhere he points to the redemptive and corrective nature of judgment on the "hubris of the violent."[8]

SIGNIFICANCE OF BOOK 2 FOR BIBLICAL WORSHIP

In book 2 (42–72) of the Psalter, worship was "noisy" and "loud" as worshipers shouted, rejoiced, sang, and engaged in movement with musical instruments and clapping hands. In short, animated worshipers expressed their exuberance for exalting God. The psalmists often offered an imperatival "call to praise" followed by a "cause of praise" that might well turn out to be praise itself. The praise reflected God's amazing acts of old as well as his current acts of deliverance that the psalmist had personally experienced. Praise blends the already with the right now. Biblical illiteracy may render contemporary worshipers ignorant of the mighty works of God described in the Scriptures, thereby hampering the historical depth of faith in their expressions of praise. Thus solid biblical teaching of God's mighty acts as described in Scripture is desperately needed in our community in order to support a robust sense of worship of our God who was engaged blending their history with ours.

The place of praise also seems to be very significant to the psalmists. They longed to go to the sanctuary/temple in Zion, the city of the great King, to join the congregation offering praise before God who rules the

---

7. Erich Zenger, *A God of Vengeance? Understanding the Psalms of Divine Wrath* (Louisville: Westminster John Knox, 1996), 92. See also from a more apologetic stance John N. Day, *Crying for Justice: What the Psalms Teach Us about Mercy and Vengeance in an Age of Terrorism* (Grand Rapids: Kregel, 2005). See also Chalmer Martin, "The Imprecations in the Psalms," *Princeton Theological Review* 1, no. 4 (1903): 537–53.
8. Zenger, *God of Vengeance?*, 66–67.

earth from heaven. How place is religiously engaged in postmodern virtual worlds has yet to be fully explored and understood.

It has been demonstrated that praise often has its roots in the depths of lament. The psalmist cries out to the great King for deliverance from the treacherous enemy and vows to praise God for his salvation. This expression of lament needs fuller expression in contemporary corporate and personal worship. This was seen on our campus when the "Catacombs" service was rebranded for a night: "Lamentacombs" followed by this invitation from Dr. Nick Rowe to our students: "Tonight we will be providing a space for anyone who is in the midst of uncomfortable and troubling times. We invite you to lament in the presence of God . . . come out and join us all to rejoice and hope again in him as we ask that his kingdom come, his will be done, here." With over one hundred thousand Christians being displaced from Mosel, Iraq, and many churches burned in Egypt and executions of Christians in Syria, lament is still of global importance to the Christian community. In Western culture, the lament caused by social isolation, family disintegration, bitter attempts to silence any type of religious expression from the public arena, and the demonization of anything designated as "Christian" leave many in a position of needing models of lament and cries for deliverance manifested in these psalms. Such cries need the hope of God's deliverance that will ultimately lead to a deepening sense of praise and thankfulness. Such lament plucks the bass strings of the heart and engages the deepest expressions of praise from worshipers (e.g., the hymn "It is Well with My Soul"). As Timothy Pierce, in his book *Enthroned on Our Praise: An Old Testament Theology of Worship*, has noted, worship and life must not be separated.[9] It is often through lament that praise and life are welded together.

It has also been demonstrated that the psalmists often wished to see the victory of God over the enemy, and that destruction of the enemy was often verbalized as something God had already done or that they were convinced the great King would do. In the imprecations, the psalmists called on God to unleash his justice and righteousness against the wicked on behalf of the vulnerable. This victory over the wicked was then woven into praise. A praise rooted in lament and arising out of imprecation against the enemy has largely been left unexpressed in the current ecclesiological worship contexts.

Finally, an underlying passion for God is what is desperately needed in an organized-for-success church obsessed with the latest leadership techniques. Without the explicit use of the word "praise," this passion for God is extolled in the opening verses of book 2. It is expressed by the psalmists in their thirst for God—thrice expressed in the refrain of hope that they would yet praise their Savior and God (42:5, 11; 43:5). Such pas-

9. Timothy M. Pierce, *Enthroned on Our Praise: An Old Testament Theology of Worship* (Nashville: B&H, 2008), 239.

sion is a necessary foundation of all expressions of praise. The flame of this passion must be fanned in contemporary corporate worship.

> As a deer pants for streams of water,
> So my soul pants for you, my God. . . .
> Put your hope in God,
> for I will yet praise him,
> my Savior and my God. (Ps. 42:1, 5, 11)[10]

BIBLIOGRAPHY

Day, John N. *Crying for Justice: What the Psalms Teach Us about Mercy and Vengeance in an Age of Terrorism*. Grand Rapids: Kregel, 2005.

Eaton, J. H. *Kingship and the Psalms.* London: SCM-Canterbury Press, 1976.

Gerstenberger, Erhard. *Psalms, Part 1: With an Introduction to Cultic Poetry.* FOTL 14. Grand Rapids: Eerdmans, 1988.

Grant, James. *The King as Exemplar: The Function of Deuteronomy's Kingship Law in the Shaping of the Book of Psalms.* Williston, VT: Academia Biblica, 2004.

Kraus, Hans. *Theology of the Psalms*. Minneapolis: Fortress, 1992.

Kuntz, J. Kenneth. "Grounds for Praise: The Nature and Function of the Motive Clause in the Hymns of the Hebrew Psalter." In *Worship and the Hebrew Bible: Essays in Honor of John T. Willis*, edited by M. Patrick Graham, Rick R. Marrs, and Steven L. McKenzie, 148–83. JSOTSup 284. Sheffield: Sheffield Academic, 1999.

Martin, Chalmers. "The Imprecations in the Psalms." *Princeton Theological Review* 1, no. 4 (1903): 537–53.

Mays, James L. *The Lord Reigns: A Theological Handbook to the Psalms.* Louisville: Westminster John Knox, 1994.

McCann, J. Clinton, Jr. *A Theological Introduction to the Book of Psalms.* Nashville: Abingdon, 1993.

Miller, Patrick D. *They Cried to the Lord: The Form and Theology of Biblical Prayer*. Minneapolis: Fortress, 1994.

Pierce, Timothy M. *Enthroned on Our Praise: An Old Testament Theology of Worship*. Nashville: B&H, 2008.

Sabourin, Leopold. *The Psalms: Their Origin and Meaning*. Staten Island: Alba House, 1969.

Tozer, A. W. *The Pursuit of God*. Abbotsford, WI: Aneko Press, 2015.

Westermann, Claus. *Praise and Lament in the Psalms.* Richmond, VA: John Knox, 1981.

Zenger, Erich. *A God of Vengeance? Understanding the Psalms of Divine Wrath.* Louisville: Westminster John Knox, 1996.

10. A. W. Tozer, *The Pursuit of God* (Abbotsford, WI: Aneko Press, 2015), passim.

CHAPTER 12

WORSHIP AS COVENANTAL DIALOGUE

Worship in Book 3 (73–89) of the Psalter

Dickson Ngama

THEOLOGY OF WORSHIP

A theology of worship in book 3 of the Psalter (73–89) involves asking what this specific portion of Scripture teaches about worship. Such a pursuit will be aided by additional questions such as: What kinds of psalms make up book 3? Who is God to the psalmists? What has God done for the psalmists? Why should the psalmists worship him? What has all this to do with the church? Answers to these questions will illuminate what Scripture is teaching about worship and thus how we are to worship in light of this segment of the Psalter. As we explore, we will find that God and Israel are in a covenantal relationship, and this portion of the Psalter builds off this relationship. In this relationship, there are expectations of how each partner is to behave. When Israel experiences the blessings of the covenant, they thank and praise God. When they experience adversity, they lament and question God. In some psalms, God also laments the behavior of Israel. God's laments recall the history of Israel and the speeches of the prophets. In the psalms we mostly hear Israel's side of the covenant dialogue. We are therefore invited to read Old Testament narratives and listen to the prophets in order to hear God's side of the covenant dialogue. Worship in Israel turns out to be a covenantal dialogue.

Philip S. Johnston has compiled an index of form-critical categorizations for all the Psalms. From Johnson's categories, we can say the following about Psalms 73–89:

> 73 (Wisdom Psalm); 74 (Lament of Community); 75 (Prophetic Psalm, Thanksgiving of the Community); 76 (Hymn of Zion); 77 (Lament of Individual or Community); 78 (Historical Psalm, Wisdom Psalm, or Hymn); 79 (Lament of the Community); 80 (Lament of the Community); 81 (Prophetic Psalm, Covenant Renewal Psalm, or Hymn); 82 (Lament of the Community, Hymn, or Prophetic Psalm); 83 (Lament of the Community); 84 (Hymn of Zion, Confidence Psalm of the Individual, or Pilgrim Psalm); 85 (Lament of the Community, Prophetic Psalm); 86 (Lament of the Individual); 87 (Hymn of Zion); 88 (Lament of the Individual); 89 (Royal Psalm, Lament of the Community).[1]

If we define worship only as praise and thanksgiving, we will end up excluding some of these psalms, and much of the entire Psalter. However, if we consider them all as psalms of worship, we will have to use a more inclusive definition of worship. Instinctively, we identify worship with thanksgiving and hymns of praise. Indeed, the Psalter is considered the hymnbook of Israel: The book of Psalms is the "'book of praises' *par excellence*," since "the psalmists turn their thoughts away from themselves and on to the object of supreme delight—the creator God, Israel's redeemer, Yahweh himself. This close correlation between theology and doxology emerges at every turn in the Psalter."[2] With regard to praise in the Psalter, James Hutchinson offers the following ten propositions:

> (1) Use of the key verb *hll* highlights the fact that praise in the Psalter is ascribed supremely to Yahweh and that he is worthy to receive it; (2) the activity of praising in the Psalter is essentially vocal; (3) the most appropriate locus of praise is a congregational setting, praise being typically conducted simultaneously on both horizontal and vertical axes; (4) praise in the Psalter is both descriptive of Yahweh's character and deeds, and declarative of his particular acts of deliverance; (5) praise has an emotional dimension; (6) praise is frequently the fruit of a transformation in outlook which the psalmist embraces in the midst of crisis or difficulty; (7) praise is considered to be a corollary of the believer's very existence; (8) praise in the Psalter arises particularly from a circumstance-defying belief that Yahweh's covenant promises will come to realization—through the arrival of the Davidic king; (9) the polemic of praise consists in the overthrow of Yahweh's rivals; (10) the Psalter insists on marrying exuberant praise not only with obedience but also with fearful trembling.[3]

These principles are reflected in Psalms 73–89 to some extent:

1. Philip S. Johnson, "Appendix 1: Index of Form-Critical Categorizations," in *Interpreting the Psalms: Issues and Approaches*, eds. David Firth and Philip S. Johnston (Downers Grove, IL: IVP Academic, 2005), 295–300, especially 298. This list is made partially with reference to the works of Gunkel (1933), Sabourin (1974), Seybold (1990), Day (1990), Bellinger (1990), Gilligham (1994), and Lucas (2003).
2. James Hely Hutchinson, "The Psalms and Praise," in Firth and Johnston, *Interpreting the Psalms*, 85.
3. Hutchinson, "The Psalms and Praise," 86–99.

1. Key verb of praise (*hll*, 74:21; 84:4)
2. Vocal praise (75:1, 9; 76:4, 7–9; 77:13–20; 81:1–3; 84:1–2; 89:1)
3. Congregational setting (75:1; 76:11; 79:13; 81:1–4; 87:7)
4. Descriptive praise (73:1; 74:12; 75:1, 7; 76:4, 7, 12; 77:10–15; 78:35, 38, 41, 56; 81:1; 84:1; 86:5, 8, 10, 13, 15; 89:1, 5–9, 13–14)
5. Declarative praise (74:13–17; 75:2–3, 8; 76:3, 5–6, 8–9; 77:16–20; 78:11–16, 23–28, 42–55, 56–71; 80:8–11; 83:9–12; 89:10–12)
6. Emotional praise (81:1; 84:1–2)
7. Transformation in crisis (73:16–17; 77:10–13; 85:12)
8. Praise and existence (73:23–26, 28; 78:33–37; 79:11–13; 80:17–18; 84:5–7)
9. Covenant hope (74:20; 77:8; 89:1–4)
10. Overthrow of enemies (73:18–20, 27; 74:10, 18, 22–23; 75:8–10; 76:4–6; 78:42–43, 51, 66; 79:6–7, 12; 81:14–15; 83:1–18; 89:22–23, 49–51)
11. Praise, exuberance, obedience, and trembling (76:7–9, 11–12; 81:14–15).

The one category that our instincts would reject as part of worship is the lament, either of the individual or of the community. Clearly, among Psalms 73–89, the lament of the community is predominant. When God failed to do what the Israelites expected him to do, they turned from praise to lament. In laments they urged him to do what he had done before or what he had promised to do. Israel did not dwell much on God in the abstract. They focused on who God was in relation to them and especially what he did or did not do, given who he was and who they were in relation to him. Philip Johnson has traced the theme of distress in the Psalter as a major cause of lament. Distress was found in personal and communal suffering. It was caused by oppressive enemies, nature and death, God, or the self due to sin. The psalmist petitioned God, who usually responded but not always immediately. When God responded, the psalmist gave thanks and praised God.[4] In their distress, Israelites cried to God for help. They

4. Philip S. Johnston, "The Psalms and Distress," in Firth and Johnston, *Interpreting the Psalms*, 63–84.

justified their prayer by an appeal to their relationship with God. God was the master, and Israel was his servant.[5] From the history of Israel as recorded in Old Testament narratives, we learn of the various distressful situations that led to all kind of prayers and laments.[6]

Since generally in worship Israel remembered the past (God's deeds) and anticipated the future (God's vision and promise), how much of this was going on in Psalms 73–89? We hear the psalmists recalling God's acts in Israel's history and lamenting the present situation of the individual or the community. Where is hope for the future? What do the psalmists anticipate? A new David? The direct reign of God? The overthrow of personal and national enemies? The psalmists give God praise for what he has done yet seem to scold him for falling asleep on the job or for remaining angry too long. They are aware of the scoffing and mockery of the enemies of Israel and of God and do not think it is good for God's reputation. So they urge God to wake up and turn his anger against the foe. But we also hear God remembering how he has been faithful to Israel yet Israel has forgotten and been rebellious. Sometimes God had given Israel over to her desires and she has reaped the consequences. Sometimes God has directly punished Israel in his anger. Yet he always ends up showing mercy, for he remembers how weak and ephemeral Israel is. We therefore have a cycle of rescue, forgetting, idolatry, wrath, destruction, remembrance, repentance, mercy, and rescue, only for that cycle to be repeated. It is like a repetition of the conditions in the book of Judges. In the book of Judges they could say they did not have a king (centralized government and worship). But did things get better with kings and temple? Maybe they did in the time of David. Solomon was not too bad, but he was no David. After that everything went downhill until all of Israel went into exile. In exile they remembered God and reminded God of his covenant with David. Certainly, the promise of the Davidic dynasty lasting forever was in question at the time of the exile. But there was hope of restoration, if the past was as they remembered it and if the promises were true. God would reign again! Zion would be reestablished and the temple rebuilt. A new David would arise.

5. "The theological setting-in-life in which all prayers for help can be read is the relation of an *'ebed* [servant] to an *'adon* [lord]. It is more important in accounting for their formation and use than particular personal situations and cultic institutions. . . . It furnishes the common identity that goes with the use of the prayers" (James L. Mays, *The Lord Reigns: A Theological Handbook to the Psalms* [Louisville: Westminster John Knox, 1994], 26–27, cited in Johnston, "The Psalms and Distress," 84).

6. "These stories thus offer us clues for understanding the laments by suggesting the kinds of opposition to which the laments allude and giving us some indication of the sorts of contexts that would have been in mind or appropriate for those psalms that cry out against the taunters of the Lord and the people" (Patrick D. Miller, *Interpreting the Psalms* [Philadelphia: Fortress, 1986], 55, cited in Johnston, "The Psalms and Distress," 75).

The Revelation of YHWH in 73–89

Psalm 73 begins with an affirmation of the goodness of God. Yet it is not goodness in abstract but as directed toward Israel: "Truly God is good to Israel, to those who are pure in heart" (73:1 ESV). The psalmist confesses that God is his strength, portion, and refuge (73:26, 28). Again we see that these attributes of God are relational. This psalmist praises God because God relates to him as the one who strengthens, protects, and provides for him. This God is his God. In Psalm 74:12, God is identified as "my king from of old" (NASB). Psalm 75:1 gives a reason for thanking God: "We give thanks to You, God; we give thanks to You, for Your name is near" (HCSB). This God is the God of Jacob, and he is the Judge (75:7, 9). God is famous in Judah (76:1). He is "radiant with light, more majestic than mountains rich with game" (76:4 NIV). In Psalm 77, God is also known as the Lord (77:2, 7, 11) and the Most High (77:10). This God is greater than any other god (77:13). Psalm 78 calls God "the Most High God" (78:35, 56), Israel's "rock" and "redeemer" (78:35), "compassionate" (78:38), "Holy One of Israel" (78:41), "the Lord" (77:65 NASB). Psalm 79 calls God "Lord" (79:5, 12) and the "God of our salvation" (79:9 NRSV). Psalm 80 recognizes God as the "Shepherd of Israel" (80:1 ESV) and the "Lord God of hosts (80:4, 19 ESV) or simply "God of hosts" (80:7, 14 ESV). Psalm 81 opens with a call to sing "to God our strength" and "to the God of Jacob" (81:1 NASB). He is again called "the God of Jacob" (81:4), and he identifies himself as "I the Lord am your God" (81:10 NASB). In Psalm 82 God addresses the gods (82:1) and call them "sons of the Most High" (82:6 NIV). In this psalm, God is presented as president and judge of the divine assembly (82:1, 8). Psalm 83 appeals to God as "God," "my God," "Lord" (83:1, 13, 16), and the "Most High over all the earth" (83:18 NKJV). In Psalm 84, God is regularly addressed as "Lord of hosts" (84:1, 3, 8, 12). He is also the Lord, the living God (84:2), my king (84:3), my God (84:3, 10), God of Gods (84:7), and God of Jacob (84:8). He is described as "the Lord God" who is "a sun and shield" (84:11 NRSV). In this psalm, the psalmist comes to the temple and revels in the name of his God. Psalm 85 mostly calls God "Lord" (vv. 1, 7, 8, 12). God is also addressed as the "God of our salvation" (85:4 ESV). In Psalm 86, the psalmist constantly cries "O Lord" (vv. 1, 3, 4, 5, 6, 8, 9, 10, 12, 15, 17 NASB). He also calls God "my God" (86:12). In this psalm we have classical descriptions of God. God is good, forgiving, kind (86:5), incomparable (86:8), and great and unique (86:10). He is "a God merciful and gracious, Slow to anger and abundant in lovingkindness and truth" (86:15 NASB). Psalm 87, which praises Zion, calls God "the Lord" (vv. 2, 6) and "the Most High" (v. 5 NIV). Psalm 88, the least hopeful of all laments, addresses God as "Lord" (vv. 1, 9, 13, 14) and "the God of my salvation" (v. 1 NASB). Psalm 89 calls God "Lord" quite often (vv. 1, 5, 6, 8, 15, 18, 46, 50, 51, 52 NRSV). He is also known as a God of "steadfast love" (vv. 1, 2, 14, 24, 28, 33, 49) and "faithfulness" (vv. 1, 2, 5, 8, 14, 24, 33, 49). The psalmist asks in 89:6–8 (NRSV):

> For who in the skies can be compared to the LORD?
> Who among the heavenly beings is like the LORD,
> a God feared in the council of the holy ones,
> great and awesome above all that are around him?
> O LORD God of hosts,
> who is as mighty as you, O LORD?
> Your faithfulness surrounds you.

To God are ascribed strength, righteousness, and justice (89:13–14). We see then that Psalms 73–89 have a rich language for the worship of God in terms of his attributes. God is worthy of worship just for who he is.

YHWH's Worthiness for Worship in Psalms 73–89

The psalmists spend more time describing or referring to God's activities than describing or referring to his attributes in the abstract. In this section, I will summarize those activities. The historical setting of Psalms 73–89 is disputed. Perhaps we should agree with Beth Tanner, who says the following: "Book Three represents every time when the world and its violence make no sense, times when we do not understand why God does not simply fix it." She calls this section of the Psalter "a poetic rendering of theodicy" whose "themes fit as well today as they did in its ancient context."[7] We will let a historical psalm and a wisdom psalm set the stage. This will be followed by hymns of Zion because they inform us of the ideal place of encounter between God and Israel. We will then look at prophetic psalms that enable us to hear what God said to the Israelites when they came to worship. Finally, we will listen to the worshipers as they relate their painful experiences as individuals or as a community before God.

Historical and wisdom psalms: Worshiping YHWH for his faithful and just actions

Psalm 78 (historical psalm, wisdom psalm, or hymn)

The psalmist is a teacher who recalls the mighty deeds of God on Israel's behalf but also reminds his students of Israel's constant forgetfulness, rebellion, and idolatry, which resulted in God's wrathful rejection of Israel. God's mighty deeds are seen in his deliverance from Egypt, provision of water, bread and meat in the wilderness, establishment of a covenant with its stipulations, conquest of the land, deliverances in the land before there was a king, and the choice of David as their monarch. This psalm is a brief summary of the history of Israel from the time of bondage in Egypt to the time of freedom under David in Jerusalem (Exodus–2 Samuel). The amazing patience of God is displayed in this psalm. It is a wonder that

7. Nancy deClaissé-Walford, Rolf A. Jacobson, and Beth LaNeel Tanner, *The Book of Psalms*, NICOT (Grand Rapids: Eerdmans, 2014), 583.

God did not destroy Israel for her forgetfulness and rebellion. The actions of God (78:33, 38–39, 42–55, 59–64, 65–72) and those of Israel (78:32, 34–37, 40–41, 56–58) are continually contrasted.[8] By recalling the deeds of Israel and of God, Israel celebrated the fact that God was faithful despite Israel's unfaithfulness.

Psalm 73 (wisdom psalm)

The psalmist laments that the wicked prosper (73:1–16) but receives revelation in the sanctuary about their eventual demise (73:17). In the sanctuary, the psalmist discerns that God has set the wicked up for failure and destruction. God has also strengthened the righteous and kept him from falling (73:18–28). The themes of this psalm are similar to those in Psalm 37 and the book of Job, except that "here the conclusion is far more lofty, for the contrast is between injustice in this world and the future glory of the righteous."[9] We see that God deals justly with the righteous and the wicked. Sometimes the individual worshiper is overwhelmed by present injustice, but when the worshiper joins others at the sanctuary, he or she is reminded of God's goodness. God has given Israel a place of worship for that purpose.

Hymns of Zion: Worshiping YHWH in his holy city

Psalm 84 (hymn of Zion, confidence psalm of the individual, or pilgrim psalm)

The psalmist longs to be in God's house, admires the birds that nest in the temple, and the pilgrims who make the journey to Zion, for prayer is heard there, and those who journey there to pray are strengthened, protected, and blessed. Those who seek favor, honor, or anything good will find it in the house of God—namely, the temple courts in Zion. The idea is that God generously dispenses good gifts at his temple to those who make pilgrimage. Therefore there is heightened expectation as the pilgrims move "from outside to inside; from the countryside to Jerusalem and to the temple; from ordinary to extraordinary; from daily concerns to sacred space."[10] You never know what blessings await you in God's house.

Psalm 76 (hymn of Zion)

The God of Israel, who reigns and judges in Zion, is to be feared and worshiped because he destroys warriors by his rebuke. Armies may busy themselves with their various weapons and strategies of war, but God has only to

8. C. Hassell Bullock, *Psalms*, vol. 2, *Psalms 72–150*, Teach the Text Commentary Series (Grand Rapids: Baker Books, 2017), 43–44.
9. Allen P. Ross, *A Commentary on the Psalms*, vol. 2, *(49–89)*, Kregel Exegetical Library (Grand Rapids: Kregel, 2013), 552.
10. Beth LaNeel Tanner, "Book Three of the Psalter: Psalms 73–89," in deClaissé-Walford, Jacobson, and Tanner, *The Book of Psalms*, NICOT653.

appear in his glory and issue a rebuke in his anger to destroy all of them. God is a warrior. In the past he demonstrated this in Zion. "No-one can resist God when he appears to judge his enemies (the psalmist continues to share themes with Nahum's opening poem). He exercises his wrath as Warrior in defense of the afflicted (the people of Israel), and thus they praise him, while those who survive his judgments are restrained in their evil."[11] The God who fights in and for Israel will be feared by all the kings of the earth.

Psalm 87 (hymn of Zion)

The psalmist celebrates God's love for Zion above the rest of Israel and other nations. God built Zion as his habitation, and that made Zion special. Zion is so special that people from everywhere wish to be registered there as citizens. The nations mentioned surrounded Israel from every direction. Egypt was in the southwest, Babylon in the southeast, Philistia to the west, Tyre to the north, and Cush to the south. Zion is in the center as a source of spiritual refreshment and spiritual citizenship.[12]

Prophetic psalms: Worshiping YHWH because of what he has done and will do

Psalm 75 (prophetic psalm, thanksgiving of the community)

The psalmist celebrates God's past deeds and his present role as the judge who promotes the righteous and demotes the wicked. Man has nothing to boast of, for cosmic stability, justice on earth, promotion, and demotion for humans come from the Lord. The wonderful deeds of the Lord are creation and judgment. As surely as God created and stabilizes the earth, he will judge the world. The wicked will drink the "cup of divine wrath (cf. Isa 51:17; Jer 25:15; Ezek 23:23). The guilty will be forced to drink of it."[13] The deeds of the Lord are both past and future.

Psalm 81 (prophetic psalm, covenant renewal psalm, or hymn)

The psalmist calls on the Israelites to praise God with music as they celebrate the fact that God rescued them from Egypt and remember that rebellion against him limits his ability to continue to rescue and to bless them. God is ever ready to protect the Israelites and to bless them, but that is conditioned on their obedience and dependence on him. The choice is between trusting God to provide and fight for them or going their own way and experiencing unnecessary hardships. God has rescued Israel in

11. Tremper Longman III, *Psalms*, Tyndale Old Testament Commentaries (Downers Grove, IL: IVP Academic, 2014), 285. See Nahum's opening poem, in which the Lord is portrayed as jealous, avenging, and furious, indignant, and angry (Nah. 1:1–6).
12. Bullock, *Psalms*, 114–15.
13. Dianne Bergant, *Psalm 73–150*, New Collegeville Bible Commentary (Collegeville, MN: Liturgical Press, 2013), 20.

the past, and he is ever ready to do it again. But will Israel listen to and obey him? This psalm looks back to the history recorded in Exodus 1–6 (Egyptian bondage) and Exodus 17:1–7 (the testing at the waters of Meribah). The assumption is that the worshipers are acquainted with their history.[14] In the very moment of praising God with jubilation, Israel reminds herself of her shortcomings and of God's disappointment with her.

Psalms of lament: Worshiping YHWH in the reality of life

Psalm 86 (lament of the individual)

The psalmist prays for God's help, grace, and salvation from ruthless enemies, and reminds God of his uniqueness, greatness, wonderful deeds, mercy, love, and faithfulness, which will enable him to fear, thank, and glorify God and walk in truth. The psalmist expresses his confidence in God's ability to answer prayer and to vindicate the innocent against his enemies. For him, who God is assures him of what God will do for him. The attributes of God are a basis for the activities of God, and that is why he fears and revels in the name of God. Knowing who God is, he asks him to listen, answer, preserve, save, be gracious, gladden, teach, unite the heart, turn, be gracious, strengthen, and give a sign (89:1, 2, 3, 4, 11, 16, 17). Even though the psalmist has confidence in God's character and in what God can do, he nevertheless asks for a sign of God's goodness. "Praying with confidence is not weakened by the desire for a sign, because the sign will more than likely be the beginning of the answer to his prayer. And once that begins, the wicked will be put to shame for their malicious ways."[15] The psalmist has one eye on God and another on his enemies, and some demonstration of God's help and compassion is what is needed.

Psalm 77 (lament of individual or community)

In the present the psalmist questions whether God has forgotten to be merciful, but he encourages himself by remembering God's former faithful deliverance, especially in the exodus from Egypt. The psalmist dramatically recalls the way God came down to lead his people out of Egypt and across the sea. He personalizes the water, which saw God and trembled, and he turns lightning and thunder into God's weapons. "The poetry is a dramatic characterization of the way in which the storm God caused the earth to tremble (vv. 16–18), divided the waters of the sea to permit an exit to freedom (v. 19), and authorized Moses and Aaron to lead God's people into the wilderness (v. 20)."[16] Walter Brueggemann and William Bellinger

---

14. Erhard S. Gerstenberger, *Psalms, Part 2, and Lamentations*, FOTL 15 (Grand Rapids: Eerdmans, 2001), 109.
15. Ross, *(49–89)*, 787.
16. Walter Brueggemann and William H. Bellinger Jr., *Psalms*, New Cambridge Commentary (New York: Cambridge University Press, 2014), 334.

notice the disparity between the lament in verses 1–10 and the memory of God's deeds in verses 11–20. The transition is in verses 11–13 (NKJV):

> I will remember the works of the LORD;
> Surely I will remember Your wonders of old.
> I will also meditate on all Your work,
> And talk of Your deeds.
> Your way, O God, is in the sanctuary;
> Who is so great a God as our God?

As in Psalm 73:17, worship in the sanctuary (77:13) changes everything. It is in communal worship and in the presence of God that the individual is reoriented.

Psalm 88 (lament of the individual)

The psalmist continually cries in desperation to the God whose anger has brought him close to death, far from his friends. The psalmist sees himself as God-forsaken. But worse, he accuses God of isolating him, placing him in a dark pit, and forgetting him there. God is not just passively ignoring him but actively terrorizing him. For the psalmist, the inactivity of God is interpreted as a negative activity. Since God is a saving God, absence of deliverance or divine silence are seen as expressions of divine wrath. This psalm is different from other psalms because it receives no resolution:

> In many other psalms discussed herein, we have seen that the laments and complaints are almost always answered; the several prayers of Israel characteristically end in satisfied resolution expressed as praise and thanks. But not here! Here prayer goes unanswered, even though the prayer is Israel's voice of urgent need, despite crisis, and passionate address to YHWH. The prayer is unanswered—YHWH never speaks or appears. The speaker receives no signal of engagement or concern on the part of the deity.[17]

This psalm teaches us to be honest in prayer and not to think of God as one who automatically answers when we call. At times there is nothing to do but wait patiently even as we make impatient demands. This requires an act of faith.[18]

Psalm 74 (lament of community)

The psalmist laments the destruction of Jerusalem, reminds God of his former deeds, and urges him to defend his cause by putting enemies/scoffers to shame. Since God had demonstrated his power in creation and in redemption (from Egypt), the present defeat of Israel must be attributed

17. Brueggemann and Bellinger, *Psalms*, 378.
18. Brueggemann and Bellinger, *Psalms*, 381–82.

to his inactivity. His inactivity is equated to his having forgotten the terms of the covenant with Israel. The deeds of God are recalled in 74:12–17. God is the Creator who calmed the sea, or more dramatically, who slew Leviathan. This drama is a poetic rendering of the creation account in which God created land and sea, day and night, summer and winter. In this section there is an obvious emphasis on God in the second person singular (you). Here we perceive "an exceptional undertone of loving intent in the alternation of the creative acts, different from but similar to an ultimate connection in the making of a livable universe and the working out of salvation (v. 12)."[19] The God who created and sustains the universe is called on to act again in history. This time to deliver Israel whose capital city Jerusalem and the temple have been devastated. The deliverance of Israel and the restoration of Jerusalem is a matter of honor for God since he is in covenant with Israel. If Israel is reviled, God is reviled.

Psalm 79 (lament of the community)

The psalmist laments the destruction of Jerusalem, the resulting mockery by surrounding nations, and asks God to turn his wrath from Israel and direct it toward their enemies with the result that Israel will thank and praise God forever. That Jerusalem has been devastated by the enemy is seen as a sign of God's displeasure with Israel. But the destruction of Jerusalem had led the enemy to mock God and surely God must respond to that by turning his wrath from Israel to the enemy. The anguished description of the destruction and resulting mockery are means of arousing God to further action. The psalmist is convinced that God is active in history. Israel's defeat by her enemies is evidence. But that same activity—namely, the expression of divine wrath—should now be turned against the enemies of Israel. "The psalm, with its appeal to divine wrath, cries for God's justice as the guaranteeing force of a world order and as a court of justice especially for the victims—and does not, as may appear at first sight, call for irrational vengeance."[20]

Psalm 80 (lament of the community)

The psalmist asks God to restore Israel by reminding him that he is the one who rescued Israel from Egypt, planted her as a vine, and now he is so quiet while the neighbors trample on his vine and continue to mock Israel. God was active in the past, but now he is passively angry, which amounts to actively giving up his people to be ravaged by their hostile neighbors. God is the shepherd of Israel and the farmer who owns Israel the vine.

---

19. Samuel Terrien, *The Psalms: Strophic and Theological Commentary*, ECC (Grand Rapids: Eerdmans, 2003.

20. John Goldingay, *Psalms*, vol. 2, *Psalm 42–89*, BCOTWP (Grand Rapids: Baker Academic, 2006), 529, citing Frank Lothar Hossfeld and Erich Zenger, *Psalms*, vol. 2, *A Commentary on Psalms 51–100*, ed. Klaus Baltzer, trans. Linda M. Maloney, Hermeneia (Minneapolis: Fortress, 2005), 307.

Israel expects protection and care from God, but she has experienced divine neglect. She is confident, however, that all God has to do is shine his face on her and she will be restored (80:3, 7, 19). Israel admits that God has the initiative for her deliverance: "This is a much repeated prayer for a renewed devotion to God, a restored loyalty to God, and a rekindled passion for God. God himself must so work in their hearts."[21]

Psalm 82 (lament of the community, hymn, or prophetic psalm)

The psalmist tells of how God presides in the heavenly assembly, rebukes the gods for their failure to rule justly, and threatens them with mortality. The psalmist urges God to judge the earth and inherit the nations. The gods were assigned nations to rule on God's behalf, and especially to care for weak, fatherless, poor and oppressed people. But they failed in their responsibility, and therefore God has to rule and judge by himself. In this mockery of the gods, Israel shows that God is in no need of assistance to care for his inheritance, the nations. But are the gods to be treated as real? Geoffrey Grogan considers four possibilities: (1) For the sake of argument they are treated as real only for their reality to be rejected; (2) maybe the are angelic beings, but angels do not die; (3) maybe they are human judges, and they are honored like gods; (4) maybe the assembly is Israel with a focus on the leaders of Israel. Grogan opts for the fourth option as the most biblical.[22] The lesson is that God is the ultimate judge, but he delegates judgment to others who often fail to be just.

Psalm 83 (lament of the community)

The psalmist reminds God that there is a grand conspiracy to destroy Israel by those who hate God, and therefore God should arise and destroy them so that they may seek him or perish forever, which will result in their acknowledging that God is supreme over the earth. God has a past record of destroying the enemies of Israel, and he is urged to do it again. In the past the enemies wanted to disinherit God. Now the enemies wish to annihilate Israel as a nation. Since the nation of Israel is God's pastureland, the present coalition deserves the same fate as the past enemies of Israel. Tremper Longman responds to those who "feel uncomfortable with the psalm because it expresses a desire to destroy the enemy." He reminds us that "the imprecations are a way of turning our anger over to God. After all, the psalmist is not asking God for resources to do it on his own, but rather petitioning God, who can decide himself how he should act."[23] The only way Israel could avoid vengeance was to transfer it to God, who avenges.

---

21. Steven J. Lawson, *Psalms 76–150*, Holman Old Testament Commentary (Nashville: Holman Reference, 2006).
22. Geoffrey W. Grogan, *Psalms*, Two Horizons Old Testament Commentary (Grand Rapids: Eerdmans, 2008), 146–47.
23. Longman, *Psalms*, 310.

Psalm 85 (lament of the community, prophetic psalm)

The psalmist asks God to stop being angry and to forgive and restore Israel as in the past so that his people may hear him speak peace and salvation, while they resist folly and become faithful, with the result that righteousness from above will encounter faithfulness from below. The psalmist recalls former national restoration, and that gives him hope for future restoration. "If people are committed to Yahweh and hold Yahweh in awe, as opposed to turning to folly (that is becoming committed to other deities), then surely Yahweh will undertake the deliverance that the people need in the first instance, restore his honor to the land, and then make it possible for them to experience well-being."[24] The psalmist looks for harmony between God and Israel with resulting prosperity in the land.

Psalm 89 (royal psalm, lament of the community)

The psalmist begins by praising God's faithfulness to David and the Davidic covenant (89:1–4), continues with praise for God's power in heaven and on earth (89:5–18), returns to God's many promises to David (89:19–37), laments the present state of affairs when the Davidic covenant is in ruins (89:38–45), and ends with a prayer asking God to keep covenant and rescue his people from the nations that mock them (89:46–52). This psalm recalls the promise of God to David in 2 Samuel 7 in light of the decline of his dynasty. It was used "to lament the low estate of David's house and to plead with God to fulfill his promises."[25] God created the world, ordered the chaotic sea to be still, rescued Israel from Egypt, and made a covenant with David. The power and authority of God is not in question. What is in question is God's current rejection of the Davidic covenant and the promises associated with it. This rejection is interpreted as a positive hiding of oneself and the exercise of divine wrath. God is being urged to act because his servant (the Davidic king) is being mocked by his enemies.

SIGNIFICANCE OF BOOK 3 FOR BIBLICAL WORSHIP

In Psalms 73–89, we hear a conversation between God and Israel. God is the Most High who rules in heaven and in Zion. He judges among the gods, and he judges on earth too. He is faithful to Israel and keeps covenant with David. He is the only hope for Israel and the nations. Israel is favored by God and is the object of his faithfulness and love. When Israel is safe and experiences blessings, with her enemies far from her, she gives thanks to God and praises him. She enjoys good harvests, pleasant fellowship, and happily goes to the temple for worship and festivities. This explains worship as a positive experience (thanksgiving and praise).

---

24. John Goldingay, *Psalms for Everyone*, part 2, *Psalm 73–150* (Louisville: Westminster John Knox, 2013), 48.
25. Keith R. Crim, *Royal Psalms* (Richmond, VA: John Knox, 1962), 105.

But this ideal life is not permanent. Even though Israel worships the Lord as the only God, she is very forgetful, straying often from him to other gods. He responds in wrath, at times punishing her directly, and at other times allowing her to reap the consequences of her choices. He punishes her with death often by means of hostile nations who destroy her and mock her and her God. She turns to him in trouble and reminds him of his covenant and of his reputation among the nations. He turns from his wrath and delivers her with the result that she praises him and the nations fear him. At times, however, Israel (or the individual in Israel) is not aware of any failure on her part and therefore puts the blame on God for his neglect of covenant obligation. Worship for Israel, according to Psalms 73–79, is a dialogue between God and Israel in good and bad times. It is a means of sustaining that relationship. Since God has covenanted with Israel, his reputation is now dependent on her behavior and her welfare. He is the God of all the earth, but he is praised or mocked as Israel is respected or despised. Such is the nature of covenant.

Worship as Covenantal Dialogue

Israel is a covenant people, and therefore we must understand its worship within a covenant relationship. Covenant is personal and communal, and therefore we can understand Israel's praise, worship, and lament as personal and communal. When Israelites lament, they claim either that they have suffered for their sins against covenant, for their faithfulness to the covenant, or for God's neglect of his part in the covenant. A resolved lament leads to understanding God and his ways in a new way (Ps. 73). Sometimes, however, the lament is not resolved and all we hear is the complaint (Ps. 88). Honest grief is part of the relationship between God and Israel, and it finds its expression in the Psalms. While God usually laments through the prophets, Israelites lament through the psalms. We can study each lament psalm as to its progress, moving from complaint to resolution and a deeper understanding of the working and nature of the God of the covenant. Maybe there is a correction from a false or shallow to a true or deep understanding of God or of Israel or the individual within Israel. Psalm 79 illustrates this covenantal understanding for the community. In all this, Israel reflects on the covenant in the history of the nation and in the daily experiences of her members. God also actively participates in the covenant. We need then to consider the rest of the Bible in order to understand the historical context of the worship of Israel in good and bad times.

Application to the Church

The God of Israel is the Father of our Lord Jesus Christ. The church is the body of Christ and also the temple of the Holy Spirit. Every Christian is a member of "a chosen people, a royal priesthood, a holy nation" (1 Peter 2:9). Unlike Israel, however, Christians do not have a central place of worship (John 4:19–26; see also Matt. 18:20). Whenever and wherever

Christians assemble for worship, they may use the Psalms to thank and praise God as the Israelites did. They may also use the Psalms to lament. God is in covenant with Christians and a covenant dialogue is in order. When things go well, the church should rejoice and when things go badly the church should lament. Just as Israel lamented when she was threatened by the nations around, or her temple was desecrated, or her people exiled, so the church may lament when parts of it are persecuted and harassed by the world. This will require local congregations to be aware not only of their own concerns but of those in distant congregations as well. As Israel longed for God to vindicate her and himself before the nations, so the church desires to bring glory to God among the nations. With regard to the individual in the Psalms, the Christian is in a similar position. Sometimes a Christian prays and his or her situation is happily and quickly resolved. But there are times when a Christian suffers for a long period with no sign of God's presence or favor, as happened to the Israelite in Psalm 88. At such a time, the congregation is called to suffer along with those who suffer, just as they rejoice with those who rejoice (Rom. 12:15). It would be a tragedy for a member of the church to experience isolation from the fellowship of believers just because God has, for his own reasons and purposes, chosen not to answer the prayers of the sufferer. While it is true that our present suffering cannot be compared with the glory that awaits us in the future (Rom. 8:18), nevertheless, the present can become unbearable if the community of believers does not "linger awhile"[26] with those who suffer, encouraging and comforting them, together sharing the sufferings of Christ in this present age (Rom. 8:17; 2 Cor. 1:5; Phil. 3:10; 1 Peter 4:13). Worship as covenant dialogue reminds us to remain close to each other (Heb. 10:25) even as we seek to be near to the God of our salvation (Ps. 88:1).

BIBLIOGRAPHY

Bergant, Dianne. *Psalm 73–150*. New Collegeville Bible Commentary. Collegeville, MN: Liturgical Press, 2013.

Bock, Daniel I. *For the Glory of God: Recovering a Biblical Theology of Worship*. Grand Rapids: Baker Academic, 2014.

Brueggemann, Walter, and William H. Bellinger Jr. *Psalms*. New Cambridge Commentary. New York: Cambridge University Press, 2014.

Bullock, C. Hassell. *Psalms*. Vol. 2, *Psalms 72–150*. Teach the Text Commentary Series. Grand Rapids: Baker Books, 2017.

Crim, Keith R. *Royal Psalms*. Richmond, VA: John Knox, 1962.

deClaissé-Walford, Nancy, Rolf A. Jacobson, and Beth LaNeel Tanner. *The Book of Psalms*. NICOT. Grand Rapids: Eerdmans, 2014.

26. The idea of lingering awhile is to be credited to Tremper Longman III and M. Daniel Carroll R. in a discussion at a session of the Evangelical Theological Society (Providence, RI, November 2017).

Gerstenberger, Erhard S. *Psalms, Part 2, and Lamentations*. FOTL 15. Grand Rapids: Eerdmans, 2001.

Goldingay, John. *Psalms*. Vol. 2, *Psalm 42–89*. BCOTWP. Grand Rapids: Baker Academic, 2006.

______. *Psalms for Everyone*. Part 2, *Psalm 73–150*. Louisville: Westminster John Knox, 2013.

Grogan, Geoffrey W. *Psalms*. Two Horizons Old Testament Commentary. Grand Rapids: Eerdmans, 2008.

Horton, Douglas. *The Meaning of Worship: The Lyman Beecher Lectures for 1958*. New York: Harper and Brothers, 1959.

Hutchinson, James Hely. "The Psalms and Praise." In *Interpreting the Psalms: Issues and Approaches*, edited by David Firth and Philip S. Johnston, 85–100. Downers Grove, IL: IVP Academic, 2005.

Johnston, Philip S. "The Psalms and Distress." In *Interpreting the Psalms: Issues and Approaches*, edited by David Firth and Philip S. Johnston, 63–84. Downers Grove, IL: IVP Academic, 2005.

Lawson, Steven J. *Psalms 76–150*. Holman Old Testament Commentary. Nashville: Holman Reference, 2006.

Longman, Tremper, III. *Psalms*. TOTC. Downers Grove, IL: InterVarsity Press, 2014.

Mays, James L. *The Lord Reigns: A Theological Handbook to the Psalms*. Louisville: Westminster John Knox, 1994.

Miller, Paul D. *Interpreting the Psalms*. Philadelphia: Fortress, 1986.

Ross, Allen P. *A Commentary on the Psalms*. Vol. 2, *(49–89)*. Kregel Exegetical Library. Grand Rapids: Kregel Academic, 2013.

Routledge, Robin. *Old Testament Theology: A Thematic Approach*. Downers Grove, IL: IVP Academic, 2008.

Tanner, Beth LaNeel. "Book Three of the Psalter: Psalms 73–89." In Nancy deClassé-Walford, Rolf A. Jacobson, and Beth LaNeel Tanner, *The Book of Psalms*, 581–684. NICOT. Grand Rapids: Eerdmans. 2014.

Terrien, Samuel. *The Psalms: Strophic and Theological Commentary*. ECC. Grand Rapids: Eerdmans, 2003.

Webber, Robert E. *Ancient-Future Worship: Proclaiming and Enacting God's Narrative*. Grand Rapids: Baker Books, 2008.

CHAPTER 13

PRAISING THE KING WHO REIGNS

Worship in Book 4 (90–106) of the Psalter

Walter C. Kaiser Jr.

CONTEXT OF WORSHIP IN BOOK 4 OF THE PSALTER: PSALMS 90–106

Perhaps the best way to demonstrate the fact that the book of Psalms has a holistic context that connects the Psalms to more than merely a social or cultural situation alone is to examine the seventeen psalms (90–106) that make up book 4 in this collection. Book 4 of the book of Psalms focuses on two key emphases: (1) there is a "permanent dwelling place" for God's people, and (2) there is a "perpetual dynasty" promised to David, even to the Messiah who is to come!

Up to this point in the psalms, in book 1 (1–41), King David faced the struggle to establish his rule against those opposed to him, or one enemy after another on earth. In book 2 (42–72), David continued this struggle to establish the Messianic kingdom, which would be known as the realm and rule of God's designated person and anointed king. In book 3 (73–89), there came the temporary defeat of this Davidic kingdom at the hands of international enemies. But now in book 4 (90–106), God himself will establish a "dwelling place" for his people, and one day soon Yahweh will rule as king over the whole earth. Thus, in one of the sharpest contrasts in the Psalter's presentations in books 1, 2, 3, this fourth book begins with the promise of a long life, and it reflects more on what it means to be the people of God under the declaration that "Yahweh reigns" (93:1; 96:10; 97:1; 99:1)—a distinctive phrase that is only found in the Psalms in book 4.

Especially in Psalm 96 there is a declaration that celebrates the historical moment when David brought the ark of God to Mount Zion and placed it in a tent he had prepared for it, which also was recorded in detail in 1 Chronicles 16, where a similar encomium broke out in praise and worship of our God. Now for the first time Yahweh's throne was situated on Mount Zion in Jerusalem, thereby bringing Yahweh's throne in close association with the promised throne of David. No wonder 1 Chronicles 16:31 exclaimed:

> Let the heavens rejoice,
> Let the earth be glad;
> Let them say among the nations,
> "The LORD reigns!"[1]

CONTEXT OF WORSHIP IN 1 CHRONICLES 16

There is a special relationship between these psalms in book 4 and the narrative in 1 Chronicles 16, a teaching that does not appear in the parallel material recorded in the books of Kings. First Chronicles 16 has at least ten passages that contain texts that involve the worship of our Lord that closely parallels the Psalms of book 4. What seemed to set off this close association between these two books was David's holy act of bringing the ark into Jerusalem. Yahweh is celebrated as the coming "King," not only among Israel, but also among the nations of the world. This, then, became the occasion for universal jubilation worldwide.

The declaration that "Yahweh reigns" (Heb. *Yahweh malak*) becomes the special emphasis of a special collection of the nine kingship psalms, Psalms 92–100. Moreover, the four announcements that "Yahweh reigns" in these nine psalms cannot be found elsewhere in Scripture besides these psalms and 1 Chronicles 16:31. But these psalms and 1 Chronicles 16 share another anomaly; the phrase "over all gods" (Heb. *'al kol 'elohim* [1 Chron. 16:25]) is also found in Psalms 95:3, 96:4, and 97:9, thus linking these psalms into a special triad. Therefore, Psalm 96 is the central hub for these nine psalms, with Psalms 95 and 97 on either side of Psalm 96 forming a triad with Psalm 96 being its epicenter.

Book 4, then, has this structure and overall plan for its grouping of these seventeen psalms: there are two introductory psalms, Psalms 90–91, which present and introduce book 4, in continuity with the other four books that initiate their books with two introductory psalms. These two psalms emphasize a long life and a dwelling place for God's people with himself. Psalm 90 also has the same author, "Moses, the man of God," as the heading of Deuteronomy 33[2] and shares the same creative work of God in "begetting" and "giving birth" as in Deuteronomy 32:18 in Psalm 90:2. These two introductory psalms are followed by a special collection of nine psalms (Psalms 92–100), which declare "Yahweh is king." Finally, book 4 concludes with two sets of triad psalms, the first three (101–3)

1. All translations here are NIV, unless otherwise noted.
2. Deuteronomy 33:1: "This is the blessing that Moses the man of God pronounced on the Israelites before his death."

praise God for David's kingship, and the second set (104–6), conclude book 4 with the first triad of hallelujah psalms that will also appear more often later in book 5.

Let us turn, then, to Psalm 96, for it has five strophes of six lines each. It is altogether appropriate that we should turn to this passage, for as George Peters observed: "the Psalter is one of the greatest missionary books in the world,"[3] but Psalm 96 is at once one of the greatest missionary psalms, as it must also be acknowledged as a special psalm for the worship of the One who is our "King" and our "dwelling place."

THEOLOGY OF WORSHIP

With this context on the relationship between book 4 of the Psalter and its relationship to 1 Chronicles 16, the following will explore Psalm 96 as a form for worship. Psalm 96 comprises thirteen verses, and it focuses on praising God for his rule and reign over Israel and over all the nations. The interrogative of this chapter is, What are the ways we can praise and worship God for his rule and reign? Here I would like to highlight the word *ways* as the reader considers their own response to the biblical challenge of this passage applied to their own lives.

The outline of this chapter has five parts, but all relate to this challenge of the *ways* in which we can praise our God in worship. First, we can praise God by declaring his glory among and over the heathen (vv. 1–3), second by announcing his transcendent glory above all and any competitors (vv. 4–6), third by adoring the Lord in the splendor of his holiness (vv. 7–9), fourth by announcing to the nations "Yahweh reigns" (vv. 10–11), and finally by joining all creation in rejoicing at his coming as Lord over all (vv. 12–13).

Worship Yahweh by Declaring His Glory among the Heathen (96:1–3)

Our anonymous author of this Psalm mandates that his Jewish audience now must "sing to the Lord." He repeats this call to "sing" three times. They are to sing a "new song," which calls for a new order of things. In fact, this new beginning is also called for in Psalm 92:1–4 as it likewise urges us to worship our God using the elements of exalting our Lord in praise of his name and all his works—namely, by making music (v. 1), by proclaiming his love and faithfulness (v. 2), by using musical instruments to praise God (v. 3), by rejoicing over all God's works (v. 4), and by singing for joy (v. 4).

The audience, just as we too are called to do so along with them, were to "proclaim his salvation day after day" and "declare [God's] glory among the nations; indeed, his marvelous deeds among all the peoples" (vv. 2b–3). Moreover, the word "declare" (Heb. *sapar* [v. 3]) appears in the imperative

3. George Peters, *A Biblical Theology of Missions* (Chicago: Moody Press, 1972), 115–16.

and intensive form only here in the whole book of Psalms.[4] Here, then, was God's mandate to make sure the good news of the gospel got around to the whole world! But this also was no less worship of the high and holy Lord we love and wish to serve.

The word to "proclaim" (Hebrew root *basar*) is the Old Testament equivalent to the New Testament word to "evangelize,"—that is, "to announce the glad tidings," "to bring good news," or "to announce the gospel." That announcement in its fullest measure was the news about the finished work of Christ on the cross. Therefore, in this context it is expressly applied to our calling to announce that same news about the suffering and ruling Messiah, who would give his life for the sins of the peoples of the world and yet would come to rule and reign over all. Evangelism was not a joy reserved only for a few, but it was a calling given to all who love the Lord. This was no mere option for believers: it was to be their chief joy and delight.

This first set of eight lines in the first strophe of Psalm 96 called Israel in that day, and all of us in our day, to sing praise in worship of the Lord and to evangelize those who do not know Christ. Israel sang this song because they saw the entrance of the ark of God being brought into Jerusalem by King David (1 Chron. 16:1–16), which evoked this extraordinary volume of praise to the Lord. This was the beginning of the anthems of praise that were to come in that final day as the Lord personally returned to earth once again and as he established his rule as the Lord who was clearly present in the ark of the covenant; but it is but a small comparison to the magnitude of joy and total delight that will come on that future day when Christ the Messiah will personally be present on this earth.

Worship Yahweh by Announcing His Transcendent Glory above All Competitors (96:4–6)

Psalm 95:3 had emphasized that "the LORD is the great God, the great King above all gods," for that was also the thrust found in these three verses (4–6) in Psalm 96 with the next eight lines of poetry. Psalm 96:4 asserted, "For great is the LORD and most worthy of praise; he is to be feared above all gods." The phrase "above/over all gods" appears not only in Psalms 95:3 and 96:4 but also in 97:9 and 1 Chronicles 16:25. Thus Psalms 95–97 form a nice triad, with Psalm 96 being the epitome and central psalm, depicting God's kingship and governing over all in this world. This theme provided us with one of the great reasons for lifting our hearts in praise of an awesome Lord.

The gods of the nations were simply and totally "nothings" (Heb. *'elilim*, "vain, insignificant, dumb nothings, zeros"). Here was a word that, no doubt, involved a wordplay on "Elohim," "God," as well. The psalmist used the Hebrew negative word *'al*, "not" (to build his wordplay on God's name)

4. The Hebrew verb *sappiru* also appears in Psalm 2:7 and in 9:1, 7–8, but not in the imperative form as it does in Psalm 96:3.

to show that the gods of the nations were merely figments of the idolaters' imagination—for they were instead just the essence of nothingness.

But over against this cacophony of nonexistent gods, there stood the Lord, Maker of heaven and earth (v. 5b). His super-terrestrial power could be seen in the splendor of his person, the majesty of his name, the strength of his might, and the glory of his persona. This was most brilliantly shown in his sanctuary (v. 6b), for these celestial attributes exceeded and transcended the very limits of space itself. Here then was a great cause for exalting the King of kings!

To whom or to what was any mortal going to compare the living God? How could any mortal say of his idol, or alleged god that he worshiped, that it was the same or of equal worth and value to the living God, when all the gods of the nations were no gods at all and things that amounted to "nothing"? Only Yahweh the Lord was Lord over all. Why mess with "nothings" when the mighty God of the universe had shown his glory, majesty, and might?

Worship Yahweh by Adoring the Lord in the Splendor of His Holiness (96:7–9)

A triple call goes out from the psalmist once again as in verses 1–2, but this time it is a call to "ascribe/give to the Lord the glory that is due his name" in verses 7–8. All the families of all the earth must listen up, for if they are even alert at all, it is time to fall down in true worship of the one and only living God. God seeks not simply to be globally famous: no, he longs to be adequately worshiped by all mortals. Steven C. Hawthorne makes this comment: "Psalm 96 shows . . . two directions of [God's] glory. God mandates a declaration of his glory to the nations in verses 2 and 3. . . . But the psalmist goes on to tell the purpose for world evangelization by describing the second aspect of God's glory: a response of glory *from* the nations toward God in verses 7–9. . . . [Then] God *reveals* his glory to all the nations in order to *receive* glory from all creation."[5]

Franz Delitzsch noted that this whole third strophe of verses 7–9 is an echo of Isaiah 60, which sees the families of the earth coming with the gifts, which they had been admonished to bring with them into the courts of the Lord as further acts of worship in the future. This strophe also shares commonality with Psalm 29 and the holy attire mentioned there, which is similar to the wedding garments spoken about in the New Testament. What a privilege to lift high the name and work of God as the heart of the evangel that is to be shared with all nations on earth. God bless all who share the good news of the evangel worldwide. What a privilege and what a joy!

---

5. Steven C. Hawthorne, "The Story of His Glory," in *Perspectives on the World Christian Movement*, eds. Ralph D. Winter and Steven C. Hawthorne, 3rd ed. (Pasadena, CA: William Carey Library, 1999), 35–36.

Worship Yahweh by Announcing to the Nations That "Yahweh Reigns" (96:10–11)

The central word, indeed the epicenter of Psalm 96 itself, is to be found in verse 10: "The LORD reigns." In fact, the prophet Isaiah had also taught, "How beautiful on the mountains are the feet of those who bring good news, who proclaim peace, who bring good tidings, who proclaim salvation, who say to Zion, 'Your God reigns'" (Isa. 52:7).

The peoples of the earth have heard the announcement of the joyful evangel that the kingdom of heaven has already begun on earth, yet it is also a taste of what is yet to come, a taste of what that final arrival of God's kingdom will be like. Meanwhile, in the world below, underneath the heavenly throne of God, which is all too often shaken by war and other types of catastrophes, there is only anarchy and upheaval in opposition to all the truth of God. There is the awful turmoil of the soul, involving crises in the areas of economics, ethics, morality, politics, and international relations, to mention just a few. But the world to come as featured in God's coming kingdom will be impossible to shake, for it stands on the foundation resting on the strength and truth of the Lord God. Here is a joy that will not only pervade the lives of all mortals but will infect the harmony and perfection of all creation as well. What joyful tidings of great joy, which shall be to all the people!

Worship Yahweh by Joining All Creation in Rejoicing in the Coming of the Lord (96:12–13)

Now even the fields and the trees of the forest join in the jubilation, bursting into song, because the Lord is returning back to earth to rule and reign as he had promised the men who stood on the Mount of Olives as our Lord ascended on high after his resurrection. Isaiah had likewise seen this same enthusiastic rejoicing on the part of mortals and nature itself over the Lord's dramatic appearance a second time:

> You will go out in joy and be led forth in peace; the mountains and the hills will burst forth into song before you, and all the trees of the field will clap their hands. (Isa. 55:12)

> Sing for joy, you heavens, for the LORD has done this; shout aloud, you earth beneath. Burst into song, you mountains, you forests and all you trees, for the LORD has redeemed Jacob, he displays his glory in Israel. (Isa. 44:23)

In Psalm 96, the commotion of unbounded joy and excitement of praise were exclusively over the arrival of the Lord, first as the ark of the covenant (the symbol of the presence of the Lord himself) was introduced into the city of David, Jerusalem, but then in that final day, as the Lord himself personally will return a second time to this earth. So important is the teaching that "he comes" (Hebrew participle *ba'*) that the psalmist repeats it twice: "He comes, he comes to judge the earth" (v. 13). Only after our Lord has come in judgment will he rule and reign in the government of his kingdom in the righteousness of mercy and in the faithfulness of his ancient glorious promises. What a day that will be!

Psalm 100: An International Finale of Praise

Psalm 100 forms the basis for William Kethe's hymn "All People That on Earth do Dwell" (1560). Its best known stanza reads as follows:

> Know the Lord is God indeed;
> Without our aid He did us make;
> We are His folk, He doeth us feed,
> And for His sheep He doeth us take.

Kethe's hymn is an example of the relationship between corporate singing (particularly in Protestant worship), the biblical text, and a proper theology of worship for the church. Worship, as has been noted throughout Psalm 96, is not primarily song, but when songs are sung by a congregation that use the biblical texts as their content, the whole body of believers is more authoritatively taught and lifted up in heart and voice in praise to the majestic name of our Lord, as men and women under the authority of the Word as we worship.

In Psalm 100 we have the grand finale of the nine psalms praising the fact that the Lord reigns. Here, all the nations are called on to "make a joyful noise unto the Lord all you lands" (Ps. 100:1). Moreover, every nation on earth in that day is to "come before the Lord with singing" (100:2). It should be clear by this time in the progress of the end times that "the Lord, he is God" (100:3). The audience is together urged to praise God's name by entering into his gates of his sanctuary with thanksgiving and into his courts with praise (100:4). Surely the Lord is extremely good and his love and faithfulness continue to endure forever (100:5). Praise his high and holy name from now and forever more!

Book four ends with two sets of triad psalms: Psalms 101–3, which focus on David as the forerunner of the Messiah, and Psalms 104–6, which sing joyfully hallelujah to the King of kings and Lord of lords!

SIGNIFICANCE OF BOOK 4 FOR WORSHIP

In the center of the nine kingship psalms, 92–100, is Psalm 96, where we can confidently be assured that "our God reigns." As Psalm 46:9–10 added, "He makes wars cease to the ends of the earth. He breaks the bow and shatters the spear. . . . He says: 'Be still and know that I am God; I will be exalted among the nations, I will be exalted in the earth.'"

It is time for the Christian church to declare and to exalt his glory among the nations so that the nations can also give back the glory that is due to our Lord both now and in that day. Our strategy here must be to focus first on giving the good news to Israel (Rom. 1:16) and then to the nations of the world. Only by following this strategy will we imitate the promise-plan of God that results in the "full number" of the Gentiles coming to Christ (Rom. 11:12–25) and the gracious surprise as our Lord returns with "all Israel [being] saved" (Rom. 11:26).

Meanwhile, all the idols and substitutes for the Lord amount to nothing. Thus we must evaluate our own heart to see whether we have allowed the worship of rival gods or material things into our lives. As we reflect on this question, we must rightfully turn our attention to Yahweh and the example set forth for us in Psalm 96. Let the songs of the redeemed be the daily joy of your life as we together worship the Lord in the splendor of his holiness.

BIBLIOGRAPHY

Delitzsch, Franz. *Biblical Commentary on the Psalms*. Grand Rapids: Eerdmans, 1959.

Goldingay, John. *Psalms*. Vol. 1, *Psalms 1–41*. BCOTWP. Grand Rapids: Baker Academic, 2006.

Hawthorne, Steven C. "The Story of His Glory." In *Perspectives on the World Christian Movement*. Edited by Ralph D. Winter and Steven C. Hawthorne. 3rd ed. Pasadena, CA: William Carey Library, 1999.

Peters, George. *A Biblical Theology of Missions*. Chicago: Moody Press, 1972.

Robertson, O. Palmer. *The Flow of the Psalms: Discovering Their Structure and Theology*. Phillipsburg, NJ: P&R, 2015.

Walton, John H. "Psalms: A Cantata about the Davidic Covenant." *JETS* 34 (March 1991): 21–31.

CHAPTER 14

RESPONDING TO THE QUESTIONS BROUGHT BY THE HIDDENNESS OF GOD

Worship in Book 5 (107–50) of the Psalter

Willem A. VanGemeren and Jinsung Seok

CONTEXT OF WORSHIP IN BOOK 5 OF THE PSALTER

In this chapter we shall look at several aspects of the fifth book of the Psalter. According to the imagery provided by Gregory of Nyssa, dwelling in the Psalms is like climbing a mountain to the summit: knowing of "the mind of Christ" and the formation of "Christ in us."[1] Climbing requires steady ascent upward through the rough terrain and challenging obstacles; yet, in his analogy, it brings the greatest of rewards. Failure, on the other hand, leaves this traveler without the growth that comes from "the sanctifying effect of God's grace." Such a climb to the summit of the Psalter offers us grand perspectives from which we may return to the first four books with greater faith and deeper apprehension of the nature of the Triune God. More than that, the "climber" becomes conformed to Jesus Christ, finding his true identity in Jesus Christ.[2]

1. Ronald. E. Heine, *Gregory of Nyssa's Treatise on the Inscriptions of the Psalms* (Oxford: Clarendon, 1995), 51. See Willem A. VanGemeren, "The Reformation and the Appropriation of Scripture: Dwelling in the Psalms" (plenary lecture given at the occasion of the International Congress of the Korean Evangelical Theological Society, Seoul, South Korea, November 11, 2017), 12.
2. For a study on our union with Christ, see Hans Burger, *Being in Christ* (Eugene, OR: Wipf & Stock, 2009). Robert David Smart, *Intentionality for Christ* (Bloomington, IN: WestBow Press, 2017).

Book 5 is collection of collections: (1) Davidic psalms[3] anchor book 5 by the opening and closing Davidic psalms (108–10; 138–45; see also 122–24; 131–33 in the Pilgrimage Songs [120–34]; incl. a Zion song [122]); (2) wisdom psalms (111–12; 119; 127–28);[4] (3) lament (see the Davidic psalms [108–9; 140–43]) and praise psalms are found throughout (the Egyptian Hallel [113–18], Pilgrimage Songs [120–34], and the Daily Hallel [146–50]).

The opening psalm of book 5 (107) associates praise with God's manifest goodness and faithfulness in the deep darkness of the exile and the Jewish Diaspora. The Babylonian exile was a period of divine hiddenness. These psalms challenge popular perceptions and address questions and doubts arising from the desolation of Jerusalem, the destruction of the temple, the pillaging and burning of the countryside, and the forced migrations. People questioned God's fidelity and goodness. Was God still good and loving? Could he forgive sin? What would be the future of God's promises and of his covenants?

The exile became a metaphor for the distance experienced by God's people awaiting their full deliverance and ultimate redemption. The last psalm of book 4 (106) brought the reader to pray for deliverance, "Save us, O Lord our God, and gather us from the nations, that we may give thanks to your holy name and glory in your praise" (106:46–47).[5] Their prayer is still ours as we wait for the coming of our Lord Jesus Christ and the reality of the promised salvation: "Let the redeemed of the Lord say this—those he redeemed from the hand of the foe, those he gathered from the lands, from east and west, from north and south" (107:2). Book 5 responds to the questions occasioned by God's hiddenness during the exilic and postexilic Diaspora experiences of God's people. It reorients these questions away from existential fears to the very character of God. When people cry out in their lostness, God is ready to deliver. The terror of the exilic experience is lessened by the reality of God's loving care in shepherding his people.

THEOLOGY OF WORSHIP IN BOOK 5

Psalm 107 as the Hinge of Books 4 and 5

Psalm 107:1–3 functions as a pointed response to the question raised in Psalm 89:49: "O Lord, where is your former great love [*hesed*, pl.]?'" Where are God's goodness and love promised in Psalm 23:6? "Surely

---

3. On the problem of interpreting superscriptions, see Willem A. VanGemeren and Jason Stanghelle, "Psalms Superscriptions and Critical Realistic Interpretation of the Psalms," in *Do Historical Matters Matter to Faith? A Critical Appraisal of Modern and Postmodern Approaches to Scripture*, eds. James K. Hoffmeier and Dennis R. Magary (Wheaton, IL: Crossway, 2012), 281–302.
4. On the structuring of wisdom connecting Psalms 107–34, see Nancy deClassé-Walford, Rolf A. Jacobson, and Beth LaNeel Tanner, *The Book of Psalms*, NICOT (Grand Rapids: Eerdmans, 2014), 810.
5. All translations here are NIV 1984, unless otherwise noted.

goodness and love [*hesed*] will follow me all the days of my life, and I will dwell in the house of the LORD forever."[6] Psalm 107 prospectively anticipates the psalms of praise (*hallel*) and of wisdom in its opening and close: "Give thanks [*hodu*] to the LORD, for he is good; his love endures forever. . . . Whoever is wise, let him heed these things and consider the great love [*hesed*, pl.] of the LORD" (107:1, 43). First, the motif of God's goodness and faithfulness connects Psalms 107–36 by the inclusive reminders of God's love (118:1–4, 29; 136 [26×]). The fuller version occurs in book 4: "Enter his gates with thanksgiving and his courts with praise; give thanks [*hodu*] to him and praise [*bareku*] his name. For the LORD is good and his love endures forever; his faithfulness continues through all generations" (100:4–5). Shorter versions may be found in 136:2, 3, 26: "Give thanks to . . . His love endures forever" and in the refrains of 118:2–4 and 136:3–26: "His love endures forever." Psalm 118, the last of the Hallel Psalms (111–13), and Psalm 136, located at the end of the Pilgrimage Songs (120–35), form a hermeneutically significant arc connecting Psalms 107–36 by the refrain that God's love endures forever.

Second, Psalm 107 anticipates the development of the motif of praise: "Let them give thanks to the LORD for his unfailing love and his wonderful deeds for men. Let them exalt him in the assembly of the people and praise him in the council of the elders" (vv. 31–32; see vv. 8, 15, 21).

Third, book 5 ties together wisdom and praise as suggested by Psalm 107:43: "Whoever is wise, let him heed these things and consider the great love of the LORD." Psalm 119, a wisdom psalm, connects the praises offered in the Egyptian Hallel (113–18) and in the Pilgrimage Songs (120–34). Moreover, Psalms 111–12 form an *inclusio* with Psalm 119 with their mutual concern with wisdom,[7] but also the Pilgrimage Songs, which center on two wisdom psalms (127–28).

As Psalm 107 opens book 5 (107–50), it also connects with Psalms 104–6, at the end of book 4 (90–106). This collection of three psalms reflects on Yahweh's wise and wondrous engagement with his world. Creation reveals God's wisdom and evokes joy and praise (104:24, 33–34). Israel's stories of redemption (105–6) also give occasion to praise and joy (105:1–3, 22; 106:1–5). Though Israel was responsible for the exilic experience, the psalms call on God's people to trust the Lord (cf. 91:2), fear him and thus grow in wisdom (cf. 90:11; 102:15; 103:11, 13, 17), and to keep

6. The term *hesed*, one of the key terms in Psalm 89 (i.e., vv. 1, 2, 15, 25, 29, 34, and 50) and Ps. 106 (i.e., vv. 1, 7, and 45 [×2]) recurs six times in Psalm 107 (vv. 1, 8, 15, 21, 31, 43), forming an *inclusio* (vv. 1 and 43). Book 5 moves from lament and doubt to the praise of God's faithfulness and goodness: "Give thanks to the LORD, for he is good; his love [*hesed*] endures forever" (107:1).

7. Willem A. VanGemeren, "Entering the Textual World of the Psalms: Literary Analysis," in *The Psalms: Language for All Seasons of the Soul*, eds. Andrew J. Schmutzer and David M. Howard Jr. (Chicago: Moody, 2013), 29–48. See also my commentary on the Psalter in *The Expositor's Bible Commentary*, vol. 5, *Psalms*, eds. Tremper Longman III and David E. Garland, rev. ed. (Grand Rapids: Zondervan, 2008).

singing his praises (*hallelujah*) (104:35; 105:45; 106:1, 48). The inclusion of all who "fear" him (103) is an invitation to the God-fearers outside of ethnic Israel, because God's kingdom includes the nations.

Book 4 develops the various forms of divine redemption beginning with a lament and prayer for divine comfort (90; 94; 102), thanksgiving and hymnic assurance of God's presence and deliverance (91–92; 93, 96–99; 100; 103; 104–6), including hymns celebrating God's cosmic kingship of justice and righteousness (93; 96–99), warning against infidelity (95), culminating in a hymn celebrating God's being the shepherd of his flock (100). The opening of book 4 (90), the middle (95), and the closing (106) situate the readers with questions regarding God's fidelity to his covenant purposes during and after the exile. The hymns and thanksgiving songs respond to and reorient the readers to God's ultimate fidelity (91–100). Psalms 101–3 introduce the readers to David's renewed commitment to a reign of justice, righteousness, and integrity (101), a petition for God's concern for people in pain (102), and a hymn in praise of God's fatherlike compassion and covenant-keeping love (103). The final three psalms detail aspects of God's fidelity as evident in his creative power and covenant fidelity in the story of Israel's early history (104–6). In conclusion, the opening call to thanksgiving in book 5—"Give thanks to the Lord, for he is good; his love endures forever" (107:1)—links up with Psalm 106:1, but also anticipates in Janus fashion the refrain in Psalm 118:1, 29; 136:1.

Book 5: The Metaphorical World of the Psalter

Psalm 107 is a thanksgiving song that invites all who suffer to draw near to God, to seek him, to experience his faithfulness, to praise him, and to discern his wisdom. The search for wisdom flows out of the vicissitudes of life. When life is complex, and God's people become disoriented, they give expression to lament, but the movement from lament to thanksgiving and praise in book 5 reveals a resilience and greater fullness of life. Hymns, thanksgiving songs, and hymnic psalms invite the students of the Psalter to enter a metaphorical world that opens a mythopoeic vision on God's kingdom and blessed presence (110; 111–13; 114; 116; 117; 118; 122; 124–26; 132; 134; 135; 136; 138; 144–45; 146–50).

The Psalter invites God's people to "see" the goodness and love (*hesed*) of their God (34:8). Special attention needs also be given to psalms that celebrate the Davidic kingship (110; 132; 144), Zion (122), and wisdom (112; 119; 127–28; 139) because they confirm God's promises in a postexilic world and invite the appropriation of the vision of the Psalter in each generation. The psalmists long for the operative power of God's instruction and wisdom (see esp. 119). They place their hope in his word (cf. 130:5–8; 119 [below]). After all, God rules over his whole creation, wherever his creatures may be found (145). His faithfulness is evident in creation and in redemption.

Biblical wisdom celebrates the reality of true peace and restoration. Wisdom provides an aperture to the supernatural. It helps people to "see" a transcendent and metaphorical world. It reveals the true reality and provides a mirror on the earthly reality. Psalm 107 delineates the journey of God's people as a second exodus in a postexilic world. God may be found by people in all the situations of life: the wilderness (vv. 4–9; cf. 68:7; 78:15–19, 40, 52; 106:9, 14; 136:16); gloomy prisons (vv. 10–16; cf. 68:6; 79:11; 102:19–20; 142:7; 146:7); folly, rebelliousness, and wickedness (vv. 17–22; cf. 109; 113; 120; 125; 129; 140, 141); or stormy seas (vv. 23–31; cf. 104:26; Jonah 1). When people cry out to the Lord, whether they are guilty or innocent, he promises to deliver them, creating an opportunity for them to praise him and to reflect on his marvelous ways: "Let them give thanks to the LORD for his unfailing love and his wonderful deeds for men" (107:8, 15, 21, 31). God's seeming absence becomes an occasion to look more intently for the supernatural manifestation of God's presence. God's silence becomes an occasion to listen more intently to his redemptive "word" of healing (107:20; cf. 143:8). Lament invites thanksgiving, hymns, and praise. Lament also invites people to discern God's wisdom. Their folly or lostness becomes an occasion to reflect on God's wisdom: "Whoever is wise, let him heed these things and consider the great love of the LORD" (107:43).

The theme of wisdom becomes more prominent in book 5. Psalms 111–13 adumbrate the excellence of Yahweh's wisdom. These psalms form a collection of three hallelujah psalms. These three psalms begin with a call to praise Yahweh (*hallelujah*), and Psalm 113 also ends on *hallelujah* (v. 9). The association of God's praise with creation becomes a focal point in the fifth book. He is to be praised forever (113:2) throughout his creation: "From the rising of the sun to the place where it sets, the name of the LORD is to be praised" (113:3). Because his glory and excellence are unique (v. 4). He is exalted (vv. 4–5), but he is also present in the redemption of people (vv. 6–9).

The creation context transforms Israel's faith from a Torah-centered focus to a sapiential reorientation. The Creator-King dwells with his people who await his deliverance. God's power and wisdom are reflected in creation. His throne is in heaven (115:3; 123:1; cf. 2:4; 102:19; 103:19) and his footstool is on earth (132:7; cf. 99:5). Particularly book 5 celebrates God's being the "maker of heaven and earth." The doctrine of the presence of the Creator fosters hope that wherever God fearers may be found, they need no longer focus on the physical temple. The psalmists adumbrate the uniqueness of Zion as they become more aware of God's universal presence in creation. He is "in heaven" and is sovereign in his governance over all creation (115:3; 135:6). He cannot be located or limited by human imagination (cf. Isa. 66:1–3). He is to be worshiped without any images, because all who bow down to images will experience death (115:1–8). But those who trust in him and fear him will experience his blessing (115:9–13; 134:3), because he is "the LORD, the maker of heaven and earth. He is their "help and shield"

(115:9, 10, 11; cf. 33:2; 89:18). He watches over and keeps his people safe (121:2, 5–8; cf. 124:8). The poet of Psalm 146 juxtaposes two aspects of God. He is "the God of Jacob" (146:5). Israel's story bears out God's deep commitment to Israel. He has been their God, but he is also the God of the nations. After all, he is "the maker of heaven and earth, the sea, and everything in them" (146:6). God comes down to meet the needs of his children wherever they are. He meets the needs of the oppressed, hungry, prisoners, the blind and handicapped, the alien, fatherless, and widows (146:7–9). His reign is everlasting and universal (v. 10). The mention of the various groups of people links with the various situations out of which Yahweh will deliver his people in Psalm 107 (cf. 68:5–10). Psalms 107 and 146 create two bookends that contribute to the poetic vision of the radical transformation from a world of folly and evil, boasting, and self-glorification to a world of wisdom, witness, and worship.

God is the ultimate answer for humanity. The Psalms point to the reality of a divine ontology. The psalmists in their longing to know God do not attempt to prove his existence. They begin with faith and discover that God, while his ways are incomprehensible and full of wonderment, is knowable. He reveals himself through the quest of the psalmists. Their words about God, their questions and incessant searching, open human eyes to the great paradox: God is exalted as the Holy One of Israel and he is present with his people. The psalmists do not yet know of the triunity of their God, but they do intimate the reality of the Trinity. God renews and restores his creation (107:32–38), and he brings transcendent justice to the earth (107:39–42). God's presence is restorative.

The Psalms open the door of hope in God's goodness and love (107:1). He is true to his promises. While the curse of exile, the perception of God's abandonment, and the harshness of life in the Diaspora were deeply felt, the fifth book of the Psalms celebrates the happiness (*'ashre*) of the godly (11×), as does book 1 (8×). The godly submit themselves to the fear of the Lord, express a wholehearted commitment to him, and delight in his instruction. They receive beatitudes (112:1; 119:1–2; 128:1) assuring them of a covenantal relationship with God and of God's presence and protection (144:15; 146:5). Further they seek and receive divine wisdom (112; 127; 128) as they await the reality of God's promises. Evidently, they suffer as they struggle with the reality of who God is (119). But in their suffering, they find their true joy in God as they walk on the sure path of wisdom (107:43; cf. 90:12). Surely, goodness and love (*hesed*) will pursue them all the days of their lives (23:6) amid their laments.

Book 5: The Journey from Lament to Hallelujah

Psalm 107: The good news is God

So far we have seen some of the links between Psalm 107 and book 4. The psalm also suggests major motifs that are developed in book 5: God's goodness, love, and salvation and human wisdom and praise. Psalm 107 provides the links connecting the shaping of the various collections in book 5. Toward the conclusion of this chapter, we will also observe the close connections between Psalms 107 and 145.

Psalm 107 opens book 5 with thanksgiving that invites the worshipers to praise the Lord and to reflect on his wisdom. God is good and faithful (107:1), and his loving acts are discerned by the wise (107:43). The subsequent Davidic laments (108–9) are reminders of the alien nature of this world in which thanksgiving and lament shape the lives of God's children.

Psalms 108–10: A new vision of the Davidic King

The two psalms that follow Psalm 107 associate David with lament (108–9). More than a fourth of the psalms in book 5 are in the form of lament. Six are associated with David in the form of individual lament psalms (109; 140–43) and one communal lament (108). Other lament psalms are by unidentified authors and are in the form of individual (120; 130) and communal (123; 129; 137) lament psalms.

In the lament psalms, the writers describe the evil circumstances of life in their prayers for deliverance, retribution, and even for the execration of the wicked (109; 137). Though they speak of feeling faint (142; 143) and of having no refuge (141; 142; 144), they look for evidences of God's love, righteousness, justice, goodness, and blessing (109; 120; 142). They may even experience divine abandonment (108; 143) as they wait for the Lord's redemption (120; 140; 141; 143). They anticipate the transformation from lament to praise and thanksgiving, from disorientation to reorientation, and from questioning to obedience and a newfound wisdom (108; 109; 140; 142). The Davidic laments (108–9) find their resolution in a royal psalm revealing God's faithfulness to David in affirming his choice of David as the priestly king in God's kingdom (110), which in turn leads to the contemplation on divine wisdom (111–12).

Royal psalms

Special attention needs to be given to royal psalms (110; 132; 144). Royal psalms occur at the opening, the middle, and the closing of book 5. They are reminders of God's commitment to David's dynasty in keeping with expectations raised in books 1 (2), 2 (72), and 3 (89). Whereas book 4 holds out the promise of God's kingdom, book 5 (144–50) affirms the certainty and blessedness of God's kingdom. It cautiously responds to the question of the future of the messianic agency after the desolation of Jerusalem and the exile of the Davidic heirs. God has promised that David's heirs will rule and establish God's kingdom on earth. But the future Davidic king will have to live up to higher expectations. He will serve God as a priestly king (110), whose commitment is to God's dwelling with his people (132) and who will experience God's miraculous deliverance (144). He is the Guardian of the theocracy.

Psalm 110, a royal psalm, reveals God's hand in reordering a world in which David will serve him as his appointed priestly ruler—"in the order of Melchizedek"—in Zion. Psalm 110 is extensively cited by Jesus, Peter, and the author of Hebrews as evidence of the messianic hope of the victorious Davidic scion (Matt. 22:44; Mark 12:26; Luke 20:43; Acts 2:35; Heb. 1:13; 5:6; 7:17, 21). This psalm together with thanksgiving songs (116; 124; 126; 138), hymns (111; 113; 114; 116; 118; 121; 125; 134; 135; 136), hymnic songs (131), liturgical psalms (115; 132), and hallelujah psalms (146–50; see below) redirect the imagination of book 5 from this world to another, more transcendent and metaphorical world. It is the world of God coming down into the world of humans with the gift of wisdom (112; 119; 127–28; 139). Major symbols of the new order are the Davidic dynasty: royalty (110; 132; 144) and Zion (122; cf. 132). The messianic king will inaugurate an era of divine blessedness (144), and God's people will be truly happy: "Blessed [*'ashre*] are the people of whom this is true; blessed [*'ashre*] are the people whose God is the Lord" (144:15). The many beatitudes (*'ashre*; lit., "happy") connect the wisdom psalms in book 5 (112:1; 119:1–2; 127:5; 128:1) with the first of the final hallelujah psalm (146:5). It forms an arc with the first beatitude (1:1) and with the beatitudes in book 1 (1:1; 2:12; 32:1–2; 33:12; 34:9; 40:5; 41:2).

Zion

The Davidic king is closely connected with the future of Zion. The one Zion psalm in book 5 celebrates the future of Zion, the city of God. It is an eschatological vision of the reality of God's kingdom on earth: a place of peace and security. Many psalms rejoice at the prospect of Zion. It is the one place where God's children are finally at home. It is where the exiles experience the reality of God's manifest presence: "The Lord reigns forever, your God, O Zion, for all generations. Praise the Lord" (146:10). See Psalms 120–34 below.

From exile to the new exodus: The Egyptian Hallel (111–18)

Three hallelujah psalms (111–13) round out the sequence from lament to praise. Psalms 111–12 open on hallelujah and are in the form of an alphabetic acrostic connecting the excellence of Yahweh (111) with the excellence of divine wisdom (112). The psalmist invites people to give thanks for God's excellence, glory, righteousness, grace, compassion, fidelity to the covenant, justice, trustworthiness, and uprightness (111:1–8). He is holy and awesome, yet his wisdom is open to all who fear him (111:9–10). The person who walks in the path of wisdom is truly happy (*ashre* [112:1]) as he and his children receive God's blessings. Their way reflects the fear of the Lord: generosity, righteousness, grace, compassion, and justice (112:1–9).

Psalm 113 has the function of a Janus psalm. It closes the three hallelujah psalms (111–13) and opens what is called the Egyptian Hallel

(113–18). This hymnic/thanksgiving collection praises the Lord for his redemptive involvement in protecting the weak and needy (113; cf. 146), in redeeming his people from Egypt; in consecrating them as his sanctuary (114; cf. 135; 136); in blessing all who fear him, in sustaining his creation, in manifesting his real presence with his people (115; cf. 104; 135; 136; 145; 147); in restoring the afflicted by his grace, righteousness, and compassion (116; cf. 107; 129); in extending his praise among the nations who witness his love and faithfulness (117; cf. 111; 115); and in manifesting the manifold evidences of his goodness and faithfulness (118; cf. 135; 136). His purposes will prevail, and he will not disappoint his children. Evil will come to an end, and his goodness will become more and more evident. God who brought his people out of Egypt is the God of the new exodus. He will bring his children home to himself.

From Torah to wisdom (119)

The hymns celebrate God's wisdom evident in his righteousness, justice, and faithfulness in the great variety of circumstances in which humans may find themselves. The central place of the word (107:20) is significantly developed in Psalm 119. The psalmist places his hope in God's Word (119:9, 11, 16, 42, 43, 49, etc.), because it confirms God's promise, the fidelity of his character, and guides the psalmist in maturity and wisdom: "Your word, O LORD, is eternal; it stands firm in the heavens. Your faithfulness continues through all generations; you established the earth, and it endures" (119:89–90; cf. v. 57). In his struggle of making sense of his world, the psalmist looks deep within his own being, while waiting for God to meet with him. He feels himself like a straying sheep who searches for the Shepherd (119:176). He seeks God wholeheartedly, but God appears so far from him. Thus the poet invites all God's children in the Diaspora to seek God and to receive his instruction. God's promises are true, but God's ways remain incomprehensible. The appropriation of God's Word includes two dimensions: the knowledge of God and of self: "It is certain that man never achieves a clear knowledge of himself unless he has first looked upon God's face, and then descends from contemplating him to scrutinize himself."[8]

From Jerusalem to Zion: Pilgrimage songs (120–34)

The collection of Pilgrimage Songs (120–34) helps to refocus the eyes of faith on Zion, the city of God. While Zion is also known as the city of David, the Psalms celebrate the true significance of the city of God (46; 48). Zion is symbolic of God's strength and presence (125), blessing (128; 133; 134), and reign (146), but also of David's kingdom (110; 122; 132). Zion is the mother city of all the nations (87). The hope of the restoration

8. John Calvin, *Institutes of the Christian Religion*, eds. John T. McNeill, trans. Ford Lewis Battles (Philadelphia: Westminster, 1960), 1.1.2.

of Zion as God's city binds the book of Psalms together (2; 72; 89; 101; 126; 146; 147; 149).

The first of the Pilgrimage Songs (120) is in the form of lament. It gives perspective on the tension between wisdom and folly, between good and evil. The poet throws light on the antithetical nature of human existence: a world of lying, deception, and war and a world of peace, truth, and justice. He entrusts himself to God's ultimate justice. The hymnic celebration of the reality of God's help and watchfulness focuses on mountains. Though he does not mention Zion, the imagery is highly suggestive of Zion. God's presence secures safety and protection, because God is "the maker of heaven and earth" (121:2). He is powerful and constant in his care wherever the people of God may find themselves. Psalm 122 is a pilgrimage song celebrating the reality of Zion and associated with David. The pilgrims rejoice in preparing for and entering Jerusalem for the sole purpose of praising their God. They hunger and thirst for God's kingdom of justice. They long for the peace that God alone can bring (vv. 7–9).

In the tension of the reality of the world and the metaphorical vision of Zion, the pilgrims lament as a community (123). They no longer look at mountains, but at God's heavenly throne (123:1; cf. Col. 3:1–3). Having endured shame and ridicule, they await his mercy. They compare themselves to the lowliness of servants who seek the favor of their master.

The lament is followed by a thanksgiving song associated with David (124). The very ground of thanksgiving lies in the assurance that their help will come from "the Lord, the maker of heaven and earth" (124:8). The attacks of the enemies have been severe and are likened to the power of Sheol, to a raging flood, to wild animals, and to a fowler (vv. 3–7). But the Creator will come to their aid.

The next song develops familiar imagery of mountains in the portrayal of the opposition of the wicked to the righteous (125). God will protect his people, so they will not be shaken. All who trust in him will enjoy the benefits of Zion. God's peace will rest on his people when the wicked perish.

Psalm 126 is a reflective thanksgiving song. The people thank the Lord for the first stages of the restoration after the exile. They were happy and grateful, saying, "The Lord has done great things for us, and we are filled with joy" (v. 3). Nevertheless, they were waiting for an even greater manifestation of his grace, as their joy was mixed with tears. The expectations raised by the prophets and poets of Israel had pointed them to great expectations.

Psalms 127 and 128 are wisdom psalms celebrating God's blessed presence in the family: mother, father, and children. Zion will be built up by the blessedness of wise children. Psalms 129–30 return to lament as a sober reminder of the evil in this world. The last of the Pilgrimage Songs (131–34) celebrate the blessedness of humility and wisdom in waiting on the Lord's salvation (131), the blessedness of David's search for a resting place for Yahweh (132), the blessedness of "brotherhood" (133), and the blessedness of God's servants who lead in blessing their God (134).

Reflections: God and Babylon (135–37)

The hallelujah psalm (135) and the thanksgiving psalm (136; also known as the great hallel) formally close the motif of God's goodness and love celebrated initially in Psalms 104–7. God has revealed himself in his being the Creator and Redeemer. He dwells with his people in Zion (135:21). But all is not well in Zion. The vision of God's powers of creation and redemption (135–36) is shattered by a most disturbing communal lament psalm that bemoans the desolation of Zion (137:1).

Has God seen the desolation of Jerusalem by the Babylonians? God cannot sit by idly and let the exile be the final word. The psalms look to God expectantly awaiting the vindication of Zion is (137:8–9). Out of the ashes of the exile arises messianic expectations when the voice of David is again heard throughout the diaspora communities.

The voice of David heard within the postexilic context (138–45)

It is significant to note that David becomes a main figure in book 5 of the Psalter by being connected with two groups of David psalms (108–10 and 138–45) at the opening and toward the close of book 5.[9] These two collections encourage a retrospective reading of the earlier Davidic collections in books 1–2 (3–41 and 51–71).

The second Davidic collection of psalms (138–45) opens on a thanksgiving song (138) followed by a reflective poem on the reality of God's presence in life. God is providentially at work in all circumstances of life (139). The four Davidic laments (140–43) express the new spirit of David in his search for rest from his adversaries. He is confident in the Lord (140), seeks his protection (141–42), and trusts in his deliverance while being open to God's instruction and counsel: "Teach me to do your will, for you are my God; may your good Spirit lead me on level ground" (143:10). The last two Davidic psalms also reveal the spirit of the new David (144–45), who sings a new song celebrating God's beneficence in renewing his people in a new song envisioning a world abundantly blessed by the Lord without war, exile, and alienation (144:9–15) and who adumbrates God's kingdom of might, goodness, righteousness, compassion, glory, might, and splendor in which God delivers all who fear him and thwarts the evildoers (145). As Abraham suffered vicariously for his descendants while awaiting the promise (Gen. 15:12–16), so David suffers for Israel in her exilic distress, oppression, and humiliation.

The final hope of David in Psalms 144–45 envisions a radical transforming vision from desolation to glorification: "The concluding collection of Davidic psalms (138–145) also prepares the reader for the final

9. He is also connected to several pilgrimage songs (122–24; 131–33).

five hallelujah psalms (146–150). David's final lament, while personal, also serves symbolically as his bearing the suffering of the people who await deliverance."[10]

Psalm 145 is to be read in close connection with Psalm 107. A close reading reveals a number of connections: (1) the praise of God—"Give thanks to the Lord" (107:1, 8, 32) // I will praise the Lord (145:1, 10, 21); (2) the mention of God's *hesed* and goodness (107:1, 8, 31 // 145:8, 13 [LXX], 17); (3) God's manifest glory—"his wonderful deeds for men" (107:8, 15) // "God's glorious splendor for men" (145:12); (4) God's exaltation of the needy and lowly—"lifting the needy out of their affliction" (107:41) // "lifting up all those who fall and those who bowed down" (145:14); (5) God's abundant provisions—"he satisfies the thirsty and fills the hungry with good things" (107:9, 36) // "you give them their food at the proper time . . . satisfies the desires of every living thing (145:15–16); (6) God's response to prayer—"Then they cried out to the Lord in their trouble, and he delivered them from their distress" (107:6, 13, 19, 28) // "God hears their cry and saves them" (145:19); and (7) God's vengeance of the wicked—"all the wicked shut their mouths" (107:42) // "all the wicked he will destroy" (145:20). Psalm 145 provides the grounds for worship. It is an anthology of the Psalter as a whole and of book 5 in particular. The usage of the nominal form of the verb for "praise" (*hll*) in 145:21 anticipates the concluding five hallelujah psalms: "My mouth will speak in praise [*tehillato*] of the Lord."

The concluding vision of God: The five hallelujah psalms (146–50)

Throughout book 5 the psalmist enjoins God's people to praise God. Seven psalms begin and close the psalm on a call to praise Yahweh (hallelujah [113, 135, 146–50]). Psalm 113 is a hymn that opens the Egyptian Hallel (113–18). Psalm 135 is a hymn at the close of the Pilgrimage Songs (120–34), celebrating Yahweh's gracious sovereignty in creation and his faithfulness in redeeming his people from Egypt and in giving Israel the land. Yahweh is truly God. Psalms 146–50 constitute the final five hallelujah psalms. Psalm 150 with its additional ten calls to praise God (*hallelu*) closes book 5 of the Psalter.

The final five hallelujah psalms again give the rationale for praising him. He is to be praised, because he is the Creator-Sustainer-Redeemer of his people, whose hope is in him. He reigns over Zion with justice and righteousness as the Father of the oppressed (146). Psalm 147 further develops the redemption theme and evokes awe for his power and wisdom that are beyond human understanding. But he has revealed his word to his people. The poet of Psalm 147 piles image on image and so impresses the readers of the Psalms with God's care. He is likened to (1) a builder—"The Lord builds up Jerusalem" (v. 2; cf. 51:18; 69:35–36); (2) a shepherd—"he gathers the exiles of Israel" (v. 2; cf. 107:1–3); (3) a physician—"He heals the

10. VanGemeren, "God's Faithfulness," 272.

brokenhearted and binds up their wounds" (v. 3; cf. 6:2–3; 30:2; 103:2–3; 109:22; Isa. 30:26; 61:1); (4) an astronomer—"He determines the number of the stars and calls them each by name" (v. 4; cf. Isa. 40:25–26); (5) a wise and powerful ruler—"Great is our Lord and mighty in power; his understanding has no limit" (v. 5; cf. Isa. 40:28); and (6) a just judge—"The LORD sustains the humble but casts the wicked to the ground" (v. 6; cf. 146:9).

Yahweh is to be praised throughout his creation in the highest heavens and on earth below: angelic beings, heavenly planets and constellations, meteorological phenomena, plants, and all earthly creatures, "for his name alone is exalted; his splendor is above the earth and the heavens" (148:13). A "new song" of joy together with music and dancing celebrate God's ultimate justice (149). The saints will rule together with God executing just judgment to earth. All creatures will ultimately praise God for his power and greatness (150).

SIGNIFICANCE OF BOOK 5 OF THE PSALTER FOR BIBLICAL WORSHIP

By now it should be obvious that worship is God-centered. It begins with a heart that desires to know the being, acts, and the glory of the living God. Since the Father has revealed his glory in the incarnate Son (John 1:14, 18) and the Son has sent the Spirit, worship is trinitarian. Worship comes to expression in all situations of life (from lament to praise), in all places on in heaven and on earth (wilderness, at sea, free or imprisoned, at home, on a pilgrimage, or in exile), and at all times (reflections on the past and prospects for the future). C. S. Lewis put it well: "Aim at heaven and you will get earth 'thrown in,' aim at earth and you will get neither."[11] The journey of the psalmists with its focus on transcendence opens up to the reality of God in Christ. It is a world of metaphors where one can enjoy God, as Hans Boersma comments, "The beatific vision, in its perpetual gaze on God in Christ, centers like nothing else on enjoying him."[12] Book 5 of the Psalms witnesses to the excellence and the glory of God. The pilgrimage goes from humans to God, from lament to praise (hallelujah), and from God to the fullness of God. Elizabeth Prentiss gave a beautiful expression of the inner transformation in the familiar hymn, "Once earthly joy I craved, Sought peace and rest; Now Thee alone I seek, Give what is best; This all my prayer shall be: More love, O Christ, to Thee, More love to Thee, More love to Thee!"

The spiritual journey begins with a desire for God much like mountain climbers are motivated to climb the Himalayas. They prepare for the journey, train for it, and anticipate the joy of climbing to the top of one peak or another until they stand on Mt. Everest. Since the book of Psalms

11. C. S. Lewis, *Mere Christianity* (New York: HarperOne, 2015), 135.

12. Hans Boersma, *Seeing God: The Beatific Vision in Christian Tradition* (Grand Rapids: Eerdmans, 2018), 5.

is composed of five books, there are five peaks to climb. Each book has its own challenges. On the journey one discovers fellow climbers who have sought God: David, the Korahites, the Asaphites, Moses, Solomon, and many other saints. Their words have become the Word of God, and their search for the fullness, glory, and beauty of God leads ultimately to the cross of the Lord Jesus Christ. He has "climbed" the peaks of the Psalms. He was tested and suffered anguish unto death. He has shown us the face of the Triune God in all aspects of life. He is the reality of God: "These are a shadow of the things that were to come; the reality, however, is found in Christ" (Col. 2:17). It is small wonder that the Desert Fathers were used to singing all 150 psalms in one day. They followed Christ as they trekked with the psalmists. They also grew in their vision of the fullness of God, the God who is one and three. True worship and prayer is trinitarian in nature. Again, Lewis expressed it well:

> An ordinary simple Christian kneels down to say his prayers. He is trying to get into touch with God. But if he is a Christian he knows that what is prompting him to pray is also God: God, so to speak, inside him. But he also knows that all his real knowledge of God comes through Christ, the Man who was God—that Christ is standing beside him, helping him to pray, praying for him. You see what is happening. God is the thing to which he is praying—the goal he is trying to reach. God is also the thing inside him which is pushing him on—the motive power. God is also the road or bridge along which he is being pushed to that goal. So that *the whole threefold life of the three-personal Being is actually going on in that ordinary little bedroom where an ordinary man is saying his prayers.*[13]

BIBLIOGRAPHY

Boersma, Hans. *Seeing God: The Beatific Vision in Christian Tradition*. Grand Rapids: Eerdmans, 2018.

Burger, Hans. *Being in Christ*. Eugene, OR: Wipf & Stock, 2009.

Calvin, John. *Institutes of the Christian Religion*. Edited by John T. McNeill. Translated by Ford Lewis Battles. Philadelphia: Westminster, 1960.

deClassé-Walford, Nancy, Rolf A. Jacobson, and Beth LaNeel Tanner. *The Book of Psalms*. NICOT. Grand Rapids: Eerdmans, 2014.

Heine, Ronald. E. *Gregory of Nyssa's Treatise on the Inscriptions of the Psalms*. Oxford: Clarendon, 1995.

Johnson, Kristen Deede. "Are We Missing the Point of Spiritual Disciplines?" *Christianity Today*, August 18, 2017. Review of *Practices of Love: Spiritual Disciplines for the Life of the World* by Kyle David Bennett (Grand

13. Cited by Kristen Deede Johnson, "Are We Missing the Point of Spiritual Disciplines?," *Christianity Today*, August 18, 2017 (book review of *Practices of Love: Spiritual Disciplines for the Life of the World* by Kyle David Bennett [Grand Rapids, Brazos, 2007]), http://www.christianitytoday.com/ct/2017/september/are-we-missing-point-of-spiritual-disciplines.html (emphases mine).

Rapids: Brazos, 2007). http://www.christianitytoday.com/ct/2017/september/are-we-missing-point-of-spiritual-disciplines.html.

Lewis, C. S. *Mere Christianity*. New York: HarperOne, 2015.

Smart, Robert David. *Intentionality for Christ*. Bloomington, IN: WestBow Press, 2017.

VanGemeren, Willem A. "Entering the Textual World of the Psalms: Literary Analysis." In *The Psalms: Language for All Seasons of the Soul*, edited by Andrew J. Schmutzer and David M. Howard Jr., 29–48. Chicago: Moody Press, 2013.

______. *The Expositor's Bible Commentary*. Vol. 5, *Psalms*. Edited by Tremper Longman III and David E. Garland. Rev. ed. Grand Rapids: Zondervan, 2008.

______. "God's Faithfulness, Human Suffering, and the Concluding Hallel Psalms (146–150): A Canonical Study." In *Building on the Foundations of Evangelical Theology*, edited by Gregg R. Allison and Stephen J. Wellum, 263–84. Wheaton, IL: Crossway, 2015.

VanGemeren, Willem A., and Jason Stanghelle. "Psalms Superscriptions and Critical Realistic Interpretation of the Psalms." In *Do Historical Matters Matter to Faith? A Critical Appraisal of Modern and Postmodern Approaches to Scripture*, edited by James K. Hoffmeier and Dennis R. Magary, 281–302. Wheaton, IL: Crossway. 2012.

CHAPTER 15

TRUSTING IN THE SOVEREIGNTY OF YAHWEH

Worship in the Hebrew Megilloth

Mark Rooker

CONTEXT OF WORSHIP IN THE MEGILLOTH

The Megilloth are a group of five scrolls that occur together in the Hebrew canon. They include Ruth, Song of Songs, Ecclesiastes, Lamentations, and Esther. These "scrolls" (books) were read in conjunction with the major Jewish festivals—Passover, Pentecost, Tabernacles, Destruction of the Temple, and Purim (Lots).

Context of Worship in the Book of Ruth

The book of Ruth begins describing how the family of Elimelech, a Judahite from Bethlehem, ventured into Moab to find relief from a famine during the time of the judges (Ruth 1:1–2).[1] While in Moab, Elimelech died and then his two sons died prematurely after they married the Moabite women Orpah and Ruth (1:3–5).[2] When Elimelech's widow, Naomi, heard that the famine in Israel was over, she planned to head back to her homeland and advised her daughters-in-law to remain in Moab because there were not likely future prospects for marriage in Israel (1:6–14).[3] Orpah heeded Naomi's advice, but Ruth, expressing unswerving loyalty, vowed that she would accept Naomi's people and would embrace the Israelite God as her own (1:15–17). This speech, Ruth's first speech in the book,

1. Famines were viewed as curses in the law (Deut. 32:24; 2 Sam. 21:1; 1 Kings 8:37).
2. According to the Aramaic Targum the deaths resulted from the intermarriages with foreign women (see Deut. 7:1–4).
3. Naomi implied there would be no possibility for levirate marriage.

may reflect treaty language wherein Ruth officially became an Israelite.[4] Chapter 1 ends with Naomi returning with Ruth to Bethlehem at the beginning of the barley harvest, bitter about what had taken place in her life since she had left for Moab with her family, only to return years later, "empty" (1:19–22).[5]

Chapter 2 opens with Ruth requesting permission from her mother-in-law to go into the fields of Bethlehem and glean among the ears of grain that the harvesters would leave in the corners of the fields (Ruth 2:2; see Lev. 19:9–10). Ruth bravely ventured into the field of Boaz, who we learn is a kinsman of Naomi (2:1). Boaz had heard of what Ruth had done for her mother-in-law and invited her to glean only in his field with his workers (2:8–11). Boaz expressed the wish that Yahweh would richly reward her for taking refuge under Yahweh's "wings" (2:12). After Boaz fed her and sent her home, Ruth reported to Naomi what had transpired and presented her with an ephah of barley (2:14–23).

In chapter 3, Naomi devised a plan for Ruth to present herself to Boaz at the threshing floor at the end of the barley harvest. Ruth's encounter with Boaz was to press the issue of marriage, as is clear from her request, "Spread your cloak over me" (3:9).[6] Boaz was agreeable to the proposal and told Ruth that he would confront the nearer kinsman to see if the nearer kinsman would take on the responsibility of next of kin (3:10–15), which would include buying back Elimelech's land. Initially the nearer kinsman agreed to purchase the land, but when Boaz reported that he would also have to marry Ruth, he refused and thereby gave legal authority to Boaz to carry out the role of the kinsman redeemer (4:5–6).

Consequently, Boaz's marriage to Ruth was quickly arranged, and soon Ruth gave birth to a son, Obed, the grandfather of the future King David. The quick meeting, romance, marriage, and pregnancy contrasts with the ten years of barrenness in the land of Moab (1:4).

Context of Worship in the Song of Songs

The title Song of Songs is taken from the opening phrase of the book, *shir hashshirim*, variously rendered "Song of Solomon," "The Song," or "Best Song." The Song of Songs has been attributed to Solomon, the last king of the united monarchy of Israel. This is for good reason since Solomon's name appears seven times in the book (1:1, 5; 3:7, 9, 11; 8:11–12).

The correct understanding of the Song is one of the real enigmas in the history of the interpretation of the Bible. As Ernst Sellin and Georg

4. Victor H. Mathews and James C. Moyer, *The Old Testament: Text and Context* (Peabody, MA: Hendrickson, 1997), 234.
5. All translations here are HCSB, unless otherwise noted. Notice that Naomi describes her earlier experiences in Judah as "full" although the family left Judah because of famine ("shortage of food").
6. See Ezek. 16:8. The Aramaic Targum explicitly comments that Ruth's request is one of marriage. The same word *kanap* is rendered as "wings" in 2:12 and frequently as "cloak," as in 3:9.

Fohrer have summarized, "The history of interpretation of the Song of Solomon is no feather in the cap of biblical exegesis."[7] Many different approaches have been proposed as the correct model for its interpretation. The two most popular are the allegorical view, which supposes that the love relationship is a metaphor for divine love, and the view that the book is about the actual love relationship between a man and a woman.

Although many Jewish and Christian interpreters have followed the allegorical method of interpretation, there is no hint in the Song itself that the male-female relationship should be understood as referring to anything else. Duane Garrett has argued that the strongest argument against the allegorical method is the sexual nature of the Song itself. The explicit language in the book would be an inappropriate way to portray the love between God and his people.[8] Thus one must conclude that as originally understood the Song of Songs was interpreted as a celebration of love and sex, and thus to read it as an allegory was a late innovation it its interpretive history.[9]

The book may divided into five sections. Each of these sections begins with the anticipation of love and the arrival of one of the lovers (1:2; 2:8; 3:6; 5:2; 8:5–6).[10] A viable alternative is to divide the Song into four sections based on it occurrence of the concluding refrain, "I adjure you, O daughters of Jerusalem" (2:7; 3:5; 5:8; 8:4). Many interpreters agree that the highpoint of the book is the lovers' consummation in marriage in 3:6–5:1.[11] Barry Webb has observed five themes in the book: (1) the summoning of the beloved (2:10–13; 4:1–7); (2) the banishment of the beloved (2:17; 4:6; 8:14); (3) the search for the beloved (3:1–5; 5:2–6:3); (4) self-worth in a hostile world (1:5); and (5) the praise of love (8:6–7).[12] Yet it should not be lost to the modern reader that in the history of interpretation, particularly as reflected in rabbinic and Jewish interpretation that the metaphor of God's love for his people was a common way to understand the book (see Eph. 5:31–32).

Context of Worship in Book of Ecclesiastes

The book of Ecclesiastes is attributed to Qoheleth, a name or term that occurs only in Ecclesiastes (1:1–2, 12; 7:27; 12:8–10). The noun *Qoheleth* is

---

7. Ernst Sellin and Georg Fohrer, *Introduction to the Old Testament*, trans. David Edward Green (Nashville: Abingdon, 1968), 300.
8. See Song 7:7–8. Duane A. Garrett, *Proverbs, Ecclesiastes, Song of Songs*, NAC 14 (Nashville: Broadman, 1993), 357.
9. G. Schwab, "Song of Songs 1: Book of Songs," in *DOTWPW*, 740.
10. See G. Lloyd Carr, "Song of Songs," in *A Complete Literary Guide to the Bible*, eds. Leland Ryken and Tremper Longman III (Grand Rapids: Zondervan, 1993), 291–92.
11. Similarly, Davidson has argued that the climax of the Song is to be found in Song 4:16–5:1, which is the exact center of the Song (sixty verses on either side) (Richard M. Davidson, "The Literary Structure of the Song of Songs *Redivivus*," *JATS* 14, no. 2 (2003): 62–64. See Paul R. House, *Old Testament Theology* (Downers Grove, IL: InterVarsity Press, 1998), 606n7.
12. Barry Webb, *Five Festal Garments: Christian Reflections on the Song of Songs, Ruth, Lamentations, Ecclesiastes, and Esther*, NSBT 10 (Downers Grove, IL: InterVarsity Press, 2000), 21.

based on the verb *qhl*, which means "convoke and assemble," or simply "to assemble." This verb occurs frequently in 1 Kings 8 concerning Solomon's gathering the people to dedicate the newly constructed temple (1 Kings 8:1–2, 14, 22, 25), and its use in Ecclesiastes would evoke the memory of Solomon.

Themes of Ecclesiastes (1:2–11)

The first major section of Ecclesiastes serves as an introduction to the book, announcing its main theme. Qoheleth began his quest by searching for human significance. The section illustrates the endless and apparently meaningless cycles of life in both nature and history. Man's labor is said to be of no profit (*yitron* [1:3; see 1:8]).

Quest for the meaning of life (1:12–6:9)

This section is written in the form of an autobiographical narrative, clearly alluding to the unique and privileged experience of King Solomon. Ecclesiastes 1:12–26 reports Solomon's experiences and reflections in his investigation of what is best for people to do during the limited days of their life (2:3).[13]

This section opens with the rather depressing note that an increase of wisdom results in an increase in sorrow, because it does not provide comprehensive answers to life (1:12–18). From this point the narrative addresses various experiences of life that are believed to lead to happiness but in fact do not bring ultimate satisfaction and meaning. These include such experiences as pleasure (2:1–11) and wisdom and toil (2:12–27). And yet, as somewhat of a consolation, opportunities to eat and drink do not come by human achievements but are gifts of God to be enjoyed (2:24–25).

Only God knows the meaning of the interaction of life's events (3:1–9). The awareness of time and eternity on the part of humanity does not bring fulfillment, for the desire to know the eternal cannot be quenched (3:11). Wisdom is no guarantee to peace and happiness; yet God blesses people with gifts that allow them to forget their hardships (5:18–20; see also 2:24–26).

Wisdom admonitions (6:10–12:8)

After an opening statement expressing man's inability to know what the future will bring (6:10–12), this third major section records several adages for appropriate behavior. This section concludes with instruction addressing the issue of youth and old age (11:7–12:8). Once again, the author returns to the futility of his toil that he mentioned at the beginning of the book (1:2–11).

The next to last verse of the section 12:1–8 states that the human spirit will return to the Lord who created it, a description of life after death (12:7). Since all life comes from God (12:1), it also must return to God.

---

13. The Aramaic Targum translation of Ecclesiastes 1:12 relates these experiences to Solomon and also identifies Solomon with Qoheleth.

Epilogues (12:9–14)

The book closes with two epilogues, the first describing Qoheleth's activities as a wise man (12:9–10), followed by instructions to the reader to be satisfied with the sayings of the wise (12:11–12). The final two verses summon Israel to heed to another level of understanding, a more fundamental duty to fear God and keep his commandments.[14] Wisdom's true foundation is trusting God and keeping his commandments.

Context of Worship in the Book of Lamentations

Because there is general unanimity regarding the theme of the book—the grief over the defeat of Judah by the Babylonians in 586 BC (2 Kings 25; Jer. 52) and the conditions of Jerusalem after the conquest—scholars are in agreement that the book was written soon after the exile began. Subsequently, it is generally agreed that the book was completed before 538, when the Persians allowed the Jews to return to their homeland. More to the point, the author of the book was completely unaware of King Jehoiachin's discharge from prison in 562 (2 Kings 25:27–30).

The book of Lamentations consists of five poems, each of which makes up one chapter. Chapters 1, 2, and 4, which all begin with the interrogative *ʾeka/ʾek* (how),[15] are funeral dirges (cf. 2 Sam 1:19, 25, 27; Isa. 1:21), and chapters 3 and 5 are lamentations and record the nation's complaint. This unique combination of funeral dirges with laments allowed the people to convey their deeply personal and tragic response to God. Chapters 1 and 5 provide summaries of the disaster while chapters 2 and 4 supply the details of the death and devastation. Chapter 3 occupies the central pivotal position in form and content as it distinctively encouraged the people to depend on the goodness of God. This chapter functions as both the literary and theological center of the book. All five poems of the book address the tragic downfall of the city and are united in stating that the reason for this tragedy was God's punishment for Israel's sins. The book reports the grief of the people as the remnant of God's people wrestled with the disaster that had overtaken their city and holy place.

Chapters 1, 2, and 4 are acrostic poems. In such a piece, each verse begins with a successive letter of the Hebrew alphabet. (Other acrostics in the OT are found in Pss. 9–10; 25; 34; 119; 145; Prov. 31:10–31; Nah. 1). Chapter 3, the central and longest poem, is a triple acrostic. The first three verses begin with the first letter of the alphabet; the next three verses begin with the second letter of the alphabet; and so on.[16] Chapter 5, the final and only nonacrostic chapter, nevertheless shares common features with the other chapters since it too has twenty-two verses (the number of letters in

---

14. See Peter Enns, "Ecclesiastes 1: Book of," in *DOTWPW*, 128–30.
15. The opening word, *ʾeka/ʾek* (how), is the traditional title of the book according to Jewish tradition.
16. F. B. Huey Jr. *Jeremiah, Lamentations*, NAC 16 (Nashville: Broadman, 1993), 445.

the Hebrew alphabet). The allusion to the entire alphabet likely conveyed the idea of completeness. The similar structure of the chapters, along with the repetition, enhances the focus on the single most tragic event in Israel's history—the fall of Jerusalem.

Since each of the five poems in Lamentations addresses the fall of Jerusalem, it does not appear that there is any necessary progression of thought in the book. In this regard, the individual poems of the book resemble the book of Psalms, whose arrangement follows no apparent evolvement. Yet many of the same themes appear dispersed throughout the book. Detailed information is provided about the destruction of the temple (1:10; 2:6–7, 20; 5:18), the sinfulness of Jerusalem (1:8; 3:39, 42; 4:6; 5:16), the horrors of famine (2:11–12, 19; 4:4, 9–10), and the hope of retribution against the enemy (1:22; 3:64, 66; 4:21). The content of each of the major poems is summarized in the opening lines of each chapter, which in effect function as a summary or title for the chapter.

Lamentations 1: Jerusalem is devastated

The first chapter depicts the anguish of Zion, moving from the eyewitness account expressed in the form of a funeral dirge (1:1–11) to the lament and outcry of the city itself (1:12–22).

Lamentations 2: The reasons for God's wrath

In Lamentations 2, the source of the nation's calamity is traced back to the Lord himself. The Lord was angry with his people (2:1). He had become an enemy (2:5). He ruined the bars of the gates enabling the enemies to invade (2:9, 13) and killed the young men and young women by the sword (2:21). As a result there was no law or vision among the people (2:9).

Lamentations 3: The city laments its devastation

Chapter 3, unlike chapters 1 and 2, is written in the first person throughout. Thus the chapter opens like an individual's lament from the Psalms (Pss. 6; 88), describing his predicament (Lam. 3:1–18) and then looking to God for relief (3:19–21). The author then expresses his faith in the goodness and compassion of God in what sounds almost like a creedal statement (3:22–24; cf. Exod. 34:6–7; Num. 14:18; Ps. 86:15).[17] The remnant turns to God in faith trusting that God hears their prayer. The poet speaks with the confidence of the coming deliverance as though it has already happened (3:61–66).

Lamentations 4: Zion's ancient glory and present misery

The horrors of the siege are depicted in chapter 4. As in chapters 1 and 2, the horrors of famine have been visited on the city. Jerusalem was worse

17. See William J. Dumbrell, *The Faith of Israel: A Theological Survey of the Old Testament*, 2nd ed. (Grand Rapids: Baker Academic, 2002), 297.

off than immoral Sodom, which was destroyed "in an instant" (4:6). The prophets and the priests, the spiritual leaders, are specifically mentioned as guilty of corruption (4:12–16).

Lamentations 5: Israel calls for God's mercy

The final poem begins with the words, "Yahweh, remember what has happened to us" (5:1), taking the form of a prayer voiced in the first-person plural. This chapter thus takes the form of a communal lament. Like the communal psalms, it concludes with an appeal to God for help (Pss. 44; 60; 74; 79; 80; 83; 89), trusting that Yahweh will hear their prayer. Lamentations 5:19–20 may be thought of as a summary of the entire book.

Context of Worship in the Book of Esther

The major purpose of Esther is to explain the origin of the Feast of Purim, the occasion for celebrating God's intervention on behalf of his persecuted people in the Persian period (Esther 9:20–32). The Jews who did not return under Cyrus (538 BC and later) and other Persian rulers thus became Persian subjects instead of Babylonian subjects (1:5).

After the introduction in chapter 1, a contest is begun to replace Queen Vashti, who had disobeyed the king. Esther providentially wins the contest and becomes the new queen. Haman, a high official in the government, has become enraged over Mordecai's impudence in refusing to pay him homage, and so he proposes to Xerxes a plan to purge the empire of the Jewish people, who are a danger to national well-being. In desperation, Mordecai informs Esther of what is going on and persuades her to use her position to prevent this massacre. As Esther was serving as queen in chapter 2, she is now in position to advocate for the Jews at the critical hour (4:14).

Esther discloses to Xerxes Haman's plan and reveals that she is a Jew and thus a target of Haman's scheme. The king orders Haman to be hanged and then sets about to arm the Jews against those who would kill them. He even authorizes the Jews to take the offensive against their enemies on an appointed day, the thirteenth day of the month of Adar (9:1, 17). The enemies of the Jews had decided to cast lots (Heb. *purim*) to determine who of the Jews should die (9:24), but now the Jews slay their tormentors in one day and rest on the next. From that day forward, days of slaughter and respite were to be commemorated as the joyous festival of Purim (9:26–28).

THEOLOGY OF WORSHIP IN THE MEGILLOTH

Despite the uniqueness of each book, the Megilloth require theological synthesis on account of their proximity in the Hebrew canon and their individual use in association with Israel's festivals. Therefore, we may seek to synthesize the messages of these books as they speak to worship while noting unique emphases as well.

Yahweh, the Sovereign

Ruth, Esther, and Ecclesiastes surely teach the sovereignty of God, which is a core presupposition for Israel's worship. In Ecclesiastes, God's sovereignty is indicated by two fundamental concepts: "all that is done under the sun is the work of God" and "humans do not understand the work of God" (3:11; 8:17; 11:5; 12:14). He is the Creator (11:5; 12:1, 7; see also 3:11, 14, 20; 7:14; 8:17), judge (3:17–18; 11:9), controller of events (3:11; 5:18–6:2; 7:13–14), benefactor (eleven times the subject of the verb "give" [2:24–26; 3:13; 5:18–20]), one to be feared (3:14; 5:1–7; 7:18; cf. 12:1) and obeyed (5:4; 7:26), and is ultimately beyond human comprehension (3:11; 8:16–9:1).

Relating to this lesson that humans do not understand the work of God, we find Ruth. Much of the story of Ruth lacks contextual detail, but what is readily evident is that God is understood as the sovereign Almighty. He causes a famine and then wills to bring it to a close (1:6), directs Ruth to Boaz's field just as Boaz was arriving from Bethlehem (2:3), and then enables Ruth to immediately conceive after her marriage to Boaz (4:13). The book of Ruth is an account of the hands of providence at work in the world.[18] The book also underscores the fact that God welcomes non-Israelites into the covenant. Ruth left her family to follow Israel's God, and this event is described in language that recalls the obedience of Abraham (Ruth 2:11; Gen. 12:1).

While God is not mentioned explicitly in the book of Esther, the sovereign hand of God is readily observable in his provision, protection, and equipping of his servants. The major theme of the book—the establishment of the Purim festival—is the "great reversal," that act of God that allowed the Jews to become the victors rather than victims—not the despised but the triumphantly delivered.[19] Another way of describing the theology of the book is under the rubric of divine sovereignty.

The specific workings of God, though masked in the Bible in language like "and it came about," may be seen in such statements as "Esther found favor in his eyes" (2:9), as well as Mordecai's challenge to Esther: "Who knows, perhaps you have come to the kingdom for such a time as this" (4:14). Also Mordecai's promotion by the king (6:10–12) eventually played a role in the Jews' victory over their enemies (9:5–16). The theme of the book is God's sovereign work in preserving the Jewish people from annihilation. The reader's unequivocal response to this sovereign work of God is to offer praise as an aspect of worship. This theme is also evident even in Lamentations in the prayer that Israel will experience future deliverance (Lam. 3:61–66).

Yahweh, the Sovereign over faithful Israelites

Explicit in the books of Ruth and Esther is God's sovereignty as seen in the narrative accounts of these women. Implicit in Ecclesiastes,

18. Robert L. Hubbard Jr., *The Book of Ruth*, NICOT (Grand Rapids: Eerdmans, 1988), 63.
19. Eugene H. Merrill, Mark F. Rooker, and Michael A. Grisanti, *The World and the Word: An Introduction to the Old Testament* (Nashville: B&H Academic, 2011), 359.

Lamentations, and the Song of Songs—while not narratives—is that God is still sovereign over the stories of those who wrote these books and lived these events. Solomon, likely author of the Song of Songs and Ecclesiastes, lived as king of Israel. In his writings, readers can see a grand progression of thought—from the ecstatic and excited newlywed, to the fatherly advice in the proverbs, to the end-of-life reflections of a master teacher working to avoid cynicism while packaging a lifetime of lessons. In each of these (and in spite of these) Solomon's story provides a backdrop to these books. Similarly, Yahweh is the Sovereign over Israel—during the exodus, as they came into the land, during the period of the judges, throughout the united monarchy, and through various rebellions leading to consequence and exile. While Lamentations does not tell the story of Israel, and was written as poetry, the poetic value of the text is enriched by the stories that surround it contextually—the story of God's people. In this, as in each of these books, we recognize that Yahweh has sovereignly guided history, often through individuals, in a manner that demonstrates his faithfulness.

Yahweh, the Sovereign over marriage

Yahweh is Creator—he is Creator and Sustainer of everyone and everything.[20] In this role, he created, inaugurated, and institutionalized marriage as a means for multiplication and discipleship. The Song of Songs is best understood as a commentary on the establishment of marriage in Genesis 1–2.[21] In some ways, it could be argued that it amplifies the first recorded words from the human race: "This one, at last, is bone of my bones and flesh of my flesh" (2:23). As such, monogamy is the assumed ethic behind the entire account (see Prov. 5:18; Eccl. 9:9; Mal. 2:14).

The Song could also be considered a corrective against all forms of sexual perversity. God has created sex, and it is not evil when enjoyed within the confines he has established (Gen. 1:26–28; 2:20–25; Matt. 19:1–12). The candor with which sexual desire and gratification are discussed within the book does not indicate a low standard of morality. The Song of Songs displays the same kind of delight in sexual union that we find in Proverbs 5:15–19.[22] The love the man and the woman have for one another displays integrity, commitment, and faithfulness. The fact that Solomon himself may not have paid particular heed to his own advice in no way undermines this message. Daniel Block contends that marriage is an ordained covenant relationship (Prov. 2:17; Mal. 2:14), the ultimate goal of which is to build a family through conception and pregnancy (Ruth 4:11).[23]

---

20. Heidelberg Catechism, q. 2.
21. The creation of man and woman as the image of God on day six was the pinnacle of the creation account (Gen. 1:27). See Kenneth D. Keathley and Mark F. Rooker, *40 Questions About Creation and Evolution* (Grand Rapids: Kregel, 2014), 227–36.
22. Webb, *Five Festal Garments*, 29.
23. Daniel I. Block, *For the Glory of God: Recovering a Biblical Theology of Worship* (Grand Rapids: Baker Academic, 2014), 119.

The New Testament, like the Song of Songs, affirms marriage as an exclusive, covenantal relationship between one man and one woman (Matt. 5:27–32; Mark 10:8; 1 Cor. 6:16; 7:1–15; Eph. 5:31). The marriage covenant served as a picture of the relationship between Yahweh and Israel in the Old Testament (Isa. 50:1; 54:4–8; 62:5; Jer. 2:2, 22–23; Ezek. 16; Hos. 1–3) and between Christ and his church in the New Testament (Eph. 5:22–23). Moreover, in the consummation the ultimate union of a believer with the Lord is described as a wedding (Rev. 19:6–8; see Isa. 62:3–5).

The institution of marriage was established for men and women to have a relationship with each other and to fulfill the creation mandate "to be fruitful and multiply" (Gen. 1:28; cf. Gen. 9:1; Exod. 1:7).

Yahweh, the Sovereign over consequence and tragedy

The people lost their land and sanctuary (Lam. 1:10) because the nation had rebelled and broken the covenant. There was thus no question among the Israelites that they deserved the punishment inflicted by the Babylonians as God's agent (Lam. 1:5, 14, 22; 4:13). Lamentations 1:5, 14, and 2:17 acknowledge that the covenant curses resulted from Israel's covenant disobedience (Lev. 26; Deut. 28). God was right to punish the sin (1:18, 22; 2:14; 3:40–42; 4:13, 22; 5:7) and unleash his wrath (1:12–14; 2:1–9, 20–22; 3:1–18; 4:6, 11). There is thus no doubt that God was ultimately responsible for the destruction since the powerful aggressors (Babylonians) are never mentioned by name.

The message of Lamentations is not entirely devoid of hope, however. Hope is expressed in Lamentations 3:22–33 that the Lord will respond to those who turn to him. Belief in Yahweh's overall sovereignty provides ability to deal with the current discipline (Lam. 3:34–38). The complaint of the lament of the city is like Job's complaint (Lam. 3:14; cf. Job 30:9). However, the author of Lamentations nowhere protests that the city is innocent (Lam. 3:39–40).

The primary themes found in the book of Lamentations are also found in the writings of the New Testament. God still disciplines his children for disobedience (Heb. 12:5–11), and those who continue in persistent rebellion can expect to be judged by God (Rom. 1:18–32; 1 Cor. 11:30) and to reap the consequences (Gal. 6:7).

Yahweh, the Sovereign over wisdom and toil

For all the skepticism expressed in the book of Ecclesiastes, Qoheleth never denies the reality of God (2:24; 3:11, 13–14), the monotheistic faith, or a meaningful role for humankind in the world. Even though man and the creation are temporal, God is sovereign (2:26; 3:14; 7:13–14; 8:16–9:1; 11:5).

Man can live and even flourish apart from having all the answers he desires.[24] The final verdict is that man should enjoy life (2:24–25; 3:12–13,

24. Craig Bartholomew, "Ecclesiastes," in *Theological Interpretation of the Old Testament*, ed. Kevin J. Vanhoozer (Grand Rapids: Baker Academic, 2008), 183.

22; 5:18; 8:15; 9:7; 11:8–9; 12:1) and fear God (12:13–14). Wisdom leads us to accept our portion (*heleq*) in life, and living day by day and enjoying the tasks that God gives us helps us to manage the uncertainty of it all.[25]

The teaching of Ecclesiastes presumes that the reader is aware of the creation and fall of Genesis 1–3. Genesis and Ecclesiastes both assume an order in the world, and God fixed this order. Human beings have a sense of eternity (Eccl. 3:1–14) as they are created in the image of God (Gen. 1:26–31). Yet man has limited knowledge since he is made from dust (Eccl. 3:20; 12:7; Gen. 2:7; 3:19). Furthermore, the fact that God has decreed that man must toil for food (Gen. 3:17–19) is everywhere assumed in Ecclesiastes with its focus on human toil (Eccl. 1:3, 13; 2:3; 3:9–10).

The desire of Qoheleth to have comprehensive knowledge parallels Eve's desire, which led her into sin. Everything about this world is marred by the tyranny of the curse that the Lord placed on all creation (Gen. 3:17–19). God made the human race upright, but they have all sinned (Eccl. 7:20, 26–29; Gen. 3). For Qoheleth, life is in many ways a curse, and this curse is especially acute not only in labor and toil but also in mental anguish (Eccl. 1:13; 2:23; 3:11; 4:7–8; 8:17; Gen. 3:17, 19). The difficulty shared by Qoheleth in the entire book can be credited to sin and its consequences.[26]

SIGNIFICANCE OF THE MEGILLOTH FOR BIBLICAL WORSHIP

The theology of worship rooted in the Megilloth takes on even deeper significance when one reflects on the reality that these books ("scrolls") were read publicly in conjunction with Israel's great festivals—Ruth at Pentecost, Song of Songs at Passover, Ecclesiastes at Tabernacles, Lamentations on the ninth of Ab, and Esther at Purim.[27] They address life in its entirety and as a result are equally relevant for the church today.

Yahweh Is Worshiped in Our Vocational and Family Life

The first institution established by God was the institution of marriage, which laid the foundation for humans to fulfill the creation mandate—"be fruitful and multiply"—as well as celebrate the intimacy of sexual love in the context of marriage (Gen. 2:23–24; Song of Songs). As indicated above the love between a husband and wife serves as a picture of God's love for his people. The love of God for his people is the focus of what is to be remembered in the Passover festival.

25. Enns, "Ecclesiastes, Book of," 129–30.

26. See Merrill, Rooker, and Grisanti, *The World and the Word*, 544–45.

27. According to the traditional *BHS* Hebrew text Ruth occurs before the Song of Songs although the Passover festival (when the Song of Songs is read) is the first festival of the year (Exod. 12:2). The reason Ruth occurs as the first Megilloth scroll is either because the contents of Ruth reflect the earliest history of the scrolls (the birth of David) or because the book of Proverbs, which immediately precedes the Megilloth scrolls, refers to the *ʾeshet hayil*, "the noble woman," in the last chapter (Prov. 31:10), and the exact same phrase is used in Ruth 3:11.

God is also to be worshiped by our work. Even though work may appear as a hardship as a result of the fall (Eccl. 1:3, 8), God allows his people to forget their difficulties (Eccl. 5:18–20; 2:24–26), providing relief in the midst by providing opportunities to eat and drink, which are gifts of God to be enjoyed (2:24–25). "Work is the principal act of worship to which humans are called."[28]

By working we reflect God's image. God provided the pattern of working six days and resting on the seventh (Exod. 20:9–11). This weekly cessation of work requires the people to demonstrate complete trust that God will provide and that they are completely dependent on him. Part of the celebration of four of the Israelite feasts, Passover and Unleavened Bread (Lev. 23:4–8), Weeks/Pentecost (Lev. 23:21), Trumpets (Lev. 23:25), and Booths/Tabernacles (Lev. 23:26–28) includes a partial prohibition of work.

Christians must recognize the dignity and value of work: it brings glory to God, it benefits others, it serves the world in which we live, and it is fundamental to our humanity. Since God has created us to do his work on earth, every legitimate occupation is God's work and done for his glory.[29] "Every project we tackle offers an opportunity not only to worship God in the work itself but also to declare our dependence on the Lord's blessing, and in the end, to give thanks for the fruits of our labor (Luke 12:22–34)."[30]

Yahweh Is Worshiped by the Way We Live

Some of the greatest examples of worshiping God by displaying a godly character are found in the book of Ruth—particularly exhibited by the characters of Boaz and Ruth. Boaz had heard of all that Ruth had done for her mother-in-law (Ruth 2:8–11) and commended her for taking refuge under Yahweh's wings (Ruth 2:12).[31]

Moreover, Boaz took the initiative to confront the nearer kinsman at the city gate who refused to take responsibility (Ruth 3:10–15; 4:5–6). In so doing the nearer kinsman became a foil to Boaz.[32]

In addition, in the epilogue of Ecclesiastes wise living is the focus. The reader is instructed to follow Qoheleth's activities as a wise man (Eccl. 12:9–10).

Yahweh Is Worshiped in Obedience

Ruth bravely entered into the field of Boaz in obedience to Leviticus 19:9–10 and received permission from Boaz, who responded obediently by allowing her to work (Ruth 2:8–11). Moreover, the book of Ecclesiastes

28. Block, *For the Glory of God*, 132.
29. Mark F. Rooker, *The Ten Commandments: Ethics for the Twenty-First Century*, NAC Studies in Bible and Theology (Nashville: B&H Academic, 2010), 100.
30. Block, *For the Glory of God*, 138–39.
31. It is not without significance that the first word uttered by Boaz is "Yahweh" (Ruth 2:4).
32. Similarly, "wicked" Haman is a foil to "faithful" Mordecai.

closes with the admonition to trust ("fear") God and keep his commandments (Eccl. 12:11–12).

Disobedience to God's commands on the other hand results in famine and apparently premature death (Ruth 1:1–5). Because of Judah's disobedience the nation went into exile and the temple was destroyed (Lam. 1:10; 2:6–7, 20; 5:18). This was the result of the sinfulness of the people (1:8; 3:39, 42; 4:6; 5:16), which brought about grief and disaster (Lam. 2:11–12, 19; 4:4, 9–10).

Yahweh Is the Only God Worthy of Worship

The use of the Song of Songs in the Passover celebration indicates the understanding that the Song expresses the love God has for his people. Ecclesiastes concludes with the affirmation that the human spirit will return to the Lord after death (Eccl. 12:7). All life comes from God and returns to him (Eccl. 12:1).

As the only being worthy of worship, God must not allow disobedience and sinfulness. (Ruth 1:1–5; Ecclesiastes; Lamentations; Esther). Rather, worshipers should be characterized by faith in the goodness and compassion of God (Lam. 3:22–24; 5:19–22).

WORSHIP IN THE MEGILLOTH: TRUST IN YAHWEH'S SOVEREIGNTY

The Bible teaches that God is the supreme ruler of the universe and thus is sovereign over human kingdoms—he raises up rulers and removes them whenever he wishes (Ps. 103:19; Dan. 4:17, 25, 34; 5:21; 7:14; Acts 14:15–17; 17:24–28). God is the "only Ruler, the King of kings and the Lord of lords" (1 Tim. 6:15 NIV; cf. Rev. 19:16). He upholds and governs the created world.[33] Only the divine Sovereign is worthy of actual worship—assuming that we understand worship as veneration of the One who is the source and sustainer of all things and on whom we are absolutely dependent.[34] The confession of the sovereignty of God should occasion the praise and glory of God and encourage a life lived in obedient love within the kingdom of the King.[35]

God is pleased and is glorified when we place our confidence in him, when we live by faith and not trust in ourselves. When we come to him like a little child we totally depend on him. Just as a parent receives great delight when the child looks to him or her for help, it is the undiluted faith that takes God at his word that gives God great delight. We must become

33. F. H. Klooster, "Sovereignty of God," in *EDT*, 1131. Verses that affirm the sovereignty of God include the following: Gen. 14:19; Exod. 18:11; Deut. 10:14, 17; 1 Chron. 29:11, 12; 2 Chron. 20:6; Neh. 9:6; Ps. 22:28; 47:2, 3, 7, 8; 50:10–12; 95:3–5; 115:3; 135:5, 6; 145:11–13; Jer. 27:5; Luke 1:53; Acts 17:24–26.
34. Block, *For the Glory of God*, 25.
35. Klooster, "Sovereignty of God," 1131.

like children to enter the kingdom of God (Matt. 18:3). Because faith involves trust, not sight (2 Cor. 5:7; Rom. 8:24).

And trust is connected to obedience. As C. S. Lewis stated, "To trust him means, of course, trying to do all that he says. There would be no sense in saying you trusted a person if you would not take his advice. Thus if you have really handed yourself over to him, it must follow that you are trying to obey him."[36] When we look to God the focus is not on ourselves, but on the one from whom all goodness comes. True worship is an expression of the believer's dependence on the Lord and submission to his will.[37]

Trust is displayed and depicted particularly in the most observed of the Israelite festivals—in ceasing from work on the weekly Sabbath. In ceasing from work on the weekly Sabbath the obedient Israelite displayed a devotion to God and complete reliance on him to provide.

In simplest terms, worship is "the human response to God. True worship involves reverential human acts of submission and homage before the divine Sovereign."[38] It must not be forgotten that every command and announcement of Jesus contained the elements of faith, trust, faithfulness, and obedience connected together inseparably.[39] A life characterized by these qualities is a life that offers worship to God, and by this God is glorified.

BIBLIOGRAPHY

Bartholomew, Craig G. "Ecclesiastes." In *Theological Interpretation of the Old Testament*, edited by Kevin J. Vanhoozer, 179–85. Grand Rapids: Baker Academic, 2008.

Block, Daniel I. *For the Glory of God: Recovering a Biblical Theology of Worship*. Grand Rapids: Baker Academic, 2014.

Carr, G. Lloyd. "Song of Songs." In *A Complete Literary Guide to the Bible*, edited by Leland Ryken and Tremper Longman III, 281–95. Grand Rapids: Zondervan, 1993.

Davidson, Richard M. "The Literary Structure of the Song of Songs *Redivivus*." *JATS* 14 (2003): 62–64.

Dumbrell, William J. *The Faith of Israel: A Theological Survey of the Old Testament*. 2nd ed. Grand Rapids: Baker Academic, 2002.

Enns, Peter. "Ecclesiastes 1: Book of." In *DOTWPW*, 121–31.

Fohrer, Georg, and David E. Green. *Introduction to the Old Testament*. London: SPCK, 1984.

---

36. C. S. Lewis, *Mere Christianity* (New York: Macmillan, 1952), 129.

37. Allen P. Ross, *Recalling the Hope of Glory: Biblical Worship from the Garden to the New Creation* (Grand Rapids: Kregel Academic, 2006), 340.

38. Block, *For the Glory of God*, 23.

39. See *pisteuō*, in *NIDNTTE* 3:767. This Greek term translates the major Hebrew corresponding word *'mn* for faith, trust, endure, obey, firm (*HALOT*, 63–64). The term *'mn* is translated by *pisteuō* in the Septuagint in virtually every occurrence of the Hebrew verb in the Old Testament (H. Wildberger, "*'mn*," *TLOT* 1:143).

Garrett, Duane A. *Proverbs, Ecclesiastes, Song of Songs*. NAC 14. Nashville: Broadman, 1993.
House, Paul R. *Old Testament Theology.* Downers Grove, IL: InterVarsity Press, 1998.
Hubbard, Robert. *The Book of Ruth.* NICOT. Grand Rapids: Eerdmans, 1988.
Huey, F. B., Jr. *Jeremiah, Lamentations.* NAC 16. Nashville: Broadman, 1993.
Keathley, Kenneth. D., and Mark. F. Rooker. *40 Questions About Creation and Evolution.* Grand Rapids: Kregel, 2014.
Klooster, F. H. "Sovereignty of God." In *EDT*, 1131–32.
Lewis, C. S. *Mere Christianity*. New York: Macmillan, 1952.
Merrill, Eugene H., Mark F. Rooker, and Michael A. Grisanti. *The World and the Word: An Introduction to the Old Testament*. Nashville: B&H Academic, 2011.
Moyer, James C., and Victor H. Matthews. *The Old Testament: Text and Context*. Grand Rapids: Baker Academic, 2012.
Reformed Church in America. *The Heidelberg Catechism*. New York: Board of Publication and Bible School Work of the Reformed Church in America, 1933.
Rooker, Mark F. *The Ten Commandments: Ethics for the Twenty-First Century*. New American Commentary Studies in Bible & Theology. Nashville: B&H Academic, 2010.
Ross, Allen P. *Recalling the Hope of Glory: Biblical Worship from the Garden to the New Creation*. Grand Rapids: Kregel Academic, 2006.
Schwab, G. "Song of Songs 1: Book of." In *DOTWPW*, 737–50.
Webb, Barry G. *Five Festal Garments: Christian Reflections on the Song of Songs, Ruth, Lamentations, Ecclesiastes, and Esther*. NSBT 10. Downers Grove, IL: InterVarsity Press, 2000.

CHAPTER 16

HEARING, RESPONDING, AND SUBMITTING TO THE VOICE OF GOD

Worship in Isaiah

John Oswalt

CONTEXT OF WORSHIP IN ISAIAH

The context in which the prophet Isaiah received his visions was one fraught with danger and all kinds of unpleasant possibilities. After some years of dormancy, the Assyrian Empire was on the move, again headed for its ultimate goal of Egypt. In order to get there, the Assyrian legions would have to pass through Canaan, that narrow territory between the Mediterranean Sea to the west and the Arabian Desert to the east. There were eight small nations in that territory. From the north they were Syria, Phoenicia, Israel, Ammon, Judah, Philistia, Moab, and Edom. In most danger were the three through whom the main trade route ran directly: Syria (Damascus), Israel (Samaria), and the Philistine cities. But the others knew that their time would not be far behind.

By 739 BC, when Isaiah began his ministry, Tiglath-pileser had been rampaging southward for at least five years. Damascus was soon to be destroyed, and Israel, having already lost most of its Galilean territories, was about to plunge into a bloodbath, with one palace coup following another during the next seventeen years. In the south, Judah had been ruled by King Uzziah, who, although confined to the palace with leprosy, was still a strong and effective king and whose presence had at least provided an illusion of security. But now he was dead, and his son Jotham, who had been his father's front man, offered no such illusion. Furthermore, Jotham would shortly be forced to take his son Ahaz, who was clearly pro-Assyrian, into a coregency.

All of this raised deep and serious theological questions for Israel and Judah (who were, despite their political separation, still one people).

Foremost among these questions was the status of their covenant with Yahweh. Surely defeat, destruction, and exile could not happen to them. Yahweh had promised to give them this land in perpetuity, to make them into a great nation, to protect them, and make them rulers of the world. Thus, if the covenant was true, what was staring them in the face *could not* happen. And if, by some awful chance it did happen, what would that mean about what they had believed?

But another, closely related question had to do with Yahweh himself. They had been taught to believe that Yahweh was not *one* of the gods, but the *only* God. Yet the Assyrians, who seemed destined to conquer the whole world, worshiped Assur and a host of other gods. If the Assyrians succeeded in destroying Samaria and Jerusalem, and dragged the leadership off into captivity, what would that say about Yahweh? Would it not say that the whole monotheistic thing had been but one more illusion?

So what should the people of Israel-Judah, faced with these terrible possibilities, do? Sadly, their first thought was not trust in Yahweh, but rather to engage in political maneuvering (Isa. 7:1–17 [cf. 2 Kings 16:5–9]; 30:1–5). But beyond that, they made two bad choices related to worship. First they chose to believe prophets who told them that they did not need to change their behavior, but only "believe." Second, they thought that they needed to be more careful to perform rituals correctly (e.g., 1:10–15).

Unfortunately, as Isaiah, Micah, and others saw with terrible clarity, these things were not at all what Yahweh wanted, and what was necessary if the tragedy was to be averted. The Yahweh that was being worshiped, whether in Jerusalem or Samaria, was one that had been subtly, but thoroughly, paganized. He existed *for* them, to supply their needs, to satisfy their longings, and to guarantee their future. The Judeans could proudly assert that unlike their northern cousins, *they* did not have any bull idols of Yahweh in *their* temple, but the biblical prophets saw right through that and argued that it was still idolatrous worship the Judeans were engaging in. They were doing the rituals so carefully—in order to receive blessings in a sort of quid-pro-quo arrangement. However, the kind of ethical living that reflected the character of Yahweh, which was not concerned with securing things from him, was largely ignored. As for "believing the promises" as proclaimed by self-called, self-indulgent, self-seeking "prophets," the people would do better to take a long look at the curses the covenant promised to those who kept surface requirements while living as though they themselves were ultimate.

In 722 BC Samaria, the last remnant of the northern kingdom, was captured, and its leadership dragged away to exile in what is today northern Iraq. It is this shocking event—the capture of much of the promised land, and the captivity of fully ten of the twelve tribes—that probably accounts for one of the distinctive features of the book of Isaiah. That feature is the remarkable breadth of vision that has chapters 40–66 speaking to people in the distant future (150 years!) from Isaiah's own times. Other prophets talk *about* people in the future, but Isaiah alone speaks *to* such people.[1]

Why would the prophet do that, or more correctly, be inspired to do that? As I just said, I believe that it is the crushing fact of the exile of the northern tribes, leaving only Judah somewhat intact. The unthinkable had happened: Yahweh had been defeated; he had broken his covenant, and all the promises were worthless.[2] But was that true? Had he been defeated? Had he broken his covenant? Were his divine promises worthless? I believe that Isaiah, having experienced the beginning of the exile, and knowing by inspiration that Judah had escaped this time, knew there was another time coming. Isaiah was impelled by the Holy Spirit to look at the implications of what had happened and to produce a holistic theological perspective that would enable the Judean people to survive their exile with their faith intact. Thus, when Yahweh did what had been previously thought impossible and opened the door for his people to return to the Promised Land, they would be a people ready and prepared.[3]

This means the cultural contexts for chapters 40–55 and 56–66 are somewhat different than for chapters 1–39. In 40–55 we see a people who are deeply discouraged and depressed. If Yahweh was not defeated by the Babylonians, he was certainly defeated by the sins of his people. In any case, it is all over. They may as well settle down and become acculturated as good Babylonians. To such a thought Isaiah speaks a resounding no. Their sin, terrible as it was, would not have defeated Yahweh, and neither

1. This feature has caused many students of the book of Isaiah to argue that Isaiah himself could not have written these chaps.. Rather someone living during the Babylonian exile (586–539 BC), and inspired by chapters 1–39, wrote chapters 40–55, while others, living during the period of the return (539–450 BC), wrote chapters 56–66. While this certainly could be the way the book reached its present form, it does not seem to be what the Bible would have us believe. It seems to say that the entire thing came to us though a single mind and heart. First, Isaiah is named at the outset, and no other author is identified; second, there is a remarkable absence of concrete historical detail about the exile and the return if chapters 40–55 and 56–66 were actually written during those times; and third, especially in chapters 41–55 there is a repeated assertion that Yahweh had specifically predicted all this in the past, something the gods could not do, and had now brought it to pass. For further reading on the subject, see Daniel I. Block and Richard H. Schultz, eds., *Binding Up the Testimony: Explorations in the Genesis of the Book of Isaiah* (Peabody, MA: Hendrickson, 2015).
2. We modern Christians, if we think about the exile at all, tend to focus on the destruction of Jerusalem in 586 BC and the ensuing Babylonian exile. But really the exile, and all the theological questions it raised, extends onward from 722 BC down across the years. Ten of the tribes were gone; what could that possibly mean?
3. But why write it so long before the event (the exile of Judah), if in fact Isaiah did do that? If the book had ended at chapter 39, the picture of Yahweh would have been incomplete. The amazing presentation of Yahweh's trustworthiness showing his power to deliver Judah from the Assyrians in 701 BC would have seemed to be invalidated by his apparent inability to deliver them from Babylon in 586 BC. Similarly, the overriding thought of chapters 1–39 is that the only hope for the deeply sinful people of God is through judgment, but how would that actually be worked out? Without chapters 40–66, the reader is left to wonder what that hope could possibly be. Thus the full-orbed message of hope through judgment needs both parts of the book.

would Babylon (or Assyria earlier). They are in captivity solely under the discipline of Yahweh, and at the appropriate time he who took them there can take them out again. In the meantime, these very people will become witnesses in Yahweh's court case against the gods. They will give the convincing evidence that he alone is God and there is no other. Far from being cast off, they are chosen (cf. 43:8–13).

If we ask how it is possible for a holy God to forgive his people's sin and to use them as the evidence of his godhood, the answer is found in chapters 49–55. They can become Yahweh's servants because of the work of *the Servant*, the one who will be for Israel what Israel could never be for herself (52:13–53:12). Thus the chapters that began in fear and uncertainty end in a great invitation to praise and worship (chaps. 54–55).

Chapters 56–66 seem to envision yet another situation, one that could easily correspond to that which existed in the chaotic situation of the return from exile. In 539 BC the short-lived Babylonian Empire fell to the Persian Cyrus and his allies, the Medes. One of the first things Cyrus did was to make a proclamation that any captive people could go home, and that his royal treasury would pay for the rebuilding of their temple.[4] People who had believed the promises of Isaiah and the other prophets in spite of all the evidence to the contrary were ready to return, and did so in a flurry of excitement. The prediction that they would go into captivity had been fulfilled, and now the prediction that they would return home, something that had never happened before, had come true. Surely all the predictions of the golden future were about to be fulfilled as well.

But it did not happen. The new temple was obviously not going to eclipse that of Solomon; it was not even going to be comparable (Ezra 3:12–13). The people who had been left behind in the land and others who had moved in were not at all happy to see these doctrinaire returnees claiming their old lands back. There was no Davidic king; they were not rulers of the world; Jerusalem was not the center of the world; it was a backwater of the edge of the great Persian Empire. Why bother to get bent out of shape about living for God when obviously he was not going to pay off? After all, the only reason God had restored them from exile was because they were the descendants of Abraham, so it did not really matter how they lived. Once again, the idea that God had called them into fellowship with himself because he wanted to share his character with them had got lost in the shuffle.

4. Recorded in short form in 2 Chronicles 36:23 and in longer form in Ezra 1:2–4. This was considered fictional until the discovery of the so-called Cyrus Cylinder, which records the general basis for Cyrus's offer not only to the Judeans but to other captive peoples as well (see J. B. Pritchard, ed., *Ancient Near Eastern Texts Relating to the Old Testament*, 2nd ed. (Princeton, NJ: Princeton University Press, 1955), 316.

THEOLOGY OF WORSHIP

Any understanding of Isaiah's theology of worship must begin with the vision in Isaiah 6. This experience shaped his entire ministry, as evidenced by the prophet's use of the appellation "The Holy One of Israel" twenty-five times throughout the book.[5] Clearly that experience of Yahweh's absolute transcendence was unforgettable. In chapter 6 we find seven elements that are essential in worship: a recognition of human inability ("In the year that King Uzziah died"); a vision of the transcendence and the immanence of Yahweh ("Holy, holy, holy . . . his glory fills the earth"); a vision of one's own utter sinfulness ("I am a man of unclean lips"); an experience of divine provision for forgiveness and cleansing ("your iniquity is taken away, and your sin atoned for"); a sensitivity to the heart of God ("whom shall I send"); a willingness to volunteer ("Here am I, send me"); and a determination to be faithful ("How long, O Lord?").

From one point of view, chapter 6 provides a template for the structure of the book as a whole. In chapters 1–39 we see both human inability and sinfulness, as both the Israelites and the Judeans are unable to protect themselves from their enemies, but yet seem incapable of any genuine trust in Yahweh, being instead inclined to trust the nations. At the same time, we have a marvelous revelation of both the transcendence and the immanence of Yahweh, focused on his fundamental trustworthiness. He is truly the Holy One, and it is his glory, and the glory of no other, that fills the earth. When he is trusted, the mightiest military power on earth is helpless before him.[6]

Then in chapters 40–55 we see God's provision for the atonement and cleansing of his servants, not only in the fire of the exile, but also in the work of the Servant (42:1–9; 52:13–53:12) on their behalf. Just as the man of unclean lips experienced a divine forgiveness and restoration, so now will the people of unclean lips experience something similar. In so doing they will be witnesses to the nations of Yahweh's unique godhood (43:10–12). They would be the evidence that not only had he predicted the exile and the return, something no god could do, but he had also fulfilled his promise.

But that display of Yahweh's glory had not been intended merely to convince the nations of the uniqueness of Yahweh. From the beginning

---

5. The phrase only occurs thirty-one times in the Bible. When the unique occurrence of "Holy One of Jacob" (Isa. 29:23) is factored in, the idea appears twenty-six times in the book. Otherwise, twice in Jeremiah, twice in the Psalms, and once in 2 Kings (parallel to Isa. 37:23).
6. The structure of chapters 36–39 seems designed to underline these points. In 36–37 we see Hezekiah finally exercising the trust that Isaiah has been enjoining since chapter 7 and receiving a marvelous deliverance. Chapter 38 might be thought to reinforce that thought if it were not for the oddity of the lament over his mortality that the healing seems to have sparked. Then, in chapter 39, when Hezekiah had a God-given opportunity to give glory to God for his healing, he instead displayed his riches and armaments to the visitors from Babylon (who had more than enough riches and armaments of their own). Instead of calling the nations to worship, which is the ultimate goal of God's revelation as made plain from chapters 2 to 66, the Judean king sought to glorify himself.

that display was intended to result in the nations turning to God in trust and coming to worship him in Jerusalem (2:1–4; 66:19–24). For that to take place, as chapters 56–66 make plain, mere forgiveness and restoration, leaving the people's sinful behavior unchanged, would not do. The true goal of the covenant—ethical transformation, the cleansing of the servant's "mouth" (life)—had to be achieved. Only then could the light of Yahweh shine out of them to the whole world (60:1–3), and the nations would flow to Jerusalem in worship.

Thus we may make the following assertions about Isaiah's theology of worship: (1) there can be no true worship without a full appreciation of the character of Yahweh, including both his transcendence and his immanence; (2) there can be no true worship without a recognition of both our deep and pervasive sinfulness, and our inability to save ourselves from it; (3) there can be no true worship unless we recognize that God alone can undo the fact of our having sinned, and alter the condition of our sinfulness; (4) there can be no true worship where the voice of God is not heard; (5) there can be no true worship where the heart of the worshiper is not moved to respond to God in service; (6) true worship results in the worshiper's abandoning himself or herself to God for whatever God might call one to.

The Character of Yahweh

Isaiah will have nothing to do with a god who exists for us. This idea is nothing more nor less than pagan religion. It makes God a part of this world subject to our control. Never! The concept that sets biblical religion apart from all the others is made plain immediately in Isaiah 6:1–3. That concept is transcendence, or holiness. Paganism recognizes that there is a mysterious, "other" quality about the spirit world, and labels that quality "holy." But as Isaiah makes so plain (along with the other prophets), the gods are not truly "other"; they are simply the forces of this world with humanlike masks on. In Isaiah 44 we find the prophet describing the process with dripping sarcasm (vv. 9–20). A man cuts down a tree, and saws it into two logs. He burns one log to cook his meal, and he makes the other log into a god, calling on it to save him! Holy? Of course not!

But Yahweh *is* Other. He is not part of the cosmos. He is not the tree, or the river, or the sun, or the stars; he is beyond all these. Thus the seraphim could declare, "Holy, holy, holy is Yahweh of Heaven's Armies" The repetition of "holy" is a way of asserting that Yahweh is the only being in the universe who is truly "other." He is not one of the host of heaven; he *made* the heavenly host (40:25–26). Thus the idea that we could manipulate him through ritual (a concept of fundamental importance in paganism) is ridiculous to Isaiah (cf. 1:10–15). If he were part of the cosmos, then what we do in the cosmos could influence him through the power of magic. But he is *not* part of the cosmos.

The Transcendent One is the Creator. Throughout the book, the contrast is continually lifted up: we did not make him, he made us (29:23). We are not the maker; he is the Maker. If our god is the work of our hands, we have to carry him! But Yahweh made us, and he will carry us all our days (46:1–4). Because he is Creator, he can be the Savior. The gods cannot save from the world because they are part of this world and are necessarily subject to it. But the Creator is not subject to his creation. He can intervene in it and do what would seem impossible; he can save (17:10; 19:20; 43:13–15; 44:22; 54:5).

But if this Transcendent One is utterly other than his creation, he is not therefore separate from it. He is everywhere present in it. That is the point of the second part of the seraphs' cry: "The whole earth is full of his glory." "Glory" in the Old Testament connotes weightiness, reality, significance (not a thin and passing glow, as is often the case in English). What is it that gives the cosmos its reality? It is the presence of Yahweh everywhere in it. All that we are and have is derived from him. To live is thus to enjoy his presence: his face shining on us (8:10; 33:17; 63:9).[7] But this sense of Yahweh's immanent presence is not limited to a few isolated references. Throughout the book the immediacy of Yahweh in human affairs is unmistakable. There is no part of life where he can be escaped. Everything that happens is under his immediate scrutiny (e.g., 25:1–9).

But what is Yahweh's "glory"? What is it that defines his reality? In the end, it is his holy character, that nature that sets him apart from all that is earthly, especially the gods, which are only reflections of humanity. Two qualities define him: truth and love. Unlike everything "under the sun" (to use the phrase from Ecclesiastes), Yahweh is absolutely true. This is the prevailing theme throughout chapters 7–39. Humans cannot be trusted; the nations cannot be trusted; the gods certainly cannot be trusted, but Yahweh *can* be. This is one of the most astounding marks of his otherness. Yes, he is other in his essence, but he is also other—holy—in his character. He is true.

Why is this so? Why can God be relied on absolutely? It is because he is completely selfless in his love. This is the theme of chapters 40–55, although it is hardly restricted to those chapters, as truth is hardly restricted to chapters 7–39. The term is *hesed*, a word that is unique to Hebrew.[8] It expresses an undying devotion of a superior to an inferior, especially when undeserved (see 16:5; 54:10; 63:7). This quality of Yahweh's love meant that even though the covenant was legally null and void because of Israel's persistent flouting of it, Yahweh would continue to keep it. This self-denying, self-giving love is what makes it possible for Yahweh to be absolutely reliable. He is not out for himself, to gain anything for himself. This is his glory.

7. Note that Hebrew lacks a word for the abstract idea of "presence." When the English word "presence" appears in a translation of the Old Testament, it is actually translating Hebrew "face."
8. The term occurs some 250 times in the OT, with about three-quarters of the occurrences referring to God.

Deep and Pervasive Sinfulness

One of the perplexing features of Isaiah is the location of the prophet's call narrative. Instead of appearing at the beginning of the book, as one would expect, it is six chapters in. Why is this? Did the prophet start preaching before he was called? No, the arrangement of the materials is not chronological, but theological. Chapters 1–5 reveal a deep and serious problem in the nation, and Isaiah offers his experience as a model for the solution of that problem.

The problem is revealed in the structure of the five chapters. That structure is one of interchange, an interchange between a very positive view of Israel's future and a very grim picture of its present condition. Chapter 1 begins with the grim picture. God's children are rebels, made so stupid by their rebellion that they are not as smart as animals, who at least know where the feed trough is (1:2–3). Far from delighting in their Holy One, they have despised him (1:4). The picture continues throughout much of the chapter. However, there are glimmers here and there of hope. They do not need to continue in this condition (1:16–20); they can yet be called "the City of Righteousness, the Faithful City." Yet the chapter closes on a grim note, accusing them of pagan worship.

Then, without any transition, 2:1–5 shows the nations coming to Jerusalem to learn the Torah of Yahweh, and we ask how this can be. Our question is deepened when we read the rest of chapters 2 and 3. Here we see a nation enamored of human greatness and as a result plunged into the deepest desolation. How can the nations learn Yahweh's ways from people in this condition?

Again, without transition, 4:2–6 depicts a Jerusalem that has been made pure and holy as a result of a fiery wind of judgment blowing through it. As a result, Yahweh's glory will be a canopy of shelter and refuge for the city. But unfortunately, this is not the conclusion of the introductory section, as we might hope. Typical of Isaiah's book, future promises are never permitted to obscure present reality.

That reality is depicted starkly in chapter 5, where Israel is compared to a vineyard that produces only bitter grapes. These grapes are arrogance, greed, self-indulgence, intentional sinning, and perversity. As a result, destruction and exile lie ahead for God's people (5:13–15).

We ask how can the brief and general promises of chapter 1 and the more expansive ones of 2:1–5 and 4:2–6 ever be realized? The answer is to be found in chapter 6. When the nation of unclean lips has an experience like the man of unclean lips did, then the light of God can shine out of a purified nation to call the nations to the worship of Yahweh and the learning of his Torah.

This picture of the sinfulness of Israel and Judah appears throughout the book up until the very last chapter. It is in stark contrast to the message of the false prophets, people who, living immoral lives themselves, promised a sinful people that everything would be well for them because they were the holders of the promises of God (28:7; 29:10; 30:9–11). If we deny the reality of our condition in the presence of God, we not only diminish his holiness but also remove ourselves from any possibility of regeneration and sanctification.

Our Hope Is in Yahweh Alone

Interestingly, Isaiah's response to his vision of Yahweh's holiness was only despair. He did not say, "I am a man of unclean lips, but I will do better." Neither did he say, "If you promise to help me, I will repent." He understood that, being what he was, and being what he had seen (and heard) the King to be, his situation was hopeless. He was like a pat of butter with the sun shining on him through a magnifying glass: he was not merely melted; he was consumed. Thus the coming of the seraph with the burning coal was entirely at the initiative of Yahweh, and as a result of his grace alone. Isaiah did not deserve this, and he did not bring it about. He was helpless to do anything to cleanse his lips and make himself fit for service.

Throughout the book, the complete helplessness of humans in the face of sin is illustrated again and again, no place more powerfully than in the final section of the book, chapters 56–66. Here Isaiah is speaking to those who will have returned from exile. Some of them would be blind in their self-righteousness, and Isaiah has harsh words for them. What they really are is idolaters and sinners (56:9–59:15; 63:7–65:16), who need a large dose of contrition (57:14–16; 66:2). However, there were others who recognized their condition, and Isaiah speaks for them (see 59:9–13; 63:15–64:12). In so doing he recognizes that apart from Yahweh, he too would be helpless in the face of sin. But he sees the one who would "tread the winepress alone" (63:3; cf. 59:16), thus climactically defeating their sin and making it possible for the light of God to shine through them to the world (60:1–3).

The Voice of God Is Heard

It was only after his lips had been cleansed that Isaiah heard the voice of Yahweh (6:8). This sequence is important; God may well have been speaking previously, but until Isaiah had received the gift of atonement, he would have been deaf to the divine speech. But now that the barrier of sin has been removed, the prophet is alert to what is one of the defining characteristics of Yahweh: he is the speaking God. The idols have mouths but cannot speak. Yahweh has no mouth, but he speaks with crystal clarity (45:18–19), including speaking the worlds into existence. It is appropriate that Isaiah would hear the voice of God at this point, for surely God's purpose in redemption is that we should be brought into a relationship with him wherein we "walk" with him through life.

If we were to catalog all the places in Isaiah where God is said to speak, or is simply quoted, the list would be very long. The point surely is that God is constantly speaking to his creatures. The words that we hear from

Yahweh may be words of condemnation (1:2; 30:1), admonition (1:16–20: 35:3), invitation (6:8; 45:22), instruction (8:11–12; 38:1), encouragement (10:12; 44:1), or forgiveness (40:2–3; 43:25).

When his people would not hear, or could not hear, he had to communicate with them through alien voices, voices that they could not understand except through the tragic consequences those voices brought on them (28:11–13; cf. 65:1–5). However, if the people came into his presence willingly and joyfully, were atoned for and redeemed, like Isaiah, they too could hear the full range of his heart to them (cf. 65:24).

Worship Entails Response

The person who has recognized Yahweh for who he truly is has recognized his own condition apart from Yahweh, has received Yahweh's provision for that condition, and has heard Yahweh's word correctly, can do nothing other than to fall on his or her face with a glad "Here am I, send me." This was true of Isaiah, and it is what Isaiah longed to see in his people.

It seems significant that in Isaiah 6, the address is very indirect. In many other places in the book, on the other hand, the address is very direct. But perhaps indirect address would be Yahweh's preferred approach. This is suggested by "Your ears will hear a voice behind you saying, 'This is the way; walk in it'" (30:21 NIV). Evidently, he would prefer not to force us onto the right path, like jerking on the bit of a "hard-mouthed" horse. Rather, in the context of true worship a tender heart is open to the softest whisper, and the gentlest suggestion.

But does divine speech always entail response? The Hebrew language seems to suggest so. It has no category whereby mental activity can be separated from action. Thus, to hear is to obey, and not to obey means not to have heard.[9] By the same token, to remember is to act in accord with what is remembered, while not to act in that way means one has forgotten (17:10; 49:14). Chapters 41–48 form a unit in which the prophet is attempting to convince the exiles that, far from Yahweh's having forgotten them, they are called to be his particular servants to give the evidence that he alone is God. But that will entail their continued belief in the return from exile and their refusal to become acculturated to Babylon. Chapter 48, which is the conclusion of the section, contains nearly a dozen occurrences of different words meaning "to hear." God has spoken; now they must "hear"—that is, believe what he has said and live accordingly. To genuinely worship Yahweh is to "hear" him, whatever he says, and to say, "Here am I, send me."

The Goal of Worship Is the Surrender of the Will

Most of the sermons one hears on Isaiah 6 end suddenly with verse 8: "Here am I, send me." We do not like to hear that the commission given to

9. Thus there are several instances where English translations will read "obey me," whereas the actual Hebrew phrase is "hear my voice" (see Exod. 19:5 NIV).

Isaiah was one of apparent failure. The truth was that if he faithfully declared the word of God to his people, it would not turn them to God but, given their heart condition, would turn them from him. Perhaps he could have engineered a superficial healing of their condition if he had "moderated" what Yahweh gave him to say, but in that case he would have disappeared from the pages of history like all the other false prophets. On the other hand, if he would be faithful, then there would appear another generation, perhaps one far in the future, that would *hear* what he had to say.

That was the challenge that faced Isaiah, and his response to that discouraging word speaks volumes. He did not ask, "Why?" or "Why me?"; he did not attempt to negotiate some other way; above all, he did not say no. What he did say was, "How long, Master?" The word "Lord" here is not the divine name; it is the word for a sovereign, an owner, or as here, a master. It is a word that necessarily involves submission. Isaiah here surrenders his will to Yahweh. He will say what Yahweh tells him to say as long as he needs to. Yahweh's response is not very comforting. Though there was a glimmer of hope at the very end (6:13) that would only come out of complete devastation.

Throughout the book, this kind of complete surrender in response to Yahweh's speech is called for. In particular, it is what the Servant gave. In contrast to the servants, who were sometimes deaf and rebellious (42:18–20), the Servant gave himself to Yahweh and to what Yahweh said without a limit (49:3–4; 50:4–6; 53:7).

SIGNIFICANCE FOR BIBLICAL WORSHIP

The implications for worship today need little explication; they should be very clear from the foregoing. But a few comments may be apropos.

Worship that is authentic must be focused on Yahweh, striking a delicate balance between his transcendence and his immanence. To fall into one or the other ditch is disastrous. Place too much emphasis on his transcendence, and worship runs the risk of being cold and formal. But when too much emphasis is placed on his immanence, as seems to be the case today, our worship can very easily become idolatrous, with the focus being on the god who exists for us.

By the same token, giving "glory" to God will need to focus more clearly on that which *is* his glory—namely, his divine character, his truth, and his love. The apostle John recognized this essential fact when he said, "We beheld his glory, glory as of the only Son of the Father, full of grace [i.e., *hesed*] and truth" (John 1:14). Jesus Christ was the full revelation of the glory of God, but again that glory is the divine character, not a glowing gossamer film.

Someone has said that the only thing that cannot be spoken of in the modern church is sin. To the degree that such a statement may be true it is a tragedy. There can be no true worship where there is no awareness that we are unclean in the presence of the Clean, rebels before the Sovereign, lost from all that is life and hope. Furthermore, we need to be reminded that there is no ground for optimism in ourselves. Our only hope is in the unmerited *hesed* of our heavenly Father made available to us in Christ Jesus. Perhaps the reason that our worship is so shallow is because we are not sufficiently aware of the pit from which we have been saved. If we could see ourselves dissolved in the glare of the Sun, and then unaccountably made clean and alive, perhaps our worship might be more profound.

If worship involves our expression of praise to the living God, as it certainly must, it must also involve our hearing from him as he speaks to us through the reading and proclamation of his word. This truth, rediscovered in the Protestant Reformation, is in danger of being obscured from two directions. From one direction, overemphasis on liturgy can obscure the Word, which becomes simply an adjunct to "the main event." But it is also possible to obscure it from another direction. I have heard a worship leader say, after the reading of Scripture, "Now let's worship," by which he meant, "Let's sing along with the band." I wanted to ask, "What has just been happening?" Worship is the expression of a relationship (see 1 John 1:3–4). As such it is unthinkable that a central aspect of the worship experience would not involve our hearing from our God. There cannot be fellowship without mutual communication.

For all too many Christian worshipers, the thought that the end of our worship is surrender of our wills to our sovereign is an alien one. Instead of total surrender, we come to enjoy the sensation of ourselves worshiping. Or we come to perform the stated rituals as a way of reminding ourselves who we are as believers. Perhaps we come to be affirmed in our choice of the Christian faith. Or we come to get our wishes fulfilled. It is hard for us to think that we come once more to have our rebel wills broken on the hard iron of the word of God. We come to reaffirm an abject surrender we may have made years ago or only last week. We come to say again that we are the slaves of the almighty One who is truth and love, whose kingdom is righteousness and justice (cf. 16:5; 65:11–16).

BIBLIOGRAPHY

Block, Daniel I., and Richard H. Schultz, eds. *Binding Up the Testimony: Explorations in the Genesis of the Book of Isaiah*. Peabody, MA: Hendrickson, 2015.

Oswalt, John N. *Isaiah*. NIVAC. Grand Rapids: Zondervan, 2003.

______. *The Book of Isaiah: Chapters 1–39*. NICOT. Grand Rapids: Eerdmans, 1986.

______. *The Book of Isaiah: Chapters 40–66*. NICOT. Grand Rapids: Eerdmans, 1998.

______. *The Holy One of Israel: Studies in the Book of Isaiah*. Eugene, OR: Cascade, 2014.

CHAPTER 17

TRUE KNOWLEDGE OF GOD AND THE TRANSFORMATION OF THE HEART

Worship in Jeremiah and Ezekiel

Gary Yates

CONTEXT OF WORSHIP IN JEREMIAH AND EZEKIEL

Jeremiah and Ezekiel served as prophets during Judah's final days as the Lord used the Babylonians as his instrument of judgment against his own people. Jeremiah ministered in the land of Judah, while Ezekiel served his fellow exiles in Babylon. King Josiah had led extensive reforms in an attempt to return the people to proper worship of Yahweh in the early days of Jeremiah's ministry, but the people soon returned to their idolatrous ways after his death in 609 BC. Improper worship was a major reason for the destruction of Jerusalem in 587 BC and the Babylonian exile. The people's central failure in worship was a refusal to repent of their sinful ways and to honor the Lord by giving him their exclusive devotion and obedience.

Jeremiah and Ezekiel remind us of the vital connection between worship and true knowledge of God. Jeremiah 9:23–24 asserts the surpassing worth of knowing God over everything that humans value, whether wealth, power, or wisdom. The Lord promises personal knowledge of himself to all who would belong to the new covenant (Jer. 24:7; 31:34). The Lord states repeatedly in Ezekiel that the purpose of his works of judgment and salvation is that "they/you will know that I am Yahweh" (Ezek. 5:13; 6:7, 10, 13, 14; etc.). This goal reflects the theocentric focus of the book of Ezekiel. Throughout Ezekiel, Yahweh reveals himself in a series of three powerful visions (Ezek. 1; 8–11; 40–43) so that his people might know him more fully and give him the honor and devotion due his name.

This chapter will develop the theology of worship in Jeremiah and Ezekiel by exploring the knowledge of God as both the focal point of worship and the motivation for worship. There could be no worship of God apart from his revelation of himself. Worship, as has been noted, is reverential submission and homage before Yahweh as our appropriate response to an infinitely holy God.[1] Jeremiah and Ezekiel confront Judah's inappropriate worship and warn that the people have brought ruin and judgment on themselves by turning from the one true God to worship gods of their own imagination. Jeremiah and Ezekiel call the people to turn away from their idolatry and to return to the Lord. They also anticipate the time when the Lord would provide the spiritual transformation that would enable his people to worship and serve him properly so that his glory and renown might extend to the nations. To be human is to worship, but to be fully human requires knowing and worshiping the one true God.

THEOLOGY OF WORSHIP

Worship as Response to God's Revelation of Himself

Jesus teaches that we must worship God "in truth" (John 4:24), and a proper understanding of the character and attributes of God is foundational to true worship. The worship of Judah turned corrupt when the people abandoned the revelation that Yahweh had given of himself and turned to idols and false gods that were merely the products of the human imagination. The people worshiped falsehood because they forfeited the ability to perceive the spiritual realities that the Lord had revealed to them (see Jer. 5:21; 7:26; 17:23; Ezek. 3:7; 12:2). While Judah's worship of false gods was not surprising in light of the surrounding cultural milieu, the degree and extent of their abandonment of Yahweh certainly was. The book of Jeremiah attests to Judah's worship of Baal and the Queen of Heaven (Ishtar?) (Jer. 7:18; 44:17–19, 25) and to the heinous practice of child sacrifice in the Valley of Ben Hinnom (Jer. 7:30–32; 19:4–7; cf. Ezek. 16:21; 23:37–39). In Ezekiel 8, the prophet sees a vision of the Jerusalem temple filled with "great abominations" that included the worship of the unidentified "idol of jealousy" (8:3–6), seventy elders bowing to images that covered the walls of the Lord's house (8:7–13), women participating in the mourning rites associated with the god Tammuz (8:14–15), and men giving homage to the sun (8:16). The beliefs of the prevailing culture had distorted the prophetic revelation of Yahweh's nature and attributes. Rather than Judah fulfilling its role of leading the nations to worship Yahweh as the one true God, the nations had influenced the people of God to worship false idols.

1. See Daniel I. Block, *For the Glory of God: Recovering a Biblical Theology of Worship* (Grand Rapids: Baker Academic, 2014), 23; and Allen P. Ross, *Recalling the Hope of Glory: Biblical Worship from the Garden to the New Creation* (Grand Rapids: Kregel Academic, 2006), 50.

The worship of false gods had diminished the people's perception of Yahweh's infinite greatness, a greatness that made him worthy of their exclusive trust and devotion. The Lord was unlike the false gods, which were nothing more than projections of various aspects of the creation itself.[2] As a corrective to the people's defective theology, Yahweh offers visions of his all-surpassing glory and transcendence in Ezekiel 1, 10, and 43. Michael McKelvey notes that the otherworldly phenomena of these visions (chariot throne, the four creatures, wheels within wheels rimmed by eyes, heavenly platform, and luminous figure on the throne) reveal that "Yahweh is above and distinct from creation, set apart from everything in such a way that it takes symbolic, supernatural 'visions' to convey what mere words cannot."[3] These images are intended to leave the prophet's audience "speechless" and filled "with wonder, fear, and amazement at the God of Israel."[4] Yahweh's presence is associated with brilliant light, and the glory of God reminds us "that he is the most important or preeminent person in this or in any other universe."[5] In turning to other gods or in conceiving of the Lord through the lens of pagan syncretism, the people had "exchanged their glorious God for worthless idols" (Jer. 2:11; cf. Rom. 1:23).

Jeremiah modeled in his own life how sustained reflection on God's revealed character and attributes in worship generates hope in the most desperate of circumstances. At Sinai, the Lord had caused his glory to pass before Moses in the aftermath of Israel's worship of the golden calf (see Exod. 34:5–7). This visual manifestation of the Lord's glory had included a verbal proclamation of his "name" and "goodness." Yahweh's self-revelation in Exodus 34 became central to Israel's understanding of the divine nature (see 2 Chron. 30:9; Neh. 9:17; Pss. 86:15; 103:8; 111:4; 145:8; Joel 2:13; Jonah 4:2; Nah. 1:3).[6] Even though it appeared that Yahweh's relationship with Israel was coming to an end, Jeremiah reminded the people that the Lord's character remained the same. As the Babylonians prepared to take the land, Jeremiah recalled Yahweh's creational power and sovereignty as he prayed for Israel's ultimate restoration and return to the land: "Ah, Sovereign LORD, you have made the heavens and the earth by your great power and by outstretched arm. Nothing is too hard for you" (Jer. 32:17 NIV). Jeremiah also echoed the confession of Exodus 34: "You show steadfast love to thousands, but bring the punishment for the fathers' sins into the laps of their children after them" (v. 18). As Jeremiah reflected on the first exodus (Jer. 32:20–23), Yahweh promised that he would accomplish a

---

2. Richard Lints, *Identity and Idolatry: The image of God and Its Inversion*, NSBT 36 (Downers Grove, IL: IVP Academic, 2015), 87.
3. Michael G. McKelvey, "Ezekiel," in *A Biblical-Theological Introduction to the Old Testament: The Gospel Promised*, ed. Miles V. Van Pelt (Wheaton, IL: Crossway, 2016), 314.
4. McKelvey, "Ezekiel," 314.
5. Ross, *Recalling the Hope of Glory*, 47.
6. Mark J. Boda, *The Heartbeat of Old Testament Theology: Three Creedal Expressions* (Grand Rapids: Baker Academic, 2017), 27–51.

second and even greater exodus by bringing his people home from exile (vv. 36–45).

Even in this time of catastrophe, the Lord remained faithful to his attributes of mercy and justice. Yahweh would pour out his anger on his people in judgment for their sins (see Jer. 4:8, 26; 7:18–20; 12:13; 21:4); yet he also would not turn away from his covenantal love and compassion for his people (31:3, 20). The prophets' vision for Israel's future was shaped by the covenantal promises that the Lord had made to Abraham (see Jer. 33:12–13; Ezek. 36:12, 24, 28, 33; 37:21–22) and to David (see Jer. 23:5–6; 30:8–9; 33:14–16; Ezek. 34:23–24; 37:24–25). God's revelation of his character, attributes, and actions offered incentive for worship in the midst of despair and provided substantive reasons for a hopeful future when present circumstances offered none.

Worship and Relational Knowledge of God

As Christopher Wright explains, knowing God in the Old Testament is always personal and relational: "It means more than just knowing what God has done (the stories), or knowing what God has said (the teachings). It means knowing the Lord in person, as a living character, knowing what his values, concerns and priorities are; knowing what brings him joy or makes him angry. And that in turn will mean living in the light of such knowledge."[7] Jeremiah and Ezekiel highlight the relational aspect of Israel's knowing Yahweh through the use of marital and parental metaphors. In Ezekiel 16, Yahweh discovers Jerusalem as an abandoned newborn and raises her as his own and then takes her as his bride when she reaches adulthood (vv. 3–8). He clothed her in fine garments and expensive jewelry as an expression of his devotion, and Jerusalem's fame and glory as the bride of Yahweh spread to the nations (vv. 9–14).

The portrayal of the covenantal relationship between the Lord and Israel as a marriage is reflective of the demand for exclusive devotion to the Lord in the opening command of the Decalogue (Exod. 20:3; Deut. 5:7). This command is a call to relational loyalty. Moses does not completely deny the existence of other gods (Deut. 4:7, 34), but instructs that Israel is to worship only the Lord because he is the one who has demonstrated his love and power on their behalf (see Deut. 4:20, 32–34, 36–38; 32:36–39).[8] The Shema in Deuteronomy 6:4–5 is "a call to exclusive and whole-hearted worship of the Lord, refusing to follow any other gods."[9] In the Prophets, especially in the second half of Isaiah, there are clear and definitive statements that there is truly only one God (see Isa. 43:10; 44:6, 8;

---

7. Christopher J. H. Wright, *Old Testament Ethics for the People of God* (Downers Grove, IL: IVP Academic, 2004), 36.
8. David L. Baker, *The Decalogue: Living as the People of God* (Downers Grove, IL: IVP Academic, 2017), 44.
9. Baker, *Decalogue*, 44.

45:5–6, 18, 21; 46:9) and that the gods of the nations are nothing more than lifeless images (see Isa. 40:18–20; 44:9–20).[10] Jeremiah asserts that the gods of the nations are "no gods" (2:11; 5:7) and that they are as worthless as "a scarecrow in a melon patch" (10:5).[11]

Judah's idolatry in Jeremiah and Ezekiel then is nothing less than spiritual adultery committed against Yahweh. The opening sermon in the book of Jeremiah (2:1–4:4) orients the entire book around the theme of the broken marriage between Yahweh and his people.[12] The prophet calls for the unfaithful wife to return to her husband and charges that she has shamelessly prostituted herself with other gods (2:20; 3:1–3, 6, 8–9). Israel "followed after" (*halak* + *'achar*) Yahweh in her youth (2:5), but then she turned to "following after" (*halak* + *'achar*) other gods (see 2:5, 8, 23, 25; 7:6, 9; 8:2). Israel's worship of other gods was more than the violation of a legal commandment; it was the betrayal of an exclusive covenantal relationship. The people had "forgotten" (*shakach*) Yahweh (Jer. 2:32; 3:21; 13:25; 18:15; Ezek. 22:12; 23:35), which involved purposeful neglect so that they could worship other gods (Jer. 23:27). In turning to these other gods, they had chosen to "abandon/forsake" (*'azav*) the Lord (Jer. 1:16; 2:13; 5:7, 19; 16:11; 17:13; 22:9). Ezekiel further highlights the relational failure of idolatry when he charges that the people have "set up idols in their hearts" (14:3–4, 7) and "went after" (*halak* + *'achar*) these idols "with their heart" (20:16).

The root cause of Judah's idolatry was a failure to "know" the Lord (Jer. 2:8; 4:22; 9:3, 6). The Lord's own people were unique among the nations in how they had changed gods (Jer. 2:11). Making the defection even more heinous, they had taken the rich blessings they received from the Lord and offered them as expressions of love and devotion to these other gods (Jer. 5:7; Ezek. 16:12–19; cf. Hos. 2:8). Worship both in ritual and lifestyle becomes corrupted when not offered from a heart that is exclusively devoted to the Lord.

In depicting the degree of Israel's relational defection against the Lord, both Jeremiah and Ezekiel employ some of the most shocking and graphic imagery in all of the Hebrew Bible. The people are unbridled in their lust

---

10. Baker, *Decalogue*, 45.

11. Jeremiah and Ezekiel both employ extensive vocabulary to express derision concerning the value of pagan gods/idols, which include (1) "vanity" (*hevel*) (Jer. 2:5; 8:19; 10:8; 14:22); (2) "detestable thing" (*shiqquts*) (Jer. 4:1; 7:30; 13:27; 32:34; Ezek. 5:11; 7:20; 11:18, 21; 20:7–8); (3) "false/falsehood" (*sheqer*) (Jer. 10;14; 16:19; 51:17); (4) "dung pellets" (*gillulim*—Ezekiel's most common word for idols) (Jer. 50:2; Ezek. 6:4–13; 22:3–4); (5) "abomination" (*to'evah*) (Jer. 16:18; Ezek. 5:9, 11); (6) idols—with idea of something insignificant and worthless (*'elil*) (Jer. 14:4; Ezek. 30:13); and (7) "despised/despised object" (*'atsiv*) (Jer. 50:2).

12. On this theme in Jeremiah, see further Gary E. Yates, "Jeremiah's Message of Judgment and Hope for God's Unfaithful Wife," *BSac* 167 (2010): 144–65. For the development of this theme in the whole of Scripture, see Raymond C. Ortlund, *God's Unfaithful Wife: A Biblical Theology of Spiritual Adultery*, NSBT 2 (Downers Grove, IL: InterVarsity Press, 2003).

for other gods and have offered themselves to the gods "on every high hill and under every spreading tree" (Jer. 2:20 NIV; 3:6; cf. Ezek. 20:28). Unlike prostitutes who were paid for their services, the people paid to give their devotion and favors to the foreign gods (Ezek. 16:30–34). Even pagan peoples found their lewd behavior shocking and shameful (Ezek. 16:25–28; cf. 23:11–20).

Focusing on the relational side of idolatry helps to specify its motivation and to clarify the contemporary application of the prophetic critique of Israel's worship of idols. Humans worship what they supremely love and value. The people worshiped the Baals and the Asherahs because they believed that these deities were able to bless them and meet their needs in ways that Yahweh alone could not. Michael Rhodes and Robby Holt remind us, "The primary attraction to Baal wasn't a pretty statue; it was an economic promise."[13] The problem of idolatry is far more encompassing than bowing down to images and worshiping pagan deities. Idolatry involves trusting in anything other than God himself as the ultimate source of meaning and security and giving that object of trust the love, loyalty, and service that belongs to God alone. Job 31 reflects this expanded understanding of idolatry when Job juxtaposes trusting in gold, rejoicing in wealth, and offering homage to the sun and moon and views all of them as "unfaithfulness" toward God (Job 31:24–28). In Colossians 3:5, Paul equates greed with idolatry. Timothy Keller offers this pastoral perspective on idolatry:

> A counterfeit god is anything so central and essential to your life that, should you lose it, your life would hardly feel like living. An idol has such a controlling position in your heart that you can spend most of your passion and energy, your emotional and financial resources, on it without a second thought. It can be family and children, or career and making money, or achievement and critical acclaim, or saving "face" and social standing. It can be a romantic relationship, peer approval, competence and skill, secure and comfortable circumstances, your beauty or your brains, a great political or social cause, your morality and virtue or even success in Christian ministry. When your meaning in life is to fix someone else's life, we may call it "co-dependency" but it is really idolatry. An idol is whatever you look at and say, in your heart of hearts, "If I have that, then I'll feel my life has meaning, then I'll know I have value, then I'll feel significant and secure."[14]

Whatever has this kind of primary importance in our lives other than of our relationship with the Lord has assumed for us the roles of Baal and Asherah.

---

13. Michael Rhodes and Robby Holt, *Practicing the King's Economy: Honoring Jesus in How We Work, Spend, Save, and Give* (Grand Rapids: Baker Books, 2018), 54–55.
14. Timothy Keller, *Counterfeit Gods: The Empty Promises of Money, Sex, and Power, and the Only Hope That Matters* (New York: Dutton, 2009), xviii.

The problem with devotion to idols is that they ultimately never satisfy and never deliver on their promises. Jeremiah's teaching on idolatry is infused with a rhetoric of futility. In preferring idols over exclusive devotion to the Lord, they have chosen cracked cisterns over the source of living water that can satisfy every need (Jer. 2:13; 17:13). In turning to Baal (*baʿal*), they have actually chosen what is "worthless" (*yaʿal*) (2:8) and have exchanged the true glory of Yahweh for "worthlessness" (*yaʿal*) as the objects of their trust and devotion (2:11). The gods they had chosen would never be able to "save/deliver" them (2:27–28; Ezek. 7:19). Richard Lints observes, "The idols could grant no protection to Israel in the face of the threats that surrounded them. Nor could they answer Israel's pleas for help and mercy."[15]

Worship given to idols not only fails to give the Lord the honor that he alone deserves; it also brings ruin and disaster into the life of the worshiper. Pursuing "worthless" (*hevel*) idols reduces the worshiper and their devotion to "worthlessness" (*hevel*) (Jer. 2:5; 10:3, 5, 18). As G. K. Beale has noted in developing the theme that humans become like what they worship, "Following after spiritually empty idols results in spiritual emptiness."[16] Idol worship becomes like drinking salt water to quench one's thirst, and Israel's pursuit of idols took on an extreme and obsessive quality since the gods were never able to deliver on their promises. Lints states, "Promising great blessing, idols created great additions."[17] Rather than enjoying life as a gift from God, they had sacrificed their children to the gods of death and would become victims of slaughter themselves in the very places they had sacrificed their children. They ended up consuming their sons and daughters (Jer. 19:4), just as Baal had done (Jer. 19:9; Ezek. 23:37–39).[18]

Two Essential Qualities of Worshipers

The fact that all of life is lived in God's presence means that worship extends beyond the rites and rituals of the sanctuary and becomes a lifestyle. A life of obedience to God's Word and devotion to the practice of prayer are two essential qualities of authentic worshipers.[19] God has revealed in his Word not only who he is but also what he expects from those who seek to honor him with their lives. Prayer is particularly the faithful

15. Lints, *Identity and Idolatry*, 82.
16. G. K. Beale, *We Become What We Worship: A Biblical Theology of Idolatry* (Downers Grove, IL: IVP Academic, 2008), 115. In following the sexually promiscuous Canaanite gods, the Judahites had themselves become sexually immoral in their behavior (Jer. 9:2; 23:10). In giving their devotion to gods that could not speak (Jer. 10:5), the people had also become spiritually dull and unable to "see" or "hear" (Jer. 5:21).
17. Lints, *Identity and Idolatry*, 89.
18. Lints, *Identity and Idolatry*, 120.
19. On the prominence of the Word of God as a theological theme in the book of Jeremiah and how the words of Jeremiah are equated with the Word of God, see Andrew G. Shead, *A Mouth Full of Fire: The Word of God in the Words of Jeremiah*, NSBT 29 (Downers Grove, IL: IVP Academic 2012).

and dependent response of those who seek to know God and to live in relationship with him.

Worship as obedience and continual repentance

Worship extends beyond rituals to a lifestyle of obedience to God's commands and instructions. The recurring charge in Jeremiah is that the people have not "listened to/obeyed" Yahweh's covenant commandments or the instructions of his prophets (Jer. 7:13, 23–28; 26:5; 29:19, 32–33; 34:14–17; 35:14–17; 36:31; 37:2; 40:3; 42:13, 21; 43:7; 44:16, 23), and the narrative accounts from Jeremiah 26–45 specifically highlight various disobedient responses to the prophetic word. Even without the prophet's indictment, the people's own words reflect their stubborn refusal to obey the Lord (Jer. 2:25–27; 18:12; 44:16–18). Manipulative scribes who altered the law's meaning (8:8) and false prophets who spoke visions from their own imagination (23:16–32; Ezek. 13:1–19) have led the people astray. By failing to obey the Lord, Judah had failed to give Yahweh the honor and renown that would lead other nations to worship and serve him (Jer. 13:11).

In his ministry to the exiles in Babylon, Ezekiel also preached to those who were "stubborn" and "rebellious" (see Ezek. 2:6–8; 3:9, 26–27; 12:2–3; 17:12; 20:8, 13, 21; 24:3). The people would gather to hear Ezekiel speak but then would treat his messages from Yahweh as nothing more than entertaining stories and parables (20:49; 33:30–33). As punishment for their disobedience to the Lord's good laws that were designed to bring life, the Lord gave them over to bad decrees, bad decrees of their own invention, including the sacrifice of their children, that brought death and ruin (20:23–24).[20] In their yawning complacency toward the prophetic word, Ezekiel's audience was as guilty of tying up and binding the prophet (3:25) as those who had angrily threatened, beaten, and imprisoned Jeremiah (cf. Jer. 20:1–6; 32:3; 37–38).[21] Passive neglect is just as much disobedience as hostile resistance.[22]

The key response to the word of God that Jeremiah and Ezekiel seek from their audiences is repentance.[23] The primary Hebrew word for "repentance" (*shuv*) means "to turn," and true repentance involves both a negative turning from idols and sinful actions and a positive turning to God and righteous behaviors (Jer. 4:1; 7:3; 25:5–6; Ezek. 14:6; 18:27–28).[24] The prophets announced that the people would be spared from exile and

---

20. These bad laws contrast to the Mosaic commands that are labeled as "my decrees . . . and laws" in Ezek. 20:11, 19, 24. See Iain Duguid, *Ezekiel*, NIVAC (Grand Rapids: Zondervan, 1999), 262n12.
21. J. Michael Thigpen, *Divine Motive in the Hebrew Bible: A Comprehensive Survey and Analysis*, Gorgias Dissertations 64 (Piscataway, NJ: Gorgias, 2015), 102.
22. This idea is highlighted in the book of Jeremiah by the juxtaposition of narratives of Jehoiakim's violent opposition to the prophetic word and Zedekiah's fearful hesitance to carry out prophetic directives in chapters 26–29 and 36–39.
23. See Mark J. Boda, *"Return to Me": A Biblical Theology of Repentance*, NSBT 35 (Downers Grove, IL: IVP Academic, 2015), 79–93.
24. Boda, *"Return to Me,"* 81.

death if they repented (Jer. 26:3–7; 36:3–8; Ezek. 3:19; 33:9, 12, 18–19), but Jeremiah 25:4–7 summarizes the people's disobedience to the prophetic word as a refusal to repent (cf. 18:11–12).[25]

Rather than turning (*shuv*) toward God in repentance, the people persisted in their "faithlessness" (*meshuvah*) of turning away from God (Jer. 3:6, 8, 11, 12, 22; 5:6; 8:5; 14:7).[26] Calls to repentance are prominent in the early chapters of Jeremiah (cf. Jer. 3:12, 14, 22; 4:1) but then gradually disappear, reflecting Judah's forfeited opportunity to experience divine mercy instead of judgment. In the course of Jeremiah's ministry, Judah went from malleable clay that the Divine Potter was willing to remold if the people would repent (18:1–12) to clay pots that would be smashed in judgment (Jer. 19:1–14).[27] The empty assurances of "peace" from the false prophets along with the misinformed belief that their status as Yahweh's chosen people guaranteed divine blessing apart from obedience emboldened the people in their refusal to turn from their sinful ways (Jer. 6:14; 8:11; Ezek. 13:10, 16, 22–23).[28] Jeremiah countered their belief in the inviolability of Zion (Jer. 7:4–8; 26:4–6), and Ezekiel warned that Yahweh had withdrawn his protective presence from the temple (Ezek. 11:22–25). The people falsely believed that the prophetic warnings did not need their attention because they were for a distant time (Ezek. 12:21–22).

Repentance is the continual posture and practice of worshipers who submit their lives to the authority of God's Word and who are sensitive to the convicting work of the Spirit. Repentance begins with honest acknowledgment and confession of sin, often a missing component in the liturgy of contemporary worship. Jeremiah provides a model confession for how the people should return to the Lord (3:20–22) and looks beyond the present situation in which the people refuse to admit their guilt (2:23, 35) and are unashamed of their sins (6:15) to a future time when the people would return to the Lord weeping over their sinfulness (31:18–19). Jeremiah twice offers confessions on behalf of the people that the Lord rejects because there is no actual turning from sin on the part of the people (14:7–9, 19–21). Ezekiel also envisioned that Israel's future restoration to the Lord would be a time when they would "loathe" their

25. Boda, *"Return to Me,"* 80.

26. Jeremiah 34:8–16 even provides an ironic account of the king and people of Judah repenting of their repentance. Zedekiah directed the people of Jerusalem to release their debt slaves in accordance with the Mosaic law (see Exod. 21:2–11; Lev. 25:39–55; Deut. 15:12–18) as an act of repentance in an attempt to gain divine favor when the Babylonian army was pressing against the city. When the Babylonians withdrew their assault, the people "repented" and took back their slaves (vv. 15–16).

27. The fact that the Lord prohibits prophetic intercession and mediation at times from both Jeremiah and Ezekiel reflects that Judah ultimately crossed a line in which their announcements of divine judgment became irrevocable (see Jer. 7:16; 11:14; 14:11; 15:1–2; Ezek. 3:24–27).

28. Thigpen, *Divine Motive*, 97.

ways and express shame for their sinful acts (Ezek. 16:60–63; 36:31–32; 43:10–11).[29]

Jeremiah charged that Judah had returned to the Lord "only in pretense" (Jer. 3:10) and that their words of repentance and devotion had not produced changes in behavior. Those who came to the sanctuary seeking God's protection apart from a lifestyle of obedience had turned the temple into a "den of robbers" (7:9–11). The incongruity of worship apart from obedient response to the Word of God is ironically highlighted in Jeremiah 36. Jehoiakim the king had called for a national day of fasting and prayer (v. 6), but when the proceedings were interrupted by Baruch's reading of the scroll of Jeremiah's prophecies, the only concerned response came from a small contingent of scribes and officials who recognized the seriousness of the prophet's warnings (vv. 8–16). Jehoiakim, who had called for the sacred fast, destroyed the scroll of Jeremiah's prophecies when they were read to him (vv. 21–26). Jehoiakim's response to the newly composed scroll was the opposite of his father Josiah's repentant and obedient response to the newly discovered "book of the law" in the early days of Jeremiah's ministry (cf. 2 Kings 22–23).[30] Josiah had modeled the Torah-observant lifestyle that the Lord desired from both kings and people (cf. Deut. 17:18–20; 2 Kings 22:2; 23:25), but his reforms were short-lived, and faithful responses to the Word of the Lord were the rare exception in Judah's final days.

Ritual and ceremony were an important aspect of Israelite worship, and the Mosaic law had provided detailed instructions concerning Israel's sanctuary, sacrifices, priesthood, rituals, and feast days. The vision of the new temple in Ezekiel 40–48 reflects how deeply ritual was woven into the fabric of Israelite worship. The larger culture of the ancient Near East stressed the importance of ritual for renewing the creation, but the Hebrew prophets also collectively warned of the dangerous idea that ritual alone was all that was needed to please God (cf. Isa. 1:10–17; Amos 5:21–24; Mic. 6:1–8). *More* than sacrifices and offerings, Yahweh was interested in a lifestyle of *obedience* to the ethical demands of the Torah. Jeremiah even emphasizes this idea with the exaggerated claim that the Lord had not even commanded Israel concerning sacrifices when they left Egypt (Jer. 7:21–26; cf. 6:20). The point was not to deny the existence of such commands but rather to minimize their importance relative to the ethical side of the law.

As in the larger prophetic corpus, obedience to God in the form of concern for the poor and oppressed is a particular focus in Jeremiah and Ezekiel. The Lord had sent the prophets to warn that the abuses of the

29. Boda, *"Return to Me,"* 91.

30. For the literary parallels between Kings and Jeremiah highlighting the contrast between the two kings and their response to the Word of God, see Charles D. Isbell, "2 Kings 22:3–23:24 and Jeremiah 36: A Stylistic Comparison," *JSOT* 8 (1978): 33–45.

monarchy and the rich and powerful were contrary to his ideals and had compromised Israel's distinctive witness to the nations. The Lord had designed Israelite society to be "geared toward the social health and economic viability of the 'lowest' units, not to the wealth, privilege, or power of the 'highest.'"[31] Ezekiel charges that Judah was no different from its sister Sodom in its view of wealth and its treatment of the poor (Ezek. 16:48–52). The Lord presents Josiah's concern for those in need rather than a lifestyle of selfish extravagance as "what it means to know me" (Jer. 22:15–17). Conversely, the pervasive dishonesty and oppression in Judah at large reflects a refusal to "know/acknowledge the Lord" (Jer. 9:4–6). To highlight the seriousness of the oppression of the poor and crimes against others as violation of the covenant with Yahweh, Jeremiah in his temple sermon twice reverses the order of the commands in the Decalogue by placing responsibilities toward others before their responsibilities toward the Lord (7:6, 9). Ezekiel does the same when he mentions first that the wicked are those who oppress the poor before stating that they also "look to idols" (Ezek. 18:12; cf. 22:29).

Turning the people to Yahweh as their exclusive object of devotion was the needed remedy for the greed and selfishness that had led to disregard for the poor. Adoration of God leads to imitation of his character. It was impossible to truly love the Lord who had released Israel from their slavery in Egypt while putting others into bondage or disregarding the needs of the widow, orphan, and alien (cf. Lev. 25:42; 26:13; Deut. 6:21). Judah's idolatry was both a cause and consequence of its greed and mistreatment of the poor. Worship of Yahweh produced a different moral and social ethic from that associated with the worship of the violent gods of the Canaanites. [32] A prophetically informed vision of the worship God desires from his people would provide a much-needed corrective to the tension between gospel proclamation and social ministry that exists in much of contemporary evangelicalism. Deeper appreciation for God's character and the blessings of living under his beneficent rule also frees the worshiper to give and sacrifice for others.[33]

Worship and the practice of prayer

Prayer enables worshipers to pour out their hearts to God in praise, confession, supplication, and intercession for others. Prayer is a prominent theme in the book of Jeremiah, which includes a series of the prophet's laments in chapters 11–20 known as his "confessions" (11:18–23; 12:1–17; 15:10–21; 17:14–18; 20:7–18). These prayers reflect the intimacy that

---

31. Wright, *Old Testament Ethics*, 55.
32. Wright, *Old Testament Ethics*, 58–61.
33. Rhodes and Holt, *Practicing the King's Economy*, 66n22. Indicators that US church members in the 2000s give less than five percent of their total income at the same time that incomes have substantially increased reflects how blighted our worship of the self-giving God has become.

exists between God and prophet. Michael Widmer comments, "Jeremiah's prayers offer a particularly rich feast of spiritual honesty, candor, and insight into the nature and ways of God."[34] In times of intense personal suffering, Jeremiah cries out to God to save him from his many enemies and his desperate circumstances (15:15; 17:14), but he also voices complaints against the Lord with surprisingly harsh language. The prophet accuses God of being a "deceptive brook" (15:18; cf. 20:7), questions why the wicked prosper (12:1–2), and complains that faithfulness to his calling has brought unceasing pain into his life (16:16–18; 17:16; 20:7–10). Despite these embittered complaints, Jeremiah's prayers also reflect a worshiper whose heart is in tune with the Lord's to the extent that his expressions of grief and anger are reflective of the Lord's own emotions toward his sinful people (see 4:19–21; 8:18–9:3; 10:17–21; 13:17–19; 14:17–18). In these expressions of raw emotion, it becomes difficult at times to distinguish the voices of God and prophet as they overlap and echo each other.[35]

Jeremiah's prayers also contain some of the harshest imprecations found in the Scriptures as the prophet angrily petitions to see God's vengeance on those who have sought his life (11:20; 12:3). Jeremiah prays for disaster to fall on his enemies and even their families as the Lord remembers their crimes (Jer. 17:18; 18:21–23; 20:11–12). The violent language of these imprecations is disturbing in many ways, but the prophet prays for divine intervention in the midst of grave injustice and personal danger. Terence Fretheim has noted that what Jeremiah asks the Lord to do to his enemies is in line with the punishments that the Lord had promised to inflict on the wicked (cf. Jer. 12:3 with 7:32; 19:6; 11:20 with 5:9, 29; 9:9; 18:21 with 6:11–12; 11:22; 15:7–9).[36] Even in these imprecations, Jeremiah prays in response to how God has revealed himself by his word.[37]

SIGNIFICANCE OF EZEKIEL AND JEREMIAH FOR BIBLICAL WORSHIP

Genuine worship comes from the heart and expresses the inward desire of the worshiper to honor God supremely and to conform one's life to his will. The fact that the Lord examines the human heart (Jer. 11:20; 12:3; 17:10; 20:12) means that he discerns the true intent and motivation of the worshiper. It was corruption of the heart that kept the people from genuinely seeking and serving Yahweh (Jer. 17:9), and the stubbornness of

---

34. Michael Widmer, *Standing in the Breach: An Old Testament Theology and Spirituality of Intercessory Prayer*, Siphrut 13 (Winona Lake, IN: Eisenbrauns, 2015), 330.
35. Widmer, *Standing in the Breach*, 330.
36. Terence E. Fretheim, "The Character of God in Jeremiah," in *What Kind of God? Collected Essays of Terence E. Fretheim*, eds. Michael J. Chan and Brent A. Strawn (Winona Lake, IN: Eisenbrauns, 2015), 306.
37. For a helpful discussion of Jeremiah's imprecatory prayers and Christian spirituality in connection with a christological rereading of these prayers from a canonical perspective, see Widmer, *Standing in the Breach*, 410–28.

their hearts led them to follow their own ways rather than the Lord's (Jer. 3:17; 5:23; 7:24; 11:8; 13:10; 17:5; 18:12; Ezek. 3:7). The sinful desires of their hearts caused them to turn to idols (Jer. 9:14; Ezek. 3:9; 11:21; 20:16), and idolatry was so prevalent because the people had erected these idols in their hearts (Ezek. 14:3–7). Sinful humanity ultimately chooses to worship the creation over the Creator (cf. Rom. 1:21–23), and the prophets also castigate the nations for the pride that causes them to make false gods of their wealth, rulers, military strength, and idols (Jer. 48:29; 49:16; Ezek. 31:10). The arrogant king of Tyre who viewed himself as a god is representative of humanity at large (Ezek. 28:2, 5–6, 17; cf. Gen. 3:5).

Transformation of the heart is necessary for sinful humans to become worshipers of the one true God. The human heart is spiritually sick and needs healing (Ezek. 16:30). When the prophets call for the people to "wash" and "circumcise" their hearts (Jer. 4:4), and even to "get a new heart" (Ezek. 18:31), they are unresponsive and unable to change. The Lord ultimately promises to do what the people could not do for themselves by providing the internal transformation necessary so that they might become faithful and obedient worshipers. The Lord would restore his people by writing his commandments on their hearts (Jer. 31:31–34), and this transforming work would provide the motivation and enablement for the people to obey his commands. The Lord would give Israel "one heart" (i.e., "a single-minded heart"), so that they would never again disobey and need divine judgment (Jer. 32:39). The writing of the law on the heart would reverse the sinfulness of the people that was etched on their hearts with an iron tool (Jer. 17:1). Werner Lemke comments, "God alone will perform the necessary operations on the human heart to make possible a reverent and abiding relationship between Israel and God."[38] Similarly, Ezekiel promises that the Lord would give the people "an undivided heart" (11:19), a "new heart" (36:26), and a "new spirit" (11:19; 36:26). The Lord would replace the old "heart of stone" that was resistant and rebellious with a new "heart of flesh" that was responsive and compliant to the Lord's directives (Ezek. 11:19; 36:26). This transformation of the people's hearts would come from God placing his Spirit within them (36:27; 37:14; 39:29), and the Spirit would empower and enable Israel's obedience to the divine commands.

Israel's turning to the Lord would also enable the nations to become worshipers of the one true God. The nations would be blessed by Yahweh as they followed Israel's example of giving him glory (Jer. 4:1–2) and they would come to Jerusalem to worship the Lord (Jer. 3:17). The same opportunities of avoiding judgment through repentance and experiencing blessing by worshiping the Lord given to Israel are extended to the

38. Werner E. Lemke, "Circumcision of the Heart: The Journey of a Biblical Metaphor," *in God So Near: Essays on Old Testament Theology in Honor of Patrick D. Miller*, eds. Brent A. Strawn and Nancy R. Bowen (Winona Lake, IN: Eisenbrauns, 2003), 314.

nations as well (Jer. 12:14–17; 18:7–8). The restoration and salvation of Israel would also restore the honor of God's reputation among the nations (Ezek. 36:22–23).[39] God would ultimately have worshipers "from every tribe and language and people and nation" (Rev. 5:9).

In turning away from Yahweh as their object of worship, Judah had not only failed to give the Lord his due honor and glory but also brought great ruin and devastation into their own lives. The Lord would remedy this situation by purging his people in judgment and then transforming their hearts so that they might become a people of worship and obedience. The Lord's renown in restoring and renewing his people would extend to the nations so that they might become his worshipers and experience the blessings of his salvation as well. The renewal of Yahweh worship would transform the broken world in which Jeremiah and Ezekiel ministered. Judgment and death would give way to joy and celebration, and a people characterized by greed and oppression would become a community of love and justice. Humanity can only thrive and fully experience all that it means to be truly human when fulfilling their ultimate purpose—to know and worship the Lord.

BIBLIOGRAPHY

Baker, David L. *The Decalogue: Living as the People of God*. Downers Grove, IL: IVP Academic, 2017.

Beale, G. K. *We Become What We Worship: A Biblical Theology of Idolatry*. Downers Grove, IL: IVP Academic, 2008.

Block, Daniel I. *For the Glory of God: Recovering a Biblical Theology of Worship*. Grand Rapids: Baker Academic, 2014.

______. *The Book of Ezekiel*. 2 vols. NICOT. Grand Rapids: Eerdmans, 1997–1998.

Boda, Mark J. *The Heartbeat of Old Testament Theology: Three Creedal Expressions*. Grand Rapids: Baker Academic, 2017.

______. *"Return to Me": A Biblical Theology of Repentance*. NSBT 35. Downers Grove, IL: IVP Academic, 2015.

Dearman, J. Andrew. *Jeremiah, Lamentations*. NIVAC. Grand Rapids: Zondervan, 2002.

Duguid, Iain. *Ezekiel*. NIVAC. Grand Rapids: Zondervan, 1999.

Fretheim, Terence E. *Jeremiah*. SHBC. Macon, GA: Smyth & Helwys, 2002.

Keller, Timothy. *Counterfeit Gods: The Empty Promises of Money, Sex, and Power, and the Only Hope That Matters*. New York: Dutton, 2009.

Lints, Richard. *Identity and Idolatry: The Image of God and Its Inversion*. NSBT 36. Downers Grove, IL: IVP Academic, 2015.

Ortlund, Raymond C., Jr. *God's Unfaithful Wife: A Biblical Theology of Spiritual Adultery*. NSBT 2. Downers Grove, IL: InterVarsity Press, 2003.

---

39. Statements concerning the nations coming to "know" Yahweh in Ezekiel generally do not appear to convey the idea of a salvific relationship (see 26:6; 28:22–26; 29:6, 9; 30:8–9). See Thigpen, *Divine Motive*, 124–26.

Ross, Allen P. *Recalling the Hope of Glory: Biblical Worship from the Garden to the New Creation*. Grand Rapids: Kregel Academic, 2006.

Shead, Andrew G. *A Mouth Full of Fire: The Word of God in the Words of Jeremiah*. NSBT 29. Downers Grove, IL: IVP Academic, 2012.

Thigpen, J. Michael. *Divine Motive in the Hebrew Bible: A Comprehensive Survey and Analysis*. Gorgias Dissertations 64. Piscataway, NJ: Gorgias, 2015.

Van Pelt, Miles V., ed. *A Biblical-Theological Introduction to the Old Testament: The Gospel Promised*. Wheaton, IL: Crossway, 2016.

Widmer, Michael. *Standing in the Breach: An Old Testament Theology and Spirituality of Intercessory Prayer*. Siphrut 13. Winona Lake, IN: Eisenbrauns, 2015.

Wright, Christopher J. H. *Old Testament Ethics for the People of God*. Downers Grove, IL: IVP Academic, 2004.

Yates, Gary E. "Jeremiah's Message of Judgment and Hope for God's Unfaithful Wife." *BSac* 167 (2010): 144–65.

CHAPTER 18

TRUE WORSHIP VERSUS FALSE WORSHIP

Worship in the Preexilic Minor Prophets

R. Alan Fuhr

CONTEXT OF WORSHIP IN THE PREEXILIC MINOR PROPHETS

Some 2,700 years ago, Micah of Moresheth asked the rhetorical question, "Who is a God like You?" (Mic. 7:18). Micah, like the other prophets of old, knew that the Lord God was "gracious and merciful, slow to anger, and of great kindness" (cf. Joel 2:13; Jonah 4:2), but also recognized that while "slow to anger," he was "great in power" (cf. Nah. 1:3). And thus, seeing the greatness of God in both his power to judge and his mercy to forgive, Micah extolls the God of incomparable grace and mercy, a God who has the power to destroy, and yet has an even greater power to forgive.

The voice of worship is a common feature within prophetic literature, and the preexilic Minor Prophets are no exception. In the decades leading up to the eighth-century Assyrian crisis and through to the Babylonian exile of the late seventh century BC, prophets such as Hosea, Amos, Micah, and Zephaniah called the people of God to depart from the worship of idols and to return to the worship of the one true God, Yahweh. Whether they were indicting the people for the sin of forsaking Yahweh and worshiping false gods, or presenting an eschatological vision of future reality wherein all people groups would worship the one true God, there is an implied sense of the value of worship throughout these books. When the people committed covenant treason by worshiping other gods, the prophets called them back to the only God worthy of worship. And where the people failed to worship Yahweh in voice, the prophets proclaimed it loud and clear. In their oracles and rhetoric, each of the preexilic Minor Prophets has a select emphasis contributing to a prophetic theology of worship.

Hosea emphasizes Israel's guilt in forsaking Yahweh to worship Baal, an act of covenant disloyalty equated with adultery. Amos reminds readers that true worship is not about the mere practice of ritual, but is rather a reflection of a righteous and just heart. Micah sees a time when the spoils of divine victory will be consecrated before the Lord, while Zephaniah envisions a day when all peoples will worship the Lord with a "pure language" (Zeph. 3:9).[1]

Meanwhile, other books canonized between Hosea and Zephaniah have their own unique contributions. Joel distinctly ties worship to repentance, while Obadiah evokes a spirit of awe over Yahweh's deliverance of Zion.[2] Jonah demonstrates that worship can be voiced by any repentant people, while Nahum celebrates Yahweh's judgment of an unrepentant kingdom with the shout of praise (Nah. 1:15; 3:19). And the prophet Habakkuk, perhaps the most liturgical of the Minor Prophets, concludes his musings over the justice of God with a full-length hymn of trust and praise (Hab. 3). The preexilic Minor Prophets do not instruct in worship or provide lengthy discourses on worship, but there is a regular, underlying emphasis on the worthiness of God throughout their writings.

THEOLOGY OF WORSHIP

True Worship: Hymnic Threads Reverencing the Name of God

The underlying theme of worship runs through the preexilic Minor Prophets like the ebb and flow of a cascading river. At times its presence is known, yet stilled up and silent, while in other places it thunders loudly through the language of the text. Some of the most prominent threads of worship flow through the hymnic units that exist within the preexilic Minor Prophets (see Amos 4:13; 5:8–9; 9:5–6; Jonah 2:2–9; Nah. 1:3b-7; Hab. 3:1–19). Through these hymnic intrusions, the prophets effectively praise the power and majesty of God. Using the language of the Psalms (perhaps in augmented quotation), the prophets express their hope and trust in the God who delivers, even while warning their readers of the awesome power of Yahweh's judgments and wrath.

There are three clear hymnic units in the book of Amos (Amos 4:13; 5:8–9; 9:5–6). In each of these, Amos uses the language of the Psalter to set forth the image of Yahweh as a God who is not like the merely localized deities of the nations, but one who "forms the mountains and creates the wind," and who "treads the high places of the earth" (Amos 4:13). His judgments "turn the day dark as night," and his mercies "turn the shadow of death into morning" (Amos 5:8). He is the God of the heavens, earth, and sea, a God who "builds His layers in the sky," who "has founded His

1. All translations here are NKJV, unless otherwise noted.
2. Although Joel and Obadiah are considered by many to reflect a chronology later than the preexilic period, they are included in this survey due to canonical arrangement.

strata in the earth," and who "calls for the waters of the sea, and pours them out on the face of the earth" (Amos 9:6). With each of these prophetic hymns, Amos concludes the unit with a clear reminder that it is the name of Yahweh that is to be revered. The reverence due to the name of Yahweh is a prominent theme that runs throughout the book of Amos; the repetition of this motif in these hymns simply reiterates in high praise the theme that is elsewhere conveyed through other prophetic subgenres (see 5:27; 6:10). In the context of Amos, the use of hymnic elements heightens the rhetoric extolling the worship of Yahweh. The function of these hymns is to remind the people that if this is the God that Amos is talking about, then woe to those who stand in opposition to him. For the people, they were prompted to consider that if this is the God they are in covenant relationship with, then they ought to give him the reverence and worship due to his name—or else.

While there is an explicit stress on the name of Yahweh in Amos, the reverence due to that great name is also found elsewhere, again through hymnic elements. We also see this thread implied in the language of warning and celebration found in Hosea. Hosea is permeated by warnings of judgment coming from the hand of God due to covenant disloyalty, and these terrors are often conveyed through rich metaphor. Yet when Yahweh's mercies and restoration commitments are realized, the reaction of the people is one of celebration—of vocal praise, loyalty, and adoration. In an eschatological state of responsive worship, those who are called "sons of the living God" (Hos. 1:10) proclaim their loyalty to Yahweh, offering the "sacrifices of their lips" and vowing no longer to worship idols ever again (Hos. 2:23; 14:2, 8). The voice of praise is given over to the God who is worthy, whose *hesed* (steadfast love) has allured his wayward bride back home (Hos. 2:14). Even though the emphasis on the worship (and fear) of that "name" is a prominent motif in the book of Amos, Hosea too calls the people to repentance in light of that "memorable name" (Hos. 12:5). And through that name, the people are one day restored to the full measure of intimacy with the God whom they come to adore (Hos. 14:1–8).

The book of Nahum also celebrates the God whose name was to be revered. In an introductory hymn, the prophet makes clear that Yahweh is a mighty God, one who is great in power, for whom "the clouds are the dust of His feet" (Nah. 1:3).[3] As with the hymnic portions of Amos, Nahum describes God as sovereign over the heavens, earth, and sea, implying great disaster for those who stand in opposition to him (1:3–6). Yet to those who are his, Yahweh is a stronghold in the day of trouble (1:7). This hymn of trust functions in the book as a precursor to the vision of the destruction of Nineveh. The Lord is powerful enough to crush the

3. The hymnic qualities of Nahum 1:2–8 are supported by the fact that this segment of the book is a partial acrostic, perhaps hinting at its origin as a portion of a preexisting hymn or psalm. See John Goldingay and Pamela J. Scalise, *Minor Prophets II*, UBCS (Grand Rapids: Baker Books, 2009), 20.

wicked Assyrians, even as he is good enough to preserve those who trust in him. Furthermore, Nahum sees in his vision a day when the God who is worshiped in hymn is ultimately praised through the celebration of his triumph over evil (1:15; 3:19).

The book of Habakkuk includes various hymnic portions that highlight a proper attitude and reverent posture for worship. While taunting Babylon with a speech of impending doom, there is a short interjection of praise, where the prophet sees a day when the whole earth will be filled with the knowledge of God (Hab. 2:14).[4] But that reality is still yet to come; in the present day, in the midst of God's judgment, the prophet reiterates that Yahweh is a God to stand in awe of—when contrasted with worthless idols, the whole earth is left speechless before the Lord (Hab. 2:20).

Although it is noteworthy to see the prophet's praise of God even while announcing judgment, the incorporation of these hymnic elements is a minor element when compared to Habakkuk 3, which constitutes a concluding psalm of worship. Set within the context of doubt turned to trust, Habakkuk sees the Lord in all his majesty. With such a vision (in the form of a psalm), the prophet's doubts are turned to praise, and his eyes are cast on the God who reigns in the heavens (Hab. 3:17–19).

Rounding out the hymnic reflections in the preexilic Minor Prophets, one must also consider the psalm of Jonah prayed from the belly of the fish. Quite in line with the literary flavor of Jonah, there is a bit of irony that qualifies this psalm. It is the pagan sailors, rather than Jonah the prophet, who cry out to God in prayer as the tempest rages on the open sea, and who offer sacrifices to Yahweh and make vows when they see God's hand calming the sea (Jonah 1:16). Yet Jonah comes to his senses later, after he is swallowed by the great fish. Only then does Jonah utter similar words of devotion, praying a psalm of trust from the belly of the fish, uttering his own devotion to Yahweh with "sacrifice" and "vows" (Jonah 2:9).

Surveying the hymns and psalms of the preexilic Minor Prophets, two complementary motifs on worship are apparent. First, there is a sense in which the worship of Yahweh flows from an appropriate fear of God. Amos sought to evoke the fear of God through hymnic reflection, and Nahum projected a God before whom no one could stand (Nah. 1:6). When the prophet Habakkuk saw a vision of the Divine Warrior, his whole body shuddered at the sight (Hab. 3:16).[5] And yet Habakkuk's hymn does not end there—the fear of the divine morphs into praise, leading the prophet to exult in the God of his salvation (Hab. 3:18). So our second motif is

4. For a brief explanation of Habakkuk 2:6–20 as "taunt song," see Richard Alan Fuhr Jr. and Gary E. Yates, *The Message of the Twelve: Hearing the Voice of the Minor Prophets* (Nashville: B&H, 2016), 232–33.

5. On the genre of Habakkuk 3:3–15 as "theophany report," see Marvin A. Sweeney, *The Twelve Prophets*, Berit Olam: Studies in Hebrew Narrative and Poetry (Collegeville, MN: Liturgical Press, 2000), 482–87.

this: the worship of Yahweh extends from appropriate fear to find a place of confidence, trust, and security. The prophet Habakkuk knew who his God was, and drew ultimate peace from this knowledge. Nahum was able to proclaim in praise that the Lord is "good, a stronghold in the day of trouble" (Nah. 1:7), and Jonah came to know that "salvation is of the Lord" (Jonah 2:9).

False Worship: Idolatry

In the preexilic Minor Prophets, Israel and Judah are not guilty of a lack of worship, but rather, they are guilty of worshiping the wrong gods. They had turned from Yahweh to the worship of Baal. Hosea is especially intense in calling Israel out for the sin of idolatry, and the whole book develops an analogous picture depicting Israel's sin of idolatry as a form of spiritual adultery. Through this picture, one sees the suffering endured by Yahweh, the jilted husband to adulterous Israel. But idolatry came not just to affect the heart of God, as troubling as that is. One sees in Hosea that misappropriated worship has collateral consequences for the nation and her children.

Having abandoned God, Israel (the nation) also came to neglect her own, and in worshiping false gods, Israel came to neglect "truth [*'emet*]," "mercy [*hesed*]," and the "knowledge [*da'at*] of God in the land" (Hos. 4:1). The whole of society therefore suffered the consequences of covenant disloyalty. Although Yahweh had blessed Israel, Israel gave their worship over to false gods—false sources of sustenance and blessing (Hos. 10:1–2). As a result, the anger of Yahweh burned fiercely against Israel (Hos. 7:13–16), and the nation was abandoned to her own devices (Hos. 4:16; 5:6–7). In judgment, Yahweh would destroy Israel along with her idols and the sanctuaries that facilitated their worship (Hos. 8:5–6). The bleak picture that Hosea paints illustrates the terrible consequences of abandoning the worship of God and giving that over to other gods who have no power to provide (cf. Joel 2:27).

What we see about worship in Hosea is always set within the context of Israel's guilt in practicing idolatry—or in the language and imagery of Hosea, spiritual adultery. But along with the other preexilic Minor Prophets, Hosea reveals a divided loyalty among the people of Israel. Syncretism envelops the spiritual consciousness of the people. In pursuing the Baals, the people still bring sacrifices to Yahweh, even in the midst of their idolatry (Hos. 5:6). The people build altars and offer sacrifices, but these are given over to the worship of false gods (Hos. 8:11–13).

Zephaniah also speaks of the sins of syncretistic worship, but now the guilt is found within seventh-century Judah (whereas Hosea primarily addressed Israel during the eighth century BC). Set in the period just prior to the Babylonian captivity, Zephaniah levels condemnation against those who worship both God and "Milcom"—even the priests are guilty of facilitating this form of syncretistic worship (Zeph. 1:4–6). Yahweh however is a jealous God, and will not share worship with another. In judgment, God would ironically prepare the priests for sacrifice (Zeph. 1:7), punishing the people and their leaders by "the fire of his jealousy" (Zeph. 1:18).

The clear message of the prophets is that God hates idolatry, and he will judge idol worshipers (Hos. 13:1–3), along with the places where idol worship is practiced (Hos. 10:7–8; 12:11; Amos 7:9; 8:3). In equal terms, God hates syncretistic worship, and it will be judged without accommodation for the "right" cancelling out the "wrong" (Amos 5:25–26). The preexilic Minor Prophets are unified in proclaiming that Israel would receive judgment for her sins of idolatry. Her sanctuaries of false worship would be destroyed, and her idols would return to their place of origination through the judgment of exile (cf. Mic. 1:7).

False Worship: Ritual Hypocrisy

Idolatry and religious syncretism were not the only misappropriations of worship noted by the preexilic Minor Prophets. They also railed against the sin of religious ritualism, which involved the practice of ritual worship that was required and regulated by the Mosaic law, but did so all the while practicing social oppression and societal neglect. Ritual hypocrisy characterized the worship of Israel and Judah during this time, and the prophets verbally blasted the hypocrisy of those who claimed to worship Yahweh all the while oppressing the least among the people of God.

Perhaps no other prophet is better known for speaking out against the sin of religious ritualism than Amos. Everything stated and implied about worship in the book of Amos should be understood in the context of religious ritualism, social injustice, and the hypocrisy of those who practiced one in plain view of the other. Worship brings honor and fame to God's name, but in Amos, social injustice is viewed as "defilement" against God's "holy name" (Amos 2:7). Israel managed to profane the sacred through her guilt of practicing injustice against the poor and the powerless (Amos 2:12).

Amos 6:5–6 provides a glimpse into the kind of hypocrisy that had come to characterize Israel during the eighth century BC. The "first-class" citizens of Israel, who had anointed themselves with the best material pleasures available, sang "idly" to the sound of stringed instruments while they paid no attention to the plight of the poor. These same individuals thought that their "feast days," "sacred assemblies," and various offerings would bring God's favor—so much so that they eagerly anticipated the day of the Lord, thinking that such a day would be a day of great blessing (Amos 5:18)! But Yahweh would have nothing to do with their hypocritical worship. Amos 5:21–24 provides a clear picture of what God really thinks of ritual worship when not accompanied by righteousness and justice. He would prefer such worship be removed from his sight, saying, "I hate, I despise your feast days" (v. 21). Furthermore, the procedures of worship are worthless when absent from righteousness: "Take away from Me the noise of your songs, for I will not hear the melody of your stringed instruments" (v. 23).

Amos even goads the guilty to practice ritual worship—and in doing so to sin all the more—if that's what they think brings honor to God (Amos 4:4–5). In encouraging them to the ongoing practice of ritualism, Amos is, of course, being sarcastic. The point is that ritual worship out of sync with the heart of God does nothing to serve the practitioner. If anything, worship outside of righteousness only heightens the guilt of the guilty.

God's displeasure with hypocritical worship eventually leads to judgment. In an ironic twist, Amos proclaims that God would take Israel's feasts and turn them to mourning, and her "songs" would become lamentation (Amos 8:10). This speaks to an appropriate and visible turn of events when God judges, where the very things that Israel trusted in would become their destruction. The places and apparatus of ritual worship in Israel would cease in the judgment of exile.

Amos is not the only preexilic minor prophet to speak of God's displeasure with religious ritualism. Where Amos preached against the ritualism of the north, the prophet Micah brought a similar message to Judah in the south. Calling the people into the courtroom of justice, the prophet asks, "What good it is to bring sacrifice in homage when sin corrupts the land?" The prophet rhetorically asks the people to testify against God, and to then defend themselves in view of the indefensible (Mic. 6:1–5). Could God really be pleased with worship and sacrifice in the face of haughty injustice? No—what God truly desires is worship that stems from a pure heart, one that values justice, mercy, and a humble posture before the Almighty (Mic. 6:6–8). A proper perspective on outward worship necessitates an inward relationship with God, a relationship that manifests itself in righteousness and justice among the people of God.

True Worship: The Voice of Repentance

Prophetic literature in the Old Testament is largely composed of indictment over sin, announcements of impending judgment, calls to repentance, and oracles envisioning an eschatological day of restoration. Regarding worship, the prophets indicted Israel and Judah for their guilt in practicing idolatry, incorporating syncretism, and engaging in hypocritical ritualism. In turn, they announced judgment in line with the consequences of covenant disloyalty. Because Israel had profaned the sacred and disavowed their covenant obligations, they would suffer the dismantling of their societal and religious edifice, eventually culminating in dispersion and exile. But through this process, they were not left without opportunity. The prophets called the people back to the worship of Yahweh, proclaiming loud and clear that "He is gracious and merciful, slow to anger, and of great kindness; and He relents from doing harm" (Joel 2:13; cf. Jonah 4:2). As the prophets beckoned the people to worship God *in* repentance, they also promised the restoration of true worship *through* repentance.

The prophet Hosea, envisioning the great struggle between God's inclination to judgment and his ultimate purposes in restoration, reveals that the goal of repentance is that Israel might return to God so as to live in God's presence—the very heart of worship (Hos. 6:1–3). As Israel turns back to God, and God in return loves them freely, the interrelationship between the restored people and their God is one of worship—there is a sense in which worship is described by Hosea as the direct result of repentance (Hos. 14:2).

The prophet Amos also ties repentance to worship. In calling the people to repentance, Amos demands that they abandon their ritual hypocrisy and return to Yahweh with a true heart. In this regard, worship is not simply the result of repentance—it is an integrated part of repentance. The people would turn from their misguided thinking that worship could take place apart from righteousness. Only through repentance would the people's worship be pure and acceptable in the sight of Yahweh (Amos 5:21–24). Joel also calls the people to repent with a pure heart, to "rend your hearts and not your garments" (Joel 2:13). Through genuine repentance, Yahweh will once again restore the fortunes of the people so that they might have the provisions to give back to the Lord offerings in worship (Joel 2:14).

Although the priests were called on to implement the elements of ritual worship to facilitate repentance (Joel 1:14), the prophets make equally clear that ritual offerings and sacrifice are not themselves the core component of repentance (Joel 2:12–17). Worship is all about God, not about sacred places, duties, or elements (Amos 5:5). Israel is called to turn back to the sacred God, not sacred places or ritual. Micah makes this very clear: God is not pleased with sacrifice apart from mercy—even ten thousand rivers of oil will not suffice (Mic. 6:7). The only worship pleasing to the Lord is that which comes from a contrite and repentant heart, one that "knows to do justly and to love mercy, and to walk humbly with God" (Mic. 6:8).

True Worship: The Celebration of Eschatological Restoration

During the time that the preexilic Minor Prophets spoke to the people, the worship of Yahweh was either compromised by idolatry and syncretism, or it constituted nothing more than misguided ritualism. Due to the abysmal condition of worship during this time, most of what these prophets had to say to their contemporaries concerning worship is negative. And while there are glimmers of celebration and devotion to Yahweh in the ancient context, most of the positive statements regarding worship in these books come within the context of eschatological restoration.[6] The prophets see a future day when Israel will fully and

6. One notable example of worship in the preexilic context is found in Nahum 1:15 and 3:19, where there is great celebration (and in context, a sense of worship) in view of God's victory over Nineveh and her wicked king. However, the prophets live during a time where worship is mainly misguided or false. Furthermore, they envision a future period (before eschatological restoration) when worship for Israel will be subdued and largely dormant (Hos. 3:4).

unabashedly approach Yahweh in full covenant restoration, residing under the headship of "David their king" (Hos. 3:5). It is only then that the true spirit of worship in Israel and among all of God's people will be fully realized (Zeph. 3:9–20).

The prophets' eschatological vision of the future held that "in that day" there will no longer be idols in the land. The idols that had so permeated society will be completely vanquished, and all worship will be given over to Yahweh. There will come a time when the people themselves will ask, "What have I to do anymore with idols?" (Hos. 14:8). Of course, there is a lot that will happen between the preexilic situation that the prophets spoke to and the eschatological cleansing that they envisioned. For the people, the day when pure worship would characterize the land would be predicated on repentance, but there is also a sense in which God would actively cleanse the land and his people of idols through the act of judgment. After all, Yahweh is a jealous God, and he will not share his glory with false idols and false worship in the established kingdom (Zeph. 3:8).

There is a sense within the prophets that the judgment of today acts as a precursor to judgment (and restoration) in the future. Micah demonstrates that current cleansing of idols from the land enacts a pattern of eschatological cleansing—as God destroys the idols of his people through the Assyrian war machine in the eighth century BC, so he will one day cleanse all nations of idols (Mic. 5:13–14). In the final judgment, the gods of the nations will be reduced to nothing, and all the people of the earth will worship Yahweh from all lands and shores (Zeph. 2:11). Micah's vision of eschatological blessing even has the Gentiles worshiping the Lord from Zion (Mic. 4:2).

The idea that God's judgments apply equally to Israel as well as the nations extends also to the scope of his grace. Through the cleansing effect of judgment all people will be prepared for the expression of worship in the day of restoration. The preexilic Minor Prophets see a day when God will gather all his people—even Gentiles—together to worship him with one "pure language" and "acceptable praise," a voice that echoes the return of creation to the goodness of God's design for humanity prior to the fall, judgment, and dispersion at Babel (Zeph. 3:9; cf. Gen. 11:1–9). All of this brings glory to the Lord of heaven and earth. God's future victory over the nations will be consecrated to the Lord—in a sense, the spoils of Israel's victory will constitute an offering consecrated to the Lord (Mic. 4:13).

Perhaps no oracle in the preexilic Minor Prophets better expresses the extent of worship in God's program for the future than Zephaniah 3:14–20. In the kingdom, worship will be a celebration of God's justice, grace, and peace, a regular and distinctive component of life enjoyed in the quietness of his love (Zeph. 3:17). As the people give praise to God and celebrate his great name, so he will reciprocate by appointing for his people praise and fame, a great name among all the peoples of the earth (Zeph. 3:19–20)!

SIGNIFICANCE OF THE PREEXILIC MINOR PROPHETS FOR BIBLICAL WORSHIP

If worship is an expression of humility, then let us not forget Hosea 13:6—the pride of self-reliance led Israel to soon forget their God, and when their God was forgotten, they soon replaced him with others. While the idolatry that corrupted the divided kingdom of the preexilic Minor Prophets may not be represented in today's society, there are still many "idols" in our day that take the pride of place before the worship of God. And while the apparatus of Israel's ancient system of worship is no longer intact, the apathy of ritualism is an easy trap to fall into as we plug worship services into our busy weekly routines. More grievous than apathy is the ever-present potential of hypocrisy in worship, where the praise of one's lips does not match the actions of one's hands. But the prophets of yesterday are still calling on God's people to repent, to posture themselves before the Lord with humility and a contrite heart, knowing that these attitudes are a prerequisite to worship that is pleasing to him (Mic. 6:6–8). Ultimately, this purity of worship will be realized by all who "go up to the mountain of the Lord" (Mic. 4:2).

BIBLIOGRAPHY

Fuhr, Richard Alan, Jr., and Gary E. Yates. *The Message of the Twelve: Hearing the Voice of the Minor Prophets*. Nashville: B&H, 2016.

Goldingay, John, and Pamela J. Scalise. *Minor Prophets II*. UBCS. Grand Rapids: Baker Books, 2009.

Sweeney, Marvin A. *The Twelve Prophets*. Berit Olam: Studies in Hebrew Narrative & Poetry. Collegeville, MN: Liturgical Press, 2000.

CHAPTER 19

REESTABLISHING RIGHTEOUS WORSHIP

Worship in Ezra

Donna Petter

CONTEXT OF WORSHIP IN EZRA

Right worship is not a matter of preference, but of obedience and true followership. This reality is evidenced throughout the history of Israelites as Yahweh disciplines his people for illicit worship as a father disciplines a son whom he loves (see Heb.12: 7–11). Sadly, the Israelites continued to fail in obeying that which was given to them in the law. Their failings were not just individual but national and systemic as well. In response to the continued hardening of the hearts of his people God sent prophets to warn the people of the pending consequences for continued rebellion (2 Kings 17:13–18; 2 Chron. 36:15–16). Yet, even these who warned were ultimately ignored, and Israel continued not only in disobedience but also in active idolatry as she pursued foreign and false gods, which furthered the pollution of right worship of Yahweh. In fact, Yahweh's abandonment of the Jerusalem temple (the departure of the "glory") and its subsequent destruction by the Babylonians was a visual aid of the serious rift in the relationship with Yahweh (Ezek. 10:18–19; 11:22–23). The temple's destruction provided a portrait of a God "who will by no means clear the guilty" (Exod. 34:5–7) since *who* you worship matters. Because of years of *wayward worship* (Ezek. 8:5–16), the prescribed way of worship (Exod. 15; 20) was tragically interrupted for roughly seventy years (Jer. 25:8–11; 27:22; 29:10). Access to and provision for a relationship with their God was strained. Ironically, because God's people blatantly engaged in wayward worship, the exile further estranged the relationship. In the words of those who experienced exile, "How can we sing the songs of the Lord while in a foreign land?" (Ps. 137:4 NIV). Not only were their identity and inheritance lost, but without the temple, God's presence in their midst, the exile impaired exclusive worship of Yahweh.

In this regard, the opening announcement in Ezra 1:1–4 of Cyrus's rise to power and his decree with the option to return and rebuild the Jerusalem temple (with its rich symbolism) would have sent waves of hope and encouragement to God's people living for decades on foreign soil in Babylon. More specifically, the king's decree would have triggered the hope of renewed worship, a restored relationship and identity with Yahweh. The Persian proclamation (Ezra 1:1) signaled a movement from warfare to worship for God's people. Israel had paid double for her sin (Isa. 40:1–2). This declaration signaled captive Israel was set free to serve the Lord after years of service to foreign powers (Ezra 9:9)! Reparation in the relationship with Yahweh was possible. True worship could now be reinstated, but it would need to be reestablished rightly and according to all that was laid out in the law.

Although Cyrus's rise to power might be deemed another move on the international political landscape of the ancient Near East (1:1), the momentous event recorded in Ezra 1:1–4 revealed otherwise. The opening verse of the book makes it crystal clear that full credit goes to Yahweh. Accordingly, he caused Cyrus to do what he did (Ezra 1:1), and the irony in so doing was that God fulfilled his own word proclaimed by Jeremiah (e.g., Jer. 25:12; 51:11; cf. Isa. 44:28; 45:13). The heart of King Cyrus was in the hand of the Lord (Prov. 21:1).

Furthermore, texts outside of Ezra offer a behind-the-scenes understanding of this moment. Jeremiah, in particular, reveals that God personally reached out to reestablish worship with wayward worshipers. "They will be taken to Babylon and there they will remain *until the day I come for them*, declares the Lord" (Jer. 27:22 NIV, emphasis added). Elsewhere he says, "When seventy years are completed for Babylon, *I will come to you* and fulfill my good promise to bring you back to this place" (Jer. 29:10 NIV, emphasis added). Through Cyrus's proclamation, God came for his people even while they were still in exile (Rom. 5:8). This is because they were still his people and he was still their God (Exod. 6:7; Hos. 2:10–11, 23). Not only is he a God who saves, but he is also a God who restores (Jer. 27:22; 29:10). Yahweh rescues his people from exile for relationship, and then equips them to return to their land and rebuild the temple which signifies their identity as his people (Exod. 6:7).

The theme of worship frames the book of Ezra. In the pre-Ezra phase (1:1–6:22) this is so due to attention drawn to the temple. Much like a church in today's context signals a spiritual hub or place of "worship," so, too, a temple in the ancient context. Worship commences in this pre-Ezra phase with the celebration of the Feast of Tabernacles (3:1–6) even before the foundation of the temple was laid (3:6) and culminates with *the* ultimate act of worship, the celebration of Passover once the temple is completed (6:19–22). The theme of worship continues in the Ezra phase of the book (7:1–10:44), the place where Ezra actually emerges on the scene (7:6). In this section worship entails reestablishing the law through the efforts of this faithful scribe, one "skilled in the Law of Moses" (7:6). Accordingly, both the rebuilt temple and the revival of the law of God constitute worship, a topic that frames the book.

Thus, understanding this multifaceted context for the worship that unfolds in Ezra remains critical especially for understanding how Ezra speaks to true worship today. Ezra shows us that God first reaches out and reenables worship with wayward worshipers for the sake of maintaining the relationship. He restores the *true* identity of his people, which derives from a relationship with him, and then this corresponds to a lifestyle of worship. The theological basis for worship that ensues in Ezra concerns divine initiative, affection, and commitment of God to wayward people.

THEOLOGY OF WORSHIP

There is a recognizable theological pattern that emerges throughout the book of Ezra. While living out consequences for sin/wayward worship, God shows up and his people experience restoration of worship, which reveals the magnitude of his mercy. For a time, renewed worshipers stay on track, but then sin resurfaces as it always does within the human condition, thus causing another breach threatening the worship relationship. In this instance, Ezra, a godly worship leader, intervenes and mediates by confessing sin and crying out for more of God's mercy. The bridge between God's justice and mercy as it relates to the human condition concerns confession of sin in hopes of an extension of God's mercy for continued worship. True worship and the reestablishing of worship arises from a deep awareness of God's character and understanding of our identity and inheritance found in him alone. Although the theology of worship that unfolds in Ezra is significant, it keeps the reader hanging because it doesn't completely fulfill the grand picture of worship promised by the prophets. But, through Ezra we see what reestablishing righteous worship entails.

Reestablishing Righteous Worship Entails Obedience

In the pre-Ezra phase (1:1–6:22) the first three chapters make it evident that returning to the land, and thus returning to Yahweh, required obedience (1:5–3:13). The first step of obedience was to submit to the call of the Lord back to the land of Israel. For in 1:5 (NIV) we are told that "everyone whose heart God had moved—prepared to go up and build the house of the LORD in Jerusalem." Just as God had worked on Cyrus's heart (1:1), so too he had worked on the hearts of his own people to prepare them for his calling back to Israel and back to worship. Willingness to return to a land that had not been occupied by these individuals for seventy years was significant, and demonstrated an obedience that in turn was itself an act of worship evidencing supreme trust in Yahweh.

This return required that a generation of Israelites who had little to no memories of their homeland give up that which they knew in hope of that which they might receive. This pursuit required changing the norms and lifestyle in pursuit of something new, something better, and something completely unknown. The Israelites not only gave up what they knew to pursue this end, they obediently gave of their finances to fund the trip and the return (1:5–6; 2:68–69). This sacrificial giving evidences a prioritization of that which God values more highly than that which was personally valuable to them in the form of the security of financial resources.

Once they made it to the land, however, the work started. It was quickly evident that this city they dreamed of was not what it once was. They continued in obedience by working. Chapter 3 summarizes how worship got underway and mentions two building projects, the altar of burnt offering (vv. 1–6) and the temple foundation (vv. 7–10). Building the altar enabled the reinstatement of daily sacrifices (v. 3), and the celebration of the Feast of Tabernacles (v. 4). Building the temple foundation allowed for a deeply emotional praise and worship service (vv. 10–13). The chapter highlights Israel's first experience of corporate worship in their homeland after the exile. The Israel of God was reunified for worship as his chosen and restored people. Their work here facilitated their ability to follow the procedural requirements for right worship.

The rally to Jerusalem in the seventh month[1] was for the unified purpose of reestablishing worship to the Lord, something years of exile had suspended. Accordingly, they wanted to do everything pertaining to worship "by the book" (3:2, 4, 11). This commitment shows that reestablishing worship entails a prescribed way of doing things in order to return to an exclusive relationship with the God of Israel. In this regard how you worship *does* matter but only as it relates to obedience, not outward conformity in worship style. Rather than understand this as a fierce legalism, doing things by the book legitimizes their reestablished worship within God given boundaries that offer freedoms. Their first building project was "to build the altar of the God of Israel" (3:2 NIV). The "altar" spoken of here is "the altar of burnt offering" first discussed in Exodus.[2] The offerings offered on this altar

1. The seventh month is significant for several reasons. First, for an Israelite the seventh month (Tishri or September/October) marked three mandatory celebrations in their calendar year. The *first* day of the seventh month is the New Year and Festival of Trumpets (Lev. 23:23–25; Num. 29:1). It kicks off and inaugurates the important events of the month whereby the *ninth*, *tenth*, and *fifteenth* days all required something special of the people. On the ninth day they were to keep their Sabbath (Lev. 23:32). The tenth day was the Day of Atonement (Lev. 23:26–31; Num. 28–29), and the fifteenth day was the start of the Feast of Tabernacles (Lev. 23:33–43; Num. 28–29). The latter extended for seven days longer and concluded roughly on the twenty-second/third day of the seventh month. In all of these celebrations sacrifices were needed and offered. The seventh month was a time of enthusiasm and deep religious reflection.

2. Exodus 27:1–8; 38:1–7. So too the Chronicler (1 Chron. 6:49; 16:40; 21:29). Solomon's "altar of bronze," a much larger rendition found in the courtyard of the temple, was the equivalent (2 Chron. 1:5–6; 4:1).

represented one's full surrender to God.[3] The emphasis here is not merely on rebuilding the altar, but the altar's purpose. The altar was vital and tied to reestablishing their relationship to the Lord via the sacrificial system.

Thus, by building and sacrificing on "the altar of the God of Israel" (3:2), Israel is given the opportunity once again to access the divine presence and experience atonement for sins. The nation and individuals could once again devote themselves entirely to the Lord in the manner called for in the law. These sacrifices officially reinstate their relationship to their God, the God of Israel, the one to whom the altar belongs, and the one to whom all worship rightfully belongs. His people were again free to offer to him their worship as responsive obedience to the type of worship he desired as made plain through the giving of the law.

Reestablishing Righteous Worship Entails Declaring the Goodness of God

As chapter 3 concludes (vv. 10–13), we do not read about the completion of the temple, as would be expected, but only about the completion of its foundation and various responses to it. This building report, quick as it is, functions as a primer for the real announcement that immediately follows: Israel then celebrated her first corporate worship service after exile. The author vividly describes this scene in the closing verses of chapter 3. Once the temple foundation is laid the personnel took their places with the sole purpose of offering up praises to the Lord. The worship personnel included the priests adorned with garments and trumpets. It also included the Levites adorned with cymbals. This arrangement was not random. It was "prescribed by David, king of Israel" (2 Chron. 23–25). The author explains this Davidic connection not deriving it from *King David* but from David, *king of Israel*. The former designation highlights the person as king, but the latter highlights the person as king of a nation thus highlighting the reinstitution of Israel as a nation of worshipers. The titular "king of Israel" speaks clearly of unity. Although the circumstances are very different, postexilic Israel is unified as in former days and is experiencing a measure of unity that she once fully enjoyed under David's leadership.

The nature of their worship at this juncture has a threefold component. First, they sang with praises and thanksgiving. The word translated "sang" is literally "answered" in reference to responsive singing or antiphonal choral singing. In other words, they are giving an answer or response

3. Burnt offerings (Lev. 1:3–17; 6:8–13 [MT 6:1–6]) come under the category of consecratory offerings along with cereal and drink offerings (Lev. 2; 6:14–23 [MT 6:7–11]; Num. 15:1–10). In very general terms, the sacrifice made with this type of offering represented an act of full surrender and commitment to God. Furthermore, the burnt offering played a primary role in the festivals of the sacred calendar and was associated also with atonement. When a person offered a sheep, goat, or bird the entire offering was consumed by the fire and deemed a pleasing odor to the Lord. The altar of burnt offering is distinct from the smaller altar of incense (Exod. 30:1–10), which was placed before the veil that screened the holy of holies and functioned differently.

to the completion of the temple foundation. Praise and thanksgiving form the content of their response. They direct their response toward the Lord, the covenant-keeping God, because he is continuing relational obligations by rescuing them from exile. Second, their praises and thanksgiving contained a specific declaration lauding the twofold nature of the Lord's character: The Hebrew literally reads, "For he is good, for forever is his covenantal loyalty" (3:11). That is, the cause for their praise is due to the fact that he is inherently good. And because he is good, he manifests his relational loyalty or faithfulness (NIV: "love") without end. His goodness and "love" are evident because the foundation of the temple was laid. And third, their song of praise identifies the recipient of his goodness. The text clearly indicates, "For forever is his covenantal loyalty toward *Israel*," the only occurrence of the phrase with "Israel" as the object. This is significant because when this same refrain appears in the biblical text often the object of his covenantal loyalty is not stated.[4] The added object here says something about their present self-awareness to be sure. The returned exiles consider themselves the new Israel. They have a renewed sense of belonging once again to the Lord. They are aware that they are his people (Israel) and he is their God (Yahweh). The assembled community is, therefore, unified in their declaration of praise, which is an affirmation of the Lord's ongoing providence. Thus their "answer" to such a display of God's goodness and love was not just a shout of praise, but "a great shout of praise!" Their praise and worship was rooted in a keen awareness of Yahweh's strong and unshakable character, without which the return from exile and the completion of the temple foundation would not have been possible.

The significance of the moment is felt by the fact that the last time the Israelite community assembled "to sing" this song or give a similar "response" was when the ark of the covenant was brought into the holy of holies upon completion of Solomon's temple (2 Chron. 5:2–14; 7:3). Prior to that David had instructed thanksgiving to be conducted after the ark was brought to Jerusalem; indeed, David was no stranger to vibrant worship (2 Sam. 6:3–16; 1 Chron. 16:1–7). The basis of David's exhortation to give thanks at that specific moment derived from this profound theological truth: "for he is good, for his steadfast love endures forever," highlighting the goodness of God's character.[5]

4. See for example Pss. 106:1; 107:1; 118:1; 136:1–26; 1 Chron. 16:34.

5. The impetus for the rich theological claims about God's goodness highlighted in the anthem sounded first by David, preexilic Israel, and now by the returned exiles here in Ezra 3:11, goes all the way back to Moses in the book of Exodus. In response to Moses's request to see God's glory (Exod. 33:18), the Lord declares that he will show Moses his total goodness (33:19). This goodness refers to God's character, his essence (33:19; 34:5–7), a description of who he is. One experiences it through covenantal relationship with Yahweh (34:5–7). One knows it by the Lord's direct and ongoing involvement in the lives of his people as he manifests his nature for their benefit. God's goodness was immediately manifested in that he forgave Israel after the golden calf incident. Moses and Israel understood God's character. Ongoing manifestations of his goodness

From the perspective of the biblical writer, the manifestation of his goodness is apparent with the temple foundation laid. Although the historical circumstances are different—there is no ark and the Second Temple has not yet been fully rebuilt—their outburst of praise at this moment represents hearts of worship, hearts that recognize the very essence of God's being as good. The exiles knew their sordid history, but they also knew the God of their sordid history. The exiles understood God's character.[6] Thus the rationale for worship derives from the theological reality that God in his very essence is good, and that his goodness knows no limits. The restored people of God understood God's character.[7]

In the closing two verses of chapter 3, the author continues the description of the worship celebration. The focal point shifts from their worship song to all the sounds associated with what appears to have been an electrifying celebration. Together with the "great shout of praise" (v. 11 NIV) others "wept aloud" and still others "shouted for joy" (vv. 12–13 NIV). On the one hand this "blended" worship service consisted of those who were optimistic, hopeful, and thus able to enter into the celebration with joy. On the other, there were those who had experienced the "glory days" of worship under David and Solomon and who thus expressed contrasting emotions (3:12). The eyewitnesses of Solomon's temple (aging senior citizens) were underwhelmed at what they saw and wept loudly (Hag. 2:3; Zech. 4:10). Although in attendance physically, their hearts and minds were not in the moment. Sadly, they were unable to recognize God's present goodness because of clinging too tightly to the past. The warning seems apparent. A denial of God's goodness (no matter how small or big it manifests itself) denies him of worship. The nature of these sounds were indistinguishable because the people "made so much noise" thus,

---

were revealed all throughout their early history. The Psalter provides evidence. In numerous *preexilic psalms*, the cause for the command to praise/give thanks to the Lord was rooted in an understanding of the Lord's character of goodness and unwavering loyalty (Pss. 100:5; 106; 107; or 136). For this reason, the psalmist, in reference to corporate Israel or as an individual worshiper, often says, "Give thanks to the LORD, for he is good, for his steadfast love endures forever" (136; 118). In fact, Psalm 136 uses the phrase as a liturgical refrain (26×) alongside recitations of Israel's early history and the Lord's ongoing providence. This song was on the tongue of the nation and people who individually experienced God's deliverance from a personal crisis. Only one who truly believes can say this.

6. 2 Chronicles 5:13; 7:3, 6, following David's instructions (1 Chron. 16:8, 34, 41; 25:1).
7. Accordingly, in various psalms after the exile, this song of praise became a standard expression of praise in the community of believers based on the return from exile. Psalm 126 states that indeed "those who sow with tears will reap with songs of joy. Those who go out weeping, carrying seed to sow, will return with songs of joy, carrying sheaves with them" (Ps. 126:5–6 NIV). The psalmist recognizes that bringing back the captives is God's work of restoration and for this reason laughter and songs of joy are on their tongues (126:2 NIV). Indeed, it was a work not only significant for Israel but one that captured the attention of those looking on: "Then it was said among the nations, "The LORD has done great things for them." God demonstrated his power to bring his people back from exile, and as a result his people extol his character of goodness and the nations recognize the Lord.

"the sound was heard far away" (3:13). Numerous times in these verses the author references the sound at the construction site. What is highlighted through this repetition is that the sound was not only loud, which indicated a renewed heart (corporately), but also that the praise reverberated outside the community, which is indicative of a renewed and unified witness (cf. Ps. 126).[8]

The power of this moment of corporate worship should not be overlooked given the backdrop and mournful tone of the exile. On the basis of Psalm 137 we know of the painful reality of no worship in Babylon: "There on the poplars we hung our harps, for there our captors asked us for songs, our tormentors demanded songs of joy; they said, 'Sing us one of the songs of Zion'" (vv. 2–3 NIV). In response to the taunt of their enemies was a self-imposed silence: "How can we sing the songs of the LORD while in a foreign land?" (v. 4 NIV). But now in glaring contrast and with the same emotional intensity as that of Psalm 137 the author captures the worshipful tone after the exile. The strong sentiment of the people manifested itself in an extremely loud and unified worship service heard from a distance. The returned exiles understood God's character.

The theology that emerges from this chapter is significant. Reestablishing worship naturally entails both a legitimate way (by the book) *and* an attitude of gratitude (awareness of God's grace). Primarily, though, reestablished worshipers are gripped by God's goodness. Ezra 3:1–13 paints a picture of unified corporate worship after tangible evidence of God's goodness to them. The only appropriate response to being on the receiving end of God's goodness is worship. In other words, to attribute this favorable outcome in their lives (opportunity to return), after a time of hardship brought on by their own wrongdoing (exile), to a natural set of circumstances (international politics) is to deny God the worship and praise he deserves. Restoration of worship may have small beginnings, but it *all* depends on God's unshakeable and unchangeable character and acknowledgment of it. This is cause for worship.

Reestablishing Righteous Worship Entails Steadfastness in Opposition

Although God's people had assistance in reestablishing worship, their efforts were met with great resistance. Opposition toward exclusive worship of Yahweh dominates the narrative of Ezra 4:1–6:12. The resistance

8. In fact, their renewed witness in the land sets the stage for the trouble described in the ensuing chapter (4:1–24). Just as the word of the Lord through Jeremiah was fulfilled regarding Cyrus's decree and the return of the exiles in chapter 1:1, so too, Jeremiah's word relative to restored worship finds fulfillment here in Ezra 3. "For in the streets will be heard the voices of those who bring thank offerings to the house of the Lord saying, 'Give thanks to the Lord Almighty, for the Lord is good, for his steadfast love endures forever.'" In other words, Jerusalem's fortunes would be restored and the visible manifestation of that would be the shift from silence to celebration, from mourning to dancing, from weeping to worship in the cities of Judah and Jerusalem (Jer. 33:10–11; 7; 9).

comes from their neighbors and those in various leadership positions, and this resistance haunts them for years (Ezra 4). But the timing of the initial resistance (4:1–4) couldn't have been worse.

When the community is barely on its feet and their identity as the renewed people of God remains fragile, opposition comes in the guise of assistance. In this instance, "neighbors" want to help them build, but these neighbors are "the enemies of Judah and Benjamin" (4:1). They self-identify as exiles, but most importantly, these exiled locals claim to seek and worship the same God (v. 2). Their boast, "We are one of you," becomes their rationale to offer assistance.

Opposition comes as an appealing offer to help at a time of need and vulnerability! Their help might have expedited the building project and made things more efficient. In addition, their claim of being like-minded spiritually could have been a temptation to which the leadership succumbed. But in a joint council session, Zerubbabel and the other leaders of the worship community responded with a united voice demonstrating discernment and uncompromising theological conviction in their worship of Yahweh for the sake of purity. Although these neighbors may consider themselves exiles, Cyrus's decree was not issued to them (v. 3; cf. 1:2). And while they *may* be seeking and worshiping Yahweh, it was not Yahweh worship exclusively (v. 3). These people were involved with other religious practices in addition to the worship of Yahweh (2 Kings 17:7–13). As such they were not wholly and exclusively devoted to the Lord. The conclusion was simple. They had neither legal nor religious grounds to participate and were, therefore, excluded.

The identity of the renewed community was fragile. Serious measures had already been taken to ensure this (cf. chaps. 2 and 3). Purity, for the sake of preserving the identity of the people of God, was the premise of rebuilding the new community. It was not a time to be "neighborly" and to hope that these neighbors could be won over to the worship of Yahweh alone. A lack of purity could not be tolerated given their sordid past, but especially in light of the second chance (return from exile) to get it right. The leadership demonstrated courage, conviction, and a sober-mindedness about the offer of help. They discerned the threat to Yahweh-alone worship and, as a result, flat-out rejected additional help. For these reasons religious intolerance, not religious tolerance, needed to be upheld. It was a time to draw a line in the sand and to say no.[9]

9. This narrative is without parallel in the entire Old Testament! With few exceptions in the annals of Kings and Chronicles Israel's leaders are not lauded for their discernment nor uncompromising stance with syncretism or idolatry. Their tendency was to be tolerant and inclusive rather than be intolerant and exclusive. This lack of passion for purity defiled the people of God and eventually led them into exile. The leaders in Ezra 4:3 may be trying to avoid the mistakes of the past by taking a hard line with those proposing help as they rebuild the covenantal community. Regardless of the unfavorable, costly results of retaliation that crippled the project for years, their courage and conviction took precedent.

Thus the theology of worship that emerges from 4:1–6:12 is critical. A theology of saying no is tantamount to religious purity regardless of taking longer to finish the God-given task of reestablishing worship. There is such a thing as righteous exclusivity of belief, and one must possess a strong conviction in the face of opposition.

Reestablishing Righteous Worship Entails Endurance in the Process

In chapter 6, a building project that endured for twenty years finally comes to completion. It is hard to imagine what this day felt like for God's people. Ezra 6:13–22 not only tells of the finished work bringing the larger pre-Ezra section on worship (Ezra 1:1–6:22) to a logical conclusion, but it also shows in a succinct summary statement how and why the temple was rebuilt (6:13–14), when it was rebuilt (6:15), and the results of rebuilding: the dedication followed by Passover (6:16–22).

The dedication of the temple marks a milestone in worship for the people of God. Joy alone characterizes the temple's dedication and ensuing celebration (6:16, 22)[10] because of the acute awareness of their restored identity and inheritance evidenced in this moment. Although the exile radically changed their circumstances, it did not redefine them. The dedication affirms they are still "the people of Israel" (v. 16), full recipients of atonement for sin and the blessings promised to the patriarchal fathers (v. 17). Their claims to Jerusalem as a spiritual hub, along with their belief in Torah, remain firm (v. 18).

Reestablishing Righteous Worship Entails a Proper Celebration

A month following the temple's dedication, the community convenes and conducts a major worship service with the celebration of Passover (Nisan: Exod. 12:6, 14; Lev. 23:5). This is not standard fare. Besides the initial Passover established during the exodus, there are only four other times the biblical writers mention observance of it, suggesting that now with the rebuilt temple, true heartfelt worship is really underway.[11]

The original Passover celebration commemorated Israel's deliverance from Egypt (Exod. 12:14). The Lamb's blood applied to their doors caused the "destroyer" to pass over each household (Exod. 12:23), and as a result they were safe from God's wrath. By "faith" they applied the blood, which demonstrated they believed they would be spared judgment. Their faith story was meant to function as a testimony to their children. Thus they were to mark their calendars so that yearly they might recall and celebrate

10. The previous worship service, however, was a mixed bag of fear (3:3), along with joy and sadness (3:12–13).

11. See Num. 9:5; Josh. 5:10; 2 Kings 23:21; 2 Chron. 30:1–2; 35:1. Second Kings mentions that before Josiah's time, "no such Passover had been kept since the days of the judges who judged Israel, or during all the days of the kings of Israel or of the kings of Judah" (2 Kings 23:21–22). Given the profound meaning of Passover, it remains unthinkable that such neglect existed.

God's rescue mission on their behalf (Exod. 12:14; 23:14–17). Passover was followed the day after with the weeklong Feast of Unleavened Bread (Exod. 12:15–20; Lev. 23:6–8). Historically, these combined feasts were intended to bring the worshiper back to God, to remind the worshiper of God's role in their lives.

The temple completion marked a major turning point for the new community. God once again "delivered" his people, but from the bondage of exile (Ezra 9:8–9). Now that opposition and the "enemies" of God's people have been put in their place (4:1–6:12), the temple's completion is both a victory and worship celebration signifying God's sovereign rule over his people. It was, therefore, appropriate to celebrate and worship Yahweh for his protection and favor in their lives.

Accordingly, measures were taken to ensure a proper celebration. The Levites take care of the meal (6:20; cf. Exod. 12:6). The emphasis lies with the purity and devotion of those partaking in the meal. Those who returned from exile secured a "cleansing" through the sin offering (6:17). Similarly, nonexiled Judeans who compromised their worship of Yahweh by engaging in "unclean practices of their Gentile neighbors" (4:2, 4) had to "separate themselves" from such practices in order to "seek the Lord, the God of Israel" in the worship of the Passover celebration (Isa. 9:13; Hos. 7:10; Zeph. 1:6; Jer. 10:21). They had to "rededicate" their lives to the Lord. They had to say yes to Yahweh and no to all other allegiances. Such devotion to "the God of Israel" required cutting all other religious ties and allegiances, something that "the enemies of Judah and Benjamin" were not willing to do, thereby barring them from participation in temple building (4:2–3). It required returning to the way of worship traditionally passed on to them. The way to be included was to be exclusive in faith and practice. Exclusive worship for an exclusive God! The worshipers were brought back to God through Passover, a reminder of his role in their lives. Indeed, the way of worship is restored.

In his concluding statement about the work on God's house (6:22), the narrator fully acknowledges that their source of joy in this worship service comes from a sovereign God who literally changed a king's heart (6:6–12). The human side of the equation (work decreed by Persian kings) operated in tandem with the divine side (work commanded by God) stretching out over a long period of time (6:14). Resistance turned into assistance. The narrative of the temple's completion ends in a joyful worship service ultimately celebrating God's assistance. The real victor here over all obstacles and opposition is not Cyrus, not Darius, but Yahweh. He alone deserves their worship.

In conclusion to this pre-Ezra phase of worship we learn much. Reestablishing worship depends on God. He draws near to us and works on hearts. In so doing he reestablishes our identity and inheritance in him. All of this takes time, energy, endurance, entails opposition and obstacles, and utter acknowledgment of his grace, eventually reestablishing *the* way of worship. The only human response to this? Loud worship declaring God's goodness, indicative of a renewed heart and renewed witness. Although the pre-Ezra phase of worship ends on a high note, and is joyous and momentous, it remains incomplete (1:1–6:22).[12] As we are about to see in the Ezra phase (chaps. 7–10), worship entails more than a rebuilt temple.

Reestablishing Righteous Worship Entails Revival of the Law

As we turn to worship in the Ezra phase of the book (7:1–10:44), where Ezra the scribe now appears on the scene (7:6), it reveals there is more to reestablishing a worship community than just a rebuilt temple. Without rules to regulate that worship, one does not have the full picture. In this regard, along with Zerubbabel years before (Ezra 1–6), and Nehemiah (Neh. 1–13) years later, Ezra (Ezra 7–10) stands in the middle of one of three movements bringing renewal of worship to Zion in this period. Although years separate one from the other, the author wishes the reader to see a panoramic view of restored worship by juxtaposing the various phases into one "book," Ezra-Nehemiah.[13] The pre-Ezra narrative (Ezra1:1–6:22) along with the attempts of Ezra to restore the community through the law in the Ezra phase of the book (Ezra 7:1–10:44) captures the heart of renewed worship more fully. Accordingly, Ezra, the priest and scribe, and the summary of his mission in Ezra 7:1–8:36 further enables worship in the community. Two items are noteworthy in this section: First, Ezra's heart posture toward worship as described by his vocation in Ezra 7:10; and second, a Gentile king's perspective about worship as described in 7:11–26.

Ezra's heart posture

Ezra's dual designation, priest and scribe (7:11, 12, 21; 10:16; Neh. 8:1, 2, 4, 9, 13), used throughout the book helps us understand him as key ministry personnel for Israel's renewed worship. As a priest and scribe, his responsibilities entailed both the oral and written communication of Israel's legal instructions. Ezra thus fulfilled an important role in the postexile phase, a role further unpacked by the statement in 7:10. Ezra had a strong resolve, or literally, "he made firm his heart" or "had set his heart" for a distinct purpose. The purpose was to study/seek/inquire, in order to practice /apply, and to teach the law of the Lord with all its requirements (statutes/decrees and ordinances/laws) in Israel. His entire life's vocation was given over to that purpose.

12. In comparison with the worship services accompanying the completion of the temple and tabernacle previously (Exod. 40:34–38; 1 Kings 8:6–11), God's glory does not fill the rebuilt temple. The anticlimactic ending to the second temple's dedication causes anticipation and expectation. This decrescendo prepares us for a crescendo as we look to the NT and the full revelation of God's plan for tabernacling with us, in Christ.
13. Ezra-Nehemiah are considered one book in the Hebrew Bible. Restored worship remains incomplete until Nehemiah. The efforts of Nehemiah to restore the city's walls and sanctity of Zion (Neh. 1:1–7:8), and his attempts to guard and protect exclusive worship of Yahweh capture the worship of Zion more fully.

Ezra's commitment toward the study, application, and teaching of the law demonstrates a lifestyle committed to worship. His work was his worship because the law (far more than a rulebook) instructed his own heart toward that end. As a minister in residence, "in Israel," his study time, which consisted mainly of the Pentateuch and perhaps some of the Prophets, was not an end but a means toward an end personally and publicly. With respect to the personal impact, his study was to produce a virtuous lifestyle, and a proper, godly way of worship. The fruit of his study was evidenced in his own application of the truths of God's law. With respect to the public impact, his study would lead to a platform of teaching others the content of the word and how to apply it to their own lives.[14]

Without a revival of the Word of God, without a tethering to Torah, attempts at restored worship remain impossible. Without the law and the lawgiver, regulating worship would not be achieved.[15] The Mosaic law, God's gift of wisdom to the nation, has now been graciously given back to them, hand-delivered through Ezra, the postexilic lawgiver's mission and commission. The height of the worship experience concerns a merger of the temple and law as in old times. The prophets envisioned restored worship with the temple as a destination for teaching that leads to worship, a place that disseminates the law as a witness to the exclusive worship of the Lord (i.e., Micah 4:2–5; Isa. 2; 40). The anticipation and hope of Ezra's mission would be nothing less than a national transformation due to the merger of these two key ingredients for worship.

Ezra's worship and the praise of life

Ezra 7:27 reads like a mini psalm of praise with the opening statement, "Blessed be the Lord, the God of our fathers." We get a peek into his devotional life with this outburst of praise in the first person. He expresses his own worship to God here as a result of Artaxerxes's favor.[16]

---

14. Ezra's public platform of teaching and urging the community in the direction of Torah is showcased twice in the book. The first concerns the problem he faces with unholy alliances (Ezra 9:1–2) and how he deals with the situation as priest/scribe (9:3–10:17). The second public platform takes place a few years later when the third group of exiles returns under Nehemiah (Neh. 8:1, 4, 5, 7–9, 13, 18). The people assemble themselves to celebrate the New Year, and Ezra leads the celebration by reading the Law. In this way, content for his teaching derived from the Law but also his lifestyle; a model for the people.

15. The law, as was originally intended in Exodus, was meant to regulate Israel's worship and relationship with the Lord.

16. Based on the comments in the Persian king's letter to Ezra, a remarkable non-Israelite point of view about worship surfaces as Artaxerxes encourages a volunteer-based movement (v. 14), sanctioned and supported financially by the government (v. 15) with tax-free benefits (v. 24) to reestablish worship in Jerusalem (The emphasis on worship is readily observed by the repetition of the term for "temple" [vv. 15, 16, 17, 19, 20, 23, 24, 27].) Artaxerxes goes out of his way to ensure that Ezra acquires proper provisions for the task. But this is because of his own understanding of the importance of law in a land, especially as it leads to worship and the exercising of justice in a nation. This Gentile king knows that the reinstatement of the law of one's God/

Ezra worships God specifically for three things. First, he worships due to the intended outcome of his mission. He was going "to bring honor to the house of the Lord" (7:27). The word "honor" is better translated as "glory" or "beauty." Outside of Ezra, only Isaiah uses this term with respect to God's house (Isa. 60:7, 13). In the restoration of Zion that Isaiah envisions, Gentile peoples and lavish sacrifices are brought to God's house, resulting in the beautification or glorification to that house. The arrival of the law of God via Ezra's mission directly affects the aesthetics of the house of the Lord in Jerusalem. Ezra attributes beauty and glory to God's dwelling as a result of the revival of the law. Second (7:28), Ezra worships because God rolled out the red carpet and extended *hesed* to him with respect to the decision made by the king and his "powerful" advisors. Ezra understood this as a manifestation of Yahweh's loyalty to him in the relationship. Last, Ezra worships because he was enabled to take action, as a result of divine intervention yet again: "the hand of the Lord my God was on me" to take action (7:28, already mentioned in 7:6, 9). The letter from Artaxerxes was a manifestation of this reality in Ezra's life. Through yet another Persian king, provision for worship of the Lord manifests itself. The law that leads to true justice and worship in the land was going forth from Jerusalem. God was restoring the beauty of his house. Thus we get a glimpse into Ezra's heart of worship. The theology of worship that unfolds in Ezra 7:1–8:36 is critical to the story. Indeed, the law regulates the worshiper's relationship to God. Without it proper worship cannot be measured or attained. Earlier in the story (1:1–5) we saw how God worked on hearts, and now we get a glimpse into Ezra's own heart posture. A properly postured heart is necessary for reestablishing worship through revival of the law.

Reestablishing Righteous Worship Entails Repentance

In Ezra 9:1–10:44 we learn of internal opposition to exclusive worship of Yahweh in the community. In the pre-Ezra phase external opposition toward exclusive worship dominated the storyline. However, after his arrival in Jerusalem, Ezra receives a report of unfaithfulness leaving this "minister in residence" to cry out for God's mercy. We witness firsthand a worship leader's response to wayward worship.

Some people, leadership included, compromised their way of worship by marrying the locals, those outside the covenantal community: "neighboring

god leads to true justice and worship and its potential to revive, restore, and give direction to a community. The picture is a secular government not only enforcing (7:13–25) but also reinforcing biblical law and principles (7:26). Is it any wonder that Ezra breaks out in worship as a result of receiving such favor (7:27)? The irony is that with few exceptions (good kings in Israel and Judah), the Israelite theocracy failed in its execution of Torah. God relentlessly raised up the prophets to reinforce covenantal law and administration in Israelite society but with abysmal results. And now the people of God have been given another chance to get it right; ironically, through the agency of a foreign government, a backing from one of the most powerful empires the ancient Near East has ever seen.

peoples," or "the people of the land" (9:1–2). These current residents are ethnically identified as "Canaanites," illegitimate residents defiling both the land and God's people based on allegiance to a deity other than Yahweh (9:1). This type of "fellowship" tampered with and polluted what was intended to be a "pure" relationship to God (Exod. 19:6; Lev. 19:2; Deut. 7:6; Isa. 6:13). A compromise in worship was already underway yet again.

The grief and guilt associated with worship choices not aligned with God's Word weighed Ezra down (9:6–7). The level of their sin and guilt is metaphorically described as limitless: "higher than our heads," "reached to the heavens" (9:6). Their guilt is comparable to their ancestors (9:7, 13) and the exile is evidence of their great guilt (v. 13), yet they stand guilty presently (v. 15) and are, in fact, *adding* to Israel's guilt (10:10).

Even after experiencing sin's consequences, even after surviving exile, Ezra's prayer (9:6–15) exposes the ongoing sin-guilt problem plaguing postexilic worshipers of the Lord. Ezra cries out to God aware of the history of his own people and God's interactions with them. Even though God graciously restored their markers of identity and showed them mercy, they sin and still are guilty. The exile with its devastating effects did not remedy the situation. Essentially, neither the exile (judgment) nor the return (mercy) fixed the heart problem, the biggest barrier in worship. No postexilic reformer, not even Ezra the lawgiver had the ability to cure the human heart's propensity to sin and associated guilt. Even the so-called righteous remnant is guilty.

From the theological perspective of a priest, one whose main concern was to regulate worship, Ezra recognizes a bigger problem. Guilty people cannot legally stand before a holy God and worship, or before a just judge without divine intervention (9:15), either mercy or judgment. It was his goodness and kindness that he had not destroyed them. Ezra's moving prayer does not call the people to action; it calls God's mercy to action. He cries out for God's mercy to triumph over judgment. He wanted to avoid experiencing more of God's wrath based on his knowledge of their history and God's word (Deut. 7:1–6, 23:2–7).[17] He knew that God's mercy is what would eventually bring the people to a place of action. As a godly worship leader Ezra understood the power of confession and God's merciful character when facing worshipers who go astray.

I would submit that Ezra's spiritual leadership here in 9:3–15, which is clearly not contrived but based on conviction, becomes the springboard for the needed change, something evidenced in the events that unfold in chapter 10. Ezra mourns in silent shame and then cries out to God for mercy in a prayer of confession, the only rightful response to the sin-guilt

17. Their ancestors' conduct provoked God to anger (5:12); God's anger awaits those who forsake him (8:22). God's anger led to the exile (9:12), and God's anger could lead to annihilation of the remnant (9:14). And there is hope presently that "the fierce anger of our God" will turn away should they take appropriate actions (10:14 NIV)—i.e., attempt to do his will.

problem. That he confesses sin and guilt, even though he was not counted among the guilty, says much of his character.

Accordingly, Ezra was a conduit for conviction in the community, a model of what to do so as to continue in worship after engaging in wayward worship yet again (10:1–11). As a leader he set a tone of conviction, not condemnation, and others responded accordingly. The common Israelites, even children, came under conviction, a recognition and admission of guilt showing the deep effects of sin in the camp (10:1). But as the story unfolds, Ezra's corporate confession and expression of grief lead not only to an admission of wrongdoing but also to a commitment to practical actions to correct the wrongdoing out of a renewed fear of God. Maintaining unbroken fellowship with God is not humanly possible. However, true worshipers can regain that sweet fellowship through conviction, confession, and repentance. Thus both confession *and* reform should be acknowledged as the will of God. The way to continued worship comes in this manner.

Ezra finds the surprising but hoped-for cooperation evidenced in the unified *and* loud voice of the assembly: "You are right! We must do as you say" (v. 12 NIV). This loud, unified voice should not be glossed over. Rarely does one see such quick admission of wrongdoing in the biblical text. They express admission of guilt and the intention to reform. They are wholeheartedly agreeing to do God's will. Moreover, they are reidentifying with him as their God. One cannot help but see their favorable response as an answer to Ezra's continued petitions to God (10:6). This is a visual aid of repentance, an integral part of reestablishing worship.

SIGNIFICANCE OF EZRA FOR BIBLICAL WORSHIP

Ezra invites us to realize that God is completely devoted to restoring his people to himself in relationship, regardless of their starting position or past failures. Metaphorically and spiritually speaking, he is in the business of restoring broken-down temples of worship. He rescues people not just once but repeatedly. No one is beyond the hope and reach of God; and this reality should result in thanksgiving and worship.

Ezra teaches us that we have a God who, through what appears to be the natural set of circumstances of life, draws wayward people back to worship—to their spiritual roots and heritage. It must be remembered that God works through the affairs of people and nations and the hearts of kings to restore regardless of the cultural circumstances and context. God works through the events of history (cf. Jer. 32:41) to bring about his will. In so doing he draws his people back to himself, which is why from Ezra we learn, it is not *how* you worship but *who you worship that matters in the end.* Because he has worked to make it all happen, we cannot possible pay him back with our work, but we can respond rightly with our worship.

We see in Ezra that worship is the only proper response to the grace-filled gifts of life, no matter how big or small they may seem. Our praise and worship acknowledges God's activity and providence over all of his domain. Just as the exiles declared the goodness of God in the first worship service after exile, so too must we preach the good news of the gospel to ourselves and declare God's goodness regularly. Improper worship, conversely, robs God of praise and worship due his name when chance is afforded the glory from our good. Reestablishing worship demonstrates renewed hearts and a renewed witness for God.

Righteous worship requires theological fidelity. Shunning that which is attractive, easy, or pleasing to the flesh requires steadfast resolve. This fight for faithfulness is not simply a one-time process. Christians must fight regularly to maintain theological fidelity in a world that is alluring (see Col. 2:8–9). Culture will routinely offer the church options that may ease temporary need but in the end will result in worship failure.

Just as the exiles needed Ezra to lead them to Yahweh and his purposes, so too the church needs godly leadership. The significance of Ezra helps us to see the role of Christian leaders in God's plan and economy for bringing wayward worshipers back to righteous worship. In the example of Ezra, we see that God raises up leaders who revere his Word and recognize its power to lead us to a life of worship. He raises up people in the church to help us follow God more faithfully. Ezra understood God's character and demonstrated restorative worship practices where he actively led the exilic community back to God. We also see through Ezra the encouragement to confess our sins and make changes in our lives, to take action in accordance with wise counsel, especially God's will revealed in his Word. The goal for continued worship is to confess sin and repent in order to avoid further difficult consequences, but especially to get our relationship with God back on track.

Ezra teaches that repentance arises as a result of experiencing God's goodness in allowing the Israelites to return to the land, rebuild the temple, and restore worship under the Persians (9:8–9). Their shameful conduct was not acceptable at any time, but especially so in light of the Lord's gracious reestablishment of worship afforded them. They deserved death and destruction, but God withheld it. The restoration they received was a visual aide of Yahweh's kindness (a restraint of destruction), a kindness that actually led guilty people to a different course of action (repentance). In this way, we learn that renewed worship in Ezra is not just a series of events (i.e., a return to the land, temple rebuilt, law restored). Renewed worship reflects a heart change. Unbroken worship and fellowship is achieved through conviction (mourning for sin), confession of wrongdoing followed by radical, visible reforms in the life of an individual or community because of one's continual awareness of God's just and gracious character. The worshiper experiences a change of heart to make things right with God. One could argue that chapters 9–10 together paint a picture of God's kindness leading people to repentance (see Rom. 2:4).

Ezra prepares the church for the reality of God's kindness expressed to us in Jesus. Through Jesus, a temple not built with human hands, God created sacred space. In the incarnation God comes to us. It was the most tangible expression of the Lord's long-term loyalty to establish a worship relationship with humankind. Rather than destroy humankind due to our miserable theological failures, he does something radical: he forgives us and gives us hope. On account of God's mercy demonstrated by Jesus at the cross he leads guilty and condemned people to conviction, confession, and a reformed life leading to worship (Rom. 2:4; 2 Cor. 7:9–10). Because God's goodness and kindness is demonstrated to us in that he withholds the wrath we deserve (Rom. 2:4), it propels people to have a change of heart. God's kindness melts our hearts and makes us want to reform for the right reasons. In him, and through Jesus's work on the cross, he saves us by performing heart surgery and fills us with the new life of his Spirit so humankind can aspire to proper worship and devotion unto God. This is cause for worship!

Rather than abandoning or forsaking us in our *present* and *ongoing* theological struggles and failures, God does something radical: he restores us regularly. The tangible expression of his present relational loyalty is God coming to us in the person of the Holy Spirit. He will not abandon us or forsake us. God comes to us in the person of the Holy Spirit so that we can worship him in spirit and in truth and experience ongoing—even daily—restoration in our individual lives and in the lives of our congregations. There is hope for the people of God. This is cause for worship!

CHAPTER 20

PROTECTING THE SANCTITY OF ZION

Worship in Nehemiah

Thomas Petter

CONTEXT OF WORSHIP IN NEHEMIAH

Originally one book, Ezra-Nehemiah concerns itself with the renewal of worship in Jerusalem during its existence under Persian rule. In 539 BC, however, the exiles were allowed to return to province of Judah (Aramaic: *yehud*). The book of Ezra is divided in two: the first return, when Zerubbabel and Joshua restored the temple (539–515 BC; cf. Ezra 1–6); and a second return, when Ezra the priest restored the faith of the people (458 BC; cf. Ezra 7–10). Nehemiah, however, began a third wave of activities some fourteen years after Ezra's return. Nehemiah's temporary career change from "cupbearer to the king" (Neh. 1:11) to Persian governor of Yehud was prompted by a *regress* report from his Hebrew brother Hanani regarding Jerusalem (7:2). His report made clear that the people suffered "great trouble and shame" because the walls of the city were broken down and the gates had been "destroyed by fire" (1:3). After several weeks of mourning, confession, and intercession (1:4–11), Nehemiah was commissioned by King Artaxerxes to return and jumpstart the restoration of the worship in Zion (2:6). Nehemiah, a Hebrew by birth, found himself as a trusted envoy with the specific mission to rebuild the desecrated city of his "fathers' graves" (2:5–6). But this task, in the eyes of Artaxerxes, was essentially ceremonial rather than political. The king's goal was not for Nehemiah to restore the city walls as a defensive fortress but instead to rebuild a sacred site and thereby restore the sanctity of Zion. Since Cyrus's decree in Ezra 1:1, the imperial policy was that nations of the empire should be able to restore their sanctuaries and to worship their regional deities. The hope of this policy was that it would result in increased tax revenue and favor from the gods for the Achaemenid rulers. Ironically, Artaxerxes is the very king who had ordered that Ezra's effort to restore worship be stopped "by force" (Ezra 4:23). In a stunning reversal, he now cancels his previous directives and appoints Nehemiah as governor of Yehud (Neh. 5:14) to restore the sanctity of Jerusalem by rebuilding it (2:6). The "God of heaven" does in fact grant Nehemiah "success" and "mercy" in the eyes of Artaxerxes (1:11) and continues to do so throughout his mission through "the good hand of the Lord" (e.g., Neh. 1:8; 13:31).

CHALLENGES TO WORSHIP IN NEHEMIAH

The actual repairing of the wall and the rebuilding of the gates (Neh. 3; cf. 2 Chron. 36:19) occupies only about half of the account in Nehemiah, which was famously rebuilt in fifty-two days (Neh. 6:15). This restoration of the wall and gate system served as a means to Yahweh's end, which was ultimately the restoration of his sacred space—the temple and its precinct. In particular, Nehemiah 8–9 brings the entire effort of the second generation into focus: Ezra and Nehemiah stood side by side to renew the Sinai covenant, thus confirming, so it appears, the restoration of Yahweh's worship in Yehud according to the Deuteronomic promise (Deut. 30:1–10). However, the reading of the covenant (Neh. 8), confession of sins (Neh. 9), and covenant renewal (Neh. 10) meant nothing unless the people were made holy and worshiped him according to his will.

Mediating right worship required an obedience to the way that Yahweh has accorded it to be done. Priests, Levites, gatekeepers, and singers were the ordained mediators, and as such they themselves must be consecrated as holy (Neh. 3, 7–12). For only those who were holy could serve Yahweh and thus those individuals who could not trace their origins to the Levitical priesthood were not allowed service in this matter (see Ezra 2; Neh. 7). The threat of a second exile due to idolatry and violation of God's law (including violating the sanctity of the Sabbath and of marriage) was very real in the minds of both Ezra and Nehemiah (Neh. 10:28, 31; 13:3, 15–27). Following the pattern that had plagued humanity beginning in the garden rebellion of Genesis 3, where sin is rebuffed by consequence, the worship rebellion of the preexilic priesthood produced similar results—a judgment to encourage repentance (Lev. 10; Judg. 17:1–13; 1 Sam 2:22; 3:12–17; Isa. 1:12–15; Jer. 7:1–7, cf. Heb. 12:4–11). The sin of their forefathers led to consequence in the form of exile, and surely the bitterness of this discipline was a present taste in the experiences of this postexilic community. With Deuteronomic obligations providing the imprimatur for the postexilic restoration, the warnings of Deuteronomy 7:3–5, previously unheeded, were at the forefront of Ezra and Nehemiah's minds. The potential for continued "canaanization"[1] through a variety of means, including illicit

1. The canaanization of Israel is the historiographic framework of the book of Judges (see Judg. 2:11–20) whereby Israel imaged more of their neighbors than their God.

unions with non-Yahwist wives (cf. Judg. 3:5–6), could not be allowed, especially from temple personnel, who were to be set apart as holy. The sanctity of Zion must be kept to include Sabbath laws (Neh. 13:17). Those who were not followers of Yahweh could not enter Yahweh's inner sanctum (Neh. 13:36–37). Modern sensitivities may be jolted by some of the drastic measures taken by both Ezra (9:3; 10:3, 19) and Nehemiah (13:25) to hold fast to the Deuteronomic obligations for corporate distinctiveness, which included the actual separation from foreign wives. However, for the community in Yehud, Yahweh's consuming fire of judgement was vividly etched in the collective memory since 586 BC. The recollection of Israelite history as a cyclical canaanization process in Nehemiah 9 underscores the seriousness of the situation (vv. 26–31). God is taken at his word that he will guard the sanctity of his mediated presence of earth and will not hesitate to unleash a new round of Deuteronomic curses if the people fail to obey his laws (Mal. 2:1–2).

Therefore, Nehemiah was tasked to restore the proper worship of Yahweh once the temple was finished. The sanctity of the Holy City must be protected by drawing a firm line of demarcation of who is allowed in and who is not (via walls and especially gates). Promises must be kept by the community to support the material demands required by the Levitical cultic apparatus: firewood, firstfruits, tithes, and physical support for the priesthood, Levites, singers, and other attendants (Neh. 10:32–39). The rest of the account in Nehemiah logically ensues: the formerly abandoned city, now regaining her status as "the Holy City," must be repopulated (leaders, descendants of Judah, Benjamin, and Levi; Neh. 11:1–24). For good measure, yet another list is provided in Nehemiah 12:1–26 to confirm every priest and Levite serving are bona fide from an ancestral perspective. The formal ceremony of purification and dedication, under the aegis of both Ezra and Nehemiah (Neh. 12:36, 38), formally closes the process: "the priests and the Levites purified themselves, and they purified the people and the gates and the wall" (v. 30). Following these purification rites, Nehemiah appointed two choirs of thanksgiving (v. 31) that are to walk on the wall. Ezra led his choir south along the wall, while Nehemiah followed his as they moved north (vv. 31, 37, 38). Both then met "in the house of God" (v. 40) and offered "great sacrifices" (v. 43). The moment serves as a climactic and fitting end to the account because the worship was reestablished at last. Notably absent, however, was the filling of the temple with the Spirit, as happened at the dedication of the tabernacle (Exod. 40:34) and the consecration of Solomon's Temple (1 Kings 8:10–11//2 Chron. 7:1–3). To restore right worship was a long process, but over the course of Ezra and Nehemiah's leadership ministry, what was started almost a hundred years earlier had founds its culmination. This culmination brought "the joy of Jerusalem [which] was heard far away" (Neh. 12:43; cf. 2 Chron. 7:10). This joy expressed in the singing on this prayer walk on the wall reaches a literal crescendo in the temple precinct (Neh. 12:46). The worship of Yahweh "as prescribed by David the man of God" (vv. 24, 36) can now resume, which also means the future Davidic king (Isa. 9; 11; 53; Ezek. 17:22–24; etc.) will be able to return to Zion. As we know, this will take some more doing and time before the fulfillment of the return of the King to Zion occurs as promised by the prophets (e.g., Luke 9:51; 19:28–40). Nehemiah thus set the stage for the next step of the return of the King, which itself unfolds in the first coming (see Mark 1:1), the outpouring of his Spirit (Acts 2), and second coming, the ultimate return of the King of kings (a known designation for the Persian kings [Rev. 19–22]). Nehemiah himself will serve as a sort of forerunner to the Elijah figure to come (Mal. 4:5; John the Baptist: Luke 1:17) when he cleansed the chambers of the temple, preparing the way for Jesus to do his own house cleaning with the money changers (Neh. 13:7–9; cf. Luke 19:45–46).

The epilogue of the book of Nehemiah, itself a bookend to the Ezra-Nehemiah corpus, punctuates the need for another covenantal framework, which amounts to a different way to worship the living God. The infrastructure provided by the Sinaitic system of worship and the accompanying uncompromising demands for holiness shows itself yet again incapable to stem the tide of stiff-necked people from the community (Neh. 9:16; e.g. Exod. 32:9). The formal commitment to organizational efficiency, unity, and the people's commitment not to "neglect the house of our God" (Neh. 10:39) was short-lived. In chapter 13, Nehemiah returned to the province in 432 BC (after his twelve-year term as governor had ended) only to find the people in blatant violation of Sabbath laws. The people stood in deep compromise, even among the family of the high priest, and engaged in illicit marriages with non-Yahwists. Yet the final word remains hope-filled. Nehemiah leans on Yahweh for "good" (Neh. 13:31) in the sense of "favor" in this context. Nehemiah's faith-filled hope is that Yahweh will not forget the good/favor that he bestowed on Nehemiah, Ezra, and all of what the returnees experienced in rebuilding Zion.

THEOLOGY OF WORSHIP

Worship in the Splendor of His Holiness

The picture of renewed worship in Nehemiah cannot take place without securing the sanctity of Zion. Nehemiah's efforts with rebuilding the wall provide protection and safety. However, safety needs to be carefully qualified. The project did not entail a rebuilding of the fortress of Zion for military purposes. The extent of the devastation of 586 BC is described via the hampered night survey by Nehemiah upon his arrival in Jerusalem (2:14). Furthermore, it's quite inconceivable that the work of the people would have produced a restored defensive structure in less than two months (3:8). Instead, and the text is quite candid about this, the project was one of consecration, literally to make holy the sacred enclosure (3:1). Gaps in the walls needed to be filled, the gates needed attention, and resources needed gathering (2:8). Ultimately this project provided the guarantee that no one unholy would be able to access the sacred precinct.

This dedication to sanctifying the site is applied with equal rigor and stringency to the people who will lead the worship in the Holy City throughout their performance, mediation, musical, or gatekeeping duties. The seemingly interminable list of priests, Levites, gatekeepers, singers, and temple servants not only provide the literary infrastructure of the second half of the book (from chapter 7 on) but also form the theological backbone of the account: the worship of Yahweh cannot be restored unless qualified personnel are in place with the proper material support from the community. To worship Yahweh costs resources and efforts on the part of the entire community. Without a consecrated priesthood and a committed community to support the worship, there is no hope for an acceptable and sustainable form of worship. Nehemiah tirelessly and sacrificially (e.g., 5:14–19) focuses his energies to restore the desecrated city of his ancestors, even as he realizes in the end that all his efforts may not leave a lasting change.

Worship according to the Word of God

Obedience to do things "by the book," in accordance with the law of Moses (Neh. 8:1) and as prescribed by David king of Israel (Ezra 3:2, 4, 10; Neh. 12:36, 45–46) provide legitimacy to worship. If holiness is a prerequisite for worship, worship according to God's law is then necessary. Therefore, renewed worship cannot happen without foundation in the law (hence Ezra is both "scribe" and "priest" in Neh. 8:1–9). Following Ezra's return to Jerusalem and bolstered by Nehemiah's presence as governor of the province some fourteen years later, the reading and renewing of the covenant in Nehemiah 8 represents the next, and *essential*, step upon which worship can be restored. The image is etched for posterity: Ezra and his Levitical attendants elevated on a platform to read the law to the congregation gathered as "one," including men, women, and children (8:2, 3). Clusters within the assembly are formed with Levites interpreting what is being read so that "the people understood the reading" (vv. 7–8). The centrality of the Word of God in worship is no mere vignette. It is anchored in steeped tradition ever since Moses addressed the congregation on the plains of Moab. The enduring image of the eschatological significance of the centrality and attractional value of the word of the Lord is captured in Isaiah *ben Amoz*'s vision of the restored Jerusalem (Isa. 2:1–4), in which God's Word serves as a point of attraction for the nations. As evidenced by Ezra and Nehemiah's own actions, genuine covenant renewal incorporates confession (Ezra 9 and Neh. 9:2–37). In fact, confession of sin and prayer drawn from the law had already framed the account in Nehemiah in chapter 1 ("I and my father's house have sinned" [1:6]).[2] Chapter 9 captures well the dynamic between worship, the reading of the law, and confession. We read, "And they stood up in their place and read from the book of the law of the Lord their God for a quarter of the day; for another of it they made confession and worshiped the LORD their God" (v. 3). The centrality of prayer in Nehemiah's own life is well known (2:4; 4:4–5; 5:19; 6:9, 14; 7:5 [by implication]; 13:14, 22, 29, 31; Ezra 9:5–15). As a final point, the awareness of the law through public reading led to the celebration of the Feast of Tabernacles (Neh. 8:1–8, 17–18) and serves as the catalyst for the long retrospective prayer in Nehemiah 9, itself imbued with impeccable knowledge of Israelite history. In short, the reestablishment of the law of God regulates people in their worship because it allows them to "understand" the will of God.

Opposition to Worship

While renewed worship becomes a reality and begins to fulfill prophetic expectations for Zion, serious opposition from the enemies of God's people is a prevailing theme in Ezra-Nehemiah. In fact, restored worship is a long-drawn-out process of fits and starts. We read of the determination of the faithful Yahwists of the first return who turned down the offer of their "adversaries'" to partner together, for they concluded, "You have nothing to do with us in building a house to our God; but we alone will build to the LORD, the God of Israel" (Ezra 4:3).

In Nehemiah, even a casual reading of the text highlights the fierce external opposition from the outset (Neh. 2:19). The opposition by neighboring governors and officials underscores how isolated and precarious the situation remained for the community of God's people during the Persian period. For they were literally surrounded and opposed on all sides (Neh. 6:1: Sanballat in the north, Tobiah from the east, and Geshem from the south). The goal on the part of the enemies of Zion was to stop the work on the wall through intimidation, fear, and threats of violence (Neh. 4:1–3, 7–8, 11). The climate of opposition continues in earnest with respect to Nehemiah's leadership. As a direct threat to the worship, the high priest himself was compromised with Yahweh's enemies when Eliashib (Neh. 13:7; see Neh. 3:1) gave a "chamber in the courts of the house of God" to Tobiah, who was aligned with Sanballat, a leader who did not want for Jerusalem what Yahweh had planned. The opposition extended even to a plot against the life of Nehemiah in order to stop that which was happening according to the plans of Yahweh (Neh. 6:19).

---

2. Baltzer alludes to the references in Nehemiah's prayer to Deuteronomic law and the prayer of Solomon in 2 Chron. 6:20, 36–39) (Klaus Baltzer, "Moses Servant of God and the Servants: Text and Tradition in the Prayer of Nehemiah (Neh 1:5–11)," in *The Future of Early Christianity*, ed. Birger A. Pearson (Minneapolis: Fortress, 1991), 125–29.

Finally, another layer of opposition to the restoration of worship comes in chapter 5.[3] The rebuilding of the wall was threatened due to a famine, which created a situation that forced small landowners to sell their land assets (and, tragically, also their children), in order to buy food (Neh. 5:1–5).[4] Technically the law did not condemn the practice of "pledge on loan" (5:3); however, in a time of famine, laws of compassion toward neighbors easily superseded the legality of selling and purchasing (which in this context amounts to profiteering). This was a delicate situation for Nehemiah and his family since they also were landowners of certain means (Neh. 5:10). After seeking divine wisdom (Neh. 5:7), Nehemiah adjudicated that restitution should be made immediately (Neh. 5:11), which the community duly acted on. Nehemiah thus averted a major crisis, and the work toward the restoration of the worship could resume (6:1).

Renewed Worship: Now and Not Yet

The book of Nehemiah represents another redemptive mission along the Exodus motif of slavery/oppression and deliverance/salvation culminating in worship. As with redemption in Exodus (i.e., 3:12, 18; 4:23; 5:3; 15:1), the worship of Yahweh was the Israelites' ultimate purpose. In Nehemiah, Yahweh redeems Israel from the Persians and brings her back to himself according to his foreordained plan, through his sovereignty. As long as Israel was exiled in Babylon under Persian rule her service was to a master other than Yahweh (cf. Ezra 9:9), and so in this return to their home, they are able to return to their ultimate vocation as worshipers. Yet the task was not yet complete so that Nehemiah functions as a signpost for more revelation of what it means to worship Yahweh. Chapter 13 especially serves the purpose to tell us that more is yet to come, since the inherent stiff-neckedness of the people is not yet healed. The "new hearts" promised by the prophet Ezekiel are yet to be evidenced in the behavior of the people (Ezekiel 36:26–27). To be sure, the presence of the "God of heaven" is felt throughout the account and reminds us of the promise of Zechariah (as they were rebuilding the Second Temple): "not by might nor by power but by my Spirit" (Zech. 4:6; Hag. 2:5). However, the filling of the new temple space with Yahweh's glory is conspicuous by its absence both at the dedication ceremony in Ezra 6:16–18 and now with the completion of the walls in Nehemiah. Nevertheless, it would not be correct to deny some activity of the Spirit related to the Second Temple (cf. Zechariah in Luke 1).

Clearly something is missing in the restoration of worship in the postexilic period, which further illustrates that more is needed in the trajectory of redemptive history: The promised presence of the King of kings

3. See H. G. M Williamson, *Ezra, Nehemiah*, WBC 16 (Waco: Word, 1985), for an excellent summation to the background of this opposition.
4. See Esther 7:8 for the sexual nature of the slavery (Williamson, *Ezra, Nehemiah*, 238).

that is yet to return to Zion. Thus, Nehemiah grounds the eschatological hope in the reestablishment of worship in Zion by restoring the sanctity of the site, as envisioned by Isaiah (58:12). By restoring pure worship now, the leaders in Judah are by implication preparing for the future of Zion, when the Davidic King will return to Zion (e.g., Jer. 33:17).

SIGNIFICANCE OF NEHEMIAH FOR BIBLICAL WORSHIP

Preparing the Way for True Worship on Mount Zion

The person and work of Christ as described and explained in the New Testament is the ultimate answer to the question of worship of the living God. Jesus is the only way to the Father (John 14:6; Acts 4:12). Consequently, Nehemiah's significance and contribution to the theme of worship from a biblical perspective must be set against the fulfillment found in Christ. Nehemiah's chronological placement in redemptive history matters since the book of Nehemiah (and Ezra) lays some of the last foundations (with Malachi) before the coming of the Messiah in fulfillment of Isaiah 40 (cf. Mark 1). In Nehemiah we see the last throes of the ongoing tensions in the sacrificial system and the worship in the Old Testament (Neh. 13). The contrast between Sinaitic worship and the direct access to the sacred space through Christ's sacrifice (Heb. 4:14–16; 1 John 4:18) is illustrated vividly in Hebrews 12:18–24:

> For you have not come to what may be touched, a blazing fire and darkness and gloom and a tempest and the sound of a trumpet and a voice whose words made the hearers beg that no further messages be spoken to them. For they could not endure the order that was given, "If even a beast touches the mountain, it shall be stoned." Indeed, so terrifying was the sight that Moses said, "I tremble with fear." But you have come to Mount Zion and to the city of the living God, the heavenly Jerusalem, and to innumerable angels in festal gathering, and to the assembly of the firstborn who are enrolled in heaven, and to God, the judge of all, and to the spirits of the righteous made perfect, and to Jesus, the mediator of a new covenant, and to the sprinkled blood that speaks a better word than the blood of Abel.

Thus, the acropolis of Zion at the time of Nehemiah (until AD 70), with the coming of the "son" (Heb. 1:1–2), turns into "the city of the living God," the "heavenly Jerusalem" (cf. Gal. 4:26). Its population (a minority in Yehud) now grows in ever-increasing numbers (in fulfillment of Isa. 2:1–4). It is now "the assembly [*ekklēsia*] of the firstborn who are enrolled in heaven" (Heb. 12:23). Zion continues to be the place where the worshiper meets "God, the Judge of all" (Heb. 12:23) now manifested through "Jesus the mediator of a new covenant" (Heb. 9:15). But instead of fear, now the picture is one of acceptance through the justification of the believer (see Rom. 8) so that they have direct access into this heavenly city, through the sacrifice of Christ (Heb. 12:23). This heavenly Zion is of course not unfamiliar to Isaiah's prophecy who so frequently refers to the new Zion both in the first and second half of his prophecy (Isa. 1:26–27; 2:1–4; 4:2–6; 10:5; 11:1–16; 25:6–9; 28:16; 30:18; 32:1; 33:5–6; 35; 40:1–31; 52–55). Nehemiah thus becomes the bridge between what Isaiah envisions and the first part of the Isaianic fulfillment in Christ's first coming until its consummation at his second coming.

Holiness Has No Expiration Date

The all-important requirements and qualifications of holiness for worship (Levitical credentials, purification and holiness—all prevailing themes in Nehemiah) and the blatant shortage of holiness on the part of his people (Neh. 13; cf. Isa. 6:3, 5; Ezek. 16) are now met by the Holy One of God himself. Jesus, God the Son, through his own sacrifice as a "guilt offering" (Isa. 53:10), met the standard no fallen human can ever meet. Paul powerfully captures the new reality (1 Cor. 1:30): "because of him you are in Christ Jesus, who became to us wisdom from God, righteousness and sanctification [*hagiasmos* = holiness] and redemption." Through our position by faith *in* Christ, we receive his holiness and have become "saints" (*hagios*) (1 Cor. 1:2; Eph. 1:1). Peter himself confirms the cancelation of the Old Testament genealogical test of worthiness (which was so important in Ezra-Nehemiah) to be qualified for worship (cf. Exod. 19:5–6): "But you are a chosen race, a royal priesthood, a holy nation, a people for his own possession" (1 Peter 2:9). However, the requirement of holiness remains a command in the new covenant (Eph. 4:24; "the will of God" [1 Thess. 4:3]; "be holy as I am holy" [1 Peter 1:15; Lev. 11:44]). We are made holy entirely outside ourselves, by faith in him (Eph. 1:4), but because God (Father, Son, and Holy Spirit) is holy, we emulate his character in every aspect of our lives out of love and loyalty to him. In Christ, the Levitical sacrificial system has been superseded by the priesthood of Christ and our worship and sacrifices become spiritual. Paul says to "offer your bodies as living sacrifices, holy and acceptable to God, which is your spiritual worship" (Rom. 12:1).

The Gathered Community

Finally, the elements of worship from Nehemiah outlined above provide continuity in New Testament forms of worship by anchoring the importance of the unity of the people gathered now fulfilled in Christ (Eph. 2:11–22). The centrality of the Word in worship (as modeled by the reading of Scripture in the synagogue in Nazareth [Luke 4:17]); confession of sin (James 5:16; 1 John 1:9); and the singing of praise and worship songs in celebratory joy (1 Cor. 14:26; Eph. 5:19–20; Phil. 4:4) have all been noted in Nehemiah. By faith in Christ and in fulfillment of the inclusion of the nations into the blessing of Abraham (Isa. 2:1–4), every nation, tribe, people, and language continue to gather in the worship of the Lamb of God and in singing (Rev. 5:6–9). God indeed has been faithful to Nehemiah's prayer to remember him and what he had done for the cause of Zion:

> And they sang a new song, saying,
> "Worthy are you to take the scroll
> and to open its seals,
> for you were slain, and by your blood you ransomed people for God
> from every tribe and language and people and nation,
> and you have made them a kingdom and priests to our God,
> and they shall reign on the earth." (Rev. 5:9–10)

BIBLIOGRAPHY

Commentaries

Allen, Leslie C, and Timothy S. Laniak. *Ezra, Nehemiah, Esther.* UBCS. Grand Rapids: Baker Books, 2003.

Baltzer, Klaus. "Moses Servant of God and the Servants: Text and Tradition in the Prayer of Nehemiah (Neh 1:5–11)." In *The Future of Early Christianity*, edited by Birger A. Pearson, 125–29. Minneapolis: Fortress, 1991.

Block, Daniel I. *Judges, Ruth.* NAC 6. Nashville: Broadman & Holman, 1990.

Boda, Mark J. *Haggai, Zechariah.* NIVAC 9. Grand Rapids: Zondervan, 2004.

Breneman, Mervin. *Ezra, Nehemiah, Esther.* NAC 10. Nashville: Broadman & Holman, 1993.

Keil, Karl F., and Sophia Taylor. *The Books of Ezra, Nehemiah, and Esther.* Sydney, Australia: Wentworth, 2016.

Kidner, Derek. *Ezra and Nehemiah.* TOTC 12. Downers Grove, IL: InterVarsity Press, 1979.

Petter, Donna, and Thomas Petter. *Ezra-Nehemiah.* NIVAC. Grand Rapids: Zondervan. Forthcoming.

Rudolph, Wilhelm. *Esra and Nehemia.* HAT 20. Tübingen: Mohr, 1949.

Smith, Gary V. *Ezra, Nehemiah, Esther.* CBC 5b. Carol Stream, IL: Tyndale House, 2010.

Williamson, H. G. M. *Ezra, Nehemiah.* WBC 16. Waco: Word, 1985.

Related Works

Alexander, T. Desmond. *From Paradise to the Promised Land: An Introduction to the Pentateuch.* Grand Rapids: Baker Academic, 2012.

Beaulieu, Paul-Alain. "Yahwistic Names in Light of Late Babylonian Onomastics." In *Judah and the Judeans in the Achaemenid Period: Negotiating Identity in an International Context*, edited by Oded Lipschits, Gary N. Knoppers, and Manfred Oeming, 247. Winona Lake, IN: Eisenbrauns, 2011.

Boda, Mark J., and Paul L. Redditt, eds. *Unity and Disunity in Ezra-Nehemiah: Redaction, Rhetoric, and Reader*. Sheffield: Sheffield Phoenix, 2008.

Briant, Pierre. *From Cyrus to Alexander: A History of the Persian Empire*. Winona Lake, IN: Eisenbrauns, 2002.

British Museum. "The Cyrus Cylinder." https://www.britishmuseum.org/collection/object/W_1880-0617-1941.

Carter, Charles E. *The Emergence of Yehud in the Persian Period: A Social and Demographic Study*. JSOTSup 294. Sheffield: Sheffield Academic, 1999.

Fried, L. S. "Something There Is That Doesn't Love a Wall: The Crisis Created by the Wall around Jerusalem." *Transeuphratène* 39 (2010): 83–84.

Jenson, Philip P. *Graded Holiness: A Key to the Priestly Conception of the World*. JSOTSup 106. Sheffield: JSOT Press, 1992.

Kitchen, K. A. *On the Reliability of the Old Testament*. Grand Rapids: Eerdmans, 2003

Klein, Ralph. "Ezra-Nehemiah, Books of." In *ABD* 2731–42.

Kline, Meredith G. *By Oath Consigned: A Reinterpretation of the Covenant Signs of Circumcision and Baptism*. Grand Rapids: Eerdmans, 1968.

Knoppers, Gary N. *Jews and Samaritans: The Origins and History of Their Early Relations*. Oxford: Oxford University Press, 2013.

Kuhrt, Amélie. *The Ancient Near East, C. 3000–330 BC*. Vol. 2. New York: Routledge, 1995.

Levenson, Jon D. *Sinai and Zion: An Entry into the Jewish Bible*. San Francisco: Harper & Row, 1985.

McConville, J. G. "Ezra-Nehemiah and the Fulfillment of Prophecy." *VT* 36 (1986): 205–24.

Na'aman, Nadav. "Text and Archaeology in a Period of Great Decline: The Contribution of the Amarna Letters to the Debate on the Historicity of Nehemiah's Wall." In *The Historian and the Bible: Essays in Honour of Lester L. Grabbe*, edited by Philip R. Davies and Diana V. Edelman, 20–30. New York: Bloomsbury, 2010.

Petter, Thomas. *The Land between Two Rivers: Early Israelite Identities in Central Transjordan*. Winona Lake, IN: Eisenbrauns, 2014.

Pittman, Holly. "Susa." In *The Oxford Encyclopedia of Archeology in the Near East*, edited by Eric M. Meyers, 106–10. New York: Oxford University Press, 1997.

Vincent, L.-H. "L'étendue de Jerusalem." In *La Palestine A L'Epoque Perse*, edited by E.-M. Laperrousaz and A. Lemaire, 121. Paris: Cerf, 1994.

Wright, Jacob L. *Rebuilding Identity: The Nehemiah-Memoir and Its Earliest Readers*. Berlin: de Gruyter, 2005.

Young, T. Cuyler. "The Iranian Migration into the Zagros." *Iran* 5 (1967): 11–34.

CHAPTER 21

RESTORING PROPER RELATIONSHIP WITH YAHWEH

Worship in the Postexilic Minor Prophets

Andrew Hill

CONTEXT OF WORSHIP IN THE POSTEXILIC PROPHETS

The books of Haggai, Zechariah, and Malachi form a distinct subcollection or literary corpus within the group of books commonly known as the Minor Prophets. In Hebrew tradition this collection of prophetic books is understood as the Scroll of the Twelve, since the twelve books were often written on a single scroll. All three prophets belong to the early Persian period of postexilic Hebrew history (dated broadly to the era between 520 and 450 BC). They are unified by literary device like the rhetorical question and the repetition of prophetic speech formulas and by theological themes like God's sovereignty over the nations, God's faithfulness to his covenant promises, repentance, temple worship, and eschatological judgment and blessing.

RESTORING PROPER RELATIONSHIP WITH YHWH

The Haggai-Zechariah-Malachi corpus is sometimes described as a narrative profile of postexilic Jerusalem recounting the spiritual history of the Hebrew restoration community. The corpus may be understood as the account of repentance and worship renewal prompting the return of the Hebrew covenant community to proper relationship with Lord God.[1] Mark Boda suggests the repeated theme of repentance in Zechariah 1:3 and Malachi 3:7 offers evidence of a "penitential redaction" of the entire

1. E.g., Paul House, *The Unity of the Twelve*, JSOTSup 97 (Sheffield: Sheffield Academic, 1990), 96–109.

Scroll of the Twelve.[2] It is clear that the Haggai-Zechariah-Malachi corpus forms a set of "bookends" with the prophets Hosea and Joel in framing the Twelve around the theme of repentance (cf. Hos. 6:1; 14:1; Joel 2:12–13).

This study assumes the Haggai-Zechariah-Malachi corpus is a positive account of God's mercy and grace in keeping his word to his people. They did return to land of ancestral promise after the Babylonian exile, the Second Temple was built, and the proper worship of YHWH prescribed by the Mosaic covenant was reinstated. Though not a comprehensive liturgical manual, the corpus does address the topics of worship, worship renewal, and spiritual formation. These last prophets of the Old Testament recognized the acute need for reestablishing temple worship (or renewing true and proper temple worship in Malachi's case) in Jerusalem. After all, it was false worship that led to the Assyrian and Babylonian exiles for the Hebrew kingdoms of Israel and Judah respectively (2 Kings 17:7–19; 22:17; 24:3–4, 20; cf. Jer. 7:1–15).[3]

For the purposes of this essay, worship may be defined simply as "God meeting with his people"[4] or "a conversation between us and God."[5] Or a more theologically refined definition like that of Marva Dawn: "Worship is our glad response to the immense grace of the Triune God."[6] In any case, worship is God's initiative; he acts and people respond. The Old Testament does not define worship as much as it describes worship. For example, the Chronicler understands worship as an attitude of humility demonstrated in the postures of bowing down and kneeling before God; and in a heart welling with thanksgiving voiced in singing praises to God as Creator and Redeemer (2 Chron. 28:27–30).

The Book of Haggai

The prophet Haggai was an advocate for the "homeless"—in this case, the "homeless" God of the Hebrew people. The Jerusalem temple had been sacked and plundered by the Babylonians nearly seventy years earlier. Regrettably, it still lay in ruins nearly two decades after the Hebrews had returned to Judah from exile in Babylonia (cf. Ezra 3:8–10; 5:16). Haggai's ministry to the Jews in Judah is reported in four related sermons dated precisely to the last four months of 520 BC, during the reign of Darius I, king of Persia (522–486 BC). Haggai's task was that of a herald sounding a wake-up call to a community that was preoccupied with personal economic concerns and overcome with spiritual lethargy (Hag. 1:2–6). He

2. Mark J. Boda, *Zechariah*, NICOT (Grand Rapids: Eerdmans, 2016), 31.
3. The "Original Setting" sections for the books of Haggai, Zechariah, and Malachi rely significantly on Richard D. Patterson and Andrew E. Hill, *Minor Prophets: Hosea—Malachi*, Cornerstone Biblical Commentary 10 (Carol Stream, IL: Tyndale, 2008).
4. Robert E. Webber, *Worship Old & New*, rev. ed. (Grand Rapids: Zondervan, 1994), 263.
5. William A. Dyrness, *A Primer on Christian Worship* (Grand Rapids: Eerdmans, 2009), 16.
6. Marva J. Dawn, *How Shall We Worship? Biblical Guidelines for the Worship Wars* (Wheaton, IL: Tyndale, 2003), xi.

was quick to point out the disparity between the desolation of the temple precinct and the comfortable homes occupied by his audience (1:4). Surely God deserved better! The book of Haggai is one of those rare "success stories" among the Old Testament prophets. The people obeyed (1:12), worked (1:14), and eventually completed the rebuilding of the Lord's temple in Jerusalem five years later, in 515 BC (cf. Ezra 6:15).

Haggai 1:1–15: Judah's leaders challenged to restore temple worship

Original setting

Haggai's first message to restore Judah is dated precisely to August 29, 520 BC (using modern equivalents). The message includes both rebuke and exhortation and is directed to the leaders of postexilic Judah; Zerubbabel, governor of Judah, and Joshua, the high priest (1:1). The sermon consists of a call to reconsider priorities (1:1–6), a charge to rebuild the temple (1:7–11), and a report of the response of the leaders and people (1:12–15).

Worship theology

Haggai's first sermon included a charge to rebuild the Jerusalem temple destroyed earlier by the Babylonians (Hag. 1:7–11). Solomon's temple was both the symbol and representation of God's presence among his people Israel. Allen Ross considers the temple not only a visible reminder of God's presence among his people but also a witness to "his saving dominion over all creation."[7] This theology of "divine presence" was initiated in God's directive to Israel to build a tabernacle, which was a portable worship sanctuary, after the Hebrews' deliverance from Egyptian oppression (Exod. 25–40). The Lord commanded Moses to build him a tent so that he might travel with and live among his people. God desired an "address" in the Hebrew community (Exod. 25:8). This launches what may be called an "Immanuel theology" in the biblical narrative, in which YHWH began to dwell with his people.[8]

The reconstruction of the Second Temple in Jerusalem contributes to this development of a biblical theology of divine presence. More importantly for the immediate context of Haggai, the Second Temple reestablished corporate worship in postexilic Judah. The Levitical priesthood was restored to their place of service as worship leaders, covenant mediators, and Torah instructors (cf. Deut. 33:8–11). Sacrificial worship was reinstated and the observation of the Sabbath, feast days, and special days of the Hebrew liturgical calendar resumed, including the pilgrimage festivals (cf. Ezra 6:19–22; Neh. 8:13–18; 13:15–22). A tangible first step was now in place for the realization of the prophetic vision of the return of God's

---

7. Allen P. Ross, *Recalling the Hope of Glory: Biblical Worship from the Garden to the New Creation* (Grand Rapids: Kregel Academic, 2006), 251.
8. See Andrew E. Hill, *1 & 2 Chronicles*, NIVAC (Grand Rapids: Zondervan, 2003), 246–47.

glory to his temple and the nations paying homage to the God of Israel in Jerusalem (Isa. 66:18–21; Hag. 2:1–9; Zech. 14:16–19).

King Solomon's prayer of dedication at the completion of the Jerusalem temple acknowledged that the God of Israel cannot be housed in the highest heavens, let alone an earthly sanctuary constructed by human hands (1 Kings 8:28; 1 Chron. 6:18). The prayer points indirectly to the New Testament and the fulfillment of the (Second) Temple in the person of Jesus the Messiah (John 2:19–22). As a result, Peter understood the church of Jesus Christ as a "building" composed of "living stones," the people of God as a spiritual house (1 Peter 2:4–5). Whether Old Testament or New Testament there is always an "interior" emphasis on the people of God as the living stones of the spiritual house, the worship of praise, and the lifestyle of doing good (Amos 5:14–15; 1 Peter 2:9–12).

Significance for biblical worship

The rebuilding of the Second Temple signaled the return of the Lord's favor to his people, but as Daniel Block notes, it also served as a test of their faith (see Hag. 1:5–11; 2:15–19; Mal. 3:10–12).[9] The Second Temple was a smaller and much less ornate structure, paling in comparison to its predecessor. The mixed response of the people of postexilic Judah, a cacophony of praising and weeping, calls attention to the disparity between Solomon's Temple and this remake of the original (Ezra 3:12–13). The despair and cynicism of the people was further compounded by the sorry state of temple worship, as worshipers cheated God in their sacrifices and tithes (Mal. 1:8). The priesthood soon became part of the problem as well, as the ministry of the apathetic priests was in need of reform. Tragically, they were actually leading the people into sin—not out of it (Mal. 2:8)! This placed a premium on the demand for ministry of faithful and righteous worship leaders. Priests and Levites, functioning as worship pastors, who were obedient to their charge to teach God's Word, instructing the people in holy living and spiritual service (Deut. 33:9–10; Mal. 2:1–9); make intercessory prayer of the people (Lev. 5:5–6); provide access to God through the sacrificial rituals (Lev. 1:3–9); and take care of the holy things associated with worship (Hag. 2:11–12).[10] Such is still in demand today!

Both the ritual sacrifice central to Hebrew religion and the prayer life of God's people were closely associated with the Jerusalem temple (1 Kings 8:29–30, 52; 2 Chron. 7:12). As time went on, the temple was increasingly identified as the "house of prayer" for Israel (Isa. 56:7; cf. Mark 11:17). This was due, in part, to the dispersion of the Hebrew people into Mesopotamia and elsewhere as a result of the Assyrian and Babylonian exiles (2 Kings 17:23; 25:11–12). The Jerusalem temple became the focus and

9. Daniel I. Block, *For the Glory of God: Recovering A Biblical Theology of Worship* (Grand Rapids: Baker Academic, 2014), 314.

10. Ross, *Recalling the Hope of Glory*, 212–14.

direction of prayer for Hebrews in the Diaspora (1 Kings 8:30, 35, 38; cf. Dan. 6:10). Following the example of King Solomon, standing with outstretched hands to heaven became one common prayer posture for the Hebrew faithful (1 Kings 8:22, 38; cf. Pss. 28:2; 63:4; 134:1–2; 135:2). Proper worship practiced at the Jerusalem temple was one way that God was glorified and reverenced among the nations in the Old Testament world (Mal. 1:11, 14; see the discussion of Mal. 1:6–2:9 below).

Haggai 2:1–9: The future glory of the Second Temple

Original setting

Haggai's second message to restoration Judah is dated precisely to October 17, 520 BC. The message includes both assurance and promise and is directed to the leaders of postexilic Judah: Zerubbabel, governor of Judah, and Joshua, the high priest, and the people of Judah (2:2). The sermon consists of an exhortation not to be afraid (2:1–5) and a promise that the glory of the Second Temple will surpass that of Solomon's Temple (2:6–9).

Worship theology

Haggai's reference to "Egypt" (2:5) sets the hortatory tone and establishes the covenant theme for this entire section. The citation is clearly a deliberate appeal to the historical traditions associated with the exodus from slavery under the pharaoh.[11] The prophet probably alludes to Isaiah's oracles announcing the second exodus and the restoration of the Hebrews from captivity in Babylon (e.g., Isa. 40:3–5; 41:17–20; 42:14–16).[12]

The clause, "when you came out of Egypt" (2:5), looks both back to the past and forward in anticipation of the future in an effort to encourage those Hebrew returnees to Judah presently in despair. This flashback to the exodus from Egypt was designed to demonstrate the continuity of YHWH's activity in history for elect Israel. Haggai's audience could be assured that the presence and power of the God who delivered the Hebrews from Pharaoh, and who delivered his people from Babylonian captivity and restored them in the land of covenant promise under King Cyrus of Persia, was still active among them.

According to Robert Webber, Christian worship "does God's story."[13] By that he means worship is a narrative that proclaims God's work in creation, his response to the fall of humanity in the judgment and redemption

---

11. Mark J. Boda, *Haggai, Zechariah*, NIVAC (Grand Rapids: Zondervan, 2004), 122–23; cf. Iain Provan, V. Philips Long, and Tremper Longman III, *A Biblical History of Israel* (Louisville: Westminster John Knox, 2003), 125–31.
12. On biblical typology and the "second-exodus" motif in Isaiah see Robin Routledge, *Old Testament Theology: A Thematic Approach* (Downers Grove, IL: IVP Academic, 2008), 43–47; and Robert B. Chisholm, *Handbook on the Prophets* (Grand Rapids: Baker Academic, 2002), 45–46, 115–16.
13. Robert E. Webber, *Ancient-Future Worship* (Grand Rapids: Baker Books, 2008), 29.

recorded in the covenant history of the Old Testament, and culminates in the incarnation of Jesus the Messiah and the redemption of all of creation in the Christ event and the establishment of the new covenant.

Hebrew worship remembers the past, especially the story of the Israelite exodus from Egypt, the redemptive event of the Old Testament (Deut. 11:1–4; Ps. 106:6–12). Hebrew worship in the Old Testament anticipates the future, and the fulfillment of the Old Testament worship prototypes in the person and work of Jesus the Messiah. The New Testament writers understood these foreshadowings typologically, identifying Jesus the Messiah as the greater Passover lamb of God (John 1:29; 1 Cor. 5:7), the very embodiment of the presence of God in the worship spaces of the tabernacle and temple (John 2:13–22; Heb. 10:11–12), and the greater High Priest and ultimate atoning sacrifice for sinful humanity (Heb. 10:11–14).[14]

Likewise, Christian worship participates in the redemptive story-shaped narrative as it remembers the past, the first advent of Jesus Christ, and anticipates the future, the second advent of Jesus Christ and the marriage supper of the Lamb (Rev. 19:6–8).[15] Robbie Castleman summarizes that worship shaped by God's redemptive story in Christ reminds worshipers "that God's story continues on life's journey through the Spirit's real presence in Word and Sacrament . . . [and] that they are not alone on life's journey but travel in the unity of Christ's body in a particular community of faith."[16] In fact, Craig Bartholomew and Michael Goheen note that "the whole point of Christianity is that it offers a story which is the story of the whole world. It is public truth."[17]

Haggai's affirmation to postexilic Judah that God's "Spirit remains among them" reminds that the Holy Spirit is active across the two testaments of the Bible (2:5). The Hebrew restoration community, including its leadership, worship, and worship renewal, was enabled by ministry of God's Holy Spirit (cf. Zech. 4:6). It is no surprise that we find the Spirit of God participating in the creation event (Gen. 1:2), the exodus event (cf. Num. 11:17, 24–25; Isa. 63:10, 14), and anointing the ministries of the Old Testament judges (e.g., Judg. 3:10; 13:25), kings (e.g., 1 Sam. 10:10; 16:13), and prophets (e.g., Ezek. 3:24–27; Mic. 3:8). Worship in the New Testament is informed and enabled by this same Holy Spirit. Jesus associated true worship with the Holy Spirit because God is Spirit (John 4:24). The apostle Paul affirmed that one can only acknowledge "Jesus is Lord," the fundamental creed of the church, by the power of the Holy Spirit (1 Cor. 12:3).

---

14. On biblical typology see Andrew E. Hill, *Enter His Courts with Praise: Old Testament Worship for the New Testament Church* (1993; repr., Grand Rapids: Baker, 1996), 233–35.
15. On *anamnesis* (remembering) and *prolepsis* (anticipating) as related to worship see Webber, *Ancient-Future Worship*, 43–44, 57–60.
16. Robbie F. Castleman, *Story-Shaped Worship: Following Patterns from the Bible and History* (Downers Grove, IL: IVP Academic, 2013), 204.
17. Craig G. Bartholomew and Michael W. Goheen, *The Drama of Scripture*, 2nd ed. (Grand Rapids: Baker Academic, 2014), 22.

So Webber comments, "The story of God is the story of the Triune God, and therefore always the story of God the Father, God the Son, and God the Holy Spirit."[18] This means Christian worship is Trinitarian, as the church raises doxology to God, offers thanksgiving to the Son, and invokes the enabling presence of the Holy Spirit as it proclaims and enacts God's redemptive narrative. As a result, for James Torrance, speaking theologically, "Christian worship is, therefore, our participation through the Spirit in the Son's communion with the Father, in his vicarious life of worship and intercession."[19]

Significance for biblical worship

Worship is the gospel enacted.[20] Along with preaching and hymn singing, this enactment can occur through the active recollection and proclamation of Christian creeds (e.g., the Apostles' Creed, the Nicene Creed). The classic creeds of the church compress historical events and theological truths into concise and memorable summary statements, and embody the story of Christ in a form to which humans can relate.[21] The regular recitation of the creeds in worship helps the members of the congregation tell the story that brings them together. They express their faith in the Triune God who has acted in history for their salvation. In so doing, congregants renew the relationship of the new covenant in Christ that the creeds rehearse and affirm. In the weekly enactment of God's redemptive story worshipers "begin to become the story."[22]

The historic structure or liturgy pattern of Christian worship reinforces the understanding of worship as a narrative. This "fourfold" worship structure is rooted in biblical teachings, especially Old Testament covenant format, and historically developed very early in church tradition as the standard worship liturgy.[23] The four movements or acts of worship in sequence feature the gathering or entrance, the service of the Word, the service of the Table, and the ending or dismissal.[24] The four elements work together to form a unified and complete worship service. William Dyrness likens the narrative of worship to a melody, with the goal of worship "to connect the melody of worship with the (often discordant) melodies of our lives, and, by the grace of God, to achieve a harmony between and among

18. Webber, *Ancient-Future Worship*, 30.
19. James B. Torrance, *Worship, Community and the Triune God of Grace* (Downers Grove, IL: InterVarsity Press, 1996), 31, as cited in Constance M. Cherry, *Worship Architect: A Blueprint for Designing Culturally Relevant and Biblically Faithful Services* (Grand Rapids: Baker Academic, 2010), 14–15.
20. Webber, *Worship Old & New*, 75.
21. See Webber, *Worship Old & New*, 75–76; Dyrness, *A Primer on Christian Worship*, 107.
22. Dyrness, *A Primer on Christian Worship*, 107.
23. See Webber, *Worship Old & New*, 150–51.
24. Cherry, *Worship Architect*, 46–47.

these various melodies."[25] Corporate worship formatted in this structure is a journey into God's presence and an invitation to join in God's story. Depending on the given Christian worship tradition, creedal recitation may be included in the second act, the service of the Word, or the third act, the service of the Table. In either case, it reminds the worshipers of their core beliefs and aids in the realization of what it speaks about since it distills the whole of the redemptive work of God.[26]

The Book of Zechariah

Zechariah's message was one of admonition, exhortation, and encouragement—a tract for troubled times. The pastoral tone for the messages of Zechariah is established in his exchange with the angel commissioned to relay the "kind and comforting words" from the Lord (1:13). The hortatory character of his sermons is seen in words of encouragement like "be strong" and "don't be afraid" (8:9, 13, 15). Zechariah's repeated appeals to the words of the "former prophets" authenticated his own ministry and assured his audience that they had not misunderstood God's earlier revelations (1:4; 7:7, 12). Haggai and Zechariah were also complementary prophets in that Haggai exhorted the people to rebuild the Jerusalem temple and Zechariah summoned the community to repentance and spiritual renewal (cf. Ezra 5:1). His task was to prepare the people for proper worship in the temple once the building project was completed.

The book of Zechariah neatly divides into two major units. The first includes the introductory verses (or superscription) with the call to repentance (1:1–6), the seven night visions (1:7–6:15), and two sermons addressing the topic of fasting (chaps. 7–8). The second part of the book consists of prophetic oracles, subdivided into two sections: the word of the Lord concerning the land of Hadrach (or Aram, chaps. 9–11), and the word of the Lord concerning Israel (chaps. 12–14).[27]

Three of Zechariah's speeches are dated to specific times during year two and year four (520–518 BC) of the reign of Darius I, king of Persia (522–486 BC). The date formula for the first speech (using modern equivalents) is October/November 520 BC. The second sermon (1:7–6:8) is dated to February 15, 519 BC, and the third sermon is dated to December 7, 518 BC. The concluding two oracles (Zech. 9–11; 12–14) are undated.

The book of Zechariah contains several passages related to Old Testament worship, including: 1:1–6 (a call to repentance); 3:1–10 (a purified priesthood); 4:1–14 (a rebuilt Jerusalem temple; see the discussion of Hag. 1:1–15); 5:5–11 and 10:1–5 (a purging of false worship); 6:9–15 (the crowning of Joshua the high priest); chaps. 7–8 (on the topics of fasting and social

25. Dyrness, *A Primer on Christian Worship*, 107.
26. Dyrness, *A Primer on Christian Worship*, 107.
27. On the literary history and structure of Zechariah see Boda, *Haggai, Zechariah*, 36–45; Boda, *The Book of Zechariah*, NICOT (Grand Rapids: Eerdmans, 2016), 16–29, 37–39.

justice); 13:1–6 (cleansing from sin, especially idolatry); and 14:16–21 (universal worship of the God of Israel as King; see the discussion of Mal. 1:6–2:9). Each text provides grist for the topic of biblical worship.

This study will examine three worship-related passages in Zechariah in more detail, including Zechariah 5:5–11, 7:8–10, and 8:16–17.

Zechariah 5:5–11: The woman in the basket

Original setting

The vision of the flying ephah, or the woman in the basket (Zech. 5:1–5), is the seventh of eight divine revelations in the visions portion of the book (Zech. 1:7–6:15). The structure of the night visions follows a standard pattern for this form of visionary literature. The basic outline includes (1) an introductory statement; (2) a description of what the prophet sees; (3) the prophet's request for an interpretation of the vision; and (4) an angelic explanation of the meaning of the vision.

The date formula (1:7) places Zechariah's experience in the second year of Darius I, king of Persia (February 15, 519 BC in modern equivalents). The precision of the fixed date indicates that the series of eight visions seen by Zechariah occurred during a single night just two months after Haggai's final two oracles. These messages promised a return of the divine presence to the Jerusalem temple and a great shaking of the cosmos (Hag. 2:10–19, 20–23). The first oracle (Zech. 2:6–9 [MT 2:10–17]) accompanying the prophet's visions anticipates the fourth vision (Zech. 3:1–10), the cleansing of the high priest as a necessary prerequisite for welcoming God's presence back to Jerusalem. The vision of the woman in the basket continues the theme of cleansing begun in the fourth vision.

Worship theology

The symbolism of the evil woman in the ephah basket represents a seductive and dangerous force that is so difficult to restrain it must be pushed back into the basket and sealed with a "heavy lid" (v. 8 NLT; lit., "lead cover" [NIV]). This evil is so potent and aggressive that it cannot be confined, but instead must be shipped back to it source, the land of Babylon, by divine decree. (v. 11).

Several interpretations of the identity of the evil woman named "Wickedness" sitting in the ephah basket are tendered. Most often the woman is understood to represent a system of evil, a culture of moral and social ills, ceremonial impurities and religious apostasy, and the injustices inherent in the political and legal institutions of Israel—all regularly condemned by the Hebrew prophets (Amos 3:14–4:1; Mic. 3:1–3, 9–11). Others regard the evil woman as a symbol of the "pagan women" brought into the Hebrew community through wrongful intermarriage with foreign people groups (an issue for Malachi 2:10–16, and one of the reform initiatives of Ezra and Nehemiah; see Ezra 9–10). It is also possible that the evil woman is a figure for "spiritual adultery" or idolatry since the vice of ritual prostitution is usually associated with idol worship in the Old Testament (e.g., Hos. 2:2; Jer. 23:10; Ezek. 16:15).[28] Regardless, God himself will both contain and remove "Wickedness" from his people and the land of Israel. Although cleansing from sin is the gracious work of God (Ps. 51:2, 7; Zech. 13:1–3), those guilty of sin and rebellion against God must turn back to him and seek his cleansing for the forgiveness of sins and a restored relationship with him (Ezek. 24:13; Zech. 1:3; Mal. 3:7).

The Old Testament associates wickedness with idolatry. It is this "wickedness of the other nations" that caused God to displace them from the land with Israel (Deut. 9:4–5). It is likely that the woman named "Wickedness" sitting in the basket represents one of the fertility goddesses of the ancient Near East.[29] The people of the kingdoms of Israel and Judah were exiled to Mesopotamia for this same "wickedness," provoking God to anger with their idolatry (2 Kings 17:16–18; 2 Chron. 36:14). The divine judgment of exile purged the Hebrews of idolatry. The postexilic prophets do not mention this form of false worship in their indictments of the restoration community. Zechariah envisions a day when God's cleansing of his people will be so thorough that the names of the idols will be banished from the land and remembered no more (Zech. 13:2).

Significance for biblical worship

False worship in Old Testament times is most commonly connected to the idolatry of the foreign nations surrounding Israel (Deut. 7:3–6). This false religion was typically characterized by homage to handcrafted images and gross misconduct, including ritual prostitution and human sacrifice (Lev. 18:6–30). The Mosaic law banned the religion of idols as a detestable and abhorrent practice before the Lord God (Deut. 7:23–26). Yet within one generation after the death of Joshua the Israelites abandon the God of their ancestors and followed the Baals. The book of Judges documents this ongoing cycle of apostasy, as the Hebrews turned away from YHWH to the false religion of Baalism (e.g., Judg. 2:11–23). Samuel records the Lord's lament that his people began forsaking him and served other gods from the day he delivered them from Egypt (1 Sam. 8:8).

Not all idol worship is as blatant as that sarcastically derided by Isaiah, the worship of images that had to be nailed to shelves to prevent them from toppling over (Isa. 41:5–7). Marva Dawn has identified several subtle idolatries of contemporary culture. These contemporary idolatries include (but are not limited to) the God of efficiency, making liturgy "clockwork"

---

28. See the discussions in Hannah K. Harrington, "Zechariah," in *The IVP Women's Bible Commentary*, eds. Catherine Clark Kroeger and Mary J. Evans (Downers Grove, IL: InterVarsity Press, 2002), 495–96; and Boda, *Book of Zechariah*, 348–49.
29. Eric M. Meyers and Carol L. Meyers, *Haggai and Zechariah 1–8*, AB 25b (New York: Doubleday, 1987), 302–3.

and stifling worship; the idolatry of money, with an appeal for churches to recognize the biblical priority of worship and the poor in their budgets; the idolatry of traditionalism, doing things the way they have always been done; the idolatry of famous people; the God of competition and the idolatry of numbers and success; and the idolatry of power.[30] She calls "the Church to both understand the surrounding culture and to resist its idolatries."[31] Like the postexilic prophets, she writes to warn the leaders and worshipers of our churches to be alert to "how extensively society's idolatries have invaded the Church and its worship."[32]

David Peterson rightly reminds us that worship is a form of spiritual warfare. More than an eschatological puzzle to solve regarding the events and details of the end times, Peterson highlights the several worship emphases in John's Revelation, including true worship, worship of the Lamb of God; and false worship, worship of the Beast, the works of Satan through the ideologies, structures, systems, and cultures of our fallen world.[33] Walter Brueggemann concurs, making a prophetic declaration regarding worship as spiritual warfare that "the act of praise is indeed world-making for the community which takes the act of worship as serious and realistic. . . . Worship is not only constitutive, but inevitably polemical. Praise (of Christ) insists not only is this the true world, but that other worlds are false. . . . The church sings praises not only toward God but against the gods."[34] Zechariah's message introduces us to the cosmic implications of true worship and the need for worshipers and worship leaders to recognize this dimension of Christian worship. "The Spirit and the Bride say, 'Come'" (Rev. 22:17)!

Zechariah 7:8–10 and 8:16–17: Administer justice

Original setting

The content of the two sermons that conclude the first half of the book of Zechariah (chaps. 7–8) are probably excerpts from messages or sermons preached by Zechariah. As such, they convey a patchwork quilt of his thought and theology.[35] The first sermon contains two messages, one condensing a response to questions concerning fasting (7:1–7), and the second a reflection on Israel's failure to practice social justice during the

30. Marva J. Dawn, *Reaching Out without Dumbing Down: A Theology of Worship for the Turn-of-the-Century Church* (Grand Rapids: Eerdmans, 1995), 41–53.
31. Dawn, *Reaching Out*, 41.
32. Dawn, *Reaching Out*, 41–42.
33. David Peterson, *Engaging with God: A Biblical Theology of Worship* (Downers Grove, IL: InterVarsity Press, 2002), 264–65.
34. Walter Brueggemann, *Israel's Praise: Doxology against Idolatry and Ideology* (Philadelphia: Fortress, 1988), 26–27; on worship as a subversive act see also, Dawn, *Reaching Out*, 57–72.
35. Peter C. Craigie, *The Twelve Prophets*, Daily Study Bible Old Testament (Philadelphia: Westminster, 1984), 2:189.

preexilic era of Hebrew history. Peter Craigie characterized chapter 8 as "an anthology of the prophet's sayings from different places and varying times."[36] This second sermon is a series of notable message excerpts joined together by a series of messenger formulas (8:4, 6, 7, 9, 14, 19, 20, 23). The two chapters are united by questions related to the topic of fasting (posed in 7:2–7 and answered in 8:18–19), and the theme of social justice (7:8–10; 8:16–17). The date formula of Zechariah 7:1 (the last in the book) places the two sermons in the fourth year of King Darius of Persia (indicating the event took place on December 7, 518 BC, using modern equivalents). This was almost two years after the vision section of the book (Zech. 1:7–6:15). It is possible that the date formula here refers primarily to the timing of the delegation seeking answers to questions on fasting (7:2–7), rather than the synopses of the prophet's messages.

Worship theology

Individual and community fasts were important acts of worship in the Old Testament. Prayers of repentance and contrition usually accompanied fasting, especially in times of personal or national crisis (cf. Esther 4:15–16; Joel 2:12–17). The question of whether to continue observing a day of fasting to mourn the destruction of Solomon's Temple was posed to the priests and prophets by a delegation from Bethel. The question about maintaining the memorial fast was of practical concern since the Second Temple was under construction, making the fast lamenting the razing of the First Temple unnecessary (7:2–3). Zechariah's direct answer to the question was delayed (cf. 8:18–19). Instead, the prophet responded with questions of his own (7:4–7). Each rhetorical question was designed to make the point that whether in their feasting or in their fasting the people were engaged in self-centered rather than God-centered activity (7:6). The point is to remember an event with an understanding of the theological significance of that event.[37]

Zechariah also offered a remedy for the self-pleasing worship and lifestyle that characterized the people (7:8–10). As an antidote to the ethos of self-interest, Zechariah proclaimed God's expectations for Israelite society with four precepts: two exhortations and two admonitions (7:9–10). The exhortations to administer true justice and show mercy and compassion echo the messages of the earlier prophets (7:12; cf. Isa. 1:17; Mic. 6:8). The injunctions against exploiting the weak and plotting evil schemes against others hearkens back to the Mosaic covenant and the command to love one's neighbor (Lev. 19:18, 34). Treating others with respect both dignifies them as people made in God's image and honors God as the Creator of all (cf. Prov. 17:5; 19:17; 22:2). This is what it meant for the Hebrew people to be ordained by God as a kingdom of priests to serve the Lord and each other (Exod. 19:6).

---

36. Craigie, *Twelve Prophets*, 2:189.
37. Craigie, *Twelve Prophets*, 2:192.

Significance for biblical worship

Zechariah calls us to rediscover the difference between the "holy day" and the "holiday." The holy day celebrates and commemorates in communal worship, whether festive or solemn and penitential, the mighty deeds of God in the redemptive history of his people. By contrast, the focus of the holiday typically involves the suspension of work routines to enable individuals to enjoy the present moment—"having a good time now." The Christian celebration of a holy day is not determined by the display of a red number on the calendar. Rather, it is a biblically informed posture toward God's involvement in time and history, toward divine mystery and worship, and divine revelation in space and time.[38]

Ross notes that fasts were special occasions for "unscheduled" worship. He summarizes that fasting is the denial of normal bodily appetites so that the worshiper might give greater attention to spiritual concerns.[39] Fasting, along with prayer and almsgiving, were core worship responses to God at the time of Jesus and later became known as the three pillars of Second Temple Judaism.[40] The Didache instructed Christians in the early church to fast regularly on Wednesday and Friday.[41] Fasting is still an important act of worship in individual and corporate Christian faith and is often included among the Christian spiritual disciplines. More important is to have a proper attitude and right motive in one's fasting, not an outward show of self-denial but fasting that is not obvious according to Jesus (Matt. 6:16–18).

The prophet Isaiah's understanding of true fasting as loosing the chains of injustice (Isa. 58:6–7) fits well with Zechariah's call to show justice, mercy, and compassion to one another (Zech. 7:8–10; 8:16–17; cf. Joel 2:12–14). The biblical messengers preached a consistent message on the imperative of social justice as a characteristic of the true worship of God (e.g., Isa. 1:10–20; Amos 5:21–24; Mic. 6:8; Matt. 25:31–40; James 1:26–27). Mark Labberton calls living out God's call to justice "the dangerous act of worship." He challenges the church to pursue "worship that enlivens and enlarges our vision for seeking and doing justice."[42] The final action or movement of corporate worship, the sending of the people of God out into the world to love and serve others, inherently includes the call to "do justice."[43]

38. See the discussion in Hill, *1 & 2 Chronicles*, 428–32.
39. Ross, *Recalling the Hope of Glory*, 239.
40. On the "three chief acts of Jewish piety" or "three pillars" of Judaism see, D. A. Carson, *Matthew*, in *The Expositor's Bible Commentary*, vol. 9, *Matthew–Mark*, eds. Tremper Longman III and David E. Garland, rev. ed. (Grand Rapids: Zondervan, 2010), 196.
41. Didache 8.1.
42. Mark Labberton, *The Dangerous Act of Worship: Living God's Call to Justice* (Downers Grove, IL: InterVarsity Press, 2007), 149.
43. Cherry, *Worship Architect*, 114–15.

The Book of Malachi

The prophet Malachi was a sensitive pastor, a lofty theologian, a stern prophet, and a spiritual mentor to the Jews regathered in postexilic Judah. He had to be, as his sermons were directed to a tough crowd that included the disillusioned, the callous, the cynical, the dishonest, the skeptical, the doubting, the apathetic, and the outright wicked. As the Lord's messenger, his essential word to Israel was profoundly simple: "'I have always loved you,' says the LORD" (1:2 NLT). Malachi's ministry to the Jews in postexilic Judah is dated broadly between 500 and 430 BC, depending on the source consulted.

Unlike Haggai and Zechariah, the book offers no date formulas for the prophet's ministry. A date for Malachi between 500–470 BC seems likely, given the similarities with Haggai and Zechariah in language and themes. Malachi's message is composed of six sermons, all delivered in the distinctive style of the disputation speech that pits God's prophet in confrontational dialogue with his jaded audience. His audience comprised expatriates resettled in Judah and the descendants of those Hebrews who survived the Babylonian sack of Jerusalem but had not been deported to Mesopotamia.

The umbrella theme of Malachi is covenant relationship with God. Specifically, he calls the people to a right understanding of God (1:2–5), a return to the practice of right worship (1:6–2:9), guarding right relationships in marriage (2:10–16), restoring right relationships in the community by seeking social justice (2:17–3:5), and honoring God in worship with right giving (3:6–12). All this will bring the people into right relationship with God (3:13–4:3).

Malachi 1:6–2:9: A call for worship renewal

Original setting

Malachi's second sermon or disputation consists of two distinct speech-acts. The first is aimed at the people and is designed to persuade these "temple-goers" that YHWH is truly Lord (1:6–14). The second speech-act is directed to the corrupt priesthood of the Jerusalem temple (2:1–2:9). The hopes raised by Haggai and Zechariah for a restoration of the Davidic dynasty rooted in the figure of Zerubbabel seemed to have disappeared by the time of Malachi. The office of provincial governor was still in its infancy, and the provincial bureaucracy was in an embryonic stage of development. The priests and Levites now served both as the religious and spiritual leaders of God's people, and they were also the political power brokers when Malachi preached to Judah.

Religiously, the Second Temple had been completed, but it paled in comparison to its Solomonic predecessor. Temple worship had been reestablished, but it was in a sorry state, as worshipers cheated God in their sacrifices and tithes. The priesthood was also in need of reform, as the ministry of the apathetic and hypocritical priests was actually leading people into sin—not out of it (Mal. 2:8)!

Socially, Malachi confronted a population given to religious cynicism and political skepticism. The disillusionment of the postexilic Jewish community was prompted by several theological misunderstandings, including the expectations for wealth that Haggai had promised once the Second Temple was rebuilt (Hag. 2:7, 18–19), the restoration of the Davidic covenant predicted by Ezekiel (34:13, 23–24), and the implementation of Jeremiah's "new covenant" (Jer. 31:23, 31–33). In the minds of many in Malachi's audience, God's word could not be trusted and he had failed his people (Mal. 3:14–15).

Worship theology

The proposition that God deserved proper worship by all people is founded on his election of Israel (1:2–5). This fundamental truth is further stressed by comparative degree in the analogies of the deserved honor due a father (1:6) and a human governor (1:8). Israel's destiny was entwined with the nations from the very beginnings of its covenant relationship with YHWH, as all the families of the earth would be blessed through Abram and Sarai (Gen. 12:1–3). The supremacy of YHWH who revealed himself to Moses (Exod. 3:1–6) as a universal deity, God of all the nations, was demonstrated convincingly in the spiritual contests against the Egyptian gods at the Hebrew exodus from Egypt (Exod. 12:12; cf. 18:10–11), and Elijah's duel with the prophets of Baal and the Canaanite gods at Mount Carmel (1 Kings 18:24, 36–39).

Malachi proclaimed the theological truth of YHWH's supremacy in a triad of verses in his first and second sermons (1:5, 11, 14). The climactic arrangement of the three declarations is often acknowledged: first, the greatness of the Lord reaches beyond the borders of Israel (1:5); then he is honored by the worship of other people groups, making his name great among the nations (1:11); and finally, YHWH is a great king, feared among the nations (1:14).

This theme of the worship of YHWH by the nations is central to the second disputation, and it fits the pattern of the universal worship of the God of Israel projected in each of the postexilic prophets (cf. Hag. 2:7; Zech. 14:16–17). More than the worship of the Diaspora Jews or even Jewish proselytes, Malachi seems to have in mind the eschatological future when the kingdom of God is established over all the earth, and the nations recognize YHWH as the true Sovereign. Malachi rightly understood that Israel's proper worship of the God of Jacob had global implications (cf. Ps. 86:9; John 3:16; Rev. 7:9–10).

Significance for biblical worship

Malachi's outrage at the worthless worship offered by the people and mediated by the priesthood led him to call for shutting the doors of God's temple and closing down the worship center (1:10). Ross comments that "if Israel would not worship him [God] properly, he would turn to the Gentiles who would honor his name in pure worship (1:11, 14). . . . Little did they expect that this would actually happen."[44] The New Testament Gospels are sprinkled with stories of Gentiles believing in Jesus as Messiah and worshiping him as Son of God. Roman soldiers (Luke 3:14; 7:1–10), a Samaritan woman (John 4), and a Greek (Syrophoenician) woman (Mark 7:24–30) serve as illustrations that Jesus is "a light for revelation to the Gentiles" (Luke 2:31–32) and the name in whom the nations will put their hope (Matt. 12:21). The church quickly became a Gentile majority after the promised event of Pentecost (Acts 2:16–21 cf. Joel 2:28–32). The Samaritans and the Gentiles also experienced the outpouring of God's Holy Spirit, their own mini Pentecosts, as validation of God's salvation being extended to all who believe Jesus is Lord (Acts 8:14–17; 19:1–8). The great commission created a global church and global worship within three decades after Jesus charged his disciples to take his gospel to the ends of the earth and make disciples of all nations (Matt. 28:16–20)—so much so that Paul could write to the church in Colossae that "the gospel is bearing fruit and growing throughout the whole world" (Col. 1:6 NIV). This is still true today. John Piper observes that "missions is not the ultimate goal of the Church. Worship is. Missions exists because worship doesn't. Worship is ultimate, not missions, because God is ultimate, not man."[45]

The global nature of the Christian church has generated new understandings and produced many challenges for the worship and mission of the global church. The interest in and appreciation for Christian worship expressions found among the many cultures of the world is sometimes labeled "ethnodoxology,"[46] John Witvliet reminds us that God is calling the nations, every tribe, language, and culture, into the kingdom of the Messiah, resulting in an ongoing fusion of Christian worship expression across the history of the church.[47] Malachi's reference to the Gentiles' worship of God (Mal. 1:10, 14) foreshadowed the expansion of the church as the people of God to the nations (Acts 1:8), and anticipated John's vision of an innumerable throng worshiping before the Lamb (Rev. 7:9–10). The reality of the global church calls us to ethnodoxology—that is, appreciating, celebrating, learning from, and joining in the "praise" of the "peoples"

44. Ross, *Recalling the Hope of Glory*, 354.

45. John Piper, *Let the Nations Be Glad! The Supremacy of God in Missions*, rev. ed. (Grand Rapids: Baker Books, 2003), 17.

46. The International Council of Ethnodoxologies (ICE) website defines ethnodoxology as "the theological and anthropological study, and practical application, of how every cultural group might use its unique and diverse artistic expressions appropriately to worship the God of the Bible" (Global Ethnodoxology Network, "Ethnodoxology = Peoples + Praise," http://www.worldofworship.org/what-is-ethnodoxology, accessed June 4, 2018).

47. John Witvliet, foreword to *Worship and Mission for the Global Church*, ed. James R. Krabill (Pasadena: William Carey Library, 2013), xxii.

of the world in the worship of the God of Israel, and the God and Father of our Lord Jesus Christ.[48]

Malachi 3:6–12: Robbing God in the tithe

Original setting

Malachi's fifth sermon is one disputation (concerning the tithe, 3:8–10) embedded within another disputation (the call to repentance, 3:6–7). The oracle is a series of three speech-acts: a divine assertion ("I . . . do not change" [3:6]), intended to assure the audience of God's constancy; a divine summons to repentance ("return to me" [3:7]), meant to persuade the audience to redirect their loyalty back to YHWH; and a divine challenge ("put me to the test" [3:10]), designed to convince the audience of God's commitment to restore his people.

The prophet accused his audience of "cheating" (NLT) or even "robbing" (NIV) God (3:8–9). The Sinai covenant introduced the requirement of the tithe of the land (grain or fruit) and the tithe of the herd and flock, returning a tenth part to God, to whom all things belong (Lev. 27:30–33). The Torah required three tithes of Israel: the annual general tithe of the land given to the Levites (Lev. 27:30–32; Num. 18:21); the eating of a portion of the tithe in conjunction with the sacred meal consecrating the payment of the general tithe (Deut. 14:23); and the tithe collected every three years for the poor (Deut. 14:28–29). Likewise, the Levites were charged to present a tithe of the general tithes they received from the people as their inheritance from the Lord (i.e., their daily sustenance [Num. 18:25–29]).

The legislation regarding the tithe is expanded in the covenant renewal ceremony at Mount Nebo with the second generation of Hebrews delivered from slavery in Egypt (see Deut. 12:11–19; 014:24–29; 26:12–15). Daniel Block states that the tithing instructions Moses delivered to Israel were both "an extraordinary privilege and a remarkably humanitarian institution."[49] He further summarizes that the calls for the tithe were accompanied by an invitation to worship (Deut. 12:12, 18–19). The laws for tithing were generous in that they provided the alternative of monetary equivalent if necessary (Deut. 14:24–26). They also served as a thanksgiving offering acknowledging God's gracious provision and afforded the opportunity to reach out to marginalized members of the community (Deut. 14:27–29; 26:12–14).[50] Most significant, the tithe highlighted the contrast between Israelite religion and Canaanite fertility religion, as the "ritual of

48. Jaewoo Kim describes this understanding of Christian worship as "glocal worship"—that is, the integration of global and local expressions of biblical worship ("The Whole World Has Gone 'Glocal,'" in Krabill, *Worship and Mission for the Global Church*, 46); see further Sandra Maria Van Opstal and Mark Labberton, *The Next Worship: Glorifying God in a Diverse World* (Downers Grove, IL: InterVarsity Press, 2016).

49. Block, *For the Glory of God*, 260.

50. Block, *For the Glory of God*, 260–61.

the triennial tithe provided an occasion for worshipers to acknowledge not only that this produce was evidence of YHWH's blessing on the land but also that the land itself was a gift (Deut. 26:15)."[51]

Worship theology

The real issue for Malachi was not the reinstitution of the legalistic giving (or payment) of the tithe in keeping with the formal obligations of the Mosaic law. Nor was the point of the message the abundant agricultural blessing promised as the outcome of testing God's faithfulness (3:10–11). No, the prophet recognized that the "robbery" of God in the failure to bring the tithe and the tithe tax was merely a symptom of a more serious disease. The stinginess of postexilic Judah was rooted in unbelief. For this reason, the charge to bring the tithe to temple worship is coupled with a call to repentance (3:7). Only by returning to a posture of faith in and reverence of God could the people begin to experience the wisdom of the sage: "Give freely and become more wealthy; be stingy and lose everything" (Prov. 11:24 NLT). Malachi understood that turning to God in spiritual renewal must begin somewhere. God himself decreed that the practical act of obedience to the Mosaic laws in bringing the tithes as an act of worship was an important first step in reasserting the community's fidelity in covenant relationship with YHWH. As Joyce Baldwin notes, "Good harvests alone . . . would not make a country *a land of delight*. . . . There were spiritual counterparts to the fruits of the soil."[52]

Malachi's invitation to postexilic Jerusalem to "test God" (3:10) should not be viewed as a contradiction with the Mosaic prohibition against "testing" God (Deut. 6:16; cf. Matt. 4:7). As Block observes, "God reserves the right to suspend his own principles and is free to invite his people to test him, to see if he will not respond positively to generous giving."[53] This is an exceptional case. Malachi 3:6–12 must be interpreted carefully, keeping in mind the covenantal context of the disputation, the community (vs. individualistic) orientation of the sermon, and the special historical, political, and socioeconomic circumstances peculiar to Judah during the early Persian period. Such an approach helps temper what has become known in contemporary American religion as "prosperity gospel," giving in worship for the purpose of getting material blessings in return. It is important to recognize that divine blessing associated with giving may include both material and immaterial or spiritual benefits (Prov. 2:9–11; 8:35). Note too that Malachi expects a reversal in the lifestyle and behavior of his audience, repudiating covenant violations like sorcery, adultery, perjury, and economic oppression (Mal. 3:5). Finally, Block reminds us that generous

51. Block, *For the Glory of God*, 261.
52. Joyce G. Baldwin, *Haggai, Zechariah, Malachi*, TOTC 24 (Downers Grove, IL: InterVarsity Press, 1972), 247.
53. Block, *For the Glory of God*, 262.

giving is the supreme expression of gratitude for grace already received and that giving in worship should always be motivated by concern for the honor and glory of the Lord.[54]

Significance for biblical worship

A significant portion of the Mosaic covenant is devoted to the giving of tithes, offerings, and sacrifices.[55] Malachi specifically speaks to the annual general tithe, the tenth-part portion of the land (produce and animals) presented to God as an act of worship acknowledging him as Lord of the earth and provider for Israel (Deut. 12:6, 11, 17; 2 Chron. 31:5–6; Neh. 12;44; cf. Gen. 14:20). The giving of the tithe is not a headline issue in the New Testament, but Jesus does admonish his religious contemporaries for failing to balance the demands of the tithing laws and the covenant principles of faith, justice, and mercy (Matt. 23:23–24). The Old Testament legislation instituting the giving of tithes and offerings demanded separating out the best one's produce and animals (see Lev. 27:30–33). Jesus may have had this teaching in mind when instructed his disciples to give (in this case alms) so that one hand is unaware of what the other is doing—that is, give to the poor without counting the personal cost (Matt. 6:3).

The worship act of giving tithes and offerings to the Lord is characterized by an attitude of joy and expressions of rejoicing in the Old Testament (Deut. 12:12, 19; 26:11). This exuberant thankfulness acknowledges God's goodness for his bountiful provision (Ps. 111:5), his faithfulness in keeping covenant with Israel (Ps. 111:9), and his lavish grace in pardoning sin and delivering his people from their enemies (Ps. 103:3). In the New Testament, Paul commended the generous giving of the Macedonian churches and encourages the Christians in Corinth to give with a similar charitable spirit (2 Cor. 8:1–15; cf. the commendation of Jesus for the widow who placed all she had in the temple treasury [Mark 12:41–44; Luke 21:1–4]). He exhorted the Corinthian church to "excel in this grace of giving" (2 Cor. 8:7 NIV), reminding them that God "loves a cheerful giver" (2 Cor. 9:7; lit., a "hilarious" giver).[56] Paul supports his teaching with the example of Christ who was rich but became poor for our sake, so that through his poverty we might become rich (2 Cor. 8:9). What better theological motivation for generous and cheerful giving than the example of our incarnate Lord?

The New Testament adds a spiritual dimension to the worship act of giving tithes and offerings, and more generally to the practice of giving to

54. Block, *For the Glory of God*, 262.

55. For a summary of sacrificial and ritual worship in the OT, see Richard E. Averbeck, "Sacrifices and Offerings," in *Dictionary of the Old Testament: Pentateuch*, eds. T. Desmond Alexander and David W. Baker (Downers Grove, IL: InterVarsity Press, 2003), 706–33.

56. See further the insert "Christian Giving," in *The NLT Illustrated Study Bible*, ed. Sean A. Harrison (Carol Stream, IL: Tyndale, 2015), 2125.

God. The Old Testament provides the seedbed for this theological understanding of giving in associating prayer with ritual sacrifice (Ps. 141:2), recognizing a broken and contrite heart as the acceptable sacrifice to the Lord (Ps. 51:17), equating doing what is right and just with ritual sacrifice (Prov. 21:3), and affirming the offering the sacrifice of praise in worship (Pss. 22:3; 100:4). So the book of Hebrews calls Christians to offer God the sacrifices of praise and doing good (Heb. 13:15–16). Ultimately, for the apostle Paul, the Christian offers one's entire life as a living sacrifice to God—this is true spiritual worship (Rom. 12:1–2).

Restoring right relationship to the Lord enables the people of God to offer him proper worship. We learn from the prophet Haggai that recognizing God's presence in our lives leads to the fear of the Lord. This reverence for God motivates obedience to his word and fosters a discipline of prayer. We learn from Zechariah that repentance is essential to restoring a right relationship with God. He also emphasizes the need for sanctified worship leaders to bring pastoral oversight to the proper worship of God in their admonition, exhortation, and instruction of his people. Both Zechariah and Malachi understand that the proper worship of God results in the practice of social justice. Last, Malachi reminds us that the proper worship of YHWH glorifies him among the nations. This is the ultimate purpose of worship—the glory of God!

BIBLIOGRAPHY

Bartholomew, Craig G. and Michael W. Goheen, *The Drama of Scripture: Finding Our Place in the Biblical Story*. 2nd ed. Grand Rapids: Baker Academic, 2014.

Bechtel, Carol M., ed. *Touching the Altar: The Old Testament for Christian Worship*. Grand Rapids: Eerdmans, 2008.

Block, Daniel I. *For the Glory of God: Recovering a Biblical Theology of Worship*. Grand Rapids: Baker Academic, 2014.

Borchert, Gerald L. *Worship in the New Testament: Divine Mystery and Human Response*. St. Louis: Chalice, 2008.

Brueggemann, Walter. *Worship in Ancient Israel*. Nashville: Abingdon, 2005.

Castleman, Robbie F. *Story-Shaped Worship: Following Patterns from the Bible and History*. Downers Grove, IL: IVP Academic, 2013.

Chapell, Bryan. *Christ-Centered Worship: Letting the Gospel Shape Our Practice*. Grand Rapids: Baker, 2009.

Cherry, Constance M. *The Worship Architect: A Blueprint for Designing Culturally Relevant and Biblically Faithful Services*. Grand Rapids: Baker Academic, 2010.

Dawn, Marva J. *Reaching Out without Dumbing Down: A Theology of Worship for the Turn-of-the-Century Church*. Grand Rapids: Eerdmans, 1995.

______. *A Royal Waste of Time: The Splendor of Worshiping God and Being Church for the World*. Grand Rapids: Eerdmans, 1999.

Dyrness, William A. *A Primer on Christian Worship*. Grand Rapids: Eerdmans, 2009.
Hill, Andrew E. *Enter His Courts with Praise: Old Testament Worship for the New Testament Church*. 1993. Reprint, Grand Rapids: Baker, 1996.
______. *Malachi*. AB 25D. New York: Doubleday, 1998.
______. *Haggai, Zechariah, and Malachi*. TOTC 28. Downers Grove, IL: IVP Academic, 2012.
Hurtado, Larry W. *At the Origins of Christian Worship: The Context and Character of Earliest Christian Devotion*. Grand Rapids: Eerdmans, 1999.
Jacobs, Mignon R. *The Books of Haggai and Malachi*. NICOT. Grand Rapids: Eerdmans, 2017.
Knowles, Michael P. *The Unfolding Mystery of the Divine Name: The God of Sinai in Our Midst*. Downers Grove, IL: IVP Academic, 2012.
McGowan, Andrew B. *Ancient Christian Worship: Early Church Practices in Social, Historical, and Theological Perspective*. Grand Rapids: Baker Academic, 2014.
Peterson, David. *Engaging with God: A Biblical Theology of Worship*. Reprint. Downers Grove, IL: InterVarsity Press, 2002.
Petterson, Anthony R. *Haggai, Zechariah and Malachi*. AOTC. Downers Grove, IL: IVP Academic, 2015.
Ross, Allen P. *Recalling the Hope of Glory: Biblical Worship from the Garden to the New Creation*. Grand Rapids: Kregel Academic, 2006.
Van Dyk, Leanne, ed. *A More Profound Alleluia: Theology and Worship in Harmony*. Grand Rapids: Eerdmans, 2005.
Webber, Robert E. *Worship Old & New*. Rev. ed. Grand Rapids: Zondervan, 1994.
______. *Ancient-Future Worship*. Grand Rapids: Baker Books, 2008.
Whaley, V. M. *Called to Worship*. Nashville: Thomas Nelson, 2009.
Witvliet, John D. *Worship Seeking Understanding: Windows into Christian Practice*. Grand Rapids: Baker Academic, 2003.
Wright, N. T. *For All God's Worth: True Worship and the Calling of the Church*. Grand Rapids: Eerdmans, 1997.

WORSHIP

in the

NEW TESTAMENT

CHAPTER 22

WORSHIP: A CONCEPT STUDY IN NEW TESTAMENT GREEK

Craig L. Blomberg and Ben R. Crenshaw

What does the New Testament teach about worship? The question sounds straightforward; however, depending on who is asking it, and in what context, it could mean several different things. It could imply that the questioner is curious about the types of gatherings and/or music used among first-century Christians. It could also be used to ask about the elements of worship. The Protestant Reformers' later definitions of "Word" and "sacraments" were elements of worship in the sixteenth century. The question may expand beyond these and find its genesis in a vision of worship as encompassing many different activities in life—in order to find scriptural support for such practices or actions. This question, while easy at face value, could have a multitude of hidden assumptions as it is asked.

The *Merriam-Webster Collegiate Dictionary* gives two primary definitions for "worship" as a transitive verb: "to honor or reverence as a divine being or supernatural power," and "to regard with great or extravagant respect, honor, or devotion." The corresponding noun, then, suggests "the act of showing respect and love for a god especially by praying with other people who believe in the same god," and "excessive admiration for someone." The New Testament, however, is written in Hellenistic Greek. Do its words that are most commonly translated as "worship" in English versions have the identical sense in this first-century language? Clearly our task is not as simple as merely looking up all the occurrences of "worship" in our preferred English translation and seeing what we learn about the concept in each context, though that could be part of our process. Concepts can appear without the specific words that flag them, just as not every use of a Greek word for "worship" may be relevant to our specific questions.

We will begin, therefore, by studying the two Greek word groups that account for the sizable majority of terms usually rendered as "worship" in English translations of the New Testament. But we will have to supplement that study by examining other texts that do not use any word that explicitly refers to worship while nevertheless disclosing something about that concept. We will focus in a bit more detail on two passages, both of them in Paul's letters, which should loom large in any conversation on biblical worship. Detailed exegesis in most instances, however, will have to be left to the contributors on the individual books and authors of the New Testament.

THE TWO KEY VERBS FOR "WORSHIP" IN THE GREEK OF THE NEW TESTAMENT

By far the most common verb for "worship" in the New Testament is *proskuneō*, which occurs a total of sixty times. Its corresponding noun, *proskunēsis*, however, does not appear at all. The noun for "worshiper," *proskunētēs*, occurs once, in John 4:23. A distant second in frequency is *latreuō*, which appears twenty times, with its corresponding noun *latreia* used in five verses. When this word group does not mean full-fledged worship, it often carries the sense of "serve" or "service," especially in the context of religious assemblies.[1] Third most common is the verb *sebomai*, with ten occurrences (cf. the cognate *sebazomai*, which appears once, in Rom. 1:26), often in the context of God-fearers (or worshipers)—Gentiles who had come to believe in the God of Israel—along with two uses of the noun *sebasma*, which is an object of worship.[2] Then we have *leitourgeō* (three times) and *leitourgia* (six times), which normally mean a person's service or ministry but can shade over into worship,[3] and *thrēskeia*, with four uses, three of which mean "religion."[4] Because of this disparity in frequency of usage, we will focus on the first two main verbs.

Proskuneō

In early classical Greek literature *proskuneō* meant to bow down, fall down and worship, or make obeisance to the gods.[5] It came from the fact that people often literally prostrated themselves, outwardly depicting their inward attitudes of subjection and humility. The word could also mean to kiss, as in the action of bowing or kneeling and kissing the hand or ring of a monarch or even the ground on which he or she stood.[6] Over time

1. Moisés Silva, "*latreuō, latreia*," in *NIDNTTE* 3:95.
2. BDAG, 917.
3. "The notion of worshipping or serving God *by means of serving one another* is thus implied" (D. G. Peterson, "Worship," in *New Dictionary of Biblical Theology*, eds. T. Desmond Alexander and Brian S. Rosner (Leicester: Inter-Varsity Press, 2000), 861 (italics original).
4. Though more narrowly than this English term often suggests. BDAG (459) defines *thrēskeia* as devotion to God or the gods, especially "as it expresses itself in cultic rites" or "worship."
5. Moisés Silva, "*proskuneō*," in *NIDNTTE* 4:150.
6. Hans Schönweiss and Colin Brown, "*proskuneō*," in *New International Dictionary of New Testament Theology*, ed. Colin Brown (Grand Rapids: Zondervan, 1976), 2:875.

the word came to refer to the adoration of the gods more generally or the loyalty and homage paid to a political ruler. When Rome established its imperial cult, the word naturally was applied to emperor worship. Here the inward concept of reverence and honor came particularly to the fore.[7]

In the Septuagint, the Greek translation of the Old Testament, about 75 percent of the time *proskuneō* denotes worship and veneration of the God of Israel, especially in explicitly religious settings. The rest of the time, deference to a human superior is in view.[8] The meaning of *proskuneō* in the New Testament continues in this same vein, except that now "it almost always denotes an action that is directed, or that should be directed to God or to Jesus Christ."[9] Its sixty appearances are by no means evenly distributed. Revelation contains twenty-four of them, and Matthew another thirteen. The gospel of John has eleven (though nine come in the four verses that constitute 4:20–23). That leaves two in Mark, three in Luke, four in Acts, two in Hebrews, and only one in all of Paul.

Three times in the New Testament, forms of *proskuneō* refer to public worship at the temple in Jerusalem (John 12:20; Acts 8:27; 27:11). In Jesus's ministry, the verb is commonly used to describe those who come to Jesus, falling on their knees or perhaps even their faces before him. Such a posture was above all an indication of acute need and a request for help. One thinks, for example, of the leper who begs for cleansing (Matt. 8:2), Jairus who is distraught over his daughter's death (9:18), and the mother of Zebedee's sons who implores that they be granted the most honored seats in Jesus's coming kingdom (20:20). While not explicitly mentioned, some kind of faith in Jesus's ability to grant the request is presupposed in each situation. In other instances, faith does emerge explicitly. John 9:38 affords a classic case: when the blind man healed by the pool of Siloam learns that Jesus is the Son of Man, he declares, "Lord, I believe,"[10] and worships him. In one summary of the significance of *proskuneō* in such passages, "obeisance is nothing less than the outward reflex action of faith: to believe means to adore Jesus, to recognize him as Lord, to render him homage as king."[11]

Of course, not every example of someone prostrating themselves before Jesus denotes worship in the sense of acknowledging his deity or universal lordship. English translations will often use other expressions in these instances to translate *proskuneō*, such as "fall down before," "kneel," "bow down," or "bow low" (and Mark and Luke may use other Greek words than *proskuneō* that mean these precise activities even when Matthew does use it—e.g., Mark 1:40 and Luke 5:12). Even when "worship"

---

7. L&N 1:217.
8. Heinrich Greeven, "*proskuneō*," in *TDNT* 6:761.
9. Silva, "*proskuneō*," 152.
10. All Scripture quotations in this chapter follow the NIV.
11. Schönweiss and Brown, "*proskuneō*," 877.

appears to be the best translation, we dare not read in post–New Testament Christology. For example, when the disciples see Jesus coming to them walking on the water and they worship him, declaring him to be the Son of God (Matt. 14:33), they could still not have articulated full-orbed Trinitarian thought or the doctrine of the two natures of Christ. Just two chapters later Jesus will praise Peter's acknowledgment of him as "the Messiah, the Son of the living God" as something new and divinely given (16:16–18), and even then he still does not have a clue about the need for Jesus to suffer and die (vv. 22–23). The disciples may well have gained an inkling of Jesus's divinity after he walked on water, but they were still ill-prepared to articulate it in any detail.[12]

All this changes quickly after Jesus's resurrection, when those who encounter him can no longer deny or explain away his spectacular power over death. There is often understandable doubt at first that it *is* Jesus they are seeing, but soon it gives way to worship (Matt. 28:9, 17; Luke 24:52–53).[13] It is significant that Jesus shows no hesitancy in accepting this worship; indeed, Hebrews 1:6 declares that even angels worship him. Conversely, when John twice in the book of Revelation appears as if he is going to worship an angelic messenger rather than Jesus himself, the angel rebukes him because John and he are merely fellow servants of Christ (Rev. 19:10; 22:8). Jesus is clearly understood as much more exalted than even the angels. This "binitarianism" that appears in places to have preceded full-blown Trinitarianism shows the astonishing impact Jesus had on staunchly monotheistic Jews, who were willing to transgress their conventional boundaries by worshiping as God someone they knew had been a man.[14]

The fact that *only* God and Jesus are ever depicted as legitimate objects of worship, however, makes identification of false gods and idolatrous worship easy. This theme is most prominent in Revelation, where in 9:20 "idols of gold, silver, bronze, stone and wood—idols that cannot see or hear or walk" are juxtaposed with "worshiping demons." Revelation 12–13 depicts the unholy "trinity" of a dragon, a beast from the sea, and a beast from the land. The dragon is explicitly identified as Satan (12:9), the ringleader of the trio. The first beast has authority delegated to it from the dragon and what looks like a fatal wound that has healed (13:2–3), an obvious attempt to mimic the death and resurrection of Jesus. The second beast "exercised all the authority of the first beast on its behalf, and made the earth and its inhabitants worship the first beast" (v. 12), just like the Spirit exercises Christ's authority to empower people to worship him.

12. See further Craig L. Blomberg, *Matthew*, NAC 22 (Nashville: Broadman, 1992), 236.
13. It is also possible to understand Matthew as claiming that some of the apostles believed, while some others hesitated (but only at first). See Blomberg, *Matthew*, 430.
14. On which see the numerous works of Larry W. Hurtado, the fullest of which is *Lord Jesus Christ: Devotion to Jesus in Earliest Christianity* (Grand Rapids: Eerdmans, 2003).

Many of the earth's inhabitants are led astray by the signs and wonders that accompany the appearance of these horrific animals, and so they worship them, saying, "Who is like the beast? Who can wage war against it?" (v. 4; cf. vv. 8, 12, 15).[15] Yet they will experience eternal punishment for their idolatry (14:9, 11; 16:2; 19:20), while those who held firm and refused to worship the image of the beast, even if it meant martyrdom, will be rewarded with new life and will reign with Christ (20:4).

Satan is indeed God's main adversary and, directly or indirectly, behind all forms of false worship. Little wonder, then, that Jesus himself had to withstand the devil during his wilderness temptations (Matt. 4:1–11 and par.) and that Satan's climactic seduction was to offer him all the world's kingdoms in return for his worship (vv. 8–9)! Jesus, however, staunchly refused, quoting Deuteronomy 6:13 on how worship was due the Lord God alone. Worship, in short, is fundamental to our relationship with God, for who or what we worship discloses our true affections and allegiance.[16]

The passage in the New Testament with the densest cluster of forms of *proskuneō* is John 4:20–24, part of Jesus's dialogue with the Samaritan woman at the well (vv. 4–42). This verb for worship occurs nine times in these five verses, as the woman brings up the long-standing debate between Jews and Samaritans over the location of true worship—Mount Zion or Mount Gerizim. Jesus's decisive reply is to refer to the new era he is inaugurating in which a specific location for worship will be irrelevant.[17] Rather, "God is spirit, and his worshipers must worship in the Spirit and in truth" (v. 24). The Greek (*pneumati kai alētheia*) can be translated "in spirit and in truth" and taken to refer to two separate qualities—from the heart rather than mere ritual, and genuine or sincere rather than sham or fake, both as a result of divine revelation.[18] But the expression seems more likely to be a hendiadys (a pair of related nouns joined by a conjunction that refer to a single concept, with one of the nouns functioning adjectivally to modify the other). In this case, the phrase would mean "the true Spirit." Given the rarity of *pneuma* in Greek meaning anything like an independent human spirit and given its consistent use in the New Testament for the Holy Spirit, this interpretation is preferable.[19] Jesus's point, then,

15. For good discussion of emperor worship as background to this imagery, see S. R. F. Price, *Rituals and Power: The Roman Imperial Cult in Asia Minor* (Cambridge: Cambridge University Press, 1984), 196–98. For similar Hellenistic practices, the classic study is Lily Ross Taylor, "The 'Proskunesis' and the Hellenistic Ruler Cult," *JHS* 47 (1927): 53–62.

16. See esp. throughout Allen P. Ross, *Recalling the Hope of Glory: Biblical Worship from the Garden to the New Creation* (Grand Rapids: Kregel Academic, 2006).

17. Indeed, the New Testament consistently "Christifies" sacred space. See esp. W. D. Davies, *The Gospel and the Land: Early Christianity and Jewish Territorial Doctrine* (Berkeley: University of California Press, 1974).

18. E.g., Gerald L. Borchert, *John 1–11*, NAC 25a (Nashville: Broadman & Holman, 1996), 208.

19. E.g., Raymond E. Brown, *The Gospel according to John I–XII*, AB 29 (New York: Doubleday, 1966), 180.

is that Spirit-guided worship is what God desires, not traveling to a specific location to be especially close to God. Neither a temple nor a church building is required, but the assembly of God's people who themselves form a temple of the Holy Spirit (1 Cor. 3:16), just as Jesus himself fulfilled the purpose of the original temple (John 2:19–21).[20]

Latreuō

The second most common New Testament verb for worship both resembles and differs from the first. In classical Greek, *latreuō* originally meant "to work for hire," but came to denote service in general, including involuntary servitude or slavery.[21] In the Septuagint, *latreuō* can be a synonym for *douleuō*, translating the Hebrew *'abad* (to serve, be a slave of). *Latreuō*, however, is employed more commonly for *'abad* where it has a religious sense—service to the tabernacle or temple and its rituals. It is also crucial to observe, nevertheless, that "it is characteristic of the OT that it is not the meticulously performed cultus which is the true worship of God, but obedience to the voice of the Lord, which grows out of gratitude for God's acts of salvation in history, although such obedience included the outward ritual of worship."[22]

In the New Testament, *latreuō* is used primarily in this sense of heartfelt service, whether of true worship toward God or of the sham worship of idols (Rom. 1:15, 25; Acts 7:42). The ritual and cultic connotations have largely fallen away.[23] Of course, Hebrews can refer back to the Old Testament sacrificial system and those who served and worshiped within it (Heb. 8:5; 9:9; 10:2; 13:10), but the epistle then goes beyond this concept by declaring that worship in the new age is through the eternal Spirit who cleanses our consciences (9:14; cf. 12:28–29) now that Jesus has made the once-for-all sacrifice for sins as our eternal high priest (7:23–28).[24] The remaining uses of *latreuō* and *latreia* in the New Testament fall into three broad categories: first, Jewish public worship (Luke 2:36–37; Acts 7:7, 42; Rom. 9:4; Heb. 9:1, 6 [including the ritual duties of the Old Testament priests]); second, service toward God whether good or bad (Luke 1:73–74; John 16:2; Rom. 1:9; 2 Tim. 1:3; Heb. 8:5; 9:14; 13:10; Rev. 7:15); and third, personal and corporate worship of God by Christian believers (Acts 24:4; 26:7; 27:23; Rom. 12:1; Phil. 3:3; Rev. 22:3). Of all these texts, probably the best known and perhaps the most important is Romans 12:1, which commands us to present our "bodies as a living sacrifice, holy and pleasing to God," which is our

20. On which, see esp. Nicholas Perrin, *Jesus the Temple* (London: SPCK, 2010).
21. Silva, "*latreuō, latreia*," 94.
22. Klaus Hess, "*latreuō, latreia*," in Brown, *New International Dictionary of New Testament Theology*, 3:550.
23. Silva, "*latreuō, latreia*," 95.
24. Cf. esp. David G. Peterson, *Engaging with God: A Biblical Theology of Worship* (Leicester: Inter-Varsity Press, 1992), 228–60.

"true and proper worship [*latreia*]." All in all, texts in which *latreuō* or *latreia* appear, just like with those using *proskuneō*, teach us more about the proper objects of worship and the holiness needed in the process than about the specific elements that constitute proper devotion.[25]

TWO KEY PASSAGES IN PAUL

To satisfy our understandable curiosity about what Christian worship services looked like in their earliest years, we have to turn elsewhere. We know that there was a somewhat liturgical form that emerged in certain places by at least the second century. This developing liturgy included a predictable sequence of prescribed prayers, hymns or psalms, an offering, Scripture readings according to a lectionary system, a homily on part or all of the Scripture read for the week, and a benediction. Here, worship followed the Jewish practices but with an expanded canon of sacred texts as the various New Testament documents were increasingly being treated as on a par with the Hebrew Scriptures.[26] The question still remains: What took place during the period of the New Testament in the first century? Acts 2:42 describes the earliest known collection of Christian practices from Pentecost onward when Luke observes that the three thousand new believers "devoted themselves to the apostles' teaching and to fellowship, to the breaking of bread and to prayer." While by no means identical to the more formal structure that would develop later, gatherings that included the four elements depicted here certainly contained practices that have almost always been central to the activity of the assemblies of Christ followers throughout church history. First, religious instruction is rooted in the apostolic tradition now deposited in Scripture; second, intimate interpersonal relationships (even to the extent that property and possessions were freely shared to help the needy fellow believers) were cultivated; third, a common meal was shared (perhaps including the Lord's Supper or Eucharist); and fourth, various forms of prayers were offered.[27]

The two main passages that take us in any significant way beyond this preliminary sketch are 1 Corinthians 14:26–40 and Ephesians 5:18–33. Each, interestingly, begins with verses that bear most directly on the nature of first-generation Christian worship, but then they continue with issues about gender roles in church and home that grow out of the worship experience. Our focus will be almost exclusively on the opening verses.

---

25. A good case can be made for many diverse forms of worship as all potentially legitimate. See, e.g., Paul A. Basden, ed., *Exploring the Worship Spectrum: 6 Views* (Grand Rapids: Zondervan, 2004).
26. For all these and related practices, see esp. Andrew B. MacGowan, *Ancient Christian Worship: Early Church Practices in Social, Historical, and Theological Perspective* (Grand Rapids: Baker Academic, 2014); and James T. Burtchaell, *From Synagogue to Church: Public Services and Offices in the Earliest Christian Communities* (Cambridge: Cambridge University Press, 1992).
27. Cf. David Peterson, "Worship in the New Testament," in *Worship: Adoration and Action*, ed. D. A. Carson (Carlisle: Paternoster, 1993), 75–77.

Every-Member Ministry (1 Corinthians 14:26–40)

The most important verse for our purposes in this passage is the very first (1 Cor. 14:26): "What then shall we say, brothers and sisters? When you come together, each of you has a hymn, or a word of instruction, a revelation, a tongue or an interpretation. Everything must be done so that the church may be built up." That Paul is speaking of a worship service is clear from the larger context. Chapter 14 is comparing and contrasting two contentious gifts of the Spirit in Corinth—prophecy and tongues. Paul's main point is to prefer prophecy to tongues because of its immediate intelligibility. The previous paragraph has just concluded by explaining the outsider or unbeliever who comes to a gathering of Christians and hears clear, convicting prophecy will fall down and will worship (*proskunēsei*) God and exclaim that he is truly among them (v. 25).[28]

What else happens at such a gathering? Here is where verse 26 provides at least a partial answer. Each person has the opportunity to use his or her spiritual gifts. The list of five items closely resembles the sample spiritual gifts Paul has enunciated in 12:8–10 and 28–30 (see also Rom. 12:6–8; Eph. 4:11–12). While hymns are not included in any of these other lists, they will reappear as part of worship in Ephesians 5:19 (see below). A word of instruction is literally a "teaching" (*didachē*), and teaching or teachers appear in 1 Corinthians 12:28, Romans 12:7, and Ephesians 4:11. A revelation (*apokalupsis*) closely resembles a message of wisdom or knowledge (1 Cor. 12:8); prophecy may likewise fall into the broader category of revelations.[29] And tongues and their interpretations clearly match the same items mentioned in 1 Corinthians 12:7 and 28–30.

The differences among the various lists of spiritual gifts suggest that none is intended to be comprehensive. The contexts of each passage demonstrate that gifts are natural or supernatural talents or abilities used by an individual for the building up of the church in all its dimensions.[30] The contents of 14:26 show that all Christians need an outlet within the congregation to utilize their uniquely God-given gifts for the benefit of the entire body (with 12:7 having already taught that every believer has at least one spiritual gift). This makes sense in a setting where the church is a collection of house congregations in a given community, and there are at least some free-flowing portions to the worship service during that anyone can contribute as they believe the Lord is leading them.[31] It becomes a much bigger challenge, and often remains unaddressed, in larger gatherings with entirely prearranged elements of worship. Smaller groups

28. Cf. Karl O. Sandnes, "Prophecy—A Sign for Believers (1 Cor. 14, 20–25)," *Bib* 77 (1996): 1–15.
29. For the probable breadth of the category of "revelation" here, see Anthony C. Thiselton, *The First Epistle to the Corinthians*, NIGTC (Grand Rapids: Eerdmans, 2000), 1136.
30. Cf. Ralph P. Martin, *The Spirit and the Congregation: Studies in 1 Corinthians 12–15* (Grand Rapids: Eerdmans, 1984), 37.
31. Cf. Gordon D. Fee, *The First Epistle to the Corinthians*, rev. ed., NICNT (Grand Rapids: Eerdmans, 2014), 765.

of many kinds then become crucial, along with mechanisms to ensure that as many church members as possible are involved in them.

First Corinthians 14:27–40 proceeds to stress that every use of what appears to be someone's spiritual gift must then be evaluated. Not every alleged prophecy actually comes from the Lord, nor is every part of even a genuine prophecy necessarily equally valid. Paul feels free to disregard portions of what was prophesied about him (specifically not to go to Jerusalem [Acts 21:4]) because he recognized that the human prophets had added their erroneous interpretation to the message they received from the Lord (if Paul goes there he will be imprisoned [v. 11]). So he goes to Jerusalem anyway (v. 13).[32] Teachers likewise make mistakes, pastors do not always counsel flawlessly, helpers may unwittingly hinder, givers may direct their money to irresponsible individuals and organizations, and so on. First Corinthians 14:27–40, therefore, provides guidelines for evaluating prophecy and for interpreting tongues (which can then be evaluated just like prophecy). In cases of debate, leadership may ultimately have to make a decision on behalf of a specific community (this *could* explain vv. 34–35), but all members are called on to weigh and assess what they have experienced (v. 29).[33] God never so controls a human being in bestowing spiritual gifts that they cannot voluntarily refrain from using those gifts if need be (vv. 32–33). At any rate, the passage ends with two clear commands: none of the gifts (not even tongues, which was proving the most divisive) is to be banned outright (v. 39), but all are to be exercised in a fitting and orderly way (v. 40).[34]

Filled with the Holy Spirit (Eph. 5:18–33)

Here is the passage in the New Testament that makes the fullest reference to singing in Christian gatherings, and even then it does not tell us a lot. Grammatically, the Greek of verses 18–23 all forms one sentence. It begins with two contrasting commands: believers should not get drunk but should be filled with (or by) the Spirit (v. 18).[35] This positive command is then modified by four subordinate participial clauses. First, they are to be "speaking to one another in psalms, hymns, and songs from the Spirit" (v. 19a); second, "sing[ing] and mak[ing] music from your heart to the Lord" (v. 19b); third, "always giving thanks to God the Father for everything, in the name of our Lord Jesus Christ" (v. 20); and fourth, "submit[ting] to one another out of reference for Christ. Verse 21 is a Janus statement,

32. On these various details in Acts 21, see esp. Wayne Grudem, *The Gift of Prophecy in the New Testament and Today*, rev. ed. (Wheaton, IL: Crossway, 2000), chap. 4.

33. Wayne Grudem, *The Gift of Prophecy in 1 Corinthians* (Lanham, MD: University Press of American, 1982), 60–62.

34. Cf. the superbly balanced conclusions in D. A. Carson, *Showing the Spirit: A Theological Exposition of 1 Corinthians 12–14* (Grand Rapids: Baker, 1987), 134–36.

35. "The Spirit is both the means and the substance of the filling" (Ben Witherington III, *We Have Seen His Glory: A Vision of Kingdom Worship* [Grand Rapids: Eerdmans, 2010], 65).

pointing both forward and backward. It supplies the last participle directly modifying the command to be filled with the Spirit, while also introducing the three subsequent pairs of relationships in which one category of individual submits to a second (5:22–6:9).[36] Verse 22, therefore, contains no independent verb in the original but carries on the thought of verse 21 by explaining, "wives to your own husbands as you do to the Lord," with "submitting yourselves" being inferred from the previous line. Verse 23, finally, supplies the rationale: "for the husband is the head of the wife as Christ is the head of the church." Verses 24–33a expand at length on the husband's responsibility, with the wife's additional responsibility (of respect for her husband) unpacked solely in verse 33b. By this time, of course, we have moved well beyond the topic of worship.

For our purposes, the most important observation to make from this text involves the relationship between the four participial clauses and the positive command to be filled with the Spirit. Three of them involve worship—reciting psalms, singing hymns and spiritual songs, and praying. The musical and poetic elements, interestingly, are to be directed both to one another and to God ("to one another . . . to God" [v. 19]). Along with appropriate mutual submission, praising and praying define what it means to be filled with the Spirit. Present-tense participles that follow a positive command given in the imperative mood regularly function in a modal, instrumental, or resultative fashion.[37] It is often not possible or necessary to choose among these three. Whether Paul had in mind the manner, the means, or the result of the Spirit's filling, the same conclusion follows: Spirit-filled people speak and sing, praise and pray, and submit to one another within the church of Jesus Christ.

Absent entirely from this passage is any necessarily "charismatic" activity, though nothing precludes such activity either. The metaphor of filling suggests simply that a person is at that time fully yielded to the power of the Spirit who lives inside of them. In the context of corporate worship, this includes a musical dimension. The debate in some circles over the use of instruments in church music cannot be settled on the basis of exegesis. The case for prohibiting musical instruments employs an odd hermeneutic that is not consistently followed elsewhere, arguing that what is not explicitly mentioned in the New Testament cannot be utilized.[38] The case for the use of musical instruments relies heavily on the continuities between

36. A rather pointless debate has pitted many complementarians (arguing that verse 21 introduces the three pairs of relationships of submission of certain categories of people to others) against many egalitarians (arguing that verse 21 enjoins mutual submission of all Christians to all other Christians in appropriate times and places). The verse functions in both ways. Each group is right in what they affirm and wrong in excluding the other interpretation.

37. See further David L. Mathewson and Elodie Ballantine Emig, *Intermediate Greek Grammar: Syntax for Students of the New Testament* (Grand Rapids: Baker Academic, 2016), 213–16.

38. See, e.g., Alan E. Highers, "Why Churches of Christ Do Not Use Instrumental Music in Worship," *Spiritual Sword* 35, no. 2 (2004): 2–24.

Old Testament and New Testament forms of worship, given the pervasiveness of instruments in ancient Jewish worship.[39]

Various attempts have been made to distinguish three categories of songs based on the three different nouns used in verse 19a—*psalmos* (psalm), *hymnos* (hymn), and *hōdē* (song). It is natural to envision the first as employing passages from the Old Testament Psalter, with the second and third distinguished on the basis of the formality or informality of the composition.[40] But these distinction run the serious risk of anachronistically imposing later meanings on words that were largely synonyms in their original context here. *Hōdais* (songs) is the one noun that has an adjective attached to it (*pneumatikais*; spiritual), leading most English translations to render the expression as "spiritual songs." If this is correct, then one might envision "psalms" and "hymns" as by definition already spiritual in their content, whereas "songs" could be a broad enough category that it has to be qualified explicitly if religious songs are in view. The NIV, however, heavily influenced here by the scholarship of Gordon Fee, opted again to see a distinctive reference to the Holy Spirit.[41] Then it is possible that the distinction between a hymn and a song from the Spirit is that the former had already been composed and become known, whereas the latter was spontaneously given to a particular singer on the spot. But it is very difficult to make any of these distinctions with great confidence; the words are simply used in too many different ways in ancient Greek for us to be dogmatic. It may be best to agree with Eduard Lohse that the three words together refer simply to "the full range of singing which the Spirit prompts."[42]

OTHER KEY PASSAGES WITHOUT AN EXPLICIT WORD FOR "WORSHIP"

Space precludes a survey of all the New Testament texts that most probably refer to worship even though their authors do not use an actual word for it. But some of the most important ones may be mentioned. In Matthew 6:1–18, Jesus berates those who give alms, pray, or fast merely for show or to gain the praise of their fellow worshipers. Returning to a similar topic in chapter 23, he rebukes a select group of Pharisees and

---

39. In fact, the early church up until the fourth or fifth century was very suspicious of instrumental music much of the time, though often for different reasons. See David W. Music, *Instruments in Church: A Collection of Source Documents* (Lanham, MD: Scarecrow, 1998).

40. E.g., Ben Witherington III, *The Letters to Philemon, the Colossians, and the Ephesians: A Socio-rhetorical Commentary on the Captivity Epistles* (Grand Rapids: Eerdmans, 2007), 312.

41. Gordon D. Fee, *God's Empowering Presence: The Holy Spirit in the Letters of Paul* (Peabody, MA: Hendrickson, 1994), 653.

42. Eduard Lohse, *Colossians and Philemon*, Hermeneia (Philadelphia: Fortress, 1971), 151. Lohse is commenting on the same triad of expressions in Colossians 3:16, a very abbreviated form of the Ephesians passage. On the Ephesians passage, see F. F. Bruce, *The Epistles to the Colossians, to Philemon, and to the Ephesians*, NICNT (Grand Rapids: Eerdmans, 1984), 158; and Klyne Snodgrass, *Ephesians*, NIVAC (Grand Rapids: Zondervan, 1996), 289.

scribes for their hypocrisy in an even broader collection of contexts. One that relates directly to worship involves their tithing of specific plants and spices beyond anything the law clearly requires while ignoring the major themes of the justice, mercy, and faithfulness of God that permeate the Torah (v. 23).[43]

In Acts 4:24–31, the gathered community of believers in Jerusalem illustrates exemplary corporate prayer after the apostles are released from the Sanhedrin's custody. They praise God, acknowledging his sovereignty over all their affairs, but then they pray not for safety but for boldness to continue proclaiming the gospel message despite the hostility against them. The result is that they are filled with the Spirit and empowered for bold witness, and they perform signs and wonders, including miraculous healings, as they had requested (cf. 5:12–16).[44]

Acts 4:32–37 immediately emphasizes the role of communal sharing that began immediately after Pentecost. This concern for impoverished fellow believers continues in a different form in 6:1–7 as the first "deacons" are chosen to help distribute food and/or money to the Hellenistic widows who had been overlooked. It takes a still different form in the special offering Paul and Barnabas deliver from Antioch to Jerusalem in 11:16–19. The diversity of mechanisms shows that none of them can be absolutized. What remains constant, however, is the early church's commitment to caring for the dispossessed in their own midst.[45] Offerings for the poor have been a part of healthy Christian worship ever since. First Corinthians 16:2–3 contains the oldest known reference to a Sunday worship service, and it is because of the collection of funds they took up that we know about it.[46]

Philippians 2:9–11 presents an intriguing allusion to Isaiah 45:23 in which every knee will bow and every tongue confess the Lord, now manifest in the person of Jesus Christ. At first glance, this sounds like universal salvation. But the larger context in Isaiah belies this impression, as verse 24 adds: "All who have raged against him will come to him and be put to shame." Whether or not unbelievers' acclamation of God or Christ should

---

43. This is not, however, justification for obligating Christians to tithe because it was given to the Jewish leaders while the age of the law was still in force. Nothing comparable to this ever appears after Jesus's death, resurrection, and the sending of the Spirit at Pentecost. For a full treatment, see David A. Croteau, *You Mean I Don't Have to Tithe? A Deconstruction of Tithing and a Reconstruction of Post-tithe Giving* (Eugene, OR: Wipf & Stock, 2010).

44. Of numerous, diverse approaches to the filling of the Spirit in Luke-Acts, probably the most exegetically compelling is Max Turner, *Power from on High: The Spirit in Israel's Restoration and Witness in Luke-Acts* (Sheffield: Sheffield Academic, 2000).

45. See throughout Christopher M. Hays, *Luke's Wealth Ethics: A Study in Their Coherence and Character* (Tübingen: Mohr Siebeck, 2010).

46. It is sometimes argued that these verses do not refer to a worship service because people could have laid aside funds weekly in their homes. But in that case, collections would still have had to be made when Paul came, the very thing he was trying to avoid. But cf. also Craig L. Blomberg, *1 Corinthians*, NIVAC (Grand Rapids: Zondervan, 1994), 324.

be called worship, both testaments do promise that it will happen when the day of the Lord comes. But for the unbeliever, the acclaim will be made under duress and compulsion, not joyfully and voluntarily. It will not be a confession of faith in or allegiance to Christ, merely the grudging acknowledgment of an undeniable reality.[47]

First Timothy 2:1–3:15 forms a major section in this pastoral epistle, in which Paul instructs Timothy "how people ought to conduct themselves in God's household, which is the church of the living God, the pillar and foundation of the truth" (3:15). Because all of the collateral activities we associate with church did not yet exist, everything in this section may be viewed as pertaining to the worship service.[48] First Timothy 2:1 specifies four necessary types of communication with God—"petitions, prayers, intercession and thanksgiving"—while verse 2 discloses both an outward and an inward focus, with prayers for those in positions of authority as well as for Christians to live peaceably and cooperatively. Verse 8 adds the command that the men pray in a holy fashion without quarreling. Presumably, that was a problem in Ephesus, just as the women may not always have been dressing with sufficient modesty (vv. 9–10).[49] These situation-specific details should caution us against drawing too many timeless principles from verses 11–15, where Paul prohibits the women from teaching or assuming authority[50] over the men, especially in view of the false teaching that was rampant in town and formed the immediate reason for this letter (1:3; cf. 4:1; 5:13).[51] Chapter 3, however, proceeds to the topic of criteria for choosing overseers and deacons, which include the foundational attributes of godliness that can be applied quite widely. In 4:13, Paul enunciates Timothy's priorities as the local pastor—the public reading of Scripture, preaching, and teaching with all diligence.

Hebrews 10:25 contains the reminder, as timely today as in the first century, that Christians should not forsake the assembling of themselves together, presumably for corporate worship and encouragement.[52] At least they may have become sporadic in attendance for fear of persecution (vv. 32–34; cf. 12:4); our excuses are far lamer. James 5:13–18 introduces the practice of anointing the very sick person with oil and praying for healing,

47. Ben Witherington III, *Paul's Letter to the Philippians: A Socio-rhetorical Commentary* (Grand Rapids: Eerdmans, 2011), 153–55.

48. George W. Knight III, *The Pastoral Epistles*, NIGTC (Grand Rapids: Eerdmans, 1992), 180–82.

49. See esp. Philip H. Towner, *The Letters to Timothy and Titus*, NICNT (Grand Rapids: Eerdmans, 2006), 201–10.

50. *Authentein* is a hotly disputed verb here, but the NIV's "assume authority" is a particularly felicitous translation because it allows for either of the word's two main uses—to exercise authority (positively) or to usurp authority or domineer (negatively). Once again debates have too often inaccurately denied the existence of one or the other of these meanings.

51. This false teaching almost certainly had something to do with Artemis worship, as Gary G. Hoag, *Wealth in Ancient Ephesus and the First Letter to Timothy: Fresh Insights from* Ephesiaca *by Xenophon of Ephesus* (Winona Lake, IN: Eisenbrauns, 2015) has recently demonstrated in detail.

52. Paul Ellingworth, *The Epistle to the Hebrews*, NIGTC (Grand Rapids: Eerdmans, 1993), 527–30.

a practice that both sides in the cessationist-continuationist debate over charismatic gifts can and should (though sadly often do not) practice.[53] First Peter 2:5 and 9–10 remind us how many of the metaphorical descriptions of the ancient Israelite assembly carry over to the Christian church. We, too, are "like living stones . . . being built into a spiritual house to be a holy priesthood, offering spiritual sacrifices acceptable to God" (v. 5) and "a chosen people, a royal priesthood, a holy nation, God's special possession, that you may declare the praises of him who called you out of darkness into his wonderful light" (v. 9).[54]

The book of Revelation, finally, is permeated with passages of worship and praise to God and the Lamb. Chapters 4–5 present the most extensive picture of heavenly worship, with repeated, explicit reasons for why God and Christ alone merit such adoration and acclamation. Throughout the apocalypse appear poetic passages of praise that were recited and perhaps even sung, articulating the glory of God's plan of salvation and judgment for the ages (7:10, 12; 11:15, 17–18; 12:10–12; 15:3–4; 16:5–7; 19:1–8). Even though everyone who ever lived is not present in the new heavens and the new earth (chaps. 21–22), at least there will be people from "every tribe and language and people and nation" (5:9; 7:9; 11:9; 13:7; 14:6).[55] Reflecting on Revelation's "hymns" helps us recall the additional fact that creedal or confessional material scattered about the epistles has likewise suggested to many the presence of early Christian hymnody, with the clearest examples being Philippians 2:5–11; Colossians 1:15–20; 1 Timothy 3:16; and 1 Peter 1:18–21; 2:21–25; 3:18–22.[56]

THE WORD AND SACRAMENTS

To the extent that preaching, baptism, and the Lord's Supper are included in one's understanding of worship, still more needs to be included in this introductory essay. Entire books have been written about each with huge theological discussions attached to them throughout church history. Here, all we can do is highlight some of our primary convictions extremely briefly. The most common form of preaching in the New Testament is the demonstration that the gospel is the fulfillment of all the deepest and truest religious hopes and aspirations of all people and most immediately of the Hebrew Scriptures.[57] This should surely continue to merit a prominent role in Christian proclamation.

53. See further Craig L. Blomberg and Mariam J. Kamell, *James*, ZECNT (Grand Rapids: Zondervan, 2008), 250–52.

54. Paul D. Achtemeier, *1 Peter*, Hermeneia (Minneapolis: Fortress, 1996), 69.

55. Cf. further Christopher J. H. Wright, *Salvation Belongs to Our God: Celebrating the Bible's Central Story*, Christian Doctrine in Global Perspective (Downers Grove, IL: IVP Academic, 2007).

56. Cf. Robert J. Karris, *A Symphony of New Testament Hymns* (Collegeville, MN: Liturgical Press, 1996).

57. See throughout Craig L. Blomberg, *A New Testament Theology* (Waco, TX: Baylor University Press, 2018).

Despite some hints to the contrary, the clearest and most consistent testimony of the New Testament is to believers' baptism, most likely by immersion. Despite some texts that superficially might seem to teach baptismal regeneration, it is better to see baptism as a metonymy (one element representing a closely related larger whole) for salvation rather than its prerequisite. If it was not absolutely *normative* for a person to be baptized to be saved in the New Testament, it was at least *normal*.[58] Debates over the meaning of "is" in Jesus's words at his Last Supper in the expressions "this is my body" and "this is my blood" accomplish little not least because in Aramaic the copula (the form of "to be") was probably left understood and not even uttered. No one seeing Jesus hold up a loaf and a cup and make these statements would have envisioned him claiming they were somehow actual extensions of his physical body; everyone would have recognized he was making a deeply symbolic statement.[59] The irony in 1 Corinthians 11:17–34 is that centuries of theological overlay here have wrestled with what it means to partake of the elements of the Lord's Supper in unworthy fashion (v. 27), while largely ignoring the answer provided in the passage itself—discriminating against the poor and needy within the very church gathering in which the rich were overeating and overdrinking (vv. 21–22)! These, and only these, are the believers who should refrain from participating in the eucharistic ceremony.[60]

CONCLUSION

The New Testament does not even come close to mandating a one-size-fits-all model for Christian worship. The key is the acclamation of God in Christ as the only Master of the Universe worthy of all praise, trust, and service. Even if we do not literally fall on our faces in church or kneel when we pray, our hearts and attitudes should recognize Jesus as so far superior to us in love and justice that the only proper response is unswerving allegiance to him. He has graciously gifted us beyond anything we could ever deserve; out of stupendous gratitude we serve him and his church with those gifts for the sake of others. Corporate worship should include prayer and praise, often accompanied by music and singing. Financial offerings are appropriate, even as are other mechanisms for sharing with the poor—a key part of what "fellowship" connotes. Biblically based preaching and teaching, the sacraments (or ordinances) of baptism and the Lord's Supper, and prayers of many different kinds should all recur regularly. After this, there is freedom for countless variations as people in

58. See the magisterial treatment by Everett Ferguson, *Baptism in the Early Church: History, Theology, and Liturgy in the First Five Centuries* (Grand Rapids: Eerdmans, 2009).

59. See further Roy E. Ciampa and Brian S. Rosner, *The First Letter to the Corinthians*, PiNTC (Grand Rapids: Eerdmans, 2010), 550.

60. "Those who disregard their responsibility to welcome and care for fellow believers in the local congregation cannot worship or serve God acceptably!" (Peterson, "Worship in the New Testament," 82).

many different cultures seek to implement and to contextualize these elements of worship in ways that will prove most meaningful to their cultures while preserving the purposes for which they were created.[61]

BIBLIOGRAPHY

Achtemeier, Paul D. *1 Peter.* Hermeneia. Minneapolis: Fortress, 1996.

Alexander, T. Desmond, and Brian S. Rosner, eds. *New Dictionary of Biblical Theology.* Leicester: Inter-Varsity Press, 2000.

Basden, Paul A., ed. *Exploring the Worship Spectrum: 6 Views.* Grand Rapids: Zondervan, 2004.

Blomberg, Craig L. *1 Corinthians.* NIVAC. Grand Rapids: Zondervan, 1994.

______. *Matthew.* NAC 22. Nashville: Broadman, 1992.

______. *A New Testament Theology.* Waco, TX: Baylor University Press, 2018.

Blomberg, Craig L., and Mariam J. Kamell. *James.* ZECNT. Grand Rapids: Zondervan, 2008.

Borchert, Gerald L. *John 1–11.* NAC 25a. Nashville: Broadman & Holman, 1996.

Brown, Raymond E. *The Gospel according to John I–XII.* AB 29. New York: Doubleday, 1966.

Bruce, F. F. *The Epistles to the Colossians, to Philemon, and to the Ephesians.* NICNT. Grand Rapids: Eerdmans, 1984.

Burtchaell, James T. *From Synagogue to Church: Public Services and Offices in the Earliest Christian Communities.* Cambridge: Cambridge University Press, 1992.

Carson, D. A. *Showing the Spirit: A Theological Exposition of 1 Corinthians 12–14.* Grand Rapids: Baker, 1987.

______, ed. *Worship: Adoration and Action.* Carlisle, PA: Paternoster, 1993.

Ciampa, Roy E., and Brian S. Rosner. *The First Letter to the Corinthians.* PiNTC. Grand Rapids: Eerdmans, 2010.

Croteau, David A. *You Mean I Don't Have to Tithe? A Deconstruction of Tithing and a Reconstruction of Post-tithe Giving.* Eugene, OR: Wipf & Stock, 2010.

Davies, W. D. *The Gospel and the Land: Early Christianity and Jewish Territorial Doctrine.* Berkeley: University of California Press, 1974.

Ellingworth, Paul. *The Epistle to the Hebrews.* NIGTC. Grand Rapids: Eerdmans, 1993.

61. It is that much more tragic that the Christian church has often been consumed by "worship wars," with everyone wanting their preferred styles of music, liturgy, or forms of worship. Our focus should be on God and on serving one another rather than having our own desires satisfied. In preparation for heavenly worship, we should want to learn as many different forms as Christians throughout the world and over time have found both true and meaningful.

Fee, Gordon D. *The First Epistle to the Corinthians*. Rev. ed. NICNT. Grand Rapids: Eerdmans, 2014.

______. *God's Empowering Presence: The Holy Spirit in the Letters of Paul*. Peabody, MA: Hendrickson, 1994.

Ferguson, Everett. *Baptism in the Early Church: History, Theology, and Liturgy in the First Five Centuries*. Grand Rapids: Eerdmans, 2009.

Grudem, Wayne. *The Gift of Prophecy in 1 Corinthians*. Lanham, MD: University Press of America, 1982.

______. *The Gift of Prophecy in the New Testament and Today*. Rev. ed. Wheaton, IL: Crossway, 2000.

Hays, Christopher M. *Luke's Wealth Ethics: A Study in Their Coherence and Character*. Tübingen: Mohr Siebeck, 2010.

Highers, Alan H. "Why Churches of Christ Do Not Use Instrumental Music in Worship." *Spiritual Sword* 35, no. 2 (2004): 2–24.

Hoag, Gary G. *Wealth in Ancient Ephesus and the First Letter to Timothy: Fresh Insights from* Ephesiaca *by Xenophon of Ephesus*. BBRSup. Winona Lake, IN: Eisenbrauns, 2015.

Hurtado, Larry W. *Lord Jesus Christ: Devotion to Jesus in Earliest Christianity*. Grand Rapids: Eerdmans, 2003.

Karris, Robert J. *A Symphony of New Testament Hymns*. Collegeville, MN: Liturgical Press, 1996.

Knight, George E., III. *The Pastoral Epistles*. NIGTC. Grand Rapids: Eerdmans, 1992.

Lohse, Eduard. *Colossians and Philemon*. Hermeneia. Philadelphia: Fortress, 1971.

MacGowan, Andrew B. *Ancient Christian Worship: Early Church Practices in Social, Historical, and Theological Perspective*. Grand Rapids: Baker Academic, 2014.

Martin, Ralph P. *The Spirit and the Congregation: Studies in 1 Corinthians 12–15*. Grand Rapids: Eerdmans, 1984.

Music, David W. *Instruments in Church: A Collection of Source Documents*. Lanham, MD: Scarecrow, 1998.

Perrin, Nicholas. *Jesus the Temple*. London: SPCK, 2010.

Peterson, David. *Engaging with God: A Biblical Theology of Worship*. Leicester: Inter-Varsity Press, 1992.

Price, S. R. F. *Rituals and Power: The Roman Imperial Cult in Asia Minor*. Cambridge: Cambridge University Press, 1984.

Ross, Allen P. *Recalling the Hope of Glory: Biblical Worship from the Garden to the New Creation*. Grand Rapids: Kregel Academic, 2006.

Sandnes, Karl O. "Prophecy—A Sign for Believers (1 Cor 14, 20–25)." *Bib* 77 (1996): 1–15.

Snodgrass, Klyne. NIVAC. *Ephesians*. Grand Rapids: Zondervan, 1996.

Taylor, Lily Ross. "The 'Proskunesis' and the Hellenistic Ruler Cult." *JHS* 47 (1927): 53–62.

Thiselton, Anthony C. *The First Epistle to the Corinthians.* NIGTC. Grand Rapids: Eerdmans, 2000.

Turner, Max. *Power from on High: The Spirit in Israel's Restoration and Witness in Luke-Acts.* Sheffield: Sheffield Academic, 2000.

Witherington, Ben, III. *The Letters to Philemon, the Colossians, and the Ephesians: A Socio-rhetorical Commentary on the Captivity Epistles.* Grand Rapids: Eerdmans, 2007.

______. *Paul's Letter to the Philippians: A Socio-rhetorical Commentary.* Grand Rapids: Eerdmans, 2011

______. *We Have Seen His Glory: A Vision of Kingdom Worship.* Grand Rapids: Eerdmans, 2010.

Wright, Christopher J. H. *Salvation Belongs to Our God: Celebrating the Bible's Central Story.* Downers Grove, IL: IVP Academic, 2007.

CHAPTER 23

A PROPER WORSHIP OF YAHWEH

Worshiping Jesus in the Synoptics

Monte Shanks

CONTEXT OF WORSHIP IN THE SYNOPTICS

The Synoptic Gospels contain important historical, literary, and cultural data. Additionally, being products of one of Jesus's disciples (i.e., Matthew), or from their close associates (i.e., Mark and Luke), manifests that they are contemporaneous accounts of the life and teachings of Jesus.[1] These facts being corroborated by the most trustworthy ancient historical sources mean that their greatest value is their collective record of the life of Jesus of Nazareth. These authors were unapologetic about their emphasis on Jesus, and their works about him are both multifaceted and complementary. Consequently, since Jesus is the singular focus of their combined efforts, if one fails to respect their cumulative message, then they will defraud these works of their fundamental purposes. Nevertheless, while this central focus of their collective efforts is acknowledged, they also provide Jesus's instructions on specific subjects; and most importantly for this chapter, they document his teachings about worship.

Entire books could be written about worship as it is portrayed in each Synoptic Gospel; consequently, a comprehensive analysis on the subject drawn from all of them is not possible since when combined they total the first sixty-eight chapters of the New Testament. Therefore, this chapter

1. On the importance of eyewitness testimony in the Gospels, see Richard Bauckham, *Jesus and the Eyewitnesses: The Gospels as Eyewitness Testimony* (Grand Rapids: Eerdmans, 2006). On Matthew's authorship of his Gospel, see Leon Morris, *The Gospel according to Matthew*, PiNTC (Grand Rapids: Eerdmans, 1992), 12–15. On the church's earliest traditions concerning the authorship of Matthew's Gospel, see Monte A. Shanks, *Papias and the New Testament* (Eugene OR: Pickwick, 2013), 193–99, 271–72.

will primarily focus on what Jesus himself taught about worship, how his disciples responded to his instructions, as well as how they related to him after his resurrection.

Worship means different things to many people; consequently, a baseline definition is hereby proposed. Authentic worship is *an appropriate response to a revelation of God that produces lasting changes in attitudes, beliefs, and behaviors in the one who has been enlightened.*[2] A more comprehensive definition will be provided in this chapter's conclusion after examining what the Synoptics impart on this subject. Regrettably, in Jesus's day, as is the case today, there was a lot of confusion about worship. This book has probably made it clear by now that the word "worship" is the umbrella term under which many different activities may fall. Worship can entail actions such as prayer and singing, but it is certainly more than just these activities.[3] This complexity is why the phrase "appropriate response" is used in the above definition. As the Synoptics reveal, when God engages an individual, it may cause any number of responses within and/or from that person. Responses such as repentance, confession, prayer, praise, meditation, singing, fasting, obedience, or proclamation can all fall under the controlling term of *worship*. This dynamic is why some find the concept of worship so difficult to define, the problem being that worship can be revealed in a diversity of expressions, both private and public. Fundamentally, therefore, worship is the volitional humbling of one's self in reverent submission to the glorious sovereignty of God. Consequently, worship initially becomes possible whenever God reveals himself through a variety of mediums, such as creation, his word, one's subjective conscience, or objective truths (e.g., moral truth, mathematical truth, philosophical truth). It is the individual's response to God, however, that reveals whether authentic worship has occurred.[4] God's revelation of himself always demands a response, and responses consistent with his will are in and of themselves acts of worship. The Synoptics provide many accounts describing worshipful activities; nevertheless, they ironically document only a few occurrences in which Jesus actually taught about the subject.

THEOLOGY OF WORSHIP

The following should aid in building a foundation for a theology of biblical worship because it exposits prominent passages involving Jesus as found in the Synoptics. This method is used to correct some common misconceptions concerning worship, many of which arise because some

---

2. The terms "authentic" and "genuine" will be used as synonyms for the concept of "biblical" worship.
3. For descriptions of various worshipful activities as found in Matthew, see Mark Allan Powell, "A Typology of Worship in the Gospel of Matthew," *JSNT* 57 (1995): 3–17.
4. Powell defines worship in Matthew's Gospel as originating from one's "attitude," which is revealed in three types of responses (Powell, "Typology of Worship," 16–17).

think that by performing a simple word search of the term "worship" while using English Bibles will provide them with a sufficient understanding on the topic. The result being that some have "christianized" the magi in Matthew 2:11 as "worshiping" the baby Jesus. The reality is that these pagan astrologists were simply showing appropriate political "honor" to a newborn king of the Jews.[5] Similarly, others have suggested that the Canaanite woman (see Matt. 15:21–28) had converted to Christianity as evidenced by her imploring Jesus to heal her daughter. Suggesting that these polytheistic Gentiles were demonstrating genuine worship is a poorly defended interpretation because it is anachronistic, as well as demonstrating a lack of knowledge about the range of nuances that the word *proskuneō* had during the composition of the Synoptics.[6] Consequently, the following approach should produce a more precise explanation of what constitutes biblical worship because it focuses on passages that document what Jesus taught about it, how his disciples understood those instructions, as well as how they responded to him during his resurrection appearances. The import of these passages is that they demonstrate that biblical worship demands fidelity to God alone; that the Scriptures are the basis and constraining influence that directs how biblical worship is to be conducted; and finally, that Jesus Christ is deserving of genuine unreserved worship that recognizes him as Lord over all to the glory of God the Father.

Fidelity in Worship

Most are familiar with the accounts of Jesus's temptations in the wilderness.[7] Mark's record of the event is sparse. Luke's account contains some minor differences from that of Matthew, but his rearrangement produces no substantial alterations.[8] Matthew's Gospel provides the most exhaustive and

---

5. R. T. France, *The Gospel of Matthew*, NICNT (Grand Rapids: Eerdmans, 2007), 75–76. For documentation of magi functioning as political emissaries, see Craig L. Blomberg, *Matthew*, NAC 22 (Nashville: Broadman, 1992), 66.
6. For further explanation, see Matthew L. Bowen, "'They Came and Held Him by the Feet and Worshipped Him': Proskynesis before Jesus in Its Biblical and Ancient Near Eastern Context," *Studies in the Bible and Antiquity* 5 (2013): 63–73. There is considerable debate over Matthew's use of *proskuneō* as compared with the other Synoptics. Some see a greater theological emphasis in Matthew. For examples see, Hak Chol Kim, "The Worship of Jesus in the Gospel of Matthew," *Bib* 93, no. 2 (2012): 227–41; Brian Renshaw, "The Worship of Jesus and the People of God in the Gospel of Matthew" (paper presented at the Southeast Regional Meeting of the Evangelical Theological Society, Louisville, KY, March 17, 2017); Powell, "A Typology," 3–17; and Heinrich Greeven, "*proskuneō*," in *TDNT* 6:763–64.
7. For a defense of this event's historicity, see Darrell L. Bock, *Luke 1:1–9:50*, BECNT (Grand Rapids: Baker, 1994), 364.
8. Concerning the differences between the accounts of Matthew and Luke, Morris asserted that one or both have "made significant alterations." Since Morris cannot provide any potential "original" source, then his conjecture is not well supported (Morris, *Matthew*, 69–70). Bock accurately described their minor differences as "theological irrelevant" (Bock, *Luke 1:1–9:50*, 365). Consequently, they can be attributed to Luke's redaction of his Matthean source while supplementing it with data gathered from his interviews of Jesus's disciples. Since Luke is often credited with

accurate description of the event.[9] All three Gospels indicate that Jesus endured this satanic attack alone; however, no one should assume that whenever Jesus trained his disciples about the realities of spiritual warfare he never detailed this encounter to them. Consequently, Matthew, being a personal disciple of Jesus, would have been privy to such conversations.[10] Mark indicates that Satan seduced Jesus throughout his time in the wilderness (Mark 1:13), while Matthew and Luke described Satan's climactic assault on him. This encounter involved three specific temptations, but it is the third and final temptation that is important for this discussion. Matthew described the event in the following manner: "Again, the devil took Him to a very high mountain and showed Him all the kingdoms of the world and their glory; and he said to Him, 'All these things I will give You, if You fall down and worship me.' Then Jesus said to him, 'Go, Satan! For it is written, "You shall worship the Lord your God, and serve Him only"'" (Matt. 4:8–10).[11] Some find this temptation by Satan rather toothless, the rationale being that since he did not create the "cosmos" then it was never his to give.[12] That Satan is not the creator is unquestionable; nevertheless, the issue is whether he possessed the right to give the kingdoms of this world to Jesus.[13] Concerning this issue, Jesus himself referred to Satan as the "ruler of this world" (John 12:31; 14:30; 16:11). Additionally, the apostle Paul called Satan "the *god* of this age" (2 Cor. 4:4, translation mine). Consequently, the biblical evidence suggests that Satan controlled the world to some degree.[14] The question, however, is merely academic because it does not change the fact that Satan claimed

---

redacting Mark, and other uncorroborated sources (e.g., Q and L), then there is no logical reason to assert that he would not treat Matthean material any differently. Consequently, Q will not be considered as a viable solution for differences found in the Synoptics. On why Luke's account differs and/or his possible use of other sources, see Bock, *Luke 1:1–9:50*, 364–66 and 7–14.

9. Donald A. Hagner, *Matthew 1–13*, WBC 33a (Dallas: Word, 1993), 62. D. A. Carson, *Matthew*, in *Expositor's Bible Commentary*, vol. 8, *Matthew, Mark, Luke*, eds. Frank E. Gaebelein and J. D. Douglas (Grand Rapids: Zondervan, 1984), 111. France, *Matthew*, 126.

10. Contra Hagner, who asserts that Matthew depended on Q (Hagner, *Matthew 1–13*, 62). Ironically, Hagner also suggests that Jesus communicated this encounter with disciples (63).

11. Unless otherwise indicated, all passages are from the NASB.

12. Bock described Satan's offer as an "oversell" and an "empty claim" (Bock, *Luke 1:1–9:50*, 363–85). Bock may be correct. It would not be the first time that "the father of lies" (John 8:44) relied on deception while offering something he had no capacity to deliver.

13. Luke's account includes Satan's claim that the kingdoms of the world had "been handed over to me, and I give it to whomever I wish" (Luke 4:6). It is ironic that someone had to "give" the world's kingdoms to Satan. This admission by Satan reveals that he knew of one who was greater than he (Robert H. Stein, *Luke*, NAC 24 [Nashville: Broadman, 1992] 147). While this temptation was real, the "theater" in which it took place was not. In modern vernacular one might say that Satan provided a PowerPoint presentation of the world's kingdoms through an "apocalyptic" vision; see David L. Turner, *Matthew*, BECNT (Grand Rapids: Baker Academic, 2008), 129; Bock, *Luke 1:1–9:50*, 374–75. It is not clear if Satan revealed only the kingdoms currently existing at that time or all of the empires throughout human history. By adding the emphasis of "all," and because "kingdoms" is plural, then Satan was not offering just the Roman Empire; therefore, it seems that the later is what was offered.

14. France, *Matthew*, 135.

authority over the world's kingdoms and therefore tempted Jesus with them. Whether they were his to give was irrelevant. The bottom line is that he tempted Jesus with them if Jesus would simply worship him.

The real temptation offered by Satan, however, was not in what he proffered to Jesus as much as what it theoretically allowed Jesus to avoid. D. A. Carson may have stated it best, explaining that Satan's suggestion provided a path enabling Jesus to "sidestep" the cross.[15] Jesus knew that the kingdoms of earth would be his after he faithfully completed a life of sacrificial obedience that would end in a tortuous and shameful death, thus fulfilling his Father's will. Satan's temptation, therefore, was an offer of global conquest via a shortcut, one that avoided the cross. Jesus's submission, however, would mean disobeying two of the Ten Commandments: "You shall have no other gods before Me," and "You shall not worship them or serve them" (Deut. 5:7, 9). Consequently, Satan's temptation was twofold, the first being to worship one who was not God, and the second being the cessation of obedience and service to the one true heavenly Father.

It was Satan's enticement to worship him that particularly offended Jesus, bringing their interaction to an abrupt end. Until that moment, Jesus willingly dialogued with his adversary by providing enlightenment on the correct interpretation and application of the Scriptures. Nevertheless, this offer instantly disgusted Jesus; consequently, he immediately commanded Satan to leave.[16] Jesus underscored the sacrilege of Satan's offer by quoting Deuteronomy 6:13. Although the verbs for worshiping and serving in Deuteronomy 6:13 are future indicatives; nonetheless, they should be understood as imperatival commands and not merely suggestions.[17]

Most recognize that Jesus's quotation of Deuteronomy 6:13 found in Matthew and Luke is different from the Septuagint, but they offer little explanation of its origin(s). The simplest explanation is not that Matthew has redacted some unknown written source, nor has he relied on an unknown variant of the Septuagint; instead he has quoted Jesus with respect to what Jesus said to Satan,[18] thus explaining the exchange of *proskunēseis* (i.e., "you shall worship") for *phobethese* (i.e., "you shall fear"), which is the original word found in Deuteronomy 6:13 in the Septuagint.[19] Satan

15. Carson, *Matthew*, 114. See also Blomberg, *Matthew*, 85.

16. Jesus's demand for Satan to retreat is in the present imperative. It is a direct command to leave at once. Concerning aspects of imperative verbs, see Daniel B. Wallace, *Greek Grammar beyond the Basics* (Grand Rapids: Zondervan, 1996), 714–17. Wallace notes this specific passage on 717n15.

17. On the imperatival force of future indicatives, especially with respect to OT quotations found in Matthew's Gospel, see Wallace, *Greek Grammar*, 569–70.

18. There is a textual variant of the quote of Deuteronomy 6:13 concerning where *proskuneseis* appears Luke's gospel. The manuscript evidence, however, supports the conclusion that Matthew and Luke's quotation of Jesus are the same in word order and vocabulary. The most significant alteration of Deuteronomy 6:13 from the MT to the LXX is the inclusion of the Greek word *mono*, which is translated as "only" or "alone." This is most likely an emphasis of Jesus as well as the LXX.

19. Contra Hagner, who conjectures Q to be the source; see Hagner, *Matthew 1–13*, 69. The change from "fear" to "worship" is preserved by both Luke and Matthew.

wanted "worship" from Jesus, and Jesus reminded him that only God rightfully deserves to be worshiped. Such a change in vocabulary is not inappropriate, since Jesus's emphasis does not damage the commandment. If anything, he has correctly interpreted its actual intent given the discussion at hand. He certainly has not changed the commandment's meaning. Moreover, if anyone had the capacity and authority to elaborate further on the commandment as originally given by God, then it would certainly be the Spirit-filled God-man, the Lord Jesus Christ.[20]

This interchange demonstrates several important aspects concerning Jesus's convictions about worship. The first is that Scripture should guide the people of God with respect to the proper practice of worship. While worship is a service that the worshiper offers to God, nonetheless the worshiper is constrained by God's written Word with respect to what constitutes its acceptable performance. Second, the singular focus of worship should be God. Genuine worship does not draw attention to the worshiper; instead, its sole focus is on God. Third, Scripture restricts all worship to be given to God alone as he has revealed himself in his Word. No others may receive worship since God has reserved all worshipful acts to be exclusively directed toward him; consequently, he is their only proper and legitimate object. He is the Creator and Sustainer of all things; consequently, he rightly demands that all worship be exclusively directed to him. Humanity, therefore, must only worship God as he has revealed himself in the Bible. People may love and respect others, they may even honor and esteem leaders, but they may only worship the one true God. And last, it is worship that infuses and energizes service to God. The term "serve" (i.e., *latreuō*) in the passage refers to the performance of deeds required by God, which as previously explained is an activity that may fall under the controlling term of "worship." Consequently, Jesus stated that God views service as a form of worship; therefore, it must be performed in a manner and attitude that is consistent with God's revelation to the worshiper. Worshiping God is primary, and service to him is its natural and expected result; therefore, the two concepts are intimately linked. Jesus affirmed that authentic worship always leads to appropriate service to God. Worship without service makes one's worship a meaningless and empty endeavor, while service without worship is rote duty that is void of spiritual life and enablement.

There is another important observation concerning this event that is often overlooked, which is that worship was a controversial issue for Jesus. The modern church vigorously avoids this reality; instead it promotes worship as a calming and peaceful experience, one that is always absent of controversy. Nevertheless, the text demonstrates that Jesus was extremely

---

20. The language that Jesus and Satan spoke is unknown. Nevertheless, Matthew has accurately recorded the correct emphases of the dialogue as he received it from Jesus. This is commonly referred to as the *ipsissma vox* of Jesus.

passionate about worship; moreover, he was hostile to the notion that worship may have a diversity of objects. And most importantly, Jesus's convictions and passion for worship was energized by his correct interpretation and application of God's Word. Consequently, Jesus's intolerance of Satan and his temptation was itself and act of worship. The Synoptics record that while there was disagreement during the first two temptations, there was still dialogue. However, with this specific enticement came division and rejection, which was instigated by Jesus and not Satan. It was Satan who suggested that it was acceptable for him, and by extension all other nondeities, to receive worship. Jesus flatly rejected this vile assertion. He was completely intolerant to the notion that it is acceptable for a diversity of beings to receive worship.[21] Jesus's intolerance on this issue is consistent with the biblical record concerning him, for throughout his ministry he passionately demanded that humanity always give "to God the things that are God's" (Mark 12:17). And as will become obvious, the Synoptics confirm that this was a fundamental passion of Jesus.

The Foundation for Worship

The next event involves a conflict between Jesus and a delegation of Pharisees. This conflict occurred in a region known as "the land of Gennesaret" (Matt. 14:34–15:9). It arose when some high-ranking Pharisees from Jerusalem arrived to confront Jesus. That they came from Jerusalem is not an irrelevant detail, and their encounter with him was not coincidental.[22] These influential Pharisees were offended that Jesus did not model for his disciples his obedience to the oral traditions "of the elders" (v. 2).[23] Conversely, Jesus was offended by their subversion of God's written word with their human-made legal idiosyncrasies (v 3). Before they could even register their offense, he provided for them a prime example of their habitual disregard of the Scriptures (v. 4). To set the table for his assertion, Jesus first quoted two commandments concerning the responsibilities of children to their parents (Exod. 20:12 and 21:17). He then focused on a pharisaic legal scheme that allowed the withholding of resources that should have been devoted to the care of aging parents. This pharisaic loophole, known as "Corban" (cf. Mark

21. The worldview that promotes multiple objects of worship is referred to as polytheism. Polytheism promotes either multiple peer deities or a multitiered creation, both spiritual and material, over which different gods exercise authority. This second option was the prevailing worldview in the first-century Roman Empire.

22. Morris, *Matthew*, 389. Mark's account reveals even greater hostility from the Pharisees: "The Pharisees and some of the scribes *gathered around him* when they came from Jerusalem" (Mark 7:1, emphasis added).

23. On the authority the Pharisees gave oral traditions, see J. Julius Scott Jr., *Jewish Backgrounds of the New Testament* (Grand Rapids: Baker Academic, 2007), 172–73, 202–6. Jesus had not broken the Mosaic Law but only misguided pharisaical extrapolations from it; see France, *Matthew*, 574–78; Robert H. Stein, *Mark*, BECNT (Grand Rapids: Baker, 2008), 338–40. Mark provided an example of their exacting additions to the law (cf. Mark 7:2–5).

7:11), alleviated adult children from their familial responsibilities under the auspices that their resources were already dedicated to God.[24]

It was at this point that Jesus leveled his most stinging rebuke, while also identifying the damning result of their marginalization of God's Word. He assessed that through their traditions they had "invalidated the word of God" (Matt. 15:6). Mark additionally documented Jesus's observation that maneuvers such as this one were a common pharisaic practice (Mark 7:13). Their proclivity for discarding God's written Word was not incidental; it was systemic. Consequently, Jesus justly identified them as "hypocrites."[25] They were hypocrites because while they claimed to be the protectors of God's Word they regularly devised convoluted traditions that provided sanctions for disobeying his commandments. Consequently, Jesus quoted Isaiah 29:13 as a prophecy of their institutionalized rejection of God's Word.[26]

Isaiah's prophecy contained four assertions, alternating between public perception and spiritual reality. Isaiah proclaimed that the Messiah's opponents would be hypocrites, stating that from God's perspective, "this people honors Me with their lips, but their heart is far away from Me. But in vain do they worship Me, teaching as doctrines the precepts of men."[27] It should be noted that although Jesus was addressing the Pharisees, he nevertheless labeled the entire nation as "hypocrites." Jesus assessed that the spiritual bankruptcy of the leadership had spread throughout the entire nation. Rarely can a people rise above those they follow. A literal translation of the first assertion from Isaiah is "This people honors Me with the lips."[28] The reason Jesus justly called them hypocrites is found in Isaiah's second assertion: "But their heart is far away from Me."[29] While the nation professed its devotion to God, its heart was nowhere near him.[30] Regrettably, the sentence's emphasis is hard to translate fluidly into English because the verb *apechō* in this context inherently means "to be away from." However, the addition of the redundant

---

24. On how Corban/Korban subverted the Torah, see Stein, *Mark*, 342–43; R. T. France, *The Gospel of Mark*, NIGTC (Grand Rapids: Eerdmans: 2002), 286–87.
25. On Matthew's emphasis on "hypocrisy," see Morris, *Matthew*, 393; France, *Matthew*, 581, 236–37. Nevertheless, Mark documented that this specific rebuke was directly from Jesus (Mark 7:6).
26. On the passage in Isaiah, see John N. Oswalt, *The Book of Isaiah: Chapters 1–39*, NICOT (Grand Rapids: Eerdmans, 1986), 524–33. Certainly, Jesus was aware that Isaiah was in like manner also rebuking his own generation. Nevertheless, Jesus clearly stated that this prophecy was ultimately fulfilled by those confronting him. Some doubt that Isaiah had any "foretelling" in mind; see France, *Matthew*, 581–2; Mark L. Strauss, *Mark*, ZECNT (Grand Rapids: Zondervan, 2014), 300.
27. The manuscript evidence reveals that the LXX quotation of Isaiah 29:13 in the Gospels of Matthew and Mark are virtually identical, with only one minor variant in word order and none in vocabulary. The Greek word for worship in this prophecy is *sebontai*, which in Jewish literature is commonly translated as "worship"; see Greeven, "*proskuneō*," 762; and BAGD, s.v. "*sebō*." On Jesus's potential knowledge of the LXX, see France, *Mark*, 284.
28. The article, the subject, the pronoun (i.e., "this"), and the verb (i.e., "to honor") are all in the singular. Translation mine.
29. Again, the subject (i.e., "heart") and the verb (i.e., "to keep away") are both singular.
30. Jesus's rightly evaluated the nation as a whole as hypocritical. He was, however, aware of individual exceptions (e.g., Luke 7:36–48; Matt. 8:1–3; Mark 10:46–52).

adverb *porrō* (meaning "far away" or "far off") means that the phrase can be more accurately translated as "But their heart retreats far, far away from Me." Regardless of what they asserted through their many professions, Jesus revealed that there was a cavernous gap between the nation and God. Moreover, the verb is not passive but active, meaning the nation and its leaders willingly worked at keeping their collective heart from God. Their aversion to God and disobedience to his Word was not accidental.

Their hypocrisy had a catastrophic impact on the value of their worship—it was all done in vain. God's evalution on the nation's worship is literally translated "And vainly they worship Me." The Greek word "vainly" simply means fruitless, without value, and/or "to no end."[31] Jesus asserted that the nation was going through the motions of worship with no real concern for experiencing its true goal. Their oblations may have appeared worshipful, but it all was robotically performed through rote duty. And the reason that the nation was misdirected into fruitless worship is found in Isaiah's last assertion: "Teaching as doctrines the precepts of men." A more fluid translation is "Having teachers *give* teachings *that are merely* the commandments of men."[32] And therein is the reason why the nation kept its heart from God: they had a predilection for musings originating from human ingenuity. In their opinion, their preference for human-made religion excused their disobedience to God's inspired commandments, not to mention their rejection of the incarnate Word of God actually standing before them (John 1:1–5, 14). They had replaced the very words of God with human thoughts, values, principles, and judgments. Moreover, Jesus made it clear that they had labored hard to achieve that end—their disobedience was not incidental; it was intentional. As it was in the garden, so it was of the Jews in Jesus's day. They believed that they had thought better than God. Their dedication to human-contrived religious principles had not only led them far away from God but also into fruitless worship. No matter how beautiful its performance or how perfect were their outward adherences to the law's requirements, it was all absent of internal devotion; consequently, it was meaningless and thus unacceptable in the eyes of God.

It should not go unnoticed that once again Jesus interjected controversy concerning worship into the discussion by redirecting the focus toward their disloyalty to God's inspired Word and the hypocrisy of their worship. The Pharisees were likely stunned at this turn in the discussion, for who could question the integrity of their worship? Surely if anyone was dedicated to proper worship, it was they. Jesus's point, however, was that from God's perspective their hearts were estranged from the very one they claimed to worship. Tragically, the same thing occurs in many churches today. People ev-

31. BAGD, s.v. "*matēn*."
32. Morris, *Matthew*, 394. See also Mark 7:8 for Jesus's emphasis that these traditions were of human origins. On Jesus's contrast between God's commandments and human traditions, see Stein, *Mark*, 341–42.

erywhere occasionally go to "worship services" where they sing wonderful songs, say loud amens, cite repetitious prayers, and make financial donations. But as they return to the secular world, many still think with unbelieving hearts and minds. They embrace secular views dealing with human sexuality, moral relativism, or religious universalism, while also simultaneously entertaining doubts about God's Word. These secular values and principles are fundamentally based on human-contrived thoughts, which for them justifies their disobedience to God's written Word. And just as Jesus condemned the worship of the Jews in his day, he would similarly condemn the worship of many modern churchgoers who embrace secular philosophies and humanistic values that countermand what God expects of them as revealed in the Bible. It was Jesus's observation that if one embraces human-engineered teachings that are contrary to the Scriptures, then it is they who have turned their hearts away from God, thus making their worship valueless. It is they who have made their worship hypocritical in the eyes of God.

The Focus of Worship

Given the previous expositions, it is now necessary to address some of the concluding passages found the Gospels of Matthew and Luke (Matt. 28:8–20; Luke 24:36–53).[33] Their significance is found in their description of how the disciples responded to the resurrected Lord. It is critical at this juncture to keep in mind Jesus's teachings concerning worship as previously discussed in order to comprehend the magnitude of what their Gospels document. Concerning the disciples, Matthew records that "after having seen him, they worshipped" (Matt. 28:17, translation mine). With respect to who they worshiped, the sentence in Greek does not provide a direct object such as "God"; consequently, the most natural reading of the passage is that they worshiped the one they saw—that is, the risen Lord Jesus Christ.[34] The text also states that they "doubted." It is not well reasoned to conclude that Matthew meant to convey that the disciples were doubting the reality of the person standing right before them while simultaneously worshiping him.[35] Such a conclusion is further unwarranted since the verb *distazō* does not mean "to not believe" but "to have concerns" or "to be hesitant."[36] Given what it means

---

33. The word "worship" is not found in the ending of Gospel of Mark. On the controversies concerning the ending of Mark's Gospel, see Stein, *Mark*, 733–37; William L. Lane, *The Gospel of Mark*, NICNT (Grand Rapids: Eerdmans, 1974), 601–5; Bruce M. Metzger, *The Text of the New Testament*, 2nd ed. (New York: Oxford University Press, 1968), 226–29.
34. However, Matthew 28:9 is more emphatic, in which Jesus is the direct object of the verb "worshiped."
35. For example, doubting in the same manner as Thomas had doubted the Lord's resurrection (John 20:24–25).
36. BAGD, s.v. "*distazō*." Donald A. Hagner, *Matthew 14–28*, WBC 33b (Nashville: Thomas Nelson, 1995), 885. France suggests that the disciples were not hesitant about who Jesus was but about "how" to respond to him. This is not convincing, however, since France also admits that they had already become accustomed to Jesus through his previous interactions with them (France, *Matthew*, 1110–12; see also Bowen, "They Came," 79). Hagner suggests that the disciples were hesitant about "what might happen next" (i.e., the future?). However, he seems to assume that Jesus had not yet begun

to genuinely worship, it is not possible, therefore, to entertain internal doubts about God while simultaneously worshiping him. God sees the heart; consequently, doubting God while also worshiping him is a fruitless endeavor (1 Sam. 16:7; 2 Chron. 16:9; Jer. 17:10; Matt. 9:4). Nevertheless, the question still remains: Why were they hesitant? The Scriptures document that Jesus made many appearances to hundreds of his followers over a forty-day period (Matt. 28:8–20; Luke 24:13–51; John 20:11–21:25; Acts 1:3–9; 1 Cor. 15:5–7). Moreover, John documented that the apostles (i.e., "the eleven" as Matthew puts it) had already met with Jesus several times, and some had even eaten with him.[37] Consequently, what the disciples doubted was not the resurrected God-man standing before them (cf. Thomas's declaration in John 20:28), but their own capacity to complete the commission that he was in the process of giving to them throughout his resurrection appearances (i.e., Matt. 28:18–20; and also John 20:21–23). They were doubting themselves, not Jesus.

It should be noted that Matthew and Luke recorded separate events in which the disciples worshiped Jesus. Matthew records Jesus's appearance to the disciples at Galilee (28:16). Thus, Matthew concludes his Gospel by recording Jesus's interactions with his disciples early or in the middle of this forty-day pre-ascension period. Luke, however, provides Jesus's interactions with his disciples in Bethany at the end of this forty-day period, which concluded with his ascension. Luke explains that having watched the Lord ascend they were "worshipping him" (Luke 24:52). Both Matthew and Luke used forms of the verb *proskuneō* (i.e., "to worship") while describing the disciples' postresurrection responses to Jesus.[38]

The salient observation concerning the descriptions of these events is that during his earthly ministry Jesus had thoroughly instructed his disciples to worship only God as mandated in the Old Testament. Consequently, for them to worship any being that was not divine not only was a breach of the entire Old Testament but also meant disregarding the objective teachings of the very one that they were worshiping. Nevertheless, that is exactly what they rightly did—they worshiped Jesus, and they did so in the same manner as they would the God of Israel.[39] This is precisely the point Luke emphasizes in Luke 24:52, which reads (emphasis added), "And they, after worshipping *Him*, returned to Jerusalem with great joy."[40]

---

commissioning the disciples until this point, which is clearly not the case; see John 20:19–23. Jesus began commissioning and instructing his apostles from the moment that he first appeared to them.

37. John documented three of Jesus's initial appearances to his disciples (John 21:14). Jesus's first appearance was during Thomas's absence; the second occurred when Thomas was present a week later; and the third was when Jesus restored Peter to apostolic ministry on the shores of Galilee.

38. Matthew uses *proskuneō* in a third-person plural aorist active, while Luke uses an aorist active plural participle.

39. Bowen, "They Came," 83.

40. Contra Kim, who rejects the majority text in favor of an obscure variant; Kim, "Worship of Jesus," 229. See Darrell L. Bock, *Luke 9:51–24:53*, BECNT (Grand Rapids: Baker, 1994), 1945–46, 1950. David E. Garland, *Luke*, ZECNT (Grand Rapids: Zondervan, 2011), 970.

Jesus would be a colossal failure and they would have been patently disobedient if they had engaged in worshiping anyone but God—just as Jesus had taught and as the Old Testament mandates. Nevertheless, this is precisely the point that both Matthew and Luke have made, which is that the very person that the disciples worshiped is the incarnate God of Israel and the Creator of the universe. Jesus is the God-man who is now the risen Savior for all humanity and ascended Lord over all the earth—to him belongs all praise, glory, adoration, and *worship*.

These incidents are considerably unlike the disciples' response to Jesus after he walked on the water (cf. Matt. 14:33), where Matthew wrote that "those who were in the boat worshipped him, saying 'You are certainly God's Son!'" Tragically, the rest of Matthew's Gospel makes it patently obvious that their momentary declaration lacked full appreciation for the reality of Jesus's true identity. For following this event, Matthew's Gospel is littered with examples of their misunderstandings, disbelief, abandonment, and even denials of association with Jesus. If the disciples had actually understood and truly believed that the one standing among them on that boat was God, then their behavior toward Jesus after their declaration on that perilous sea would have been considerably different.[41] It would have resembled how they responded to Jesus after his resurrection, but it did not. They still did not fully comprehend who Jesus really was—the God-man worthy of their complete submission, loyalty, and worship. Although they called him "lord," they still believed that he was just like them—merely a man susceptible to death. How wrong they were. It is only after his resurrection and instructions to them concerning precisely who he is and why he came (Matt. 28:18–20; Luke 24:36–49; and also Acts 1:4–8) that they appropriately comprehended and rightly responded to him as he alone deserves. It was only then that they genuinely worshiped Jesus as God incarnate.

SIGNIFICANCE OF THE SYNOPTICS FOR BIBLICAL WORSHIP

Jesus held unalterable convictions about worship. He believed that only God, as he has revealed himself in his Word, should receive worship. Moreover, he asserted that if anyone knowingly lives disobediently toward God and his Word, then their worship is not only in vain but also hypocritical. Consequently, if anyone realizes that they are living sinfully toward God, then their first mandatory response would be to immediately repent and begin obeying him, which itself would be the only appropriate worshipful

41. Contra Kim, "Worship of Jesus," 229–30; Greeven, "*proskuneō*," 764. Mark's Gospel only mentions that the disciples were "astonished," and asserts that they did not fully comprehend Jesus's identity at that moment (Mark 6:51–52). It is best to see Matthew's description as a nascent understanding that Jesus was uniquely related to God, one about which they would inevitably comprehend, and thus appropriately act on after Jesus's resurrection; see Morris, *Matthew*, 384–85; Hagner, *Matthew 14–28*, 424–25. On Matthew's record of the disciples faithlessness toward Jesus after this event, see Matt. 16:13–23; 26:31–35, 56, 69–75.

response. Jesus asserted that authentic worship produced and energized genuine obedience and service to God. Genuine obedience is sincere conformity to God's will that starts within the heart and inevitably transforms all areas of one's life. And finally, as a result of the incarnation, crucifixion, and resurrection of the Lord Jesus Christ, worship now starts through faith in him, and it continues with adoration and devotion to him alone.

Jesus never promoted a style of worship, nor did he teach his disciples how to generate "an atmosphere" that would encourage it. Moreover, he did not leave behind a single song to foster it. In fact, when combined the Synoptics only record a single event in which Jesus and the disciples even sang (Matt. 26:30; Mark 14:26). By today's standards, therefore, Jesus would be an abject failure with respect to promoting worship. Regrettably, however, many have missed the Lord's entire emphasis concerning authentic worship. In an attempt to manufacture worship, many churches focus on singing, musical performance, human emotions, and the atmosphere of the moment instead of lifelong obedience to the Lord.[42] The product of this type of focus is hypocritical participants engaging in vain worship instead of maturing, loyal, and devoted worshipers of the Lord Jesus Christ.

If the words "music" and "singing" are what first comes to mind when the word the word "worship" is heard, then there is little understanding of what Jesus actually taught about it. Consequently, a definition of what constitutes genuine worship as recorded in the Synoptics is now provided. *Authentic worship is an appropriate and sincere response to God through faith in Jesus that produces in the one who has been enlightened lasting changes in attitudes, beliefs, and behaviors; all of which are constrained by conformity to the Scriptures and submission to the lordship of Jesus Christ.* Anything that emphasizes the performance of the moment instead of enduring obedience to the Lord has missed the essential point of what Jesus taught about worship. As Jesus himself might say to the modern church, "Why do you worship me as 'Lord,' but do not do as I say?" (see Luke 6:46). Singing one's self into a trance to the point of emotional exhaustion is no proof that authentic worship has occurred. Only a life sacrificed to greater loyalty to the Lord Jesus Christ confirms the occurrence of genuine worship. No matter how worshipful the momentary expression may be, if it does not result in greater objective devotion to the lordship of Jesus and obedience to the Scriptures in one's private and public life, then it is hypocritical and thus empty of value in the eyes of our God and Savior, the Lord Jesus Christ.

---

42. One example of this common misguided emphasis is observable in an evangelical quarterly with the cover title: "SING: Why Corporate Worship Matters." The anchor article on the topic of "corporate worship" contains more than 1,600 words, within which words associated with songs, singing, music, choir, performance, and hymns occur more than 120 times, whereas the words "obedience" and "devotion" with respect to the Lord Jesus Christ are conspicuously absent. See Bob Smietana, "Finding Our Voice: Why the Decline of Congregational Singing Matters—and How to Fix It," *Facts & Trends*, Winter 2017, 12–17.

BIBLIOGRAPHY

Bauckham, Richard. *Jesus and the Eyewitnesses: The Gospels as Eyewitness Testimony*. Grand Rapids: Eerdmans, 2006.

Blomberg, Craig L. *Matthew*. NAC 22. Nashville: Broadman, 1992.

Bock, Darrell L. *Luke 1:1–9:50*. BECNT. Grand Rapids: Baker, 1994.

______. *Luke 9:51–24:53*. BECNT. Grand Rapids: Baker, 1994.

Bowen, Matthew L. "'They Came and Held Him by the Feet and Worshipped Him': Proskynesis before Jesus in Its Biblical and Ancient Near Eastern Context." *Studies in the Bible and Antiquity* 5 (2013): 63–73.

Carson, D. A. *Matthew*. In *The Expositor's Bible Commentary*, vol. 8, *Matthew, Mark, Luke*, edited by Frank E. Gaebelein and J. D. Douglas, 1–599. Grand Rapids: Zondervan, 1984.

France, R. T. *The Gospel of Mark*. NIGTC. Grand Rapids: Eerdmans, 2002.

______. *The Gospel of Matthew*. NICNT. Grand Rapids: Eerdmans, 2007.

Garland, David E. *Luke*. ZECNT. Grand Rapids: Zondervan, 2011.

Greeven, Heinrich. "*proskuneō*." In *TDNT* 6:758–66.

Hagner, Donald A. *Matthew 1–13*. WBC 33a. Dallas: Word, 1993.

______. *Matthew 14–28*. WBC 33b. Nashville: Thomas Nelson, 1995.

Kim, Hak Chol. "The Worship of Jesus in the Gospel of Matthew." *Bib* 93, no. 2 (2012): 227–41.

Lane, William L. *The Gospel of Mark*. NICNT. Grand Rapids: Eerdmans, 1974.

Metzger, Bruce M. *The Text of the New Testament*. 2nd ed. New York: Oxford University Press, 1968.

Morris, Leon. *The Gospel according to Matthew*. PiNTC. Grand Rapids: Eerdmans, 1992.

Oswalt, John N. *The Book of Isaiah: Chapters 1–39*. NICNT. Grand Rapids: Eerdmans, 1986.

Powell, Mark Allen. "A Typology of Worship in the Gospel of Matthew." *JSNT* 57 (1995): 3–17.

Renshaw, Brian. "The Worship of Jesus and the People of God in the Gospel of Matthew." Paper presented at the Southeast Regional Meeting of the Evangelical Theological Society, Louisville, KY, March 17, 2017.

Scott, Julius J., Jr. *Jewish Backgrounds of the New Testament*. Grand Rapids: Baker Academic, 2007.

Shanks, Monte A. *Papias and the New Testament*. Eugene OR: Pickwick, 2013.

Smietana, Bob. "Finding Our Voice: Why the Decline of Congregational Singing Matters—and How to Fix It." *Facts & Trends*, Winter 2017, 12–17.

Stein, Robert H. *Luke*. NAC 24. Nashville: Broadman, 1992.

______. *Mark*. BECNT. Grand Rapids: Baker Academic, 2008.

Strauss, Mark L. *Mark*. ZECNT. Grand Rapids: Zondervan, 2014.

Turner, David L. *Matthew*. BECNT. Grand Rapids: Baker Academic, 2008.

CHAPTER 24

JESUS AS THE TEMPLE AND THE FULFILLMENT OF THE FEASTS

Worship in John

Donald Roe Love III

CONTEXT OF WORSHIP IN THE GOSPEL OF JOHN

Do you not see all these things? Truly I say to you, not one stone here will be left upon another, which will not be torn down" (Matt. 24:2).[1] With Jesus's coming, things were about to change and the disciples knew it. But they dared not speak of such things within earshot of the Pharisees and Sadducees. Whatever he meant by this omen of destruction, speaking against the temple was a serious offense.[2] A blasphemy that they need not risk.[3] They would have to wait until they were safely outside the city before discussing such matters.

As they traveled through the Kidron Valley, the disciples likely turned the implications of all Jesus was predicting over in their minds. Temple worship was central to the sacred rhythms of every observant Jewish family. The temple was the dwelling place of God's glory, the place where heaven met earth, and where sin was remembered no more. Unlike other nations, Israel was afforded no other temple, and by Mosaic law, this was the place for sacrifice and festival celebration. The last time that their temple was destroyed, God exiled Israel from the land of his blessing. Jesus's prediction, therefore, would have been a matter that served as a disturbing harbinger of a coming age.

1. Unless otherwise noted, all Scripture quotations are from the NASB.
2. Unlike other religions that allowed for worship in many temples, within Judaism there was only one temple. To attempt to establish another was considered a sinful act (1 Kings 12:29; Josh. 22:16).
3. The relationship between blasphemy and speaking against the temple is seen in Jesus's court trials (Mark 14:58) as well as in the accusations against the apostles in Acts (16:3).

Once safely outside the city walls on the Mount of Olives, overlooking the Eastern Gate and the temple, the disciples pressed Jesus for details: "Tell us, when will these things happen, and what will be the sign of your coming, and of the end of the age?" (Matt. 24:3). Jesus, knowing their hearts, responds with words of warning concerning the things to come. Wars, rumors of wars, earthquakes, and famines would all remain. The world would persecute and kill them because of Jesus's name. Many would fall away and betray one another and hate one another and most people's love would grow cold. But the one who endured to the end would be saved. False christs and false prophets would arise and show great signs and wonders, so as to mislead, if possible, even the elect (Matt. 24:3–35).

As John heard these ominous words, there would have been no way for him to know that his brother James would be the first of their number to die by the sword (Acts 12:2). Or that all the other disciples would follow until John alone was left. He would remain as a witness of the fulfillment of Jesus's words. He would live on as the Flavian Caesars, Vespasian and Titus, would pillage the treasure of the temple, carrying out of Judea their sacred menorah and the law of God.[4] He would live on as the most holy place of Jewish worship was set ablaze and dismantled stone by stone as every ounce of molten gold was pillaged. John would live on to watch in horror as his people were violently removed from the Promised Land. In this dark moment, it would become clear to those expelled from the land that God's kingdom would not come in the way that they had expected. The Torah had prophesied that this era was when the Messiah would come, but now the unthinkable had happened. They were in exile, again.

To add insult to injury, the Flavian Caesars were now claiming to be the true fulfillment of the Jewish messianic expectations. Vespasian compiled a list of signs to evidence his divine right to rule over Rome.[5] And as he learned of the well-known, widespread Jewish belief that *men coming out of Judea would rule the world*, Vespasian would take this upon himself along with his sons Titus and Domitian. As the three of these participated in the triumphal procession coming out of Judea with the spoils of war, Vespasian and his sons, in the minds of the citizens of Rome, became the christs that were predicted by the Hebrew Scriptures.[6] But, in truth, they were among the false christs that Jesus himself had predicted.

---

4. Josephus, *Jewish War* 7.148–52, in *The Works of Josephus: Complete and Unabridged*, trans. William Whiston (Peabody, MA: Hendrickson, 1987).
5. Suetonius, *Life of Vespasian.*
6. Roman acceptance of this belief is likely due to the Flavian dynasty's own application of it to themselves, based on their military triumph over Judea in AD 70. Josephus recounts that the temple articles were the focal point of this procession (Josephus, *Jewish War* 7.148–52). In their triumphal entry to Rome from Judea, all three Flavians participated in the procession (see Josephus, *Jewish War* 5.132). This triumph proved to be an important factor in securing Flavian succession. See discussion in Allen C. Myers, "Titus," in *The Eerdmans Bible Dictionary*, ed. Allen C. Myers (Grand Rapids: Eerdmans, 1987), 1008.

At the time of Vespasian's death, the Senate voted to recognize Vespasian's deity.[7] By implication, this made Vespasian's two sons "sons of God." Titus would be immortalized in his death as one who ascended into heaven on the wings of an eagle. And upon his death, this royal succession would continue through the Flavian line with the throne passing to Domitian (the third of the Flavian Caesars who *came out of Judea with the spoils of the temple*). This Caesar, too, was considered a "son of God" due to his father's deification. Not content with this, he expressed the desire to be acknowledged as a god-man, being called "Lord God."[8]

Clearly, to those who knew the Scriptures, the Flavians did not meet all of the biblical criteria of messiahship. They were not virgin-born as Isaiah 7:14 predicted, of the tribe of Judah, or born in Bethlehem as Micah 5:2 predicted. Nonetheless, they were fulfilling the expectation that the Messiah would rule the whole known world predicted in Isaiah and Daniel and either due to the ignorance of the masses or the power of their rule, the citizens of Rome accepted them as the messiahs who were to come. Surely Christians and Jews alike, who were familiar with the prophecies of the Jewish Scriptures, would not be easily deceived. But as the Jewish Historian Josephus explains, "This oracle certainly denoted the government of Vespasian, who was appointed emperor in Judea. However, it is not possible for men to avoid fate, although they see it beforehand."[9]

A shift was occurring. The world would now look to Rome and the divine Flavian dynasty as the fulfillment of the Jewish Scriptures. Jews and even professing Christians would be tempted to doubt their messianic beliefs. And those who became convinced of Flavian messiahship would grow increasingly hostile to the Judeo-Christian message. After all, wasn't

7. The Arch of Triumph records the Senate's deification of Titus and Vespasian in AD 81. These reliefs depict the Flavians triumphing out of Judea with the temple spoils (the ark of the covenant and golden lampstands), Titus ascending to heaven on eagle's wings, and the inscription *Senatus Populusque Romanus divo Tito divi Vespasiani filio Vespasiano Augusto* (The Roman Senate and people to the divine Titus Vespasianus Augustus, son of the divine Vespasian).
8. James M. Scott suggests that this claim may be why John records Thomas's declaration of Jesus as Lord and God in John 20:28. See "Heavenly Ascent in Jewish and Pagan Traditions," in *Dictionary of New Testament Background: A Compendium of Contemporary Biblical Scholarship*, eds. Craig A. Evans and Stanley E. Porter (Downers Grove, IL: InterVarsity Press, 2000), 447. Contra Warren Carter, who states that this connection is unsustainable because the titles are not the same in Greek. Dio Cassius refers to Domitian as "Lord and God" (*despotēs kai theos*), not as "My Lord and my God" (*Ho kurios mou kai ho theos mou*) in John 20:28. See *John and Empire: Initial Explorations* (New York: T&T Clark, 2008), 196.
9. Josephus continues, "The Jews took this prediction to belong to themselves in particular and many of the wise men were thereby deceived in their determination" (Josephus, *Jewish War* 6.5.4). Likewise, Tacitus states, "This mysterious prophecy [that men coming me out of Judea would rule the world] really referred to Vespasian and Titus, but the common people, true to the selfish ambitions of mankind, thought that this exalted destiny was reserved for them" (Tacitus, *Histories* 5.13). Suetonius reflects, "This prediction, as it later proved, referred to the two Roman Emperors, Vespasian and his son Titus; but the rebellious Jews, who read it as referring to themselves" (Suetonius, *Life of Vespasian* 4).

Caesar the son of God who came out of Judea, ruling the whole world? The message of Christ, like never before, would appear to be a message of foolishness. In their minds, Jesus was simply one among many hopeful messianic candidates who met his end at the hands of the Romans like so many others. Furthermore, if the Jews, his own people who knew the Scriptures, rejected him, then why should any reasonable person accept a crucified Jew over Caesar as God and ruler of the world?

John watched this all unfold as he ministered to the churches in Asia. One can imagine that all of these happenings seemed reminiscent of Jesus's prophecy from the Mount of Olives so long ago. All others who had stood with John on that day were put to death by those thinking they were doing a service for God. Now, not only had the temple been destroyed by war, but the enemies who had destroyed it had, in effect, convinced the world that they were the ones predicted by the ancient prophecies. The false messiahs had come with a list of signs validating their rule by divine right, and the world was coming to worship them in droves. The historians of Rome had become their false prophets, and so much had happened to fulfill all that Jesus said would happen within that generation.

Therefore, for John, the temple's destruction was not a sudden and surprising event. For most Jews, however, the temple's ruin and their own exile from the Promised Land would prove to be a fundamentally ground-shaking event for their faith. For with the Flavian destruction of the temple, worshipers would find themselves untethered not only from the central place of worship but also from the messianic hope that many of these rituals embodied, which in turn would result from an even greater sense of being cut off from God's presence.[10] Following these events, all who anticipated a Jewish messiah were now in a position to reexamine the question that John the Baptist asked during his imprisonment: Was Jesus the one to come, or should we expect someone else (see Matt. 11:13)? And, to be sure, many would be tempted to abandon hope in a Jewish messiah and begin joining Rome in looking to the Flavian Caesars as their messiah. It is out of this this context that John writes, refocusing the sacred rhythms of worship for this post-temple generation in light of the knowledge that Jesus is the Messiah, the Son of God.

THEOLOGY OF WORSHIP

John's understanding of Jesus's teaching concerning the temple empowered him not only to endure the temple's absence but also to celebrate its absence in light of its obsolescence. For a time was coming and then was when Jesus, and not a temple made and destroyed by human hands,

---

10. While he does not address the implications of the temple's destruction, Andreas Köstenberger also views the temple's destruction as the occasion for John's Gospel. See Köstenberger, "The Destruction of the Second Temple and the Composition of the Fourth Gospel," *TJ* 26 (2005): 205–42.

would be the focus of all worship. John explains in Revelation 21:22–22:1 that in the new Jerusalem there would be no need of the temple, for the Lord God Almighty and the Lamb (Jesus) are its temple. No longer would there be need to seek the shekinah glory of God on the Temple Mount and to seek to be cleansed by ritual waters, for the Lamb's light shines like the sun and a river of life flows out of him. Similarly, by means of Old Testament allusions to light, water, and Jewish festival fulfillment, John's gospel refocuses worship onto Jesus, presenting his incarnation as the inbreaking of the eschatological temple.

Jesus as Temple

Two temple allusions are found in the first chapter of John's gospel. The first begins as early as John's prologue. Here we see John's writing replete with references to Jesus's incarnational ministry being categorized as shining light and bringing life into the world. He explains that "life was in him and he was the light of men" (1:4), and "that this light shined in the darkness, and the darkness did not overcome it" (1:5). For Jesus was "the true light, who gives light to everyone," and that light "was coming into the world" (1:9). This light that John is referring to could be linked to the light that emanated from the temple that John speaks of in Revelation 22. This connection between light and temple is strengthened by two other temple allusions in the prologue. First, John describes Jesus's incarnation as tabernacling (*eskēnōsen*) among us (1:14). With his use of the word *eskēnōsen*, John is calling the mind of his readers to the tabernacle (*skēnē*) that served as the temple from the time of Moses through the time of David. By making this connection between the tabernacle and Jesus's incarnation, John is presenting Jesus's body as a wilderness-wanderings-like temple. Second, John explains that "we beheld his glory." This reference to Jesus's glory is another allusion to the tabernacle where the shekinah glory of God dwelt. John drives home the monumental nature of this indwelling presence when he states, "Out of his fullness we have all received grace in place of grace already given. For the law was given through Moses; grace and truth came through Jesus Christ. No one has ever seen God, but the one and only Son, who is himself God and is in closest relationship with the Father, has made him known" (1:15–18 NIV). This statement looks back to when Moses asked God, "Show me your glory!" and the Lord explained that no one can behold his face and live (Exod. 33). Together, these allusions serve to present Jesus's body as an incarnational temple of God where the glory of God dwelt and the light of life shined. This "tabernacling" presence emanated an incarnational grace that surpassed even that which Moses and the tabernacle could provide under the old law.

The second temple allusion occurs within Jesus's conversation with Nathanael (1:47–51), where Jesus alludes to Jacob's experience at Bethel. This allusion commences with Jesus calling Nathanael an Israelite promising him that he would "see the heavens opened and the angels ascending and descending on the Son of Man" (1:51). This imagery reaches back into Genesis, when Jacob (whose name is later changed to Israel) receives a vision of angels ascending and descending on a ladder from heaven. Jacob called that place Bethel, meaning "the house of God." Bethel is traditionally believed to be the place where the temple in Jerusalem would later be built. Thus Jesus's claim is that he himself is Bethel! He is the house of God and the ladder to heaven. Jesus then travels to Nathanael's hometown and uses water to miraculously reveal his glory to the disciples (2:11). Because this sign comes directly after Jesus's Bethel allusion with Nathanael and occurs in Nathanael's hometown of Cana of Galilee, it serves as a partial fulfillment of Jesus's promise to show him "greater things" (1:50–51). Also of significance is that Jesus used Jewish ceremonial washing jars to perform this sign—perhaps to foreshadow that Jesus's water of the Spirit would surpass the ceremonial washings of the temple (John 2:6).[11] In this way, Jesus's manifestation of his glory in this sign reveals to his disciples that the glory of God dwells in him in an even more powerful and personal way than it did in the tabernacle of Moses or the temples of Solomon or Herod.

The third temple allusion arises when Jesus is challenged by the Jewish leaders to produce a sign to validate his authority to cleanse the temple. Jesus asserts, "Destroy *this* temple [referring to his body], and I will rebuild it in three days" (2:19). Jesus refers to himself as temple, thereby emphasizing his body as the place of the Spirit's indwelling presence.[12] John explains that it was only after Jesus's resurrection that his disciples would come to understand Jesus was referring to his body as the temple (John 2:21). This claim, too, amounts to a front against the temple, and had the religious leaders understood in the moment, this claim would have amounted to a capital offense. Had they realized Jesus was presenting himself as a temple, thereby shifting the focus of worship from the Jerusalem temple to himself, they would surely have found Jesus guilty of blasphemy and would have dealt with him decisively.

This temple allusion is coupled with Jesus's night meeting with Nicodemus, when John presents Jesus as the origin of light and the water of life. Nicodemus, a ruler of the Jews and a Pharisee, comes to Jesus as a result of his temple signs and acknowledging that no one can do such signs unless they come from God (2:23; 3:1–2). Jesus explains that Nicodemus needs to be born of water and Spirit (3:5). As he does so, he looks ahead to his glorification on the cross where he would accomplish a work similar to what

---

11. D. A. Carson makes a similar observation. See Carson, *The Gospel according to John*, PiNTC (Grand Rapids: Eerdmans, 1991), 208–9.
12. It is of note that Jesus refers to himself as the *naon* (the inner sanctuary of the Holy Spirit), instead of using the word *hieron* (the whole temple complex). See discussion in Joel R. Wohlgemut, "Where Does God Dwell?," *Direction* 22 no. 2 (1993): 87–93. See also Alan R. Kerr, *The Temple of Jesus's Body: The Temple Theme in the Gospel of John*, JSNTSup 220 (London: Sheffield Academic, 2002), 93.

Moses accomplished in the wilderness with the serpent on the pole (3:14). He is able to do this because he is the light that comes into the world and anyone who lives by the truth will come to this light (3:19–21).

Finally, a fourth temple allusion arises in Jesus's conversation with the Samaritan woman (4:1–26). As she begins to discern that Jesus is a prophet, she asks him what was likely her most burning question: "Our fathers worshiped on this mountain [Mount Gerizim], and you Jews say that in Jerusalem [Mount Zion] is the place where one ought to worship" (4:20). Implicit in this statement is the question, "What am I to do if I as a woman and a Samaritan am forbidden to worship at the place that God has commanded us to worship?" As a woman and a non-Jew, she would only be able to enter as far as the marketplace of the temple. Jesus's response tears down this wall of separation: "Woman, believe Me, an hour is coming when neither in this mountain nor in Jerusalem will you worship the Father. You worship what you do not know; we worship what we know, for salvation is from the Jews." He explains, "an hour is coming, and now is, when the true worshipers will worship the Father in spirit and truth; for such people the Father seeks to be his worshipers. God is spirit, and those who worship Him must worship in spirit and truth" (4:21–24). Jesus's response effectively shifts the focus of worship from the place of worship to the mode of worship. For, if Jesus is a temple, it follows that worship need no longer be centralized in Jerusalem.

Furthering this temple connection is John's presentation of Jesus as giver of water of life that surpasses that of the Jews. John makes this explicit by introducing the conversation as occurring at "Jacob's well" (4:6) and by repeating this connection in the Samaritan woman's question, "Are you greater than our father Jacob who gave us this well and used it to water his whole family and livestock?" (4:12). Jesus explains that whoever drinks the water that he gives will never thirst but will have a fountain of water spring up into everlasting life (4:14). The fourth gospel's presentation of Jesus's baptism of the living water of the Spirit culminates in John 7, when Jesus extends this invitation publicly on the last and greatest day of the Feast of Tabernacles. On this last day, the day when water offerings had just ceased, Jesus cries out saying, "Whoever believes in me, as Scripture has said, rivers of living water will flow from within them" (7:38 NIV). John explains, "By this he meant the Spirit, whom those who believed in him were later to receive. Up to that time the Spirit had not been given, since Jesus had not yet been glorified" (7:39 NIV). Together, these passages in John concerning water and Spirit present Jesus's Spirit baptism as a cleansing work within the believer. This seems to be in fulfillment of Ezekiel's promise, "Then I will sprinkle clean water on you, and you will be clean; I will cleanse you from all your filthiness and from all your idols. Moreover, I will give you a new heart and put a new spirit within you; and I will remove the heart of stone from your flesh and give you a heart of flesh. I will put My Spirit within you and cause you to walk in My statutes, and you will be careful to observe My ordinances"

(Ezek. 36:25–27). In this way, John presents Jesus as the one to come who would baptize with the water of the Spirit that would purify the hearts of all who would receive this cleansing river within them through belief in the Son who has come from the right hand of the Father. This cleansing would surpass John's baptism and the ritual washings of the Jews—whether it be that of John's baptism, that of the Jewish washing pots, Jacob's well, or even the libations of the temple. Now more than ever, true worshipers of the living God have access to the Spirit of God and his cleansing ministry. Living water would now flow out of them like the waters of the temple of the kingdom (Ezek. 47:1–2; Rev. 22:1).

Together these four Johannine temple allusions demonstrate that Jesus's incarnation is a kind of tabernacling among us that reveals the glory of God in an even greater way than God revealed to and through Moses. By Jesus's own self-pronouncements, he is the new Bethel (house of God), a new *naon* (dwelling place of the Spirit), and with his coming the Mosaic requirement to worship at Mount Zion is no longer in effect, for God is spirit and he seeks worshipers who will worship in sprit and truth. Out of this temple Jesus, the true light, shines into the darkness and living water flows into all who would receive it. This water that he offers is far greater than that offered by the Jewish purification rituals because it is the water of the Spirit promised long ago by the prophets.

Jesus as the Focus of Festival Celebration

The feasts of the Jews were an essential part of Jewish temple worship. The law of Moses required all Jewish males celebrate Passover, Tabernacles, and Pentecost at the temple (Deut. 16:16). In his gospel, John presents the messianic worship rituals of Passover and Tabernacles as finding their fulfillment in Jesus.[13] This refocusing of festival worship is an extension of John's fulfillment motif, where he presents Jesus not only as the temple but as the fulfillment of the temple feasts as well. The first temple feast that Jesus fulfills is that of the Passover. This, by far, is the feast that John most focuses on throughout his gospel. He mentions Jesus's participation in three Passovers throughout his gospel. In the first, discussed above, Jesus cleanses the temple and declares himself to be a temple of the Holy Spirit (2:13–25). This temple cleansing represents Jesus's first act of recentering of Jewish worship, and his self-pronouncement looks ahead to the more pervasive eschatological reformation to come, where there will be no more temple, because the lamb is the temple (Rev. 21:22–22:1). This refocusing of worship continues within the other two Passover feasts later in John, with Jesus presenting himself as replacing the elements of this feast. In John 6:22–71, after feeding the five thousand, Jesus presents himself as

13. Perhaps Pentecost was not included because it was fulfilled by the coming of the Holy Spirit in Acts 2. This motif may be present in the Feast of Dedication as well. See Gerald L. Borchert, *John 12–21*, NAC 25b (Nashville: Broadman & Holman, 2002), 328.

the bread of life—the new manna from heaven. All who eat his body and drink his blood would have eternal life. Jesus's attribution of his body as bread coming down from heaven as food and his blood as drink during Passover links Jesus's ministry as the fulfillment of the feast.

Similarly, in 12:1–19:42, Jesus is presented as the Passover Lamb. This theme begins in the first chapter, where Jesus is introduced as "the Lamb of God who takes away the sin of the world" (1:29). Now as Jesus's final Passover approaches, John crafts his narrative with care to include important historical details paralleling Jesus's life with the that of Passover lamb. First, like this lamb, Jesus's death would save the lives of others (11:52). Second, Jesus's anointing occurred six days before the Passover—the same day when the lamb would be chosen for the meal (12:1). Third, Jesus was handed over to be crucified at the time when the Passover lambs were beginning to be sacrificed in the temple (19:14). Fourth, Jesus's bones were not broken, in fulfillment of Exodus's prohibition of breaking the bones the Passover lamb (19:36; Exod. 12:46). Finally, the removal of Jesus's body before dawn parallels Deuteronomy's command for the removal of the Passover lamb's carcass (19:31; Exod. 12:10).

The second temple feast that John records Jesus fulfilling is the Feast of Tabernacles (7:1–8:59). Here Jesus makes two significant self-pronouncements concerning his identity that take on special significance when occurring during this feast. First, John notes that "on the last day and greatest day of the feast" Jesus presents himself as the giver of living water (7:37). On this last day of the feast, water offerings, commemorating the water that flowed from the rock of Horeb during the exodus, ceased to be offered. This was to cause the worshiper anticipate a day when the Lord would pour out living water to purify his people.[14] It is at this time that Jesus cries out, "If anyone is thirsty, he should come to Me and drink! The one who believes in Me, as the Scripture has said, will have streams of living water flow from deep within him" (8:37–38 HCSB).[15] With this in view, Jesus's comment is most certainly messianic. Second, it is at this same feast that Jesus declares himself to be "the light of the world." Many believe that this self-declaration was also made during the Feast of Tabernacles. If so, the festival context may add to its messianic significance. During this feast, a single candelabra was left unlit in the temple courtyard in recognition that the full light of God had not yet been given. This candelabra would, therefore, remain unlit during the festival until the messiah was revealed to Israel.[16] Therefore, Jesus's self-declaration as the light of the world could be viewed as Jesus's public declaration of himself as the expected Messiah who would lead the people into the kingdom of God.

14. See the Talmud (y. Sukkah 5:1).

15. Possible OT references that Jesus is alluding to are Isa. 12:3; 44:3; Ezek. 36:25–27.

16. Craig L. Blomberg, *The Historical Reliability of John's Gospel* (Downers Grove, IL: InterVarsity Press, 2001), 141.

Summary

In the wake of the temple's destruction by false messiahs (the so-called Flavian sons of God), much of John's Gospel serves to shift the focus of worshipers from the Flavians and human-made temples to Jesus and the temple of his body. For just like the tabernacle, the Spirit of God moved with him. And like the eschatological temple, water poured out of him like living water flowing into the disciples. And while Jewish law required temple observance of certain Jewish feasts, John recounts that Jesus taught that this requirement was no longer binding and presented himself as the fulfillment of these feasts. For a time had come when it no longer mattered where one worshiped—only whether one worshiped in spirit and in truth. Empowered with these beliefs, John re-forms worship for post-temple worshipers using Jesus's words, with his amazing evangelistic message for all whose messianic hopes were lost with the temple's destruction.

SIGNIFICANCE OF THE GOSPEL OF JOHN FOR BIBLICAL WORSHIP

The conversation of Jesus and the woman at Jacob's well and Jesus's water-to-wine miracle at Cana serve as pantomimes of the post-temple worshiper's internal conversation with Jesus. The water of Jacob's well and the ceremonial washing pots of the wedding feast represent the old way of Jewish worship that Jesus has come to replace with living water and celebratory wine.[17] This new form of worship, like new wine, cannot be contained within the confines of the old wineskins of a human-made temples and traditions. As Jesus's blood and water was poured out like wine, the temple curtain tore—redefining worship as God's Spirit is now unleashed, filling true worshipers with living water and making them the temple of the Holy Spirit. This spiritual reality is central to the goal of Jesus's finished work on the cross. It is therefore essential for all who seek to worship Jesus in spirit and truth to consider what it means to be the temple of the Holy Spirit and to consider the implications of the christocentric meaning of the Jewish feasts in relation to our own sacred rhythms of worship.

Worship from the Sanctuary of the Soul

If the Gospel of John teaches that Jesus was the temple during his earthly ministry and Revelation teaches that Jesus will be the temple in the new Jerusalem, what is the application of this truth for the people of John's day and ours? Perhaps the first, most straightforward implication is that we are no longer under the old covenant Mosaic mandate of the law that worshipers must worship at a single geographical location. So, Jesus's answer to the Samaritan woman's question of which mountain to worship on still rings true today: "Believe me, a time is coming when you will worship the Father neither on this mountain nor in Jerusalem. You

17. See discussion in Carson, *John*, 208–9.

Samaritans worship what you do not know; we worship what we do know, for salvation is from the Jews. Yet a time is coming and now has come when the true worshipers will worship the Father in Spirit and in truth, for they are the kind of worshippers the Father seeks. God is spirit, and his worshipers must worship in the Spirit and in truth" (John 20–24 NIV).

With the coming of Jesus and the temple's destruction, the time has come for us to move our focus off of holy places to worshiping the Father in spirit and truth. Only some translators capitalize the word "Spirit," as there is debate as to whether Jesus is referring to God's Spirit (the Holy Spirit) or our own spirit. In other words, is Jesus's admonition for his followers to worship the Father from the depths of our spirits or through the Holy Spirit? Both reflect an interpretation that accords with other Scripture passages. What is clear from the whole of the gospel of John is that Jesus is seeking to refocus worship from the Father's house, to the Father himself. In the end, while it might not be clear which meaning is intended, *both* are essential elements within the Trinitarian worship that Jesus is advocating.

Just as the temple was the way to God in the old covenant, Jesus is now offering himself as the way to the Father saying, "I am the way, and the truth, and the life; no one comes to the Father but through Me" (John 14:6). And he explains that he was going to the Father and he was not going to leave them as orphans, but would send them the Spirit of truth (14:18; 16:12). This Spirit of truth would guide the disciples into all truth and would not speak on his own accord, but only what he heard from the Father and the Son (16:12–13). This ministry of the Spirit most certainly comes into play when it comes to spirit-and-truth worship, for Jesus also explains that God's word is truth and that the Spirit is going to lead the disciples into *all truth* (17:17; cf. 16:13). Thus the ministry of the Holy Spirit is not merely to illuminate the truth of Scripture but also to illuminate the lives of the disciples as their mighty counselor who remains with them forever to lead and guide them (14:16; 16:13). Jesus promises that this Spirit is with them and will be in them (14:17). This seems to be fulfilled as Jesus, after his resurrection, breathes on them and says, "Receive the Spirit" (John 20:22). With all of this in view, the Holy Spirit (the Spirit of truth) most certainly plays an important role in spirit-and-truth worship as his ministry is closely related to guiding in the truth of God's Word and in leading in truth.

The spirit of the individual likewise plays a role in spirit-and-truth worship. John 4 emphasizes both God and worshipers when it says that "the Father is spirit" and "his worshipers" must worship in spirit and truth (John 4:24). Jesus is calling worshipers to encounter a spiritual God with their own spirit. In other words, one does not need a physical temple to worship a God that is spirit. Rather you need to encounter his Spirit with your own spirit. Certainly, because we live and function within a physical world, it may become difficult to consider how one enters into such a state that our spirit is not eclipsed by the physical aspects of worship. John's gospel offers a few helpful insights on this matter. First, all throughout John's Gospel, Jesus is portrayed as not doing his own will, but doing the will of his Father. He explains, "Very truly I tell you, the Son can do nothing by himself; he can do only what he sees his Father doing, because whatever the Father does the Son also does" (5:19 NIV). Thus Jesus's ministry can be described as extended time of Jesus listening to the Father and then doing his will.

As Jesus breathed on his disciples, he imparted the indwelling of the Holy Spirit, thereby making them temples of the Holy Spirit as well (20:22). The Holy Spirit would guide them not only from the outside but also now from inside. By listening to the Spirit they, too, could listen to the Father and be empowered to do greater works than Jesus (14:12).

So, returning to the question at hand, how does this relate to the worshiper of John's day and today? The apostle Paul extends Jesus's teachings applying this to all believers, saying, "Do you not know that your bodies are temples of the Holy Spirit, who is in you?" (1 Cor. 6:19 NIV). The same question should be asked of worshipers today. Do *you* not know that *your* body is the temple of the Holy Spirit within *you*? This indwelling could therefore be described as the sanctuary of the soul, the most holy place where heaven meets earth—inside of us. It is this indwelling presence that empowers our spirit to worship God in truth. It is within this inner sanctuary that the Spirit of truth disciples us in true worship of the true and living God.

This indwelling presence is similar to what Adam experienced in the garden of Eden as he walked with God. Just as God breathed the breath of life into him (Gen. 2:7), now he has breathed his Spirit into us. We therefore do not need to wait until the new Jerusalem to be revealed for the Lamb's light to shine on us and for the river of life to flow into us. We are now God's temple, and we now have access to "boldly approach his throne of grace that we might obtain mercy and find grace to help in time of need" (Heb. 4:16). It is therefore essential that we as worshipers diligently seek to learn how to enter into and dwell in this sanctuary of the soul where the Spirt of God now resides. As we meet him in this inner sanctuary his light will shine brightly out of our innermost being and his living water will flow unceasingly from the depths of our souls.

In order to enter this sanctuary, it is essential that we seek to love the Lord our God with all of our heart, soul, and mind (Matt. 22:27). The Jewish leaders were concerned with the scriptures and protecting the temple, but they missed the work of the Holy Spirit through the incarnate Jesus. Jesus said of them, "You study the Scriptures diligently because you think that in them you have eternal life. These are the very Scriptures that testify about me, yet you to come to me to have life" (John 5:39–40 NIV). These leaders feared the death that Rome could bring to their country and their temple more than they sought the life Christ could bring to their souls (11:48). We need to continually balance spirit and truth, always cautious that we do not get so caught up in our studies of the Scriptures that we neglect the more soulish practices of the heart that help us enter into the sanctuary of the soul where our spirit abides with the Spirit of the living God.

Worship through Christian Celebrations of Jewish Feasts

Even before Jesus's ministry, it was recognized that the Jewish feasts not only celebrated the past but also looked to a future messianic hope. As Jesus spoke during these feasts, he claimed that he was the fulfillment of these feasts, infusing them with a renewed messianic dimension. With this in view, it should not be seen as a return to the Mosaic law when Christians celebrate these feasts as lasting memorial of Jesus's teachings—something that Christians celebrate in remembrance of him. In fact, Jesus himself said of the Passover meal, "As often as you do this, do in remembrance of me" (Luke 22:19; 1 Cor. 11:24). While this has become a part of the liturgy of many denominations, all too often our remembrances are just a shadow of the Passover meal, stripped of the fuller significance of Jesus being our Passover Lamb (1 Cor. 5:7). Perhaps it is time that Christians reconsider the Christocentric meaning of the Jewish feasts and how these could once again become remembrances as part of our sacred rhythms as well. Could celebrating messianic versions of the Passover Feast more fully capture the spirit of Jesus's idea of remembrance than that of our traditional Communion alone? Likewise, perhaps it would be helpful to celebrate the Feasts of Tabernacles, Dedication, and Pentecost along with the renewed significance that comes with the history surrounding them in the New Testament.

BIBLIOGRAPHY

Blomberg, Craig L. *The Historical Reliability of John's Gospel*. Downers Grove, IL: Inter Varsity Press, 2001.

Borchert, Gerald L. *John 1–11*. NAC 25a. Nashville: Broadman & Holman, 1996.

______. *John 12–21*. NAC 25b. Nashville: Broadman & Holman, 2002.

Carson, D. A. *The Gospel according to John*. PiNTC. Grand Rapids: Eerdmans, 1991.

Carter, Warren. *John and Empire: Initial Explorations*. New York: T&T Clark, 2008.

Kerr, Alan R. *The Temple of Jesus's Body: The Temple Theme in the Gospel of John*. JSNTSup 220. London: Sheffield Academic, 2002.

Köstenberger, Andreas. "The Destruction of the Second Temple and the Composition of the Fourth Gospel." *TJ* 26 (2005): 205–42.

Myers, Allen C. "Titus." In *The Eerdmans Bible Dictionary*, edited by Allen C. Myers. Grand Rapids: Eerdmans, 1987.

Scott, James M. "Heavenly Ascent in Jewish and Pagan Traditions." in *Dictionary of New Testament Background: A Compendium of Contemporary Biblical Scholarship*, edited by Craig A. Evans and Stanley E. Porter. Downers Grove, IL: InterVarsity Press, 2000.

Wohlgemut, Joel R., "Where Does God Dwell?" *Direction* 22, no. 2 (1993): 87–93.

CHAPTER 25

LIFE TOGETHER IN THE LAST DAYS

Worship in the Acts of the Apostles

Brian J. Tabb

CONTEXT OF WORSHIP IN ACTS

The book of Acts presents the worship and life of the people of God in a period of unique redemptive-historical transition. Luke's second book begins where his first book ends: The Lord Jesus presents himself alive to his apostles and provides foundational teaching and commands before his ascension into heaven (Luke 24; Acts 1:1–11). Luke explains that his gospel deals with "all that Jesus *began* to do and teach" (Acts 1:1), which implies that Acts recounts what Jesus *continues* to do and teach through his Spirit-empowered witnesses following his ascension.[1]

Jesus's last words in Acts 1:8 set forth the church's mission between his ascension and his return (cf. 1:11): "But you will receive power when the Holy Spirit has come upon you, and you will be my witnesses in Jerusalem and in all Judea and Samaria, and to the end of the earth." As many commentators have recognized, this verse offers a "programmatic statement" or "advance summary" of the book's focus on the spread of the message of salvation.[2] Luke's narrative begins in Jerusalem (Acts 1:12; 5:28; 6:7), moves to Judea and Samaria when the believers are scattered by

1. On this point, see Alan J. Thompson, *The Acts of the Risen Lord Jesus: Luke's Account of God's Unfolding Plan*, NSBT 27 (Downers Grove, IL: IVP Academic, 2011), 48–49.
2. Craig S. Keener, *Acts: An Exegetical Commentary*, vol. 1, *Introduction and 1:1–2:47* (Grand Rapids: Baker Academic, 2012), 708–10.

persecution (8:1, 4; 9:31),[3] and then Paul and his coworkers proclaim the gospel throughout the Gentile world as far as Rome (19:21; 23:11; 28:14).[4]

In the context of the gospel's advance to the end of the earth, Acts describes early Christian worship in a variety of ways.[5]

1. The key term *latreuō* occurs infrequently in Acts to refer to Israel's true and false cultic service in the Old Testament (7:7, 42) and Israel's earnest worship in the first century (26:7). Paul stresses during his trial that he worships "the God of our fathers" in accordance with the Law and Prophets (24:14) and later states that he belongs to and worships God (27:23).

2. Similarly, the verb *proskuneō* conveys an attitude or posture of submission or homage before a deity or a superior. Strikingly, the disciples worship the Lord Jesus after his ascension (Luke 24:52). The Ethiopian eunuch and Paul both travel to Jerusalem to worship in the temple (Acts 8:27; 24:11). Cornelius falls down and worships Peter before being reprimanded (10:25). Stephen recounts that God sent Israel into exile for bowing down before images (7:43).

3. *Leitourgeō* and the related noun *leitourgia* denote priestly service to God in Luke 1:23, Hebrews 10:11, and regularly in the Septuagint. Acts 13:2 refers to prophets and teachers in Antioch (and perhaps the whole church) "worshiping [*leitourgountōn*] the Lord and fasting." The "worship" of gathered Christians here is closely linked to the exercise of spiritual gifts such as prophecy and teaching (v. 1) and prayer (v. 3).

4. The verb *sebomai* and its cognates refer to worship and devotion to God (13:43; 16:14; 18:7, 13) or to pagan deities (17:23; 19:27).

5. Believers live in "the fear of the Lord" (9:31). Fear (*phobos* or *phobeomai*) conveys the profound awe and reverence people

---

3. On the link between persecution and mission, see Brian J. Tabb, "Salvation, Spreading, and Suffering: God's Unfolding Plan in Luke-Acts," *JETS* 58 (2015): 51–53.

4. Rome is not strictly speaking "the end of the world" (1:8) but serves an anticipatory or proleptic function in Acts "as representative of the whole world," according to C. K. Barrett, *Acts 1–14*, ICC (Edinburgh: T&T Clark, 1994), 80. "The end of the earth" in Acts 1:8 and 13:47 alludes to Isaiah 49:6 and carries theopolitical connotations of the inclusion of the Gentiles within God's people, according to David W. Pao, *Acts and the Isaianic New Exodus*, BSL (Grand Rapids: Baker Academic, 2002), 91–96.

5. This paragraph is informed by the surveys in I. Howard Marshall, "How Far Did the Early Christians Worship God?," *Chm* 99 (1985): 217–20; Steve Walton, "Your Praise Reaches to the End of the Earth: Worship in the Book of Acts" (paper presented at the Deep Calls to Deep Worship Symposium, London School of Theology, 2008).

experience in response to manifestations of God's power and presence (5:5, 31; 19:17).

6. Acts refers to believers glorifying (*doxazō*), praising (*aineō*), and magnifying (*megalynō*) God (2:47; 3:8–9; 4:21; 10:46; 11:18; 21:20), the word of the Lord (13:48), and the name of the Lord Jesus (19:17).

Luke also frequently depicts people praying (*proseuchomai*), petitioning (*deomai*), and thanking (*eucharisteō*) God.[6] For example, the disciples devote themselves to prayer after Jesus's ascension (1:14) and pray for guidance regarding Judas's successor (1:24). The believers in Jerusalem respond to opposition and threats with a model prayer for continued boldness (4:24–31). Peter and Paul receive revelatory visions while praying (10:9–10; 16:9; 18:9; 22:17). The church gathers in Mary's home to offer earnest petitionary prayer for Peter while he is in prison (12:5, 12). Believers pray and fast when commissioning Paul and Barnabas for a new work and appointing elders in the churches (13:3; 14:23). Paul and Silas pray and sing hymns to God while in custody in Philippi (16:25). Believers pray together before saying goodbye to Paul (20:36; 21:5). Peter prays for Dorcas, and Paul prays and lays hands on Publius's father, and both are healed (9:40; 28:8). God's people pray to express their devotion, gratitude, and dependence on God, who consistently and powerfully acts in response to these petitions.

THEOLOGY OF WORSHIP

Acts contributes significantly to the New Testament's theology of worship by describing the preaching and practices of the earliest Christians following Jesus's ascension. At least five significant redemptive-historical transitions inform and shape how and why Christ's followers gathered for worship: (1) the *object* of worship, (2) the *time* of worship, (3) the *people* who worship, (4) the *places* of worship, and (5) the *manner* of worship.

The Object of Worship

Jesus affirms the Old Testament insistence on worshiping Yahweh alone. The divine Son resists Satan's calls to "worship me" by citing Deuteronomy 6:13: "You shall worship [*proskynēseis*] the Lord your God, and him only shall you serve [*latreuseis*]" (Luke 4:8). In Acts 18:13, the Jews accuse Paul of "persuading people to worship [*sebesthai*] God contrary to

6. For examples and discussion, see Joel B. Green, "Persevering Together in Prayer: The Significance of Prayer in the Acts of the Apostles," in *Into God's Presence: Prayer in the New Testament*, ed. Richard N. Longenecker, McMaster New Testament Studies (Grand Rapids: Eerdmans, 2001), 183–202; J. Gary Millar, *Calling on the Name of the Lord: A Biblical Theology of Prayer*, NSBT 38 (Downers Grove, IL: IVP Academic, 2016), 191–200.

the law." Acts repeatedly shows that these charges are baseless and that Paul and early Christians worship God faithfully and truly. For example, Paul asserts during his hearing before Felix the governor, "I worship [*latreuō*] the God of our fathers, believing everything laid down by the Law and written in the Prophets" (24:14; cf. 24:11; 26:7; 27:23).

Acts sharply distinguishes between the true God, who alone is worthy of worship, and human beings, who are made to give—not receive—praise. In Acts 10:25–26 and 14:11–15, Peter, Paul, and Barnabas rebuff expressions of worship by insisting that they are merely men.[7] In 12:22–23, King Herod receives idolatrous praise from the people and is struck dead "because he did not give God the glory."

At the same time, "Luke is clear that worship of the God of Israel entails worship of the risen Jesus as Lord."[8] The closing verses of the third gospel state that Jesus "was carried up into heaven" and his disciples "worshiped him [*proskynēsantes auton*] and returned to Jerusalem with great joy" (Luke 24:51–52).[9] They then continue "blessing God" in the temple (v. 53). It is striking that the only other occurrences of *proskyneō* in Luke's gospel come in the temptation narrative (4:7–8), where Jesus affirms that the Lord only is worthy of worship.[10] Further, Luke 24:52–53 presents no tension between "worshiping" Jesus and "blessing" God. These expressions of praise, adoration, and devotion are complementary and fitting given Luke's repeated identification of Jesus as *kyrios*, "the Lord," which signals his "shared identity" with the God of Israel.[11] Jesus not only shares Yahweh's designation as *kyrios*; he acts as only Yahweh can act and thus is worthy of worship reserved for Yahweh alone. When the disciples in Luke 24 worship the ascended Lord Jesus, it signals that they "have, at last, recognized Jesus for who he is."[12] This passage also highlights what David

7. Alan J. Thompson, "The Trinity in Luke-Acts," in *The Essential Trinity: New Testament Foundations and Practical Relevance*, ed. Brandon Crowe and Carl Trueman (Leicester: Apollos, 2016), 68.
8. Dennis Hamm, "The Tamid Service in Luke-Acts: The Cultic Background behind Luke's Theology of Worship (Luke 1:5–25; 18:9–14; 24:50–53; Acts 3:1; 10:3, 30)," *CBQ* 65 (2003): 230. Similarly, Peterson writes, "The exalted Lord Jesus is the object of devotion in the early churches" (David Peterson, *Engaging with God: A Biblical Theology of Worship* [Leicester: Inter-Varsity Press, 1992], 159).
9. It is remarkable that there is no discussion of Luke 24:51–53 in the massive study of biblical worship by Allen P. Ross, *Recalling the Hope of Glory: Biblical Worship from the Garden to the New Creation* (Grand Rapids: Kregel Academic, 2006). Daniel Block offers scant treatment of Luke 24:52 in a single footnote and an appendix table, in *For the Glory of God: Recovering a Biblical Theology of Worship* (Grand Rapids: Baker Academic, 2014), 15n46, 363. Block imprecisely states that 24:52–53 presents "God" as the object of worship (p. 363). Rather, the disciples bless God in verse 53 and worship the exalted Jesus in verse 52.
10. Alan J. Thompson, *Luke*, Exegetical Guide to the Greek New Testament (Nashville: Broadman & Holman, 2017), 380.
11. C. Kavin Rowe, *Early Narrative Christology: The Lord in the Gospel of Luke*, BZNW 139 (Berlin: de Gruyter, 2006), 77. For a similar stress, see Richard B. Hays, *Reading Backwards: Figural Christology and the Fourfold Gospel Witness* (Waco, TX: Baylor University Press, 2014), 64–66.
12. Joel B. Green, *The Gospel of Luke*, NICNT (Grand Rapids: Eerdmans, 1997), 862.

Peterson dubs "the paradox of early Christian worship": the disciples venerate Jesus, the glorified Messiah, apart from the traditional context of Jewish worship, yet they continue to praise God in the Jerusalem temple (Luke 24:52–53).[13]

The Time of Worship

The second crucial redemptive-historical transition that affects the church's worship in Acts is the dawning of "the last days" and the inauguration of the kingdom of God. Alan Thompson has rightly argued that the book of Acts is best understood within the framework of "inaugurated eschatology."[14] The Scriptures present the Creator God as the rightful King of Israel and the whole world, who will one day reestablish his dominion, judge his enemies, save his people, and restore lasting justice and peace.[15]

In Luke's Gospel, Jesus announces that the kingdom of God "has drawn near" (*ēggiken* [10:9, 11]), "arrived" (*ephthasen* [11:20]), and is "in your midst" (*entos hymōn* [17:21]). He also announces a future "coming" of the kingdom (11:2; 22:18).[16]

The book of Acts opens and concludes with references to God's kingdom (1:3, 6; 28:23, 31), which suggests that Luke frames his narrative around this crucial theme.[17]

The ascension of Jesus, narrated in Luke 24:51 and Acts 1:9–11, does not mark the absence or deferral of the kingdom of God but rather a new stage of its inaugurated fulfillment. Peter declares in Acts 2:33, "Being therefore exalted at the right hand of God, and having received from the Father the promise of the Holy Spirit, he has poured out this that you yourselves are seeing and hearing." Earlier in his speech, the apostle interprets the remarkable events of Pentecost as proof that God has fulfilled his ancient promise: "But this is what was uttered through the prophet Joel: 'And in the last days it shall be, God declares, that I will pour out my Spirit on all flesh'" (Acts 2:16–17, citing Joel 2:28 [3:1 LXX]). The phrase "in the last days" comes not from Joel but from Isaiah 2:2 (LXX): "For *in the last days* the mountain of the Lord shall be manifest . . . and all the nations shall come to it" (NETS).

Thus Peter makes clear that the Lord Jesus has begun to reign at God's right hand and has poured out the Holy Spirit to fulfill God's ancient promises through the prophets (Joel 2:28–32) and his own words to his followers (Luke 24:49; Acts 1:4–5). Acts 2:17 also signals that God's people

13. Peterson, *Engaging with God*, 147.
14. Thompson, *Acts of the Risen Lord Jesus*, 125.
15. This paragraph adapts material from Brian J. Tabb, *Suffering in Ancient Worldview: Luke, Seneca, and 4 Maccabees in Dialogue*, LNTS 569 (London: Bloomsbury T&T Clark, 2017), 190.
16. John Nolland, "Salvation-History and Eschatology," in *Witness to the Gospel: The Theology of Acts*, eds. I. Howard Marshall and David G. Peterson (Grand Rapids: Eerdmans, 1998), 68–70.
17. Thompson, *Acts of the Risen Lord Jesus*, 44–48; Michael Wolter, "'Reich Gottes' bei Lukas," *NTS* 41 (1995): 541.

now live in the eschatological time of restoration and renewal that the prophets referred to as "the last days."[18]

Jesus's heavenly ascension and pouring out of the Spirit in Acts 1–2 serve as foundational events in Luke's narrative that have direct bearing on the church's identity, mission, and worship. Beale has convincingly shown that the Spirit's coming in Acts 2:1–4 reflects a theophany, particularly God's paradigmatic self-revelation at Sinai (Exod. 19:16–20; 20:18).[19] In Exodus 19, God's awesome presence descends on Mount Sinai and only Moses is allowed to come up to the mountain's top while the people stand fearfully at its foot. But Acts 2 depicts God's Spirit coming to rest on his people, which leads them to proclaim his mighty deeds of salvation.

Acts explains that Jesus, the true messianic king, has ascended to heaven and poured out the end-time Spirit on his people, which recalls Ezekiel's prophecy that Yahweh's servant David will reign over Israel, and Yahweh will set his sanctuary in their midst forever (Ezek. 37:24, 26).[20] The allusion to Isaiah 2:2 in Acts 2:17 further signals that "in the last days," God is establishing his end-time temple ("the mountain of the house of the Lord"), from which the word of God will go forth and to which the nations shall come (Isa. 2:2–3).[21] The events of Pentecost make clear that God's Spirit inhabits not the Jerusalem temple but everyone who calls on the name of the Lord Jesus (Acts 2:21, 38). According to Acts, God is fulfilling his ancient promises and gathering his people from among the nations through the Spirit-empowered witness of his people (1:8). Thus the dawning of the last days in Acts directly influences who gathers to worship, where they worship, and how they worship.

The People Who Worship

Acts stresses that the events of the last days have brought about a change in marks and membership of the people of God in fulfillment of the Old Testament hopes. The apostle announces that Jesus has poured out the Spirit "on all flesh" (Acts 2:17), which recalls the prophetic expectation that "all flesh shall see the salvation of God" (Luke 3:6; Isa. 40:5 LXX). Moreover, Peter declares that Christ is "Lord of all" (Acts 10:36), a sweeping designation stressing his authority over all peoples, Jews and Gentiles. This spread of the gospel to new places and peoples occurs just as Jesus promised (1:8). In Acts 8, Philip proclaims "the Messiah" in the city of Samaria (v. 5), and the people receive the Word of God and the Holy Spirit (vv. 14–17). Samaria's response to the gospel of Christ signals not only the geographic spread of the Christian mission but also the fulfillment of

18. See Keener, *Acts 1:1–2:47*, 877–81.

19. G. K. Beale, *The Temple and the Church's Mission: A Biblical Theology of the Dwelling Place of God*, NSBT 17 (Downers Grove, IL: InterVarsity Press, 2004), 204–5.

20. Similarly Thompson, *Acts of the Risen Lord Jesus*, 148–49.

21. Beale, *The Temple and the Church's Mission*, 209.

God's promises to restore and reunite the divided kingdoms of Israel under a Davidic sovereign (Ezek. 37:22, 24).[22]

After preaching about Christ in Samaria, Philip meets an Ethiopian eunuch who "had come to Jerusalem to worship" and "proclaims to him the good news about Jesus" (8:26, 35). Luke refers to the man as "the eunuch" five times in Acts 8:27–39. This recalls the law's ban on eunuchs entering the assembly of God's people (Deut. 23:1) as well as the prophecy of salvation and inclusion for eunuchs and foreigners in Isaiah 56.[23] The prophet anticipates a day when the Lord would give to eunuchs "an everlasting name that shall not be cut off" (v. 5) and make foreigners joyful in his house of prayer (v. 7). Isaiah declares that Yahweh will gather "the outcasts of Israel" and "others" as well (v. 8). While the eunuch makes a pilgrimage to Jerusalem (Acts 8:27), where he would have been prevented from worshiping in the temple due to his physical condition, he experiences true joy after hearing the good news about Jesus and being baptized (v. 39). Thus Acts 8 signals that God is assembling the outcasts, such as Samaritans and a eunuch, in accordance with his promises.[24]

God also reveals to Peter that he "shows no partiality" by sending him to Cornelius's house and pouring out the Holy Spirit on the Gentiles (10:34, 44–45). This gift of the Spirit to Gentile believers unequivocally marks them as equal and full members of God's people (11:17–18). In Acts 15, the apostles and elders clarify *how* Gentiles will participate in God's saving plan.[25] They decide that Gentile believers do not need to be circumcised or keep the Mosaic law to be saved (15:1, 5); rather, Jews and Gentiles alike "will be saved through the grace of the Lord Jesus" (v. 11). James confirms that God promised to take from the Gentiles "a people for his name" by appealing to "the words of the prophets" (vv. 14–15). He cites Amos 9:11–12 (LXX), where God promises to rebuild and restore David's fallen tent, "that the remnant of mankind may seek the Lord, and all the Gentiles who are called by my name" (Acts 15:16–17). The renewal of the Davidic dynasty through Jesus's resurrection and heavenly reign thus leads to the Gentiles' full inclusion in God's eschatological people.[26]

Acts thus makes clear that "in the last days" God's people include men and women from every nation who are saved by Jesus, baptized in the name of Jesus, and receive the promised Holy Spirit. Those who experience eschatological salvation and blessing through Christ consistently respond by rejoicing and glorifying God. When Philip proclaims the good

22. Thompson, *Acts of the Risen Lord Jesus*, 114–16. Cf. Pao, *Acts and the Isaianic New Exodus*, 127–29.
23. Thompson, *Acts of the Risen Lord Jesus*, 116–18.
24. David Seccombe, "The New People of God," in Marshall and Peterson, *Witness to the Gospel*, 360.
25. Thompson, *Acts of the Risen Lord Jesus*, 120.
26. For support of this interpretation of Acts 9:11–12 and discussion of the hermeneutical and textual complexities, see Edward W. Glenny, "The Septuagint and Apostolic Hermeneutics: Amos 9 in Acts 15," *BBR* 22 (2012): 1–26.

news in Samaria, "there was much joy in that city" (8:8). When Paul and Barnabas announce that they are turning to the Gentiles with their message of salvation in fulfillment of Isaiah 49:6, the Gentiles "began rejoicing and glorifying the word of the Lord, and as many as were appointed to eternal life believed" (13:46–48). The churches in Phoenicia and Samaria experience great joy when they learn of the Gentiles' conversion (15:3), and the Antioch church rejoices when they receive the letter from Jerusalem (15:31). Likewise, the Philippian jailer is baptized and "rejoiced along with his entire household that he had believed in God" (16:33). Thus genuine joy characterizes the worship of God's people from every nation who are saved and baptized in Jesus's name.

The Places of Worship

The early chapters of Acts repeatedly reference the Jerusalem temple as a place of worship, prayer, revelation, and ministry for the apostles and the early church. Acts 2:46–47 summarizes the early practice of Jesus's followers who "day by day" attended the temple, broke bread in their homes, praised God, and enjoyed favor with the people. Acts twice specifies that the early Christians gathered together at Solomon's Colonnade on the east side of the temple's outer court (3:11; 5:12).[27]

Peter and John went to the temple "at the hour of prayer, the ninth hour" (3:1). While it is reasonable to infer that the apostles and early Christians participated in the traditional prayers in the temple, the narrative focuses on their preaching about Jesus and healing in his name, not their Jewish piety or allegiance to the temple cult.[28]

Acts 3:7–8 describes the lame man "leaping" and "praising God" as he entered the temple with language that recalls the prophecy of eschatological renewal in Isaiah 35:6, as well as Jesus's description of his ministry in Luke 7:22.[29] This healing and the proclamation of salvation in Jesus's name alone put the apostles in direct conflict with the temple authorities (Acts 4:1–22). This conflict intensifies in Acts 5, when an angel leads the apostles out of prison and directs them to return to the temple to teach "all the words of this Life" (v. 19–20). The Jewish council interrogates the apostles then beats them and prohibits them from speaking in Jesus's name, but the apostles rejoice that they suffer for Jesus and resume their teaching and preaching "every day, in the temple and from house to house" (vv. 40–42).

Stephen's opponents falsely accuse him of speaking words "against this holy place and the law" and of saying that Jesus would destroy the temple and change their customs (6:11–13). In his extensive speech before

---

27. David G. Peterson, *The Acts of the Apostles*, PiNTC (Grand Rapids: Eerdmans, 2009), 162.
28. Geir Otto Holmås, "'My House Shall Be a House of Prayer': Regarding the Temple as a Place of Prayer in Acts within the Context of Luke's Apologetic Objective," *JSNT* 27 (2005): 404; Thompson, *Acts of the Risen Lord Jesus*, 152–53.
29. Thompson, *Acts of the Risen Lord Jesus*, 155–56.

the Jewish council, Stephen ironically and incisively turns these charges back on his accusers, who have not grasped the temple's true nature and purpose and have not heeded the law themselves (7:53).[30] He strikingly refers to the temple as "made with hands" (*cheiropoiētos*)—a term always used of idols in the Septuagint—because it has become for them idolatrous (7:48).[31] Climactically, in 7:55–56 Stephen looks to heaven and beholds the glory of God and Jesus standing at his right hand. Thompson writes, "In pointing to Jesus, therefore, Stephen points away from the temple, not just because God is bigger than the temple but because in the kingdom of God, which Jesus inaugurated, Jesus is the one who fulfills the goals of the temple."[32] True worship does not require a temple or shrine but genuine repentance and proper understanding of God as he has revealed himself most definitively by raising Jesus from the dead (vv. 30–31).[33]

The proper *place* of worship relates directly to Jesus as the proper *object* of worship, the new *time* for worship "in the last days," and the multiethnic *people* who worship God. Jesus declares that the temple has become "a den of robbers" instead of "a house of prayer" (Luke 19:46).[34] However, the vision of "a house of prayer for all peoples" (Isa. 56:7) is realized as Jesus's followers gather to pray and praise God in the temple (Luke 24:53; Acts 2:46–47), as well as in homes (Acts 1:14; 12:12), public locations (16:13), and even prison cells (16:25). The church prays in every place, and the good news about Jesus brings great joy to all peoples, including Samaritans, Gentiles, and eunuchs (8:8, 39; 13:48, 53; 16:34). This suggests that Isaiah's prophecy does not point merely to the reform of the Jerusalem temple but to its replacement. Acts and other New Testament writings present *Jesus* as the true temple.[35] Peter refers to Christ as "the cornerstone" (4:11, citing Ps. 118:22); he is the only one in whose name salvation and forgiveness may be found (Acts 2:38; 4:12; cf. Luke 24:47). The Lord Jesus reigns in glory and power, receives prayer, and grants forgiveness and access to God's heavenly presence (Acts 7:56, 59–60).[36] Moreover, Jesus pours out the divine Spirit "on all flesh," which means that Jews and Gentiles alike may worship God in Jesus's name with equal standing and access.

---

30. Adapted from Tabb, *Suffering in Ancient Worldview*, 132.
31. See Beale, *The Temple and the Church's Mission*, 224–25
32. Thompson, *Acts of the Risen Lord Jesus*, 170.
33. Brian J. Tabb, "The Nature of True Worship: Reading Acts 17 with Seneca, Epistle 95," in *Paul and the Greco-Roman Philosophical Tradition*, ed. Joseph Dodson and Andrew W. Pitts, LNTS 527 (London: Bloomsbury T&T Clark, 2017), 272.
34. On Jesus's appeals to the OT, see David W. Pao and Eckhard J. Schnabel, "Luke," in *Commentary on the New Testament Use of the Old Testament*, eds. G. K. Beale and D. A. Carson (Grand Rapids: Baker Academic, 2007), 357–60.
35. Walton, "A Tale of Two Perspectives? The Place of the Temple in Acts," in *Heaven on Earth: The Temple in Biblical Theology*, eds. T. Desmond Alexander and Simon J. Gathercole (Carlisle: Paternoster, 2004), 144–46.
36. Thompson, "The Trinity in Luke-Acts," 77–78.

In Acts, believers meet together for prayer, fellowship, instruction, and worship in a variety of locations. In addition to Solomon's Colonnade, the churches regularly gather in believers' homes. This pattern begins in 1:13–14, when the disciples gather to pray in "the upper room" at a Jerusalem home. After Pentecost, believers continue meeting together in homes in Jerusalem (2:46; 5:42), including the house of John Mark's mother (12:12). Paul states that he teaches the whole counsel of God "in public and from house to house" (20:20), which includes ministry in various synagogues[37] and at the homes of believers such as Lydia in Philippi (16:15, 40), Jason in Thessalonica (17:5–7), and Titius Justus in Corinth (18:7). After experiencing opposition in the synagogue in Ephesus, Paul meets daily for two years with Jewish and Gentile disciples in the hall of Tyrannus (19:9–10). Thus we see early Christians gather for prayer, worship, and instruction in a variety of places, including the Jerusalem temple, synagogues, homes, and public spaces.

The Manner of Worship

Acts offers occasional glimpses into the patterns and priorities of believers' corporate gatherings. In particular, Acts 2:41–47 and 13:1–3 offer important insights into the manner of worship in the early church.

In 2:41, three thousand people receive Peter's word and are baptized and added to the community of Jesus's followers.[38] Luke then highlights four important features of the gatherings of believers beginning in verse 42: "And they devoted themselves to the apostles' teaching and the fellowship, to the breaking of bread and the prayers."

First, Luke's summary begins appropriately with the early church's persistent attention to apostolic teaching or instruction (*didachē*). The risen Jesus instructed the apostles, opened their minds to understand the Scriptures, and designated them as his "witnesses" (Luke 24:44–48; Acts 1:1–8). Luke records the apostles' resolute devotion to prayer and the ministry of the Word (Acts 6:4) and the church's devotion to their instruction (2:42). The apostles teach in the name of Jesus and proclaim that he is the Messiah (5:28, 42). Their ministry of instruction includes "testimony to the resurrection of the Lord Jesus" in the power of the Holy Spirit (4:33; cf. 1:8, 22; 4:2). Acts concludes by highlighting Paul's continued ministry of the word during his house arrest in Rome, "proclaiming the kingdom of God and teaching about the Lord Jesus Christ with all boldness and without hindrance" (28:31).

---

37. On the role of the synagogue in Paul's mission strategy, see Eckhard J. Schnabel, *Paul the Missionary: Realities, Strategies and Methods* (Downers Grove, IL: IVP Academic, 2008), 288–93.

38. While many commentators outline Acts 2:41 with the preceding section (following the NA[28] and most English translations), the introductory marker *hoi men oun* signals that this verse begins a new section that depicts believers' life together. Cf. Barrett, *Acts*, 159; Peterson, *Acts*, 158; Keener, *Acts 1:1–2:47*, 991.

Second, Acts highlights the early Christians' devotion to "the fellowship" (2:42). The term *koinōnia* connotes "close association involving mutual interests and sharing,"[39] and verses 44–47 describe several characteristics of this *koinōnia.* The believers "were together" (*epi to auto*), formally translated "in the same place." They "had all things in common" (*koina*), selling possessions to meet one another's needs (cf. 4:32). Further, they continue "together" or "with one mind"; the term *homothymadon* suggests that believers are not simply in the same place but have "a shared commitment of heart and mind."[40] The early Christians thus regularly met together and generously shared their material goods with one another "as an expression of the unity of the community in common allegiance to the Lord Jesus."[41]

Third, the believers persisted in "the breaking of bread" (v. 42). Some interpreters argue that "breaking of bread" designates the Lord's Supper, appealing to the words of institution in Luke 22:19 and the gathering to break bread "on the first day of the week" in Acts 20:7.[42] However, Luke explains in 2:46 that they broke bread "in their homes" and "received their food with glad and sincere hearts" (NIV). Thus, while "the breaking of bread" probably evokes "memories of Jesus,"[43] the primary thrust in Acts 2 is on the early Christians eating regular meals together.[44] Similarly, in 20:11 Paul breaks bread, eats, and converses with the believers, which suggests an ordinary meal and most likely clarifies the reference to breaking bread in 20:7.[45] Likewise, in 27:35 Paul initiates a meal with the sailors by thanking God, breaking the bread, and beginning to eat. Thus in Acts "the breaking of bread" refers primarily to believers' shared meals together, which powerfully express their unity and fellowship.

Fourth, Luke refers to the early Christians devoting themselves to "the prayers" (v. 42). The plural use of "prayers" may refer to observing

---

39. BDAG, 552.
40. Steve Walton, "*Homothymadon* in Acts: Co-location, Common Action or 'Of One Heart and Mind'?," in *The New Testament in Its First Century Setting: Essays on Context and Background in Honour of B. W. Winter on His 65th Birthday*, eds. Peter J. Williams, Andrew D. Clarke, Peter M. Head, and David Instone-Brewer (Grand Rapids: Eerdmans, 2004), 101. Cf. 1:14; 4:24; 5:12.
41. Alan J. Thompson, *One Lord, One People: The Unity of the Church in Acts in Its Literary Setting*, LNTS 359 (London: T&T Clark, 2008), 67.
42. For summaries of scholarship on meals and the Lord's Supper in Luke-Acts, see François Bovon, *Luke the Theologian: Fifty-Five Years of Research (1950–2005)*, 2nd ed. (Waco, TX: Baylor University Press, 2006), 563–65; Keener, *Acts 1:1–2:47*, 1003–11. Second-century Christian writers employ "breaking bread" as a technical expression for the Lord's Supper (e.g. Didache 14.1; Ignatius, *To the Ephesians* 20:2; Irenaeus, *Against Heresies* 5.2.2). For a nuanced discussion of "the first day of the week" in Acts 20:7, see Max Turner, "The Sabbath, Sunday, and the Law in Luke/Acts" in *From Sabbath to Lord's Day*, ed. D. A. Carson (Grand Rapids: Zondervan, 1982), 128–37.
43. Fiona J. Robertson Gregson, *Everything in Common? The Theology and Practice of the Sharing of Possessions in Community in the New Testament* (Eugene, OR: Pickwick, 2017), 50.
44. Peterson, *Acts*, 160. cf. Luke 24:30, 35; Acts 27:35.
45. Longenecker comments that breaking bread in 20:7 "must surely mean 'to celebrate the Lord's Supper'" but says that the same phrase in 20:11 signifies "an ordinary meal" (Longenecker, "Acts," 1024).

regular times of prayer according to traditional Jewish practice (cf. 3:1).[46] Alternatively, this may express "a more general commitment to prayer," which recalls the prayer gathering of Jesus's followers in 1:14 and anticipates later depictions of the Jerusalem church's characteristic practice of prayer (4:23–31; 6:6; 12:12).[47] In 2:47, the believers praise God while eating together in homes. Acts presents believers praying and praising God in a variety of contexts and situations. God's people ask God for healing (9:4; 28:8), guidance (1:24; 13:3), deliverance (12:12), boldness, and power (4:29–30). They pray to express their devotion to God (10:9; 22:17), submission to his will (21:14), and gratitude for his provision and blessing (27:35; 28:15). In his Pentecost sermon, Peter declares that "everyone who calls upon the name of the Lord shall be saved" (2:21, citing Joel 2:28 [3:5 LXX]). Later, believers draw on Joel's prophecy to describe themselves as "those who call upon the name of the Lord" (9:14, 21), which suggests the fundamental place of prayer in the early church.[48]

Acts 13:1–3 offers an important glimpse into the worship and ministry at the church in Antioch. Verse 1 names a diverse group of five leaders in the church of Antioch who are designated "prophets and teachers." Barnabas, the Jewish Christian from Cyprus, was sent by the Jerusalem church to Antioch to encourage and instruct the new believers there, and Barnabas brought Saul from Tarsus to join him (11:22–26). Simeon's nickname "Niger" probably refers to his dark complexion,[49] while Lucius hails from Cyrene in North Africa and may have come to Antioch to evangelize the Greek speakers (11:20). Manaen was a person of high social status, who was brought up with Herod Antipas and would have been at least sixty years old.[50]

Luke presents those gathered in Antioch "worshiping [*leitourgountōn*] the Lord and fasting" when the Holy Spirit directs them to set apart Barnabas and Saul for a new work (13:2). It is unclear whether this verse describes a regular meeting of the church or only the prophets and teachers mentioned in verse 1, though the former is likely for several reasons.[51] Verse 1 situates the prophets and teachers "in the church at Antioch." Luke's earlier depiction of the Antioch church refers to Barnabas and Saul meeting "with the church" (*en tē ekklēsia* [11:26]). Similarly, when prophets come from Jerusalem to Antioch, Agabus "arose" and delivered his prophetic word concerning the famine by the Spirit (11:27–28). Luke's

46. Keener, *Acts 1:1–2:47*, 1011. Cf. "the hour of prayer" in 3:1.
47. Millar, *Calling on the Name of the Lord*, 192. Cf. Holmås, "My House Shall Be a House of Prayer," 402–3.
48. Green, "Persevering Together in Prayer," 194–95; Millar, *Calling on the Name of the Lord*, 194.
49. BDAG, 672. For a nuanced discussion, see Craig S. Keener, *Acts: An Exegetical Commentary*, vol. 2, *Acts 3:1–14:28* (Grand Rapids: Baker Academic, 2013), 1984–87.
50. Keener, *Acts 3:1–14:28*, 1988–90.
51. For the former view, see Eckhard J. Schnabel, *Acts*, ZECNT (Grand Rapids: Zondervan, 2012), 554–55. For the latter, see Barrett, *Acts*, 604–5.

presentation suggests that Agabus stands and speaks this prophecy when the Antioch church is assembled;[52] "the disciples" then respond to this revelation by acting "every one according to his ability" (v. 29). Returning to 13:2, it is most likely that the Spirit's call to set apart Barnabas and Saul comes as a revelation to one of the prophets when the church is gathered for prayer and worship. As in 11:29, it is probably the assembled believers and not simply the leaders mentioned in 13:1 who respond to the Spirit's revelation with prayer, fasting, and commissioning (v. 3).

Acts 13:2 is the only place where Luke clearly applies the language of worship to a Christian gathering.[53] In extrabiblical Greek, *leitourgeō* may refer to the work of public officials or other acts of service.[54] In the Septuagint, *leitourgeō* regularly denotes the ministerial duties of the priest (e.g., Exod. 28:35; Deut. 10:8). Elsewhere in the New Testament, *leitourgeō* refers to priestly service under the old covenant (Heb. 10:11) and to Gentile Christians serving Jewish believers by sharing material blessings (Rom. 15:27).

Commentators interpret "worshiping" in this verse in at least three ways. (1) Some argue that it refers to praying, since verse 3 pairs "fasting and praying." Thus I. Howard Marshall asserts that "prayer is regarded as the 'cultic' activity of the church."[55] (2) Alternatively, Eckhard Schnabel interprets this reference to worship more broadly to encompass various aspects of the church's life together such as prayer, teaching, and the breaking of bread.[56] (3) Peterson offers a third option, suggesting that the prophets and teachers (v. 1) employ their gifts for the benefit of other believers as "a specific way of serving or worshiping God under the new covenant."[57] Some combination of the second and third interpretations is most likely.

While *leitourgeō* may include prayer, it is overly restrictive to limit "worshiping" to praying. Rather, "worshiping the Lord" serves as a summary reference to the believers' devotion to, delight in, and dependence on the Lord as expressed in corporate petition, thanksgiving, and praise. In 20:19, Paul refers to his teaching ministry in Ephesus with the similar expression "serving the Lord" (*douleuōn tō kyriō*), so "worshiping the Lord" in 13:2 may include teaching, prophesying, and exercising other spiritual gifts in the context of the church's life together.

Acts gives precious little detail regarding the external forms or structures of the church's corporate gatherings. The narrative regularly presents

52. Keener, *Acts 3:1–14:28*, 1853.

53. David G. Peterson, "The Worship of the New Community," in Marshall and Peterson, *Witness to the Gospel*, 388.

54. LSJ, 1036.

55. I. Howard Marshall, *Acts: An Introduction and Commentary*, TNTC 5 (Downers Grove, IL: IVP Academic, 1980), 229.

56. Schnabel, *Acts*, 554–55.

57. Peterson, *Engaging with God*, 151. Similarly F. F. Bruce, *The Book of the Acts*, rev. ed., NICNT (Grand Rapids: Eerdmans, 1988), 245.

believers together for teaching, prayer, fellowship, and breaking bread (e.g., 2:42). Their communal life together is marked by radical generosity, unity, and love for each other (2:44–45; 4:32, 34); the fear of God (5:5, 11); joy and perseverance even in suffering (5:41; 14:22); earnest, God-centered prayer (4:23–30); and bold proclamation in Jesus's name (4:31). In particular, Luke highlights the centrality and priority of the apostles' teaching in the community of God's people. Luke's depictions of the early Christian community "show that God was truly among his people."[58]

Summary

While Acts occasionally uses common Greek verbs for worship (e.g., *latreuō, proskyneō, leitourgeō*) and praise (e.g., *aineō*), the book's treatment of the early church's worship cannot be reduced to the occurrence of such terms and must be situated within the context of the substantial redemptive-historical transition "in the last days" (Acts 2:17; cf. Isa. 2:2).

First, Luke presents Christians praising and praying to the exalted Lord Jesus and declaring that salvation is available in his name alone (Luke 24:52; Acts 4:12; 7:59–60). The God of Israel has fulfilled his ancient promises and revealed himself through the person of Jesus Christ, such that Christians fittingly venerate Jesus as the object of their worship.

Second, Acts makes clear that by ascending into heaven and pouring out the Holy Spirit on his people, Jesus has ushered in "the last days" about which the prophets spoke (2:17, 33).

Third, Acts presents a decisive transition in the marks and membership of the people of God, as Jews, Samaritans, and Gentiles call on the same Lord, experience the same baptism, and receive the same Spirit.

Fourth, Luke narrates a transition in the role of the Jerusalem temple and a decentralization of worship for the people of God. For a season, Jesus's followers continue gathering in the temple following his ascension (Luke 24:53; Acts 2:46). The narrative does not stress believers' devotion to Jewish worship practices but their allegiance to and adoration of the exalted Lord Jesus, who realizes the temple's goals and thus relativizes its role as the centralized place for worship. The early Christians gather in a variety of locations, including the temple, synagogues, homes, and public spaces.

Fifth, Acts does not elaborate on the external forms or structures of the early church's corporate meetings but stresses three key features of their life together: (1) steadfast devotion to the apostles' teaching about Jesus; (2) bold, God-centered prayers; and (3) radical fellowship characterized by unity, love, sharing of material blessings, and eating together (2:42–47; 4:23–37).

SIGNIFICANCE OF ACTS FOR BIBLICAL WORSHIP

According to Peterson, "Worship in New Testament terms means responding with one's whole life and being to the divine kingship of

58. Seccombe, "The New People of God," 355.

Jesus."[59] He adds that for the early church, "'worship' was a way of life with Jesus at its centre."[60] These summaries rightly capture the stress in Acts on the centrality and supremacy the Lord Jesus Christ, which has far-reaching significance for every area of our lives, not simply corporate "worship services" on Sunday mornings. For example, the opponents of the early church claimed that the believers "turned the world upside down . . . saying that there is another king, Jesus" (17:6–7). At the same time, Luke's descriptions of believers' communal life together have significant implications for how Christians today conceive of the church and its priorities. Walton explains that Luke's summary in Acts 2:42–47 is programmatic for the corporate life of the early church and suggests that this portrait invites readers "to identify with those believers and to live and respond to God in similar ways."[61]

Believers' whole lives are marked by a commitment to worship and serve the Lord Jesus, and they regularly express their devotion to and dependence on Christ by meeting together. According to Acts, such worship gatherings should be marked by (1) commitment to apostolic teaching, (2) constant prayer and praise, and (3) radical unity, love, and joy.

Apostolic Teaching

Acts stresses the priority and centrality of preaching and teaching to the church's life together. The early church did not simply gather to consider a weekly sermon; they were constantly committed to hearing and heeding sound teaching. The apostles unceasingly taught and proclaimed Jesus "every day, in the temple and from house to house" (5:42). Similarly, the Bereans thoroughly studied the Scriptures daily (Acts 17:11), and Paul reasoned daily with the disciples in Ephesus (19:9) and taught "in public and from house to house" (20:20). Such teaching and preaching about Jesus is an expression of true worship (13:2; 20:19). This ministry of the word not only gives birth to the church (19:20) and furthers Jesus's mission plan to the end of the earth (1:8); it also edifies and strengthens the souls of believers (11:23; 14:22; 20:32).[62] The Holy Spirit empowers the apostles to testify to the resurrection of Jesus Christ and steward the commands of Jesus for his people (1:2, 8, 22). Both men and women respond to the apostolic gospel message by repenting of their sins, being baptized in Jesus's name, and joining the believing community devoted to the apostles' teaching and true worship (2:37–42; 5:14; 17:12). The church's obedient response to divine revelation about Jesus distinguishes its worship

59. Peterson, *Engaging with God*, 144.

60. Peterson, *Engaging with God*, 150.

61. Steve Walton, "A Spirituality of Acts?," in *Reading Acts Today: Essays in Honour of Loveday Alexander*, eds. Steve Walton, Thomas E. Phillips, Lloyd K. Petersen, and F. Scott Spencer, LNTS 427 (London: Bloomsbury T&T Clark, 2011), 200.

62. For similar emphases, see Peterson, *Engaging with God*, 153; Thompson, *Acts of the Risen Lord Jesus*, 66.

from that of Gentiles, who ignorantly worship lifeless idols instead of the living God (14:15; 17:23, 29), and from unbelieving Jews, who condemned Jesus because they were ignorant about his true identity as revealed by the prophets (13:27; cf. 3:17). In contrast, the church offers acceptable worship in response to redemption in Jesus's name, revelation by the Holy Spirit, and instruction from the apostles, prophets, and teachers (2:47; 13:2). The worshiping church should be a people of the word.

Constant Prayer and Praise

Acts presents constant prayer and praise as hallmarks of biblical worship. Jesus's followers pray to express their devotion, gratitude, and dependence on God, who consistently and powerfully acts in response to these petitions. In Acts, believers "call upon the name of the Lord" Jesus to be saved (2:21). On several occasions, they also pray to Jesus as the divine Lord who knows hearts, rules over his people, and grants forgiveness and access to God's presence (1:23–24; 7:59–60).[63]

Acts 4:24–31 offers an extended example of the early church's practice of prayer, and this passage informs our perspective on worship in several ways. First, their prayer is deeply God-centered and shaped by the Scriptures. The church "lift[s] their voices together to *God*" and addresses him as "sovereign Lord" (v. 24). They recognize God's awesome power as creator of heaven and earth (v. 24), employing the language of Psalm 146:6 (145:6 LXX). The believers acknowledge that God has revealed his word to his servants by the Holy Spirit (vv. 25–28; cf. Ps. 2:1–2). They also rehearse the outworking of God's sovereign plan in Jesus's suffering and their own trials (vv. 27–28).

Second, Jesus's followers pray in response to suffering and adverse circumstances.[64] Luke does not specify that this gathering takes place on a Sunday; rather, the church unites in prayer when they hear the apostles' report about the threats made by the Jewish leaders (vv. 23–24). The church does not pray that God would deliver them from adversity but that he would help and embolden them to continue speaking about Christ amid adversity (vv. 29–30).

Third, believers ask God to act in response to their prayers. The appeal "look upon their threats" expresses their belief that God is attentive to his people's plight (v. 29; cf. Exod. 2:25). They also petition God to continue to stretch out his hand to grant healings, signs, and wonders in Jesus's name. God then immediately and powerfully responds to his people's prayers by manifesting his presence, filling his people with the Spirit, and enabling them to persevere in bold preaching (v. 31). The model prayer in Acts 4:23–31 thus signals that the worshiping church should be a people of prayer and praise.

---

63. Thompson, "The Trinity in Luke-Acts," 76–78.
64. Geir Otto Holmås, *Prayer and Vindication in Luke-Acts: The Theme of Prayer within the Context of the Legitimating and Edifying Objective of the Lukan Narrative*, LNTS 433 (London: T&T Clark, 2011), 182; Tabb, *Suffering in Ancient Worldview*, 170.

Unity, Love, and Joy

Finally, Acts presents unity, love, and sharing as essential characteristics of the worshiping church. The believers in Acts are constantly "together," meeting at the temple, in homes, or wherever there is available space. We have seen that Christ's followers devoted themselves to the apostles' teaching and to prayer, but they also expressed their unity, love, and commitment to fellowship by regularly eating together and sharing their resources. In the ancient world, meals "established a relationship among those who partook," and the early church's *koinōnia* entailed sharing meals and material possessions (2:42–46; 4:32).[65] Jesus's followers eat together "with glad and sincere hearts" (2:46); these communal meals are occasions for joy and express their unity and common devotion to their risen Lord.

Moreover, the believers "were of one heart and soul" and sacrificially shared their resources with one another (4:32). Luke writes, "There was not a needy person among them," recalling the biblical vision for God's people expressed in Deuteronomy 15:4 (LXX). Acts does not present a form of "primitive communism," nor does it avoid recounting examples of corruption or neglect in the early church (5:1–2; 6:1). Rather, the early church "held their possessions lightly as in trust from God," ready to share what they had to meet the needs of their fellow believers.[66] In Acts 11:29–30, the disciples in Antioch send relief to "every one according to his ability" to express their solidarity with and support for believers in Judea affected by famine. In contrast to customary Roman practice, assistance comes not from a few wealthy patrons but from the whole community.[67]

The salvation offered in Jesus's name creates a prayerful, joyful, generous, dependent community of believers committed to carrying out his mission. Acts does not prescribe set times and forms for Christian worship; rather, it presents us with a compelling narrative of God's people submitting to Jesus's lordship and offering true worship marked by biblical teaching, God-centered prayer, and radical fellowship in Christ.[68]

BIBLIOGRAPHY

Barrett, C. K. *Acts 1–14*. ICC. London: T&T Clark, 1994.

Beale, G. K. *The Temple and the Church's Mission: A Biblical Theology of the Dwelling Place of God*. NSBT 17. Downers Grove, IL: InterVarsity Press, 2004.

Block, Daniel I. *For the Glory of God: Recovering a Biblical Theology of Worship*. Grand Rapids: Baker Academic, 2014.

65. Keener, *Acts 1:1–2:47*, 1006.
66. Steve Walton, "Primitive Communism in Acts? Does Acts Present the Community of Goods (2:44–45; 4:32–35) as Mistaken?," *EvQ* 80 (2008): 109.
67. Bruce W. Winter, "Acts and Food Shortages," in *The Book of Acts in Its Graeco-Roman Setting*, eds. David W. Gill and Conrad H. Gempf, BAFCS 2 (Grand Rapids: Eerdmans, 1994), 75–76.
68. I am grateful to Steve Walton, Alan Thompson, Hernan Wu, and Matt Denzer for offering comments and suggestions on this essay.

Bovon, François. *Luke the Theologian: Fifty-Five Years of Research (1950–2005)*. 2nd ed. Waco, TX: Baylor University Press, 2006.
Bruce, F. F. *The Book of the Acts*. rev. ed. NICNT. Grand Rapids: Eerdmans, 1988.
Glenny, Edward W. "The Septuagint and Apostolic Hermeneutics: Amos 9 in Acts 15." *BBR* 22 (2012): 1–26.
Green, Joel B. *The Gospel of Luke*. NICNT. Grand Rapids: Eerdmans, 1997.
______. "Persevering Together in Prayer: The Significance of Prayer in the Acts of the Apostles." *Into God's Presence: Prayer in the New Testament*, edited by Richard N. Longenecker, 183–202. McMaster New Testament Studies. Grand Rapids: Eerdmans, 2001.
Gregson, Fiona J. Robertson. *Everything in Common? The Theology and Practice of the Sharing of Possessions in Community in the New Testament*. Eugene, OR: Pickwick, 2017.
Hamm, Dennis. "The Tamid Service in Luke-Acts: The Cultic Background behind Luke's Theology of Worship (Luke 1:5–25; 18:9–14; 24:50–53; Acts 3:1; 10:3, 30)." *CBQ* 65 (2003): 215–31.
Hays, Richard B. *Reading Backwards: Figural Christology and the Fourfold Gospel Witness*. Waco, TX: Baylor University Press, 2014.
Holmås, Geir Otto. *Prayer and Vindication in Luke-Acts: The Theme of Prayer within the Context of the Legitimating and Edifying Objective of the Lukan Narrative*. LNTS 433. London: T&T Clark, 2011.
______. "'My House Shall Be a House of Prayer': Regarding the Temple as a Place of Prayer in Acts within the Context of Luke's Apologetic Objective." *JSNT* 27 (2005): 393–416.
Keener, Craig S. *Acts: An Exegetical Commentary*. Vol. 1, *Introduction and 1:1–2:47*. Grand Rapids: Baker Academic, 2012.
______. *Acts: An Exegetical Commentary*. Vol. 2, *3:1–14:28*. Grand Rapids: Baker Academic, 2013.
Kilgallen, John J. *The Stephen Speech: A Literary and Redactional Study of Acts 7, 2–53*. AnBib 67. Rome: Biblical Institute, 1976.
Longenecker, Richard N. "Acts." In *The Expositor's Bible Commentary*, vol. 10, *Luke–Acts*, edited by David E. Garland, 665–1102. Rev. ed. Grand Rapids: Zondervan, 2007.
Marshall, I. Howard. *Acts: An Introduction and Commentary*. TNTC 5. Downers Grove, IL: InterVarsity Press, 1980.
______. "How Far Did the Early Christians Worship God?" *Chm* 99 (1985): 216–29.
Millar, J. Gary. *Calling on the Name of the Lord: A Biblical Theology of Prayer*. NSBT 38. Downers Grove, IL: IVP Academic, 2016.
Nolland, John. "Salvation-History and Eschatology." In *Witness to the Gospel*, edited by I. Howard Marshall and David G. Peterson, 63–81. Grand Rapids: Eerdmans, 1998.
Pao, David W. *Acts and the Isaianic New Exodus*. BSL. Grand Rapids: Baker Academic, 2002.

Pao, David W., and Eckhard J. Schnabel. "Luke." In *Commentary on the New Testament Use of the Old Testament*, edited by G. K. Beale and D. A. Carson, 251–414. Grand Rapids: Baker Academic, 2007.

Peterson, David G. *The Acts of the Apostles*. PiNTC. Grand Rapids: Eerdmans, 2009.

______. *Engaging with God: A Biblical Theology of Worship*. Downers Grove, IL: InterVarsity Press, 2002.

______. "The Worship of the New Community." In *Witness to the Gospel: The Theology of Acts*, edited by I. Howard Marshall and David G. Peterson, 373–96. Grand Rapids: Eerdmans, 1998.

Ross, Allen P. *Recalling the Hope of Glory: Biblical Worship from the Garden to the New Creation*. Grand Rapids: Kregel Academic, 2006.

Rowe, C. Kavin. *Early Narrative Christology: The Lord in the Gospel of Luke*. BZNW 139. Berlin: de Gruyter, 2006.

Schnabel, Eckhard J. *Acts*. ZECNT. Grand Rapids: Zondervan, 2012.

______. *Paul the Missionary: Realities, Strategies and Methods*. Downers Grove, IL: IVP Academic, 2008.

Schreiner, Thomas R. *The King in His Beauty: A Biblical Theology of the Old and New Testaments*. Grand Rapids: Baker Academic, 2013.

Seccombe, David. "The New People of God." In *Witness to the Gospel: The Theology of Acts*, edited by I. Howard Marshall and David G. Peterson, 349–72. Grand Rapids: Eerdmans, 1998.

Sweeney, James P. "Stephen's Speech (Acts 7:2–53): Is it as 'Anti-temple' as Is Frequently Alleged?" *TJ* 23 (2002): 185–210.

Tabb, Brian J. "The Nature of True Worship: Reading Acts 17 with Seneca, Epistle 95." In *Paul and the Greco-Roman Philosophical Tradition*, edited by Joseph Dodson and Andrew W. Pitts, 263–78. LNTS 527. London: Bloomsbury T&T Clark, 2017.

______. "Salvation, Spreading, and Suffering: God's Unfolding Plan in Luke-Acts." *JETS* 58 (2015): 43–61.

______. *Suffering in Ancient Worldview: Luke, Seneca, and 4 Maccabees in Dialogue*. LNTS 569. London: Bloomsbury T&T Clark, 2017.

Thompson, Alan J. *The Acts of the Risen Lord Jesus: Luke's Account of God's Unfolding Plan*. NSBT 27. Downers Grove, IL: IVP Academic, 2011.

______. *Luke*. Exegetical Guide to the Greek New Testament. Nashville: B&H Academic, 2017.

______. *One Lord, One People: The Unity of the Church in Acts in Its Literary Setting*. LNTS 359. London: T&T Clark, 2008.

______. "The Trinity in Luke-Acts." In *The Essential Trinity: New Testament Foundations and Practical Relevance*, edited by Brandon Crowe and Carl Trueman, 62–82. Leicester: Apollos, 2016.

Turner, Max. "The Sabbath, Sunday, and the Law in Luke/Acts." In *From Sabbath to Lord's Day*, edited by D. A. Carson, 99–157. Grand Rapids: Zondervan, 1982.

Walton, Steve. "Primitive Communism in Acts? Does Acts Present the Community of Goods (2:44–45; 4:32–35) as Mistaken?" *EvQ* 80 (2008): 99–111.

______. "Your Praise Reaches to the End of the Earth: Worship in the Book of Acts." Paper presented at the Deep Calls to Deep Worship Symposium. London School of Theology, 2008.

______. "A Tale of Two Perspectives? The Place of the Temple in Acts." In *Heaven on Earth: The Temple in Biblical Theology*, edited by T. Desmond Alexander and Simon J. Gathercole, 135–49. Carlisle: Paternoster, 2004.

______. "A Spirituality of Acts?" In *Reading Acts Today: Essays in Honour of Loveday Alexander*, edited by Steve Walton, Thomas E. Phillips, Lloyd K. Petersen, and F. Scott Spencer, 186–201. LNTS 427. London: Bloomsbury T&T Clark, 2011.

______. "*Homothymadon* in Acts: Co-location, Common Action or 'Of One Heart and Mind'?" In *The New Testament in Its First Century Setting: Essays on Context and Background in Honour of B. W. Winter on His 65th Birthday*, edited by Peter J. Williams, Andrew D. Clarke, Peter M. Head, and David Instone-Brewer, 89–105. Grand Rapids: Eerdmans, 2004.

Winter, Bruce W. "Acts and Food Shortages." In *The Book of Acts in Its Graeco-Roman Setting*, edited by David W. Gill and Conrad H. Gempf, 59–78. BAFCS 2. Grand Rapids: Eerdmans, 1994.

Witherington, Ben, III. *The Acts of the Apostles: A Socio-rhetorical Commentary*. Grand Rapids: Eerdmans, 1998.

Wolter, Michael. "'Reich Gottes' bei Lukas." *NTS* 41 (1995): 541–63.

CHAPTER 26

UNITY IN CHRIST

Worship in the Corinthian Church

Benjamin L. Gladd

CONTEXT OF WORSHIP IN FIRST AND SECOND CORINTHIANS

If one ancient church is analogous to the modern church in the West, it is the church at Corinth. Many at Corinth were marked by strife, sexual immorality, and pride, to name a few. In sum, they were "worldly." At the heart of Paul's letters is the need for the Corinthians to rally around the crucified Messiah and embrace a wisdom that stands at odds with their pagan neighbors. The church at Corinth must embrace a threefold, cross-centered approach to public worship: adopt the creational pattern of gender distinctions between a husband and a wife, fulfill their calling as true, united Israel in the Lord's Supper, and serve one another through the gifts of the Spirit. Remarkably, these three areas of concern remain an issue in the modern church, and we would do well to heed Paul's admonitions.

Paul's correspondence with the church at Corinth was substantial, and many scholars are convinced that we have evidence of at least four letters to the church. The letter known as "1 Corinthians" appears to be the second epistle, whereas "2 Corinthians" seems to be the fourth. So, by tracking Paul's interaction with this church we learn a great deal about his apostleship and the inner workings of the Corinthian church. One aspect that comes into particular focus in 1 Corinthians is the nature of the church's public worship. In 1 Corinthians 11–14, Paul expends a significant amount of energy on several problematic areas. First Corinthians 11–14 gives us incredible insight into the nature of public worship, covering a wide range of topics, from head coverings to speaking in tongues. I will endeavor to articulate the nature of public worship at Corinth, highlighting three central aspects—falling into step with the pattern of creation, adhering to unity in the Lord's Supper as end-time Israel, and promoting ecclesiastical unity with spiritual gifts.

Division at Corinth

To understand the nature of worship at Corinth, we must first grasp the occasion of 1 Corinthians as a whole. The church at Corinth is strained from within, suffering from self-inflicted wounds. Much of Paul's letter to the Corinthians can be boiled down into two interrelated problems: First, the largely Gentile church is enamored with the surrounding pagan culture. Based on a few comments in the letter, it appears that many within the church at Corinth are recent converts (e.g., 6:9–11). Keep in mind that Paul founded the church and ministered in Corinth for roughly a year and a half (Acts 18:11). Paul writes 1 Corinthians a few years later from Ephesus around AD 54–55, so many at Corinth have only been believers for a handful of years. Therefore, the Corinthians are still coming to grips with how they relate to the surrounding pagan culture while embracing the crucified Christ. Gordon Fee famously argues, "Although they were the Christian church in Corinth, an inordinate amount of Corinth was yet in them."[1]

Second, one concrete way in which the Corinthians continue to keep in step with the pagan culture pertains to their factional behavior. Many consider factions and egotistical behavior to be an impetus, if not the root cause, for Paul's entire epistle. Wisdom, so treasured at Corinth, is likely a type of sophistic wisdom. The exact contents of this wisdom are quite difficult to ascertain, but it is probably safe to assume that sophistic wisdom was alluring, philosophical, and human-centered. Rhetorically gifted individuals paraded this wisdom, hoping to gain a following by their persuasive rhetoric. The Corinthians are jockeying with each other by aligning themselves with one sophist over another, thus pitting the leaders (and themselves) against each other. The net result is a party-line division between the house churches (1:13–16). These house churches are not divided over theological lines but personal rifts—a clash of ecclesiastical titans. If that was not enough, the wealthy within the church disparage the poor within the church, excluding them from fellowship.

Worship and Creation (11:2–16)

Chapter 11 divides roughly into two sections. Both concern the Corinthian worship service: head coverings (11:2–16) and the Lord's Supper (11:17–34). The first section, on head coverings is, at the core, a discussion of gender roles during the worship service. We should remain cautious as we tread here, as we are attempting to explicate a passage that is culturally situated. Many cultural nuances in Corinth in the middle of the first century are simply lost to us.

Paul prefaces this section with praising the Corinthians for "remembering" him and for "holding to the traditions" that he "passed on to them" (11:2).[2] Verses 2–16 must, therefore, be somehow tied to these "traditions"

1. Gordon D. Fee, *The First Epistle to the Corinthians*, NICNT (Grand Rapids: Eerdmans, 1987), 4.
2. Unless otherwise noted, all biblical translations are from the NIV.

that Paul previously taught them. So, in what follows, Paul is convinced that it is necessary to remind his audience once more of the role of men and women during their weekly assembly.

The contrastive "but" (*de*) at the beginning of 11:3 probably qualifies his praise of the Corinthians. Verses 3–16 are a veritable hornet's nest of exegetical and theological issues. It is probably not an understatement to claim that this is one of the most difficult and debated passages in all the New Testament. Given the restraints of this essay, we simply lack the space to unpack each option. Suffice to say, my own view is that Paul here argues for a functional distinction between men and women within the worship gathering. While men and women are ontologically equal and are one in Christ (Gal. 3:28), they enjoy differing roles in public worship.

The apostle Paul first outlines a principle and then applies that principle to their circumstances. The principle is that "the head of every man is Christ, and the head of every woman is man, and the head of Christ is God" (11:3). Some opt for the translation "source" rather than "head," but this is probably incorrect.[3] The term *kephalē* most often means "head" or "authority" (e.g., Eph. 1:22; Col. 2:10). Therefore, this hierarchy is then concretely applied to the Corinthian situation. Males are not to "pray or prophesy" with their heads covered because it "dishonors" them (11:4), because head coverings in worship gatherings generally symbolize honor and respect.[4]

In pagan Roman culture, males covered their heads with their toga during religious ceremonies, demonstrating their superior status over the other worshipers.[5] Women, too, wore head coverings or veils in the culture, symbolizing their marriage and dependence on their husband. David Garland surmises that a head covering "communicates to others in public that the woman is demure, chaste, and modest, and that she intends to stay that way."[6] Therefore, if a Corinthian man dons a head covering during a Christian worship service, then he is declaring superiority to all those gathered. Such an act of superiority undermines his subordination to Christ (11:2). If a married Corinthian woman fails to wear a head covering, then she is symbolically declaring independence from her husband and, as a result, brings shame on him (11:2). Again, contrary to the rising

---

3. For a survey of views regarding this difficult and complex debate, see Anthony C. Thiselton, *The First Epistle to the Corinthians*, NIGTC (Grand Rapids: Eerdmans, 2000), 812–20.
4. Some commentators only discern gender distinctions here in 11:2–16 and not any reference to authority structures and subordination (see L. Ann Jervis, "'But I Want You to Know . . .': Paul's Midrashic Intertextual Response to the Corinthian Worshipers (1 Cor 11:2–16)," *JBL* 112 [1993]: 231–46). While Paul is primarily concerned with gender distinctions in worship, the authority structure outlined in 11:3 must be upheld. See Thomas R. Schreiner, "1 Corinthians 11:2–16: Head Coverings, Prophecies and the Trinity," in *Recovering Biblical Manhood and Womanhood*, eds. Wayne Grudem and John Piper (Wheaton, IL: Crossway, 1991), 117–32.
5. David W. J. Gill, "The Importance of Roman Portraiture for Head-Coverings in 1 Corinthians 11:2–16," *TynBul* 41 (1990): 245–60.
6. David E. Garland, *1 Corinthians*, BECNT (Grand Rapid: Baker Academic, 2003), 510–11.

tide of many contemporary commentators, subordination seems to be the issue at stake. Moreover, this principle seems to apply to women in general during worship and not simply married women (11:10, 15).

Underpinning Paul's exhortation to the Corinthians is Genesis 1–3. Paul takes a contemporary issue (11:4–6), a situation that is culturally tied to a specific time and place, and appeals to the Old Testament for authority. But Paul reaches beyond Mosaic legislation and taps into the fountainhead of the entire storyline of the Bible—Genesis 1–3. Three specific passages are probably alluded to in the immediate context: Genesis 1:26–27, 2:22–23, and 3:16. Paul alludes to Genesis 3:16 in the programmatic 11:3, whereas in 11:8–9 he underscores the sequence of creation. Charting the similarities is helpful here (all quotations taken from NASB, emphases added):

1 Corinthians 11:3: "Christ is the head of every man, and the *man is the head of a woman*, and God is the head of Christ."	Genesis 3:16b: "Yet your desire will be for your husband, *And he will rule over you*."
1 Corinthians 11:7: "For a man ought not to have his head covered, since he is the *image* and glory of *God*; but the *woman* is the glory of *man*."	Genesis 1:26–27: "Then *God* said, 'Let Us make *man* in Our *image*, according to Our likeness; and let them rule over the fish of the sea and over the birds of the sky and over the cattle and over all the earth, and over every creeping thing that creeps on the earth.' *God* created *man* in His own *image*, in the *image of God* He created him; *male and female* He created them."
1 Corinthians 11:8: "For man does not originate from woman, but *woman from man*."	Genesis 2:22–23: "The LORD God fashioned into a *woman* the rib which He had *taken from the man*, and brought her to the man. The man said, 'This is now bone of my bones, and flesh of my flesh; she shall be called Woman, because *she was taken out of man*.'"

Why bring Genesis 1–3 to bear on his discussion with men and women during a public worship service? The apostle attempts to return the Corinthian church back to its creational intention, particularly as it is applied to "head coverings." Paul's explicit mentioning of "man" being in the "image and glory of God" forces us to reflect a bit on men and women being created in God's image in Genesis 1–2.

As God's images, the first couple represents him on the earth and serves on his behalf (Gen. 1:26–28). But the serpent allures them to cast off God's image and become independent of God and function at the divine level. The temptation, at heart, is to become like God—to rule and to think like God. Notice that the serpent first tempts Eve and strategically bypasses Adam. According to the narrative, Adam is created first (Gen. 2:7, 20) and appears responsible for leading, teaching, and representing his family (cf. Gen. 4:20; 2 Cor. 11:3; 1 Tim. 2:13). Recall in Genesis 3:9 that God approaches Adam and not Eve to give an accountability for their actions. Adam is thus the representative head of all humanity. By approaching Eve, the serpent is attempting to dismantle the family structures God originally set in place. Adam, who appears to be within an earshot (Gen. 3:6), should have immediately intervened. Moreover, the second part of the curse reads, "Your desire will be for your husband, yet he will rule over you" (3:16b HCSB). The language is difficult here, but the verse appears to say that discord will emerge within the marriage relationship. The fall did not destroy Eve's identity as queen, but it did affect how she would rule. Instead of ruling the created world together and preserving the internal structure of marriage, Eve would attempt to "rule" over her husband and wrest control from him.[7]

The apostle Paul, then, exhorts the Corinthians to maintain the prefall pattern of creation. Christ is functionally (and temporally) subordinate to God in the incarnation, and men are functionally subordinate to Christ, and women are functionally subordinate to their husbands. Men and women are both created in God's image and enjoy identical worth and value, but the way in which they relate to one another differs. Equal yet interdependent.

Worship and Christ's Death (11:17–34)

Paul devotes the second portion of chapter 11 to the problem of divisions during the Lord's Supper (11:17–19). Instead of using the meal as an opportunity to remember Christ's life and anticipate his return (11:23–26), some of the Corinthians, particularly the wealthy and more prominent members, perhaps ate together in a private room and left the poor to eat alone, resulting in another form of division within the church (11:21–22).

This section begins with a startling admission by Paul: "In the following directives I have *no praise* for you, for your meetings do more harm than good" (11:17, emphasis added). Paul's words are stunning, especially in light of the previous passage, where he praised them (11:2). The first half

7. Victor P. Hamilton argues, "It [3:16b] means a desire to break the relationship of equality and turn it into a relationship of servitude and domination. The sinful husband will try to be a tyrant over his wife. Far from being a reign of co-equals over the remainder of God's creation, the relationship now becomes a fierce dispute, with each party trying to rule the other" (*The Book of Genesis: Chapters 1–17*, NICOT [Grand Rapids: Eerdmans, 1990], 202).

of this section outlines the pernicious problem taking root in the church. The nub of the issue is found in 11:20–21: "when you come together, it is not the Lord's Supper you eat, for when you are eating, some of you go ahead with your own private suppers." Though we lack some finer details, we can fill in some of the details about what is transpiring.

The church at Corinth, like many churches in the first century, probably consisted of house churches (see Rom. 16:3–5; 1 Cor. 16:19; Col. 4:15; Philem. 2). Wealthy Christians in Corinth hosted the worship gatherings in their private homes, and some of these homes consisted of many rooms and a dining room (triclinium) and an atrium. Larger homes could host fifty or so,[8] whereas smaller one may host far less. Here, though, in 1 Corinthians 11 it appears that the entire church has come together in a single home (11:18), possibly the home of Gaius (cf. Rom. 16:23).[9]

When the church at Corinth assembled in a single house, the rich within the congregation probably feasted in the dining room and relegated the poor during the Lord's Supper to outside in the atrium.[10] Verses 21–22 read, "when you are eating, some of you go ahead with your own private suppers. . . . [D]o you despise the church of God by humiliating those who have nothing?" Instead of celebrating the death of Christ in the Eucharist, the wealthy were using it for their own personal advancement. Paul, though, would have none of it (11:22b).

At the heart of Paul's exhortation lies his quotation of a well-known saying of Jesus:

> For I received from the Lord what I also passed on to you: The Lord Jesus, on the night he was betrayed, took bread, and when he had given thanks, he broke it and said, "This is my body, which is for you; do this in remembrance of me." In the same way, after supper he took the cup, saying, "*This cup is the new covenant in my blood; do this, whenever you drink it, in remembrance of me.*" For whenever you eat this bread and drink this cup, you proclaim the Lord's death until he comes. (11:23–26, emphasis added)

The relationship between this saying and the Synoptics need not deter us here, though the Synoptics were likely written after 1 Corinthians. In any case, our question is, *Why* does Paul quote Jesus? What do the words of Jesus have to do with an unsettling division at Corinth? Notice that 11:23 begins with "for" (*gar*) and 11:27 opens with "so then" (*hōste*). The point is that the quotation provides the *basis* for Paul's argument before (11:17–22) and after (11:27–32). Clearly, then, the saying is essential for Paul's admonition.

8. Jerome Murphy-O'Connor, *St. Paul's Corinth: Texts and Archaeology* (Collegeville, MN: Liturgical Press, 1983), 156–58.
9. Mark Button and Fika J. Van Rensburg, "The 'House Churches' in Corinth," *Neot* 37 (2003): 25n38.
10. Murphy-O'Connor, *St. Paul's Corinth*, 158–59.

Scholars are quick to underscore the considerable role of the Old Testament in this saying of Jesus. Old Testament texts such as Exodus 24:8, Isaiah 52:13–53:12, Jeremiah 31:31, 34, and Zechariah 9:11 are some of the more prominent ones in mind. Two of these texts, Jeremiah 31:31, 34, and Zechariah 9:11, are worth considering, especially in light of Paul's admonitions to the church at Corinth.

Jeremiah 31, a classic Old Testament passage concerning the nature of the new covenant, is filled with references to the unification of the twelve tribes of Israel. Israel paid dearly for her idolatrous behavior by living in Babylonian exile, but God promises to bring them back to the promised land. Their arrival back in the land will be marked with several eschatological events, and central to these events is the unification of the tribes. Jeremiah 31 is explicit here: "I will be the God of all the families of Israel" (31:1); "I will plant the kingdoms of Israel and Judah" (31:27); "I will make a new covenant with the people of Israel and with the people of Judah" (31:31). Though not quite as pointed, Zechariah 9 states that "the eyes of all the tribe of Israel are on the Lord" (v. 1). A few verses earlier, in the previous chapter, Zechariah claimed, "Just as you, Judah and Israel, have been a curse among the nations, so I will save you, and you will be a blessing" (8:13).

As we turn back to 1 Corinthians 11, these references to the eschatological restoration of all the tribes of Israel are quite helpful. Jeremiah 31 and Zechariah 9 predict that the arrival of the new covenant will apply to *all* of Israel (cf. Ezek. 36:24–27; 37:15–28). At the Last Supper, part of Jesus's reasoning for echoing Jeremiah 31 and Zechariah 9 is to announce the eschatological regathering of Israel. So, by quoting the saying of Jesus, Paul underscores Jesus's words to the disciples. The time has come for God to regather the exiled Israelites and usher them into his presence. Christ inaugurated the fulfillment of these prophecies in his work, and the church at Corinth is participating in their fulfillment.

When the Corinthians come together and participate in the Lord's Supper but divide according to social standing, they are turning back the redemptive-historical clock. In Christ, the Corinthians are true Israel and all barricades have been torn down. They are one people group in Christ. But by shunning the poor, though, the wealthy at Corinth have fallen out of step with a cardinal eschatological reality—the unity within the covenant community.

Worship and the End-Time Spirit (12:1–14:40)

Our third and final section, chapters 12–14, is quite complex, and scholars debate nearly every exegetical and hermeneutical nuance of this section. Space precludes a thorough investigation, so we will instead focus on Paul's central thrust. Chapters 12–14 are dedicated to the topic of spiritual gifts during public worship at Corinth. Above all, these Spirit-enabled gifts are for the community as a whole (12:12–31) and not to be utilized for self-adulation. Without love, these gifts become useless (13:1–13).

Tongues, though very attractive to the Corinthians, ought to be done in private (14:3, 14–17), unless they are interpreted, resulting in the edification of the body (14:5). Prophecy, on the other hand, is much more public and beneficial for the community (14:1, 3, 5–12, 20–33), since the church understands the message and is edified.

The pouring out of the Spirit at Pentecost signaled a new chapter in the Bible's grand storyline. God's people now enjoy a unique Spirit-filled experience, an experience that was previously limited to only prophets, priests, and kings in the Old Testament. The Spirit's ministry enables believers to bear witness to the risen Christ to those outside the church and serve one another within the church. To unbelievers, Spirit-enabled gifts testify to the risen Christ. Such gifts, when properly employed, also promote unity and harmony within the covenant community.

Paul begins his discussion of spiritual gifts with the ultimate goal of unity (12:4–6). Whether a "message of wisdom," special "knowledge," "healing," "prophecy," or "different kinds of tongues," the Spirit distributes each gift for the well-being and unity of the church (12:11). Each member of the church, whether Jew or Gentile, equally participates in the "one Spirit." Believers are "the body of Christ, and individual members of it" (HCSB). Gifts are intended to promote unity among the church members, even members from various social backgrounds and ethnicities. Paul tempers the role of gifts with "love" in the following chapter. Without love, any gifting becomes unfruitful because it fails to edify the church (13:1–13). Paul uses himself as a hypothetical example to show that even his gifts would be worthless without love (13:1–3).

After instructing the congregation on the goal of the gifts and the motivation that propels their use of them, Paul highlights some trouble spots within the Corinthian congregation during their worship service. Speaking in "tongues"—that is, personal revelations—is a private endeavor and edifies only the individual. Unless tongues are interpreted in a public gathering (14:5, 13–17), they ought to remain private (14:2, 4). "Prophecy," on the other hand, is designed for public consumption, edifying the church as a whole (14:3). Prophecy is to be preferred, as it strengthens and unifies the entire congregation (14:6, 18–19).

One of the more remarkable aspects of 1 Corinthians is Paul's discussion of tongues. In 13:1–2, Paul associates tongues, angels, and mysteries (emphases added): "If I speak in the tongues of men or of *angels*. . . . If I have the gift of prophecy and can fathom all *mysteries*." Once again in 14:2 Paul states, "anyone who speaks in a *tongue* does not speak to people but to God. Indeed, no one understands them; they utter *mysteries* by the Spirit." In several early Jewish texts, we find the visionary joining the angels in their heavenly veneration of God. One passage in the Dead Sea Scrolls is strikingly similar to Paul's discussion: "And the offering of their *tongues* . . . *seven mysteries of knowledge* in the wonderful *mystery* of the seven regions of the hol[y] of holies. . . . The *tongue* of the first will be strengthened seven times with the *tongue* of the second to him" (4Q403 1 II, 26–28).[11] Angels and Jewish worshipers at Qumran jointly praise God with their "tongues" in God's heavenly sanctuary, celebrating deep knowledge or "mysteries." If part of Paul's understanding of tongues resembles this Jewish outlook, then the worshipers at Corinth are participating in the angelic praise of God in heaven. Such a conclusion resonates with Paul's enigmatic statement that a "woman ought to have authority over her own head, *because of the angels*" (11:10). Public worship is not simply a local gathering of believers but a cosmic event.

What Paul hints at here in 1 Corinthians the book of Revelation explicitly develops. The book of Revelation claims that the faithful church on earth is represented in the heavenly temple and before the throne of God. While the church is the temple of God and his presence dwells in believers on earth, his full presence is found in the heavenly temple, where the deceased saints and angels gather in worship. In the incarnation, Christ irreversibly opened up access to God's heavenly presence. He bridged the heavenly and earthly realities. Through Christ's work, God's presence in heaven extends down to earth, allowing the church to enjoy his glory. To use a sci-fi metaphor, Christ is the portal between these two locations. The physical and spiritual dimensions now intersect with one another through Christ.

We see glimmers of this reality in Revelation 5:

> And when he had taken it, the four living creatures and the twenty-four elders fell down before the Lamb. Each one had a harp and they were holding golden bowls full of incense, which are the prayers of God's people. And they sang a new song, saying: "You are worthy to take the scroll and to open its seals, because you were slain, and with your blood you purchased for God persons from every tribe and language and people and nation. You have made them to be a kingdom and priests to serve our God, and they will reign on the earth." (Rev. 5:8–10; cf. 4:4–11)

Identifying the twenty-four elders sitting on heavenly "thrones" in 4:4 and 5:8 has been the subject of much debate. The most satisfying view identifies them as angelic representatives of the people of God throughout the ages. They are angels who represent the covenant community in the Old and New Testament—twelve for the people of God under the old covenant (the twelve patriarchs) and twelve for those under the new covenant (the twelve apostles).[12] What's critical, though, is how they are functioning here in 5:8: "Each one had a harp and gold bowls filled with incense, which are the prayers of the saints." These twenty-four angels are understood as serving the church in a priestly capacity before the throne. Just as the priests offered up incense to God in the temple (Exod. 30:7–8), so too the

11. Quotation taken from Florentino García Martínez and Eibert J. C. Tigchelaar, *The Dead Sea Scrolls Study Edition*, 2 vols. (Leiden: Brill, 1997–1998).

12. Grant R. Osborne, *Revelation*, BECNT (Grand Rapids: Baker Academic, 2002), 229.

angels offer up the incense of the prayers of God's people on earth. The point is that the suffering church, though on earth, is represented in heaven before the throne. Through angelic representation, believers on earth participate in heavenly worship before God. Our worship is their worship.

THEOLOGY OF WORSHIP

First Corinthians contributes to our understanding of worship in a few ways. First, Paul is concerned that the church maintain the pattern of creation as outlined in Genesis 1–3. The creation of Adam and Eve and their relationship to one another is absolutely foundational to the remaining chapters of the Bible's storyline. The marriage relationship does not come under the microscope here in 1 Corinthians 11; rather, Paul is concerned for the preservation of male and female roles in public worship. For Paul the early chapters of Genesis are paradigmatic on multiple levels, such as corporate worship (11:7–9), marriage (Eph. 5:31–32), and the nature of our resurrection (1 Cor. 15:42–49) to name a few. The church would do well to mediate on Genesis 1–3 and glean from Scripture what God has achieved in his Son and what desires from his people today.

Second, the apostle Paul's quotation of Jesus's words in 11:24–25 demonstrates the need for continued reflection on the gospel and the four gospels at large. The quotation of Jesus appears to be just as authoritative as other Old Testament quotations throughout 1 Corinthians (e.g., 1:19; 1:31; 2:9; 2:16; 3:19; 3:21; 6:16; 8:4), suggesting that the words of Jesus are the very words of God. Paul probably learned about Jesus's life, death, and resurrection through other apostles, and he felt compelled to "pass on" that same message to the Corinthians (emphases added):

> I praise you for remembering me in everything and for holding to the traditions just as I *passed them on* to you. (11:2)
> For I received from the Lord what I also *passed on* to you. (11:23)
> For what I received I *passed on* to you as of first importance. (15:3)

The bedrock of the Christian faith is the gospel—the death and resurrection of Jesus. Paul pleads with the church to hold fast unswervingly to that truth and live in light of it.

The quotation of Jesus in 11:24–25 also reveals that Jesus is the ultimate fulfillment of the Passover celebration. The Last Supper celebrated the annual Passover meal. The institution of Passover finds its roots in Exodus 12. Each year, an Israelite family must find a perfect male lamb and slaughter it at twilight. It is an atoning sacrifice. Then the families are to eat it a certain way and dress accordingly. They are to take blood from the lamb and apply it to the doorframes of their houses (Exod. 12:1–50; Pesahim 10:5). The Passover lies deep within the heart of the Jewish nation, symbolizing God's redemption and deliverance. It recalls God vanquishing Pharaoh and the Egyptians and anticipates what God will do in the future. Remarkably, Jesus identifies himself as the ultimate Passover Lamb. He is also the Lord who promised to liberate Israel from slavery. In other words, Jesus is *both* the sacrificial lamb and Israel's God in the flesh. Celebrating the Eucharist in the context of public worship is essential for nourishing the faith of believers, and one concrete expression of such nourishment is promoting unity among the people of God. The hallmark of new covenant believers lies in their solidarity with one another as they worship the crucified Christ.

Third, a hallmark of the Spirit's presence in the life of the church is supreme cooperation between diverse people groups. The prophet Joel foresaw a time, though, when all within Israel receive the Spirit and serve in the capacity of prophets, priests, and kings. But Joel 2 is part of a larger expectation that began in the early stages of Israel's career. According to Numbers 11, Moses pleads with God to furnish him with leaders to share in the burden of the people (11:11, 17 [cf. Exod. 18:13–27]). God orders Moses to gather "seventy men from the elders" and "bring them to the tent of meeting, and let them take their stand there with you. Then I will come down and . . . will take of the Spirit who is upon you, and will put Him upon them" (11:16–17 NASB). Moses obeys God: "He gathered seventy men of the elders . . . and stationed them around the tent. Then the Lord came down in the cloud . . . and took of the Spirit who was upon him [Moses] and placed Him upon the seventy elders. And when the Spirit rested upon them, they prophesied" (11:24–25). They then stopped prophesying, but two elders at another location continued to prophesy. When Joshua heard about this, he asked Moses to stop them. Moses declined, replying, "Would that all the Lord's people were prophets, that the LORD would put His Spirit upon them!" (11:29). What began with a wish from Moses was transformed into a formal prophecy by the prophet Joel.[13] The Spirit's gifts, previously restricted to sanctioned kings, priests, and prophets, is universalized to all of God's people. Jews and Gentiles, young and old, and male and female enjoy a restored image of God. A church that is often reminded of these spiritual truths is a church that embodies God original intent—all nations will one day worship and enjoy God's presence in the new creation.

SIGNIFICANCE OF THE CORINTHIAN CORRESPONDENCE FOR BIBLICAL WORSHIP

In light of our three points of theological reflection, we will now explore three points of application. One way in which we can apply Paul's admonitions about males and females in 11:2–16 is to reaffirm gender distinctions in family, home, and in our culture. The church has come under attack in its conviction of marriage and gender. Though marriage is not Paul's primary concern here in 1 Corinthians 11, I do think it is not out of Paul's purview.

13. G. K. Beale, *The Temple and the Church's Mission: A Biblical Theology of the Dwelling Place of God*, NSBT 17 (Downers Grove, IL: InterVarsity Press, 2004), 210.

The church must remain clear on this issue: God has, from the beginning, intended marriage for men and women. This union in marriage in Genesis 2 is incredibly important to the spread of God's glory (Gen. 1:28). It is the means by which the divine commission will be accomplished and God's glory will reach the ends of the earth. This marriage is also is the template for every subsequent Israelite union (Mal. 2:15; Matt. 19:5; Eph. 5:31; etc.) and the pattern for Yahweh's relationship with his people. The marriage between Adam and Eve, a male and a female, is unquestionably held out as a model for the proper union. This explains why we get the wording: "That is why a man leaves *his father and mother* and is united to his wife, and they become one flesh" (Gen. 2:24, emphasis added). Adam and Eve did not have a father and a mother! We live in a culture that is hostile to the biblical definition of marriage, but Christians must not be vague or acquiesce.

Pastors must affirm gender distinctions in worship gathering. This is becoming more problematic in light of the tectonic shift in how our culture understands human sexuality. The lines between males and females are quickly becoming blurred. Though the teaching 1 Corinthians 11:2–16 is intended to confront a cultural issue in the Corinthian church, I do think a principle carries over today. Consider the vast cultural differences between the original audience of the Pentateuch and the audience of 1 Corinthians. Yet Paul unflinchingly extracts a moral principle from Genesis 1–3 and expects the church of Corinth to take heed. The church at Corinth is true Israel in Christ and we, too, must embrace our identity as true Israel in Christ. When the apostles give moral admonitions to their original audience, those same admonitions apply to us. Therefore, even though we are two thousand years removed from 1 Corinthians, the church today must do its best in maintaining gender distinctions in all of life and worship. What this looks like will differ from culture to culture, but we must continue to embrace the Bible's teaching even in the face of hostility.

The church must also reflect on the nature of the new covenant, especially during the celebration of the Lord's Supper. We learned that one dimension of the Lord's Supper is the unification of the twelve tribes of Israel. Paul is convinced that the church of Corinth, though largely made up of Gentiles (12:2), is the restored people of God—namely, true Israel. Israel in the Old Testament was marked by division and strife, whereas eschatological Israel in the New Testament is marked by ecclesiastical unity. Pastors should strive to maintain unity in their congregations by reminding each member of their identity in Christ. Paul puts it so aptly in Galatians 3:28: "There is neither Jew nor Gentile, neither slave nor free, nor is there male and female, for you are all one in Christ Jesus." Perhaps during the Lord's Supper pastors could underscore the bond of unity that exists between all of God's people. There is one God and one people group. Pastors should be mindful of how their congregants relate to one another not just during the Lord's Supper but in the church at large. Is racism ignored or tolerated? What about those who are financially distressed and in society's fringes? Are they being cared for and loved? Our tendency is to wait for problems to flare up rather than proactively pursue peace and harmony among the flock.

The theme of unity is again pervasive in chapters 12–14. What we discover here, though, is how each individual is uniquely gifted. But differing gifts should not lead to pride or abuse. They should lead to service. The Spirit furnishes an array of gifts for the edification of the whole body. There is strength in diversity. It is tempting in any culture to elevate and promote those endowed with public gifts (e.g., preaching and teaching) and minimize those who work behind the scenes. Church leaders must earnestly recognize the gifts that each member possesses and encourage them accordingly. This principle requires pastors and leaders to get to know their people well and discover where they are gifted and how they can serve the church. There is not shortcut here: church leaders must spend quality time with their congregations and nurture the church's spiritual gifts.

CONCLUSION

The church in the West today resembles the church at Corinth. We are struggling with gender distinctions in worship, erecting walls between the rich and the poor, and abusing our spiritual gifts to promote ourselves. Paul argues against such ungodly behavior by upholding the pattern of creation and drawing the church's attention to their unity in Christ. As the end-time people of God, the church must hold fast to their identity and shine brightly in a fallen world.

BIBLIOGRAPHY

Beale, G. K. *The Temple and the Church's Mission: A Biblical Theology of the Dwelling Place of God*. NSBT 17. Downers Grove, IL: InterVarsity Press, 2004.

Button, Mark, and Fika J. Van Rensburg. "The 'House Churches' in Corinth." *Neot* 37 (2003): 1–28.

Fee, Gordon D. *The First Epistle to the Corinthians*. NICNT. Grand Rapids: Eerdmans, 1987.

Garland, David E. *1 Corinthians*. BECNT. Grand Rapids: Baker Academic, 2003.

Gill, David W. J. "The Importance of Roman Portraiture for Head-Coverings in 1 Corinthians 11:2–16." *TynBul* 41 (1990): 245–60.

Hamilton, Victor P. *The Book of Genesis: Chapters 1–17*. NICOT. Grand Rapids: Eerdmans, 1990.

Murphy-O'Connor, Jerome. *St. Paul's Corinth: Texts and Archaeology*. Collegeville, MN: Liturgical Press, 1983.

Osborne, Grant R. *Revelation*. BECNT. Grand Rapids: Baker Academic, 2002.

CHAPTER 27

WORSHIP ROOTED IN DOCTRINE *FOR* LIFE

Worship in Galatians and Romans

Kenneth Berding

CONTEXT OF WORSHIP IN GALATIANS AND ROMANS

Paul's letter to the Galatians offers fewer glimpses into the theme of worship than does his letter to the Romans, so less space will be devoted to our discussion of this theme in Galatians. Paul's primary purpose in Galatians is to warn about those who distort the gospel (1:8–9). As such, Galatians tends to be more polemical, and thus includes fewer signposts to Paul's understanding of worship than will be encountered in Romans.

Cultural Context of Worship in Galatians

A few interpreters have tried to argue that the pressures of obligatory emperor worship is an important cultural background for what Paul writes in his letter to the Galatians.[1] If so, it might provide a backdrop for understanding worship in Galatians. Separately, a few other interpreters have attempted to situate Paul's concerns in pagan worship of some sort.[2] Again, such would be relevant to our discussion if it were the case. But

1. E.g., Justin K. Hardin, *Galatians and the Imperial Cult: A Critical Analysis of the First-Century Social Context of Paul's Letter*, WUNT 2/237 (Tübingen: Mohr Siebeck, 2008); N. T. Wright, *Paul in Fresh Perspective* (Minneapolis: Fortress, 2005), 59–79; Bruce W. Winter, *Seek the Welfare of the City: Christians as Benefactors and Citizens* (Grand Rapids: Eerdmans, 1994), 123–43.
2. Troy Martin, "Apostasy to Paganism: The Rhetorical Stasis of the Galatian Controversy," in *The Galatians Debate: Contemporary Issues in Rhetorical and Historical Interpretation*, ed. Mark D. Nanos (Peabody, MA: Hendrickson, 2002), 73–94; Susan Elliott, *Cutting Too Close for Comfort: Paul's Letter to the Galatians in Its Anatolian Cultic Context*, JSNTSup 248 (London: T&T Clark, 2003), 13.

both suggestions falter on what actually appears in the text; neither the imperial cult nor paganism is explicit in Galatians, whereas Jewish practices are. Paul's central concern in the book of Galatians appears to focus on those who are trying to convince the young Galatian believers that they have to be circumcised and live according to the law if they want to fully engage in their Christian faith (6:12–13). This also suggests that the agitators in Galatia pitted the law-observing believers against those who did not observe the Mosaic law. Consequently, Paul's argument is primarily polemical, theological, and sociological, and thereby connects less frequently than some of his other writings (such as the Corinthian letters and Romans) with a theology of worship. There is no extended reflection on worship in Galatians; Paul only offers bits and pieces. But together these morsels are helpful in guiding us toward a few key ideas about worship.

Cultural Context of Worship in Romans

Romans is somewhat less personal than many of Paul's letters. Unlike the specific instructions and emotional connections that appear in Paul's correspondence with the churches in Corinth, Galatia, Philippi, and Thessalonica, Paul's letter to the Roman Christians is a bit less situational. This is not to say that Paul lacks specific knowledge about the Roman house churches; the contrary is evident in his pastoral counsel in chapters 14–15 and in his greetings to the various house churches in chapter 16.[3] But background appears to be less relevant to a study of worship than it would be, say, in the Corinthian context. There are four cultural observations, though, that can be drawn from the letter to the Romans that probably connect in some way with Paul's theme of worship when it appears in this wonderful letter.

1. Paul is apparently writing against the backdrop of widespread idolatry in the broader culture. This may have relevance to his comments in chapter 1.

2. Paul seems aware of Jews who display hypocritical tendencies. This may have relevance to his comments in chapter 2.

3. Paul knows that there are sacrifices being offered both by Jews in the temple in Jerusalem and by Gentiles in various pagan temples across the Roman Empire.[4] This may have relevance for his comments at the beginning of chapter 12.

---

3. At minimum, five separate house churches are discernible in Rom. 16, including (1) the church in the house of Prisca and Aquila (16:5); (2) those in the household of Aristobulus (16:10); (3) those in the household of Narcissus (16:11); (4) the "brothers" of 16:14; and (5) the "saints" who gather with the people mentioned in 16:15.
4. Lesly F. Massey, "Paul and Christian Worship in light of Romans 12:1," *Chm* 130 (2016): 108.

4. There appear to be tensions between Jewish Christians and Gentile Christians.[5] This seems to underlie various issues in Romans, but especially Paul's pastoral counsel concerning the "weak" and the "strong" regarding food and days in chapter 14 and the early verses of 15.

THEOLOGY OF WORSHIP

Focused on the Glory of God

Worship should focus *on God*. It should be unto his glory and filled with praise, thanksgiving, fear, reverence, rejoicing, declaration, and submission. All of these responses are acknowledgments of God's innate worth and our need to glorify him.

Centered on the glory of God

After Paul greets the Galatians ("grace and peace") and mentions "the will of our God and Father," he exclaims, "to whom be the glory forever and ever. Amen" (Gal. 1:4–5). For Paul, the glory of God is central to worship. In Galatians 1:10, Paul comments, "For am I now seeking the approval of man, or of God?" A dominant concern of Paul throughout his ministry is to focus on the approval of God, not of humans. In Galatians 1:22–24, Paul recounts that in the first years after his conversion he was not personally known to the churches in Judea, though they knew that the former persecutor was now preaching the faith he tried to destroy. Paul then adds, "And they glorified God because of me." Again, the glory of God takes center stage.

Thanksgiving

In Romans 1:8, Paul says that he thanks his God through Jesus Christ for the Roman Christians. Since this statement comes on the heels of Paul blessing the Roman Christians with grace and peace (1:7), it is worth noting the wordplay. Grace and thanks are cognates, suggesting that thanksgiving can be thought of as a grateful response to God's grace.[6]

"Boasting" as praise

Paul "boasts" in the cross of Christ and refuses to boast in anything else (Gal. 6:14).[7] His renunciation of the world ("by which the world has

---

5. See James C. Walters, *Ethnic Issues in Paul's Letter to the Romans: Changing Self-Definitions in Earliest Roman Christianity* (Valley Forge, PA: Trinity Press International, 1993).
6. John Paul Heil, *The Letters of Paul as Rituals of Worship* (Eugene, OR: Cascade, 2011), 77. For more on the theme of thanksgiving in Paul, see David W. Pao, *Thanksgiving: An Investigation of a Pauline Theme*, NSBT 13 (Downers Grove, IL: InterVarsity Press, 2002). Pao argues that thanksgiving is closely tied to worship and praise, and thus finds its explication in Old Testament passages that declare the honor and deeds of a God who is Lord of all.
7. Remember that the cross was a symbol of violence and shame, not something anyone would have thought to "boast" about in the ancient world. See Douglas J. Moo, *Galatians*, BECNT (Grand Rapids: Baker Academic, 2013), 395.

been crucified to me") is a basic posture for worship and stands in contradistinction to any sort of human boasting. "Boasting" in the cross of Christ in this passage appears to be synonymous to praising Christ for what he did on the cross.

No grounds for self-boasting

The subtheme of self-boasting shows up first in Romans 2:17 and appears again in 2:23, 3:27, 4:2, and 15:17 (cf. 5:2–3, 11). In 11:20 Paul writes, "So do not become proud, but stand in awe" (cf. 11:25). In Romans, Paul's point is that no one possesses any grounds of boasting in God's presence. The rejection of boasting in the presence of God is a key posture related to worship as well. Paul does present positive counterparts to boasting in Romans, but such references might be better described with a different word than "boasting." In 5:2–3, 11, Paul mentions confident rejoicing in our access and reconciliation to God, even allowing us to rejoice in our sufferings. In 15:17–21 Paul says that he has reason to be proud of his work for God, but refuses to speak of anything except what Christ has done through him. I have already observed that in Galatians 6:14 Paul has asserted that if he is going to boast, it will only be in the cross. But when it comes to self-boasting, there is no place for it whatsoever in the presence of a glorious God.

Proclaiming God's honor

In Romans 2, we see that some Jews boast in the law but "dishonor" God when they break the law (2:23). Paul then includes a loose citation of Isaiah 52:5 in 2:24: "The name of God is blasphemed among the Gentiles because of you." In other words, God intended his glory to be proclaimed to the nations through his people, but first-century Jews who live hypocritical lives (saying one thing and doing another [2:17–22]) are not proclaiming God's honor. In fact, they are doing just the opposite; they are dishonoring God. The Gentiles of Romans 1:21 are castigated for failing to honor God; in 2:23 the Jews are lumped in with Gentile sinners for doing precisely the same thing.[8]

Seeking and fearing God

Paul pulls together a pastiche of quotations from the Old Testament in Romans 3:10–18 to drive home his major point that everyone is a sinner. The verses he draws on exhibit a curious connection with worship, as John Paul Heil notes:

> Paul goes on to insist that not only the ungodly but all, Jews as well as Greeks, are under the devastating power of sin (3:9). So pervading is this power that it

8. "Perhaps Paul intends the reader to see the irony in having responsibility for dishonoring God's name transferred from the Gentiles to the people of Israel" (Douglas J. Moo, *The Epistle to the Romans*, NICNT [Grand Rapids: Eerdmans, 1996], 166).

> deprives even their organs of speech of the ability to worship God, as indicated by a subsequent list of scriptural citations that confirm this scathing indictment: "Their *throat* is an opened grave; with their *tongues* they deceive [Ps. 5:9]; the poison of asps is under their *lips* [Ps. 140:3]; their *mouth* is filled with cursing and bitterness [Ps. 10:7]." In other words, instead of praising, blessing, or glorifying God with their throat, tongues, lips, and mouth (3:13–14, 19), the scriptural list concludes that "there is no reverence of God before their eyes [Ps. 36:1]" (3:18).[9]

Early in this compendium of sins, Paul says that no one seeks God (3:11, citing Pss. 14:2; 53:2) and closes by commenting that before their eyes there is no fear of God (3:18, citing Ps. 36:1). A proper relationship to God, including one's worship, includes both seeking God and fearing (that is, reverencing) God.

The "glory of God"

Is Romans 3:23, "for all have sinned and fall short of the glory of God," relevant to our discussion? What is the meaning of "fall short of the glory of God"? It is not uncommon to hear people in our churches paraphrase this clause as falling short of God's righteous standard. But where else does Paul use the word "glory" to describe a standard God has set forth? Although a variety of views have been suggested for "glory of God,"[10] I consider one of the following two views to be most likely: either (1) people have fallen short of the glorious humanity that God intended for Adam and Eve when he created them, but that was lost in the fall and now (and fully in the future) is renewed in Christ (cf. various Jewish texts[11]); or (2) people have fallen short of giving God glory (similar to the exchange of glory and failure to worship God in Romans 1:21–25, Abraham giving God glory in Romans 4:20, the Gentiles glorifying God in Romans 15:9, and the final doxology of the letter in Romans 16:27, where glory is given to God).[12] The advantage of the second interpretation is that it is contextually linked to what came before in Paul's massive argument in Romans in which he calls everyone a sinner starting in 1:18. It also comports with the repeated warnings against idolatry that permeate the biblical record and that are referenced in chapter 1.

9. Heil, *Letters of Paul*, 78–79.
10. See Ben C. Blackwell, "Immortal Glory and the Problem of Death in Romans 3.23," *JSNT* 32 (2010): 286–292, for a summary of views.
11. Commonly suggested texts are Life of Adam and Eve 20–21 (also known as Apocalypse of Moses); Targum Pseudo-Jonathan Gen. 2.25; 3.7; 3 Baruch (Greek) 4.16; Genesis Rabbah 12.6; and Apocalypse of Sedrach 6.5. See Blackwell, "Immortal Glory," 288–89, for English translations.
12. Taken as an objective genitive ("glory to God"). See Peter Abelard in *The Letter to the Romans*, trans. and eds. Ian Christopher Levy, Philip D. W. Krey, and Thomas Ryan, The Bible in Medieval Tradition (Grand Rapids: Eerdmans, 2013), 112; Carey C. Newman, *Paul's Glory-Christology: Tradition and Rhetoric*, NovTSup 69 (Leiden: Brill, 1992), 225.

If this second interpretation is correct, then this well-known verse becomes important for our theme of worship. In one of the most succinct verses about the need for justification, Paul summarizes humanity's sin by writing that everyone has failed to do what God created them to do—that is, to worship him. Failure to worship God, in this verse, is tantamount to saying "all have sinned." But the reader should be reminded that the expression "glory of God" in Romans 3:23 is debated and so may not connect with our theme.

Equal Access in the Presence of God

Paul is clear in both Galatians and Romans that in the presence of God it makes no difference whether one is a Jew or Greek, circumcised or uncircumcised. There are no racial, ethnic, or gender distinctions before God. Instead, there is equality in worship before God, and believers should recognize, embrace, and lean into this reality as we worship together.

No distinctions before God

In Galatians 3:28 Paul remarks that all who have faith are included in Christ; there is no limitation based on ethnicity ("neither Jew nor Greek"), social status ("neither slave nor free"), or gender ("neither male nor female"). Paul wrote these words into a region where there were many ethnic and class tensions.[13] Like Romans 5:1, this means that all who are in Christ have open access to God. Here in Galatians 3:29–4:7 our access to God is like that of a child to his father and even includes inheritance rights. This comports with Paul's earlier interjection in Galatians 2:6, where Paul states bluntly, "God shows no partiality."

Members of a body glorifying God

Following of the heals of Paul's well-known injunction to present ourselves as living sacrifices (Rom. 12:1, see below), we see that Paul's understanding of worship is tied to another theme, that of various members in one body serving one another in the places of ministry to which God has appointed them (Rom. 12:3–21).[14] Though worship can be individual, we are all members of a corporate entity and thereby glorify God together.[15] Paul makes this explicit in Romans 15, where he writes, "May the God of endurance and encouragement grant you to live in such harmony with one another, in accord with Christ Jesus, that together you may with one voice glorify the God and Father of our Lord Jesus Christ.

13. E. Randolph Richards and Brandon J. O'Brien, *Misreading Scripture with Western Eyes* (Downers Grove, IL: IVP Academic, 2012), 68.
14. Not exercising their purported special abilities, as popular teaching would have it, but serving one another in the ministry roles God has given them. See Kenneth Berding, *What Are Spiritual Gifts? Rethinking the Conventional View* (Grand Rapids: Kregel Academic, 2006), 93–101.
15. Western Christians in particular need to reinvigorate the idea of corporate worship because of our culturally conditioned tendency to radicalize individual expression. See discussion in Richards and O'Brien, *Misreading Scripture*, 95–112.

Therefore welcome one another as Christ has welcomed you for the glory of God" (vv. 5–7).

Gentile inclusion in worship

One of the key passages on worship in Romans is 15:8–12, where Paul quotes from four Old Testament passages (Ps. 18:49 [= 2 Sam. 22:50]; Deut. 32:43; Ps. 117:1; Isa. 11:10) regarding the inclusion of the Gentiles in what God is doing with his people. The first three of these quotations (Ps. 18:49; Deut. 32:43; Ps. 117:1) come from worship contexts. These uses of the Old Testament remind us of what we have already observed about there being no distinctions of persons in the presence of the Lord. In addition, a few verses later, Paul adds to the worship context by using cultic language to describe his ministry; he serves like a priest to the Gentiles (15:15–16).[16] Gentiles, along with Jews, are invited into the grand purposes of God that all might worship him.

Idolatry

Worship, according to Paul, must be focused on God, and only on God. As is clear throughout Scripture, worship of anything other than the one true God must be properly removed from the hearts and practices of God's people. Idolatry is a distortion and perversion of God's primacy in worship.

Freedom from slavery

Paul asserts that before the Galatians knew God, they were "enslaved to those that by nature are not gods" (4:8). In so doing, he invokes the well-known theme of idolatry. But his point is to warn the Galatians not to turn back and become slaves again, since now they have come to know God and be known by him (4:9–11). And even though Paul uses the language of idolatry, his point is to warn about reversion to Jewish practices.[17] When Paul launches into the second main section of Galatians, he exclaims, "For freedom Christ has set us free; stand firm therefore, and do not submit again to a yoke of slavery" (5:1; cf. 5:13). We have been freed, among other things, to genuinely and freely worship the one true God.

Idolatry as a work of the flesh

Galatians 5:20 is the only time the specific word *idolatry* appears in either Galatians or Romans (it only appears elsewhere at all in Paul's letters

16. Paul uses the imagery of temple, sacrifice, and service throughout his letter, anticipating what he will write in Romans 15:15–16. See William A. Simmons, "Priest—Sacrifice—Life as Worship: A Pauline Matrix for Understanding Romans," *BSac* 172 (2016): 85–99.
17. "What is astonishing is that Paul equates subjection to Torah with paganism. One can only imagine the shock the Pauline assertion would have given the Judaizers!" (Thomas R. Schreiner, *Galatians*, ZECNT [Grand Rapids: Zondervan, 2010], 278–79).

in 1 Cor. 10:14 and Col. 3:5), though one of Paul's most important discussions of idolatry anywhere is Romans 1:18–25 (see below). Here idolatry is one of many other sins listed among the "works of the flesh" (5:19–21). "Idolatry to Paul is the very antithesis of the worship of God."[18]

Idolatry and the failure to worship God

The central passage about idolatry for the theme of worship is Romans 1:18–25. Paul says that that God has manifestly announced the truth of his invisible attributes through what he has made ("plain" [1:19]; "clearly perceived" [1:20]), but people have suppressed that truth. As a result, they are without excuse (1:20). Paul even includes the audacious proclamation that sinners "knew" God (1:21; cf. 1:25, 28, 32), but suppress that knowledge (1:18; cf. 1:21, 23, 25, 28, 32). Therefore, God "gave them up" (1:24, 26, 28) to do what they want to do anyway. And what is it that they want to do? They want to worship something other than themselves.

But Paul particularly penetrates the theme of worship in verse 21. Paul says that "they did not honor him as God," displaying the centrality of honoring God in the life of a Christian. Furthermore, they did not "give thanks to him," highlighting the importance of thanksgiving. Moreover, they "exchanged the glory of the immortal God for images resembling mortal man and birds and animals and reptiles" (v. 23). In other words, they transferred the focus that should have been on God's glorious attributes and began to worship human and beastly images.

The text furthermore states that God's giving them over to permissive judgment (that is, to do the things that they want to do but that function as destructive judgment on them) is "because they exchanged the truth about God for a lie" (v. 25), repeating the language of evil exchange already surfaced in verse 23. Finally, using the explicit language of worship, we read that they "worshiped and served the creature rather than the Creator" (v. 25).[19] Worshiping and serving the creature is probably another way of saying that they engaged in idolatrous acts with creature-like images, but may also include a suggestion that their worship was human-centered, connecting with the statement in verse 23 that they went after "images resembling mortal man" in addition to the other images. There is a sharp distinction between the Creator and the creature in Paul's thought. But here Paul says that these people have broken down that distinction by worshiping creatures.[20]

---

18. Tony Costa, *Worship and the Risen Jesus in the Pauline Letters*, StBibLit 157 (New York: Lang, 2013), 129.

19. Romans 1:23 and 25 seem to contain various allusions to OT texts that focus on the golden calf incident, including Ps. 106:19–20; Jer. 2:11b (cf. 2:20–28); and Hos. 4:7. See G. K. Beale, *We Become What We Worship: A Biblical Theology of Idolatry* (Downers Grove, IL: IVP Academic, 2008), 204–11.

20. Costa, *Worship and the Risen Jesus*, 76–79; Ronald E. Man, "False and True Worship in Romans 1:18–25," *BSac* 157 (2000): 27–28.

Toward the end of Paul's description of what happens when people fail to worship God in Romans 1, Paul writes that "since they did not see fit to acknowledge God, God gave them up" (1:28). Acknowledging God—whether in worship or life—might be viewed a shorthand summary of worship.

Theology for Worship

Galatians and Romans contain a lot of theology in a concentrated space. The relationship between sound theology and worship appears repeatedly in Galatians and Romans. This is noticeable, since Paul emphasizes the importance of sound doctrine in these two letters probably more than in any of his other letters. Thus we see that worship is theological. This is a key takeaway from this chapter—right theology is foundational for right worship.

Calling out attributes of God the Father or Jesus the Son

Though not worship itself, nor even a reflection on worship, Paul's opening volley in Romans concerning the gospel includes shout-outs such as we would expect in worship of Jesus. Paul proclaims that Jesus "was declared to be the Son of God in power according to the Spirit of holiness by his resurrection from the dead, Jesus Christ our Lord" (1:4). This pattern of calling out attributes of God or of Jesus continues throughout Romans (in such diverse contexts as 1:20; 2:4–5; 3:4, 24–26; 4:17; 9:14–18; 11:33–36; 14:9; 15:5, 8).

Peace with God, access to God, and rejoicing

In 5:1–2, Paul emphasizes that because we have been justified by faith, (1) we have peace with God,[21] (2) we have access to God via the one who introduces us into God's courtroom, Jesus Christ, and (3) we "rejoice in hope of the glory of God." All of these are not only crucial for being in right relationship with God but are also basic for our worship of God. Once again, "glory of God" is ambiguous. But in this case, because it is linked with hope, the expression probably points toward future glory that God will give his people.[22]

Rejoicing and hoping

In Romans 5:3–5 we rejoice in our sufferings because of the endurance, character, and hope that are produced in us by God's pouring his love into our hearts through the Holy Spirit. There are a few key ideas that

21. This does not mean that we have a feeling of peacefulness; rather, "God is no longer against him but for him, and he does not suffer God's resistance but experiences God's endowing work" (Adolf Schlatter, *Romans: The Righteousness of God*, trans. Siegried S. Schatzmann [Peabody, MA: Hendrickson, 1995], 119).

22. Joseph A. Fitzmyer, *Romans*, AB 33 (New York: Doubleday, 1993), 396–97.

are important for worship as well in these three verses. We can rejoice (in the presence of God, for where else is our rejoicing directed?) when we suffer. One of the reasons we rejoice is found in Romans 5:11: we rejoice because we have been reconciled to God! These verses also remind us to look forward to what God will do ("hope"), both now and in the future. Furthermore, these verses show us that we rejoice and hope in this way because God's love has been poured out into our hearts through the Holy Spirit. In other words, he initiates and we respond.

Directed toward God through Jesus

In Romans 7:25, Paul interrupts his flow of thought with an outburst of praise: "Thanks be to God through Jesus Christ our Lord!" Regardless of how one interprets the struggle of the "wretched man" (7:24; see 14–25 for fuller context)—whether as the struggle of a believer, as the struggle of an unbeliever or pious Jew, as a grand analogy describing the change from the old age to the new age, or as something else—7:25 is viewed by most interpreters as the cry of a believer.[23] And what do we learn about worship from this verse? We learn that thanks is directed to God through Jesus Christ. Like Romans 5:2, Jesus is the basis for our access to God, and is, moreover, the grounds of the thanksgiving we exclaim.

No condemnation

In Romans 8:1, Paul launches one of the most-loved chapters in the Bible with the declaration, "There is therefore now no condemnation for those who are in Christ Jesus." We already know from this letter that we have access to God's presence through Christ (5:2); now we learn that when we stand in his presence, we stand uncondemned. "It follows that if condemnation as an objective reality has been removed, there is no legitimate place for condemnation as a subjective experience."[24] This is crucial when we stand or bow in worship in the presence of a holy God.

The Holy Spirit

Throughout the first twenty-seven verses of Romans 8, the role of the Holy Spirit is highlighted as central in the life of a believer. In Romans 8, Christians (1) walk in the Spirit (8:4), (2) set their minds on the things of the Spirit (8:5–7), (3) put to death the deeds of the body by the Spirit (8:13), (4) are led by the Spirit (8:14), (5) know the Fatherhood of God by the Spirit (8:15–17), (6) hope in the Spirit (8:18–25), and (7) pray in the

---

23. "There are difficulties regarding this verse on any view, but 'Thanks be to God' is certainly the cry of the believer" (Leon Morris, *The Epistle to the Romans*, PiNTC [Grand Rapids: Eerdmans, 1988], 286).

24. Robert H. Mounce, *Romans*, NAC 27 (Nashville: Broadman & Holman, 1995), 174.

Spirit (8:26–27).[25] Each of these is important in the context of worship. A few highlights from this rich passage for thinking clearly about worship include the leading of the Spirit, which is crucial in worship (8:14); the focus on our adoption instead of our fears when we worship (8:15a)—to such a degree that we cry out "Abba! Father!" (8:15b; cf. Gal. 4:6); the direct witness of the Spirit to/with our spirit that we are children of God and heirs (8:16–17); the groaning along with the rest of the creation as we lament the distance between our current state and the redemption of our bodies (8:18–25); and, perhaps most importantly, the work of the Spirit in helping us in our weakness when we pray by interceding for us with wordless groanings (8:26–27). In all of this, the Holy Spirit is central.

Abba! Father! via the Spirit

In Galatians 4:6, the Holy Spirit has been sent into our hearts, and he is the one who cries, "Abba! Father!" This is nearly the same in Romans 8:15, except in Romans we cry, "Abba! Father!" by the Spirit. Because of the similarities between the two passages, I think it likely that the two passages view the same worship activity from two different perspectives—one from the perspective of what we do by the Spirit (Rom. 8:16) and one from the perspective of what the Spirit does in us (Gal. 4:6). That is, we cry out in acknowledgment of our adoption along with the Holy Spirit, who cries out with us, interceding *with* us and *for* us at the same time (cf. Rom. 8:26–27).[26] This is all based on our new relationship with God; he is now our adoptive Father, and we need the Spirit to help us accept and respond appropriately to our adoption (Gal. 4:1–6). This is the only place where worship or prayer is associated with the Holy Spirit in Galatians. The Holy Spirit's role is to help us address God as Father. Never is the Holy Spirit the recipient of worship in Paul's writings, even though in Galatians and Romans the Holy Spirit figures prominently in other contexts. "While many doxologies glorify God generally, without specifying a person within the Trinity, the focus is usually on God the Father and in some cases on Jesus Christ."[27]

Worship through declaration

Romans 8:31–39 offers an example of worship through declaration of truth. It is not simply doctrinal content that is awe-inspiring in this section; it is the passion and the God-focus—the implicit worship—that permeates the climax of Romans 8. Included in this outpouring of truth-affirmation is that no one and nothing can stand against us when God is for us and when the

25. For more on the role of the Holy Spirit in Rom. 8:1–27, see Kenneth Berding, *Walking in the Spirit* (Wheaton, IL: Crossway, 2011), 15–112.
26. Berding, *Walking in the Spirit*, 74–75.
27. Daniel I. Block, *For the Glory of God: Recovering a Biblical Theology of Worship* (Grand Rapids: Baker Academic, 2014), 50. See also Boris Paschke, "Praying to the Holy Spirit in Early Christianity," *TynBul* 64, no. 2 (2013): 299–316.

crucified Christ is interceding for us (8:31–34). These truths are conjoined in a stunning crescendo where Paul utterly denies that anything in heaven or earth is capable of separating us from the love of Christ (8:35–39).[28]

Sovereignty and initiative of God

Paul places great emphasis on the sovereignty of God throughout Romans 9 (emphatically so), and continues the theme into Romans 10, even though in chapter 10 he also emphasizes the need for people to confess the Lord Jesus and believe in him (vv. 9–10).[29] The upshot for worship is that we venerate a God who both knows and plans all that will take place, something we as humans cannot fathom. In chapter 10 the theme of sovereignty extends to a focus on the initiative of God (vv. 18–21), something that is important to know regarding salvation, but also is crucial in worship. God is the initiator; we, the responders.

Faithfulness to his promise

A theme that runs through chapters 9–11 is that God is faithful to his promises. A key verse is 11:29: "For the gifts and the calling of God are irrevocable"—that is, if God has made promises to Israel, and since he has called them as his people, he will make good on his promises (cf. 15:8).[30] This is a theological truth that we can take with us into worship.

Eschatological worship

Eschatological worship is implied in Paul's quotation of Isaiah 45:23 in Romans 14:11: "As I live, says the Lord, every knee shall bow to me, and every tongue shall confess to God." In the immediate context, though, Paul's purpose is to communicate that each of us must stand on our own before God (14:12).

Doxology

In two sections of Romans, Paul breaks out into doxological praise. Just as Paul closed a former section (end of chap. 8) by affirming truths about God, at the end of another main section (11:33–36), Paul simply breaks out in praise. Paul lauds the wisdom and knowledge of God and acclaims the truth that God is the source of all things and the one to whom all

---

28. "In these verses [38–39] the confidence of the apostle is expressed in the strongest language. He heaps words together in an effort to set forth fully the absolute inability of all created things, separately or united, to frustrate the purpose of God, or to turn away his love from those whom he has determined to save" (1886; repr., Charles Hodge, *Commentary on the Epistle to the Romans* [Grand Rapids: Eerdmans, 1950], 291).
29. "The predestinarian statements in ch. 9 are not revoked in our entire chapter [ch. 10]. They are unflinchingly adopted in the appeal to Scripture" (Ernst Käsemann, *Commentary on Romans*, trans. and ed. Geoffrey W. Bromiley [Grand Rapids: Eerdmans, 1980], 297).
30. "His gifts are the privileges he bestowed on Israel, which are listed in 9:4–5" (John R. W. Stott, *The Message of Romans*, The Bible Speaks Today [Leicester: Inter-Varsity, 1994], 306).

worship belongs ("from him and through him and to him are all things"). Throughout, Paul emphasizes that God is wholly other in his essence—far too great for humans to understand.[31] He then closes with: "To him be glory forever. Amen" (11:36). There is one central thing to underscore about worship in this context: Paul, to this point in Romans, has been engaging with some deep doctrinal issues, some of which are too large for humans to fully comprehend. This suggests that spending reflective time in worship is an appropriate thing to pair with teaching of doctrine.

Appropriately, Paul closes his magnificent letter with a doxology (16:25–27). In it, he highlights the themes of God's faithfulness to his promise, the proclamation of the gospel to the nations, and the sovereignty of God. He concludes by focusing on God's wisdom and glory: "to the only wise God be glory forevermore through Jesus Christ! Amen" (16:27).

Worship Is Life

Worship is more than just an action carried out on special occasions. Worship is a posture and a lifestyle. The one who would worship as a lifestyle lives with a posture of yieldedness and dependency on God, resisting the lure to conform to the world, and applying a God-glorifying heart to the practicalities of life.

A lifestyle of worship

In Galatians 2:19–20, Paul explains that he died to the law so that he "might live to God." He follows up with a reflection on his co-crucifixion with Christ and explains that he only lives to God because Christ lives in him, accessed by faith. In verse 20, he reflects on "the Son of God, who loved me and gave himself for me." In other words, Paul's lifestyle is a type of worship ("I live to God"), and he is empowered by Christ to live out that posture of worship in daily life. Jumping ahead in the book, the theme of life as worship appears also in Galatians 6:7, where Paul comments that "God is not mocked" and connects how one lives ("sows") to whether God is mocked or is not mocked. In other words, through the way we conduct our lives, God is either extolled or held up for derision.

Presenting ourselves to God

In Romans 6:13, 16, and 19, Paul introduces us to the idea of the presentation of self to God, a theme that will burn brightly in 12:1.[32] Paul

---

31. Costa, *Worship and the Risen Jesus*, 43–44.
32. "The language of Romans 6:13 . . . specifically anticipates 12:1. . . . The verb is the same but the imagery is that of ownership and servitude in chapter 6, rather than sacrificial offering" (David Peterson, "Worship and Ethics in Romans 12," *TynBul* 44 [1993]: 278). "This integration of worship and holiness is borne out further, by the opening verses of chapter 12, where Paul echoes chapter 6 but within an explicit appeal" (N. T. Wright, "Worship and the Spirit in the New Testament," in *Spirit in Worship—Worship in the Spirit*, eds. Teresa Berger and Bryan T. Spinks [Collegeville, MN: Liturgical Press, 2009], 19).

instructs us to stop presenting ourselves to unrighteousness, but rather to present ourselves to God (6:13). Similarly, he says that we should stop presenting the members of our bodies (that is, ourselves) to sin as though we are slaves to sin; rather, we should view ourselves as slaves of righteousness (6:16–19). All this is rooted in our union with Christ and in our identification with him in his death and resurrection, all of which have been unpacked by Paul in 6:1–10. Presentation of the members of our body to God for righteousness is the natural posture of people whose bondage to sin has already been broken. This is also the basic posture of worship. We repeatedly present ourselves to God (yield, submit, surrender). We view ourselves as dead to sin and alive to God in Christ Jesus (6:11). As such, worship becomes a way of life.

Living sacrifices

In Romans 12:1, we encounter what is perhaps the most important "therefore" in all of the Bible, and it leads into perhaps Paul's most important (or second only to 1:18–28) comments about worship in the book of Romans. In fact, 12:1–2 parallels (antithetically) in many ways Romans 1:18–28.[33] Paul's basis for these comments is everything he has already written about sin, justification, faith, access to God, sanctification, the Holy Spirit, sovereignty, and the inclusion of Gentiles with Jews in God's plan of salvation—"therefore" (!)—"I appeal to you . . . brothers, by the mercies of God, to present your bodies as a living sacrifice, holy and acceptable to God, which is your spiritual worship." There are three important issues to note about worship here. First, worship is based on the "mercies of God" (shorthand for all that Paul has already written to this point in Romans). That is, there is a doctrinal/positional basis on which we worship, a basis that has already been established in Romans 1–11. Second, we are to "present" our bodies to God. This, of course, is reminiscent of Paul's discussion in 6:13, 16, 19. (The idea that someone could offer his or her body to God would have been foreign to most Greek thought in the first century, which tended to view the body as evil or as imprisoning the soul.) Third, we are to approach God as though we are sacrifices to be offered on an altar. This, he says (depending on the translation you are using), is a "worship" or "service" that is "spiritual" or "reasonable." I would like to suggest that we understand the "worship" or "service" as either a "worshipful serving" or a "service-oriented worship." That works well with the already-observed tendency of Paul to describe a life of sanctification in worship terms. It is hard to determine whether the adjective should be "reasonable/rational" or "spiritual."[34] Perhaps these, too, should not be regarded as mutually exclusive. Regardless, a key concept for understanding

33. Beale, *We Become What We Worship*, 216–18.
34. See balanced discussion in C. E. B. Cranfield, *The Epistle to the Romans*, ICC (Edinburgh: T&T Clark, 1979), 602–5.

worship is the connection between worship and life. Worship and ethics cannot be separated from one another.[35]

Not conformed to this world

Paul continues to connect this posture of worship with the way the Roman Christians are supposed to live in the world (12:2), signifying once again that worship is not just something that happens in a worship service but is part and parcel of a Christian's entire life. Indeed, Christian ethics flow out of and is part and parcel of a life of worship.[36] Christians are to daily resist conformity to the world and constantly be being transformed in their thinking and in their discerning of the will of God.

Worship in daily life

Worship as ongoing lifestyle appears also in Romans 14:6, where Paul writes, "The one who observes the day, observes it in honor of the Lord. The one who eats, eats in honor of the Lord, since he gives thanks to God, while the one who abstains, abstains in honor of the Lord and gives thanks to God." Paul goes on to write in 14:7–8, "For none of us lives to himself, and none of us dies to himself. If we live, we live to the Lord, and if we die, we die to the Lord." Paul wants us to know that our entire orientation in life should be focused on thanking God and giving him the honor that is his due.

SIGNIFICANCE OF GALATIANS AND ROMANS FOR BIBLICAL WORSHIP

How are Paul's letters to the Galatians and Romans important for the practice of worship? I will limit my comments to five themes that show up in Galatians and/or Romans that can help us to become more faithful worshipers and worshiping communities.

1. The focus of our worship should be the glory of God based on the atoning work of Christ by which we have access to God. The Holy Spirit's role is to guide us, help us when we are weak, and empower us in such worship. Although no true theological problem exists with praying to the Holy Spirit, especially when emphasizing the works ascribed to him in Scripture ("guide us, convict us, comfort us"), we should seek for our worship to ordinarily follow the pattern laid down in Scripture, that of glorifying God based on what Christ has done.

---

35. "The worship of which God is worthy is not adequately expressed in symbols, rites, rituals, and token offerings, but rather in practical daily ministry to human need in the context of routine life and mundane activities, a life-ethos that serves the interests of God in the world" (Massey, "Paul and Christian Worship," 105).

36. Ernst Käsemann, "Gottesdienst im Alltag der Welt (zu Rm 12)," in *Judentum Urchristentum Kirche: Festschrift für Joachim Jeremías*, ed. W. Eltester (Berlin: Töpelmann, 1960), 165–71.

2. Paul emphasizes both in Galatians and Romans that in the presence of God it doesn't matter whether one is a Jew or Greek. This theme of inclusion should encourage us to be intentionally inclusive in our worship services, making no distinctions based on ethnicity either for those who join together with us in worship or those who lead our times of worship.

3. Paul has strong words to say about idolatry in Romans 1. Ironically, the way we tend to structure our contemporary worship services means that we often place the focus squarely on the worship leader and thereby risk subverting the worship of God. In contemporary worship, too much emphasis is often placed on the worship leader, including the expectation that such a leader will wear the appropriate (cool) attire, play only the best possible guitar (or other instrument), be illuminated by the brightest spotlight in the room, perform the music flawlessly, and sing only the most up-to-date songs (and if the songwriter is well-known, make that person rich off worship-song royalties). The risk, of course, is that all this will lead to idolatry, and that the honor due God alone will be placed on something or someone else.

4. The relationship between sound theology and worship bubbles to the surface regularly in Galatians and Romans. This is noticeable, since Paul emphasizes the importance of sound doctrine in these two letters probably more than in any of his other letters. I believe that more insipid and incorrect theological ideas get introduced into our churches through worship songs than through any other means. Paul's letters to the Galatians and Romans are a constant reminder that we must emphasize sound and robust doctrine in all our corporate gatherings, including in our song selection. Even if only one out of ten worship songs being composed today could be described as doctrinally robust (and I am not making such a claim), there would still be plenty of deep, insightful, and truly worshipful songs for worship leaders to choose from. Worship leaders should choose doctrinally faithful songs, and only doctrinally faithful songs.

5. Finally, worship for Paul is clearly not just what happens when God's people gather to sing, pray, and learn from God's Word. Worship is life. Paul envisions people who live out the regular stuff of daily life in the presence of God. Christians should view themselves as living sacrifices who ardently avoid conformity to the world. Throughout their days they keep presenting themselves to God as available for his service. Just like a worship service, so are their lives.

BIBLIOGRAPHY

Beale, G. K. *We Become What We Worship: A Biblical Theology of Idolatry*. Downers Grove, IL: IVP Academic, 2008.

Berding, Kenneth. *What Are Spiritual Gifts? Rethinking the Conventional View.* Grand Rapids: Kregel Academic, 2006.

Blackwell, Ben C. "Immortal Glory and the Problem of Death in Romans 3.23." *JSNT* 32 (2010): 285–308.

Block, Daniel I. *For the Glory of God: Recovering a Biblical Theology of Worship*. Grand Rapids: Baker Academic, 2014.

Costa, Tony. *Worship and the Risen Jesus in the Pauline Letters.* StBibLit 157. New York: Lang, 2013.

Cranfield, C. E. B. *The Epistle to the Romans.* ICC. Edinburgh: T&T Clark, 1979.

Elliott, Susan. *Cutting Too Close for Comfort: Paul's Letter to the Galatians in Its Anatolian Cultic Context.* JSNTSup 248. London: T&T Clark, 2003.

Fitzmyer, Joseph A. *Romans*. AB 33. New York: Doubleday, 1993.

Hardin, Justin K. *Galatians and the Imperial Cult: A Critical Analysis of the First-Century Social Context of Paul's Letter*. WUNT 2/237. Tübingen: Mohr Siebeck, 2008.

Heil, John Paul. *The Letters of Paul as Rituals of Worship.* Eugene, OR: Cascade, 2011.

Hodge, Charles. *Commentary on the Epistle to the Romans.* 1886. Reprint, Grand Rapids: Eerdmans, 1950.

Käsemann, Ernst. *Commentary on Romans.* Translated and edited by Geoffrey W. Bromiley. Grand Rapids: Eerdmans, 1980.

______. "Gottesdienst im Alltag der Welt (zu Rm 12)." In *Judentum Urchristentum Kirche: Festschrift für Joachim Jeremías*, edited by W. Eltester, 165–71. Berlin: Töpelmann, 1960.

Levy, Ian Christopher Levy, Philip D. W. Krey, and Thomas Ryan, trans. and eds. *The Letter to the Romans.* The Bible in Medieval Tradition. Grand Rapids: Eerdmans, 2013.

Man, Ronald E. "False and True Worship in Romans 1:18–25." *BSac* 157 (2000): 26–34.

Martin, Troy. "Apostasy to Paganism: The Rhetorical Stasis of the Galatian Controversy." In *The Galatians Debate: Contemporary Issues in Rhetorical and Historical Interpretation*, edited by Mark D. Nanos, 73–94. Peabody, MA: Hendrickson, 2002.

Massey, Lesly F. "Paul and Christian Worship in Light of Romans 12:1." *Chm* 130 (2016).

Moo, Douglas J. *The Epistle to the Romans.* NICNT. Grand Rapids: Eerdmans, 1996.

______. *Galatians*. BECNT. Grand Rapids: Baker Academic, 2013.

Morris, Leon. *The Epistle to the Romans.* PiNTC. Grand Rapids: Eerdmans, 1988.

Mounce, Robert H. *Romans*. NAC 27. Nashville: Broadman & Holman, 1995.

Newman, Carey C. *Paul's Glory-Christology: Tradition and Rhetoric*. NovTSup 69. Leiden: Brill, 1992.

Pao, David W. *Thanksgiving: An Investigation of a Pauline Theme*. NSBT 13. Downers Grove, IL: InterVarsity, 2002.

Paschke, Boris. "Praying to the Holy Spirit in Early Christianity." *TynBul* 64, no. 2 (2013): 299–316.

Peterson, David. "Worship and Ethics in Romans 12." *TynBul* 44 (1993): 271–88.

Richards, E. Randolph, and Brandon J. O'Brien. *Misreading Scripture with Western Eyes*. Downers Grove, IL: IVP Academic, 2012.

Schlatter, Adolf. *Romans: The Righteousness of God*. Translated by Siegried S. Schatzmann. Peabody, MA: Hendrickson, 1995.

Schreiner, Thomas R. *Galatians*. ZECNT. Grand Rapids: Zondervan, 2010.

Simmons, William A. "Priest—Sacrifice—Life as Worship: A Pauline Matrix for Understanding Romans." *BibSac* 172 (2016): 85–99.

Stott, John R. W. *The Message of Romans*. The Bible Speaks Today. Leicester: Inter-Varsity Press, 1994.

Walters, James C. *Ethnic Issues in Paul's Letter to the Romans: Changing Self-Definitions in Earliest Roman Christianity*. Valley Forge, PA: Trinity Press International, 1993.

Winter, Bruce W. *Seek the Welfare of the City: Christians as Benefactors and Citizens*. Grand Rapids: Eerdmans, 1994.

Wright, N. T. *Paul in Fresh Perspective*. Minneapolis: Fortress, 2005.

______. "Worship and the Spirit in the New Testament." In *The Spirit in Worship—Worship in the Spirit*, edited by Teresa Berger and Bryan T. Spinks, 3–24. Collegeville, MN: Liturgical Press, 2009.

CHAPTER 28

DOING ALL THINGS IN THE NAME OF THE LORD

Worship in the Prison Epistles

A. Chadwick Thornhill

CONTEXT OF WORSHIP IN THE PRISON EPISTLES

Though Paul's letters have been mined vigorously for their theological insights for centuries, an underemphasized dimension of Paul's theological purposes is that of worship.[1] Perhaps this is because linguistically Paul only uses the major Greek verb for "worship" (*proskuneō*) once in his letters (1 Cor. 14:25). If worship, as Daniel Block has suggested, is "reverential submission and homage" to God, then we must look not just for the words for "worship" in Paul's letters, but rather for those ideas that fit within the conceptual framework of worship throughout Scripture.[2] With a wider definition in view, we find not that Paul rarely speaks of worship but rather that his letters are permeated with a call to his recipients to wholeheartedly devote themselves to God, through Christ, and in the power of the Spirit—in other words, to worship. As John Paul Heil recognizes, "We often neglect to give [Paul] the full consideration he deserves as the preeminent and paradigmatic person of prayer and worship. . . . [His

1. As Heil notes (John Paul Heil, *The Letters of Paul as Rituals of Worship* [Eugene, OR: Cascade, 2011], 3), some exceptions are David Peterson, *Engaging with God: A Biblical Theology of Worship* (Leicester: Inter-Varsity Press, 1992); Larry Hurtado, *At the Origins of Christian Worship: The Context and Character of Earliest Christian Devotion* (Grand Rapids: Eerdmans, 1999); Hurtado, *Lord Jesus Christ: Devotion to Jesus in Earliest Christianity* (Grand Rapids: Eerdmans, 2003); Gerald L. Borchert, *Worship in the New Testament: Divine Mystery and Human Response* (St. Louis: Chalice, 2008).
2. Daniel I. Block, *For the Glory of God: Recovering a Biblical Theology of Worship* (Grand Rapids: Baker Academic, 2014), 23.

letters] were originally performed publicly in a liturgical assembly . . . [to] frame the issues and problems that Paul addressed through them within a context of communal worship . . . to enable and facilitate the worship of the assembly."[3] Put in this light, Paul's letters are thoroughgoing acts of worship intended to facilitate both the private and public worship of the congregations to whom he wrote. It is with this concept of worship in mind that we turn to the Prison Epistles.

The Pauline Prison Epistles, though commonly grouped together with the understanding that they were produced from a similar setting during Paul's ministry, each address diverse and divergent issues stemming from the unique social settings of each of Paul's congregations. Contained within this grouping are circular letters, letters to local churches, and a personal letter to a friend of Paul as well. Just as the forms of the letters are diverse, so too are the contexts and needs of their audiences, as well as the theological emphases found within them.

Ephesians

The letter to the Ephesians belongs to the group of "disputed" Pauline Letters,[4] meaning that scholars debate whether these letters came from Paul himself or from either a later student of Paul's or a pseudonymous author. For this epistle, suggested reasons for doubting Pauline authorship are its unique stylistic differences from Paul's other letters, unique theological emphases (e.g., a supposed "realized eschatology," a more developed ecclesiology, and absence of "justification" language, among others), and unique vocabulary in comparison with Paul's other letters. Adding to the difficulty of this letter is the relative lack of details about the intended audience within the letter as well as the absence of the phrase "in Ephesus" in several early and important manuscripts. This creates the possibility either that the letter was actually the letter to the Laodiceans mentioned in Colossians 4:16, or that it was intended as a circular letter for a region rather than a specific local church community, though it is possible to read the "in Ephesus" as authentic as well. Regardless of the identity of the original audience, as Ben Witherington has argued, there are reasonable explanations for these challenges to Pauline authorship, especially given the regional dialectic differences that Paul, or his amanuensis, may have accounted for in writing, as well as the epideictic rhetoric (i.e., focused on praise rather than argumentation) that is adopted here and not used in the "accepted" Pauline Letters.[5] Given the potential circular nature of the letter, Paul's encouragements and admonitions within it, especially of unity

3. Heil, *Letters of Paul as Rituals of Worship*, 1.
4. Included typically within this grouping are Ephesians and Colossians as well as the Pastoral Epistles (1–2 Timothy and Titus), and sometimes 2 Thessalonians as well.
5. Ben Witherington III, *The Letters to Philemon, the Colossians, and the Ephesians: A Socio-rhetorical Commentary on the Captivity Epistles* (Grand Rapids: Eerdmans, 2007), 219–24.

between Jews and Gentiles within the church,[6] may more be a means of reinforcing the churches in the region rather than correcting major issues as in, for example, Galatians or 1 Corinthians.

Philippians

The letter to the Philippians falls into the category of Paul's undisputed letters, meaning virtually no scholar doubts that it originated from the apostle Paul. Paul likely wrote the letter toward the end of his life and ministry, and the letter evidences the special relationship between the apostle and this community of believers. Paul writes to the Philippians out of gratitude for their support for his ministry as well as to encourage them in the midst of social pressures and possible persecutions they were experiencing from outsiders, particularly from the local Romans and pagans, since Philippi was a Roman city.

Colossians

Colossians, like Ephesians, finds itself included among the group of "disputed" Pauline Letters. In that it shares many themes and stylistic similarities with Ephesians, a similar approach to authorship is warranted, meaning that Paul, or his amanuensis, likely wrote in an Asiatic style that would be fitting for the recipients.[7] Colossae was a Greek city, home to Jews and Gentiles, and thus to both Diaspora Judaism and local and imperial cults. This letter does take more of an argumentative tone (deliberative rather than epideictic)[8] than Ephesians, addressing several teachings and practices that Paul finds out of step with the acceptable norms of Jesus's community of followers. Of chief target for Paul are the adherence of certain Jewish practices among Gentile Christians, particularly with ascetic and mystical activities in mind. Paul sees such practices as devised by humans rather than God and encourages the Colossian believers to live a life transformed by the power of the Spirit of God and the word of Christ.

Philemon

The last of the four Prison Epistles in the New Testament canon, Philemon diverges slightly from the form of the previous three letters in that it is largely a personal letter written to a person named Philemon, largely concerning an appeal Paul makes concerning Philemon's slave Onesimus. It is clear from the letter that some point of tension had arisen between Onesimus and his master Philemon, though there is debate among scholars as to what exactly created this conflict. Whether Onesimus deserted or defrauded Philemon, or appealed to Paul for some other reason, he

6. See A. Chadwick Thornhill, *The Chosen People: Election, Paul, and Second Temple Judaism* (Downers Grove, IL: IVP Academic, 2015), 179–85, 218–28.
7. Witherington, *Letters*, 100–102.
8. See Witherington, *Letters*, 103–7.

seeks the apostle's help in reconciling with Philemon. Paul's response is grounded in the radical ethic of Jesus. which offered a countercultural vision to social relationships, in this instance between a master and his slave.

Summary

Though the purpose and form of each of these letters differ, sometimes drastically, they share in common that Paul is identified as "imprisoned" in each of them. Within these letters, Paul often recounts his own sufferings, not as a means of acquiring sympathy from his recipients, but rather as a means of rejoicing at the progress of the gospel as well as to encourage his hearers to continue pressing on in their journeys of faith in the midst of their own difficulties. The number and locations of Paul's imprisonments are debated, largely because of the limited historical evidence we possess, and the fact that Paul likely experienced varying degrees of restrictions during his imprisonments.[9] At times Paul was actually imprisoned in stocks and beaten, while at other times he was placed more on "house arrest," with restrictions to his travel imposed. Paul ultimately sees his imprisonment as to Christ and not Rome (e.g., Eph. 3:1; Philem. 1, 9), reinforcing his trust in Christ as the ultimate judge, his embracing of the sacrificial and humble identity of a follower of Christ, and his willingness to suffer for Christ for the sake of the advancement of the gospel.

THEOLOGY OF WORSHIP

Following Block's taxonomy of worship, we find that the biblical texts see worship of God (i.e., "reverential human acts of submission and homage")[10] as involving one's disposition, cultic (i.e., "formal religious") service, and devotion of resources/life.[11] In other words, all of life, lived as God prescribes, is an act of worship and service, showing honor and covenantal fidelity to the gracious Creator God. These three dimensions of worship attested throughout Scripture can likewise be found in the Prison Epistles of Paul.

Christlike Virtue as Worship

The Prison Epistles are replete with admonitions to express Christlike virtues in the life of the believer, both in private and personal conduct. Paul understood the Christian life as one that emulated Christ through identification, communion, and union with Jesus. Paul praises the Ephesians for their faith(fulness) (*pistis*) to the Lord and love for God's people (Eph. 1:15–17; 2:8). He likewise prays that this faith(fulness) will sustain the indwelling presence of Christ in their midst through the working

9. For a brief discussion, see Stanley E. Porter, *The Apostle Paul: His Life, Thought, and Letters* (Grand Rapids: Eerdmans, 2016), 61–69.
10. Block, *For the Glory of God*, 23.
11. Block, *For the Glory of God*, 26.

of the Spirit, and that, on the basis of their foundation of love, they will come to know God more deeply and fully in Christ (Eph. 3:16–19). He then admonishes the Ephesian believers to embody the virtues of humility, patience, love, forgiveness, and peace,[12] which, through the work of the Spirit, will bind the community together in unity of faith (Eph. 4:1–6, 13; 4:32–5:2). Paul offers a similar admonition to the Colossians, where his list of virtues includes patience, thankfulness, faith(fulness), compassion, kindness, humility, love, and forgiveness 51-(Col. 1:10–12; 2:6–7; 3:12–15).

These virtues are to be embodied in the life that emulates God as revealed in Christ Jesus. While these virtues have an important place in the church body, Paul shows their embeddedness in the life of the family household as well. As Michael Gorman summarizes Paul's admonitions in Ephesians 5:21–33, "The church is the place where believers embody the virtues of the messianic era of peace as a foretaste of the full and future reign of the messiah's peace, for Christ *is* our peace—present tense."[13] Though English stylistic conventions can obscure the structure of this passage in our translations, Paul's admonitions in Ephesians 5:21–24 are a grammatical continuation of his earlier command to "be filled with the Spirit" (Eph. 5:18) as well as the participle of 5:21 ("submitting to one another in the fear of Christ," HCSB), which governs the rest of 5:22–24.[14] What this demonstrates is that the radical transformation which Paul envisions is possible only in the submission of the believer to the working of the Spirit in their lives and that the social relationships of believers are to be governed by a mutual submissions, seeking the good of others and not just the good of the self. The cultivation of these virtues requires nothing less than the total transformation of their patterns of thinking (Eph. 4:23–24) and their affections (Col. 3:1–4), which Paul assures may be accomplished through setting their thoughts on heavenly realities, meditating on the rich truths of the gospel, and enacting the practices that flow from them (Phil. 4:8–9; Col. 3:1–4).

Religious Activity as Worship

We likewise find various descriptions of "cultic service" in the prison epistles. Paul describes and prescribes instructions concerning formal religious activities for the gathered body of believers. As Gorman reminds us, "The church needs appropriate ecclesial practices to sustain its holiness and harmony."[15] The concrete practices outlined in the New Testament do

12. As Gorman notes, "The task of the Christian community is not first of all to *make* peace but to *keep* the peace it has been given in the gospel . . . [which] requires the same kind of cruciform love (4:2; cf. 4:31–5:2) that created the church. Without forbearing, forgiving love, there is no hope for peace" (Michael J. Gorman, *Becoming the Gospel: Paul, Participation, and Mission* [Grand Rapids: Eerdmans, 2015], 196).
13. Gorman, *Becoming the Gospel*, 202.
14. Unless otherwise noted, all biblical translations are from the NIV.
15. Gorman, *Becoming the Gospel*, 197.

not merely function to offer thanks to God, but in actuality shape the kind of people the worshipers become, both as individuals and as the corporate body, the church.

Paul references on several occasions in these letters the public reading and performance of Scripture. In Ephesians 4:11–12, Paul states that those who proclaim and explain the word of God in the assembly of believers do so in order to build up and unify the body of Christ and bring them to conformity to Jesus's image. Similar to the theme of unity, in Colossians 3:15–17, Paul sees the teachings of Christ as functioning to bring peace and thankfulness to God's family. Part of the means by which the message of Christ is made to dwell among believers is through their singing songs of praise to God together. At the conclusion of the letter to the Colossians, Paul instructs the congregation to have this letter publicly read in the church of the Laodiceans and for the Colossians to read the Laodiceans' letter as well (Col. 4:16). In each of these examples, the public reading and singing of Scripture was to function to both give praise to God and to cultivate unity, maturity, peace, and thankfulness within the body of believers.

Paul also describes financial giving as an important part of the worship practices of believers. Grounded, no doubt, in his Christ-hymn of Philippians 2, Paul sees sacrificial giving, a giving of oneself for the good of others, as the pattern to which the lives of believers should conform, based on the pattern of life offered to them through Jesus's own life of other-oriented love and self-sacrifice (Phil. 4:10–19).

Paul describes the Philippians' gift to him as "an acceptable sacrifice, pleasing to God" (Phil. 4:18). Paul uses here a term (*thusia*) common in the Greek version of the Old Testament to refer to various sacrifices offered to YHWH (e.g., Gen. 4:3; 31:54; Exod. 10:25; 18:12; Lev. 2:1–15; Lev. 17:5–8; Deut. 12:27; Judg. 6:18; Pss. 49:5–8, 14, 23; 50:18–21). This represents an example of the spiritualizing of sacrifices in the New Testament, which finds some precedent in the Old Testament as well.[16] The gift of the Philippians to Paul was an act of sacrificial worship on their part, requiring financial sacrifice to provide for his needs.[17] Giving here, again, does not just constitute a good practice (though it is that), but actually functions transformatively to cultivate a heart of charity and service to

16. Paul opens his Letters to the Ephesians and Colossians by addressing them as "saints" (*hagios*), a term with cultic/liturgical implications, which designated things consecrated to the service of God. These believers do not just participate in services or acts of worship, but themselves are dedicated wholly to the service of God and his people.

17. "All of these above-mentioned actions, which are described in sacrificial terms, are part of that total response to the living God which is called for in Rom. 12:1. In this comprehensive exhortation believers are urged to present themselves totally ('your bodies') as *living* sacrifices that are 'holy and acceptable' to God. Their wholehearted presentation of themselves is their 'reasonable or spiritual service' and involves living their total lives in obedience to him" (Peter Thomas O'Brien, *The Epistle to the Philippians*, NIGTC [Grand Rapids: Eerdmans, 1991], 542).

others within the life of the church. By supporting Paul and by giving of their own finances, the Philippians lived out the reality of Jesus's own self-sacrificial love within their own life circumstances.

The Prison Epistles are also replete with prayers, both with references to Paul's own prayers and the prayers of his companions (Eph. 1:16–21; 3:14–21; Phil. 1:3–6, 9–11; 4:10; Col. 1:3–4, 9–12; 1:24; 4:12; Philem. 4–7), references to and commands for the prayers of his recipients (Eph. 6:18–20; Phil. 1:19; 4:4–7; Col. 4:2–4), and prayers included in the letters as well.

Paul customarily opens his letters with a brief word of prayer for his recipients (Phil. 1:2; Col. 1:2; Philem. 1:3). In Ephesians, however, Paul's opening prayer (1:2) transitions into a full-blown prayer of thanksgiving for the gracious interventions of God for his people (1:3–14). Here Paul thanks God for the gracious blessings of being chosen, adopted, redeemed, forgiven, and receiving God's riches, revelation, and hope.

Similarly in Colossians 1:3–14, Paul offers a prayer of thanks for the faith and love that had taken root among the Colossians as a result of their embrace of the gospel. Paul then asks God to fill them with wisdom and understanding in order that they might live thankful lives worthy of the Lord Jesus.

Though quite short, Paul's letter to Philemon also opens and closes with prayers for Paul's recipient. In Philemon 4–7, Paul thanks God for the love and faith of Philemon and asks God that he might increase further still in his faith and effective service. Of this section, Heil comments: "The closing prayer-greeting . . . forms a literary inclusion with the opening prayer-greeting . . . to envelope the entire letter within a context of communal worship. Paul thus ends the letter to Philemon with a prayer that the church in his house may continue to experience the divine grace they have already experienced (v. 3), and Paul hopes that they will continue to experience the effects of this saving grace through the "good" that Philemon can do for Onesimus, Paul, and his house church."[18]

In Ephesians 4:4–6, Paul mentions "one baptism" (along with "one body," "one Spirit," "one faith," "one Lord," and "one God and Father of all") as a unifying activity for the believer. Paul here emphasizes the necessity of the believing community to pursue unity and peace in their midst, and sees baptism as a means of cultivating those virtues. While Paul does not explain its inclusion in the list of unifying beliefs and activities, the rite of baptism offered a visualization of the identification of the believer with the death and resurrection of Jesus. While divisions festered among early Christian communities concerning certain beliefs, practices, and other markers of identity, Paul reminds the Ephesians that their immersion into the Lord Jesus Christ is what unifies them.[19] Jesus's death and resurrection stand at the center of the Christian faith, not just as doctrines to hold, but as a way of life for those who follow him in cruciform love.

18. Heil, *Letters of Paul as Rituals of Worship*, 99.

19. See Clinton E. Arnold, *Ephesians*, ZECNT (Grand Rapids: Zondervan, 2010), 235–36.

This reality is made more explicit in Colossians 2:12, where Paul refers to the Colossian believers "having been buried with him in baptism, in which also you were raised together with him through faith in the working of God, who raised him from among the dead." As N. T. Wright notes, baptism thus means "that being a Christian means dying with Christ to the old solidarities and habits and coming alive to the new family of God and its new lifestyle."[20] The ritual of baptism thus constitutes not just a public act of worship but also serves as a transformative event in which believers completely place their life stories into the story of Jesus and take up his crucified and resurrected identity as their own.

Paul, finally, commends the singing of praise to God as a fitting act of worship for the community of believers. In two passages that closely parallel one another (Eph. 5:18–20; Col. 3:15–17), Paul offers a description of three types of songs fitting to be used in the collective worship experience of believers: psalms (*psalmois*), hymns (*hymois*), and spiritual songs (*odais pnematikais*).

While Colossians 3 offers the more detailed version of the teaching, there is rough parallelism between the two passages. The main additions in the Colossians text are the framing of the unit by calling the Colossians to peace and unity in Christ and the specific connection of the didactic function of these songs to reinforce the teachings of Jesus. In Colossians, Paul directs the songs "to God," while in Ephesians it is to the Lord (assumedly Jesus), and in Colossians, Paul commands thankfulness in his introduction, while in Ephesians he commands being filled with the Spirit. Both units close, however, with giving thanks to God in the name of the Lord Jesus, and though Colossians adds doing everything, not just singing, in the name of the Lord, the central materials are roughly parallel.

Colossians	***Ephesians***
Col. 3:15a: "Let the peace of Christ rule in your hearts, since as members of one body you were called to peace."	
Col. 3:15b: "And be thankful"	Eph. 5:18: "be filled with the Spirit"
Col. 3:16a: "Let the message of Christ dwell among you richly"	
Col. 3:16b: "as you teach and admonish one another with all wisdom through psalms, hymns, and spiritual songs, singing to God with gratitude in your hearts."	Eph. 5:19: "speaking to one another with psalms, hymns, and spiritual songs. Sing and make music from your heart to the Lord"

20. N. T. Wright, *Colossians and Philemon*, TNTC 12 (Downers Grove, IL: InterVarsity Press, 1986), 112.

Colossians	**Ephesians**
Col. 3:17a: "And whatever you do, whether in word or deed, do it all in the name of the Lord Jesus"	Eph. 5:20b: "in the name of our Lord Jesus Christ."
Col. 3:17b: "giving thanks to God the Father through him."	Eph. 5:20a: "always giving thanks to God the Father for everything."

The three types of songs mentioned have connection to common Old Testament terminology for songs and poems. As Allen Ross notes, "psalms" (*psalmois*) refer to poems sung to instrumental accompaniment.[21] "Hymns" (*hymnois*) refer in the Old Testament to special songs of praise sung to YHWH, which, in contrast to a psalm, often focused more on the nature of God than one's personal experiences.[22] The third collection, "spiritual songs" (*odais pneumatikais*), is more frequently taken as "new songs that set forth the believer's spiritual enjoyment of life under God."[23] Here, again, the songs function both to offer thanks and praise to God and to transform the minds and hearts of believers as they sing and set their attention on the message of Christ. Finally, Block notes the Trinitarian shape of Paul's admonition in Ephesians 5:18–20 and Colossians 3:15–17.[24] It is the message of Christ that provides the content of the songs and the name of the Lord Jesus that provides the means by which praise and thanks are given. God is the recipient of these offerings of thanks and praise, and the Spirit is the empowering agent who fills and leads the church as they commune with their God.

Complete Devotion as Worship

Finally, as referenced above, Paul not only sees one's attitude and formal religious activities as constituting worship of God but also prescribes the complete devotion of one's life, body, and resources to the Lord as an act of worship. Paul's letters are replete with such references, which are sometimes read in passing and thus easy to overlook. In the letter to the Ephesians, Paul states that believers exist "for the praise of his glory" (1:12) and constitute a "dwelling place for God" (2:22 BSB), and Paul describes himself as a slave of the gospel (3:7). In the letter to the Colossians, Paul admonishes his recipients to "live a life worthy of the Lord and please him in every way" (1:10) and to do everything in the name of Jesus with thanks (3:17).

21. Allen P. Ross, *Recalling the Hope of Glory: Biblical Worship from the Garden to the New Creation* (Grand Rapids: Kregel Academic, 2006), 439.
22. Ross, *Recalling the Hope of Glory*, 439.
23. Ross, *Recalling the Hope of Glory*, 440.
24. Block, *For the Glory of God*, 233.

Similarly, Paul refers to believers in Philippians 3:3 as those who serve God by the Spirit, using a term (*latreuō*) common in liturgical contexts in the Old Testament. As Nijay Gupta suggests, Paul's focus here is on the identity of the true worshipers of God, whom he identifies as those who worship by the Spirit and in Christ.[25] His comments against the "dogs" and "mutilators" can be taken then as warnings against following the Torah but missing Christ (cf. Phil. 3:7–10; Rom. 10:1–4). It is in Christ that God was "summing up all things" (cf. Eph. 1:10). To miss Christ is to miss the point of Torah itself, which is to love and worship God (cf. Deut. 10:12–16).[26] This love of God involves, of course, feelings of affection for God, but beyond that is a wholehearted, covenantal commitment of the individual to life with God. Paul can thus speak of himself and his recipients as slaves, servants, and worshipers of God to indicate the expectation that the entirety of the believer's life, action, resources, and commitments are wholly devoted to God and to loving him and loving their neighbors.

The pinnacle of Paul's expression of a life lived in total devotion and commitment to God is found in the Christ hymn of Philippians 2:6–10. Paul sees in Jesus the chief example of a life of self-sacrificial love that believers are to emulate. Paul's hymn, which is a poetic expression of the story of Jesus's incarnation, death, resurrection, and exaltation, was likely a common creed known and shared among Christians in the ancient world. Though theologically important, Paul includes it in the letter to the Philippians to provide a theological grounding for his commands in Philippians 2:1–5 for the church to be unified and live in humility, seeking the good of one another rather than only their own. Paul refers to this as the "mind-set of Christ." Though sharing fully in the divine nature, Christ humbled himself by taking on human flesh and becoming a slave.[27] He exemplified trusting obedience to God, being obedient even to death on a cross. He was vindicated by God, being raised from the dead and exalted above every name. As Rodney Reeves says, "This pattern of humiliation leading to exaltation is the essence of the gospel according to Paul. Messianic suffering must precede messianic glory. Death gives life. Loss becomes gain. Shame morphs into honor.

25. Nijay K. Gupta, *Worship That Makes Sense to Paul: A New Approach to the Theology and Ethics of Paul's Cultic Metaphors* (Berlin: de Gruyter, 2010), 145. As Gupta continues, he notes that the irony of Paul's debate about circumcision is a hidden symbol of covenant membership had been turned into publicized symbol to maintain one's honor and communal standing. Paul contrasts this with the public shame of Christ, which he admonishes the Philippians to emulate in their service to God and one another (Gupta, *Worship That Makes Sense to Paul*, 147).

26. Note that Paul uses a form of the same verb (*latreuō*) in Philippians 3:3 as does the Septuagint translation of Deuteronomy 10:12.

27. So, Gorman writes, "Christ chose not to exploit something he could have exploited . . . [offering] a pattern of non-self-centered, self-giving obedience" (Michael J. Gorman, *Apostle of the Crucified Lord: A Theological Introduction to Paul and His Letters*, 2nd ed. [Grand Rapids: Eerdmans, 2017], 507).

The cross explains the resurrection. This is the divine paradigm of the cruciform life."[28]

For Paul, this paradigm is not just something Jesus did but also something believers are to inhabit as they live "in Christ." They live their lives in total dedication to God, committed to loving him and sacrificially loving others like Christ. As Gorman summarizes, "Paul interprets Christ's death not only as an act of love but as an act of (voluntary!—cf. 2:6) obedience, and he expects such voluntary obedience to be the pattern of the believers' existence, too. The story of the Messiah is one of radical vulnerability and downward mobility."[29]

We have thus seen that Paul follows in the Prison Epistles the larger biblical pattern of seeing worship as expressing Christlike virtues, participating in formal religious activities, and offering complete devotion of one's life, body, and resources to the Lord for his good purposes. While Paul's theological framework grows out of the Old Testament, his encounter with Christ, and his own cultural context, there nonetheless remain several important implications of the theology of worship in the Prison Epistles that the church can implement today.

SIGNIFICANCE OF THE PRISON EPISTLES FOR BIBLICAL WORSHIP

Paul's letters offer helpful reminders that though our formal religious activities and services are an important dimension of a biblical approach to Christian worship, they by no means exhaust it. Paul's theology of worship evidences conformity with the larger biblical patterns whereby Christian worship means nothing less than the total commitment of the believer to God and to his ways, evidenced in their gratitude, obedience, and moral transformation through the power of the Spirit of God. While often Christian traditions emphasize the importance of the various acts of worship Paul commends and commands, less often do they emphasize the transformative effect these rites are intended to have on their participants. While worship offers praise to God, who is certainly worthy to receive it, participation in these worshipful activities creates a giving, thankful, humble, and peaceful spirit within the believer. These practices act as a means of spiritual formation, not as a legalistic checklist of spiritual activities to climb the spiritual ladder, but rather as a means of living out the faithful and humble obedience of Jesus that has taken root in their own hearts through the gracious gifts of God.

One notable feature of Paul's instructions for public singing in the church is the didactic function Paul assigns it. While evangelical churches and worship gatherings often emphasize the emotional impact of corporate

---

28. Rodney Reeves, *Spirituality according to Paul: Imitating the Apostle of Christ* (Downers Grove, IL: IVP Academic, 2011), 35.

29. Gorman, *Apostle of the Crucified Lord*, 508.

worship, for Paul, teaching and instruction in the message of Christ was a central part of the singing of his early churches. This means that Christian leaders must not only carefully reflect on the doctrinal content of their songs but also see part of the purpose of corporate singing as instruction. Corporate singing thus should function as a means of discipleship (teaching obedience to Jesus's commands) in the church.

Paul's vision of Christian worship is also largely a public affair. Paul's spiritual activities certainly include certain private practices that believers can and should carry out on their own (prayer, singing, reading Scripture, etc.), but in their first-century context the concrete practices Paul describes are mostly public and communal, being performed in the assembly of believers and/or in the public square. In the Prison Epistles, this includes public prayer, the public reading of and meditation on Scripture, financial giving and support of Christian ministers and "missionaries," baptism, and singing "to one another."

Finally, Paul's vision of Christian worship is also pervasive. Paul sees thankful expressions of obedience, praise, and gratitude to God as permeating all of the Christian life, from relationships, to home life, to corporate worship, to eating and drinking, and to work, to name a few specific examples. As Witherington has stated, "There are no secular moments in a Christian life."[30] Too often modern Christians can easily fall into the trap of seeing worship as an event we attend, and even more narrowly, the singing of songs in attendance at these gatherings. For Paul, as for the rest of the canonical witness, worship is a mind-set for the entirety of life, bringing our attention to God in the midst of every activity, from our meals and social interactions, to our work and play, our finances, our hobbies and habits, and yes, even to our corporate gatherings. Worship is a mind-set cultivated not just in moments of emotional and exhilarating singing but also in the quiet of an evening stroll or the tilling of a garden bed. All of life is a gift from God, and thus every moment of life is an opportunity for gratitude and worship.

Paul's Prison Letters transport us to another time and place. The setting of the New Testament may seem strange to us, as we see early followers of Jesus wrestling with issues of how Gentile Christians fit into this Jewish movement, how to follow Christ in the midst of pagan and imperial pressures, or how slaves and masters should now relate in the Lord, along with a host of other questions and challenges. Though our challenges may differ in substance, these letters also provide a helpful reminder that the gift of life, with its challenges and all, offers opportunities in all things to give thanks to God and to commit ourselves as Christians in the present age to doing all things in the name of the Lord.

30. Ben Witherington III and Darlene Hyatt, *Paul's Letter to the Romans: A Socio-rhetorical Commentary* (Grand Rapids: Eerdmans, 2004), 337.

BIBLIOGRAPHY

Arnold, Clinton E. *Ephesians*. ZECNT. Grand Rapids: Zondervan, 2010.

Block, Daniel I. *For the Glory of God: Recovering a Biblical Theology of Worship*. Grand Rapids: Baker Academic, 2014.

Borchert, Gerald L. *Worship in the New Testament: Divine Mystery and Human Response*. St. Louis: Chalice, 2008.

Gorman, Michael J. *Apostle of the Crucified Lord: A Theological Introduction to Paul and His Letters*. 2nd ed. Grand Rapids: Eerdmans, 2017.

______. *Becoming the Gospel: Paul, Participation, and Mission*. Grand Rapids: Eerdmans, 2015.

Gupta, Nijay K. *Worship that Makes Sense to Paul: A New Approach to the Theology and Ethics of Paul's Cultic Metaphors*. Berlin: de Gruyter, 2010.

Heil, John Paul. *The Letters of Paul as Rituals of Worship*. Eugene, OR: Cascade, 2011.

Hurtado, Larry. *At the Origins of Christian Worship: The Context and Character of Earliest Christian Devotion*. Grand Rapids: Eerdmans, 1999.

______. *Lord Jesus Christ: Devotion to Jesus in Earliest Christianity*. Grand Rapids: Eerdmans, 2003.

O'Brien, Peter Thomas. *The Epistle to the Philippians*. NIGTC. Grand Rapids: Eerdmans, 1991.

Peterson, David. *Engaging with God: A Biblical Theology of Worship*. Downers Grove, IL: InterVarsity Press, 2002.

Reeves, Rodney. *Spirituality according to Paul: Imitating the Apostle of Christ*. Downers Grove, IL: IVP Academic, 2011.

Ross, Allen P. *Recalling the Hope of Glory: Biblical Worship from the Garden to the New Creation*. Grand Rapids: Kregel Academic, 2006.

Thornhill, A. Chadwick. *The Chosen People: Election, Paul, and Second Temple Judaism*. Downers Grove, IL: IVP Academic, 2015.

Witherington, Ben, III. *The Letters to Philemon, the Colossians, and the Ephesians : A Socio-rhetorical Commentary on the Captivity Epistles*. Grand Rapids: Eerdmans, 2007.

Witherington, Ben, III, and Darlene Hyatt. *Paul's Letter to the Romans: A Socio-rhetorical Commentary*. Grand Rapids: Eerdmans, 2004.

Wright, N. T. *Colossians and Philemon*. TNTC 12. Downers Grove, IL: InterVarsity Press, 1986.

CHAPTER 29

THE WORD, PRAYER, AND PRACTICE

Worship in the Pastoral Epistles

Ray Van Neste

D. A. Carson opens an essay on worship with this caution: "To construct a theology of worship turns out to be a difficult task."[1] This can be seen in the numerous attempts at a faithful, biblical definition of worship in works of biblical theology on worship.[2] The word *worship* at its root means to ascribe worth to something, thus Ralph Martin's simple definition is helpful: "To worship God is to ascribe to Him supreme worth, for He alone is worthy."[3] When we look to the Scriptures we see that ascribing such worth to God involves private adoration, gathered worship, as well as daily obedience and commitment. Worship is tied to love, and Jesus clearly states that to love him is to obey him. Thus Christian worship incorporates all of life.

However, one of our tendencies is to think of worship in only one of its arenas. Some think only of their private, personal devotional life. Others think only (or primarily) of the expressions of corporate worship. Still others, often in reaction to the previous two groups, think only of worship as a broad category encompassing all of life. Careful thinking, however, is

1. D. A. Carson, "Worship under the Word," in *Worship by the Book*, ed. D. A. Carson (Grand Rapids: Zondervan, 2002), 11.
2. See Allen P. Ross, *Recalling the Hope of Glory: Biblical Worship from the Garden to the New Creation* (Grand Rapids: Kregel Academic, 2006); Carson, *Worship by the Book*; David Peterson, *Engaging with God: A Biblical Theology of Worship* (Grand Rapids: Eerdmans, 1993); Daniel I. Block, *For the Glory of God: Recovering a Biblical Theology of Worship* (Grand Rapids: Baker Academic, 2014).
3. Ralph P. Martin, *Worship in the Early Church*, rev. ed. (Grand Rapids: Eerdmans, 1974), 10. For a very useful, though quite long, definition of worship see Carson, "Worship under the Word," 26.

rarely reactional thinking. We need our wide-angle lens when we think about the act of worship. Since worship is an expression of love, there is an analogy here in marriage. A truly loving husband will tell his wife he loves her, privately and before others, with a variety of words and behaviors. He will also demonstrate this love in the way he loves his wife in practically every area of his life. Because this love is not merely a passing fancy but central to who he is, this love cannot be limited to certain areas but permeates how he thinks of and pursues his job, his hobbies, his familial responsibilities, and his engagement with others. Then, to come full circle, this husband, precisely because this love shapes how he lives, will not think of leaving this love unexpressed. He must speak it.

It is precisely the same with worship. For the Christian, expressing the supreme worth of God is the only reasonable response to his amazing grace to us in Christ (Rom. 12:1–2). This will manifest in privately speaking to and praising God. It will come forth in gathering with other believers to worship as well. Then, because it is the response of an all-consuming love, it will shape all of life. Specifically, obedience is an act of worship, and all we do is done with the aim to please God and to demonstrate his worth.

Therefore, in this chapter I will look not only for mentions of acts of devotion typically associated with private or corporate worship but also for expressions of the greatness of God, obedience, and shaping life according to the ways of God.[4]

CONTEXT OF WORSHIP IN THE PASTORAL EPISTLES

For many, the Pastoral Epistles (1 Timothy, 2 Timothy, Titus) have been lumped together in analysis. More recently scholars have begun to emphasize the distinctiveness of each letter. This is a valuable turn. Second Timothy is significantly different from 1 Timothy and Titus, and Titus is much more than simply a shortened version of 1 Timothy. At the same time, some have now swung to the opposite extreme, seeming to resist any connection between these letters. While they are unique, individual letters, they do share more in common with one another than with any other letters in the New Testament. They are the only letters of Paul to his coworkers. We know from Acts and his other letters that Paul relied on a circle of coworkers, but only in these letters do we see inside these relationships. Not surprisingly, therefore, there is a shared set of vocabulary and ideas among these three letters. So, in this essay I will consider these letters together while attending to the specific nuances of each letter.

---

4. Some have suggested the presence of creeds or hymns (1 Tim. 2:5–6; 3:16) in these letters as well as allusions to baptism (Titus 3:5) and the Lord's Supper (1 Tim. 4:3). However, since the identification of these items is uncertain (and largely dubious in my mind) and are not developed in any way, they will not be dealt with here. Paul F. Bradshaw, *The Search for the Origins of Christian Worship: Sources and Methods for the Study of Early Liturgy*, 2nd ed. (Oxford: Oxford University Press, 2002), 47–53, helpfully warns against drawing more conclusions than warranted from the limited information given in the NT texts.

In each of these letters Paul is writing to an apostolic delegate who is functioning in a way very similar to a pastor today (Titus in Crete, Timothy in Ephesus). Timothy is serving a well-established church in Ephesus, and Titus is serving relatively new churches in Crete. (Notice that elders have not yet been appointed in all of the Cretan churches [1:5].) Contrary to common misperception, Paul is not writing to provide a church order in these letters. He is addressing specific issues in the respective churches, instructing his delegate in how to address these issues. These are, however, the only letters we have written directly to individuals serving in a pastoral role, so they do stand out in pastoral instruction.

These letters are largely about ethics, how Christians should live in light of the gospel. Commentators have frequently pointed out that the critique of false teachers does not provide many details on the content of their teaching. Instead, the focus is on their behavior. Similarly, although people commonly describe 1 Timothy 3 and Titus 1 as "job descriptions" for pastors and deacons, the passages turn out to say very little about the work of these offices. Rather the focus is on their behavior. In fact, I often describe these letters as calls to gospel-shaped living as Paul instructs masters and slaves (1 Tim. 6:1–2), the rich (1 Tim. 6:9–10, 17–19), widows and their families (1 Tim. 5:3–16), and different age groups within the church (Titus 2:1–10) in how they should behave. That this ethical instruction is rooted in the gospel is seen clearly, for example, in how Titus 2:11–14 (a gospel summary) grounds 2:1–10 (ethical instruction).[5] Furthermore, the contrast between Titus 1:16 and Titus 2:1 is significant. In 1:16 the false teachers claim to know God but their behavior exposes this claim as untrue. In contrast ("But you"), Titus is to teach people the manner of living that affirms a claim to know God. Additionally, in 1 Timothy 3:14 Paul explicitly says he writes so that the Christians might know how they ought to behave. Thus, behavior is an important aspect of worship in these letters. Proper living is evidence that one knows God.[6] Worship involves our humble, honorific response to the grace of God, and that response is here clearly shown to involve holiness and obedience to God.

Making such ethical demands and rooting those in a theological basis was odd in the first century. Greco-Roman religions tended to focus on ritual actions and observance of special days with little concern for ethics. The philosophers who speak to ethical concerns typically rooted those in the avoidance of shame, not in robust theological truths like Paul does. Shame is a consideration in the Pastorals (e.g., 1 Tim. 5:14, 6:1; Titus 2:5, 7–8), but the concern is for the reputation of God and his message rather

5. Similarly, note how Titus 3:3–7 grounds 3:1–2.

6. The Greek word *eusebeia* is significant on this theme in the Pastorals, but space does not allow us to pursue this specific word here. Note the significant excurses in I. Howard Marshall, *The Pastoral Epistles*, ICC (Edinburgh: T&T Clark, 1999), 135–44; Philip H. Towner, *The Letters to Timothy and Titus*, NICNT (Grand Rapids: Eerdmans, 2006), 171–74.

than personal shame as in the Greco-Roman philosophical writings. Thus, this tying together of belief, behavior, and worship was a distinctively Christian trait in the first century.[7]

THEOLOGY OF WORSHIP

Adoring and Thanking God (Reflecting on the Character and Work of God)

At the core of these letters are gospel summaries (1 Tim. 1:14–16; 2:3–6; 3:16; 2 Tim. 1:9–11; 2:8–10; Titus 2:11–14; 3:3–7).[8] These doctrinal statements provide the basis for all the other instruction in the letters. Additionally, scattered throughout the letters are various references to the character and majesty of the Triune God. These are significant for our topic, since Christian worship is a response to the character and work of God. As Carson has stated, "If you wish to deepen the worship of the people of God, above all deepen their grasp of his ineffable majesty in his person and in all his works."[9]

This can especially be seen in the doxologies found in these letters (1 Tim. 1:17; 6:15–16; 2 Tim. 4:18). Here we see examples of Paul himself at worship. In 1 Timothy 1:17 he writes, "To the King of the ages, immortal, invisible, the only God, be honor and glory forever and ever. Amen." Paul praises God for his greatness, ways in which he is beyond us. Nothing is said about what God has done. Rather the focus is on the majesty of his being. But the reason Paul pauses to express this praise is in response to God's saving work, even for such a sinner as Paul knew he was (1:16). Thus Paul praises the character of God in response to the saving work of God. Furthermore, this paragraph begins as a thanksgiving to Christ Jesus for his mercy (1:12–13).[10]

In 1 Timothy 6:15–16 Paul refers to God as "he who is the blessed and only Sovereign, the King of kings and Lord of lords, who alone has immortality, who dwells in unapproachable light, whom no one has ever seen or can see. To him be honor and eternal dominion. Amen." Again the praise focuses on God's majestic character. There are several parallels or repetitions from the previous doxology. This outburst of praise is not connected

---

7. Larry Hurtado's *Destroyer of the Gods: Early Christian Distinctiveness in the Roman World* (Waco, TX: Baylor University Press, 2016) is excellent on this point. Hurtado states, "The strong theological bases for behavior in early Christian texts comprise a distinguishing feature in comparison with most philosophical texts of the day" (155).
8. For a discussion of how these passages serve as the core of the letters see my *Cohesion and Structure in the Pastoral Epistles*, LNTS 280 (London: T&T Clark, 2004).
9. Carson, "Worship under the Word," 31.
10. Robert Yarbrough refers to this verse as "a celebration of the divine largesse that had given Paul's life transcendent meaning over thirty stressful years and that could also galvanize Timothy in his own daunting circumstances" (*The Letters to Timothy and Titus*, PiNTC [Grand Rapids: Eerdmans, 2018], 130).

explicitly to the past work of Christ but to his future return. The awareness of the greatness of God informs this paragraph's call to perseverance in the face of difficulty. Here worship not only honors God but aids in perseverance. And last, in 2 Timothy 4:18 he concludes, "To him be the glory forever and ever. Amen." This doxology is much simpler than the previous two, simply ascribing eternal glory to God without elaboration on his character. It comes in response to Paul's faith that just as God has delivered him in the past, so now he will continue to deliver him, eventually bringing him safely home to heaven. So, this praise is in response to the faithful character and work of God. It also appears to function as a basis for perseverance.

In addition to these doxologies, Paul praises God elsewhere in these letters. For example, in 1 Timothy 1:11 (NASB), Paul does not simply refer to "the gospel" but to "the glorious gospel of the blessed God." This is worship language.[11] The use of the word "glory" (*doxa*) can be interpreted differently. In the ESV translation cited, it describes the gospel as itself glorious. I think the better interpretation is that "glory" is the content of the gospel—that is, the gospel speaks of the glory of the blessed God. To say that God is "blessed" is to assert that God fundamentally has within himself all blessedness and is therefore the source of all true blessing.[12] Thus, on either reading of "glory," Paul, when pointing to the gospel in contrast to false teaching, pauses to extol the beauty of God as shown in the gospel. This is a helpful example of worship not as a separate activity but as one that arises naturally as a believer engages the world around him in light of the gospel. Worship just spills out of Paul when he considers God and his blessings.

Similar language is found in the gospel summary in Titus 2:11–14. In verse 13 Paul references the return of Christ, but he expresses himself not in the efficient, sparse language of a reporter but in the expansive, extravagant language of a lover. We are not simply waiting for the return of Christ. Rather it is the "great God and Savior Jesus Christ" for whom we are waiting.[13] And it is not just his return but his "appearing," indeed "the appearing of [his] glory"![14] And this appearing is our "blessed hope." The

---

11. Paul Jeon says this language is "not only a summons for the audience to recall God's salvific blessings but also—and much more—to respond by blessing God" (*1 Timothy: A Charge to God's Missional Household* [Eugene, OR: Pickwick, 2017], 1:106).

12. Only in the Pastorals is *makarios* used of God. See Marshall, *Pastoral Epistles*, 273–74, for a thorough discussion of the word and its use in the NT.

13. Whether one or two persons of the Godhead are in view here is a matter of significant debate. This distinction is not crucial to our point here, but for the argument that Father and Son are in view (and thus Jesus is not referred to as "God") see Gordon Fee, *Pauline Christology: An Exegetical-Theological Study* (Peabody, MA: Hendrickson, 2007), 440–48. For the view taken here that only Jesus is in view (and thus Jesus is referred to as "God") see Murray J. Harris, *Jesus as God: The New Testament Use of Theos in Reference to Jesus* (Grand Rapids: Baker, 1992), 143–85.

14. The use of "glory" here is similar to that in 1 Timothy 1:11. Some understand the phrase as "the glorious appearing." However, I believe the ESV gets it right here. Paul refers to the appearing of Jesus's glory. The One who is maligned and misrepresented by the false teachers will appear in his glory, and Paul relishes this certainty.

sense of longing, exuberance, and affection is palpable in this language. This is the language of worship. As Paul expounds the gospel hope he is moved to worship. As in the previous passage, we see that worship is a natural response to contemplating the gospel. A Christian does not have to step aside from daily life to worship. Rather he worships amid daily life as he contemplates the gospel to help him live. Here also this worshipful consideration serves to aid in perseverance.

Ethics as Worship

As stated earlier, 1–2 Timothy and Titus are particularly centered on the idea that the gospel should shape all of life. The letters are replete with ethical instruction for Timothy (1 Tim. 4:6–16; 2 Tim. 2:14–26), Titus (Titus 2:7–8), church leaders (1 Tim. 3:1–13; Titus 2:5–9), and various groups within the church (1 Tim. 5:1–6:2a; Titus 2:1–10). A key problem with the false teachers is that they indulge in speculation and empty discussions but do not produce love (1 Tim. 1:3–7; similarly, Titus 1:10–16). Furthermore, the behavior called for is explained as the proper response to God's saving work in Christ (1 Tim. 4:10; Titus 2:11–14; 3:3–7). Proper behavior is thus worship. It proclaims the worthiness of God, or as Paul says it, this behavior "adorn[s] the doctrine of God our Savior" (Titus 2:10).[15]

The ethical exhortation given in these letters is framed by the identity of the church, which is most directly addressed in 1 Timothy 3:15, where the church is described as the "household of God, which is the church of the living God, a pillar and buttress of the truth." This is a rich and profound ecclesiological statement.[16] The first thing to note for our purposes is that this description is couched in worship language. The first two phrases identify the church as, among other things, the new temple. "House of God" echoes the common Old Testament language for the temple (See esp. Isa. 6:1–8; also 1 Chron. 9:13; Pss. 55:14 [54:15 LXX]; 65:4 [64:5 LXX]; Eccl. 5:1; See also Matt. 12:4).[17] In the second phrase, "living God" is a common phrase in the Old Testament pointing to the Lord as the true God as opposed to idols (1 Sam. 17:26; Isa. 37:4; Jer. 10:10; see also Acts 14:15; 1 Thess. 1:9). It is also used to point to God's real presence among his people (Josh. 3:10; Ps. 42:2). Thus the church is the assembly

15. That Paul says this specifically of the behavior of slaves, those lowest on the social scale, is particularly significant.

16. Raymond Collins states, "This verse [v. 15] contains of the most succinct ecclesiological formulations in the entire New Testament. . . . The profound theological understanding of the Christian community expressed in the triad is unmatched by any other early Christian text" (*I & II Timothy and Titus*, NTL [Westminster John Knox Press, 2002], 102).

17. Several translations render this phrase as "household of God," which obscures this connection. See especially Jens Herzer, "Rearranging the 'House of God': A New Perspective on the Pastoral Epistles," in *Empsychoi Logoi—Religious Innovations in Antiquity: Studies in Honour of Pieter Willem van der Horst*, eds. Alberdina Houtman, Albert de Jong, and Magdalena Misset-van de Weg (Leiden: Brill, 2008), 547–66.

where the presence of God is truly manifested, like the temple in the Old Testament. Paul is concerned about how Christians "ought to behave" (3:14) as the new temple. Their identity as the people among whom God is worshiped should shape their behavior. Ethics is significantly shaped by worship—or should be.

Instructions for Corporate Worship

The most significant text on corporate worship in these letters is 1 Timothy 2. The context of worship is indicated by the reference to various worship activities and the number of people involved in these activities together. These practices are encouraged to occur "in every place" (2:8), so we have Pauline exhortation concerning worship for all churches.[18]

Prayer is the primary act of worship called for here with a compilation of terms: supplications (*deēsis*), prayers (*proseuchē*), intercessions (*enteuxis*), thanksgivings (*eucharistia*). It is clear that Paul expects a praying church.[19] The fact that this call to prayer is the first directive given for the church in the letter likely suggests its importance as well.[20] Two specific points about prayer are stated. First, the gathered church is to pray for "kings and all who are in high positions, that we may lead a peaceful and quiet life, godly and dignified in every way" (2:2). So the church in its gathered worship is to pray for the common good of the society around it by interceding for political leaders. This command is prominent since not many other specifics of the prayer are mentioned. Thus, on the one hand churches are not allowed to be insulated from the concerns of their culture, and on the other hand they are not to be reduced to political activism since the call is to pray for a peaceful setting in which the Christian faith can be lived out.

Second, the prayer prescribed here is on behalf of "all people" to the end that there might be peace and that people might be saved (implied by vv. 3–4). The peace the church prays for (noted above) is not isolationist (merely peace to be left alone) but is to serve the advance of the gospel (peace to live out and speak the gospel).

Note as well that the call for prayer is rooted in the person and redemptive work of the Father and Son. This is made clear in 2:5–6 by grounding ("for"; Greek *gar*) the call to prayer in the fact that there is only

18. Everett Ferguson, "Topos in 1 Timothy 2:8." *Restoration Quarterly* 33, no. 2 (1991): 65–73, makes a compelling case with Jewish background for understanding *topos* as referring to "place of worship." Fee (*Listening to the Spirit in the Text* [Grand Rapids: Eerdmans, 2000], 152–53) and Jeon (*1 Timothy*, 173n91) accept the reference to places of worship but restrict the reference to all the places where the Ephesian Christians gather. However, this misses the allusion to Malachi 1:11 and the broader universal theme permeating the passage.

19. J. N. D. Kelly, *A Commentary on the Pastoral Epistles*, Thornapple Commentaries (Grand Rapids: Baker, 1963), 60, also suggests the piling up of terms demonstrates emphasis.

20. Cf. Marshall, *Pastoral Epistles*, 418–19. The Greek phrase translated in the ESV as "first of all" could also be translated "above all."

one God and only one way to him. Since there is only one God and one Mediator, there is no other way of salvation. And since this one true God desires "all people to be saved" (2:4), Christians must pray that people come to know him.

This leads to one more important point: worship practices grow out of gospel realities. The character and purpose of God directs the discussion of worship. There may, in the end, be various expressions of these practices, but the consideration of what things the church ought to do in worship is fundamentally rooted in who God is, what he is like, and what he is doing.

Paul continues the discussion of prayer in 2:8–15, instructing that there should be no hindrances or distractions from this prayer, whether anger, quarreling, showy clothing, or subversion of the created order in regards to leadership roles.[21] This concern for safeguarding corporate prayer demonstrates its importance. Additionally, the men are instructed to pray with hands uplifted (v. 8), which was a common posture for prayer among the Jews (e.g., Exod. 9:29; Ps. 28:2). More important than the posture, though, is the purity.[22] Men are to pray, lifting up "holy hands."[23] This may be an allusion to the priestly practice of handwashing before temple service, but it is certainly a reference to approaching God with reverence and purity.[24] Thus prayer is a key aspect of public worship where we should pray for all people, asking for peace and the propagation of the gospel. Furthermore, both the content of our prayer and the manner in which we pray is shaped by the God whom we address. Because he is holy, we must approach him in purity and reverence, and because he desires to save, we pray for the salvation of people from all over the world.

First Timothy 4:13 is another significant text on the public ministry of the Word. This verse is in the middle of two paragraphs of instruction to Timothy about his own behavior and ministry. In the context of discussing Timothy's teaching ("put these things before the brothers" [4:6]; "Command and teach these things" [4:11]), Paul specifically exhorts Timothy to devote himself to three things: "public reading of Scripture," "exhortation," and "teaching."[25] What is in view here is not Timothy's private study but

---

21. The interpretation and modern application of 1 Timothy 2:11–15 is a subject of significant debate, though it does not significantly impinge on this point.
22. Jeon says "the phrase ["lifting up holy hands"] highlights not only the men's total focus on the person to whom they are praying—God—but also a comprehensive devotion to him while they are praying" (*1 Timothy*, 174).
23. See Stanley E. Porter, "1 Timothy 2:8: Holy Hands or Holy Raising?," in *Linguistic Analysis of the Greek New Testament: Studies in Tools, Methods, and Practice* (Grand Rapids: Baker Academic, 2015), 339-46, for the argument that "holy" refers to the men rather than the hands.
24. "Paul is specifically concerned about the holiness and demeanor of men when they pray" (Towner, *Letters to Timothy and Titus*, 201).
25. "The use of the article with each of the three following nouns indicates that these are familiar, recognized activities in the congregational meeting" (Marshall, *Pastoral Epistles*, 562). The first item is just one word in Greek (*anagnōsis*), which basically means "reading." However, it is com-

the public ministry of the Word. Paul expects corporate worship to include the public reading of Scripture and the preaching of that Scripture in a way which instructs and exhorts. A similar point is made in 2 Timothy 4:1–3, where Timothy is exhorted to "preach the word" in every situation, giving faithful instruction whether people approve of it or not.

This fits well with the high view of preaching and teaching seen in 1 Timothy 5:17, where Paul calls for double honor for elders who rule well, "especially those who labor in teaching and preaching." The work of expounding Scripture is highlighted as particularly worthy of honor, indicating its importance in the life of the church.[26] The proper teaching of Scripture is demanding work (*kopiaō*),[27] and those who labor in this way for the community ought to be appreciated.

Aspects of Personal Worship

The primary aspects of personal or private worship Paul mentions in these letters are in the realm of prayer. Christians are to receive their food with thanksgiving (1 Tim. 4:3–5). Prayer is a mark of a mature, godly woman (5:5), and Paul prays night and day for Timothy (2 Tim. 1:3). Thus prayer not only is reserved for the public meeting but is a personal practice as well. No doubt the private and the public are intended to reinforce and shape one another.

Furthermore, the call to give thanks for food (1 Tim. 4:3–5) is in contrast to false teachers who forbid marriage and certain foods. Thus true worship will include grateful reception of appropriate pleasures, rather than legalistic asceticism. While we must say no to sin (Titus 2:12), but joyful embrace of God's good provision is also an important aspect of honoring God. Worship involves recognizing daily provisions (dare we call them mundane?) as evidence of God's gracious care and responding in gratitude and joy.[28]

Death as Worship

Paul portrays his impending death as an act of worship in 2 Timothy 4:6: "I am already being poured out as a drink offering." The verb translated "poured out" (*spendomai*) refers to pouring a liquid as a sacrifice

---

monly used in Jewish literature to refer to the public reading of the Law. The similar use of this word elsewhere in the NT (Acts 13:15; 2 Cor. 3:14) leads most scholars, rightly, to understand this as a reference to the public reading of Scripture.

26. On the meaning of the Greek word *malista* I was previously convinced by the argument by T. C. Skeat, "'Especially the Parchments': A Note on 2 Tim. 4:13," *JTS* 30 (1979): 173–77, understanding it to mean something like "that is." However, I have been convinced of the traditional understanding ("especially") by Vern Sheridan Poythress, "The Meaning of *Malista* in 2 Timothy 4:13 and Related Verses," *JTS* 53 (2002): 523–32. Hong Bom Kim argues the same point as Poythress but less convincingly in "The Interpretation of *Malista* in 1 Timothy 5:17," *NovT* 46 (2004): 360–68.
27. "The implication is that teaching is demanding work" (Marshall, *Pastoral Epistles*, 612).
28. C. S. Lewis's seventeenth letter to Malcolm is a great reflection on this point (*Letters to Malcolm: Chiefly on Prayer* [New York: Harcourt, Brace & World, 1964], 88–93). "I have tried," Lewis states, "to make every pleasure into a channel of adoration" (89).

or as an accompaniment to a sacrifice (Lev. 23:13; Num. 15:5; 28:7).[29] It is clearly sacrificial language, and thus the language of worship. The idea is that Paul's death will not be a defeat, but will serve to glorify God and advance his kingdom. "His life blood will be poured out as a sacrifice for the sake of the gospel."[30] This seems to be an extension of what Paul had earlier said to the Romans, that Christians should present their bodies to God as living sacrifices (Rom. 12:1). Having lived as a sacrifice for years, it is fitting that his death also serve as worship.[31] This statement along with its thematic connection to Romans 12:1 emphasizes again the idea of all of life as worship. Christians are to live as sacrifices to God and then to die as such as well. Our aim should be for the worthiness of God to be displayed by our life and by our death.

SIGNIFICANCE OF THE PASTORAL EPISTLES FOR BIBLICAL WORSHIP

With all this, what then do these letters say about our gathered, corporate worship? We have seen that in 1 Timothy 2 Paul stressed the importance of prayer, connecting it to societal well-being, missions, and personal holiness. Of all the things Paul addresses in 1 Timothy, corporate prayer comes first. It may be that in our debates over the role of women in ministry leadership (cf. 2:11–15) we have rushed past this emphasis on prayer. Do we give enough attention to corporate prayer in our worship services? Paul clearly indicates its importance here, but does it slide down in the list of priorities when public worship is considered today? Protestant church services vary widely, but in general, I do not think most evangelical worship services in the West today give evidence of prayer being a primary purpose of our gathering. Our missional impotence and lack of holiness are common topics of discussion. Since these are tied to prayer in 1 Timothy, could our lack of progress in these areas be tied to our lack of attention to prayer?

Perhaps this lack of attention to prayer in our public worship is related to our commonly lamented weakness in private prayer. Eugene Peterson helpfully describes his realization that as a pastor his chief educational task was to teach people to pray, to meaningfully engage with God.[32] Surely he is right. In the Pastoral Epistles (as elsewhere in his letters), we see Paul himself praying, which in turn provides a model for his hearers.

We have also seen that the public reading of Scripture was singled out as a significant element of public worship. This continued as an important

---

29. See Marshall, *Pastoral Epistles*, 805, for further examples of this use in ancient literature, Greek and Jewish.
30. Marshall, *Pastoral Epistles*, 806. Similarly, Towner, "Above all, the passive voice and the sacrificial imagery underline that this death is not a meaningless but rather a necessary event in the furtherance of the work of the gospel" (*Letters to Timothy and Titus*, 611).
31. Yarbrough, *Letters to Timothy and Titus*, 443.
32. Eugene Peterson, *The Contemplative Pastor: Returning to the Art of Spiritual Direction* (Grand Rapids: Eerdmans, 1993), 89.

element of public worship through most of the history of the church. Writing around AD 140, Justin Martyr described Sunday worship in Rome this way: "All who live in cities or in the country gather together in one place, and the memoirs of the apostles or the writings of the prophets are read, as long as time permits; then, when the reader has ceased, the president verbally instructs, and exhorts to the imitation of these good things."[33] Similarly, Tertullian, writing in the late second or early third century, described Christian worship this way: "We assemble to read our sacred writings . . . with the sacred words we nourish our faith, we animate our hope, we make our confidence more steadfast."[34] Examples could be multiplied, but it is clear that public reading of Scripture played a significant role in Christian worship all the way through the Reformation.[35] Today, however, this practice has fallen on hard times in many evangelical churches, where only a brief passage or single verse is ever read. It is particularly odd for churches who talk much of the importance, power, and truthfulness of the Scripture to read so little of it in the gathered worship. In a time of steadily declining biblical literacy, we would do well to reclaim this historic practice, which is commanded by Paul in the Pastoral Epistles. What would it look like for the public reading itself to be a significant element of corporate worship?[36]

Last, for public worship, these letters hold up the importance of the preaching and teaching of Scripture. This is generally recognized today, but it is important to note the prominent place this theme holds in these letters. The hard work of preaching and teaching is central to the role of pastors. This is a key means for the congregation to be shaped for behavior that conforms to Christ and sound doctrine. And it is the primary way for believers to be reminded of the great truths of God's saving work in Christ, which is the reason for worship. If we lose sight of this truth or grow cold to it, we will lose our motivation to pray, to be thankful, to worship.

Related to this point, we should note from our examination of the doxological passages that worship is driven by love. Worship is love expressed to God. Thus if churches or individuals are lacking in worship, they are lacking in love and need to repent, as the church in Ephesus is commanded to do in Revelation 2:1–5. Working on techniques and acquiring new equipment can improve the show but cannot inspire worship. Too easily today we confuse a show with worship. The only way to move forward with worship is to engage afresh with the amazing truth that "Christ Jesus came into the world to save sinners, of whom I am the foremost" (1 Tim. 1:15). We

33. Justin Martyr, *First Apology* 47 (*ANF* 1:186).

34. Tertullian, *Apology* 39 (*ANF* 3:252).

35. The directories for worship from the Reformation give ample evidence of this. See for example Luther's "Concerning the Ordering of Divine Worship in the Congregation," *The Middleburg Liturgy* (1586, English Puritans), and Westminster Directory for Public Worship (1645).

36. For a helpful discussion of the background of 1 Timothy 4:13 and its contemporary application, see Philip Towner, "The Function of the Public Reading of Scripture in 1 Timothy 4:13 and in the Biblical Tradition," *SBJT* 7, no. 3 (Fall 2003): 44–53.

must "remember Jesus Christ, risen from the dead, the offspring of David" (2 Tim. 2:8), and that though "we ourselves were once foolish, disobedient, led astray, slaves to various passions and pleasures . . . he [God] saved us not because of works done by us in righteousness, but according to his own mercy" (Titus 3:3, 5). Biblical worship is always a response to the glorious character and saving work of God. Remembrance and realization of these truths stirs the hearts of believers to worship. Perhaps this is why worship is so often related to perseverance in these letters. Defection occurs when love grows cold. Proper worship keeps before us the incredible mercy of God, stirs our hearts and minds afresh, reminding us of the who this great God is. Thus, also, powerful worship is not dependent on the size of a crowd or on the use of certain instruments.

Furthermore, what has been stated so far connects to our obedience as worship. The gospel truths that compel us to worship also compel us to obedience (Titus 2:11). Obedience, like worship—indeed as an element of worship—flows out of love. These letters show us a posture of worship composed of gratitude and humility, mixed with adoring awe. This is one reason Paul exhorts Timothy to "remind them of these things" (2 Tim. 2:14). We need regular reminders of the glorious gospel to thaw and soften our cold hearts and tune them for worship.

Last, we should give further thought to Paul's portrayal of his death as a sacrificial offering. Historically faithful Christian worship has directly addressed death regularly, recognizing its certainty and its defeat in Christ. Classic hymns typically deal with death and resurrection as church leaders recognized that dying well in faith was an essential aspect of discipleship and thus of our worship. We have noticed in this study that worship often was connected to perseverance. Too many believers today are caught off guard by the death of loved ones. Robust worship, which raises the realities of life and death, prepares us to face these realities in light of the gospel. As J. I. Packer has stated,

> "Our people die well," said John Wesley somewhere, commending Methodist Christianity. Dying well, as the final climactic step in living well, was a prominent theme in older Roman Catholic, Protestant, and Orthodox teaching on the Christian life and in some places may still be so. But in the West death has become the great unmentionable, like sex in Victorian times, and little is taught to Christians in these days about preparing for it. Instead, we live as if we shall be here forever. . . . This being so, and knowing as we do that life in this world is a terminal condition, it is surely most important that our catechesis should promote readiness for dying. When the late Dag Hammarskjold wrote that only one who knows how to die can know how to live, he was absolutely right, and our churches are much at fault in having forgotten it.[37]

37. J. I. Packer, "Reflection and Response," in *J. I. Packer and the Evangelical Future: The Impact of His Life and Thought*, ed. Timothy George (Grand Rapids: Baker Academic, 2009), 177.

Can we consider a worship service fully Christian if it does not address death and the hope of the resurrection?

Furthermore, how ought this effect how we conduct the funerals of Christians? My point is not to call for more celebration. Already we have a tendency to hide from deep sorrow and the place of lament. Rather, what can we do in funeral services to recognize the closing of a faithful life as worship? This is just one of many areas where we could benefit from a more thoughtful approach to funerals.[38]

CONCLUSION

Beyond the role of preaching, the Pastoral Epistles are not often considered significantly in discussions of worship.[39] I hope this study has demonstrated significant ways in which these letters should inform our understanding of worship, both private and public. With the rising awareness of a need for renewal in worship, it is too easy to turn first to technique and hype. The Pastorals remind us that worship arises in response to the truths of God's gracious saving work. Worship renewal then must begin with faithful gospel proclamation, which leads to life transformation. We must not allow public worship to become a show that is disconnected from daily life. Worship is not escapism. Deepening awareness of our great need and God's even greater provision should lead to growth in holiness and vibrant private prayer, individually and corporately.

BIBLIOGRAPHY

Block, Daniel I. *For the Glory of God: Recovering a Biblical Theology of Worship*. Grand Rapids: Baker Academic, 2014.

Borchert, Gerald L. *Worship in the New Testament: Divine Mystery and Human Response*. St. Louis: Chalice, 2008.

Bradshaw, Paul F. *The Search for the Origins of Christian Worship: Sources and Methods for the Study of Early Liturgy*. 2nd ed. Oxford: Oxford University Press, 2002.

Carson, D. A. "Worship under the Word." In *Worship by the Book*, edited by D. A. Carson, 11–63. Grand Rapids: Zondervan, 2002.

Collins, Raymond. *I & II Timothy and Titus*. NTL. Louisville: Westminster John Knox, 2002.

Fee, Gordon. *Listening to the Spirit in the Text*. Grand Rapids: Eerdmans, 2000.

38. Thomas Long's *Accompany Them with Singing: The Christian Funeral* (Louisville: Westminster John Knox, 2009) is a helpful and provocative resource on this point.

39. So also Gregory J. Stiekes, "Liturgy in the Pastoral Epistles," *Artistic Theologian* 2 (2013): 38. Stiekes's article is very helpful, though his aim is a little different from mine. He examines more fully the role of public prayer and proclamation in light of the challenge of false teaching evident in the letters. Gerald Borchert's treatment of the Pastorals in *Worship in the New Testament: Divine Mystery and Human Response* (St. Louis: Chalice, 2008), 159–75, says little actually about worship, providing rather a brief running commentary.

______. *Pauline Christology: An Exegetical-Theological Study*. Peabody, MA: Hendrickson, 2007.

Harris, Murray J. *Jesus as God: The New Testament Use of Theos in Reference to Jesus*. Grand Rapids: Baker, 1992.

Herzer, Jens. "Rearranging the 'House of God': A New Perspective on the Pastoral Epistles." In *Empsychoi Logoi–Religious Innovations in Antiquity: Studies in Honour of Pieter Willem van der Horst*, edited by Alberdina Houtman, Albert de Jong, and Magdalena Misset-van de Weg, 547–66. Leiden: Brill, 2008.

Hurtado, Larry. *Destroyer of the Gods: Early Christian Distinctiveness in the Roman World*. Waco, TX: Baylor University Press, 2016.

Jeon, Paul. *1 Timothy: A Charge to God's Missional Household*. 2 vols. Eugene, OR: Pickwick, 2017.

Kelly, J. N. D. *A Commentary on the Pastoral Epistles*. Thornapple Commentaries. Grand Rapids: Baker, 1963.

Long, Thomas. *Accompany Them with Singing: The Christian Funeral*. Louisville: Westminster John Knox, 2009.

Marshall, I. Howard. *The Pastoral Epistles*. ICC. Edinburgh: T&T Clark, 1999.

Martin, Ralph P. *Worship in the Early Church*. Rev. ed. Grand Rapids: Eerdmans, 1974.

Peterson, David. *Engaging with God: A Biblical Theology of Worship*. Grand Rapids: Eerdmans, 1993.

Peterson, Eugene. *The Contemplative Pastor: Returning to the Art of Spiritual Direction*. Grand Rapids: Eerdmans, 1993.

Ross, Allen P. *Recalling the Hope of Glory: Biblical Worship from the Garden to the New Creation*. Grand Rapids: Kregel Academic, 2006.

Stiekes, Gregory J. "Liturgy in the Pastoral Epistles." *Artistic Theologian* 2 (2013): 37–50.

Towner, Philip H. "The Function of the Public Reading of Scripture in 1 Timothy 4:13 and in the Biblical Tradition." *SBJT* 7, no. 3 (Fall 2003): 44–53.

______. *The Letters to Timothy and Titus*. NICNT. Grand Rapids: Eerdmans, 2006.

Van Neste, Ray. *Cohesion and Structure in the Pastoral Epistles*. LNTS 280. London: T&T Clark, 2004.

Yarbrough, Robert. *The Letters to Timothy and Titus*. PiNTC. Grand Rapids: Eerdmans, 2018.

CHAPTER 30

THE SUPERIORITY AND WORSHIP OF CHRIST

Worship in Hebrews

Dickson Ngama

CONTEXT OF WORSHIP IN HEBREWS

The book of Hebrews provides an intentional contrast between Old Testament worship and worship in the new covenant. Whereas Old Testament worship was centered on sacrifices and services at the tabernacle with its Levitical priesthood, worship in the new covenant centers on Jesus Christ the Son of God. He is introduced as worthy of worship (1:6) because of his divine status (1:8) and his willingness to become a human being for the salvation of humankind (2:14–15). The book of Hebrews stresses God's final revelation in the Son (1:2), Jesus's superiority to Israelite heroes of faith (chap. 11), and his superiority to the Levitical high priest (chap. 7). The new covenant he ushers into the world will be shown to be superior to the covenant God made with Israel at Sinai. In view of Jesus's superior status and high priesthood, Hebrews' Jewish Christian audience is encouraged to persevere in its commitment to, confession of, and witness to Jesus Christ in spite of opposition resulting in discouragement. For this Jewish Christian congregation, Jesus the Son of God is irrevocably included in the worship of the God of Israel.

From the very beginning of the church, in the 30s AD, Jewish Christians found themselves in conflict with non-Christian Jews. This is surely evidenced both by Paul's hostile pursuit of early Christians and indeed by Jesus's own crucifixion by Roman authority at the instigation of Jewish leaders. Such disputes did not slow down as the early church spread throughout the Roman Empire. Most of this friction was theological in that Jews held tightly to the Old Testament traditions while Jewish and

Gentile Christians accepted a new covenant. Larry Hurtado refers to these skirmishes as conflicts over Christ devotion. "This opposition, from devout defenders of Jewish religious practices concerned with the uniqueness of God, likewise seems to have been directed against the Christ-devotion of Christian Jews, because it was seen as a dangerous development."[1] It appears that the earliest Jews and Christians differed, not in their respect for Jewish Scriptures, Jewish heroes of the faith, or Jewish institutions such as temple and priesthood, but in the special place they gave Jesus next to the God of Israel. This was rather unexpected because the God of Israel had, as Richard Bauckham has explained, a "unique identity," which God could not share with any other being.[2] This identity included the following qualities: (1) God is the sole Creator of all things (all others are created by God); (2) God is the sole sovereign Ruler over all things (all others are subject to God's rule); (3) God is known through his narrative identity (that is, who God is in the story of his dealings with creation, all nations, and Israel); (4) God will achieve his eschatological rule (when all creatures acknowledge YHWH's sole deity; (5) The name YHWH names God in his unique identity; (6) God alone may and must be worshiped (since worship is acknowledgment of God's sole deity); and (7) God alone is fully eternal (self-existent from past to future eternity).[3] It is clear that early Christians attributed all of these qualities to Christ.

Several forces worked together to produce Christ devotion. God had commanded Israel to worship only one God. Jesus himself had made claims and done things that made him controversial before and after his death and resurrection. The Holy Spirit had given Jesus's followers experiences and insights into the meaning of Jewish Scriptures. The Jewish and pagan environments surrounding the followers of Jesus forced them to clarify their worship practices with reference to God and Jesus. Much as they loved the Jewish way of life and its exclusivist worship of God, Jewish Christians could no longer worship God without reference to Jesus since God had revealed to them in various ways that Jesus was also worthy of worship.

What we find then in Hebrews is that Jesus is considered the final and ultimate revelation of the God of Israel, who had previously and in various ways revealed himself to the fathers by means of the prophets (1:1). While the author of Hebrews sees Jesus as the final revelation of God, he continues to appeal to Israel's Scriptures in support of Jesus as superior to angels, to Abraham, Moses, and Aaron. Jesus, a priest in the order of Melchizedek, is greater that the Levitical high priest at the tabernacle, and

1. Larry W. Hurtado, "Pre–70 C.E. Jewish Opposition to Christ-Devotion," in *Ancient Jewish Monotheism and Early Christian Jesus-Devotion* (Waco, TX: Baylor University Press, 2017), 207.
2. Richard Bauckham, "The Divinity of Jesus Christ in the Epistle to the Hebrews," in *The Epistle to the Hebrews and Christian Theology*, eds. Richard Bauckham, Daniel R. Driver, Trevor A. Hart, and Nathan MacDonald (Grand Rapids: Eerdmans, 2009), 16.
3. Bauckham, "Divinity of Jesus Christ," 16.

he inaugurates a new covenant that is better than the old one made with Israel. The death of Jesus is declared to be a sacrifice superior to any sacrifice offered by Levitical priests. The ascension to and session at God's right hand are superior to the endless service of priests in the tabernacle. The blood of Jesus, which was shed once on the cross, is more effective for purification than the blood of animals shed at the temple. Hebrews then does not reject past revelation but continually appeals to it to illustrate the surpassing superiority of Jesus as Son of God, High Priest, founder and perfecter of our faith, and mediator of a new covenant.

THEOLOGY OF WORSHIP

In the book of Hebrews, Jesus shares a unique identity with God, a likeness that nothing else has. "He is the radiance of the glory of God and the exact imprint of his nature" (1:3). Jesus is the Son of God and the ultimate revelation of God. He is superior to the angels (1:5–14), to Moses (3:1–2), to Aaron, and to the high priest (7:1–2). According to Murray J. Harris, one can derive an implicit Christology from Hebrews where Christ has divine functions as creator (1:2) and sustainer (1:3). He has divine status as eternally existent (11:26), perfect revealer (1:1–3), and object of worship (1:6). Hebrews also has an explicit Christology where the author cites the Old Testament in order to apply qualities of Yahweh to Jesus. Hebrews highlights Jesus's character (1:11–12), his worthiness of worship (1:6), and his work in creation (1:10). Jesus is given divine titles such as Son of God (1:2) and God (1:8).[4] Robert Bowman and Ed Komoszwski give evidence for Jesus's divine nature. Jesus shares divine honor with God (3:3–4), glory (13:20), and worship (1:6). He shares the attributes of God, for he is eternal (1:2, 10–12; 7:3), uncreated (1:2, 10–12), and immutable (1:10–12; 13:8). He is given the name of God (Heb. 1:8), and the deeds of God are attributed to him such as creating (1:2–3), sustaining (1:10), and saving (5:9). Jesus occupies God's throne (1:3, 13; 8:1; 10:12–13; 12:2). He also governs with God's rule over all and forever (1:2; 2:8; 1:8).[5] All of this evidences the author's theological convictions that Christ is superior, and the covenant instituted by Christ is also superior. This conviction then forms the basis for what Hebrews has to teach the church today regarding worship.

Léon Vaganay has a five-theme outline, and with some modification it serves well for an exploration into a theology of worship within the book of Hebrews.[6] Here he divides the book as follows: (1) Jesus superior to the angels (1:5–2:18); (2) Jesus, compassionate and faithful high priest (3:1–5:10);

---

4. Murray J. Harris, *Jesus as God: The New Testament Use of Theos in Reference to Jesus* (Grand Rapids: Baker, 1992), 315–17.
5. Robert M. Bowman Jr. and J. Ed Komoszwski, *Putting Jesus in His Place: The Case for the Deity of Christ* (Grand Rapids: Kregel, 2007), 268, 281–88.
6. Léon Vaganay, "Le Plan de l'Épître au Hébreux," in *Mémorial Lagrange* (Paris: Gabalda, 1940), 269–77, cited in William L. Lane, *Hebrews 1–8 Hebrews 1–8*, WBC 47a (Dallas: Word, 1991), lxxxvi.

(3) Jesus, source of eternal salvation, perfected priest, high priest like Melchizedek (5:11–10:39); (4) perseverance in the faith (11:1–12:13); and (5) the need to be holy (12:14–13:21). In the following, we will lean on most of this structure but combine sections 4 and 5. We will pay special attention to how these themes contribute to a theology of worship. Certainly, Jesus is praiseworthy for his superiority to angels, for being a compassionate and faithful high priest, a perfected priest, and a high priest like Melchizedek. But, again, one can be praiseworthy without being worthy of worship. In Judaism and in Christianity, only God is worthy of worship. No man or angel can qualify for worship since God forbids the worship of created beings. Jesus has a special relationship with God, however.

Introducing the Superiority of Christ (1:1–4)

In the beginning of Hebrews, God introduces his Son as his ultimate means of revelation. All the prophets, in various ways and at various times, pointed forward to the Son of God.[7] The Son is "the radiance of the glory of God and the exact imprint of his nature" (1:3). The Son is creator and upholder and heir of all things (1:2, 3). In Jewish thought, only God is considered the creator and upholder of the universe. This must mean that Jesus is on the side of God as the uncreated Creator. This uncreated Creator is also the Savior from sin and now sits at the right hand of God in a position superior to any angel and having a name above that of every angel (1:4). Here we are introduced, in a few words, to the Creator who became a Savior. The details of how he accomplished this come later. The Son is worthy of worship from the very start because he shares with his Father such qualities as uncreated creator and sustainer of the universe. All that comes after will substantiate these claims.

First Theme: Jesus Is Superior to the Angels (1:5–2:18)

God commands that all the angels worship his Son (1:5–6).[8] In effect, God is the one who, having commanded Israel never to worship any other God, now commands that the worship of the one true God include Jesus. Henceforth, worship of God means worship of God the Father and the Son. God is thereby declaring that Jesus is not a created being but an eternal being. God is revealing that the unity of God is a complex unity, for God addresses the Son as God even as he calls himself the God of the Son (1:8–9). God is one, and yet this oneness includes at least two distinct persons, the Father and the Son. All religious Jews believed that only the God

7. Lane, *Hebrews 1–8*, 6, notes the alliteration in verse 1: *polymerōs, polytropōs, palai, patrasin, prophētais*. The writer begins with an explosion of plosive constants to contrast Old Testament revelation with revelation through Son (*en Huiō*) in v. 2.

8. In the Old Testament, verse 6 could be citing Psalm 97:7 (96:7 LXX) or Deuteronomy 32:43. In the former case, the gods are commanded to worship the Lord and in the latter the sons/angels of God are urged to worship God. See Bruce, *The Epistle to the Hebrews*, NICNT (Grand Rapids: Eerdmans, 1990), 56–57.

of Israel was worthy of worship. God's angels were agents and messengers and servants worthy of admiration, but they could not be worshiped. No matter how exalted, they were creatures of God. There was only one God, the Creator, and a lot of creatures, the most exalted among whom were angels. If Jesus was worthy of worship, he could not be counted among the angels. He had to be superior, not just in rank, but also in kind. He was not one of the creatures but had to be on the side of the Creator.

It is true that Jesus became superior to angels after his resurrection. Jesus had become inferior to angels when he became a human being. He was made a little lower than angels for a little while so that he may share the frailty of humanity and become a merciful and sympathetic high priest. In his humiliation he provided deliverance from the fear of death perpetrated by the devil and salvation from sin. Jesus was worthy of worship because of his willingness to identify with humanity and success in saving them from the fear of death and the damnation of sin. When he rose again from the dead and ascended to heaven, he regained his former position as superior to the angels. What needs to be made clear is that he did not lose his divinity by becoming a human being, but rather submitted himself to the Father's will for the sake of our salvation (2:5–18). Having gained that salvation, he returned to his former glory at the right hand of God.

Second Theme: Jesus, Compassionate and Faithful High Priest (3:1–5:10)

Jewish worship was carried out ideally at the tabernacle or in the temple where the high priest was the chief official. Since worship involved devotion to or relationship with God by means of various ritual activities at the tabernacle or the temple, the high priest was the person closest to God. He was the only one privileged to perform certain rituals on behalf of the worshipers. Not even the king could perform the duties assigned to the high priest. How then could Jesus be considered superior priest to the high priest in matters of worship?[9] Jesus must have had qualities that the surpassed those of any high priest.[10] What we see is that Jesus was more faithful than Moses, who inaugurated the priesthood of the tabernacle. Moses was only a faithful servant among God's people, while Jesus was the faithful son among God's

9. Eric F. Mason, *"You Are a Priest Forever": Second Temple Jewish Messianism and the Priestly Christology of the Epistle to the Hebrews*, STDJ 74 (Leiden: Brill, 2008), investigates backgrounds to the priesthood of Jesus. He considers background theories such as the originality of the author of Hebrews, early Christian exegesis, Gnostic ideas, and Judaism. He is most persuaded by the similarity between Hebrews and Dead Sea Scrolls on priesthood and Melchizedek.

10. Here Jesus is the apostle and high priest of our confession (*Apostolon kai Archierea tēs homologias hēmōn Iēsoun.* Both "high priest" and "apostle" are unusual titles for Jesus. Hebrews will further explicate the high priesthood of Jesus. Jesus is an apostle because he is "one who is sent." Our confession may refer to a creed, a body of faith, or public witness. See Philip Edgcumbe Hughes, *A Commentary on the Epistle to the Hebrews* (Grand Rapids: Eerdmans, 1977), 126–29.

people (3:1–6).[11] Jesus was superior to any high priest in that he completely understood our sinful condition yet he himself was not a sinner.[12] The high priest first offered sacrifices for himself before he could represent other worshipers at the tabernacle. Jesus represents worshipers in the very presence of God as he eternally mediates on their behalf. Further, Jesus was not presumptuous in becoming a high priest because he was appointed to his role as high priest by God just as Aaron was. Jesus performed his role as priest in obedience and reverence and thereby became the source of salvation for the worshipers. He, however, was appointed priest in a different priestly order, the order of Melchizedek, which, as the audience learns later, was superior to the order of Aaron. Christian worshipers needed therefore to confess that the Son of the living God was their high priest before God, redeemer from the devil, and savior from sin. For his role as High Priest is an eternal role, and thus stands on our behalf throughout the entirety of our lives. Christian worshipers could approach God's throne with confidence for the grace that was made available because of the service of Jesus their heavenly high priest.

Third Theme: Jesus, Source of Eternal Salvation, Perfected Priest, High Priest Like Melchizedek (5:11–10:39)

In order to appreciate the superiority of the high priesthood of Jesus, the worshipers needed to recall just how great Melchizedek was. He was a priest of the Most High God and king of Salem and was recognized as such by Abraham. Abraham honored him by giving a tithe of all his gains from war, and Melchizedek blessed Abraham. Since Abraham was the ancestor of Aaron the high priest, then Aaron paid tithes to Melchizedek when Abraham did. Jesus belongs to the order of Melchizedek since God swore to him, "You are a priest forever, after the order of Melchizedek" (7:17, 21).[13] The greater priest of necessity had a greater covenant and a more effective sacrifice. The Aaronic priesthood was ineffective in that the priests were sinners and mortal and therefore needed to be replaced regularly. Jesus was sinless, and yet he died once as a sacrifice for sins he

---

11. Philip Church, *Hebrews and the Temple: Attitudes to the Temple in Second Temple Judaism and in Hebrews*, NovTSup 171 (Leiden: Brill, 2017), 312n7: "1 En. 89:36 depicts Moses with an angel-like status; in Ezek. Trag. Moses sits on the throne of God in heaven as God's vicegerent; Sir 45:2 compares him with the angels in glory; in Philo *Somn.* 2:188–189; *Mos.* 2.70 Moses is in some sense divine; in 4Q374 9 3 and 4Q 377 1 recto 11 5 Moses is God's 'anointed' (*msyh*). Many of these texts can be traced back to the influence of Exod 7:1 where Moses is 'God/a god' to Pharaoh. This text does not feature in Hebrews."

12. That Jesus was sinless and fully shared our humanity means that sin is not a necessary part of humanity. We should recall Adam before the fall. See David Peterson, *Hebrews and Perfection: An Examination of the Concept of Perfection in the "Epistle to the Hebrews,"* SNTSMS 47 (Cambridge: Cambridge University Press, 1982), 188–90.

13. Jesus was from the tribe of Judah, and therefore had a genealogy that disqualified him from becoming a priest in Israel. Melchizedek, lacking a genealogy and therefore resembling (*apōmoiōmenos*) the Son of God, had an eternal priesthood. An eternal priesthood is superior to a temporal one. See Donald Guthrie, *Hebrews*, TNTC 15 (Downers Grove, IL: InterVarsity Press, 1983), 160.

was raised from death never to die again. He became an immortal and perfect priest who never needed to be replaced. He lived in God's presence and had a perpetual ministry of intercession for worshipers. The covenant he established was not a new invention but the same one promised by God through the prophets (Jer. 31:31–34). Israel had failed to keep the old covenant as is evident in many prophetic woe oracles. Repeated sacrifices and observances at the temple had not produced a holy people who could approach God with confidence. God found fault with the people and declared the need for a new covenant.[14] As soon as God promised a new covenant, the old one was declared temporal, and in good time it would disappear. Further, the tabernacle of the old covenant, with its equipment, sacrifices, and services, was found to be a copy and a shadow of a heavenly reality.[15] This covenant was of limited efficacy, in that its sacrifices did not cleanse the conscience of worshipers no matter how often they were made. Jesus, in contrast, is a high priest who performed one act of sacrifice, presented his own blood as a sacrifice once for all in the heavenly sanctuary, and obtained eternal salvation for worshipers. This one sacrifice took away sins, cleansed the conscience of worshipers, and sanctified those whom God had saved. Those who became members of the new covenant were made holy and had confidence to approach God in worship and to live by faith despite their challenging circumstances. Attraction to the old covenant for people of the new covenant would be misguided because it would lead to the repudiation of the new. Once the audience of Hebrews truly understood that the old covenant, even if it had been given by God, was now surpassed by the new covenant, they would seek to worship God in a new way. No longer would they see the service of the priests in the same way. No longer would they view the temple as the only place to approach God. All the holy convocations of the old covenant would have only a symbolic value pointing to the superior priestly work of Jesus. The people would know that in the new covenant, one priest had done what generations of Levitical priests could not do. One priest had finally presented a sacrifice for sin that could not be repeated. One priest was now in the presence of God interceding for the people of God.

Fourth Theme: Perseverance in Faith and Holiness (11:1–13:21)

A list of ancient heroes of faith was given to show that throughout history there had been those who believed in God's promises, trusted and obeyed God, no matter their circumstances (chap. 11).[16] This list of the

14. Some manuscripts state that God found fault with it, meaning the covenant. See Lane, *Hebrews 1–8*, 202.
15. Church, *Hebrews and the Temple*, 1, prefers "symbolic foreshadowing" to "copy and shadow." For him, the "referent is not the tabernacle but the temple, and the sense of the expression is that the temple anticipates God's eschatological dwelling with his people."
16. The author repeats the word "faith" twenty-three times in this chapter. Steven Ger calls the chapter a "textbook example of rhetorical anaphora, the concentrated repetition of a key word at

ancient heroes also showed the audience of Hebrews that they lived in continuity with famous people found in the Hebrew Bible and in Jewish history. These were examples to emulate. In view of those demonstrations of enduring faith, worshipers were urged to consider their life of faith as an athletic contest that required endurance. In their athletic contest, it was good to encourage themselves with the examples of those who had run the race and completed it with success. Yet in the end, they were to look to Jesus as the "founder and perfecter of our faith" (12:2). Their sufferings and persecutions were also evidence of their legitimacy as God's children who needed to be trained in holiness in order to become partakers of God's holiness. Worship required faithful endurance with holiness as a goal.

As God's children, they have come to Mount Zion, the heavenly Jerusalem (12:22).[17] Yet they are being disciplined and trained in holiness in preparation for heavenly worship in the Mount Zion, the heavenly Jerusalem, where others like them have gone before and where angelic hosts await them in the presence of God and Jesus their Mediator (12:14–29).[18] In the meantime, they are to practice love among themselves, hospitality for strangers, concern for prisoners, chastity, contentment, concern for their leaders, faithfulness to Jesus, praise of God, benevolence, obedience to their leaders, prayer for the author of the book and his companions (13:1–19). The author of the book offers a benediction on behalf of the audience (13:20–21). Worship then involves discipline for the purpose of divine holiness, focus on the heavenly city, and godly practices on the way.

Conclusion (13:22–25)

The author identifies his book as a word of exhortation.[19] The goal is to encourage the worshipers who may be feeling discouraged and are in danger of giving up their personal commitment to Jesus, congregational identification with him, and their public confession of him. He gives them the good news of Timothy's release and the possibility of his visit with

---

the beginning of a sentence or clause for heightened effect. Other examples in Jewish literature include the apocryphal Sirach, which repeats "let us now praise famous men and our fathers that begat us" and 1 Maccabees, which has "a catalogue of biblical personalities." See Steven Ger, *The Book of Hebrews: Christ Is Greater* (Chattanooga, TN: AMG, 2009), 187.

17. David L. Allen, *Hebrews*, NAC 35 (Nashville: B&H, 2010), 590, notes that the verb use here, "you have come" (*proselēluthate*), is in the perfect tense. The Christians then "are converted and have a permanent place of eternal relationship with God." But it could mean that "the readers have drawn near but have not yet arrived." See Allen, *Hebrews*, 590n504.

18. Mount Zion, the heavenly Jerusalem, is contrasted, not with the earthly Jerusalem where the temple was located, but with Mount Sinai, the place where God gave the law to Moses.

19. Word of exhortation (*logou tēs paraklēseōs*). This expression is used in Acts 13:5; A plural form (*logous paraklēseōs*, words of encouragement) is used in 1 Maccabees 10:24. In 1 Timothy 4:13, *paraklēsei* is translated as exhortation or sermon. Lane considers it a practice of the synagogue and the early church to have an "exposition and application of the Scriptures that had been read aloud to the assembled congregation" (William L. Lane, *Hebrews 9–13*, WBC 47b [Dallas: Word, 1991], 568).

them. He requests greetings for their leaders and fellow worshipers and sends them greetings from their countrymen.[20] Finally, he wishes them God's grace. This ending of the book demonstrates an aspect of worship—namely, concern for the welfare of fellow worshipers. Ideally, worship is a communal activity.[21]

SIGNIFICANCE OF HEBREWS FOR BIBLICAL WORSHIP

Once the author of Hebrews has established the divine status of Jesus, it follows logically that Jesus is superior to such ancient Israelites as Moses and Aaron. The priesthood of Jesus is superior to that of the high priests of the tribe of Levi. The sacrifice Jesus made is superior to all the sacrifices made by priests at the sanctuary. The access to God that Jesus made is superior to the limited access priests have in the earthly sanctuary. The new covenant Jesus establishes is superior to the old covenant. The heavenly sanctuary where Jesus now serves is superior to the earthly tabernacle where earthly priests serve. The heavenly city, Mount Zion, where Jesus resides now is superior to the earthly Mount Sinai. Focus now must not be on the original place of the law but on the heavenly Mount Zion, where worship takes place in the company of the angels and all the saints of the God who is forever associated with Jesus on his throne. Jesus is one with God the Father, and therefore he is equally worthy of worship. The book of Hebrews contributes to worship by showing how Jesus, in his incarnation, life, ministry, death, resurrection, ascension, session, and intercession at God's right hand, is worthy of the kind of devotion previously given to the God of Israel alone. In every way, the worship of God the Father and his Son Jesus Christ is urged. Private commitment to, ecclesial confession of, and public witness to Jesus as Son of God and high priest cannot be compromised without dire consequences because drifting away from Jesus will result in falling away from the living God.

In view of the fact that Jesus the Son of God had come and inaugurated the new covenant promised to Israel (Jer. 31; Heb. 8), the old covenant was declared old and passing away and it had no future. No matter what persecution or the troubles that Jewish Christians were to experience because of their allegiance to Jesus, there was no going back since there was nothing to go back to. To fall away from following Jesus was the same as falling away from the living God. There was no God to go to other than the Father of the Lord Jesus Christ. God and Jesus were forever united: the God of Abraham, Isaac, and Jacob was the Father of Jesus Christ.

---

20. All along we have assumed that audience was a Jewish Christian house church in Rome, Italy, such as is addressed by Paul in Romans 16. See Lane, *Hebrews 9–13*, lviii–lx.
21. Larry W. Hurtado, "Worship, NT Christian," in *The New Interpreter's Dictionary of the Bible*, ed. Katharine Doob Sakenfeld (Nashville: Abingdon, 2006–2009), 5:910–11: "In the NT, and in Christian tradition generally, although prayer and praise can be offered by individuals privately, Christian worship is more characteristically set in the gathered *ekklēsia*."

Throughout Scripture, when human beings come face-to-face with the angels of the Lord there is a temptation to bow and worship. Time and again, however, these mortals are instructed not to worship these angels for worship only belongs to the Father (e.g., Rev. 22:8–9, cf. Matt. 4:9–10). It is clear, through the author's contrast of Christ being superior to the angels that he then is worthy of all praise.

Hindrances to Proper Worship

The warning passages in Hebrews indicated the need for Jewish Christians to remain faithful to God through Jesus Christ, to persevere in their confession of and witness to Jesus Christ. They were to persist in congregational meetings in order to encourage each other in their pilgrimage to the heavenly city where ancient Israelite heroes of faith had already arrived and where uncountable angels, Jesus, and God the Father were waiting for them. They needed to consider their troubles as training for the race set before them and as evidence that God considered them to be legitimate sons in need of discipline. If they heard and heeded the exhortation, then they would be made fit for heavenly worship. Indeed they could now participate in it by coming to God by the way that Jesus had established in his death, resurrection, and ascension to the right hand of God.

The worshipers are warned of five dangers: drifting from messianic faith (2:1–4); disobedience and doubt (3:7–4:13); spiritual stagnation (5:11–6:20); the inferior lifestyle of faithlessness (10:26–31); and spiritual insensitivity (12:25–29). These warnings of danger, however, must be balanced with assurances of the eternal salvation given elsewhere (Heb. 5:9; 6:19; 7:25; 9:12, 15; 10:14; 13:20).[22] At any rate, we need to consider each of the warnings to determine how they affect worship.

Drifting from messianic faith (2:1–4)

God gave the law by means of angels.[23] He gave the message of salvation initially through the Lord and later through those who heard the Lord. He confirmed the message by miracles and gifts of the Holy Spirit. Also, by this time the audience was familiar with the fact that angels had been commanded to worship the Son of God and are sent out by God in service of those who inherit salvation. The argument was that if disobeying or transgressing the lesser message was punished severely, how much more severely would those be punished who drifted away from or neglected the greater message? Proper worship required listening to and accepting the message of salvation. Part of worship was acknowledging

22. Ger, *Hebrews*, 55–59.

23. Did God speak directly to Moses or did he speak indirectly through angels? There is no mention of angels in Exodus 19 and 20. But Moses mentions that a great company of holy ones came with God (Deut. 33:2). Psalm 68:17 gives the number of God's chariots as thousands upon thousands. See Hughes, *Hebrews*, 74–75.

that the message of salvation given by the Lord, passed on by his disciples, and confirmed by the Holy Spirit was superior to the law given by angels.

Disobedience and doubt (3:7–4:13)

Jesus was more glorious than Moses in that while Moses had been a faithful servant among God's people, Jesus was a faithful son. The people that Moses led out of Egypt failed to enter the land of promise where they would find rest. Their unbelief and disobedience were their undoing. The Holy Spirit warned Jewish Christians against hardening their hearts as their ancestors did in the wilderness.[24] Jewish Christians risked worse consequences if they fell away from the living God. They needed to hold on to their original confession of Jesus and to encourage each other daily. In that way, they would enter God's rest, a rest that had eluded their ancestors. As part of Christian worship, mutual exhortation to confess Jesus continually was a sure way to avoid sin and to enter God's rest.

Spiritual stagnation (5:11–6:20)

These Jewish Christians, even though saved and instructed in basic Christian doctrines, seemed to have become stuck in a state of immaturity, like children who fail to move from milk to solid food. The author of Hebrews reminded them of the impossibility of renewal to repentance for anyone who, having been enlightened, tasted the good things of heaven and shared in the Holy Spirit, falls away from the son of God.[25] That would be like contemptuously putting Jesus on the cross again. Such people were comparable to a field sown with good seed only for it to produce weeds. Such a field was only good for burning. The evidence that those addressed had not fallen away was that they continue to serve each other in love. However, they needed to develop in hope, faith, and patience. Their hope was to be founded on and assured by Jesus their high priest. Their faith and patience would enable them to inherit the promises of God. By developing their love, hope, faith, and patience, they would mature and have greater confidence in their worship, which included a commitment to, confession of, and a witness to the crucified Jesus. The antidote for apostasy was maturity.

---

24. Psalm 95:7–11 is cited by the author of Hebrews as a word from the Holy Spirit for today. Today is every day. It is remarkable that now we have another divine speaker—namely, the Holy Spirit. Bruce, *Hebrews*, 95n23: "The Holy Spirit is viewed as the author of the OT revelation not only in words, as here (cf. 10:15), but also in its material content such as the plan for the construction of the wilderness tabernacle (9:8)."

25. The big question here is whether people who were once saved could become apostates, lose their salvation, and thereby enter damnation. Lane, *Hebrews 9–13*, 142, explains the impossibility of repentance fro apostasy as follows: "The apostate repudiates the only basis upon which repentance can be extended. . . . To repudiate Christ is to embrace the 'impossible.'"

The inferior lifestyle of faithlessness (10:26–31)

Even though the law of Moses had provision for sins through sacrifices, certain deliberate sins were not covered and capital punishment resulted for those found guilty.[26] Christ made one sacrifice for sins that would not be repeated. Those who persisted in deliberate sin were in effect rejecting the only means of salvation available and could only expect God's judgment. The way to avoid that state of affairs was to confidently and continually approach God by the way Jesus has provided, to persistently confess Jesus, and to encourage each other to attend communal worship (10:19–25).

Spiritual insensitivity (12:25–29)

When God established the covenant at Sinai, the manifestation of God's presence and the sound of his voice frightened Moses and the people of Israel.[27] The God who shook the earth and issued severe warnings was the same who dwelt in Mount Zion with Jesus, angels, and saints (12:18–24). This awe-inspiring God, who was also a consuming fire, warned that he would shake the heavens and the earth. Since Christians were receiving a kingdom that could not be shaken, they ought to have heeded God's voice, been grateful to him, and reverently offered him acceptable worship.

Summary and Conclusion

The author of Hebrews insisted that the God of Israel shared his identity with his son Jesus Christ. God the Father commanded angels to worship Jesus. Jesus also shared identity with human beings. Having become a man, he demonstrated willing obedience to his Father and sympathetic service to his brothers as a high priest. He was superior to Moses in his faithfulness and superior to Aaronic high priests in his sinless life. His one sacrifice was superior to the many offered by Levitical priests, and his blood more effective in cleansing human sin and human conscience. Having provided atonement for sins, he sat down at the right hand of God and continued to intercede for believers. His new covenant with Israel was not a new idea but a fulfillment of what God had promised through the prophets. Jewish Christians therefore had no reason to drift away from Jesus, disobey or doubt, become spiritually stagnant, accept an inferior lifestyle of faithlessness, or become spiritually insensitive to the voice of God.

---

26. Ger, *Hebrews*, 179: "The Torah's legislation made no provision for those guilty of willful, deliberate sin, that sin defiantly committed with a rebellious, high-handed attitude (Num. 15:29–31), such as idolatry, murder, adultery, or blasphemy. There was no available Levitical sacrifice for covenant infidelity of such magnitude that it warranted capital punishment."

27. Guthrie, *Hebrews*, 264–67, sees references to Exodus 20:19 and Haggai 2:6. Israel was so frightened by God's presence and voice that they begged God to stop speaking and use Moses as a mediator (Exod. 20:19). Yet these same Israelites became insensitive to God's word through the mediator. The danger is that Christian Jews may also become insensitive to the heavenly voice.

Rather, they could confidently approach the throne of God for mercy and grace in times of need. They were to grow in love, faith, hope, and patience as they journeyed to Mount Zion their heavenly home. Since they had continual access to the throne of God, they were exhorted to encourage one another to persevere in their personal commitment to Jesus, public confession of Jesus, and communal worship of God the Father and his Son Jesus Christ.

BIBLIOGRAPHY

Allen, David L. *Hebrews*. NAC 35. Nashville: B&H, 2010.

Bauckham, Richard. "The Divinity of Jesus Christ in the Epistle to the Hebrews." In *The Epistle to the Hebrews and Christian Theology*, edited by Richard Bauckham, Daniel R. Driver, Trevor A. Hart, and Nathan MacDonald, 15–36. Grand Rapids: Eerdmans, 2009.

Bowman, Robert M., Jr., and J. Ed Komoszwski. *Putting Jesus in His Place: The Case for the Deity of Christ*. Grand Rapids: Kregel Academic, 2007.

Bruce, F. F. *The Epistle to the Hebrews*. NICNT. Grand Rapids: Eerdmans, 1990.

Carson, D. A., and Douglas J. Moo. *An Introduction to the New Testament*. 2nd ed. Grand Rapids: Zondervan, 2005.

Church, Philip. *Hebrews and the Temple: Attitudes to the Temple in Second Temple Judaism and in Hebrews*. Leiden: Brill, 2017.

Dunn, James D. G. *Christology in the Making: A New Testament Inquiry into the Origins of the Doctrine of Incarnation*. 2nd ed. Grand Rapids: Eerdmans, 1996.

Ger, Steven. *The Book of Hebrews: Christ Is Greater*. Chattanooga, TN: AMG, 2009.

Grindheim, Sigurd. *God's Equal: What Can We Know about Jesus's Self-Understanding?* LNTS 446. London: T&T Clark, 2011.

Guthrie, Donald. *Hebrews*. TNTC 15. Downers Grove, IL: InterVarsity Press, 1983.

Hagner, Donald A. *Encountering the Book of Hebrews: An Exposition*. Grand Rapids: Baker Academic, 2002.

Harris, Murray J. *Jesus as God: The New Testament Use of* Theos *in Reference to Jesus*. Grand Rapids: Baker, 1992.

Heil, John Paul. *Worship in the Letter to the Hebrews*. Eugene, OR: Wipf & Stock, 2011.

Hughes, Philip Edgcumbe. *A Commentary on the Epistle to the Hebrews*. Grand Rapids: Eerdmans, 1977.

Hurtado, Larry W. "Worship, NT Christian." In *The New Interpreter's Dictionary of the Bible*, edited by Katharine Doob Sakenfeld, 5:519–23. Nashville: Abingdon, 2006–2009.

______. "Pre–70 C.E. Jewish Opposition to Christ-Devotion." In *Ancient Jewish Monotheism and Early Christian Jesus-Devotion*, 185–208. Waco, TX: Baylor University Press, 2017.

______. “The Origin and Development of Christ-Devotion: Forces and Factors.” In *Ancient Jewish Monotheism and Early Christian Jesus-Devotion*, 211–38. Waco, TX: Baylor University Press, 2017.

Landgraf, Paul David. “The Structure of Hebrews: A Word of Exhortation in Light of the Day of Atonement.” In *A Cloud of Witnesses: The Theology of Hebrews in its Ancient Contexts*, edited by Daniel Driver, Nathan MacDonald, Richard Bauckham, and Trevor Hart, 19–27. LNTS 387. New York: T &T Clark, 2008.

Lane, William L. *Hebrews 1–8*. WBC 47A. Dallas: Word, 1991.

______. *Hebrews 9–13*. WBC 47B. Dallas: Word, 1991.

Loke, Andrew Ter Ern. *The Origin of Divine Christology*. SNTSMS 169. Cambridge: Cambridge University Press, 2017.

Macleod, Donald. *The Person of Christ*. Contours in Theology. Downers Grove, IL: InterVarsity Press, 1998.

Mason, Eric F. *“You Are a Priest Forever”: Second Temple Jewish Messianism and the Priestly Christology of the Epistle to the Hebrews*. STDJ 74. Leiden: Brill, 2008.

Morrison, Michael D. *Who Needs a New Covenant? Rhetorical Function of the Covenant Motif in the Argument of Hebrews*. Princeton Theological Monograph Series. Eugene, OR: Wipf & Stock, 2008.

Peterson, David. *Hebrews and Perfection: An Examination of the Concept of Perfection in the “Epistle to the Hebrews.”* SNTSMS 47. Cambridge: Cambridge University Press, 1982.

Wellum, Stephen J. “The Deity of Christ in Apostolic Witness.” In *The Deity of Christ*, edited by Christopher W. Morgan and Robert A. Peterson, 115–49. Theology in Community. Wheaton, IL: Crossway, 2011.

CHAPTER 31

GROUNDED IN ALLEGIANCE TO CHRIST AND AFFECTION FOR GOD

Worship in John's Letters

Andreas Köstenberger

CONTEXT OF WORSHIP IN JOHN'S LETTERS

Most likely, John the apostle, the author of the gospel that bears his name, wrote the three letters included in the New Testament in the years following the publication of his gospel.[1] While the gospel was written primarily to set forth the case that Jesus is the Messiah by providing a narrative account of Jesus's works and signs (John 20:30–31), the letters are written to various churches in a pastoral vein, dealing with a variety of issues needing to be addressed.[2] In the case of 1 John, false teachers had unsettled the church but recently departed (2:19), so that John likely felt a need to reassure believers as they were still processing what had happened. John's other two letters likewise deal with specific issues, such as the question of extending hospitality to false teachers and the excesses of a dictatorial pastor named Diotrephes.[3]

1. For introductory matters pertaining to John's letters, see L. Scott Kellum, "The Johannine Epistles: 1–3 John," chapter 19 in Andreas J. Köstenberger, L. Scott Kellum, and Charles L. Quarles, *The Cradle, the Cross, and the Crown: An Introduction to the New Testament*, 2nd ed. (Nashville: B&H Academic, 2016).
2. For a literary-theological reading of John's letters, see Andreas J. Köstenberger, *A Theology of John's Gospel and Letters: The Word, the Christ, the Son of God*, BTNT (Grand Rapids: Zondervan, 2009), 263–72.
3. However, I will only discuss 1 John in this essay, as 2 and 3 John do not feature the theme of worship in any significant way.

While "worship" terminology is absent from John's letters,[4] it will be possible in the study below to unearth entailments for proper worship by positing a more extended definition. In this way, John's letters can be seen to make a valuable contribution to our understanding of proper worship. In what follows, I will provide a reading of John's first letter with special focus on passages that have at least an indirect bearing on our understanding of worship. In this way, various emphases will emerge that combine to set worship into a Johannine framework, which, in turn, will provide some unique parameters for a biblical theology of worship.

THEOLOGY OF WORSHIP

Personal Experience

John's first letter starts out on a worshipful note. John writes, "That which was from the beginning, which we have heard, which we have seen with our eyes, which we have looked at and our hands have touched—this we proclaim concerning the Word of life" (1:1 NIV). John's worship of Jesus—the Word of life—is grounded in *personal experience*. John had encountered the Word that had become flesh in Jesus—the life-giving Word—and had come to embrace him as the God-sent Messiah and God-given atonement for the sins of the world and placed his faith in him. This personal relationship with the Lord Jesus Christ, the Son of the Father, in turn, became the ground of fellowship with others and of the message John proclaimed (vv. 2–3).[5] Thus, properly understood, worship—defined as recognizing the true worth of God's gift in Jesus and a believing response to it—is at the root of Christian *fellowship* and *proclamation*.

First, John worships God—and Jesus—as *holy*: "God is light, and in him is no darkness at all" (v. 5).[6] Anyone who lives in moral darkness

4. Note that treatments such as Judith M. Lieu, *The Theology of the Johannine Epistles*, New Testament Theology (Cambridge: Cambridge University Press, 1991), have little to say about worship in John's letters. John Paul Heil, *1–3 John: Worship by Loving God and One Another to Live Eternally* (Cambridge: James Clarke, 2015), despite its title, does not really discuss worship as a significant theme in John's letters. In John's gospel, the word "worship" (*proskyneō*) occurs especially in the conversation between Jesus and the Samaritan woman about true worship "in spirit and truth" (4:20–24 [8×]; see also "worshiper," *proskynētēs*, in 4:23) as well as in 9:38 and 12:20. The word is almost ubiquitous in the book of Revelation, where it appears twenty-four times. S. Johnson Samuel, "'Neither on this Mountain Nor in Jerusalem': The Johannine Understanding of Worship," *Bangalore Theological Forum* 19 (1987): 121–29, focuses on John 4:19–23 while mentioning 1 John only twice briefly in passing.

5. The word "fellowship" (*koinōnia*) occurs in 1 John in 1:3, 6, and 7. It is not found in the Gospels and appears in the NT first in Acts 2:42. The word connotes the idea of sharing together or holding in common.

6. Cf. John 1:5: "The light shines in the darkness, and the darkness has not overcome it"; and John 3:19: "the light has come into the world, and people loved the darkness rather than the light because their works were evil." In these passages, "the light" is Jesus (cf. 8:12; 9:5), and "the darkness" is the evil realm of the world apart from God (cf. 12:35). For a discussion of light and darkness in John's gospel and letters see Köstenberger, *Theology of John's Gospel and Letters*, 283–84.

while claiming to have fellowship with Christ and the believing community fails to live out the truth (v. 6). True worshipers of God and followers of Christ must pursue *holiness* because their object of worship and vital allegiance is holy through and through, without even a hint of darkness. Any claim to live in fellowship with God while practicing immorality is therefore unmasked as a lie; right belief and right practice—orthodoxy and orthopraxy—go hand in hand and cannot be separated. True worship takes place with our hearts *and* minds, with our beliefs *and* actions, and above all in our relationships with others. Proper follow-through in our relationship with God is therefore vital—only if we exhibit holiness in our dealings with others have we fully absorbed and given expression to the reality of our relationship with God in Christ.

The true Christian experience, therefore, is this: "If we walk in the light, as he is in the light, we have fellowship with one another, and the blood of Jesus cleanses us from all sin" (v. 7). This reference is critical as it highlights the centrality and foundational nature of the *blood of Jesus* in the Christian's day-to-day experience of living out the Christian life. The world's claim to have no sin is tantamount to self-deception (v. 8; cf. v. 10). Conversely, those who know themselves to be sinners and confess their sin will find God faithful and righteous; he will forgive their sin and cleanse them from all unrighteousness (v. 9). Any claim that Christians no longer need to confess their sin is therefore baseless and unscriptural. As Jesus told Peter when the latter refused to have his feet washed, symbolizing his need for ongoing cleansing from sin, "If I do not wash you, you have no share with me" (John 13:8). Believers in Jesus are continually pruned by the divine vinedresser so that they bear even more fruit (John 15:2; cf. vv. 8, 16).

Propitiation

In fact, Jesus is the *propitiation* (*hilasmos*) of the sins of the entire world (2:2; cf. 4:10)—he is God's Lamb who took away the sins of the world (John 1:29, 36) and removed God's wrath from believers. Worshipers, therefore, are saved sinners who live in fellowship with God and others because their sins have been taken away and God's wrath has been removed from them by the propitiatory blood of Christ. Apart from the blood of Christ, there is no efficacious means of forgiveness for human sin. Not only this, believers in Jesus experience the power and efficacy of Christ's atoning blood in their daily lives as they continually engage in the process of exercising repentance and receiving forgiveness and cleansing. In this way, they remain in Christ, without whom they can do nothing (John 15:5). Jesus died on the cross for our sins in history past, but his work continues—he is our advocate (*paraklētos*) with the Father, "Jesus Christ the Righteous One" (2:2).[7] Yet while sinless perfection in this life is an impossibility, God's love is perfected

7. In the Gospel, the term "Advocate" (*paraklētos*), without exception, refers to the Holy Spirit (John 14:26; 15:26; 16:7); this is the only place in John's writings where the expression refers to Jesus.

in human *obedience* (2:5). The true Christian keeps Christ's commandments, of which none is greater than the "new commandment"—to love one's fellow believers (2:3–4; cf. John 13:34–35).[8] We must "walk" as Jesus walked (2:6),[9] which, in context, means living a life of obedience inspired by and grounded in the love of God.

Earlier, John has denounced the spurious claim of a person enjoying fellowship with God while walking in darkness (1:6). Now he specifies this general assertion by providing a concrete instantiation of such a contradiction in terms: "Whoever says he is in the light and hates his brother is still in darkness" (2:9; cf. vv. 10, 11). Such fraternal hatred, which in Cain's case led to fratricide (the example used by John at 3:12), is demonically inspired and devoid of the Spirit, who is a Spirit of love. John's point can be viewed as two sides of a single coin: If we truly love others with the love of Christ, this validates our claim of being Christ-followers.[10] Conversely, if we hate others, this belies any such claim and shows that we are truly unregenerate—for only those who possess the indwelling Holy Spirit can love the way Christ loves. A life of worship is therefore a life of *love*.

We've already discussed the likely occasion for John's letter above, which John will mention shortly (cf. 2:19). Suffice it to say here that John's purpose is not to establish a series of tests to see whether his readers are true believers. More likely, his primary purpose for writing his first epistle is that of assuring his readers that, no matter what their detractors have been telling them, they are in fact genuine Christians. "You're not a Christian because you sin"—not true; all Christians still sin. But, in Christ, they have a means of propitiation for all sins past, present, and future. In 2:11–14, John writes to various groups in the congregation he addresses—fathers, children, young men—that their sins are forgiven; that they know both God the Father and his Son, the Lord Jesus Christ; that they are strong, God's Word lives in them, and that they have overcome the evil one. Worship is thus grounded in the *certainty* that one is a child of God—forgiven and living in close fellowship with God in Christ and in community with other believers (cf. 5:13).

Love

We've already seen that, for John, a life of worship is a life of love. In many ways, a person worships that to which he or she attaches his or her

8. The statement in 2:7–8 that this is in fact no "new commandment" but an old one appears to be a formal contradiction with John 13:34–35 but can be reconciled when one understands that John here is merely seeking to point out that in the ultimate analysis God's love truly is eternal and thus the imperative to love is likewise grounded in eternal realities—the nature of God.

9. The word "walk" (*peripateō*) regularly in the NT refers metaphorically to a person's lifestyle or habitual conduct. In Paul, see, e.g., Rom. 6:4; Gal. 5:16; Col. 1:10. In John's letters, the word occurs in 1 John 1:6, 7; 2:6, 11; 2 John 4, 6; 3 John 3, 4.

10. In 4:7, John asserts that "whoever loves has been born of God and knows God." That is, true love validates a person's regeneration and provides irrefutable evidence of the genuineness of their relationship with God.

affections.[11] This is the topic of John's passionate appeal in 2:15: "Do not love the world or the things in the world. If anyone loves the world, the love of the Father is not in him." In this statement, John contrasts love for the world and the things in the world with love of God the Father. The passage stands in intriguing contrast to the signature verse of John's gospel, where the evangelist asserts that "God so loved the world that he gave his one and only Son" (John 3:16 NIV). While the world is therefore the object of God's redemptive love, which prompted him to send and sacrifice his unique, one-of-a-kind Son (echoes of Abraham being prepared to offer his one-of-a-kind son Isaac [Gen. 22]), believers are not to love the world—understood in opposition to God's will and purposes—or attach undue affections to it. "For all that is in the world—the desires of the flesh and the desires of the eyes and pride of life—is not from the Father but is from the world" (2:16). Many have seen in this passage a thinly veiled allusion to the fall narrative, which depicts Satan as tempting and deceiving Eve by appealing to her senses: "When the woman saw that the fruit of the tree was good for food and pleasing to the eye, and also desirable for gaining wisdom, she took some and ate it" (Gen. 3:6 NIV). The parallels can be laid out as follows:

1 John 2:16	*Genesis 3:6*
The desires of the flesh	Good for food
The desires of the eyes	Pleasing to the eye
The pride of life	Desirable for gaining wisdom

Figure 1. Echoes of the Fall Narrative in 1 John 2:15–17

Similarly, the temptation narratives of Jesus in Matthew and Luke—though not included in John's gospel—focus on temptations related to the desires of the flesh: "If you are the Son of God, tell this stone to become bread" (Matt. 4:3 NIV; Luke 4:3) and the pride of life: "All this I will give you if you will bow down and worship me" (Matt. 4:9 NIV; Luke 4:7). In response, Jesus quoted two passages of Scripture from the book of Deuteronomy: "It is written: 'Man shall not live on bread alone, but on every word that comes from the mouth of God'" (Matt. 4:4 NIV; Luke 4:4; cf. Deut. 8:3), and "It is written: 'Worship the Lord your God, and serve him only'" (Matt. 4:10 NIV; Luke 4:8; cf. Deut. 6:13).

Perhaps 1 John 2:15–17, then, in keeping with his love ethic that finds eloquent articulation in his gospel,[12] is John's attempt to probe the essence

11. See G. K. Beale, *We Become What We Worship: A Biblical Theology of Idolatry* (Downers Grove, IL: IVP Academic, 2008); James K. A. Smith, *You Are What You Love: The Spiritual Power of Habit* (Grand Rapids: Brazos, 2016).
12. On the Johannine love ethic, see Köstenberger, *Theology of John's Gospel and Letters*, chap. 13.

of temptation as a failure to devote one's love and affection to the only object that is truly deserving of such love: God the Father himself. Rather than loving the world—which "is passing away along with its desires"—believers ought to love the Father, knowing that "whoever does the will of God abides forever" (2:17). In many ways, then, 2:15–17 constitutes the climactic passage in John's theology of worship, which centers on the contrast between appropriate love of God the Father in contrast to inordinate love for the things in the world.[13]

Spiritual Warfare

Not surprisingly in view of the likely allusion to the devil in 2:15–17, John's thoughts next turn to the antichrist and the numerous preliminary manifestations of antichrists already at work (2:18–27; cf. 2 John 7). One such manifestation furnished the likely occasion for writing John's first letter—namely, the recent departure of false teachers from the congregations in John's sphere of influence (2:19). Essentially, John argues, these false teachers were demonically inspired and lacked spiritual regeneration. Reassuring the recipients, John writes, "But you have been anointed by the Holy One, and you all have knowledge" (2:20; cf. v. 27). Rather than claim possession of esoteric knowledge, as the false teachers apparently did while denying that Jesus is the Messiah, believers simply need to hold onto the message they've heard from the beginning—the apostolic gospel of salvation in the Lord Jesus Christ (2:24; cf. 1:1).[14] Worship thus takes place in the context of *spiritual warfare* and attempted satanic deception including his use of false teachers as his instruments.[15]

Worship also takes place against an *eschatological backdrop* and, as mentioned, is undergirded by certainty as to believers' status as children of God. Believers in Jesus can have confidence at Christ's return and will not shrink back in shame (2:28); they are likewise confident that they are the recipients of God's love and that they are his children (3:1). What is

13. Note that Paul's theology is very similar in this regard. See esp. the vice list in 2 Timothy 3:1–5, which characterizes people in the last days among other things as "lovers of self," "lovers of money," "not loving good," and "lovers of pleasure rather than lovers of God."

14. Note that this exhortation to affirm that Jesus is the Christ in verse 22 closely parallels the purpose statement in John's gospel (20:30–31). For an excellent treatment of the nature of the false teachers, see Daniel R. Streett, *"They Went Out from Us": The Identity of the Opponents in First John*, BZNW (Berlin: de Gruyter, 2011).

15. See Andreas J. Köstenberger, "The Cosmic Trial Motif in John's Letters," in *Communities in Dispute: Current Scholarship on the Johannine Epistles*, eds. R. Alan Culpepper and Paul N. Anderson, Early Christianity and Its Literature 13 (Atlanta: SBL Press, 2014), 157–78. Note the use of the word "deceive" (*planaō*) in 2:26 and 3:7, which invokes Satan's deception of the woman at the fall (Gen. 3:1–7; see also verse 16: "The serpent deceived me"; cf. the use of cognate verbs in 2 Corinthians 11:3 and 1 Timothy 2:14). Again, Paul's letters to Timothy and Titus furnish poignant parallels to the depiction of false teachers as Satan's instruments and as demonically inspired. See Andreas J. Köstenberger, *Commentary on 1–2 Timothy and Titus*, BTCP (Nashville: B&H Academic, 2017), 516–21.

more, they will be like Jesus, because they will see him as he is (3:2). In keeping with Jesus's words, "Blessed are the pure in heart, for they shall see God" (Matt. 5:8), believers will also purify themselves just as Jesus himself is pure (3:3). This cleansing, as already mentioned, involves confession of sin (1:9) and takes place in the company of other believers in the context of Christian fellowship. The practice of sin is contrary to Jesus's purpose of coming into the world, which was to take away sins (3:5; cf. John 1:29, 36), just as he himself is free from sin (3:5; cf. John 8:46). Conversely, sinning aligns oneself with the devil, who is the prototypical sinner (3:8).

In the Johannine universe, as in Scripture in its entirety, there are only two kinds of children—children of God and children of the devil—the distinguishing mark between them being *spiritual rebirth* (3:9; cf. John 1:12–13; see also 8:39–47). Not that God's children no longer sin, yet they do not *keep on* sinning but confess their sin and are cleansed by the blood of Christ (2:4–10). Again, John stresses that the mark of the true believer is love for others, which is living proof that believers have passed from death into life (3:14; cf. John 5:24). This love, in turn, is exemplified by deeds of charity (3:17).[16] As John categorically states, "Whoever does not love abides in death" (3:14). Thus, for John, there are only two spheres of human existence: love—leading to eternal life—and death. Hatred, for its part, reveals a murderous heart, and no one with an unregenerate, murderous heart has eternal life (3:15; cf. Matt. 5:21–22). John's insistence that love be expressed not merely "in word or talk but in deed and in truth" (3:18) echoes Jesus's teaching (Matt. 7:24–27) and resembles James's exhortation (likely echoing Jesus's teaching as well) that believers be "doers of the word, and not hearers only" (James 1:22).

Confession

John's assertion that true believers know that God abides in them "by the Spirit whom he has given us" (3:24) transitions seamlessly to the warning not to "believe every spirit" but to "test the spirits to see whether they are from God" (4:1).[17] In his gospel, John included Jesus's assertion that true worshipers must worship "in spirit and truth," because God is spirit (John 4:23–24), while later in the present letter, John affirms, "By this we know that we abide in him and he in us, because he has given us of his Spirit" (4:13). Here, he registers the caveat that nor every spirit is from

16. The reference in 3:16, "By this we know love, that he laid down his life for us, and we ought to lay down our lives for the brothers," echoes the footwashing in John 13 and Jesus's subsequent instruction of his followers.

17. The teaching on the two spirits—namely, "the Spirit of truth and the spirit of error" (4:6)—bears a certain resemblance to the beliefs of the Qumran community (e.g., 1QS 3:13–4:26). See James H. Charlesworth, "A Critical Comparison of the Dualism in 1QS 3:13–4:26 and the 'Dualism' Contained in the Gospel of John," in *John and Qumran*, ed. James H. Charlesworth (London: Chapman, 1972), 76–106 (though Charlesworth's conclusion that John borrowed some of the dualism from Qumran is tenuous, as is noted by Lieu, *Theology of the Johannine Epistles*, 38n23).

God but only the one who confesses Jesus as Messiah (4:2).[18] There are other spirits, however, who do not confess Jesus as Messiah; these spirits—demonic spirits—inhabit the many "false prophets" (4:1) who are active in this world and who serve as preliminary manifestations of the "spirit of the antichrist" (4:3) prior to the coming of the antichrist himself. As the following chart demonstrates, the vital point to derive from this is that proper worship is contingent on right *confession* (*homologeō*)—specifically, right confession as to the identity of Jesus as Messiah.[19]

Reference	*Object of Confession*	*Consequence*
1 John 2:23	the Son	has the Father
1 John 4:2, 3	Jesus Christ has come in the flesh / Jesus	is from God
1 John 4:15	Jesus is the Son of God	God abides in him
2 John 7	Jesus has come in the flesh (negative)	deceiver/antichrist

Figure 2. Right Christological Confession in John's Letters

Love Revisited

In 4:7–5:3, John cycles back around and once again extols the supreme virtue of *love*. In the original context—the recent departure of the false teachers (2:19)—John's emphasis on love fulfills the dual purpose of reassuring believers of the genuineness of their relationship with God and of exposing the actual nature of the false teachers as not truly knowing God. In distinguishing between true believers and false pretenders, love can serve as a crucial test: If anyone truly loves others from the heart, they are born again and love God; if they hate others, they are unregenerate and hate God. John seems to assume that the believers left behind in the church are examples of the former, while the false teachers fall into the latter category. Not that believers' love originates in their own hearts; rather, it is given to them by God, who in his very essence is love (4:8) and who sent his one and only Son into the world to serve as the propitiation for our sins (4:10; cf. 2:2).[20] John himself says it best: "We love because he first loved us" (4:19).

18. For this understanding of 4:2, see Streett, *They Went Out from Us*, passim.

19. See Andreas J. Köstenberger, "Orthodoxy," in *The Encyclopedia of Christian Civilization*, ed. George T. Kurian (Malden, MA: Blackwell, 2011), 3:1735–43, where I point out that ultimately the right confession of Jesus is at heart of the Christian understanding of orthodoxy versus heresy. In addition to the above-listed references, *homologeō* occurs also in 1 John 1:9 with regard to believers' confession of sin. See also the references to confession in John 1:20 (the Baptist is not the Messiah); 9:22 (confession of Jesus as Messiah leading to synagogue expulsion); and 12:42 (many authorities believed but did not confess Jesus out of fear that they would be put out of the synagogue).

20. See the discussion above.

In 4:12, we find an intriguing parallel to a statement made by John in his gospel. Consider the similarity:

1 John 4:12	*John 1:18*
No one has ever seen God;	No one has ever seen God;
if we love one another, God abides in us	the only God, who is at the Father's side,
and his love is perfected in us.	he has made him known.

Figure 3. Parallels between 1 John 4:12 and John 1:18

As can be seen in the figure above, the underlying premise in both statements is identical: No one has ever seen God. In the gospel, John goes on to assert that Jesus, himself being God, has made God known (i.e., Jesus made God visible in human form as the Word-become-flesh, God's tangible self-expression; cf. 1:1, 14). Thus, while God, being spirit, is in and of himself invisible to human eyes, Jesus closed the communication gap, as it were, by making the invisible visible. In John's first letter, John then develops the same underlying premise in a different direction. While no one has seen God, John maintains, "if we love one another, God abides in us, and his love is perfected in us."[21] This is to say that the outside world—which cannot otherwise see God—can see him in and through believers' love for one another!

In this way, the circle is closed. While God's own love prompted him to send Jesus into the world to procure redemption from sin, those who received redemption and became children of God now have the amazing opportunity and privilege—similar to Jesus—to make God, and his love for sinful humanity, visible to those who are in the world. How will this happen? It will take place through loving relationships among believers in the congregation. In terms of worship, this means that love for one's fellow believers is vital if one is to truly worship. Worship is not an individualistic affair. We cannot truly worship God in a way that pleases him if we fail to love our fellow believers or those outside the walls of the church. Thus, worship and love are inseparable and inextricably linked.

Faith

There is one more important ingredient to God-honoring worship: world-overcoming, victorious *faith* in Jesus the Son of God (5:4–5). The Spirit, Jesus's baptism, and his death on the cross all testify to Jesus's genuine joint humanity and divinity (5:6–8). Faith thus places its trust and

21. Note that not only does perfect love serve as a tremendous witness to unbelievers, but it also instills confidence for the day of judgment (4:17) and drives out fear (4:18).

confidence, not in the testimony of mere humans, but in the testimony borne by God himself (5:9). Those who don't believe in effect make God a liar, because they fail to accept his testimony regarding Jesus (5:10). This unbelief is a grave offense to God and has eternal consequences. John has woven references to the reality of God's future judgment into the latter part of his letter (4:17). Life is found only in the Son; no Son, no life (5:12). This is a momentous assertion and realization. Worship thus is contingent on faith, faith in Jesus the Son of God, both human and divine—the historical person of Jesus Christ who as the eternal Word entered human history as the God-man at the incarnation, who was baptized by John the Baptist at the inception of his ministry, and who died a real human death as our sinless substitute on the cross, shedding his blood for the forgiveness of our sins on Calvary.

The only God-honoring and God-pleasing worship is thus predicated on this kind of faith—*faith that accepts God's testimony regarding his Son*. Such trusting reception and affirmation, in turn, yields assurance of faith (5:13) and confidence of answered prayer (5:14–15).[22] True worship, therefore, is tied to a person's settled assurance of salvation and a firm belief in the power and privilege of *prayer*. It is also aware of one's need for spiritual *protection* from the evil one in and through Christ (5:18) and cognizant of the fact that the entire world is under the control of the evil one (5:19). As those who are assured of victory in Christ, believers must guard themselves from idols and remain "in him who is true . . . his Son Jesus Christ. He is the true God and eternal life" (5:20).

SIGNIFICANCE OF THE JOHANNINE EPISTLES FOR BIBLICAL WORSHIP

Worship in John's first epistle is placed within the orbit of several factors, including personal experience, propitiation, love, spiritual warfare, confession, and faith. At the outset, John grounds his witness in his *personal experience* of knowing and following Christ. He proceeds to affirm the reception of *propitiation* in Christ's blood as the basis on which he can enter fellowship with God and with others in the congregation. At the heart of John's theology of worship is *love*. Because God is love, and because believers love since God first loved them, the Christian life is lived in the orbit of love, and lack of love is evidence that a person is not a

22. Prayer, that is, which is not asking God to forgive "a sin leading to death" (5:16). It is unclear what specific kind of sin John has in mind in this statement. The reader is referred to the commentary literature for the various interpretive options. See, e.g., I. Howard Marshall, *The Epistles of John*, NICNT (Grand Rapids: Eerdmans, 1978), 245–51; and more recently, Robert W. Yarbrough, *1–3 John*, BECNT (Grand Rapids: Baker Academic, 2008), 306–13. See also Marianne Meye Thompson, "Intercession in the Johannine Community: 1 John 5:16 in the Context of the Gospel and Epistles of John," in *Worship*, Theology and Ministry in the Early Church: Essays in Honor of Ralph P Martin, eds. Michael J. Wilkins and Terence Paige, JSNTSup 87 (Sheffield: JSOT Press, 1992), 225–45.

Christian at all. This invalidates all claims of worship by those who hate believers and others around them.

Worship also takes place in a context of *spiritual warfare* and conflict, which require God's protection from Satan, the ruler of this world. This cosmic conflict, in turn, renders proper christological confession vital. Specifically, true worshipers must *confess* that Jesus is the Messiah and that he came to provide propitiation by his blood. *Faith* in Jesus—in conjunction with confession of sin and continual cleansing—is thus an indispensable prerequisite for worship. For John, proper worship of God is grounded in attaching one's *love* and affections to the one who alone is worthy of exclusive allegiance and supreme honor and praise. All genuine believers are not to love the world, or the things in the world, but to love God the Father and to do his will which abides forever. They should guard against idols and worship only the true God—God the Father and the sender of the Lord Jesus Christ.

BIBLIOGRAPHY

Beale, G. K. *We Become What We Worship: A Biblical Theology of Idolatry*. Downers Grove, IL: IVP Academic, 2008.

Charlesworth, James H. "A Critical Comparison of the Dualism in 1QS 3:13–4:26 and the 'Dualism' Contained in the Gospel of John." In *John and Qumran*, edited by James H. Charlesworth, 76–106. London, 1972.

Heil, John Paul. *1–3 John: Worship by Loving God and One Another to Live Eternally*. Cambridge: James Clarke, 2015.

Kellum, L. Scott. "The Johannine Epistles: 1–3 John." In *The Cradle, the Cross, and the Crown: An Introduction to the New Testament*, edited by Andreas J. Köstenberger, L. Scott Kellum, and Charles L. Quarles, 781–808. 2nd ed. Nashville: B&H Academic, 2016.

Köstenberger, Andreas J. *Commentary on 1–2 Timothy and Titus*. BTCP. Nashville: B&H Academic, 2017.

______. "The Cosmic Trial Motif in John's Letters." In *Communities in Dispute: Current Scholarship on the Johannine Epistles*, edited by R. Alan Culpepper and Paul N. Anderson, 157–78. ECL 13. Atlanta: SBL Press, 2014.

______. "Orthodoxy." In *The Encyclopedia of Christian Civilization*, edited by George T. Kurian, 3:1735–43. Malden, MA: Blackwell, 2011.

______. *A Theology of John's Gospel and Letters: The Word, the Christ, the Son of God*. BTNT. Grand Rapids: Zondervan, 2009.

Lieu, Judith M. *The Theology of the Johannine Epistles*. New Testament Theology. Cambridge: Cambridge University Press, 1991.

Marshall, I. Howard. *The Epistles of John*. NICNT. Grand Rapids: Eerdmans, 1978.

Samuel, S. Johnson. "'Neither on This Mountain Nor in Jerusalem': The Johannine Understanding of Worship." *Bangalore Theological Forum* 19 (1987): 121–29.

Smith, James K. A. *You Are What You Love: The Spiritual Power of Habit.* Grand Rapids: Brazos, 2016.

Streett, Daniel R. *"They Went Out from Us": The Identity of the Opponents in First John.* BZNW. Berlin: de Gruyter, 2011.

Thompson, Marianne Meye. "Intercession in the Johannine Community: 1 John 5:16 in the Context of the Gospel and Epistles of John." In *Worship, Theology and Ministry in the Early Church: Essays in Honor of Ralph P Martin*, edited by Michael J. Wilkins and Terence Paige, 225–45. JSNTSup 87. Sheffield: JSOT Press, 1992.

Yarbrough, Robert W. *1–3 John.* BECNT. Grand Rapids: Baker Academic, 2008.

CHAPTER 32

GOD'S SPIRITUAL HOUSE

Worship in 1 Peter

Karen Jobes

CONTEXT OF WORSHIP IN 1 PETER

The English word "worship" may evoke various images to the modern churchgoer. It may suggest quiet spaces of prayer, hymns, candles, organ music, and perhaps stained glass. In contemporary evangelical America it more likely suggests rousing singing perhaps accompanied by guitars and drums, a time of *fellowship* (i.e., coffee and sweets), and a hopefully Bible-based sermon or message to inspire living in the week ahead. In the Reformation era, listening to the sermon, which was understood to be a word from God, was the centerpiece of Protestant worship—in contrast to the Roman Catholic liturgy of the Mass, a symbolic reenactment of the sacrifice of the body and blood of Jesus. I would guess that this Reformation-era ideal is not common, and most churchgoers today would not identify the sermon as the essence of Sunday worship on the first mention of the word.

When we enter the biblical world, we find forms of worship in the Old Testament based on the sacrificial killing and butchering of animals in a sacred spot by a specially designated group of people, the priesthood. Because of the once-for-all sacrifice of Jesus on the cross, the Christian church did not continue animal sacrifice into the New Testament era, but the vocabulary and images of ritual animal sacrifice were sometimes used to redefine Christian worship of God.

We find no instructions or teaching explicitly about worship in 1 Peter. The most frequently used Greek words that are translated "worship" in the New Testament—such as *proskuneō*, *sebeomai*, and *phobeomai*—do not occur in 1 Peter.[1] This makes it difficult to agree with John Heil that

1. Words in L&N's semantic domain G Worship, Reverence (53.53–53.64).

worship is the "main theme of 1 Peter."[2] Nevertheless, there is a powerful metaphor in this letter, which can inform our understanding of what Peter thought the worship of God involved for the Christian. That metaphor is from the sacrificial practices of ancient Israel's temple and priesthood (1 Peter 2:5, 9). Peter describes a new temple built on the Living Stone, the risen Lord Jesus Christ, writing, "As you come to him, the living Stone—rejected by humans but chosen by God and precious to him—you also, like living stones, are being built into a spiritual house *to be a holy priesthood*, offering *spiritual sacrifices* acceptable to God through Jesus Christ" (1 Peter 2:4–5, emphasis added).[3] After quoting verses from the Old Testament that speak of the stone God has laid in Zion, a stone precious to him but rejected by so many, Peter declares once more in 2:9 (emphasis added), "But you are a chosen people, a royal *priesthood*, a holy nation, God's special possession, that you may declare the praises of him who called you out of darkness into his wonderful light." Peter contrasts those people referred to in 2:18 who stumble and fall because they disobey the Living Stone with those who come to the Living Stone (2:5) and are built into a "spiritual house" to be a priesthood to offer spiritual sacrifices. Whatever Peter says in this letter that is relevant to the topic of worship begins with this understanding of the Christian believer in relation to Christ, to God the Father, and to other believers. There is a new temple, so to speak, a new priesthood, and new sacrifices that constitute Christian worship.

The quotations in 1 Peter 2:6–8a come from Isaiah 28:16, Psalm 118:22, and Isaiah 8:14, verses understood even before the advent of Christ to be messianic, as evidenced, for instance, by the Old Greek translation of Isaiah 28:16.[4] Peter understands these prophetic verses to have been fulfilled spectacularly by the resurrection of Jesus Christ, who was God's precious means of true redemption taking the place of sacrificial animals, and whose victory over death creates a new place of worship that deems the Jerusalem temple, its priesthood and sacrifices no longer necessary. That ancient cultic model of worship became for the New Testament writers a means of explaining the significance of Jesus's death and resurrection.

THEOLOGY OF WORSHIP

The Jerusalem temple was the place where God chose to meet humankind, the place where sin was cleansed by blood sacrifice, and the place of prayer and singing of psalms. After his resurrection, Jesus himself becomes the "place" of worship, the place where all sin is cleansed by his

2. John Paul Heil, *1 Peter, 2 Peter, and Jude: Worship Matters* (Eugene, OR: Cascade, 2013), 23.
3. Unless otherwise noted, all Scripture quotations in this chapter are from the NIV.
4. Karen H. Jobes, "The Septuagint Textual Tradition in 1 Peter," in *Septuagint Research: Issues and Challenges in the Study of the Greek Jewish Scriptures*, eds. Wolfgang Kraus and R. Glenn Wooden, SCS 53 (Atlanta: Society of Biblical Literature, 2006), 311–33, esp. 320; Jan de Waard, *A Comparative Study of the Old Testament Text in the Dead Sea Scrolls and in the New Testament*, STDJ 4 (Leiden: Brill, 1965), 54–60.

own blood, and where God incarnate meets humanity. Peter presents this new place of worship as a temple founded on the Living (i.e., resurrected) Stone, Jesus Christ. From this understanding, Peter writes, "As you come to him, the living Stone—rejected by humans but chosen by God and precious to him—you also, like living stones, are being built into a spiritual house to be a holy priesthood, offering spiritual sacrifices acceptable to God through Jesus Christ." Reflection on this metaphor yields insight into the nature of Christian worship in 1 Peter.

The Living Stone (*lithon zōnta*) and the living stones (*lithoi zōntes*)

The parallel between the Living Stone—the resurrected Jesus Christ—and the living stones implies much about Christian life and worship. As Peter envisions it, the Christian community is a temple ("a spiritual house") implying that the church universal is the place of God's earthly dwelling by the Holy Spirit and the place of true worship and sacrifice acceptable to God through Christ (cf. John 4:23–24).[5] As I have written elsewhere, "In Peter's imagery, Christ is included in the spiritual temple alongside believers, but as the foundational, first, and preeminent stone in the new temple, a stone that holds a unique place. Christ is the foundation stone of this new temple; apart from him the new temple would not exist."[6]

From this we learn that *true Christian worship is grounded in Jesus Christ*. Just as a building under construction is plumbed to be square with the foundation stone, giving the building strength, stability, and integrity, the Christian temple of which Christ is the cornerstone must be squared to and conformed to Jesus Christ. Through the work of the Holy Spirit, those who have a place in the corporate church universal must be plumbed and squared to the character of Jesus to be his strong, stable, and authentic presence in the world.

Think of stone temples or other buildings you may have seen, with stones of various sizes and shapes, each taking its place and giving the building strength, integrity, and beauty. The image of living stones taking their places in God's new temple as they come to Christ has implications for Christian worship in relationship to other believers. As we are joined to Christ, we are at the same time joined to all those living stones who have come to him, past, present, and future, locally and around the globe. Notably, Peter does not present an image of these living stones as lying about in idle isolation or disorder. They are neither heaped in a pile nor scattered across a field. In the Lord's spiritual house, each is put in a specific place to bear its own weight, and to function in its unique "architectural" purpose. It is worth noting here that if ever there were a place where

5. Although this understanding of *oikos* as temple enjoys a majority, see John H. Elliott, *A Home for the Homeless: A Sociological Exegesis of 1 Peter, Its Situation and Strategy* (Philadelphia: Fortress, 1981), for a different reading.
6. Karen H. Jobes, *1 Peter*, BECNT (Grand Rapids: Baker Academic, 2005), 148.

the apostle Peter could have exploited the nickname that Jesus had given him, "the rock" (or stone), this would have been it (cf. John 1:42; Matt. 15:18). However, there is not even a hint here that Peter thought of himself as being a special stone, much less a foundational stone in the church.

The image of God's spiritual house speaks to the unity, significance, and purpose of the *corporate* body of Christian believers, apart from which no true worship can occur. The significance and purpose of the individual Christian is realized in community with other believers. God's presence sanctified the Jerusalem temple, and it is his presence through the Holy Spirit that sets apart the Christian church universal as the place where the Lord God dwells on earth. It is the presence of the Spirit that unifies all living stones into *one* structure. This means that worship is a corporate experience for all those in whom the Holy Spirit dwells, even if only two or three individuals are gathered, for those few are part of the much larger spiritual house that includes all Christians through all time. This corporate understanding of the nature of worship corrects any individualistic, just-Jesus-and-me attitudes that seem so prevalent in North American Christianity. And so, *true Christian worship is corporate worship*.[7] This does not mean merely gathering in a building on Sunday morning, but the convergence of the lives of believers lived for the glory of God. The Sunday gathering is but an expression and reflection of the corporate nature of the new temple built on Christ.

William Barclay recounts the legendary story of an ancient Spartan king boasting to a visiting monarch about the great walls of Sparta. However, the visitor could see no walled city and asked, "Where are the renowned walls of Sparta?" The Spartan king pointed to his army and replied, "These are the walls of Sparta, every man a brick."[8] Peter's idea of a spiritual house comprising individual believers is similar. Only at the end of human history when Christ's kingdom is revealed will the structure of God's house be completed. All of human history will be seen to have been the scaffolding of God's construction site, as divine providence working through every stage of history and in every place around the world built living stones into the spiritual house. Just as the men of Sparta were trained to function as one for the defense and well-being of the city, God's spiritual house is built of the lives of those who come to Christ and join together as one to offer spiritual sacrifices acceptable to God through Jesus Christ.

A Spiritual House (*oikos pneumatikos*)

In 1 Peter 2:5, Peter uses the general word *oikos* in the phrase "a spiritual house," which introduces a purposeful ambiguity that segues into

7. As also J. Ramsey Michaels, *1 Peter*, WBC 49 (Waco, TX: Word, 1988), 101.
8. William Barclay, *The Letters of James and Peter*, rev. ed. (Philadelphia: Westminster, 1976), 195–96.

Peter's next thought of Christian believers as a priesthood.[9] For *oikos* was used in the Greek Old Testament to refer to a kinship of people as well as to a building for deity. For instance, in Exodus 19:3–6 (LXX) God addresses the "house" (*oikos*) of Jacob, clearly referring to Jacob and his progeny. In that same passage God declares that his obedient people who keep his covenant will be "a kingdom of priests" (v. 6).

Because 1 Peter 2:6–7 refers to a cornerstone, the living stones are understood to be part of a building, and the reference to a priesthood specifically implies the building is a temple. However, Peter could have used a more specific word such as *naos* (temple) or *hieron* (sanctuary) if he wished to limit the image to a building where deity dwells. The two senses of *oikos*, as both a building and as a related group of people, suggest Peter employs it here as a metonymy that easily shifts from the temple image to the people it houses, a holy priesthood. As Peter Davids observes, "It is a 'spiritual house' in that the Spirit forms it and especially in that it is not physical."[10] This means the Christian church is not primarily a social organization but the place where the consecrated lives of believers are offered as sacrifice to the glory of God.

Holy Priesthood (*basileion herateuma*)

If modern readers have any concept of priesthood, it is probably that of Roman Catholic parish priests who oversee the sacraments and instruct the local congregation. However, priesthood as referred to in 1 Peter must be understood within the concepts of ancient priesthoods, which represented the deity to people through oracles and other forms of revelation, and represented the people to the deity, mostly through animal sacrifices and prayer. The modern title *priest* as used in Roman Catholicism still connotes that idea of sacrifice where the Mass is thought of as a resacrificing of Christ's body.

An ancient priesthood was to be consecrated and set apart from the people at large for their ministry to the deity, to whom they had special access (see Lev. 21:1–22:16 for rules regulating priests in ancient Israel). In Peter's description, the priesthood of the Christian church is composed, not of a special few, but of everyone who comes to Christ—that is, *every* Christian. Israel's priestly function in the world based on Exodus 19, especially verse 6, may have stimulated Peter's understanding of the Christian church in similar terms. For all who embrace the new covenant in Christ are called to a holy consecration with respect to the world ("a holy nation") and set apart for purity and a purpose demanded by God. This is what the

---

9. The Greek of 1 Peter 2:5 presents several exegetical issues, discussion of which are beyond the scope of this chapter. See Jobes, *1 Peter*; Torrey Seland, "The 'Common Priesthood' of Philo and 1 Peter," *JSNT* 57 (1995): 87–119; Peter H. Davids, *The First Epistle of Peter*, NICNT (Grand Rapids: Eerdmans, 1990).
10. Davids, *First Epistle of Peter*, 87.

famous Reformation phrase "the priesthood of all believers" refers to. It is not a matter of ecclesial authority, but a consecrated difference in character and lifestyle that is to set Christians apart from the world for the purposes of God. Consecration to God, the King of the universe, makes the priesthood both holy and royal.

Spiritual Sacrifices (*pneumatikas thysias*)

Peter further describes the holy priesthood of the Christian church as offering spiritual sacrifices acceptable to God (2:5), a royal priesthood declaring the praises of him who called his people out of darkness (2:9). With no further need for animal sacrifice after the crucifixion of Jesus, the sacrifices of this priesthood are spiritual sacrifices in that they are not material and they are works of the Holy Spirit. Many commentators refer to "the loving service of Christians to God, their deeds of charity to each other, and their praises and thanksgiving to God" as instances of such spiritual sacrifices.[11] Scot McKnight mentions in passing that the spiritual sacrifices in view are something "like the list of behaviors typical of early Christian churches (e.g., 4:7–11)."[12] J. Ramsey Michaels considers spiritual sacrifices "first of all something offered up to God as worship (*anenegkai*) and, second, a pattern of social conduct. The two aspects cannot be separated."[13]

Just as the function of the ancient priesthood was to mediate God's presence to the people and to represent the people to God, the ministry of the corporate church universal is to bring Christ to the world and the world to Christ. First Peter 2:9 specifies that the purpose of the priesthood is to "declare the praises of him who called you out of darkness into his wonderful light." The verb translated "declare" (*exaggeilēte*) has the connotation to preach, proclaim, or declare in a public venue and therefore is toward the world, not toward God. This is not a reference to singing praise choruses to God during times of Sunday worship but to the testimony of believers in the world. In our times, public proclamation of the gospel is often done by professional clergy and missionaries through church programs and mission agencies, but Peter describes a priesthood that involves *every* living stone built into God's house, every Christian believer. This points to a lifestyle evangelism consistent with Peter's exhortation later in 2:11–12: "Dear friends, I urge you, as foreigners and exiles, to abstain from sinful desires, which wage war against your soul. Live such good lives among the pagans that, tough they accuse of doing wrong, they may see your good deeds and glorify God on the day he visits us."

The apostle has already exhorted readers in 2:1 to "rid yourselves of all malice and all deceit, hypocrisy, envy, and slander of every kind." This suggests that the spiritual sacrifices Peter has in mind have to do with the

11. Seland, "Common Priesthood," 87–119, esp. 113.
12. Scot McKnight, *1 Peter*, NIVAC (Grand Rapids: Zondervan, 1996), 107.
13. Michaels, *1 Peter*, 101.

ethics and morality of a life lived in consecration to God. It is within the context of a consecrated life that relationships with others develop and provide an opportunity to share the gospel.

As I have written elsewhere, “The spiritual sacrifices in view [in 1 Peter 2:5] may be understood as all behavior that flows from a transformation of the human spirit by the sanctifying work of the Holy Spirit (1:2).”[14] But how is this form of worship a *sacrifice* in any sense of that word? Peter explains as he continues in chapter 2. The example of Jesus as the one in whose footsteps Christians are to follow suggests that choosing to suffer rather than to sin is at the heart of spiritual sacrifice (2:11–3:17). Peter writes that the Christian, in following Christ, is called to unjust suffering (2:19) and to suffering for doing good (3:17). Peter was writing to Christians living at a time when it was likely that expressions of belief in Christ, whether in word or deed, would result in social ostracism and perhaps even more systematic persecution by the ruling authorities. The suffering involved in living for Christ constituted a spiritual sacrifice acceptable to God. To the extent that Christians in any time or place live in such hostile social circumstances, we too are called to choose faith in Christ, offering up the spiritual sacrifice of suffering for our faith should that be the consequence (3:17). After all, we follow the *Suffering* Servant. Heil, too, writes, “That the sufferings of Christ function as both a model and means for worship indicates that the worship of God for life is ‘through the sufferings of Jesus Christ.’”[15]

But if worship in 1 Peter involves offering spiritual sacrifices of suffering what are they for those of us who are not persecuted for our faith in Christ? Peter’s encounter with Jesus in Matthew 16:21–27 may suggest an answer. After Peter tries to turn Jesus away from the path that would lead to his death in Jerusalem, Jesus declares, “Whoever wants to be my disciple must *deny themselves* and take up their cross and follow me.” To be consecrated to Christ in the holy priesthood of all believers (1 Peter 2:5, 9) requires the self-denial of all needs, wants, and wishes that are in conflict with God’s revealed will. Self-denial hurts, and that is where authentic Christian sacrifice begins. It is better to suffer by denying oneself than to indulge in sin in order to avoid suffering unfulfilled needs, wants, and wishes (3:17). For example, a student may be tempted to cheat on a test rather than suffer the humiliation of failure. But it is better to suffer the humiliation of failure than to sin (“Rid yourselves of all deceit, hypocrisy” [2:1]). A husband or wife might be tempted to infidelity driven by legitimate unmet needs, but self-denial demands the sacrifice of suffering with those unmet needs rather than sin (“Abstain from sinful desires, which wage war against your soul” [2:11]). The act of self-denial is countercultural in modern America, where all sort of sin is justified in the name of

14. Jobes, *1 Peter*, 151.
15. Heil, *Worship Matters*, 25.

human fulfillment. In other words, Peter understands that the way we live our days is our priestly offering of spiritual sacrifices acceptable to God through Jesus Christ and constitutes authentic worship of God beyond the walls of a church sanctuary. Paul speaks similarly in Romans 12:1, where he urges readers "to offer your bodies as a living sacrifice, holy and pleasing to God—this is your true and proper worship." The transformation of our character and lives *is* our declaration of praises of him who called us out of darkness into his wonderful light. This is the essence of authentic Christian worship.

SIGNIFICANCE FOR 1 PETER FOR BIBLICAL WORSHIP

With this Petrine theology of worship in mind, it is important ask how these views inform the more common sense of the word as it is practiced in churches and lived throughout our lives. *The Pocket Dictionary of Theological Terms* defines worship as "the act of adoring and praising God, that is, ascribing worth to God as the one who deserves homage and service."[16] Attendance at a formal church service should be an expression of our relationship with God through Christ, a relationship that goes far beyond and far deeper than prayers, praise, and songs during an hour-long church service. Nothing done inside a church building is acceptable worship if the life of the worshiper does not reflect reverence and adoration for the Lord throughout each day of the week.

Does this view of worship encourage a disturbing trend among believers to forgo weekly gathering? After all, if authentic Christian worship is offered throughout the week in all of life, why attend worship services at a specific time and place? Although there are times due to travel, illness, or other such circumstances when worshiping alone is the best we can do, Peter's description of the living stones built into a spiritual building suggests that worship acceptable to God is worship together. Peter does not portray the living stones scattered about in splendid isolation but *purposefully placed* by the Master builder into the Lord's house. When Christians gather in one place to experience together singing, prayer, confession, sacrament, and preaching of the Word, we are acknowledging the unity and integrity of the Lord's spiritual house because of its cornerstone, Jesus Christ. We are recognizing that the Lord has put us in *this* time in *this* place with *these* people, and the presence of each one of us is significant to him.

Therefore, each living stone has a function in the Lord's spiritual house offering spiritual sacrifices. Often those functions are active and expressed by various forms of service in the church and wider community. But stones in a building contribute to the purpose of the building just by their presence. A ministry of presence is not insignificant, for by being with others we become of aware of the strength in numbers, of the

16. Stanley J. Grenz, David Guretzke, and Cherith Fee Nordling, eds., *Pocket Dictionary of Theological Terms* (OakTree Software, 2001).

needs of others, of the inadequacy of individualism, and of the presence of Christ among his people. We cannot love one another (1 Peter 1:22), offer hospitality to one another (4:9), relate in humility to one another (5:5), or greet one another (5:14) in absentia. Only by being present do we bear our weight as a living stone in God's spiritual building, first, by taking our place in the church and, second, by staying in the church. Our presence in the church with all that entails throughout decades of life is itself a witness to the world, proclaiming "the praises of him who called you out of darkness into his wonderful light" (2:9).

No one can worship God without first coming to Christ, for it is by coming to Christ that a stone is enlivened and is built into the Lord's spiritual house. No one can worship, no matter how many praise choruses they sing, without consecrating their life to Christ and embracing the self-denial that such consecration demands. Worship is just empty chatter without ridding ourselves "of all malice and all deceit, hypocrisy, envy, and slander of every kind" (2:1). Worship as 1 Peter defines it is expressed every day, in every hour, in every encounter throughout a lifetime. What we call *worship* on Sundays is a celebration of what God has done and is doing in us and through us, a time for the Spirit to reenergize believers for a new week of worship ahead.

BIBLIOGRAPHY

Barclay, William. *The Letters of James and Peter*. Rev. ed. Philadelphia: Westminster, 1976.

Davids, Peter H. *The First Epistle of Peter*. NICNT. Grand Rapids: Eerdmans, 1990.

de Waard, Jan. *A Comparative Study of the Old Testament Text in the Dead Sea Scrolls and in the New Testament*. STDJ 4. Leiden: Brill, 1965.

Elliott, John H. *A Home for the Homeless: A Sociological Exegesis of 1 Peter, Its Situation and Strategy*. Philadelphia: Fortress, 1981.

Heil, John Paul. *1 Peter, 2 Peter, and Jude: Worship Matters*. Eugene, OR: Cascade, 2013.

Jobes, Karen H. *1 Peter*. BECNT. Grand Rapids: Baker Academic, 2005.

______. "The Septuagint Textual Tradition in 1 Peter' in *Septuagint Research: Issues and Challenges in the Study of the Greek Jewish Scriptures*. SCS 53. Atlanta: Society of Biblical Literature, 2006.

McKnight, Scot. *1 Peter*. NIVAC. Grand Rapids: Zondervan, 1996.

Michaels, J. Ramsey *1 Peter*. WBC 49. Waco, TX: Word, 1988.

Seland, Torrey. "The 'Common Priesthood' of Philo and 1 Peter." *JSNT* 57 (1995): 87–119.

CHAPTER 33

WORSHIP AS RESISTANCE AND EMBRACE

Worship in 2 Peter and Jude

Greg Couser

CONTEXT OF WORSHIP IN 2 PETER AND JUDE

Worship is a weighty term. Reverence, homage, submission, adoration, and the like are its conceptual friends. Kneeling, bowing low, lying prostrate, and standing out of respect are some of its physical postures. Even when you hear someone use it irreverently, as in "I worship the ground you walk on," its weight makes it useful for expressing a type of deep affection that is all-consuming. It implies that the one loved is utter perfection. Worship is not only the appropriate response but also deep affection and reverence that extends to anything associated with them. Whatever they touch has somehow been taken up into their perfection so that it itself is perfected.

Worship gains its heft because it fundamentally belongs to the discussion about the relationship between God and humanity. It is one of those terms, maybe the most central, used to describe how any individual should respond to what is ultimate, what stands as reality's supreme, final, and fundamental generating source and governing authority. Indeed, in the Scriptures, worship is something reserved for God and God alone. It is an activity that differs in extent, in terms of its attitudes and actions, from anything appropriate to any other being, no matter what their rank or position. Explicitly in the New Testament, it is always a Spirit-enabled response to God's revelation of himself in word and deed,[1] a revelation that comes to its fullest

1. Daniel Block, in dealing with the Scriptures as a whole, likewise emphasizes worship as a response to God's revelation of himself: "True worship involves reverential human acts of submis-

expression in the life and work of Christ. Awakened by the Spirit to God's good greatness and astounding love displayed in Christ, the true worshiper is overtaken by a deep sense of awe and wonder that springs forth into a life of love, a life of grateful, delighted, humble, and unreserved homage, trust, and obedience. Were this type of reverence given to any other person or thing other than the Triune God, it would be idolatrous.[2]

Interestingly, when we come to the books of Jude and 2 Peter, books held together in the study of the New Testament due to their literary connection,[3] there is much we can learn about worship. Though these books are relatively short and the explicit terminology for worship is largely absent, the amount of material bearing on our subject still means that we will only be able to handle the material selectively. In particular, Jude (vv. 24–27) and 2 Peter (3:18) both end with an act of worship, a doxology, expressed in terms that respond uniquely to the situations occasioning the letters. These doxological endings, in turn, suggest that the contents of the letters grow out of and direct the readers toward the kind of attitudes and actions commensurate with a due regard for God. In fact, with the concluding "amen" the authors' are giving "the readers an opportunity to make the message of praise their own . . . as well as unite with one another through their simultaneous utterance of this liturgical acclamation. The unified 'amen' is a means for promoting the corporate spirit of worship."[4] It may not be too much to say that 2 Peter and Jude are both acts of worship and directions for worship.

Second Peter and Jude are written against the backdrop of communities under threat. The threats and responses share much in common yet differ in significant ways. The specific identity of the opponents is not clear, but there is enough information provided in each to sketch out their characteristics and impact. For both letters, worship and directions for worship involve both resistance and affirmation. Fealty to the Sovereign is a must.

Cultural Context of Jude

Jude addresses a community infiltrated by individuals bent on exploiting them financially and sexually ("secretly slipped in" [v. 4]).[5] These outsiders have succeeded in insinuating themselves right into the heart of the church's communal life. Even as the community gathers to celebrate communion

---

sion and homage before the divine Sovereign in response to his gracious revelation of himself and in accord with his will" (Daniel I. Block, *For the Glory of God: Recovering a Biblical Theology of Worship* [Grand Rapids: Baker Academic, 2014], 23).

2. Cf. Richard Bauckham, *Jesus and the God of Israel: God Crucified and Other Studies on the New Testament's Christology of Divine Identity* (Grand Rapids: Eerdmans, 2008), 131.
3. For a concise and convincing discussion of the literary and chronological relationship between 2 Peter and Jude, see Terry L. Wilder, J. Daryl Charles, and Kendall Easley, *Faithful to the End: An Introduction to Hebrews through Revelation* (Nashville: B&H Academic, 2007), 148–54.
4. J. L. Wu, "Liturgical Elements," in *DLNT*, 661.
5. Unless otherwise noted, all Scripture quotations in this chapter are from the NIV.

and share a common meal to reflect and celebrate their deep bonds of affection in their common allegiance to Christ (their "common salvation" [v. 3; cf. v. 2]), these individuals join in as wolves in shepherd's clothing (v. 12). The opponents are not what they profess to be (vv. 12–13). The very fact that they change "grace . . . into a license for immorality" (v. 5) suggests that they use "Christian lingo," but only as a ruse. Very likely their denial of the authority of Jesus is done in the name of Jesus. Indeed, Jude grants that they are dazzling orators who "flatter others for their own advantage" (v. 16). Additionally, the influence of their teaching is linked to the religious insights and experiences that supposedly came to them in their dreams or visions (v. 8). In other words, these false teachers present themselves as knowing spiritual savants. Their mouths march fearlessly into realms where angels fear to tread (vv. 9–10). They are bold in their arrogant irreverence (vv. 12, 16). On the authority of their charismatic experiences they overturn and reappropriate God's expressed Word, whether that be the Old Testament or its extension through the apostles. The received standards for belief and life are being used to endorse and commend the kind of gross sexual immorality and shocking irreverence that the Scriptures, as received and extended through apostolic teaching, condemn.

The effect on the community is as predictable as it is tragic. The community is divided (v. 19). Some are wavering in doubt as the ground is shifting under their feet. Others are flirting with the fires of God's judgment, and sadly, some have come under his judgment as they have capitulated altogether (vv. 22–23). The "faith," both in terms of belief and practice, "once for all entrusted to the saints" (v. 3; cf. v. 20) is becoming the "once held but now abandoned" faith for some. The words and acts of the "ungodly" false teachers (v. 15) are replacing the truths that mark out the boundaries of God's love—the path where believers find the provision and protection from God necessary for their flourishing (v. 21). Richard Bauckham sums the situation up nicely:

> Jude's opponents are a group of itinerant charismatics who have arrived in the church(es) to which he writes. Everything else Jude tells us about them is related to their antinomianism, which is the target of his attack. They reject all moral authority, whether that of the law of Moses (vv. 8–10) or that of Christ himself (vv. 4, 8), even though they claim to be followers of Christ. . . . In line with their rejection of moral authority, they indulge in immoral behavior, especially sexual misconduct (vv. 6–8, 10); in this they may be deliberately flouting accepted standards of Jewish morality and conforming to the permissiveness of pagan society.[6]

Though the threat in Jude comes cloaked in Christianese, Jude wants the church to know that it is a threat that is motivated and directed by the

6. Richard Bauckham, *2 Peter and Jude*, WBC 50 (Waco, TX: Word, 1983), 25.

fallen, disordered passions of the false teachers (vv. 7, 10, 16, 19). Their teaching and lifestyle have nothing to do with promoting God's saving work in and through them. He wanted to write in celebration of God's saving work (v. 3) but had to deal with something threatening it instead. Jude steps into this situation with a plan. He begins by establishing identity (who he is, who they are, and what resources they have to enjoy—a concise but surprisingly full expression of the place of favor and security they have been given by God [vv. 1–4]). He continues by offering an analysis of the problem and by warning them of how God has treated this kind of thing in the past (what the threat is to their experience of God's favor [vv. 5–7]). He then dedicates a large portion of his letter to identifying and pronouncing judgment on those encouraging them to abandon the path of God's favor (vv. 8–16). He concludes with specific guidance for maximizing their enjoyment of God's favor toward the fulfillment of God's calling on their lives (vv. 17–25).

Cultural Context of 2 Peter

The readers of 2 Peter are also under threat from false teachers. While Jude seems to denounce infiltrators who became influential insiders within the community, Peter seems to suggest a movement in the opposite direction (see 2:1–3, 20–22). His language depicts the false teachers as insiders on the way out. They have rejected the apostolic teaching on the character of the future and replaced it with their own version (1:20; 2:3; 3:4). In particular, Peter suggests that what the apostles taught about the future coming of Christ and the accompanying judgment of humanity were being treated as myths (1:16; cf. 3:3–4a).[7] Whether the false teachers' eschatological skepticism created an open door for a licentious lifestyle or their lifestyle drove their "theology," the eclipse of the eschatological vision found in the Old Testament prophets and the apostolic teaching lies at the heart of Peter's concern. This decisively distinguishes the opponents in view here from those in Jude. Though their behavior overlaps that of Jude's opponents and most likely accounts for Peter's creative and selective appropriation of Jude, the skewed "theology" accompanying their licentious lifestyles differ significantly.

Peter warns his readers that, despite the fact that the false teachers at one time professed to know the "Lord and Savior Jesus Christ," the teaching and behavior of these teachers make it clear that they are rejecting Christ's rule and have become "slaves of depravity" (2:19; cf. vv. 10, 12; 3:3). In fact, though Peter, like Jude, sees that false teachers as denying Christ (2:1; cf. Jude 5), for Peter that charge is heightened and emphasized. First, this

7. For a concise overview of the skewed eschatology of the false teachers in 2 Peter and Peter's response, see Frank Thielman, *Theology of the New Testament: A Canonical and Synthetic Approach* (Grand Rapids: Zondervan, 2005), 522–25. For a detailed treatment of Peter's ultimate eschatological vision in 3:1–18, see Craig Blaising, "The Day of the Lord Will Come: An Exposition of 2 Peter 3:1–18," *BSac* 169 (2012): 387–401.

heightening appears in his clear emphasis on the deity of Christ that bookends his letter. Though both forms of expression are rare in the New Testament, Peter opens the letter affirming that "Jesus Christ" is "our God and Savior" (1:1)[8] and closes his letter with a doxology addressed to Christ: "To him be glory both now and forever! Amen" (3:18). Second, and most poignantly, he stresses that their rejection of the apostolic vision of the future is a direct affront to what Christ revealed to him, a revelation of his deity that confirmed and extended the Old Testament prophetic vision of the future (1:19).[9] Peter appeals to what was revealed to him at the transfiguration of Christ, both by the voice of the Father and in the person of Christ, as his initial defense of Christ's future coming (1:16–18). "Apparently he conceived of the transfiguration as a proleptic and prophetic indication of the glory and power of Christ that would be displayed at this future coming."[10] Consequently, their bold and arrogant rejection of the Old Testament and apostolic vision of the future, and consequently of the life consistent with that vision in the present, is first and foremost a bold affront to Christ.

Peter contends that what the false teachers are saying with such bravado and bluster is really nothing more than a cover for their greed and lust in an attempt to gain a platform of influence within the community from which to exploit its members. In fact, at the time of writing these men are taking the opportunity provided by communal meals to prey on the immature who have recently come into the Christian community (2:14, 18). Peter warns that the "knowledge" they offer is rooted in ignorance (2:12) and is devoid (2:17–18) of the spiritually nourishing and mission-enabling knowledge of "our Lord Jesus Christ" that comes to the people of God through the Old Testament and apostolic teaching (1:3, 8, 19–21; 3:2, 13, 15). Peter recounts and defends the nature and authority of the Old Testament prophetic and apostolic visions of the future (1:16; 3:1–10). He wants to remind the community of what are "the great and precious promises" that are the divine means through which believers become partakers of God's own nature and fulfill his mission in the world.[11] At the same time, he also wants to arm them so that they can escape the corrupting effects of the world around them (1:4)—effects, unfortunately, that are being played out before their eyes in the lives of the false teachers and those being deceived by them.

Peter ends by urging his readers to "be on their guard" against destructive "error" and to "grow in the grace and knowledge of our Lord and Savior Jesus Christ" (3:17–18). In other words, the path of God's favor,

8. Daniel B. Wallace, *Greek Grammar beyond the Basics* (Grand Rapids: Zondervan, 1997), 276–77.
9. With Gene L. Green (*Jude & 2 Peter*, BECNT [Grand Rapids: Baker Academic, 2008], 226–27) Peter's statement in 1:19 most likely refers to how the transfiguration event confirms the OT prophetic word with regard to the future rather than vice versa.
10. Thomas R. Schreiner, *1, 2 Peter, Jude*, NAC 37 (Nashville: B&H Academic, 2008), 312.
11. Peter H. Davids, *Living in Light of the Coming King: A Theology of James, Peter and Jude*, BTNT (Grand Rapids: Zondervan, 2014), 212.

for the present age and the age to come, is the path including the eschatological vision revealed by the Old Testament prophets and confirmed and further delineated by Christ through the apostles. Christ will return to judge and vindicate. The divine resources the righteous presently enjoy in Christ and the divine judgment presently being meted out on the wicked are but a foretaste of the complete rescue of the righteous and the consummate condemnation of the wicked that will mark Christ's certain return (1:10–11; 2:9–10; 3:7, 12–13).

A SHARED THEOLOGY OF WORSHIP IN JUDE AND 2 PETER

For both Jude and 2 Peter the nature of the problems they confront and their strategy of confrontation share many points in common. In particular, both call their readers to worship God by maintaining a holistic fealty to the Triune God of the Scriptures in the face of calculated misrepresentations of what God has revealed about himself and his purposes (Jude) or in the face of their flat denial (2 Peter). In addition, though with differing levels of emphasis, this holistic fealty is particularly directed to Christ (esp. in 2 Peter). In support of this call to fealty, both audiences are reminded that they inhabit a space where God's saving blessings have been mediated to them through Christ by the Spirit.

Both Peter and Jude operate from the assumption that God creates worshipers and sustains their worship by bringing them into his saving riches in Christ. God's saving acts in Christ lay as the assumed foundation supporting Peter's and Jude's calls to worship (Jude 1, 21, 24–25; 2 Peter 1:1, 3, 16–18, 21; 2:1, 20). Positively, God initiates and sustains worship as he invites believers into this place of blessing and security (2 Peter 1:10; Jude 1) as his acts are explained (2 Peter 1:21) and applied by the Spirit (Jude 19–20). In 2 Peter, God initiates worship as he is the one who enabled them to believe in response to his call so that they enjoy his blessing (1:1). While in Jude, he is the one who will sustain their worship so that they securely reach the goal for which he has called them (v. 24; cf. 2 Peter 1:3–4). At the same time, negatively, he enables worship by freeing believers from the idolatry of self-worship. What marks off the opponents in both letters is an enslavement to their base desires.[12] In Jude, this is why the opponents co-opt terms associated with God's person and acts and distort their meaning. It is a part of a calculated strategy to hide their greed and lust under a gilding of orthodoxy. God is being used to construct a persona that will allow them to exploit the community for their own evil ends. In 2 Peter, God is simply shouted down and dismissed. Christ, in effect, is being told how things are and how they will turn out. The scoffers are defying what God by his Spirit has said through the Old

12. See Green's helpful and clarifying comments on the "base desires" at work driving the activities of the opponents in both letters and, in 2 Peter, on how the false teachers appeal to those desires to entice others (*Jude & 2 Peter*, 109, 128, 294–95, and 299).

Testament prophets and via Christ through the apostles (2 Peter 1:12–21). In the end, these opponents represent everything contrary to the heart of a true worshiper. Their take on the world (2 Peter 3:4) and their ecstatic experiences (Jude 8) become their authorities and supersede the authority of God's revelation of himself.

In addition, since God's acts in Christ by the Spirit are the assumed foundation on which the life of worship is built and sustained, God's nature and acts (past, present, and future) set the expectations informing worship and determine its character this side of the eschaton. Worshipers "look forward" in anticipation of the consummation of all things at Christ's return (Jude 21, 24; 2 Peter 3:11–13). In the meantime they "guard" and "grow" (2 Peter 3:17–18) or they "contend" and "build up" (Jude 3 [cf. v. 21], 20). Within God's timeline, they exist in a moment that calls for resistance and embrace in order to give God his due, know his blessing and further his saving mission in the world.

In sum, for both authors salvation is provided for, initiated, explained, applied, sustained, directed, and consummated by the Triune God; it is wholly a work of God. At the same time, while believers are secure in that place of affection secured by God's saving acts in Christ by the Spirit, for both authors personal and communal spiritual flourishing and mission effectiveness require steadfast adherence to what God has revealed about himself and his purposes (2 Peter 1:5–7; Jude 20). For the believer to "grow in grace" (2 Peter 3:18) or to keep herself in the path of God's affection (Jude 21) this means that the Old Testament as read through and extended by apostolic teaching represents a given and settled deposit of truth that must be kept alive as the sole charter for God's people. Both letters are replete with commands calling for an active appropriation and holistic embrace of what God has revealed about himself and his purposes. Peter famously urges his readers to appropriate what God has granted them in Christ so that they can progressively reflect God's character and faithfully fulfill their duties toward God (1:3–4).[13] Jude urges his readers to actively struggle to stay within the path of God's affection by remembering what God has revealed, by "building themselves up" in the revealed "faith," and by praying in a manner consistent with the Holy Spirit's revealed character and acts (vv. 17–21).[14] For both authors, these pretenders trying to displace

13. Green, *Jude & 2 Peter*, 182.

14. In both Peter and Jude, the urgent commands to affirm the truth and resist falsehood raise questions about just what is under threat. Are the authors' worried that genuine believers will apostatize—i.e., return to a status of an unbeliever by rejecting Christ? This seems unlikely for both authors, but especially for Jude (on Peter, see Schreiner's comments on 2:1, 17–22 [*1, 2 Peter, Jude*, 331, 355–65] and J. Daryl Charles, *Virtues amidst Vice: The Catalog of Virtues in 2 Peter 1*, JSNTSup 150 [Sheffield: Sheffield Academic, 1997], 152). Jude urges his readers to "keep themselves in" (v. 21) as those who are "kept" (vv. 1, 24). They have been brought into a settled and sustained place of affection and security with God through Christ by the Spirit. Their place in God's affection is secure. However, the nature of their experience of God's love in the present

the Sovereign's charter—by their lives and their teaching—must be resisted. Believers must resist by not only denouncing them as false teachers verbally, but even more so by fully submitting and living into their new identity and mission in contradistinction to these false teachers. On the one hand, worship calls for resistance to what transposes or denies God's revelation of himself and his purposes. On the other hand, worship calls for affirmation coupled with faithful appropriation of what God has provided for the worshiper's spiritual sustenance and mission effectiveness.

SIGNIFICANCE FOR BIBLICAL WORSHIP FROM JUDE: WORSHIP AND GRACE

Jude writes to rescue grace from the hands of those presuming upon it (v. 4). He wants to reclaim it as a force that leads to the worship of Christ.[15] Grace, as we will see, is a force that would enable an acceptance of Christ's deity and authority and a humble submission to his will. What is happening among the false teachers is just the opposite; they are denying Christ his rightful place in their lives. For the believer, grace allows them to turn (and keep turning) in love toward Christ in response to the love experienced from God in Christ by the Spirit.

Biblical Worship Surrenders to Divine Grace

But before we get into Jude's response, we need further clarity regarding what is meant by "presuming on grace." First, we need to think more about just what it means to be "graced" by God. To be graced by God is to know his favor and, for the believer, to be put in a unique place of favor.[16] In a general sense, God's favor is aimed at moving all his creatures—human beings and spiritual beings—into the relationship with their Creator for which they have been made. With respect to believers, his grace disposes them

(and, for Peter, the type of welcome they will enjoy in the eschaton [2 Peter 1:11]) is what is in question. In other words, the keeping actions of the believer are not to maintain a place in God's affections as if their ultimate salvation is dependent on their efforts and the ultimate outcome is in doubt. Rather, Jude is concerned that they maintain God as their chief affection and so lovingly and tenaciously adhere to what God has revealed about himself and his purposes toward them. Not only is such activity indicative of genuine conversion (Jude 20; cf. 2 Peter 1:10; 3:14), but it is absolutely necessary for the believer to enter into the blessing and protection, in life and service, of the saving grace they have come to know in Christ in this time up until the consummation of all things at Christ's return.

15. References to "grace" bookend Peter's letter (1:2; 3:18). God's favor is presented as a resource that sustains and promotes growth in the new life made possible by Christ's gift of faith (1:1, 3–4). Not only does it come through a relationship with Christ (1:2), but it also enables the believer to deepen that relationship with Christ (3:18). In this light, the opponents in 2 Peter are resisting grace by thwarting God's purposes and cutting themselves off from his saving resources. However, the attack on grace is indirect. In other words, he does not present the opponents as libertines who are presuming on grace. Grace is not their watchword or their cover. Their moral debauchery and destructive activity within the church are tied to the eschatological skepticism that frees them from the threat of future judgment.

16. See Green, *Jude & 2 Peter*, 59–60.

toward and fits them for an intimate relationship with God made possible by Christ's work and effected by the power of the Spirit. In other words, the favor of God is aimed at taking the believer toward what he has created them to be and is redeeming them to become. For this restoration to take place grace is needed to reorient and transform the one "graced" so that they can increasingly live into their created identity that is being restored in Christ. The consummate effect of this transformation is worship.

To presume on grace is to reject and resist grace's intent and substitute the goals you chose. In addition, you attempt to co-opt the place of favor you enjoy as an excuse for neglecting God's claims and even attempt to use it as a lever to force God's hand. Instead of submission and worship you attempt to use him to satisfy your own evil desires and so get where you want to go when and how you want to get there, versus where, when, and how he wants to take you. Presuming on grace is the little boy who is running away because he chafes at his parents' authority and demands. The parents would argue that the place he occupies is a place of favor arising out of their love for him. They are exercising their authority and setting boundaries intending to protect him from harm and bring him more and more into who he needs to be. Proofs of their love are everywhere—in the clothes on his back, the roof over his head, the food on the table, the unique access he has to them, the lock on the cabinet door where the hazardous cleaning chemicals are stored, and so much more. They want him to see the evidence of their love that surrounds him so that he will trust them and fully draw on their wisdom and resources. Nonetheless, he knows that his parents don't know what's best for him; *he* does. Their "love" is misguided, even suffocating. So he demands his way or he's going to run away. Rather than leaning into the kindness of his parents and experiencing the life-giving effects that would follow (cf. Rom. 2:4), he presumes on the grace of his parents by using his place of favor as a mechanism to manipulate and coerce them. He thinks, "I'll show them. If they don't give me what I want I'll hit them where it hurts. I'm leaving! You will regret your decision. You'll see. You'll be coming back to me crawling on your hands and knees begging me to come back! Then, once we establish who's running the show, we'll get this ship sailing in the right direction—mine!"

And so Jude begins the body of his "grace-rescue" letter with some reminders. In other words, he begins with truths they are fully aware of since these truths come from the teaching that has been handed down to them. Here we find that there is a recognized body of teaching that bears authority within this community of believers. It can be cited against the backdrop of a common regard for its place within the community. A case is not being made for its place of authority; it is being assumed. It stands as judge and guide for their experience, not vice versa. Jude (see also 2 Peter 1:12–21) turns to the Scriptures with confidence to navigate the crisis in front of him. The Scriptures articulate the path of grace so that the believers can locate and follow the voice of the Spirit in the face of the false teachers' beguiling misrepresentations.

This, succinctly, is a clear picture of the place and role of Scripture within the life of worship. It is the "touchstone" (standard, measure, model) for life as it is the words of God given to his people for their guidance and blessing through his Spirit-inspired (and so authorized) messengers. The Old Testament as read through and extended in the teaching of the resurrected Christ through his apostles is the authority that must be consulted to determine the rightness or goodness of any "new" teaching brought to them by these charismatic leaders who have arrived on the scene. It is the guide that allows the believers to "keep" themselves "in God's love" as they "wait for the mercy of our Lord Jesus Christ to bring" them "to eternal life" (v. 24).

Biblical Worship Rejects Distortions of Grace

Beginning in verse 5 Jude draws on scriptural teaching to provide three groups as examples of what transposing grace looks like and of how God responds. The first is the group within God's chosen people who distrusted God in the face of his covenant blessings and promises and were judged nonetheless.[17] The second is the group of angels with all of their privileged access to God who rejected God's boundaries on their activity and were judged nonetheless.[18] And the third is two pagan cities, Sodom and Gomorrah, which knowingly spurned the Creator's prescribed

17. God had delivered his people from bondage in Egypt (Exod. 6–14), an act of grace if there ever was one! Yet just because God had decisively saved them did not mean that they could presume on his grace and mercy by using their place of favor to deny God's rightful authority and to try to manipulate and coerce him toward their own ends. They fought God's appointed leaders. They doubted and challenged God's goodness ("he brought us out here to kill us!"). They grumbled in disagreement with his plan and wanted God to do it their way (they wanted to eat what they wanted, to go where they wanted, to get the Promised Land the way they wanted to get it). He judged them for such presumption. All, with the exception of Joshua and Caleb, were kept from entering the Promised Land (Num. 14:29–30; Deut. 1:32–36; 2:15; cf. 1 Cor. 10:1–5). They wandered in the wilderness until they died. In the same way, Jude tells his readers, don't presume on God's grace experienced in Christ.
18. Jude's second example and warning with respect to presuming on grace deals with angels who stepped outside of God's prescribed boundaries for them. This could refer to Genesis 6:1–4 (cf. 2 Peter 2:4). If this is the case, it refers to angels who did not keep their assigned station. They had sexual liaisons with human women and so stepped out of their assigned sphere of authority and activity. Unlike the angels now in service of God (who do not "marry or give in marriage" [Matt. 22:30]), they stepped outside God's boundaries for their existence as his creatures. The other option is a reference to the rebellion of Satan and the fallen angels with him that preceded the temptation of Adam and Eve. Whatever the specific instance, the point here seems to be that even angels who share this heavenly status and privilege—both in terms of their nature (spiritual beings who worship God) and role (willing servants of the Most High) as angels—could not presume upon these privileges. When they contravened God's boundaries, God held them accountable and judged them. Here it seems to be a situation of arrogance that moved them to stand over against God and step outside the prescribed sphere for their existence (with, in the first possible understanding, overtones of sexual debauchery). Despite their great privileges, their place of favor with God, they were imprisoned eternally for the egregious contempt of God and his order (see Schreiner, *1, 2 Peter, Jude*, 447–51).

boundaries for sexual expression (cf. Rom. 1:24–27) and infamously distinguished themselves from their pagan surroundings in their headlong pursuit of sexual debauchery. They not only swept up the surrounding cities into their debauchery but also succeeded in making their cities the archetypical example of God's consummative judgment (vv. 5–7).[19] Jude links these Old Testament examples to the false teachers because none of the varied places of favor they enjoyed protected them from judgment when they resisted the loving intent of God's favor. Likewise, the false teachers of Jude's time, and those who follow them, cannot presume on God's favor by thinking that God's favor was something they could count on no matter how they lived. Succinctly, these Old Testament examples show what presuming on grace looks like and stand as a warning of its consequences. The Scriptures allow Jude to cut a straight path for the truth through the falsehood coming to his readers, even though it came cloaked in dazzling rhetorical flourishes and backed up by visions and dreams.

This is the procedure we, as the people of God today, need to emulate in our moment to evaluate contemporary claims about where God's grace is found, especially when these claims come to us liberally sprinkled with biblical phraseology and grounded in the experience of the speakers. To put it in our moment, maybe we can think of how biblical concepts like "love," "holiness," "faith," "salvation," "heaven," "hell," and the like are often stripped of their biblical context and content and co-opted to describe and endorse something that redefines the persons of the Godhead and dismisses their demands. For a popular example, consider the song by two worship leaders turned country-music stars titled "H.O.L.Y." Throughout the song, biblical terms, phrases, and concepts are used with abandon even while they are co-opted to describe sexual pleasure. In the process, sex, a gift to be enjoyed within God's boundaries, is twisted into something to be worshiped in place of God. Sex is distorted and profaned under the banner of "holy." Or, think of how "love," redefined on the basis of some new spiritual insight gained from personal experience or the experiences of others, is used to affirm sexual perspectives and behaviors that God explicitly warns against and wants to redeem people from (cf. 1 Cor. 6:9–11, 19–20). In particular, in the name of "love" Christians are increasingly urged to adumbrate and even repudiate a biblical vision for human sexuality so that "love" can "win"—with some of the most strident and insistent voices arising from within the church. To affirm God's created design for sex, a design reaffirmed by Christ and made possible to reclaim from sin's distortion in Christ, has become something hateful in certain corners of the church.

19. That Jude refers to the sexual deviancy prevalent in these cities, with an emphasis on homosexuality, see Schreiner, *1, 2 Peter, Jude*, 452–53, and sources cited there. For the OT backdrop of Jude's reference here, with special reference to Ezekiel 16:49–50, see Brian Neil Peterson, "Identifying the Sin of Sodom in Ezekiel 16:49–50," *JETS* 61, no. 2 (2018): 307–20.

Biblical Worship Leans Into God's Definition of Grace

Though the threat in Jude, and to the church perennially, comes in Christianese, Jude wants his church to know that it is a threat that is motivated and directed by the base desires of the false teachers. Despite their Christian-sounding language, Scripture makes it clear that they are misrepresenting God and challenging his expressed will and, thus, his authority. They are not leaning into grace. Rather, they are pushing people to change their allegiances, to change kingdom loyalties. In particular, the false teachers are using their experience to reshape Christ and deny him his rightful claim to their allegiance and obedience.

Jude shows us that the life of worship is a life that looks to Scripture to define the nature and intentions of God's grace and then leans into that grace. True worshipers "go all out for grace" not just outside the walls of the church, but inside as well. Many of the churches in the New Testament faced mortal threats from within. Jude wants us to know that our loving God will not and cannot let us use our place of favor with him on our own terms and, thus, presumptuously. His favor, his grace, is directed by his love and is meant to take us toward what he has created us, and is redeeming us in Christ by the Spirit, to become. When we presume upon that favor as if it is a lever to manipulate and co-opt God toward ends that are contrary to his loving goals for us, God's loving favor will be expressed in warning and discipline. When we presume upon that favor and tell others that God extends his favor to those who reject his loving will (whether that be to increase our wealth, slake our lust, or enhance our standing), we step outside the path of God's favor, invite our neighbors down a path of destruction, and forfeit his peace for ourselves and our neighbor. God's love, and the love of those who truly love in his name, remains steadfastly committed to his expressed, loving will. For Jude, the true worshiper teaches, persuades, commends, urges, and warns each person with the intent to move them toward a free, willing embrace of wherever it is that God's will leads and his blessings lie.

As we conclude, perhaps reflecting on his letter in the form of questions can help us clarify and adjust our own posture toward God's grace. First, do we live from the perspective of a delight in God's favor expressed in his full rescue in Christ from everything that truly threatens us? Do we live out of gratitude for all he has done, is doing, and will do? Second, do we have an increasing sense of our need for God's favor, his loving provision, so much so that we yearn for others to know him? In turn, do we feel grieved and even fear for those who spurn his grace altogether or, with fellow believers, who treat it with contempt? Third, do we live assuming God is there even though he has become like elevator music in the background of our lives—something that we largely neglect, maybe even get annoyed about, but we certainly don't listen to or enjoy? Fourth, do we speak to God and think of him as if he exists to make our plans work? That we get to determine what is best for us and then get mad at God or try to coerce him to get on our side when what we want is not happening? Fifth, are we letting his expressed, loving will shape our loves, or are we letting our experiences (or those of others) be our authority and then we cover our move with words of "grace," "love," and so on? For example, are we willing and ready to update the embarrassing, old-fashioned notions of God revealed in Scripture so that we can bring them into line with what we, or the voices around us, think is best? Do we think we need to update God's views on sex and gender? On success? On what makes us important? On the real problem with us and others (i.e., sin)? On the real solution for us and others (i.e., faith in Christ)? Jude answers these questions by calling us to be worshipers who lean into grace and not users of God who presume upon his favor. It is only then that we can join Jude in worship as we say together, "To him who is able to keep you from stumbling and to present you before his glorious presence without fault and with great joy—to the only God our Savior be glory, majesty, power and authority, through Jesus Christ our Lord, before all ages, now and forevermore! Amen" (vv. 24–25).

BIBLIOGRAPHY

Bauckham, Richard. *Jesus and the God of Israel: God Crucified and Other Studies on the New Testament's Christology of Divine Identity*. Grand Rapids: Eerdmans, 2008.

______. *Jude-2 Peter*. WBC 50. Waco, TX: Word, 1983.

Blaising, Craig. "The Day of the Lord Will Come: An Exposition of 2 Peter 3:1–18." *BibSac* 169 (2012): 387–401.

Block, Daniel I. *For the Glory of God: Recovering a Biblical Theology of Worship*. Grand Rapids: Baker Academic, 2014.

Charles, J. Daryl. *Virtues amidst Vice: The Catalog of Virtues in 2 Peter 1*. JSNTSup 150. Sheffield: Sheffield Academic, 1997.

Davids, Peter H. *Living in Light of the Coming King: A Theology of James, Peter and Jude*. BTNT. Grand Rapids: Zondervan, 2014.

Green, Gene L. *Jude & 2 Peter*. BECNT. Grand Rapids: Baker Academic, 2008.

Martin, Ralph P. "The Theology of Jude, 1 Peter, and 2 Peter." In *The Theology of the Letters of James, Peter and Jude*, edited by A. Chester and Ralph P. Martin, 63–163. New Testament Theology. Cambridge: Cambridge University Press, 1994.

Schreiner, Thomas R. *1, 2 Peter, Jude*. NAC 37. Nashville: B&H Academic, 2003.

Thielman, Frank. *Theology of the New Testament: A Canonical and Synthetic Approach*. Grand Rapids: Zondervan, 2005.

Wilder, Terry L., J. Daryl Charles, and Kendall Easley. *Faithful to the End: An Introduction to Hebrews through Revelation*. Nashville: B&H Academic, 2007.

Wu, J. L. "Liturgical Elements." In *Dictionary of the Later New Testament and Its Developments*, edited by Ralph P. Martin and Peter H. Davids, 660–65. Downers Grove, IL: InterVarsity Press, 1997.

CHAPTER 34

HALLELUJAH, WHAT A SAVIOR!

Worship in the Apocalypse

Edward E. Hindson

CONTEXT OF WORSHIP IN REVELATION

The book of Revelation is the most fascinating book ever written.[1] In the pages of the apocalypse we are swept up in a spirit of worship as we are transported to heaven to gain a glimpse of the future where worship will never end. This final book of the biblical canon is the capstone of divine revelation. In its pages, the risen Christ appears to the apostle John at the end of the first century AD to open the door to heaven and reveal the glorious future that awaits every believer.

It was on a Sunday, the Lord's Day—resurrection day. John had been exiled to the island of Patmos in the Aegean Sea off the coast of Asia Minor. That's when it happened. A booming voice broke the silence, announcing, "I am the Alpha and Omega . . . who is and was and is to come" (Rev. 1:8).[2]

When John turned to see who was speaking to him, he saw the risen Christ in all of his divine glory and heavenly splendor. The divine Intruder had come for his disciple with a vision of the future and a message of hope for his church.

---

1. The numerous commentaries on Revelation cannot do literary justice to this amazing book. But the reader may want to consult some of the following: G. R. Beasley-Murray, *The Book of Revelation*, NCB (London: Marshall, Morgan, & Scott, 1978); G. K. Beale, *The Book of Revelation*, NIGTC (Grand Rapids: Eerdmans, 1998); Edward Hindson, *Revelation: Unlocking the Future* (Chattanooga, TN: AMG, 2002); Bruce Metzger, *Breaking the Code: Understanding the Book of Revelation* (Nashville: Abingdon, 1993); J. Ramsey Michaels, *Interpreting the Book of Revelation* (Grand Rapids: Baker, 1992); Leon Morris, *The Revelation of St. John*, TNTC (Grand Rapids: Eerdmans, 1969); Robert H. Mounce, *The Book of Revelation*, NICNT (Grand Rapids: Eerdmans, 1987); Grant Osborne, *Revelation*, BECNT (Grand Rapids: Baker Academic, 2002); C. Marvin Pate, *Interpreting Revelation and Other Apocalyptic Literature* (Grand Rapids: Kregel, 2016); Merrill Tenney, *Interpreting Revelation* (Grand Rapids: Eerdmans, 1957).
2. Unless otherwise noted, all Scripture quotations in this chapter are from the NASB.

And what an incredible future it would be! As John was ushered down the tunnel of time through the corridors of eternity, he would witness the unfolding plan of God for all the ages, which would culminate in his final appeal: "Even so, come, Lord Jesus" (22:20).

As John turned to get a glimpse of the voice that called to him, he saw seven golden lampstands—probably in the shape of a Jewish menorah (1:12). These were representative of the seven churches to which the book is addressed (1:20). In the middle of the menorah, John saw the Savior dressed in the high priestly garments—the floor-length robe with the golden sash (cf. Exod. 39). The rest of his description follows a sevenfold pattern:

1. Hair: white like wool
2. Eyes: blazing fire
3. Feet: burnished bronze
4. Voice: sound of many waters
5. Right hand: holds seven stars
6. Mouth: sharp two-edged sword
7. Face: shining like the sun

David Hocking observes, "To say that His appearance is unique is an understatement: it is supernatural, a glorious description that could be given to God alone."[3] The grandeur of this portrait points to the majesty, purity, and authority of the One described. This is the risen Savior, the glorified Christ. This is the coming King!

John, the beloved disciple, collapses at the Savior's feet. He lays prostrate on the ground before the King of kings, the High Priest of heaven. He cannot stand in his own strength before his divine King. Remember, this is one of Jesus's dearest and closest disciples. If he cannot stand before him, how dare we think we can! But as John looked up, he saw the Savior looking down. "I was dead, and behold, I am alive forevermore," he announced (1:18). It was in this position of worship, as John lay prostrate before the Savior, that he would receive the commission to write the book of Revelation.

THEOLOGY OF WORSHIP

The theological focus of the Apocalypse emphasizes the sovereignty of God over both earthly and heavenly realms. He is orchestrating the events of the past, present, and future in regard to his ultimate plan for the universe. Merrill Tenney states, "The primary concern of the Apocalypse is not with social and economic conditions, but with the spiritual interpretation of life."[4] Its focus is thus on the supernatural purposes of the revelation of God. It is not written to mystify, but to explain the truth of God, which leads to the worship of God.

---

3. David Hocking, *The Coming World Leader* (Portland, OR: Multnomah, 1988), 35. Hocking contrasts Jesus Christ with the Antichrist.
4. Tenney, *Interpreting Revelation*, 23.

The Ultimate Perspective

G. R. Beasley-Murray writes, "It is evident that a new beginning in the book of Revelation is made at 4:1. A door in heaven is opened to enable the prophet to enter its portals and see what transpires in heaven, that he may understand what takes place on earth."[5]

This is the *key* to interpreting Revelation. It provides us with a heavenly perspective on human events. And it reassures us that God is in control of it all. He is still on the throne! His sovereign will shall be done. His eternal purposes will be accomplished. And his ultimate triumph is certain.

The "vision of heaven" (chaps. 4–5) serves as the fulcrum of the Apocalypse. It is the pivot on which the entire book turns our attention from earth to heaven and from time to eternity. Chapters 4 and 5 contain a double vision: (1) God the Creator and (2) Christ the Redeemer. In chapter 4, all of heaven worships God the Father for creating the world. In chapter 5, all of heaven worships Christ, the Lamb of God, for redeeming the world from the curse of sin. Beasley-Murray observes, "A single motif binds together the double vision of Chapters 4–5, namely that the God of creation is the God of redemption, accomplishing His gracious will through the crucified and risen Christ."[6]

The "Jewishness" of Revelation 4–19 is so strong that some critics have objected that the Apocalypse is little more than a "weakly Christianized Judaism."[7] In reality, the Christology of Revelation is quite "advanced." The book constantly ascribes the attributes of God to Christ. The Savior is confessed as Alpha and Omega (22:13). He is the mediator of creation (3:14), redemption (5:9), and of the final kingdom (19:11). As in John 1:1, he is called the "Word of God" (19:13). He is also depicted as the Lamb of God (5:6). In the final vision of the book, the eternal state is pictured as jointly ruled by God and the Lamb as a unity. Beasley-Murray comments, "The Lamb remains the mediator of judgment and redemption, yet he is inseparable from the God who enacts his works of judgment and redemption through him."[8]

Transported to heaven

"Come up here" (4:1). John is about to be temporarily "raptured" to heaven "in the Spirit." He suddenly sees a door opened in heaven. The force of the original Greek text emphasizes that the door was already opened and that it remains open.[9]

The purpose of John's "translation" into heaven was to provide him with a divine perspective on what was presently occurring behind the

5. Beasley-Murray, *Book of Revelation*, 108.
6. Beasley-Murray, *Book of Revelation*, 108.
7. Cf. Rudolf Bultmann, *Theology of the New Testament* (London: SCM, 1955), 2:175; C. H. Dodd, *The Apostolic Preaching and Its Development* (London: SCM, 1944), 40.
8. Beasley-Murray, *Book of Revelation*, 23–25. He emphasizes the inseparability of the Christology from the eschatology of Revelation.
9. Metzger, *Breaking the Code*, 47.

scenes of the human dilemma and what would occur on earth in the future. The reference to "heaven" is in the singular, as are fifty-one of the fifty-two uses of the term in Revelation. Here it refers to the dwelling place of God Almighty.

The invitation to "come up here" (Greek *anaba*) is used by the same voice of authority ("like the sound of a trumpet") that John heard from the glorified Christ in 1:10. The speaker further announces, "I will show you what must take place after these things." Therefore, Christ himself issues the invitation and promises to reveal the future to the apostle.

Transfixed by the throne

The focal point of what John saw in chapter 4 is the One seated on the throne, not the throne itself. The throne merely symbolizes his great authority, power, and position. It is the One seated on the throne, God the Father, who is the focus of attention in this chapter.

John's description of the One seated on the throne is that of his shekinah glory. John was overcome by the presence of the glory of God. He became transfixed on the indescribable occupant on the throne of the universe. He sees the One of whom he himself said, "No man has seen God at any time" (John 1:18). Therefore, John's description is limited to that of his glorious appearance. Other than the references to his sitting on the throne (4:2) and to his holding the scroll in his right hand (5:1), there are no other anthropomorphic descriptions of the Father.

There were also twenty-four elders seated on twenty-four lesser thrones surrounding the throne of God (v. 4). They are described as robed in white (righteousness) and wearing "golden crowns" (rewards). Together they depict the courtroom of heaven. Their number is significant since there were twenty-four courses (shifts) to the Old Testament Levitical priesthood (cf. 1 Chron. 24:7–19). The church is also described as a "royal priesthood" (1 Peter 2:5–9). We, like they, are "elders" in the economy of God. Many believe the elders represent the raptured church since they already have white robes and golden crowns, indicating the judgment seat of Christ has already taken place (cf. 2 Cor. 5:10).[10]

Songs of Worship

The declaration "Holy, holy, holy" recognizes the Triune nature of God. Just as Isaiah the prophet (6:3) heard this declaration in the throne room of heaven, so John the apostle hears it as well. This is but one of the numerous interconnections of the divine revelation of Old and New Testament Scripture, indicating that the symbols of the Apocalypse are drawn from the biblical record.

---

10. Charles Feinberg, "Revelation," in *Parallel Bible Commentary*, eds. Edward E. Hindson and Woodrow Michael Kroll (Nashville: Thomas Nelson, 1982), 2868.

Robert Coleman points out that the expressions of praise and worship in Revelation are the "songs of heaven."[11] He finds fourteen of them in the pages of the Apocalypse, beginning with 4:8. God's holiness is thrice proclaimed, and he is exalted as the One who was, and is, and is to come. Coleman views the angelic creatures as the guardians of the throne exclaiming, "only God is great!" His nature is holy. His kingdom is divine. His rule is just. And his will shall be done. He alone is worthy of our worship. Each of the fourteen songs is an expression of worship.

Songs of the Apocalypse: Praise and Worship in Revelation
1. The Anthem of the Triune God *Revelation 4:8*
2. The Creation Hymn *Revelation 4:11*
3. The New Song of Redemption *Revelation 5:9–10*
4. The Angels' Chorale *Revelation 5:12*
5. The Crescendo of the Universe *Revelation 5:13–14*
6. The Martyrs' Canticle *Revelation 6:10*
7. The Song of Salvation *Revelation 7:10*
8. The Antiphonal Amen *Revelation 7:12*
9. The Kingdom Carol *Revelation 11:15*
10. The Psalm of Judgment *Revelation 11:17–18*
11. The Shout of the Overcomers *Revelation 12:10–12*
12. The Song of Moses and the Lamb *Revelation 15:3–4*
13. The Hallelujah Chorus *Revelation 19:1–4*
14. The Symphony of the Marriage Feast *Revelation 19:6–7*
Adapted from Robert Coleman, *Songs of Heaven* (Old Tappan, NJ: Fleming H. Revell, 1980), 9.

11. Robert Coleman, *Songs of Heaven* (Old Tappan, NJ: Fleming H. Revell, 1980), 29–37. This is the best work ever done on the songs of the Apocalypse.

Chapter 4 ends with the elders (the redeemed) on their faces before God, casting their golden crowns before him and singing, "worthy art thou." The term *worthy* is the basis of our English word *worship*—to ascribe "worth-ship" or honor to someone greater than ourselves. The term *worthy* (Greek *axios*) was used in biblical times to attribute praise when the emperor marched in a triumphal procession. For Christians to ascribe this term to God was their way of saying that he and he alone deserved their worship. No human emperor could compare nor dare compete with him.

The crescendo of praise exalts God the father as the Creator of the universe. He receives praise for his glory, honor, and power. The chapter closes with a hymn of praise to our Creator—the One on the throne. It reminds us that the world is never out of his control.

Worthy Is the Lamb!

Jesus Christ is the central figure of chapter 5. He appears suddenly and dramatically at the center stage of heaven. He comes to claim his rightful inheritance fro his Father's hand. He is the heir of the line of Jewish royalty—the "Root of David." He comes with divine authority to receive the title deed to the world and to enact the eternal purposes of God Almighty.

He appears in the courtroom of heaven as the Lamb of God. Here the emphasis is on his atonement for our sins. The symbolism is that of the Old Testament lamb slain for the sins of humankind. It is the same terminology John the Baptist used when he first saw the Messiah and proclaimed, "Behold the Lamb of God who takes away the sin of the world!" (John 1:29).

As John the apostle turns to see Christ, he recognizes the Savior as having been "slain" (5:6). There in the midst of the throne, John sees the only human-made things that will even enter heaven: the wounds of Christ! He and the other apostles had seen them before on the risen Christ in the upper room (John 20:20–27). But now, the apostle sees them in the glorified Christ in heaven. The nail prints and the spear mark are still there to remind us of God's eternal love.

Walter Scott writes, "The memories of Calvary are treasured in heaven. John the *Baptist* first points out Jesus on earth as the 'Lamb of God.' John the *apostle* now beholds him in that same character on high. But how different the position! *There*, wounded and slain; *here*, the center of heaven's strength and glory, yet bearing in His Person the marks and scars of the cross."[12]

John's attention is initially focused on the book (Greek *biblion*, "scroll") in the right hand of God Almighty. Since bound books as we know them today developed much later, it is best to understand this document as a rolled papyrus scroll sealed with seven seals across the outer edge. It is

12. Walter Scott, *Exposition of the Revelation of Jesus Christ* (Grand Rapids: Kregel, 1962), 135. Scott's commentary on Revelation is one of the most worshipful and majestic ever written.

possible that the seals were affixed throughout the scroll at the longitudinal ends so that it could be unrolled section by section. However, this arrangement of seals is virtually unknown in ancient documents.

John weeps because no one is found "worthy" to open the seals of the scroll and fulfill God's plan for human history (5:3–4). Worthiness, as in 4:11, implies deity—worthy of our worship. Those falling short of this nature are described in three locations:

1. In heaven (angelic)
2. On the earth (human)
3. Under the earth (demonic)

At this point, one of the "elders" interrupts John to announce that the "Lion that is from the tribe of Judah" and the "Root of David" has prevailed to open the book (5:5). Therefore, he tells John, "Stop weeping." John's crying indicates there are tears in heaven but they shall later be wiped away (Rev. 21:4). The symbolism of the "Lion that is from the tribe of Judah" comes from Genesis 49:9–10. The lion served as the symbol of Israel's messianic tribe.

Hearing this startling announcement, John brushes his tears aside and turns to see the Deliverer. Bruce Metzger writes, "What follows is altogether unexpected. John looked to see the Lion, the king of beasts, and instead he sees a Lamb with the marks of slaughter upon it (5:6)!"[13]

The symbolism of the lamb emphasizes the ultimate triumph of the sacrificial death of Christ. The symbol of the lamb appears twenty-eight times in Revelation. His death is the only atonement for sins that God the Father will accept. The issue is not whether your religion satisfies you, but whether it satisfies God! And God is only satisfied with the blood atonement of Jesus Christ, his Son. That sacrifice alone can pay for the sinner's debt, satisfy the demands of divine justice, and set the sinner free.

His death is our triumph! He alone has overcome every obstacle by his death on the cross. Thus he alone has the unchallenged right to approach the throne of God on our behalf, take the scroll from the hand of the Almighty, and effectuate the counsels of God. Indeed, the whole scope of Revelation tells us that the Lamb that was slain shall become King of kings and Lord of lords.

In Jesus Christ alone the majesty and might of the lion and the meekness and sacrifice of the lamb are combined in one glorious person. He is at the center of the universe, and all of heaven waits breathlessly as he approaches the throne of God. The Lamb who once stood silent, meek, and humble before his accusers now marches boldly through the throngs of heaven. He who was rejected shall rule and reign in righteousness. He who was spat on shall sit on the throne of David. He who was crowned with thorns shall be crowned with the diadem of the Almighty.

13. Metzger, *Breaking the Code*, 52.

God's Son approaches the Father's throne and all of heaven bows before him. The nail-pierced, thorn-scarred, spear-marked Son of the Almighty comes with his wounds of love crying out for the redemption of humankind. He has come to claim the heathen for his inheritance (Ps. 2:8), and he will not be denied. His innocent blood, which flowed like a river of mercy at Calvary, has paved the way into the heavenly courtroom. The title deed is his, and his alone.

The Lamb of God reaches forth his nail-scarred hand to receive the scroll from the eternal Father. Who can deny such love? Such sacrifice? Certainly not the God of the universe! For he himself is love (1 John 4:16). In that one incredible moment, the love of the Father meets the love of the Son. The scroll is passed and the triumph is secured. The Lamb of God now holds the title deed to the universe. Hallelujah! What a triumph!

Scott writes, "Now the self-same Lamb bearing in His person the marks of His passion is here seen as the object of heaven's worship. No voice is, nor can be silent when the slain Lamb appears."[14] What follows are the greatest hymns of triumph in all of Scripture. The heavenly hosts break into songs of praise and worship that clearly portray Christ as deity.

The picture of the Savior in 5:1–7 underscores the great culmination of messianic expectation in the New Testament. The Messiah did not come as a conquering hero, but as a wounded lamb. He did not come to destroy the enemies of Israel, but to love his enemies into submission to his kingdom. He did not come to condemn the world, but to save the world (John 3:17).

The New Song

Coleman has written a superb study on the songs of Revelation titled *Songs of Heaven*.[15] He finds fourteen such songs (a double seven) throughout the last book of the Bible. He calls attention to the fact that the heavenly choir bursts forth with a "new song of redemption" in this atmosphere of holy communion. He writes, "It is called a 'new song' because that which Christ has accomplished is wholly different and superior to the old covenant; nothing like it has ever existed before."[16]

The new song is one of praise and worship to Jesus Christ, the Lamb. It acknowledges that he is also "worthy" (Greek *axios*) of our worship. The fact that the song of praise to the Lamb follows the song of praise to the Creator emphasizes the deity of both. Only that which is divine deserves our worship ("worth-ship"). There can be no doubt that this emphasis is intended to underscore the deity of Christ. He, like the Father, is "worthy" of our worship.

---

14. Scott, *Exposition*, 137.
15. Coleman, *Songs of Heaven*, 47.
16. Coleman, *Songs of Heaven*, 47. Coleman points out that the word "new" (*kainen*) used here is the same word used for "new creation," "new heaven," "new earth," and "new Jerusalem."

All of the redeemed people of heaven sing, "Worthy art Thou to take the book, and to break its seals; for Thou wast slain, and didst purchase for God with Thy blood men from every tribe and tongue and people and nation" (5:9 NASB 1977). This is the song of redemption sung only by the saved. It is the expression of the "prayers of the saints" (5:8). No angel can sing this song. They can only bow down in wonder and amazement that the Son of God would become the Lamb of God who died for the sins of the world.[17]

Coleman notes, "Christ's worthiness in carrying out the divine purposes rests upon His sacrificial death, by which mankind was purchased for God. Without the offering up of His own life on Calvary, there could have been no redemption of the world, and Christ would have entered heaven alone."[18] The words of praise and worship that follow emphasize the divine nature of the Lamb who is worshiped in a manner equal to the Father.

The elders who are expressing these words of praise are representative of the whole church because they are described as having been redeemed "from every tribe and tongue and people and nation" (5:9). Such a host cannot be limited to the Old Testament saints alone, although it may include them. What is clear is that this host must include the New Testament church, and that they are already in heaven prior to the judgments that are about to fall on the earth.

The Angelic Choir

Chapter 5 ends with myriads of angels joining the elders to praise the Lamb. Their innumerable host is described as "myriad of myriads, and thousands of thousands" (5:11). The best modern equivalent would be "millions." The angels are not redeemed because they are not fallen creatures. Therefore, they could not sing redemption's song. But now they join the redeemed in singing praise to the Lamb for who he is.

Angels play a prominent role in the Apocalypse. An angel dispatched the message to John (1:1). Each of the seven churches is said to have an angel (1:20). An angel asked if someone was worthy to open the scroll (5:2). Angels are pictured as the proclaimers and executors of God's judgments in chapters 8, 9, 10, 12, 14, 15, 16, 17, 18, 19, and 20. They are also told to seal the elect (7:1–4) and to assist in their prayers (8:3–5). In eternity, they unveil the new Jerusalem (21:10) and guard the gates of the city (21:12).

The expression "worthy is the Lamb" places the worship of Christ equal with that of God the Father. God is worshiped as Creator in chapter 4, and Christ is worshiped as Redeemer in chapter 5. The combined impact of these two chapters leaves no doubt as to the deity and divine nature

17. See David Jeremiah, *What the Bible Says about Angels* (Sisters, OR: Multnomah, 1996).
18. Beasley-Murray, *Book of Revelation*, 127–28.

of Christ. He is to be worshiped as equal in essence to the Father, while the Holy Spirit draws our attention to both because "he will not speak on His own initiative" (John 16:13).

The worship of the Lamb is based on his sevenfold worth to receive the following:

1. Power (*dunamis*, "unlimited ability")
2. Riches (*ploutos*, "unconditional wealth")
3. Wisdom (*sophia*, "mental excellence")
4. Might (*iskus*, "superhuman power")
5. Honor (*timē*, "praise of character")
6. Glory (*doxa*, "majestic radiance")
7. Blessing (*eulogia*, "thanksgiving")

Each of these qualities is recognized in the Lamb himself. They are also blessings that he bestows. But their emphasis here is on the qualities he possesses. They begin with a focus on his power and might (points 1–4) and move to the more usual sequence of doxologies: honor, glory, and blessing (points 5–7). These rapid-fire expressions of praise and worship leap from the lips of the angelic host with the spontaneous recognition of who he is and what he has done. These thrilling crescendos lead to the grand finale of praise.

The chapter ends with all of creation praising both God ("Him who sits on the throne") and the Lamb, equally ascribing "blessing and honor and glory and dominion" to both. These songs express an exuberance of praise and adoration for all that God has dome through the Lamb. Leon Morris says it so well: "There cannot be the slightest doubt that the Lamb is to be reckoned with God as God.[19]

The four "living creatures" add their final "Amen." And the twenty-four elders prostrate themselves in worship. What a picture! All of heaven is on its face before the Father and the Son. Praise resounds in crescendos, and worship exudes from every heart. The Lamb has taken possession of the title deed to the universe. He holds the divine contract in his nail-scarred hands. He stands ready to open the seals, pronounce the judgments, and take possession of his rightful kingdom on earth. By the end of the Apocalypse the heavenly chorus breaks into a triumphal hymn of praise (19:10) for the righteous judgments of God that have triumphed over the fallen world. They reach a crescendo in four hallelujahs that praise the salvation, glory, and power of God "for the Lord our God the Almighty reigns" (19:1–6). The final cantata of praise calls our attention to the marriage of the Lamb as he and his triumphant Bride take center stage, Hallelujah—what a Savior!

19. Morris, *Revelation*, 102.

SIGNIFICANCE OF REVELATION FOR BIBLICAL WORSHIP

The concept of worship is expressed in the Apocalypse by the term *axios* (worthy) and its relationship to *hagios* (holy). That which is holy is worthy of our worth-ship (as in 4:11; 5:2, 4, 9, 12). This expression of "worth" is focused on God the Father and God the Son (the Lamb). All of heaven (angels, creatures, and the redeemed) fall down and worship both the Creator and the Redeemer as equally worthy of our worship. The scene reaches its climax when a doxology rings out over the halls of the heavenly scene: "Holy, holy, holy, is the Lord God, the Almighty, who was and who is and who is to come" (4:8). This is followed by the crescendo of the universe as the myriads sing, "Worthy is the Lamb" (5:12–14).

The Apocalypse is filled with numerous verbal and physical responses of worship. These include falling down (1:17; 4:10; 5:8; 7:11; 11:16; 19:10; 22:8); casting crowns (7:10); being carried in the Spirit (1:10; 21:10); crying aloud (7:10); blessing God (4:13); fearing God (14:7); giving glory to God (4:9; 11:13; 14:7; 12:20; 21:24); saying hallelujah (19:1, 3, 4, 6); saying amen (5:14; 19:4; 20:20); listening to the Spirit (2:7, 11, 17, 29; 3:6; 13; 22), playing trumpets (8:2, 7, 8, 10, 12; 9:1, 10; 11:15); playing harps (14:2); waving palm branches (7:9); praising God (5:11–12; 19:5); praying (4:8; 8:3); prophesying (10:11; 11:3); reigning with Christ (20:4; 22:5); rejoicing (12:12; 18:20); repenting (2:5, 16, 22; 3:19); singing (4:8, 11; 5:9–10, 12, 13–14; 6:10; 7:10, 12; 11:15, 17–18; 12:10–12; 15:3–4; 19:1–4, 6–7); serving (7:15; 22:3); shouting (5:12; 7:2, 10; 11:15); responding in silence (8:1); testifying (11:7; 12:11, 17; 22:16); walking with Christ (3:4); weeping (5:4); writing (1:19; 2:1, 8, 12, 18; 3:1, 7, 16); and inviting people to come to Christ (22:17).

CONCLUSION

Worship in the Apocalypse is the exuberant response of all believers. They worship the Triune God in adoration of his person, acknowledgment of his sovereignty, appreciation for his redemption, and anticipation of his coming and the fulfillment of his eternal purposes. In summary, the Apocalypse is one of the most significant and passionate expressions of worship in all of Scripture. In its pages we see the heart of worship on display as the redeemed respond with their hearts, hands, and minds to the amazing grace of the Kings of kings and Lord of lords.

BIBLIOGRAPHY

Beale, G. K. *The Book of Revelation*. NIGTC. Grand Rapids: Eerdmans, 1998.

Beasley-Murray, G. R. *The Book of Revelation*. NCB. London: Marshall, Morgan, & Scott, 1978.

Bultmann, Rudolf. *Theology of the New Testament*. London: SCM, 1955.

Coleman, Robert. *Songs of Heaven*. Old Tappan, NJ: Fleming H. Revell, 1980.

Dodd, C. H. *The Apostolic Preaching and Its Development.* London: SCM, 1944.
Feinberg, Charles, L. "Revelation." In *Parallel Bible Commentary*, edited by Edward E. Hindson and Woodrow Michael Kroll, 1774–1831. Nashville: Thomas Nelson, 1982.
Hindson, Edward. *Revelation: Unlocking the Future.* Chattanooga, TN: AMG, 2002.
Hocking, David. *The Coming World Leader.* Portland, OR: Multnomah, 1988.
Jeremiah, David. *What the Bible says about Angels.* Sisters, OR: Multnomah, 1996.
Metzger, Bruce M. *Breaking the Code: Understanding the Book of Revelation.* Nashville: Abingdon, 1993.
Michaels, J. Ramsey. *Interpreting the Book of Revelation.* Grand Rapids: Baker, 1992.
Morris, Leon. *The Revelation of St. John.* TNTC. Grand Rapids: Eerdmans, 1969.
Mounce, Robert H. *The Book of Revelation.* NICNT. Grand Rapids: Eerdmans, 1987.
Osborne, Grant. *Revelation.* BECNT. Grand Rapids: Baker Academic, 2002.
Pate, C. Marvin. *Interpreting Revelation and Other Apocalyptic Literature.* Grand Rapids: Kregel Academic, 2016.
Patterson, Paige. *Revelation.* NAC 39. Nashville: B&H, 2012.
Scott, Walter. *Exposition of the Revelation of Jesus Christ.* Grand Rapids: Kregel, 1962.
Swindoll, Charles R. *Insights on Revelation*, SNTI. Grand Rapids: Zondervan, 2011.
Tenney, Merrill. *Interpreting Revelation.* Grand Rapids: Eerdmans, 1957.

EPILOGUE

Biblical Worship for the Glory of God

Benjamin K. Forrest and Vernon M. Whaley

We are surrounded by a great cloud of witnesses who spent their lives joining in the story of worship (cf. Heb. 11–12:1). The faithfulness of these witnesses has left us a heritage that should encourage us along in our own worship. To hear their admonition, however, we must listen well to the pages of Scripture. In listening to these pages, we hear notes and sequences repeated, combining into melodies and harmonies that make up the song of the redeemed. These individual pieces contribute to a unified whole that points toward a coming climax, but they continually require our remembrance as we press on in our day-to-day journeying. As JoAnna Hoyt has reminded us, the Israelites saw the future as behind them because it could not yet be seen, while the past was in front because it was known through remembrance.[1] Such a mindset positions worshipers well, for in remembrance we worship for what we have seen while knowing by faith what is yet to come. As we remember God's faithfulness in the past and recall his promises as unchanging, we are able to press on and finish the race that is set before us.

This race regularly includes what Paul calls the "affairs of this world" (1 Cor. 7:33). These ordinary affairs, however, are not second-class events but the daily context for a worship-filled life. They are locations and occasions to be set apart and consecrated for God's glory. Throughout this history of worship, we see how ordinary spaces, places, practices, people, and times are all made sacred by being set apart. And the sacralization of ordinary places and spaces affirms our position as new covenant worshipers because the presence of God tabernacles within believers who worship in Spirit and in truth (John 4:24). Biblical worship for the glory of God is

1. See chapter 4, "The Calendar for Worship in Ancient Israel: Worship in the Feasts and Celebrations."

the theological framework that reconfigures the ordinary aspects of our lives—our work (Eccl. 9:10; Col. 3:23), our relationships (Phil. 2:1–8), our eating and drinking (1 Cor. 10:31)—as an offerings to the Lord for his glory and the honor due his name (Ps. 29:2; 96:8).

Just as the story of redemption is woven throughout Scripture, God's plan for worship has been spoken through patriarchs, prophets, poets, and the people of God who are committed to following the resurrected Christ. The stories of redemption and worship consistently point to Jesus and the joy of the Father to reconcile humanity to himself through the gift of his Son. While this text has just spent more than 200,000 words attempting to articulate a biblical theology of worship, the story of worship is both simpler than we have made it and still woefully incomplete. Simply, worship is the acknowledging the ontological worthiness of our God. But profoundly, only eternity will provide humanity the opportunity to fully express his worthiness.

We have learned much on this journey exploring the Word of God for the magnification of the worth of God. Perhaps we are even more aware of our inadequacies in telling this story, but we recognize that we are only a single voice in this choir that has stretched from creation to today, and will continue throughout eternity. We rejoice, however, that in spite of our shortcomings, we have been invited to join with heaven and history in the worship of the One who is worthy. A conclusion to this project deserves a Handelian crescendo, but our prose is insufficient to communicate a rightfully climactic conclusion to the worship of our God, who is "of himself infinite in being, glory, blessedness, and perfection; all-sufficient, eternal, unchangeable, incomprehensible, everywhere present, almighty, knowing all things, most wise, most holy, most just, most merciful and gracious, long-suffering, and abundant in goodness and truth."[2] And so with the witnesses already singing in the presence of God, we conclude by practicing now what will be our heavenly refrain through all eternity:

> Hallelujah!
> For our Lord God Almighty reigns.
> Let us rejoice and be glad
> and give him glory!
> For the wedding of the Lamb has come,
> and his bride has made herself ready. (Rev. 19:6–7 NIV)

Soli Deo Gloria

2. Westminster Larger Catechism (1647–1649), Q. 17.

SCRIPTURE INDEX

Leviticus

Numbers

Deuteronomy

Joshua

Proverbs

Ecclesiastes

Song of Songs

Isaiah

Jeremiah

Lamentations

Amos

Jonah

Micah

Nahum

Habakkuk

Zephaniah

Haggai

Zechariah

John

Acts

Romans

1 Corinthians

2 Corinthians

Galatians

Ephesians